W9-DIR-382

Iberia and
the Americas

Other Titles in ABC-CLIO's

Transatlantic Relations Series

Iberia and
the Americas

Culture, Politics, and History

A Multidisciplinary Encyclopedia

VOLUME I

EDITED BY

J. Michael Francis

Transatlantic Relations Series

Will Kaufman, Series Editor

A B C ⬙ C L I O

Santa Barbara, California   Denver, Colorado   Oxford, England

Library of Congress Cataloging-in-Publication Data
Iberia and the Americas : culture, politics, and history : a multidisciplinary encyclopedia / edited by J. Michael Francis.
  p. cm. — (Transatlantic relations series)
 Includes bibliographical references and index.
 ISBN 1-85109-421-0 (hardcover : alk. paper) — ISBN 1-85109-426-1 (ebook) 1. America—Relations—Spain—Encyclopedias. 2. Spain—Relations—America—Encyclopedias. 3. America—History—Encyclopedias. 4. Spain—History—Encyclopedias. 5. North America—History—Encyclopedias. 6. Latin America—History—Encyclopedias. 7. South America—History—Encyclopedias. 8. America—Politics and government—Encyclopedias. 9. Spain—Politics and government—Encyclopedias. I. Francis, J. Michael (John Michael) II. Series.

 E18.75.I24 2005
 303.48'2181204603--dc22
        2005025407

08 07 06 05 10 9 8 7 6 5 4 3 2 1

303.482
IBE

This book is also available on the World Wide Web as an e-Book. Visit abc-clio.com for details.

ABC-CLIO, Inc.
130 Cremona Drive, P.O. Box 1911
Santa Barbara, California 93116-1911

This book is printed on acid-free paper ∞.
Manufactured in the United States of America

CONTENTS

ADVISORY BOARD

Professor Michael Burns, Mount Holyoke College
Professor Charles Forsdick, University of Liverpool
Dr. Yves Laberge, Laval University
Professor Jocelyn L'tourneau, Laval University

SERIES EDITOR'S PREFACE

The transatlantic relationship has been one of the most dynamic of modern times. Since the great age of exploration in the fifteenth and sixteenth centuries, the encounters between the Old World and the New have determined the course of history, culture, and politics for billions of people. The destinies of Europe, Africa, North and South America, and all the islands in between have been intertwined to the extent that none of these areas can be said to exist in isolation. Out of these interconnections comes the concept of the "Atlantic world," which Alan Karras describes in his introductory essay to *Britain and the Americas* in this series: "By looking at the Atlantic world as a single unit, rather than relying upon more traditional national (such as Britain) or regional (such as North or South America) units of analyses, scholars have more nearly been able to re-create the experiences of those who lived in the past." This perspective attempts to redefine and respond to expanding (one might say *globalizing*) pressures and new ways of perceiving interconnections—not only those rooted in history ("the past") but also those that are ongoing. Just one result of this conceptual redefinition has been the emergence of transatlantic studies as an area of inquiry in its own right, growing from the soil of separate area studies, whether European, North American, African, Caribbean, or Latin American. Students and scholars working in transatlantic studies have embarked on a new course of scholarship that places the transatlantic dynamic at its heart.

In this spirit, the Transatlantic Relations Series is devoted to transcending, or at least challenging, the boundaries of nation/region as well as discipline: we are concerned in this series not only with history but also with culture and politics, race and economics, gender and migration; not only with the distant past but also with this morning. The aim, in a phrase, is to explore the myriad connections and interconnections of the Atlantic world. However, although the Atlantic world concept challenges the isolation of smaller, national perspectives, nations do continue to exist, with boundaries both physical and conceptual. Thus this series acknowledges the intractability of the national and the regional while consistently focusing on the transcending movements—the connections and interconnections—that go beyond the national and the regional. Our mode of operation has been to build an approach to the Atlantic world through attention to the separate vectors between the nations and regions on both sides of the Atlantic. We do this by offering the six titles within the series so far commissioned, devoted respectively to Africa, Britain, France, Germany, Iberia, and Ireland in their engagements with the Americas. In each case, the transatlantic exchanges are those of all kinds: cultural, political, and historical, from the moment of the first contact to the present day. With this organizing principle in mind, the object is to offer an accessible, precisely focused means of entry into the various portals of the Atlantic world.

Finally, a word about this series' origins: in 1995, Professor Terry Rodenberg of Central Missouri State University invited scholars and teachers from eighteen universities on both sides of the Atlantic to establish an educational and scholarly institution devoted to encouraging a transatlantic perspective. The result was the founding of the Maastricht Center for Transatlantic Studies (MCTS), located in the Dutch city whose name, through its eponymous treaty, resonates with transnational associations. Since its foundation, MCTS has continued to bring together students and scholars from a host of worldwide locations to explore the intricate web of Atlantic connections across all disciplines. It has been a dynamic encounter between cultures and people striving to transcend the limitations of separate area and disciplinary studies. I am pleased to acknowledge the extent to which the Transatlantic Relations Series grows out of the discussions and approaches articulated at MCTS. Therefore, although the separate titles in the series carry their own dedications, the series as a whole is dedicated with great respect to Terry Rodenberg and the students and scholars at Maastricht.

Will Kaufman
University of Central Lancashire
Maastricht Center for Transatlantic Studies

EDITOR'S PREFACE

Few events in world history have sparked as much curiosity, imagination, and at times visceral anger as the Iberian "discovery," conquest, and colonization of the New World. Yet however one chooses to characterize the meeting between Iberia and the Americas, the historical significance and the lasting legacy of that encounter are undeniable. The pages that follow set out to explore the remarkably diverse, rich, and complex relationship that has characterized Spanish and Portuguese relations with the Americas, from Tierra del Fuego to Canada, since 1492.

From the earliest voyages of discovery and conquest to the nineteenth-century wars of independence, from the end of the slave trade to the start of the cold war, and from the Treaty of Tordesillas to the Turbot fishing dispute, *Iberia and the Americas* aims to elucidate the manifold connections between the New World and the Old. The entries that make up these volumes explore the many political, economic, social, and cultural connections and interconnections between the two worlds, addressing a wide range of topics and themes. I hope that through this unique lens, readers will gain a renewed appreciation for topics already familiar to them, such as the American Revolution, the cold war, the Enlightenment, World Wars I and II, the Mexican Revolution, and the Spanish Civil War. Likewise, I hope to introduce readers to subjects that perhaps are less common in reference works of this nature, thus exposing them to the richness of recent trends in different academic disciplines, as well as the many levels at which Iberians and Americans interacted. For that reason, my approach is more thematic than event-driven. Readers will notice that there are no biographical entries; instead, most topics are intentionally broad in scope and multidisciplinary in perspective. Readers will move from entries on art and architecture to poetry and fiction, from science and education to migration and medicine, from music and dance to religion and economics. This approach, I hope, will reveal the extensive influence of the encounter on both sides of the Atlantic.

It is important to acknowledge the limitations inherent in such an ambitious project. In spite of its length and breadth, the pages that follow do not pretend to offer a comprehensive examination of all aspects of Iberian-American relations. Readers will recognize that the work is heavily weighted in the colonial period, in recognition of the importance of Iberian-American relations during colonial rule. This emphasis can, however, be somewhat misleading; perhaps one of the important lessons to learn from the entries that follow is that Iberian-American relations did not cease after the independence movements of the nineteenth century, in spite of the relative paucity of scholarly work on the subject. Still, the constraints of time and space dictate that there are important omissions and unfortunate silences, further testimony to the richness and complexity of five hundred years of transatlantic encounters. Those who wish to pursue specific topics in more detail will find useful references at the end of each entry.

Perhaps the greatest satisfaction in taking on a project of this nature comes from the relationships, both personal and professional, that develop through the process of recruiting contributors and editing their entries. It has been an absolute pleasure to work with such a remarkable group of distinguished scholars, representing more than twenty countries from around the world and a wide range of academic disciplines. My own understanding and appreciation of Iberia and the Americas have been enriched greatly through reading their work. For that reason, I would like to extend my sincere gratitude and appreciation to everyone who contributed valuable time and expertise in writing the entries that appear in these volumes. In particular, I would like to thank Kendall Brown, John Schwaller, and Robert Jackson for contributing so much of their knowledge to the project. Special mention also should be given to Victoria Cummins, Scott Eastman, Sasha Pack, Fernando Lopez-Alves, and John Farrell for agreeing to take on entries at the last minute and for finishing them so quickly. I am grateful to my colleagues at the University of North Florida, who have offered generous support and encouragement ever since I arrived in Jacksonville in 1997. I thank Tom Leonard and Aaron Sheehan-Dean for agreeing to contribute to the project, and my department chair, Dale Clifford, deserves special thanks. I am also grateful to my friends, colleagues, and enthusiastic contributors Matthew Restall, Kris E. Lane, Renée Soulodre–La France, Juliette Levy, Lina Del Castillo, Heather McCrea, Jason Frederick, Robert Whitney, and Jane Landers.

At ABC-CLIO I would like to thank Peter Westwick for his thoughtful comments and suggestions. I also thank Ron Boehm and Elaine Vanater. I reserve special gratitude for Project Editor Wendy Roseth, whose patience and infectious enthusiasm helped me throughout every stage of the process. And although he no longer works at ABC-CLIO, Simon Mason's assistance was invaluable during the early stages of this project.

Working with Will Kaufman has been a rare privilege; his constant encouragement, valuable advice, and endless supply of good humor helped to make this project such a rich and rewarding experience.

Finally, I could not have completed this project without the unfailing support of my wife and dearest friend, Annie. It is to her that I gratefully dedicate these volumes.

J. Michael Francis
University of North Florida

TOPIC FINDER

General
Armies—Colonial Brazil
Armies—Colonial
   Spanish America
Armies—Modern Latin
   America
Defense—Colonial
   Brazil
Defense—Colonial
   Spanish America
Guerrillas
North Atlantic Treaty
   Organization
   (NATO)
Rebellions—Colonial
   Latin America
Terrorism
Weapons

Mines and Mining
Emeralds
Gold
Mining—Gold
Mining—Mercury
Mining—Silver
Potosí
Silver

Philosophy
Enlightenment—Brazil
Enlightenment—Spanish
   America
Environment
Fin de Siècle
Liberation Theology
Syncretism

Places (see Geography)
Amazon
Argentina
Belize

Bolivia
Borderlands
Brazil
California
Chile
Colombia
Costa Rica
Cuba
Ecuador
El Dorado
El Salvador
Florida (La Florida)
French Guiana
Gran Colombia
Guatemala
Guyana
Hispaniola
Honduras
Mexico
Nicaragua
Panama
Paraguay
Peru
Puerto Rico
Suriname
Trinidad and Tobago
Uruguay
Venezuela

**Political, Social, and
Economic Concepts**
Communism
Conquest and the Debate
   over Justice
Crime
Democracy
Human Rights
Liberalism
Nationalism
Populism
Positivism

**Race, Gender, and
Ethnicity (see Slavery)**
Creoles
Hidalgo
Jews—Colonial Latin
   America
Jews—Modern Latin
   America
Ladino
Mestizaje
Moors
Mulatto
Native Americans I—
   Amazon
Native Americans II—
   Brazil
Native Americans III—
   Caribbean
Native Americans IV—
   Mesoamerica
Native Americans V—
   Central and Southern
   Andes
Native Americans VI—
   Northern Mexico
Native Americans VII—
   Northern Andes
Native Americans VIII—
   Southeastern North
   America
Race
Women—Brazil
Women—Colonial Spanish
   America
Women—Modern Spanish
   America

Religion
Beatas
Cannibalism
Catholic Church in Brazil

CHRONOLOGY OF IBERIA AND THE AMERICAS

1419	Between 1419 and 1451, Portugal lays claim to Madeira and the Azores, two uninhabited archipelagos in the Atlantic. The success of sugar and wine production on the islands will spark further Atlantic exploration and later influence Portuguese colonization in Brazil.
1441	Portuguese merchants begin to trade for slaves in sub-Saharan Africa. By the 1450s, hundreds of African slaves are entering Europe each year.
1469	Queen Isabella of Castile marries King Ferdinand of Aragon. Later dubbed the Catholic Monarchs (in Spanish, *Reyes Católicos*) by Pope Alexander VI, they will witness the development of the central institutions that will serve to govern Spain and its American colonies.
1478	The Holy Office of the Inquisition is formally founded in Spain.
1479	The Treaty of Alcáçovas ends the war between Spain and Portugal and gives Castile sovereignty over the Canary Islands.
1492	On January 2, the Catholic Monarchs, Isabella and Ferdinand, defeat the last

Muslim kingdom in Spain and triumphantly enter the city of Granada.

The Acts of Expulsion force Spain's Jewish population to either convert to Christianity or leave Spain; many Spanish Jews flee to neighboring Portugal.

On April 17, Isabella and Ferdinand draft an agreement with Christopher Columbus. Known as the *Capitulaciones de Santa Fe,* it contains certain promises to Columbus if his venture proves successful.

On August 4, three vessels, the *Niña,* the *Pinta,* and the *Santa Maria,* depart from the Spanish city of Palos, under the command of Christopher Columbus. On September 9 the three ships leave the Canary Islands, and one month later, on October 12, Columbus and his men sight land.

On December 25, the *Santa Maria* strikes a reef and sinks. With the assistance of a local chieftain (or cacique) named Guacanagarí, the crew salvages most of the ship's cargo.

Europeans first learn about the use of tobacco when the Taino Indians show them the leaves.

1493   Papal bulls issued by Pope Alexander VI grant to Castile title to the lands Columbus has discovered and charge the monarchy with Christianizing the inhabitants of those lands.

Columbus embarks on his second of four voyages to the Americas. Outfitted to establish a European colony, Columbus's ships carry a wide variety of Old World grains, grasses, vegetables, and livestock. Sugar is also introduced to Hispaniola.

Columbus returns to Hispaniola to find that the fortress he established at La Navidad has been destroyed, and the Spanish garrison killed.

1494   On June 7, following careful negotiations between Portugal and Castile, the Treaty of Tordesillas is signed; the treaty establishes a designated line 370 leagues west of Cape Verde. Spain is permitted to claim territories to the west of that line, and Portugal receives authority to claim territories to the east of the boundary.

1496   Portugal's King Dom Manuel issues an expulsion order for all Jews who do not convert to Christianity.

Columbus builds the first American caravel on the island of Hispaniola.

1498   Christopher Columbus departs on his third voyage to the New World, charged with carrying colonists and supplies to Hispaniola as well as conducting further exploration. Among the colonists are thirty women.

1499   Spanish explorer Alonso de Ojeda sets out from Spain to conquer and explore the northeastern coast of South America.

1500   Pedro Álvarez Cabral claims Brazil on behalf of the Portuguese Crown.

1501   Gaspar Corte Real explores the northeast coast of Newfoundland and the coast of Labrador. Reports of rich fish stocks in the Great Banks encourage Iberian fishermen, mainly Basques, to establish small processing plants in villages that still bear Portuguese and Spanish names.

From this date, Muslims, Jews, and heretics, as well as their children, are forbidden to travel to the New World.

1502   Nicolás de Ovando arrives as governor of Hispaniola.

The explorer Amerigo Vespucci maps the northeastern coastline of the Southern Cone.

Christopher Columbus embarks on his fourth and final voyage to the New World.

1503   The House of Trade (Casa de Contratación) is established in Seville, charged with supervising and regulating the traffic of goods and peoples between Spain and Spanish America.

1504   Queen Isabella dies, leaving Ferdinand king of Aragon and regent of Castile.

1508   Pope Julius II grants the privilege of *patronato real* (royal patronage) to the Spanish monarchy, which gives the Crown the right to appoint bishops and parish priests in the New World.

1511   The first American *audiencia* (high court) is established at Santo Domingo.

The conquest of Cuba repeats the economic model established earlier on the island of Hispaniola—plunder, followed by gold mining and agriculture with forced labor.

1512   The Laws of Burgos are issued by King Ferdinand of Spain to regulate relations between Spaniards and the indigenous inhabitants of Hispaniola.

1513   Juan Ponce de León becomes the first Spaniard to explore La Florida; he will return to colonize the region in 1521, but will die during the campaign.

Blasco Núñez de Balboa informs the Crown of the existence of the Pacific Ocean, which he claims for Castile.

Pope Leo X authorizes the creation of the New World's first ecclesiastical see at Santo Domingo.

1514 Alessandro Geraldini, the first bishop in the Americas, oversees the construction of the cathedral of Santo Domingo.

1516 Juan Díaz de Solís lands briefly in what is now Argentina.

The archbishop of Toledo, Francisco Jiménez de Cisneros, awards the Dominican friar Bartolomé de Las Casas the title of "universal defender and protector of the Indians."

1517 Diego Velásquez de Cuéllar, the governor of Cuba, authorizes Francisco Hernández de Córdoba to lead a voyage of exploration of the Yucatán Peninsula. The discovery of Mayan cities will spark a second voyage the following year, this one led by Juan de Grijalva.

Charles I becomes king of Aragon and Castile.

Alfonso Manso, the bishop of Puerto Rico, becomes the first inquisitor in the New World.

1518 A smallpox epidemic devastates the Indian population of Hispaniola.

1519 Cuba's governor Diego Velásquez de Cuéllar commissions Hernando Cortés to lead an expedition west, building on the previous expeditions of Francisco Hernández de Córdoba (1517) and Juan de Grijalva (1518).

Governor Velásquez's efforts to remove Cortés from command are too late, and on February 18, Cortés sets sail from Cuba, with over 500 men, 11 ships, 16 horses, and some artillery.

Scuttling all but one of his ships (which he dispatches to Spain), Cortés and his forces march inland, initiating the conquest of the Aztec Empire.

Pedro Arias de Ávila is appointed governor of Panama; he immediately relocates the capital to the Pacific side, near present-day Panama City.

Ferdinand Magellan anchors in the bay of what is now Montevideo, Uruguay; he then sails past the entire region and through the straits that today bear his name.

King Charles I is elected Holy Roman Emperor Charles V.

1520 On June 30, Cortés and 450 of his men make their escape from Tenochtitlan during the *Noche Triste* (Night of Sorrows). More than 900 Spaniards are captured and killed, as are 1,000 of Cortés's Tlaxcaltecan allies.

A major smallpox epidemic ravages central Mexico.

1521 Hernando Cortés launches a direct assault on the Aztec capital city of Tenochtitlan, with the assistance of 20,000–30,000 Indian allies. Tenochtitlan falls to Cortés's forces, ending ninety-three years of Aztec imperial domination. Mexico City is founded on the ruins of the former Aztec capital.

On the island of Hispaniola, Wolof slaves lead the first recorded slave revolt in the Americas.

1522 A Spanish law restricts emigration to the New World to Castilian Old Christians.

Gil González Dávila leads the Spanish conquest of Nicaraguan territory.

1523 Pedro de Alvarado, a lieutenant of Hernando Cortés, arrives in Central America with a force of 400 Spaniards and hundreds of Tlaxcaltecan allies to conquer the Maya of highland Guatemala.

1524   The Council of the Indies is established, entrusted with the administration of Spain's imperial affairs.

         Twelve Franciscan friars arrive in Mexico City to begin the "spiritual conquest" of Mexico's Indian population.

1525   The Inca Huayna Capac, ruler of the vast Inca empire, and his chosen heir both die unexpectedly, sparking a violent civil war between Huascar and Atahualpa. Francisco Pizarro will be able to exploit the bitter divisions when he arrives in the region seven years later.

1526   In order to protect ships and regulate trade, Spanish vessels are required to travel in fleets; over the next few decades a system will develop that dispatches an annual convoy to Mexico (the *flota*) and another to Panama for Peru (the *galeones*).

1527   Pánfilo de Narváez leads an expedition of 400 men and 40 horses into northwestern Florida. Only 4 men will survive, including Alvar Núñez Cabeza de Vaca, who will later record his eight-year ordeal as a captive and his remarkable overland journey from East Texas (near modern-day Galveston) to New Spain (Mexico).

1528   The second audiencia (high court) in the Americas is established in Mexico City.

1529   A special ceremonial bullfight is celebrated in Mexico City to mark the anniversary of Hernando Cortés's conquest of Tenochtitlan (Mexico City) eight years earlier.

         The Caribbean city of Santa Marta (Colombia) is founded.

         Francisco Pizarro obtains royal authorization to launch an expedition of exploration and conquest in Peru.

1531   Francisco Pizarro founds the city of San Miguel de Piura on the northern coast of Peru, commencing the invasion of Inca territory.

1532   On November 16, a band of Spanish adventurers under the command of Francisco Pizarro capture the Inca ruler Atahualpa and hold him hostage in the city of Cajamarca. After collecting a rich ransom for the Inca's release, Pizarro orders that Atahualpa be executed.

1533   The Caribbean city of Cartagena de Indias (Colombia) is founded.

1534   Jauja, the first capital of Spanish Peru, is formally founded; the capital is then moved to Lima, the City of Kings.

         Sebastián de Benalcázar founds the city of San Francisco de Quito, amid the smoldering ruins of the conquered Inca city.

1535   The legendary Inca general Rumiñahui is captured and executed.

         Sebastián de Benalcázar establishes the port city of Guayaquil.

         The first viceroyalty in the Americas is established in New Spain (Mexico).

         Diego de Almagro, a veteran of the conquest of Peru and a former partner of Francisco Pizarro, organizes his own expedition to move south to conquer Chile. Not finding any gold, a disgruntled Almagro and his men will return to Cuzco in 1537.

         Vasco de Quiroga, the Franciscan bishop of Michoacán, argues that because the Indians failed to establish a civil society (as defined by Europeans), the lands of the New World were unoccupied and available to peoples capable of creating such a society.

         Gonzalo Fernández de Oviedo y Valdés, King Charles I's official chronicler of the Indies, publishes his *Historia General y Natural de las Indias*.

1536   Manco Inca assembles an army of 100,000 and lays siege to the city of Cuzco. In early 1537, with his forces dwindling, Manco will withdraw northward to Vilcabamba; the effort to drive the Spaniards out of Peru will have failed.

Spanish conquistador Gonzalo Jiménez de Quesada leads an expedition into Colombia's eastern highlands, leading to the conquest of the Muisca Indians and the establishment of the new Kingdom of Granada.

In Mexico City, the Franciscans open a college for Indian students called Santa Cruz of Tlatelolco; there, young Indian nobles study Spanish, Latin, rhetoric, logic, theology, music, and medicine.

With the papal bull *Cum ad nil magis,* the Portuguese Inquisition is formally established to police the behavior and the beliefs of the subjects of the Portuguese Crown.

1537   Pope Paul III, in *Sublimis Deus,* confirms the basic humanity of the Indians, meaning that they are capable of becoming Christians; he forbids their enslavement and the seizure of their lands or property.

The port of Guayaquil is formally founded.

1538   Christopher Columbus's son Fernando publishes his *Historia del Almirante,* a biography of his father.

The Audiencia (High Court) of Panama is established.

King Charles I issues a royal decree allowing the foundation of the first brothel in Mexico City.

1539   Hernando de Soto undertakes the first extensive land exploration of La Florida. Three years later, de Soto will fall ill and die on the west bank of the Mississippi River.

The first printing press in the Americas begins operation in Mexico City.

Francisco de Vitoria delivers his *Relectio de Indis* at the University of Salamanca in Spain; in the speech, Vitoria declares

himself against the belief that the pope has the authority to donate the lands in the New World to Spain and Portugal and argues that the Indians are the rightful owners.

1540   Pedro de Valdivia, a friend or relative of Francisco Pizarro, is granted permission to conquer Chile. He sets out with 1,000 Peruvian Indians and roughly 150 Spaniards. In February of the following year, he will found the city of Santiago del Nuevo Extremo.

The Society of Jesus (Jesuit order), bulwark of the Catholic Counter-Reformation, is founded.

1542   The New Laws of 1542 prohibit further *encomiendas* (grants of rights to collect taxes and enjoy the labor of conquered indigenous communities) and order the reversion to the Crown of all encomiendas upon the death of the current *encomendero.* The New Laws also ban the enslavement of Indians. Widespread resistance to the laws will lead to some revisions, restoring the right to pass encomiendas to an heir; nevertheless, the ban on personal service will be preserved.

Bartolomé de Las Casas's influential and highly controversial text, the *Brevísima Relación de la Destrucción de las Indias* (Very Brief Account of the Destruction of the Indies) is first published.

Spanish explorer Juan Rodríguez Cabrillo becomes the first Spaniard to explore the territory that will later become California.

Viceroy Don Antonio de Mendoza leads a force of 500 Spaniards and 50,000 Indian allies to defeat the Mixtón Indians, ending the 1541–1542 Mixtón War.

Hernando Pérez de Quesada leads an ill-fated expedition in search of El Dorado.

Francisco de Montejo leads the conquest of the Yucatán Peninsula.

1543   The Consulado (Merchant Guild) of Seville is established to help organize fleets to the New World and supervise the loading and unloading of vessels.

1544   The viceroyalty of Peru is established; the first viceroy, Blasco Núñez Vela, arrives with orders to enforce the New Laws of 1542. Two years later, when Núñez Vela attempts to impose his authority by force, Gonzalo Pizarro will have the viceroy captured and executed.

1545   Pope Paul III convokes a general council of the Catholic Church to respond to the challenges of the Protestant Reformation and initiate reforms within the Church. The council meets in the northern Italian city of Trent, and in 1563 the Council of Trent will promulgate its decrees, which will profoundly influence Catholicism in Iberia and the Americas.

The rich silver mines of *Potosí* are discovered, sparking a boom in silver mining in the viceroyalty of Peru.

1547   Santo Domingo becomes the metropolitan see of the Indies.

1548   Silver is discovered in Zacatecas, Mexico.

1549   The Portuguese Crown appoints Tomé de Sousa as Brazil's first governor-general.

The first missionaries arrive in Brazil, as well as Brazil's first paid troops, known as the *tropas de primeira linha.*

The city of La Paz is founded in present-day Bolivia (originally named Nuestra Señora de la Paz).

1550   The Audiencia (High Court) of Santa Fe is established, with jurisdiction over most of present-day Colombia and Venezuela.

Silver mining begins at Guanajuato, Mexico.

1551   Brazil's first diocese, centered in Salvador, is established.

The University of San Marcos in Lima, Peru, is founded.

1552   Francisco López de Gómara's *Historia general de las Indias* is published in Zaragoza, Spain.

Aztec healer Martín de la Cruz produces his *Codex Badianus,* an illustrated manuscript that describes indigenous botanical medicine; the work is translated into Latin by his collaborator, Juan Badiano.

The University of La Plata is founded in Sucre, in modern Bolivia.

1553   Mexico's Royal and Pontifical University opens, with a curriculum based on that of the University of Salamanca.

The Hospital Real de Naturales (Royal Indian Hospital) is founded in Mexico City.

The Jesuit Bernabé Cobo writes his *Historia del nuevo mundo;* however, the work will not be published until 1890–1895.

1554   Pedro de Cieza de León's *Descubrimiento y conquista del Perú* (Discovery and Conquest of Peru) is published.

Peruvian rebel Francisco Hernández Girón is captured and executed by viceregal forces.

1555   Bartolomé de Medina invents a method of refining silver ores through amalgamation, a process that makes it possible to refine lower-grade ores. The new technology spreads quickly throughout Spanish America.

1556   King Charles I (Holy Roman Emperor Charles V) abdicates the Spanish throne in favor of his son, Philip II.

The Augustinians found the University of San Fulgencio in Quito.

1558   The Jesuit order founds its first university in the Americas, the Universidad de Santiago de La Paz in Santo Domingo.

1559   A royal decree of June 12 creates the Audiencia (High Court) of Charcas (also known as Upper Peru), with jurisdiction over much of the territory of modern Bolivia.

1561   Under the reign of King Philip II, Madrid is made into the imperial capital city.

1562   The discovery of idolatrous practices in Yucatán sparks a violent response from the resident Franciscans at Maní, who interrogate more than 4,000 Mayas, 158 of whom die from the torture.

1563   The Audiencia (High Court) of Quito is created.

1564   Spaniards begin to mine the rich mercury deposits at Huancavelica, Peru.

1565   Under the command of Pedro Menéndez de Avilés, the Spanish establish a small colony at Saint Augustine, Florida.

1566   Florida's first Jesuit missionaries arrive.

1567   The city of Rio de Janeiro is founded.

1568   On his third voyage to the New World, English naval commander John Hawkins anchors in the Mexican port of Veracruz. Attacked by Spanish forces, Hawkins flees, leaving behind 114 of his English and Irish crew. Within the next three years, many of these exiles will be tried as heretics by the Mexican Inquisition. At least three will be burned at the stake; the others will convert to Catholicism.

1569   The Holy Office of the Inquisition is established in Mexico City and in Lima.

Francisco de Toledo begins his tenure as Peru's fifth viceroy. Between 1569 and 1581, Toledo will work to reorganize and revive the colony.

1570   The Audiencia (High Court) of Guatemala, extending from Chiapas to Costa Rica, is established.

1572   A group of escaped slaves (*cimarrones*) in Panama help Francis Drake, at this time an English privateer, capture a treasure in Spanish silver.

Túpac Amaru, the ruler of the neo-Inca state established at Vilcabamba, is captured and executed.

1574   Spanish King Philip II codifies the Crown's right to patronage in the Ordinances of the Royal Patronage. The decree reserves for the king the right to appoint bishops, canons, and priests.

1575   At the age of twenty-seven, the Italian painter and Jesuit Bernardo Bitti arrives in Peru. Bitti will establish himself as one of the pioneers of painting in Peru, Ecuador, and Bolivia.

1576   Juan de Betanzos completes his *Suma y narración de los Incas,* a meticulous history of the Inca elite. Betanzos is married to an Inca princess, and possesses a rich knowledge of the Quechua language.

1577   Sir Francis Drake sets sail on his legendary voyage of piracy and discovery through the Straits of Magellan, along the Pacific coast of South America, and north to Drake's Bay, beyond present-day San Francisco.

1578   Luis de Camões pens his monumental narrative of the Lusitanian (Portuguese) nation, *Os Lusíades.*

1580   Following the death of Cardinal-King Henrique, the most powerful claimant to the Portuguese throne is Spain's Philip II. For the next sixty years, the Iberian Peninsula will be united politically under Habsburg rule.

The city of Buenos Aires is founded (named the Ciudad de la Santísima Trinidad y Puerto de Santa María de los Buenos Ayres).

The Dominicans found the Universidad Tomista de Santafé in Bogotá (in modern Colombia).

1582   The Jesuits found the College of San Gregorio in Mexico City to educate the sons of the indigenous elite.

Philip II makes the town of San Juan, Puerto Rico, a presidio, giving it front-line military status within the Spanish defenses.

1585   The church hierarchy declares that Indians cannot be ordained priests because they are unsuitable for the religious life. The ban will continue until the eighteenth century.

1587   Thomas Cavendish, English navigator, manages to seize a so-called Manila Galleon off the coast of Mexico.

1590   The Jesuit José de Acosta writes his *Historia natural y moral de las Indias.*

1595   The Spanish Crown grants the first true *asiento,* a formal contract for a monopoly on the introduction of slaves into Spanish America. The initial nine-year grant is awarded to Pedro Gomes Reynal.

King Philip II issues a decree disallowing the cultivation of new vineyards in the Americas; however, the decree proves ineffective.

Walter Raleigh, favorite of Queen Elizabeth, poet, historian, and navigator, attacks and plunders Trinidad in his search for El Dorado, the legendary City of Gold.

1596   King Philip II decrees that Indians shall not be forced to learn Spanish and that no parish priests can be appointed unless they speak the language of their parishioners.

1598   Philip III becomes king of Spain.

Araucanian Indians in southern Chile revolt, taking scores of Spanish women and children hostage, and displaying the severed head of Spanish governor Martín García Oñez de Loyola.

1599   Diego de Ocaña, a friar from the monastery of Guadalupe in Extremadura, Spain, begins his lengthy journey through Spain and Spanish America. He later publishes his *Un viaje fascinante por la América Hispana del siglo XVII* (A Fascinating Journey through Seventeenth-Century Spanish America).

1601   Bento Teixeira, who flees across the Atlantic to escape the Inquisition, writes *Prosopéia.*

1603   The *Ordenações filipinas* establish clear procedures that govern marriage and inheritance in Brazil.

1607   The Jesuits begin to establish missions in the Río de la Plata region.

1608   A record 200 ships depart from Seville to the New World, marking a high point during Spanish colonial rule.

1609   The masterful *Comentarios reales de los Incas* (Royal Commentaries of the Incas), by the mestizo El Inca Garcilaso de la Vega, is published.

Before a large crowd gathered in Lima's main square, Spanish priest Francisco de Ávila burns a collection of confiscated native gods and ancestral mummies; he also publicly whips the Andean religious teacher Hernando Paucar. The event marks the beginning of a series of visitations near Lima, aimed at extirpating Indian idolatry.

Following the Basque witch persecutions, the Spanish Inquisition's supreme council (the Suprema) concludes that witchcraft is a superstition and not a demonic pact and that claims to the contrary should be treated with skepticism and restraint.

1610   The Holy Office of the Inquisition is established in Cartagena de Indias.

1616   Still searching for El Dorado, Sir Walter Raleigh angers King James I by attacking a Spanish settlement in present-day Guyana.

1618 The Thirty Years' War begins.

1621 The Jesuit Pablo José Arriaga completes his *Extirpación de la idolatría en el Perú* (The Extirpation of Idolatry in Peru), a text critical to the study of religion in the Andes.

Philip IV becomes king of Spain.

The Jesuit order establishes six separate institutions: La Javeriana in Bogotá (Colombia), Córdoba in Córdoba (Argentina), San Francisco Xavier de Carcas in Sucre (Bolivia), San Miguel in Santiago (Chile), San Gregorio Magno in Quito (Peru), and San Ignacio de Loyola in Cuzco (Peru).

1623 Aleixo de Abreu writes his *Tratado de las siete enfermedades* (Treatise of the Seven Diseases), making him one of the first authors of a work on tropical medicine.

1626 Gonzalo Correas's *Arte grande de la lengua española castellana* is published.

1628 Dutch privateer Piet Heyn captures the entire Spanish treasure fleet in Matanzas Bay, Cuba.

1631 In an effort to avoid further silver diversion away from the Atlantic system, the Crown bans all trade between New Spain (Mexico) and Peru.

1632 Bernal Díaz del Castillo's rich account of his experiences during the conquest of Mexico, titled the *Historia verdadera de la conquista de Nueva España* (The True History of the Conquest of New Spain), is published.

1638 Juan Rodríguez Freile's *El carnero* is published; the account chronicles the conquest of Colombia, as well as telling lurid fictional tales of prostitutes, witches, and murderers.

1640 Under the new Bragança dynasty, Portugal regains its independence from Habsburg Spain.

1648 The Peace of Westphalia brings the Thirty Years' War to an end, although Spain's struggles against France continue until the 1659 Peace of the Pyrenees, by which time Spain's economic decline is clear.

A Creole (that is, of European descent born in Spanish America) priest by the name of Miguel Sánchez publishes the first written narrative of the Virgin of Guadalupe apparition story; a Nahuatl version by another Creole priest, Luis Laso de la Vega, will be published the following year.

1652 In Brazil, a general law prohibits the felling of the *madeiras de lei* (timbers under the law), which are prized for their utility in shipbuilding, construction, and furniture.

1665 Charles II becomes king of Spain, the final Habsburg monarch to rule Spain before the Bourbon accession in the early eighteenth century.

1670 The Treaty of Madrid grants England the title to Jamaica.

1671 Henry Morgan sacks Panama City.

1672 In Saint Augustine, Florida, the construction of the stone fortress, the Castillo de San Marcos, begins.

1676 The University of San Carlos in Guatemala is founded.

1679 The port city of Cádiz is authorized to conduct limited trading operations with the New World.

1680 King Charles II promulgates the *Compilation of the Laws of the Indies*.

The Pueblo revolt gives independence to New Mexico's Pueblo Indians; twelve years later Diego de Vásquez will return to reassert Spanish authority.

The Universidad San Cristóbal de Huamanga, in Ayacucho, Peru, is founded.

1690   England claims the first recorded landing on the uninhabited Falkland Islands off the coast of Argentina.

Infortunios de Alonso Ramírez, by Carlos de Sigüenza y Góngara, is published.

1694   João Ferreira da Rosa of Brazil publishes his *Tratado único da constituição pestilental de Pernambuco* (Lone Treatise on the Pestilential State in Pernambuco), which is the first book to describe yellow fever in detail.

1695   The world's greatest gold rush prior to 1849 begins when gold is discovered in the interior highlands north of Rio de Janeiro.

1696   A second Pueblo revolt proves unsuccessful.

1697   The Jesuits establish the first chain of missions in Baja California.

In Guatemala's Petén region, the last Maya kingdom, the Itzás, surrenders to the Spanish.

1700   The death of Charles II ends the Habsburg dynasty in Spain; Philip V becomes the designated heir, placing Spain under the control of the French Bourbons.

1702   Fearing a Franco-Spanish dynastic alliance that would reverse the English commercial inroads into Spanish America and threaten the English colonies of North America, King William III brings England into the War of the Spanish Succession, known in North America as Queen Anne's War.

1703   The Methuen Treaty between Britain and Portugal grants commercial preference to British merchants in Brazil. In return, England guarantees a market for Portuguese wine.

1709   A large basilica in honor of the Virgin of Guadalupe is built in Mexico City.

1712   The Tzetzel Revolt begins in the Chiapas village of Cancuc.

1713   The Treaty of Utrecht, ending the War of the Spanish Succession, grants to Britain the *asiento,* the monopoly on importing slaves from Africa to the Spanish possessions in the Americas.

The Royal Academy of the Spanish Language is founded to guard and preserve the language.

1714   The first coffee plantation is established in Suriname. Production quickly spreads west to Venezuela and then south to Brazil.

1716   Gold from Brazil supports the foundation in Portugal of a music school and the expansion of the royal chapel to a patriarchal chapel, which attracts numerous foreign musicians, including Domenico Scarlatti.

1717   The House of Trade (Casa de Contratación) is transferred from Seville to Cádiz.

The Crown monopolizes tobacco distribution in Cuba, introducing the Real Factoría de Tabacos (Royal Tobacco Company).

1724   A convent for noble indigenous women is founded in Mexico City.

1728   The Caracas Company (known in Spanish as the Real Compañía Guipozcoa de Caracas) is granted exclusive trade rights over commerce between Spain and Venezuela, an agreement that will last until 1780.

1739   The Viceroyalty of New Granada is established.

During the War of Jenkins' Ear (1739–1742), the British attack Spanish shipping and ports in the Caribbean; together with their Indian allies, the British launch assaults on Spanish forts in Florida.

1744   The Capuchins seek intervention from the Spanish Crown to keep the Jesuits out of their territory on the Meta River (Colombia).

1748   Antonio de Ulloa and Jorge Juan publish their five-volume work entitled *Relación histórica del viage a la América Meridional* (literally, Historical Account of a Voyage to South America, published in English in 1758 as *A Voyage to South America*).

1749   In an effort to invigorate and modernize its administration, Spain's Bourbon monarchs introduce the intendancy system in the New World.

1750   Through the Treaty of Madrid, Spain buys back the *asiento*—the Atlantic slave-trading monopoly—from Britain for £100,000. The terms of the treaty also cede some of the Jesuit mission territory to Portugal.

1751   French scientist Charles La Condamine's *Journal d'un voyage* (Journal of a Voyage) describes his investigations in Quito as well as his subsequent exploration of the Amazon.

1755   Brazil's powerful royal minister Sebastião José de Carvalho e Melo (titled the Marquis of Pombal) declares the Indians of Brazil free of Jesuit authority.

1756   The Seven Years' War, known in North America as the French and Indian War, begins.

1757   The missionary Miguel Vanegas writes his *Noticia de la California,* a hybrid history and compilation of travelogues.

1759   Portuguese king Dom João I (in English, John I) expels the Jesuits from Portugal and Brazil and seizes their substantial holdings.

1761   Spain enters the Seven Years' War and within a year suffers major defeats at the hands of the British in Havana and Manila.

1762   A British invasion force arrives at Cojímar (fifteen miles east of Havana, Cuba) to challenge Spanish dominion; a ten-month British occupation of Havana follows. Britain also seizes the Spanish stronghold of Manila in the Philippines.

1763   The Treaty of Paris among France, Britain, and Spain ends the Seven Years' War. France cedes to Britain all its territory east of the Mississippi River. Britain returns the key islands of the French West Indies but gains important Windward Islands such as Grenada and Dominica. Spain cedes Florida to Britain in order to secure the return of Havana. Britain is required to protect the Catholic institutions of the territories it acquires.

La Cabaña, the largest fortress built in the Americas, is constructed in Havana, based on the designs of the French engineer Sebastien Le Prestre, Seigneur de Vauban.

Brazil's capital is moved from Salvador to Rio de Janeiro.

1766   The first (temporary) British settlement is established on the Falkland Islands.

In Madrid, the Hat and Cloak Riots directly precipitate the expulsion of the Jesuits the following year.

1767   In an attempt to undermine their political and economic power, the Spanish Crown expels the Jesuits from Spanish America; Jesuit lands and wealth are confiscated by the Crown.

1768   New Spain's viceroy José de Gálvez seizes two Jesuit-built ships and confiscates the Jesuit shipyard at San Blas, Mexico, where he builds vessels to explore Alta California.

1769   Following reports of increased Russian activity in Alaska and James Cook's expedition to Polynesia, New Spain's viceroy José de Gálvez organizes an expedition to colonize California.

Uruguayan poet José Basílio da Gama writes his epic poem *O Uruguai.*

1773   In his July papal brief, *Dominus Redemptor,* Clement XIV suppresses the Jesuit order in all of Christendom; many ex-Jesuits take refuge in Prussia and Russia.

1774   Colonial officials erect a poorhouse in Mexico City, aimed at containing and educating the poor and transforming them into productive members of society.

1775   The Monte de Piedad, a state-sponsored pawnshop, opens in Mexico City, providing low-interest loans.

1776   The Viceroyalty of the Río de la Plata is established, assuming jurisdiction over the districts of Tucumán, Paraguay, Buenos Aires, and Cuyo, as well as the territory that makes up most of modern Bolivia.

1778   The Decree of Free Trade abolishes the Spanish fleet system (the *flota*), opening trade to several ports in Spain and Spanish America.

The *Real pragmática de matrimonios,* issued by the Spanish Crown, requires prospective marriage partners to obtain parental consent, although parental decisions could be challenged in court.

1780   José Gabriel Condorcanqui, a wealthy *kuraca,* or chief, from the central Andes, leads a massive Indian uprising in Peru. Taking the name of Túpac Amaru, the ruler of the neo-Inca state established at Vilcabamba in the sixteenth century, Condorcanqui organizes a massive army that threatens Spanish presence in the Andes.

1781   The Comunero Revolt in New Granada (Colombia) is indicative of the frustrations felt by many over the fiscal reforms of Spain's Bourbon monarchs. More than 20,000 rebels protest increases in local taxes.

1782   New Granada's archbishop-viceroy Antonio Caballero y Góngora agrees to sponsor José Celestino Mutis's proposal for a natural survey in New Granada. Mutis, a Spanish priest, had introduced Copernican astronomy at the Colegio del Rosario in Santa Fe (Colombia), sparking decades of debate with adherents of the Ptolemaic cosmovision.

1783   The Treaty of Paris recognizes the independence of the United States and establishes the borders of the new republic with the British territories to the north, the French to the west, and the Spanish to the south. Spain regains Florida.

1784   Following the Túpac Amaru revolt, the *repartimiento de comercio* (forced distribution of goods) is abolished, although it reappears illegally in some provinces.

1785   Venezuelan revolutionary Francisco de Miranda establishes a base in London, where much of the planning for the eventual independence of Latin America is carried out.

The Caracas Company is liquidated, with investors' remaining stock being transferred to the Philippine Company.

Colonial officials erect a poorhouse in Quito, aimed at containing and educating the poor and transforming them into productive members of society.

1786   Britain acquires logging rights from Spain in what becomes British Honduras (now Belize).

1787   In an effort to gain a stronger foothold in Honduras, Spain recruits more than 1,200 settlers from Asturias, Galicia, and the Canary Islands to settle the northern Honduran coast; nearly one-fourth die en route to their new homes.

Native Totonacs of Papantla Veracruz launch a revolt against local Spaniards; the district magistrate is badly injured, and 287 Spanish troops are called in to restore order.

1790   The House of Trade (Casa de Contratación) is abolished as part of the liberalization of intra-imperial trade.

1791	The Haitian Revolution begins, eventually leading to the world's first successful slave revolt and the creation of the first independent state in Latin America.
1792	Portuguese-born poet Tomás Antonio Gonzaga writes his pastoral love poem, *Marília de Dirceu.*
1795	The Treaty of Bâle forces Spain to withdraw from Sainte-Domingue and Santo Domingo; Spanish authorities evacuate more than 700 black officers to other areas of the empire that require soldiers and settlers.
1796	In Britain's final serious attempt to take Puerto Rico from Spain, Admiral Sir Henry Harvey, General Ralph Abercromby, and 7,000 regulars are stopped by the Creole militia at San Juan. The British forces withdraw after thirteen days.
	A British naval force captures Trinidad, belonging to the Audiencia of Venezuela.
1802	Under the terms of the Peace of Amiens, Spain cedes Trinidad to Great Britain.
1806	An unauthorized British force of nearly 2,000 occupies Buenos Aires, Argentina, in a bid to block both French designs and Spanish authority in Latin America; the invasion stirs the patriotism of the Creole population of Buenos Aires.
	A campaign by Creole militia under Santiago de Liniers to break the occupation of Buenos Aires ends with a British surrender.
1807	After having captured Montevideo, Uruguay, British forces again attack Buenos Aires. Again, a Creole counterattack forces a British retreat and capitulation.
	British diplomats help to persuade the Portuguese royal family to flee a French invasion force and seek exile in Brazil. The Royal Navy escorts the Portuguese court from Lisbon to Brazil, and Brazil becomes the official center of the Portuguese empire.

	The Act for the Abolition of the Slave Trade is passed by Parliament, outlawing the slave trade among British subjects throughout the British Empire.
1808	The French emperor Napoleon invades Spain and seizes the Spanish Crown, holding King Charles IV and his son Ferdinand VII in forced exile in France. Napoleon installs his brother Joseph on the Spanish throne; the invasion provokes a constitutional crisis in the Spanish Empire.
	The so-called Peninsular War (1808–1814) begins.
	Brazilian ports are fully opened to foreign trade.
1809	Quito becomes the first Spanish American city to declare autonomy, the city's municipal government proposing to govern itself in the name of Ferdinand VII until the Spanish monarch returns to the throne; however, Royalist forces fight back, and the autonomists will be defeated by the end of 1812.
1810	Simón Bolívar, the Latin American revolutionary leader, bases himself in London.
	The Cortes (Parliament) of Cádiz is established in an effort to resist the French occupation of Spain, and to govern in the king's absence.
	Miguel Hidalgo y Costilla's *Grito de Dolores* (Cry from Dolores) begins the armed struggle for Mexican independence.
1811	Paraguay gains its independence.
	In Venezuela, an elected congress declares independence, and in December of the same year produces a constitution.
	Miguel Hidalgo y Costilla is captured by the Spanish royal army and executed by firing squad; Hidalgo will later be seen as one of the great heroes of the independence period.

1812   The Cortes of Cádiz adopts Spain's first written constitution, which introduces constitutional governance to Spain and Spanish America.

In Cuba, a group of slaves and free people of color launch a general uprising, known as the Aponte Rebellion; fourteen of the main conspirators are executed, and sixty-three followers are banished to Saint Augustine, Florida.

1814   Napoleon's forces are defeated and driven from Spain; King Ferdinand VII returns from exile and attempts to restore absolute monarchy. He dissolves the Cortes of Cádiz, abrogates the constitution of 1812, and restores the Council of the Indies, which the Cortes of Cádiz had abolished in 1812.

France cedes Saint Lucia, Tobago, and Dominica to Britain at the close of the Napoleonic Wars.

In Bahia, Brazil, 250 slaves rise up and attack the city of Salvador.

Pope Pius VII reinstates the Jesuit order.

1815   A royal charter elevates Brazil to the status of kingdom within a new United Kingdom of Portugal, Brazil, and the Algarve region.

1816   Haiti's president Alexandre Pétion provides supplies and finances to Simón Bolívar, enabling the independence leader to launch another campaign that year.

1817   Chile's ports are opened following the overthrow of Spanish rule, in which the Royal Navy under Admiral Thomas Cochrane has participated. Cochrane will eventually be drummed out of the Royal Navy and take the command of the Chilean navy.

1818   In the battle of Maipú in April, Chilean forces under Bernardo O'Higgins and José de San Martín inflict a devastating blow on Spanish troops; and although Spanish resistance will continue for several years, the battle virtually ensures Chile's political independence from Spain.

1819   Spain signs the Adams-Onís Treaty, which transfers ownership of Florida to the United States.

In the aftermath of the decisive battle of Boyacá (Colombia), the Congress of Angostura announces the creation of Gran Colombia, a political union among modern-day Colombia, Ecuador, Panama, and Venezuela.

1820   Liberals in Spain revolt, demanding that the king restore the 1812 constitution; the unrest prevents Spain from sending more reinforcements to the Americas to combat the independence movements.

Mexico and Peru both declare the abolition of their Inquisitions.

1821   Portugal's Inquisition is abolished.

Mexico achieves its independence from Spain.

Central America declares its independence from Spain.

The Inquisition at Cartagena de Indias ceases to exist.

Antonio José de Sucre commands the forces that defeat the Spanish army on the slopes of the Pichincha Volcano above Quito, thus securing Ecuador's independence from Spain.

Occupying Lima, on July 28 José de San Martín declares Peru independent; San Martín emancipates all children born of slaves, abolishes Indian tribute and *mita* (a draft system of forced labor), expels all Spaniards, and confiscates their property; however, military conflict will continue until 1826.

1822   Brazil wins independence from Portugal, assisted by British mercenaries and Royal Navy forces under Admiral Lord Thomas Cochrane. Pedro I, the son of the Portuguese king, becomes head of Brazil's constitutional monarchy.

1823   U.S. president James Monroe enunciates the Monroe Doctrine in a message to Congress, declaring that the United States will not interfere in the affairs of Europe, nor will it seek to overturn existing European colonies in the Americas, but it will vigorously resist any further European incursions into the Western Hemisphere.

An assembly representing Guatemala, Honduras, El Salvador, Nicaragua, and Costa Rica declares independence for the isthmus under the banner of the United Provinces of Central America.

1824   After the battle of Ayacucho, Peru achieves its independence from Spain.

Following the U.S. recognition of key Spanish American states in 1822, British foreign secretary George Canning renounces the 1808 policy of propping up Spain and recognizes the independent states in Spanish America, thus delivering the coup de grâce to Spain's empire.

With the loss of most of its prized colonies, Spain's empire in the Americas is reduced to Cuba and Puerto Rico.

1825   Upper Peru (Bolivia) becomes the final region in mainland Spanish America to gain its independence from Spain.

1827   Spaniards are expelled from Mexico.

1829   Spain attempts to recapture Mexico with 3,000 troops; however, they are defeated by Mexican general Antonio López de Santa Ana.

1830   Uruguay gains its independence.

Gran Colombia, the political union of Ecuador, Colombia, Panama, and Venezuela, officially dissolves because of regional differences.

1833   The American Anti-Slavery Society is founded on the heels of the New England Anti-Slavery Society. Both are modeled on the British Anti-Slavery Society (founded 1823), with which common links are established.

Mexico's liberal reformers order the closure of Mexico's Franciscan missions, which they perceive as colonial anachronisms.

Britain establishes a naval command post on the Islas Malvinas (Falkland Islands), expelling the Spanish-speaking inhabitants and preventing further migration from the mainland.

1834   The Council of the Indies is dissolved.

1836   Diplomatic relations between Spain and Mexico are restored.

Texas achieves its independence from Mexico.

1838   The emancipation of African slaves in British Guiana is completed.

The first indentured servants from India arrive on Trinidad.

1840   Ecuador and Spain sign a treaty of peace and friendship in Madrid. The treaty officially recognizes Ecuador's independence and paves the way for closer economic ties between the two countries.

1841   Jesuits are permitted to return to Brazil.

1843   Mexico signs its first treaty with Portugal.

1844   Slavery is abolished in Santo Domingo.

1847   The prolonged Maya peasant rebellion, known as the Caste War, erupts in Yucatán.

The United Provinces of Central America, a political union among Guatemala, El Salvador, Nicaragua, Honduras, and Costa Rica, officially dissolves after more than two decades in existence.

1848   Paraguay's government closes the surviving ex-Jesuit missions in the Río de la Plata region and confiscates remaining assets.

1850   Brazil officially outlaws the importation of slaves. Slavery itself, however, will continue in Brazil until 1888.

Slavery is legally abolished in Peru.

1853   Portugal recognizes Paraguay's independence.

1857   Brazilian poet and novelist José de Alencar writes the novel *O Guarani.*

1864   The five-year War of the Triple Alliance (Paraguayan War) breaks out between Paraguay and the combined forces of Brazil, Argentina, and Uruguay.

1866   Spain officially recognizes Argentina, almost five decades after Argentina declared its independence.

Manuel Araújo writes the epic poem *Colombo,* which extols European expansion in the figure of Columbus.

1867   When Benito Juárez executes Archduke Maximilian of Austria (who had been Napoleon III's choice as Mexican emperor), Spain and Portugal sever diplomatic relations with Mexico.

1868   Cuba's first war for independence begins; known as the Ten Years' War, the movement has been initiated by disgruntled plantation owners, slaves and former slaves, and a new generation of nationalist youths from all social classes.

1870   Spain passes the Moret Law, which initiates the gradual emancipation of Cuba's 370,000 slaves.

Brazilian poet and novelist José de Alencar celebrates the horseman as a national hero in his *O gaúcho.*

1871   Spain renews diplomatic ties with Mexico (severed in 1867).

1872   The epic poem by José Hernández, *Martín Fierro,* identifies the gaucho as the soul of Argentine civilization, sparking a heated debate with turn-of-the-century Spanish intellectuals such as Miguel de Unamuno.

1878   Cuba's Ten Years' War comes to an end with the signing of the Treaty of Zanjón, which promises Cubans greater representation in Madrid; the treaty also guarantees freedom to slaves who fought for the rebels, and it guarantees safe passage to rebel leaders.

Mexico's labor federation, the Gran Círculo de Obreros, is founded, modeled after Spain's Confederación Nacional del Trabajo (National Confederation of Labor, or CNT).

1879   The three-year War of the Pacific pits Chile against Peru and Bolivia.

1880   Spain officially recognizes Paraguay's independence.

1882   The Knights of Columbus, the world's largest organization of Catholic laity, is established; by the end of the twentieth century, the order will have over 1.5 million members.

1884   Portugal restores diplomatic relations with Mexico (broken in 1867) and opens a Mexican consulate in Lisbon.

In Brazil, parliament passes the Saraiva-Cotegipe Law, effectively freeing all slaves over the age of sixty.

1885   The Iberian-American Union (Unión Ibero-Americana) begins to promote trade relations and closer cultural interaction between Spain and Spanish America.

1886   Spain abandons its policy for the gradual emancipation of slaves and abolishes the institution in Cuba.

1888   Brazil abolishes African slavery, making it the last country in the Western Hemisphere to do so.

The Universal Exposition is held in Barcelona, the first time Spain has hosted the world's fair.

1889   Brazil becomes a republic.

1893   To commemorate the four-hundred-year anniversary of Christopher Columbus's first landing in the West Indies, the city of Chicago stages a six-month world's fair, attracting more than 27 million visitors.

1895   Cuba's second war of independence begins, leading to U.S. intervention in the conflict in 1898.

1898   The U.S. battleship *Maine* explodes mysteriously in the harbor of Havana, Cuba. When war erupts between Cuban nationalists and Spain, the United States supports the Cubans and declares war on Spain. The conflict ends in a U.S.-Cuban victory, and Spain is forced to relinquish its sovereignty over the island. Puerto Rico, Guam, and the Philippines are ceded to the United States.

1901   The U.S. government passes the Platt Amendment.

1902   One of the principal works of turn-of-the-century Brazilian literature, Euclides da Cunha's *Os Sertoes,* is published.

1903   With the assistance of the United States, which desires to construct a canal across the isthmus, Panama achieves its independence from Colombia.

1910   Ecuador rejects a Spanish proposal to resolve a territorial dispute with Peru over vast territory in the upper Amazon Basin. Final resolution will not be reached until 1998.

The Mexican Revolution begins after fraudulent elections return Porfirio Díaz to office; between 1910 and 1919, 1,477 foreigners will die in the conflict, 209 of whom are Spaniards.

1913   In Chile, a group of artists labeled the Generation of Thirteen shock the academy with an exhibition of colorful, impressionistic paintings influenced by Spanish professor Fernando Álvarez de Sotomayor.

1914   Following the outbreak of World War I, U.S. president Woodrow Wilson offers to mediate among Britain, Germany,

and other belligerent powers. Spain maintains a position of strict neutrality.

The Panama Canal opens, just one week after the start of World War I.

1917   Portugal enters World War I on the side of the Allies.

Following the Russian Revolution, pro-Soviet dissidents from the Argentine Socialist Party form the International Socialist Party.

Arthur Zimmermann, Germany's foreign secretary, promises to return to Mexico all lands lost to the United States in the nineteenth century if Mexico offers assistance to the Germans. Mexican president Venustiano Carranza declines, and Mexico remains neutral.

Madrid threatens to withdraw its recognition of Mexico in protest of Mexico's 1917 constitution, which secularizes education and marriage, bans public religious worship, and imposes strict controls on the clergy. Portugal actually cuts diplomatic ties with Mexico (which will not be restored until 1929).

1918   The armistice ending World War I is signed.

With the Argentine University Reform movement, Latin American students rebel against the "colonial" and "medieval" institutions they have inherited from Spain.

1921   The Partido Comunista de España (Communist Party of Spain, or PCE) is founded.

1928   Spanish cleric Josémaría Escrivá de Balaguer founds Opus Dei; the transnational lay Catholic organization expands rapidly, with more than 30,000 members in Latin America and 80,000 members worldwide.

1930   The first World Cup is hosted by Uruguay in Montevideo, applying the universalized rules of England's Football Association.

1932   Women earn the right to vote in Brazil.

1936   The Spanish Civil War erupts when a contingent of Spanish officers (including Francisco Franco) move to overthrow Spain's Popular Front government.

The outbreak of the Spanish Civil War rekindles relations between Latin American and Spanish artists, creating an Ibero-American surrealist community that bridges the Atlantic.

In Paraguay, pro-Franco sentiment in the Catholic Church, the military, and nationalist circles sparks a generation-long admiration between Franco and Paraguay, perhaps best articulated in the long dictatorship of Alfredo Stroessner (1954–1989).

Mexican president Lázaro Cárdenas offers military aid to the Loyalist government in Spain.

1939   In March, Francisco Franco and his Nationalist Army defeat the Popular Front, thus ending the Spanish Civil War. Following the war, thousands of Republicans make their way across the Atlantic; approximately 20,000 Spaniards move to Mexico.

1940   Formal diplomatic ties between Mexico and Spain are broken.

1941   Japanese forces attack the U.S. Pacific Fleet at anchor in Pearl Harbor, Hawaii.

The United States declares war on Japan; the Axis powers declare war on the United States.

1942   Japan occupies East Timor, a Portuguese colony, which influences Portugal's gradual entry into World War II.

A German submarine torpedoes and sinks a Mexican tanker (the *Potrero de Llano*) in the Caribbean; ten days later, the Germans torpedo another Mexican tanker (the *Faja de Oro*). Mexico declares war on Germany.

Brazil decides to lend support to the United States; Argentina remains neutral.

1943   Portuguese dictator António Sálazar opens military bases on the Azores Islands for Allied use.

1944   Under the terms of the Portuguese-American agreement signed on November 28, the United States accepts Portugal's participation in Pacific operations and in the restoration of East Timor to Portuguese control. In return, Portugal authorizes the United States to construct and use an air base on the island of Santa Maria. The agreement marks a significant shift in Portuguese foreign policy and signals a new alliance with the United States.

1945   Mexico hosts José Giral's Spanish government-in-exile, and works to isolate Francisco Franco diplomatically; Mexico successfully sponsors a United Nations resolution to have member nations withdraw their ambassadors from Madrid until Spain returns to democracy.

1948   The Organization of American States is founded.

The UN Economic Commission for Latin America is founded.

1949   The North Atlantic Treaty Organization (NATO) is established in Washington. Article 5 of the founding treaty declares that an attack against any NATO member will be considered an attack against all the countries in the Alliance. Portugal is among the founding member states.

Eva Duarte (Evita) of Argentina visits Spain and offers Francisco Franco financial support to purchase Argentine food.

Spanish exiles in Mexico found El Ateneo Español de México.

1955   Spain is incorporated into the United Nations.

1961   On January 22, opponents of Portugal's Salazar regime hijack a Portuguese cruise liner, the *Santa Maria,* off the Venezuelan coast. The dissidents surrender to Brazilian officials thirteen days later.

1962   British Guiana becomes the independent nation of Guyana.

The Cuban Missile Crisis further divides Cuba and the United States.

1966   Spain becomes Cuba's closest trading partner after the USSR, allowing Francisco Franco to demonstrate his independence from U.S. policy.

1967   Lisbon becomes the headquarters for NATO's Iberian Atlantic Command (IBERLANT), which is responsible for the territory that stretches from Portugal to the Azores and the Tropic of Cancer.

André Gunder Frank, a German-born, University of Chicago–trained economist, publishes *Capitalism and Underdevelopment in Latin America.* Frank's book becomes the most widely read and influential treatise on dependency theory.

1968   The term "Liberation Theology" is first used in a talk by Father Gustavo Gutiérrez at a conference of Peruvian Roman Catholic priests in Chimbote, Peru.

1969   John Dos Passos publishes *The Portugal Story: Three Centuries of Exploration and Discovery.*

1973   Right-wing military officers in Chile launch a successful coup against elected president Salvador Allende.

1975   Spanish dictator Francisco Franco dies.

1976   British Commonwealth member Trinidad and Tobago becomes a republic, and replaces Queen Elizabeth with a president as head of state.

Portugal's transition to democracy ends Europe's oldest authoritarian regime; a new democratic constitution is created.

1977   Mexico and Spain restore diplomatic ties, severed more than thirty-five years earlier in 1940.

1980   A group of armed men take over the Spanish embassy in Guatemala City to protest their own government's atrocities. Guatemalan security forces attack the embassy, and thirty-seven people die. As a result, Spain severs its diplomatic ties with Guatemala. Days later, groups take hostages and occupy Spanish embassies in El Salvador and in Peru.

1981   Belize—formerly British Honduras—declares independence.

The state of Antigua and Barbuda declares independence.

1982   With the election of Prime Minister Felipe González, Spain completes its transition to democracy.

Spain joins NATO.

A group of Argentine scrap-metal dealers lands on the British island of South Georgia and hoists the Argentine flag. The Falklands War begins with Argentina's military seizure of the Falkland and South Georgia Islands. Britain declares the 200-mile Falkland Island Maritime Exclusion Zone.

British air attacks cripple and sink the Argentine submarine *Santa Fé.* A Royal Marine assault force captures Argentine positions on South Georgia, and Britain commences air attacks on Argentine positions at Port Stanley and Goose Green.

An Argentine Exocet missile sinks HMS *Sheffield,* while British marines and special forces begin a sustained ground assault on East Falkland Island. The Argentine air force attacks Royal Navy positions.

British forces move from their beachhead for the final assault on Port Stanley. The Falklands War ends with the surrender of Argentine forces at Port Stanley. The war has claimed approximately 650 Argentine and 250 British lives.

1983   The United States and supporting Caribbean forces invade Grenada to overthrow the hard-line Marxist regime of Bernard Coard.

1986   Spain joins the European Economic Community.

1992   The city of Seville hosts Expo 92 to commemorate the quincentenary of Columbus's discovery of the Americas.

1994   In Toronto, the first monument is erected to honor Canadian volunteers who died during the Spanish Civil War (1936–1939).

1995   A fishing dispute between Canada and Spain intensifies when Canadian warships seize Spanish fishing vessels in international waters. The master of one Spanish trawler, the *Estai,* is arrested and charged with using illegal nets.

1996   Pope John Paul II sends a letter to Dominican bishops commemorating the baptism of Juan Mateo (Guaticaba) on September 21, 1496, the first baptism in the Americas.

1997   The National Geographic investigation into the 1898 explosion of the USS *Maine,* which killed 226 U.S. soldiers, is unable to determine if the explosion was the result of an accident or a deliberate act of sabotage.

1998   Former Chilean president Augusto Pinochet is arrested in London, following an extradition request by the Spanish High Court in order to try Pinochet for human rights violations. Senior English law lords hearing Pinochet's appeal fail to reach a decision.

2000   According to the U.S. Bureau of the Census, approximately 35 million Hispanics live in the United States.

2001   Islamist militants fly hijacked airliners into the World Trade Center in New York and the Pentagon in Washington, DC. A fourth hijacked plane crashes in a Pennsylvania field. The Organization of American States (OAS) adopts an Inter-American Convention Against Terrorism.

2002   Pope John Paul II canonizes Juan Diego, the Indian before whom the Virgin Mary is said to have appeared in 1531.

2004   Moroccan terrorists inspired by or linked to al-Qaeda set off ten explosions aboard four commuter trains in Madrid, killing 192 people and wounding more than 1,800.

INTRODUCTORY
ESSAYS

IBERIA AND THE ATLANTIC WORLD

Kris Lane

For hardscrabble Iberians, the vast Atlantic, or "Ocean Sea," as it was called in Columbus's day, offered promise of a better life. There were prospects in fishing and whaling, trade, and colonization. Occasionally, opportunities arose for missionary work or military service. In the midst of Iberia's recovery from the Black Death (1347–1349), the crusade was taken to North Africa by the Portuguese in 1415. In these same years, sweet wines (see WINE) flowed north from Portugal and southwestern Spain to satiate England's growing thirst. Thus, from the beginning of early modern times, Atlantic ventures offered restless Iberians the promise of wealth, fame, and possibly salvation (see ATLANTIC ECONOMY; CATHOLIC CHURCH IN BRAZIL; CATHOLIC CHURCH IN SPANISH AMERICA; CONQUISTADORS; MIGRATION—FROM IBERIA TO THE NEW WORLD).

Spain's Atlantic endeavors mostly followed Portugal's, but there were pockets of seafaring dynamism in the Basque country, Catalonia, and select Mediterranean and Atlantic ports. After many years of exploiting distant cod banks, hunting whales, and exporting Castilian wool to chilly North Atlantic markets, the Basques in particular developed sturdy, maneuverable ships. Such vessels were copied by others, and navigational innovations and pilotage notes were openly exchanged with the Portuguese. With magnetic compasses, charts, and a variety of devices for measuring latitude in widespread use by the early fifteenth century, sailing far from land was no longer the frightening prospect it had once been for Iberian mariners (see NAVIGATION; SHIPS AND SHIPBUILDING). Meanwhile, by the 1450s, Portuguese farmers had settled distant volcanic island chains discovered by intrepid fishermen: the Azores, Madeiras, and Canaries. Only the latter archipelago was inhabited, and dominion over it was ultimately to fall to the Spanish.

It should be remembered that Scandinavians had ventured out across the rough waters of the North Atlantic in late medieval times, but their efforts were stymied by a variety of factors, including the onset of the Little Ice Age. With these efforts in eclipse, Atlantic dynamism had shifted southward to Iberia. A confluence of events and trends here—spanning politics, religion, technology, and demography—meant that, among western Europeans at least, Iberians were uniquely poised and motivated to carry their expansion overseas. Despite some internal disagreements, something akin to national unity was achieved in Portugal after 1400 and in Spain by 1500. Neither crown would invest significant capital in overseas projects directly, but support in the forms of monopoly licensing and royal blessings (titles) proved essential to success. At home and abroad, Iberians in early modern times followed medieval patterns of vassalage. As a result, Spanish and Portuguese colonialism would bear more traces of the medieval period than later European ventures in the Americas. A series of sympathetic popes also backed, or at least blessed, Iberian ventures, giving them added impetus (see PAPACY).

Nature also aided Iberians in their overseas ventures. Just as the Indian Ocean has its monsoons, the Atlantic Ocean enjoys fairly predictable winds and currents. Without them, transatlantic trade and colonization projects in the presteam era would have been all but impossible. The wind system of the Atlantic, like that of the larger Pacific, is a result of the interaction between Earth's rotation and its lagging atmosphere over a more or less flat surface. Winds circulate clockwise north of the equator, and counterclockwise to the south. These "trade winds," as they came to be known among mariners, linked not only Iberia to the Americas, but Africa with both. The latter proved a fateful "triangular" connection, making the slave trade all too easy.

Dangerous by-products of the trade winds in the North Atlantic are hurricanes, great cyclonic storms that draw energy from tropical waters warmed by summer as they roll westward from Africa. Despite Columbus's preference for early autumn departures, transatlantic sailing during hurricane season was soon abandoned. Aside from tempests, sailors also feared entrapment among the doldrums, persistent calms found around the equator (see FLEET SYSTEM).

Currents abound throughout the Atlantic as well, most of them tending to flow along trenches abutting the continents. The current system results primarily from regional differences in ocean temperature, and hence water density, combined with ocean floor geography. Some currents can be quite strong and extensive. Perhaps most important to Spanish and later English, French, and Dutch shippers in the Atlantic was the Gulf Stream, a powerful warm-water current flowing from the Gulf of Mexico northward along the shores of eastern North America, then out to sea and all the way to Europe. Much of northwestern Europe would in fact be significantly colder and dryer minus the Gulf Stream effect. Cold, usually polar, currents encouraged fish procreation, as in the Newfoundland Banks. As a general rule, winds and currents along the west coast of Africa and in the South Atlantic were less helpful to early modern sailors. It took Iberians, primarily the Portuguese, nearly a century to master them.

North Atlantic winds and currents enabled the Spanish to reach their overseas colonies with relative speed. The Canaries could be reached from southwest Spain in two weeks or less, and the larger Caribbean islands and ports in another one to two months. Columbus's first Atlantic crossing from the Canaries, not far from Morocco, took only thirty-three days. Strong contrary winds in the Caribbean and Gulf of Mexico, along with the treacherous passage through the Florida Straits and a jog north to catch prevailing westerlies, rendered the return trip from the Americas to Europe nearly twice as long. The voyage from Veracruz, Mexico, to Sanlúcar de Barrameda, in Andalusia, averaged four months. With stops at Havana and other delays, it could take much longer.

The length of Portuguese voyages to Brazil varied widely according to season and destination, but the same tendency for significantly longer return trips prevailed. More problematic, as in western Africa, was efficient coastwise sailing in Brazil. Winds and currents conspired against it, and nothing but time- and energy-consuming tacking could be done in response. Only the transatlantic crossing from western central Africa to Brazil proved relatively speedy, often taking only a month. This convenient phenomenon enabled Portuguese colonization in Congo and Angola, and of course greatly facilitated the slave trade to Brazil (see SLAVE TRADE; SLAVERY I–IV).

Captive Angolans in the seventeenth and eighteenth centuries were said to have considered the Atlantic crossing a deep-river passage, a kind of final journey. Many believed they were being shipped away for slaughter and consumption by the Portuguese, which was at least partly true. As another consequence of slavery and the slave trade, African and Afro-Iberian sailors became omnipresent and indispensable throughout the Atlantic world. Afro-Iberian trade intermediaries also came to dominate slaving ports throughout western Africa, along with offshore island chains such as the Cape Verdes. Meanwhile, the Portuguese language became the Atlantic lingua franca.

An often-overlooked limitation of early modern overseas exploration regards provisioning. Sealing and food preservation technologies, although not ineffective, were at best imperfect in early modern times. Aside from occasional opportunities for seine fishing and collection of rainwater, sailors depended almost entirely on pickled, desiccated, and otherwise preserved food stores. The growth of the Portuguese sugar economy in the East Atlantic islands enabled fruit preservation, and salt for meat and pickles was available in large quantities in both Portugal, at Setúbal, and the Cape Verde Islands (see FOOD; SUGAR). Water was most difficult to preserve beyond a week or two, leaving sailors to slake their thirst with a modest daily ration of wine. Interestingly, scurvy, or generalized tissue breakdown due to long-term vitamin C deprivation, did not afflict Iberian mariners to the same extent that it did northern Europeans. It is possible that Portuguese and Spanish conserves contained significant traces of citrus fruits.

Iberians followed two basic models of colonization in the course of early modern Atlantic expansion: (1) the fortified trading post and (2) the settlement colony. For the most part, the Portuguese adhered to the former model, which derived from Italian experiences in the Mediterranean. The Spanish subscribed mostly to the latter, which was somewhat more in line with the patterns seen in the Spanish reconquest of the land ruled by the Moors in the Iberian Peninsula. Some scholars have argued that this apparent divergence reflected differences in early national character, the Portuguese being "a trading people," the Spanish "a nation of conquerors."

However tempting such essentialisms might be, there is more than enough contrary evidence in both cases to render such sweeping characterizations useless. As was true of later northwest European competitors, Iberians abroad tended to act logically, if not kindly; Atlantic colonization schemes matched perceived local moneymaking potentials with the parent country's—or more often private sponsor's—ability to staff, settle, or defend the site (see COLONISTS AND SETTLERS I–VI; CONQUEST I–VII; DEFENSE—COLONIAL BRAZIL; DEFENSE—COLONIAL SPANISH AMERICA). For example, even as they settled Madeira and participated in the conquest of Ceuta, the Portuguese established trading posts, or *feitorías,* all along the west coast of Africa. Prefiguring in some ways later imperial policies, Portugal's chronic shortage of colonizers was sometimes met by orphans and convicts shipped abroad by the state. Transatlantic colonization, in short, would always be a multipronged affair.

Pushed along by royal sponsors such as Prince Henry "the Navigator" (1394–1460), the Portuguese gained a considerable lead over the Spanish in their Atlantic endeavors (see MONARCHS OF PORTUGAL). Their ultimate interest, which the Spanish and other Christian Europeans shared, was finding a sea route to Asia. Muslim princes and merchant families controlled trade in North Africa and the Middle East by the early fifteenth century, and the Ottoman conquest of Constantinople in 1453 provoked an almost messianic response among some Westerners. Also, the closing of the Hellespont left numerous Christian Mediterranean cities without access to captive Slav (whence "slave") laborers. While churchmen and neocrusaders wrung their hands, hardheaded European merchants complained mostly of the costs of dealing with middlemen in general, regardless of faith. They wanted more direct access to Asia's fabrics and spices, and to Africa's gold, pepper, and ivory (see GOLD; SILVER). Now that Eastern Europeans could not be had as slaves, a trade in sub-Saharan captives developed. The Portuguese pioneered this nefarious business, beginning in 1441.

Competition from the Spanish first emerged in the Canaries, or Fortunate Isles, where missionaries, conquerors, and settlers of varying nationalities had been active since the early fourteenth century. Ultimately the pope sided with the Spanish, who gained uncontested possession of the Canaries in 1479 under the Treaty of Alcáçovas. Portugal's claims in the rest of the East Atlantic, however, were not in question, and with Columbus's 1492 westward voyage, Spanish overseas endeavors focused primarily on American shores.

In oceanic terms, the Portuguese continued to dominate African shores, and eventually the South Atlantic more broadly. The Spanish dominated the North Atlantic, at least for a time, as well as the eastern Pacific. In 1494, six years prior to the Portuguese discovery of Brazil, an imaginary line was drawn between Spanish and Portuguese claims 370 leagues west of the Cape Verde chain. Once Brazil's coastline was discerned in the decade after 1500, this line was found to run roughly from the mouth of the Amazon to near the mouth of the Río de la Plata. The pope-sanctioned Treaty of Tordesillas, as this landmark agreement was called, was not recognized by other European monarchs, including Catholic ones (see TORDESILLAS, TREATY OF).

Africans and Native Americans, along with most native Canary Islanders and some Spanish and Portuguese subjects, resisted Iberian imperial claims on territory and of course bodily imprisonment. The resistance of subject peoples consistently shaped policy and checked imperial expansion in one way or another throughout the Atlantic Basin. Of equal concern, however, were threats from northern Europeans against Iberian overseas sovereignty. The French were first, threatening Spanish ships returning from Columbus's third voyage off Madeira in 1498, and landing dyewood traders along the coast of Brazil by 1503. French harassment in the form of privateering and colony planting continued until the late 1560s, when Fort Caroline, Florida, and "Antarctic France," near modern Rio de Janeiro, were destroyed (see PIRATES AND PIRACY).

Greater threats were mounted in subsequent years by the English and the Dutch, the former doing most harm to the Spanish trade, the latter doing most to the Portuguese. The Atlantic was vast, and communication slow. Furthermore, European conflicts over religion, boundaries, and other matters flowed into it all too readily. Once Portugal and Spain were united under Habsburg rule in 1580, English and Dutch rivals felt freer than ever to attempt to "singe the King of Spain's beard," as the English privateers put it (see HABSBURGS; MONARCHS OF SPAIN). Privateering would eventually give way to formation of settlement colonies and trading posts, the English somewhat following the Spanish model, and the Dutch following the Portuguese one. Once again demography and patterns of investment, rather than the innate character of these peoples, seem to have been the main factors explaining this divergence.

The Spanish and Portuguese immediately reacted to these external, transoceanic threats by better arming their vessels, gathering them together into convoys, and fortifying key ports. Indefensible sites and sometimes whole regions, such as the Haitian side of Hispaniola, were abandoned, and trade outside the fleet system was made illegal (see CONTRABAND; HISPANIOLA). In general, the Spanish, having vast quantities of gold and silver to lose if they failed, made more concerted efforts than the Portuguese to protect their fleets and ports. This was much more evident in the Atlantic than the Pacific sphere, as distance from Europe naturally sheltered the latter.

During the period when Spain and Portugal were united under one ruler (1580–1640), the Spanish proved their dedication to ultramarine defense by driving Dutch attackers away from Brazil in 1624. The Spanish force was the largest transatlantic fleet to date, for defense or any other purpose, and it proved almost as costly as the Armada that failed in its attack on England in 1588. Ultimately, Spain's active defense of its Portuguese dominions overseas was to no avail, as northeast Brazil and many key African ports were in the end captured and managed by the Dutch West India Company between 1630 and 1654. Still, the Dutch soon discovered, as the English did later in the Caribbean and elsewhere in the circum-Atlantic, that maintaining overseas colonies, even valuable, cash-producing ones, was no small business.

Meanwhile, nonstate piracy became a matter of growing concern for all parties. With the development of sugar islands such as Martinique and Jamaica, any nation interested in protecting its own Atlantic trade and colonies had to think twice before sponsoring or harboring pirates. Freelance sea robbers could be good for business in the short term, perhaps, but usually proved bad in the long. First, they tended to prey on alleged friends in lieu of sworn enemies, and second, their social practices were seen as destabilizing. Mocking Old World conventions of race, status, and gender, the sea robbers represented a threat to colonial hierarchy, the key to order in lieu of martial law (see LAWS—COLONIAL LATIN AMERICA). For the Spanish and Portuguese, Atlantic piracy had never been beneficial, although contraband traders (some of them pirates, such as Francis Drake) did occasionally offer desired goods at discount.

In the course of the seventeenth century, Spanish and Portuguese sea dominance waned. In their stead there emerged the English and the French, with the Dutch a close third. The Spanish and Portuguese had set the mold for overseas affairs in the Atlantic basin, and even with new powers on the scene it was not soon broken. The English Royal Navy suppressed Atlantic piracy in the 1710s and 1720s, and English merchants won entry into Spain's closely held monopoly trade system (see MONOPOLIES).

But this shift in power was not the end of Spain and Portugal in the Atlantic. Spanish-American mining and trade were revitalized by the second half of the eighteenth century, and the discovery of gold and diamonds in Brazil around 1700 elevated that colony to the status of viceroyalty for the first time (see MINING—GOLD; MINING—SILVER). Rio de Janeiro emerged as an important Atlantic hub. In both the Spanish and Portuguese Atlantic spheres, the volume of trade in money, raw commodities, luxury goods, and slaves grew exponentially in the eighteenth century, falling off only amid the Napoleonic wars (see NAPOLEONIC INVASION AND LUSO-AMERICA; NAPOLEONIC INVASION AND SPANISH AMERICA). The early modern Atlantic system pioneered by the Spanish and Portuguese was simply taken to new levels in the twilight of the colonial era. Finally, Spanish America's transatlantic ties suffered extraordinary rupture with independence, whereas Brazil's did not (see INDEPENDENCE I–VI). This was especially true of the South Atlantic, where Brazilian and Angola-based merchants continued the slave trade until 1850. Then the age of sail gave way to the age of steam, ushering in a new phase of Atlantic history.

References

Brooks, George E. *Eurafricans in Western Africa: Commerce, Social Status, Gender, and Religious Observance from the Sixteenth to the Eighteenth Century.* Athens: Ohio University Press, 2003.

Coates, Timothy. *Convicts and Orphans: Forced and State-Sponsored Colonizers in the Portuguese Empire, 1550–1755.* Stanford, CA: Stanford University Press, 2001.

Fernández Armesto, Felipe. *Before Columbus: Exploration and Colonization from the Mediterranean to the Atlantic, 1229–1492.* Philadelphia: University of Pennsylvania Press, 1987.

Parry, John H. *The Age of Reconnaissance.* New York: Mentor, 1963.

Pérez-Mallaína, Pablo. *Spain's Men of the Sea: Daily Life on the Indies Fleets in the Sixteenth Century.* Translated by Carla Rahn Phillips. Baltimore: Johns Hopkins University Press, 1998 (Spanish edition 1992).

Phillips, Carla Rahn. *Six Galleons for the King of Spain: Imperial Defense in the Early Seventeenth Century.* Baltimore: Johns Hopkins University Press, 1986.

Phillips, William D., and Carla Rahn Phillips. *The Worlds of Christopher Columbus.* New York: Cambridge University Press, 1992.

Sweet, James H. *Recreating Africa: Culture, Kinship, and Religion in the African-Portuguese World, 1441–1770.* Chapel Hill: University of North Carolina Press, 2003.

Symcox, Geoffrey, and Blair Sullivan. *Christopher Columbus and the Enterprise of the Indies: A Brief History with Documents.* Boston: Bedford St. Martin's, 2004.

SPAIN AND SPANISH AMERICA

Kris Lane

More than any other European imperial power, Spain developed in tandem with its overseas colonies. This complex symbiotic relationship lasted three centuries with the Spanish American mainland (ca. 1520–1820), and four centuries with the Caribbean islands of Cuba and Puerto Rico (1492–1898). Although it was perhaps coincidental that late medieval political, religious, and cultural consolidation of the Iberian Peninsula overlapped with overseas exploration and conquest, the two projects soon became closely intertwined, each feeding off the other.

As happened elsewhere in early modern Europe, Spain's internal centralization and overseas expansion projects both offered new opportunities for institution building, revenue collection, and religious proselytizing. Most significantly, American treasure soon came to sustain the colonizing mother country, with manufactured goods and European political charisma offered in exchange (see ATLANTIC ECONOMY; SILVER). Unequal as this relationship was, considerable violence was required to sever it in the nineteenth century (see INDEPENDENCE I–VI).

Afterwards, despite British, French, and U.S. political and commercial intervention in Spanish America, significant cultural links with Spain were maintained, particularly with regard to religion, arts, and letters. Spain's long and brutal civil war (1936–1939) revived transatlantic political ties in the twentieth century, and in more recent times, massive business investment and reverse migration have marked Spain's relationship with its former colonies (see SPANISH CIVIL WAR AND LATIN AMERICA). Various legacies of the colonial relationship have persisted on both sides of the Atlantic.

Imperial Consolidation

The roots of modern Spain may be traced to the 1469 marriage of Isabella of Castile and Ferdinand of Aragon. Dubbed the Catholic Monarchs (*Reyes Católicos*) by Pope Alexander

VI in 1494, Isabella and Ferdinand attempted to centralize authority on the peninsula. Despite some groping and rearranging, it was during their reign (1469–1516) that the main institutions of governance for both Spain and its American colonies were established. These institutions, which included viceroyalties (see VICEROYALTIES), regional appeals courts, district magistracies, and various investigative and administrative arms of the Catholic Church, underwent rapid development and then gradual devolution in the following two

centuries of Habsburg rule (see ADMINISTRATION—COLONIAL SPANISH AMER-
ICA; CATHOLIC CHURCH IN SPANISH AMERICA; HABSBURGS). Considerable
negotiation between Crown and subjects, both in Spain and abroad, became standard practice by the early seventeenth century, and it persisted for some time. Violent rebellions in
the Low Countries, Portugal, and even the Catalonian city of Barcelona further challenged
the authority of the Spanish Crown by 1640.

Following a long succession war with England and its allies (1702–1713), Spain's new
Bourbon monarchs faced declining revenues and growing foreign competition (see
BOURBON REFORMS; MONARCHS OF SPAIN; WAR OF THE SPANISH SUC-
CESSION). As a result, they and their ministers enacted major government renovations
along French absolutist lines. The armed forces were professionalized, district boundaries
were redrawn, the power of the Catholic Church was curbed, and crown monopolies were
placed on luxuries such as tobacco, brandy, and playing cards (see ALCOHOL; DE-
FENSE—COLONIAL SPANISH AMERICA; MONOPOLIES; TOBACCO). Fiscal
reform, in particular, was violently resisted throughout Spain itself in Bourbon times.
Riots rocked Madrid and other cities in the 1760s. Resistance to the Bourbon project
proved more serious still in the American colonies, yet unlike neighboring British North
America, Spanish American colonies did not immediately seek independence (see RE-
BELLIONS—COLONIAL LATIN AMERICA).

Colonial relations grew most strained during the reign of Charles III (1759–1788).
Prominent advisers to the king, such as José de Gálvez, who had spent considerable time
in Mexico, argued that Spain's American possessions were not quasi-kingdoms, as envisioned by the neomedieval Habsburgs, but rather dependent satellites. Church and local
elite power was to be curbed without negotiation, and revenues were to be raised at any
cost. Colonial commercial activity was to be strictly controlled and taxed, and all men
identified as "Indians" were to be reminded of their tribute and draft labor obligations (see
ALCABALA; NATIVE AMERICANS I and III–VIII).

By the 1760s colonists of virtually every color and rank faced rising taxes, new trade
restrictions, and increasingly limited access to government posts. To make matters worse,
they also faced a variety of natural disasters and epidemics. Rebellions erupted sponta-
neously throughout the colonies in the last decade of Charles III's rule. Despite widespread discontent, however, even the most vocal colonial critics called for a return to
Habsburg-style negotiation, not revolution or separation.

Frightened by popular rebellions, colonial elites flatly rejected independence until after
Napoleon Bonaparte's 1808 invasion of Spain. King Charles IV (1788–1808), a bumbling
incompetent by comparison with his father, was forced to abdicate (see NAPOLEONIC
INVASION AND SPANISH AMERICA). He and his son, the future Ferdinand VII, were
exiled to France. With a pretender, Bonaparte's brother Joseph, on the throne, both colonial and Spanish peninsular governance reverted to town councils and parliaments (*cabildos* and *cortes*) (see CABILDO; CORTES OF CÁDIZ).

The cabildos of Buenos Aires and Caracas happened to be led by independence-
minded elites. Meanwhile, the Cortes of Cádiz—the parliament that was elected to act in
lieu of the exiled king—soon alienated colonial elites, breeding sympathy for the inde-

pendence cause among both liberals and conservatives. Still, securing independence from Spain required over a decade of bloody and destructive civil war (1810–1825), finally guaranteed by British naval and financial assistance. Too weak to reclaim its mainland colonial possessions, Spain clung only to Cuba, Puerto Rico, and the Philippines, all of which were lost to the United States at the turn of the twentieth century (see CUBA; PUERTO RICO).

Administrative Reorganization

Ferdinand and Isabella pursued three key objectives in the years leading up to Columbus's famous voyage, all of which had lasting consequences. First, the customary rights of towns and nobles were sharply curbed, particularly in the larger and richer kingdom of Castile. Second, Granada, the last Islamic kingdom in Iberia, was conquered with joint royal sponsorship (1488–1492). And third, the Holy Office of the Inquisition was instituted to root out and punish alleged infidels (1478) (see INQUISITION—SPANISH AMERICA). Iberian Jews were consequently persecuted in a series of vicious pogroms, among the harshest of them taking place in the year 1492 (see JEWS—COLONIAL LATIN AMERICA; MOORS). Powerful as it was in such shrill and intolerant times, the Catholic Church was subordinated to the Crown by 1501 through royal patronage (*patronato real*), an arrangement that gave Spanish monarchs control of tithe collection and high-level clerical appointments. In the colonies, the Spanish monarchy exercised even more power over church affairs (see ORDENANZA DEL PATRONAZGO).

Meanwhile, *corregidores* (Crown-appointed magistrates) and other district-level bureaucrats answering directly to the sovereign proliferated, many of them men of low birth trained in Spanish universities such as Salamanca and Alcalá de Henares (see CORREGIDOR/CORREGIMIENTO; EDUCATION—COLONIAL SPANISH AMERICA; HIDALGO; UNIVERSITIES). "Lettered men" (*letrados*) in fact constituted a new professional class in early modern Spain and its growing empire. The letrados and their posts were a departure from feudal models of governance and patronage, in that career advancement was at least ideally based on education and honorable service in office, rather than upon battlefield triumphs.

As further evidence of professionalization, lettered bureaucrats in Spain and the colonies periodically investigated one another, reporting back to peninsular oversight councils, and even to the king (see VISITA). Spain's early modern bureaucracy was not as complex or professionalized as that of China during the same period, but it was more far-flung. Both were obsessed with collecting taxes in silver, a money commodity that Spanish America produced in abundance.

Despite a tradition of independent monarchs, the Spanish state and Roman Catholic Church remained closely intertwined throughout early modern times. Church affairs in fact sometimes trumped political ones, particularly in the baroque era. In these years of eminent, sometimes ostentatious piety, archbishops frequently served double duty as colonial viceroys. Although significant curbs on church authority were instituted in late Bourbon times, Spanish imperialism in the Habsburg era was a near realization of medieval schoolmen's dreams: a merit-based theocracy.

War and American Treasure

The providentialist mystique so cultivated by Habsburg monarchs such as Philip II (1556–1598) and his successors died hard. Events such as the 1571 defeat of the Ottoman fleet at Lepanto seemed only to confirm divine approval. With the conquest of the Philippines (1565) and the union of the Spanish and Portuguese Crowns (1580–1640), Spain's Catholic empire was the world's first empire upon which "the sun never set," as used to be said of the British Empire. And of Philip II it was said that, for his ambition, "the world is not enough." The 1588 defeat of the Armada at the hands of the English and Dutch was a harsh reminder that divine will could go both ways, and defending the world's first global empire proved a nearly impossible task (see CONTRABAND; PIRATES AND PIRACY).

What made ambitions like Philip's possible in the first place was American silver. The colonies in fact served as the main account upon which expansionist Habsburg monarchs such as Charles I (1516–1556) and Philip II and later Bourbons such as Philip V (1700–1746) and Charles III (1755–1788) drew. The silver supply seemed inexhaustible, which led perhaps inevitably to irresponsible spending and a general lack of investment in industry in both the colonies and mother country. Some have argued that Spain and Spanish America remained underdeveloped through modern times as a result of their own good fortune.

The Indies also served as Spain's principal moral and political testing ground, each experiment in colonial governance and resource exploitation watched, often with groans and grimaces, by the entire world. Spanish treatment of Native American peoples was the first crucial issue, and the resulting *Black Legend* of wanton Spanish cruelty has remained perhaps the most persistent of all colonial legacies (see CONQUEST AND THE DEBATE OVER JUSTICE). As early as the sixteenth century, the Black Legend was a key pretext for invasion among Protestant European challengers such as the Dutch and English (see PROTESTANT REFORMATION).

Spanish Roots of American Conquest

In order to understand the forces at play, it is necessary to go back even further in Spanish history. Long before Columbus's day, Iberians engaged in an on-again, off-again *guerrilla,* a "little war," that mostly pitted Christians against Muslims. There were also occasional cross-religious alliances and long periods of relative peace (often called *convivencia,* "coexistence"). Though not described thus at the time, this nearly eight-century-long territorial struggle, eventually called the *Reconquista,* ended with Christian dominance in Iberia.

In the course of reconquest, the Christians adopted Saint James "the Moor-Slayer" as patron, and a protonationalist cult was born. By the early 1510s, "Santiago!" (the form "Saint James" took in Spanish) was the battle cry of the conquistadors of the Caribbean fringe (see CONQUEST I, III–VII). But whereas the war that culminated in Ferdinand and Isabella's seizure of Granada's palace-fortress of the Alhambra in 1492 was played up as a righteous, nationalist crusade, the greater Reconquista was less ideological, and less organized. Still, several patterns affecting later relations with the Americas were firmly established.

First, raids were mostly organized by private citizens and sanctioned only after the fact by monarchs or princes (see CONQUISTADORS). Royal sponsors received a portion of booty in exchange for land grants or titles of nobility. This medieval clientage approach to warfare produced occasional open battles, with some key ones fought in Castile and Valencia by the famous eleventh-century Christian raider, Ruy Díaz "El Cid" of Bivar, but more often the Reconquest resembled organized banditry. Still, paramilitary raiders traversed great distances and often struck with lightning speed. Learning from their Muslim foes, Christian Spaniards adopted the techniques of light cavalry *(jinete),* which later proved devastating in parts of Europe and the Americas.

A second relevant pattern established in the Reconquest concerned the redistribution of land, captives, and goods taken by successful raiders. A portion, usually a fifth, was reserved for powerful princes, the remainder being doled out to the war captain or head raider himself, then afterwards to each of the lesser participants according to "investment." Investment might include such intangibles as rank or seniority, but usually consisted of weapons, rations, horses, and other quantifiable contributions to the expedition. Captives were variously enslaved, ransomed to relatives, or left in place to carry on their agricultural or pastoral endeavors as tributaries (see ENCOMIENDA; HORSES; REPARTIMIENTO; WEAPONS).

Spanish overseas expansion before Columbus was limited in scope, but it could be argued that experiences in the Canary Islands, in Columbus's day still inhabited by Neolithic peoples whom the Spanish called Guanches, prefigured the American experience. Somewhat after the Reconquest model, the Guanches were dispossessed of their territories, enslaved if they rebelled, forced to convert to Christianity, and generally subjected to the whims of a new class of pious European proprietors devoted to export agriculture. Sugar proved immediately viable, followed by sweet wines (see SUGAR; WINE). Both sugar and wine grapes were eventually planted in the Americas and harvested by slaves (see SLAVERY II–IV).

Given the rigid orthodoxy of their Catholic monarchs, Spanish subjects abroad based all new land claims on religious grounds first, only appealing to Roman and other ancient principles of possession later. The most famous artifact of this approach to colonization was the so-called *Requerimiento* (Requirement), a legal disclaimer to be read aloud to native enemies (occasionally through an interpreter) prior to battle (see REQUERIMIENTO). It essentially excused the slaughter and enslavement of anyone so bold as to challenge the sovereignty of the Universal Church and its earthly representatives, the pope and the kings of Spain (see PAPACY). At one level a quaint reminder of Spanish regalism, for many conquistadors the Requerimiento constituted a license to pillage the Indies. In a way that would have shocked their European authors, legal documents could take on a fetishistic quality abroad, particularly among semiliterate subject peoples.

Native American Policy

The emphasis on religious proselytizing, however, was taken seriously, so much so that enslavement of indigenous Americans was all but outlawed in the Spanish Indies by the time of the conquest of Peru in the 1530s (see RELIGIOUS ORDERS). Despite its religious orthodoxy, Spain's university culture could pit skeptical humanists against more rigid scholastics. Contrary to the Black Legend, all was not obscurantism and rigid adherence to tradition. The condition of Amerindian subject peoples remained a prime concern among Spain's men of letters, but it proved particularly salient in the first half of the sixteenth century. The issue peaked when the University of Salamanca staged debates between the proindigenous activist Bartolomé de las Casas and his Aristotelian foe, Juan Ginés de Sepúlveda.

Although too late for most Caribbean islanders, these exercises accompanied a raft of laws (especially those of 1542–1543) meant to improve the lot of native subjects of the Spanish Crown (see NEW LAWS OF 1542). A compromise with the Aristotelians was to declare Amerindians legal minors, and hence subject to labor demands and payment of tribute. An inadvertent effect of this partly well-meaning, partly exploitative legislation was the formalization of the misnomer *Indian* as a hard, protoracial category (see RACE). A similar elision soon occurred with the terms *negro* and *slave*. Apartheid-like legislation soon followed, although always with the ostensible aim of protecting Indians (see CONGREGACIONES). In matters of race, however, the state proved much weaker than its laws; powerful "white" colonists almost always won out (see LAWS—COLONIAL LATIN AMERICA). Neither could peoples of mixed heritage, an increasingly significant group not really foreseen by Spanish lawmakers, be suppressed (see MESTIZAJE; MULATTO).

Urban Settlement and Administration

If "Indians" proved more legally complicated than conquered Muslims or Jews, so also did patterns of settlement in the so-called Indies. One legacy from medieval and ancient times was the importance of towns, each one founded and incorporated by a group of presumably upstanding citizens (*vecinos*) (see CITIES). Following trends in Spain itself, Spanish towns in the Americas were not granted much autonomy by the sovereign, nor were they allowed much freedom in terms of planning. Nevertheless, colonial and peninsular householders occasionally disagreed with the sovereign, sometimes violently.

All Spanish American towns were ordered to be laid out on a perfectly rectilinear grid, centered on a plaza and surrounded by church, town council house, and other government buildings. According to sixteenth-century ordinances, the municipal water supply was to be clearly channeled and guaranteed, and butcheries and tanneries located well downstream. Nearby woods were also to be protected from overexploitation, and common pastures maintained for visitors. As in Reconquest Spain, the Christian town in the New World was the nucleus of both colonization and civilization. The countryside remained suspect.

Despite frequent proclamations of loyalty to the Crown, Spanish American town councils, cabildos, served as the base unit of colonial political life, a function that regained importance in the era of independence. The Spanish town was also distinct from the overwhelmingly indigenous countryside. Still, there were mandated Indian towns and *barrios* (neighborhoods), all of them subject to neighboring Spanish settlements. Indigenous towns soon developed Spanish-style structures of governance, with chieftains and aldermen in charge (see ALTEPETL; CAH). Surviving symbols from New Mexico to Chile include the staff of office, *bastón de mando.* In shape, symbolism, and function, many early modern urban trends have persisted in both Spain and Spanish America. The shape of new towns in the Peruvian Amazon is a case in point, as are the demands for autonomy still being made by old Spanish towns such as Bilbao and Barcelona.

Effectively tying the motherland to the colonies was no small task, given the enormous distances and primitive communications methods involved (see FLEET SYSTEM). Still, Spanish America remained remarkably consistent in its overall loyalty. The explanation for this seeming paradox lies in the unique qualities of the Habsburg system. Habsburg monarchs such as Philip II treated the Spanish Indies as second-tier kingdoms, each with certain medieval-style rights and privileges.

Colonial society, like Spanish society itself, was broken into numerous corporate units, among them various arms of the church, military orders, the civil service, and other social groupings. All, including Amerindians and occasionally slaves, competed for the king's ear. Foreign attacks and other matters of state had to be considered from time to time, but everyday politics consisted in mediating disputes among these various subject parties. This job was too much for any king, and hence it was carried out by Spanish-born and often university-trained bureaucrats.

Above the level of the town council were crown-appointed officials called variously *corregidores, gobernadores,* and *alcaldes mayores.* Each had a substantial jurisdiction, usually encompassing several large towns. What was later called corruption was virtually assured, since bureaucratic salaries were tied to the gathering of tributes and other imposts. Above these regional appointees were councils of judges called *audiencias,* basically appeals courts, but also capable of certain legislative and executive functions (see AUDIENCIAS). A peninsular model was the Audiencia of Granada; the first American one was the Audiencia of Santo Domingo (est. 1511). Many others followed, most of them located in what are now Spanish American national capitals.

Audiencia judges overwhelmingly were sent from Spain, although Creoles made inroads in the seventeenth and early eighteenth centuries (see CREOLES). With the exception of Panama, audiencias ruled large jurisdictions, many of which formed the basis of later nation-states. Jurisdictions frequently overlapped, and the dozen or so audiencias in place by 1600 were ranked. The overlaps and rankings encouraged competitive wrangling rather than cooperation.

Above the audiencias were the viceroyalties, first established in New Spain (1535), and then Peru (1544). New Spain, or Greater Mexico, had authority even over the distant Philippines, yet the Viceroyalty of Peru was much larger and initially wealthier. The Viceroyalty of Peru would eventually be split into three parts, with a new viceroy at Bogotá (1739), then Buenos Aires (1776). With the rearrangement of trade routes throughout the course of the eighteenth century, Lima was reduced to a jurisdiction not much larger than modern Peru.

Above the viceroys was the Council of the Indies, essentially the king's advisory board on colonial affairs, created in 1524 (see COUNCIL OF THE INDIES). The king himself saw only very special appeals and reports, although thousands of such documents were addressed to him directly by disgruntled or hopeful subjects of all colors and classes.

Madrid, made into an imperial capital only in 1561, under Philip II, grew largely in relation to the wealth of the Indies.

Migration and the New Culture

From the time of Columbus, people flowed mostly from Spain to the Americas, not in huge waves, but steadily (see MIGRATION—FROM IBERIA TO THE NEW WORLD). With the exception of the African slave trade, mass migration only began around the turn of the twentieth century (see SLAVE TRADE). Some successful early migrants, called variously *indianos* and *peruleros,* returned (see PERULEROS). Many others sent money home to support relatives, much as migrant populations do today. Spain differed from other European colonizing powers, however, by closely monitoring and controlling emigration. Only so-called Old Christians (persons said not to have descended from Jews or Muslims) were supposed to be allowed, with Gypsies, Moors, recently converted Jews and Muslims, and other potentially polluting groups barred. The idea was to protect Amerindians from exposure to all but the purest Catholics.

With the passing of time, Spanish colonists came to see themselves as both Spanish and colonial. Those of mostly Spanish descent born in the New World came to be known as Creoles to distinguish them from those born in Spain. That is, they maintained a sense of cultural superiority derived from their ancestry, even as they developed a local identity and culture (see CULTURE). Indigenous and African terms entered Creole speech, just as indigenous and African men and women entered Creole households (see LANGUAGES). Crossovers occurred constantly, despite sumptuary laws and other self-conscious attempts to prevent "pollution." Foodways and modes of dress were by necessity adapted to different climates and cultural milieus (see ARCHITECTURE—COLONIAL SPANISH AMERICA; ART AND ARTISTS—COLONIAL SPANISH AMERICA; FOOD; MUSIC AND DANCE II–V; SYNCRETISM).

The result by the seventeenth century was not only a mixed culture but a colonial consciousness distinct from that of peninsular Spaniards. For their part, Spaniards born on the Iberian Peninsula consistently considered themselves superior to their colonial counterparts. Some advanced theories of tropical degradation, which they felt applied even to settler families of impeccable pedigree. Tension between the two groups, peninsulars and Creoles, and with plebeians of color besides, ultimately fueled the riots and independence movements of the later Bourbon era (see ENLIGHTENMENT—SPANISH AMERICA).

Postcolonial Relationships

With few exceptions, relations between Spain and Spanish America ranged from weak to strained to mutually hostile for much of the nineteenth century. U.S. hemispheric security proclamations were not a significant factor at first, but they became so by the end of the century. For their part, Spanish Americans were frequently embroiled in internal and regional conflicts. Only certain religious organizations, such as the revived Jesuit order, maintained transatlantic links (see JESUITS—IBERIA AND AMERICA). New international missionary orders, such as the Salesians, also made their way to Spanish America's undeveloped margins. In political and economic terms, though, it was first British, then U.S. interests that largely displaced the former mother country, extending credit, influencing political parties and caudillos, redrawing borders, and extracting resources (see CAUDILLOS; LIBERALISM). In the early twentieth century, relations with Spain improved, only to be sidetracked by the worldwide depression and the Spanish Civil War.

The long dictatorship of Francisco Franco (1939–1975) followed, drawing few admirers but many imitators in Spanish America (see GUERRILLAS; TERRORISM). With Spain's return to democracy in the late 1970s, ties with the former colonies expanded once again (see DEMOCRACY). Even Communist Cuba came to be viewed in a relatively positive light. Since about 1990, Spanish business and cultural interests in the Americas have grown exponentially, with huge investments in everything from telecommunications to colonial church restoration projects. Tourism has ballooned (see TRAVEL AND TOURISM). This neoliberal shift has produced unintended consequences, as well. Spain's own economic expansion since joining the European Community in 1986, coupled with a falling birth rate, has produced a reversal of colonial migration patterns: as of 2004, over a million Spanish Americans, primarily from Andean countries, have migrated to Spain to work, largely in the service sector.

Despite this general trend toward reintegration with the former colonizer, many Spanish Americans still regard their relative poverty as deriving at least in part from colonial legacies. Many such legacies have been argued, if not conclusively proven. Persistent patterns of irresponsible resource exploitation, unequal race and gender relations, political corruption, and religious intolerance are but a few of the alleged "colonial" sources of modern Spanish American ills. Increasingly, however, scholars are framing Spain and Spanish America's long and troubled colonial and postcolonial relations in terms of broader patterns of global integration. Theirs has been but one variant of the larger story of world capitalist expansion.

References

Adelman, Jeremy, ed. *Colonial Legacies: The Problem of Persistence in Latin American History.* New York: Routledge, 1999.

Alpert, Michael. *A New International History of the Spanish Civil War.* New York: Palgrave, 2004.

Altman, Ida D. *Transatlantic Ties in the Spanish Empire: Brihuega, Spain, and Puebla, Mexico, 1560–1620.* Stanford, CA: Stanford University Press, 2000.

Barton, Simon. *A History of Spain.* New York: Palgrave, 2003.

Brading, D. A. *The First America: The Spanish Monarchy, Creole Patriots, and the Liberal State, 1492–1867.* Cambridge: Cambridge University Press, 1991.

Elliott, J. H. *Imperial Spain, 1469–1716.* New York: Penguin, 1963.

Gibson, Charles. *Spain in America.* New York: Harper and Row, 1966.

Haring, C. H. *The Spanish Empire in America.* New York: Harcourt, Brace, 1947.

Lockhart, James, and Stuart B. Schwartz. *Early Latin America.* Cambridge: Cambridge University Press, 1984.

Parry, J. H. *The Spanish Seaborne Empire.* Berkeley and Los Angeles: University of California Press, 1967.

Ruiz, Teofilo. *Spanish Society, 1400–1600.* New York: Longman, 2001.

Stein, Stanley J. *Apogee of Empire: Spain and New Spain in the Age of Charles III, 1759–1789.* Baltimore: Johns Hopkins University Press, 2003.

IBERIA AND THE CARIBBEAN

Heather L. McCrea

Iberia and the Caribbean were brought together through an arrangement between the Crown of Castile and Christopher Columbus in April of 1492. Columbus utilized the knowledge gained by Genoese merchants and sailors during previous explorations of Mediterranean and Atlantic coast routes in the late thirteenth century. A hunger for material wealth, especially gold, slaves, and spices, largely motivated the expeditions of Columbus and his predecessors (see CONQUISTADORS; SLAVE TRADE). At the same time, however, the Catholic monarchs on whom Columbus relied for financial and political support were motivated by a desire, once they had reconquered all European lands taken by the Muslims in 711, to spread Christianity beyond the European continent.

With their Iberian goals largely accomplished, the Spanish monarchs looked at Columbus's expeditions as a means to spread their power and Christianity beyond the European continent and into Asia. Indeed, Columbus, thinking he had arrived in Asia via a new shortcut, had no idea he had discovered a "new world," which led him to mistakenly label the first Caribbean islands on which he landed the "Indies." On his first voyage, Columbus bypassed the Bahamas and headed for the north coast of the island of Hispaniola (now divided between Haiti and the Dominican Republic) (see HISPANIOLA). Once there, his crew established a small settlement, which they called La Navidad. Columbus subsequently departed for Spain in September of 1493. Returning to Hispaniola in 1494 after exploring the southern coast of Cuba during his second voyage, he found La Navidad in chaos. Native peoples had resisted or fled, and many had been subdued into slavery under horrible conditions (see NATIVE AMERICANS III—CARIBBEAN). Supplanted as governor of Hispaniola, Columbus was required to explain his activities to Crown authorities.

By the early sixteenth century, the Portuguese had acquired the lucrative Spice Islands, or Moluccas, in what is now Indonesia, and many of the Pacific routes for trade

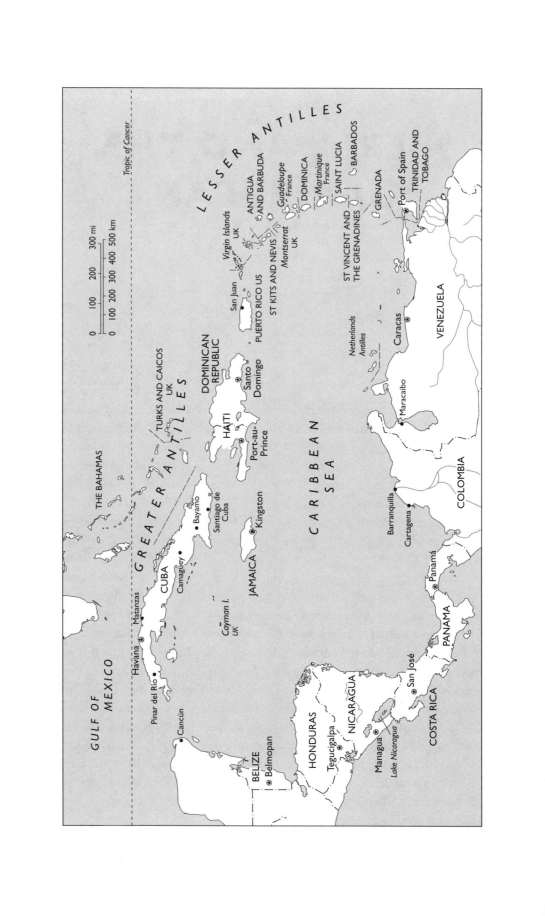

were under their control. Initially, the Spanish Crown claimed possession of Cuba, Hispaniola, Antigua and Barbuda, Jamaica, and Puerto Rico. However, the movements of the Portuguese into South America and the Caribbean prompted Pope Alexander VI to divide the world into Spanish and Portuguese spheres to minimize conflict between the two prominent Christian nations. The 1494 Treaty of Tordesillas outlined the terms of conquest for the Iberian rivals (see TORDESILLAS, TREATY OF). Most immediately, the treaty protected Spain's claim to its Caribbean islands. More broadly, it divided the world into Portuguese and Spanish spheres, and thereby provided a regulatory framework for future exploration and claims.

The drive for political, economic, and spiritual conquest that motivated Columbus set into motion profound changes for the peoples of the Americas, Europe, and Africa (see CATHOLIC CHURCH IN SPANISH AMERICA; SLAVERY II—CARIBBEAN). Throughout the fifteenth and sixteenth centuries, Iberian colonizers enslaved the indigenous populations of the Caribbean. Though the colonizers' physical abuse killed many of the indigenous peoples they enslaved, it was not the only—nor perhaps even the most important—cause of the high death rate. In explaining the devastation inflicted on the indigenous population, the Black Legend, as the myth of the unique cruelty of the Spanish is called, tends to assign most of the blame to the brutal Hispanic colonizers and slave drivers for the destruction of the Indies (see CONQUEST AND THE DEBATE OVER JUSTICE; CONQUEST III—CARIBBEAN). However compelling this version of the story is, reexaminations of the first encounters between Iberian and Amerindian populations have drawn into question the overall validity of this argument. Indeed, disease proved even more deadly than the grim conditions of slavery (see COLUMBIAN EXCHANGE—DISEASE). The indigenous inhabitants of the Caribbean died at a rapid rate from European diseases, particularly smallpox and measles, as well as typhus and influenza. Smallpox accompanied Columbus's second voyage to the Caribbean in 1493. Another smallpox outbreak in 1518–1519 wiped out much of the region's indigenous population. Hispaniola's population declined from approximately 62,000 in 1509 to about 28,000 by 1514 and 15,600 during the 1518 smallpox epidemic. Similar losses have been calculated for neighboring islands. Iberian settlers also suffered from smallpox and various deadly infections. The Caribbean islands then entered into an exchange of illnesses, vegetation, and livestock, known as the Columbian exchange; this process significantly shaped centuries of Iberian-Caribbean interaction (see COLUMBIAN EXCHANGE—AGRICULTURE; COLUMBIAN EXCHANGE—LIVESTOCK).

Colonization of the Caribbean utilized and relied on supervisory systems such as *encomiendas* and *repartimientos* (see ENCOMIENDA; REPARTIMIENTO). These administrative tools centered on an exchange: the Spanish Creoles (American-born Spaniards) and *peninsulares* (Spaniards born in Spain) offered protection to the Amerindians in exchange for tribute and labor (see CREOLES; RACE). Spaniards needed workers to mine, cultivate, and harvest the natural resources of the islands; the encomienda and repartimiento provided ways to meet those demands.

The caste system that developed in the Caribbean attributed a specific social value to each race. As the colonial period progressed, however, social divisions based on race became complicated by an increase in mixed-race offspring. The racial mixtures in the Caribbean included a significant African presence (established through the Caribbean's integration into the slave trade), thus differentiating the Caribbean population from the mestizo (of indigenous and European ancestry) population of New Spain (Mexico) and Peru (see MESTIZAJE).

Together with Iberian political and economic domination of the Caribbean, conversion of the native population to Catholicism also intensified in the early sixteenth century. However, spiritual goals often proved inconsistent with economic objectives. Many New World evangelizers, including Dominicans, Franciscans, Augustinians, and Benedictines, clashed with Spanish entrepreneurs and explorers over the treatment of the natives (see RELIGIOUS ORDERS). King Ferdinand, worried about productivity in Hispaniola, was reluctant to be swayed by the passionate words of Dominican friars Bartolomé de Las Casas and Antonio de Montesinos. Nevertheless, he authorized formal discussions regarding the treatment of New World natives in Burgos in 1512. Debate centered on the intelligence of native populations and their capacity for conversion to Christianity. Ultimately swayed by the argument that all the natives were free, the monarch's special committee drafted the Laws of Burgos in 1512 (see LAWS OF BURGOS). These statutes mandated that native labor requirements not obstruct religious conversion, and in the process they established the precedent for Spanish monarchs to regulate the movements of their distant colonial subjects. The New Laws of 1542, informed by arguments made by Las Casas in his *Very Brief Account of the Destruction of the Indies,* carried the logic of the 1512 decrees even further. They commanded, "That with regard to the lading of the said Indians the *Audiencias* [governors] take especial care . . . that it be in such a manner that no risk of life, health and preservation of the said Indians may ensue from an immoderate burthen." (Stevens 1893) (see LAWS—COLONIAL LATIN AMERICA; NEW LAWS OF 1542).

Debates continued throughout the sixteenth and seventeenth centuries in Spain and the Caribbean regarding the proper treatment and conversion of the indigenous populations. Ultimately, the indigenous populations of the Caribbean were given separate status as members of the República de Indios (Republic of Indians) and afforded certain protections by Spanish Crown authorities (see REPÚBLICA DE INDIOS). However, these protections did not extend to providing opportunities to gain real positions of power in the colonial apparatus. Individuals of mixed ancestry and indigenous peoples remained on the margins of power at best. Moreover, by the middle of the sixteenth century, the Inquisition had been extended to Spain's Caribbean and American colonies and focused on the native populations. Often accused of idol worship and fomenting resistance while in the grip of "possession by demons," the Caribbean's indigenous peoples at times were subjected to tortures that forever marred their relations with the Spaniards.

The rise of nation-states in Europe by the sixteenth century and the ensuing interstate rivalries further affected Iberian-American relations. In 1580, King Philip II (1556

–1598) sat on both the Spanish and Portuguese thrones, thanks to his father's abdication from the Spanish throne in 1556 and the death of his mother, the queen of Portugal, in 1580 (see MONARCHS OF PORTUGAL). For much of the sixteenth and seventeenth centuries Portugal remained a part of the Iberian Empire. The Iberian Peninsula was united under one monarch for sixty years, securing Spanish domination over the lucrative Caribbean possessions in the process. The Crown of Castile controlled the economy of its colonial possessions in the Caribbean (and the rest of Latin America) through the Casa de Contratación (House of Trade) (see ATLANTIC ECONOMY; CASA DE CONTRA-TACIÓN; TRADE—SPAIN/SPANISH AMERICA). Located in Seville, the Casa de Contratación provided the Crown with official leverage to augment royal revenues and increase taxes (see ALCABALA). Most of Spain's wealth came from mineral extraction in the colonies of New Spain (Mexico) and the South American Andes (see MINING—GOLD; MINING—SILVER). The Crown received an automatic one-fifth of all metal profits. Over the course of the next two centuries, the Spanish Crown concentrated on protecting valuable mineral extracts from their continental colonies.

However, Spain's New World wealth was quickly drained by fighting in a succession of European conflicts that also extended to the Caribbean. The Thirty Years' War (1618–1648) seriously disrupted Spain's economy, weakening its trade and compromising the security of Spain's Caribbean possessions (see THIRTY YEARS' WAR). After years of rivalry between the Spanish and the Dutch (1609–1621), the Dutch initiated the West India Company; by 1622 Spanish maritime trade had declined both in volume and value. Shipments of goods between Spain and the Indies fell 60 percent between 1606 and 1610 and between 1646 and 1650 (Bakewell 1997, 212).

By the mid-seventeenth century, Spain's power was in decline, and European competition for Spanish island possessions soared. Jamaica was lost to England, the western portion of Hispaniola went to France, and by 1697 France had claimed the rest of the island. A significant loss, the island of Hispaniola was a rich sugar colony (see SUGAR). By the end of the eighteenth century, several smaller islands in the eastern Caribbean were lost to European rivals, particularly Holland, France, and England (see PIRATES AND PIRACY).

Despite alarming dips in Spanish power and its imperial economy, the Spanish Caribbean islands of Puerto Rico and Cuba emerged as epicenters of sugar production (see CUBA; PUERTO RICO). In Cuba, sugar was planted early in the colonial period; it was not until the 1780s, however, that overseas demand and production reached a pinnacle. Puerto Rico utilized free or "coerced" contract labor early in its agricultural development of sugar. By the mid-nineteenth century, Puerto Rican and Cuban landowners imported both African slaves and Chinese contract workers to maximize production (Curtin 1990, 176–177). Ultimately the number of non-African laborers working on sugar plantations throughout the Caribbean surpassed the number of illegally imported African slaves at the end of the nineteenth century. Spanish settlers understood that depending on already devastated indigenous populations for such labor-intensive activities pitted them against the evangelizing goals of the Church. To avoid this conflict, Spanish colonizers imported African slaves to meet labor demands.

Spanish participation in the transatlantic slave trade had already reached a high level in the mid-seventeenth century. Annually, approximately 5,000 African slaves were brought to the Spanish-American colonies, until the 1780s, when the numbers reached about 6,000 per year. Almost all African slaves were initially brought to large markets in Cuba and Puerto Rico, where they were sold and shipped to other destinations. Although British and French participation in the slave trade ended at the turn of the nineteenth century, the transport of slaves to Cuba and Puerto Rico skyrocketed to 32,000 slaves annually by 1820; by the 1840s Cuban sugar production surpassed Jamaican and Brazilian crop yields, thus cornering 41 percent of world production (Klein 1986, 92). The intense cycles of boom and bust, typical of the sugar-producing islands of the Caribbean, meant that labor needs were perpetually tied to world demand for the crop. The sugar economy fostered a reliance on the million or so slaves who worked in one aspect or another of the plantation economy. By the late eighteenth century, the interconnectedness of slavery, sugar, and the Caribbean economy was undeniable. The Caribbean plantation system simply could not survive the abolition of slavery and the cessation of the slave trade.

With Spain in decline, the Spanish Crown implemented crucial changes in its colonial system. Indeed, the Crown itself was changing. The War of the Spanish Succession (1702–1713) saw the Spanish Habsburgs replaced by the Bourbons, the same royal family that ruled France (see HABSBURGS; WAR OF THE SPANISH SUCCESSION). Influenced by the methods that France's Louis XIV and his bureaucrats used when centralizing the power of the national government during the seventeenth century, Spain's Bourbon king Philip V (1700–1746) overhauled colonial administrative tactics (see BOURBON REFORMS). To prevent the further hemorrhaging of New World colonial spoils to piracy and the black market, the new Bourbon Spanish monarchy tightened its grip on the trade and taxation in its colonial possessions. The Bourbons were determined to reassert the imperial trade monopoly (see MONOPOLIES).

Nonetheless, events in Spain continued to conspire against effective colonial control. In part inspired by the American Revolution of 1776, Enlightenment philosophies heralding an age of liberation swept across the Americas and the Caribbean at a particularly vulnerable juncture for the Spanish and Portuguese Empires (see AMERICAN REVOLUTION; ENLIGHTENMENT—BRAZIL; ENLIGHTENMENT—SPANISH AMERICA). In 1804 residents of the western portion of Hispaniola (Haiti) successfully won their independence from French colonial rule. Under the dynamic leadership of Toussaint L'Ouverture and Jean-Jacques Dessalines, Haiti became the Western Hemisphere's first black nation and the first to declare independence from European colonial rule within the orbit of Spain's and Portugal's American possessions (see HAITIAN REVOLUTION). When Napoleon Bonaparte invaded Portugal in 1807 and placed his brother-in-law on the throne the following year, the reverberations from this hostile takeover were felt in the Spanish and Portuguese colonies (see NAPOLEONIC INVASION AND LUSO-AMERICA; NAPOLEONIC INVASION AND SPANISH AMERICA). By 1821 New Spain (Mexico) had wrested itself free from the yoke of Spanish colonial rule, and Spain's South American colonies were liberated by the mid-

1820s. Between 1808 and 1824, Spain lost almost all of its colonial possessions, and by 1824 the Spanish Empire had been reduced to Cuba and Puerto Rico (see INDEPENDENCE I–VI).

Cuba, however, hoped to join the ranks of former Spanish colonies in short order. A long, but ultimately failed, decade-long rebellion that erupted in 1868 was crushed by Spanish forces. In the years following, Cubans endured increased political repression and growing poverty, which further fueled revolutionary desires. Between 1880 and 1892, exiled Cuban nationalist José Martí organized the Cuban Revolutionary Party, recruiting men and money from his base in the United States. In 1894, Martí had his chance. The Cuban economy had fallen victim to a new U.S. tariff that raised duties on imported sugar shipments to the United States, thereby shutting Cuban sugar out of the lucrative U.S. market and forcing the island's economy into a tailspin. With Cuban unrest increasing, Martí's revolutionaries opened another drive for independence on February 24, 1895. The Spanish response to the Cuban rebellion was overpowering. Under General Máximo Gómez, a veteran of the 1868–1878 war, the Cubans were outnumbered (approximately 30,000 Cubans to 200,000 Spanish) and lacked adequate weapons and supplies. Nonetheless, the determined Cubans fought on, even after Martí's death shortly after the outbreak of hostilities. Although the rebels were unable to win independence, a weakened Spain was also unable to suppress the rebellion. In short order, the economic, political, and humanitarian costs of the rebellion soured Spanish-U.S. relations and ultimately resulted in the Spanish-American War of 1898, a decisively one-sided affair, which saw Spain lose its last two colonies in the Western Hemisphere (as well as its Pacific possession, the Philippines) (see SPANISH-AMERICAN WAR).

During the first half of the twentieth century, Spain's relationship with Caribbean nations was minimal. As a result of the Spanish-American War, Cuba received its independence. The relationship between Spain and Cuba endured, largely because Cuba had continued as a Spanish colony for seventy years longer than other Spanish American colonies. However, the U.S. expulsion of Spain from Cuba was also followed by a U.S. military occupation and then by an "independent" Cuban government whose formation was heavily influenced by the occupation authorities. Moreover, the U.S. government passed the so-called Platt Amendment in 1901, which listed certain conditions that Cuba had to abide by before it would be granted independence (see PLATT AMENDMENT). These conditions included allowing the United States to post naval bases on the island and to intervene in Cuban affairs. Indeed, before his death, Cuban revolutionary leader José Martí had become vehemently anti-American, warning against a U.S. policy that arrogantly treated Latin American countries as dependencies. Such fears seemed to be realized through the terms ending the occupation, which established a tense beginning to Cuban-U.S. relations at the dawn of the twentieth century.

Spanish nationals living in Cuba during the years following the Spanish-American War were allowed to keep their property. In fact, by 1934 almost 300,000 Spaniards lived in Cuba. Cuban leaders struggled during the reconstruction after the war to achieve economic and political stability. In September of 1933 a coup led by Fulgencio Batista overthrew Cuban president Gerardo Machado (1924–1933), laying the groundwork for almost twenty-five years of dictatorial rule. Spain's relatively minor participation in Caribbean affairs during the first few decades of the twentieth century can be attributed to its own internal disruptions, which culminated in the eruption of the Spanish Civil War in July 1936 (see SPANISH CIVIL WAR AND LATIN AMERICA). This war initiated thirty-eight years of Fascist leadership under General Francisco Franco and claimed more than 500,000 lives. Defeating the Republican forces in 1937, General Franco and his German and Italian allies set into motion an influx of refugees, mostly to Mexico but also to Caribbean and South American nation-states.

Two attempts to oust Fulgencio Batista, in 1957 and 1958, failed. There were also attempts to assassinate him, but they too failed. In the summer of 1958, Batista's army tried to defeat the rebel forces training in the Sierra Maestra Mountains. Led by University of Havana–trained Dr. Fidel Ruz Castro, the rebels issued a detailed declaration calling for less dependency on the United States, as well as education and public health reforms. By the end of 1958, the United States began an arms embargo against the Batista regime. Batista was forced to flee on January 1, 1959, to escape the rebellion that had swept the country. He fled to the Dominican Republic. Meanwhile, Castro and his forces took over Havana on January 8, 1959; the rebels took full control of Cuba within a few hours after Batista fled. About a month and a half later Castro became the prime minister. Once Castro began the expropriation of Spanish-owned businesses and investments during the early phases of the revolution, and the expulsion of several Spanish clergy from the Cuban Catholic Church, relations between Cuba and Spain disintegrated. Despite their political and ideological differences, though, both dictators shared a common distrust of U.S. foreign interventions and democracy, and they openly repressed independent labor organization. Indeed, the relationship between the two dictators has been defined as "very special," principally expressed in a week of mourning mandated by Castro after Franco's death in 1975 (Geyer 1991, 35).

The Spanish-American War also resulted in Puerto Rico's severance from the Spanish empire. Unlike Cuba, Puerto Rico was annexed by the United States and remains a U.S. territory. Puerto Ricans suffered through the depression of the 1930s; and under U.S. orbit, Puerto Ricans were exposed to "Operation Bootstrap," a program designed to modernize the island, generate jobs, and improve public health and education.

Until General Franco's death in November 1975, trade between Spain and the Caribbean nations stagnated. However, foreign relations between Spain and the Caribbean took a new form in the post-Franco era. With the constitution of 1978, Spain transitioned to a socialist democracy with a parliamentary monarchy. In 1982, Spain joined NATO (see NORTH ATLANTIC TREATY ORGANIZATION). In 1992, at the close of the quincentennial celebration of Columbus' landfall in the Americas, the voices of mixed-heritage peoples were heard against a new sociopolitical backdrop of multiculturalism. Today, many Caribbean peoples feel strong connections to their Spanish colonial past as well as their indigenous and African heritage. Spain and its former Caribbean colonies share a past that indelibly links the nations and its peoples together in a unique way.

References

Bakewell, Peter. *A History of Latin America: Empires and Sequels, 1450–1930.* Oxford: Blackwell, 1997.

Cook, Noble David. *Born to Die: Disease and New World Conquest, 1492–1650.* Cambridge: Cambridge University Press, 1998.

Cook Sherburne F., and Woodrow Borah. *Essays in Population History: Mexico and the Caribbean.* Vol. 1. Berkeley and Los Angeles: University of California Press, 1971.

Crosby, Alfred W., Jr. *The Columbian Exchange: Biological and Cultural Consequences of 1492.* Westport, CT: Greenwood, 1972.

Curtin, Philip. *The Rise and Fall of the Plantation Complex: Essays in Atlantic History.* New York: Cambridge University Press, 1990.

Geyer, Anne. *Guerilla Prince: The Untold Story of Fidel Castro.* Kansas City: Little, Brown and Company, 1991.

Hennessy, Alistair. "Spain and Cuba: An Enduring Relationship." Pp. 360–374 in *The Iberian–Latin American Connection: Implications for U.S. Foreign Policy,* edited by Howard J. Wiarda. Boulder, CO: Westview, 1986.

Klein, Herbert S. *African Slavery in Latin America and the Caribbean.* Oxford: Oxford University Press, 1986.

Offner, John L. *An Unwanted War: The Diplomacy of the United States and Spain over Cuba, 1895–1898.* Chapel Hill: University of North Carolina Press, 1992.

Stevens, Henry, ed. *The New Laws of the Indies.* London: Chiswick, 1893. Excerpts posted by Paul Halsall as "Modern History Sourcebook: The New Laws of the Indies, 1542," July 1998, http://www.fordham.edu/halsall/mod/1542newlawsindies.html.

Suchlicki, Jamie. *From Columbus to Castro and Beyond.* Washington, DC: Brassey's, 2002.

Thornton, John. *Africa and Africans in the Making of the Atlantic World, 1400–1680.* New York: Cambridge, 1992.

Winn, Peter. *Americas: The Changing Face of Latin America and the Caribbean.* New York: Pantheon, 1992.

PORTUGAL, BRAZIL, AND THE ATLANTIC WORLD

Ivana Elbl

The Atlantic Ocean has played a fundamental role in the history of Portugal ever since the country was established as an independent political entity in the twelfth century. A key waterway and an important source of raw materials, the ocean provided a gateway to commerce, settlement opportunities, and empire building. In time, Portugal, and later Brazil, came to serve western and northern Europe as notable suppliers of tropical and subtropical commodities, while offering lucrative markets for European exports (see ATLANTIC ECONOMY). This multilateral relationship eventually expanded to include North America.

Historically, Portugal played a distinctive dual role in the Atlantic world. In Europe it was one of the lesser powers, wisely avoiding most of the political upheavals that shook the continent over the centuries. In the South Atlantic it sought to build a maritime empire (see BRAZIL). The independence of Brazil in the nineteenth century and of Portugal's former African colonies in the second half of the twentieth century brought the imperial era to an end, leaving in its place Portuguese-speaking countries that do not always look primarily to each other but to regional Atlantic partners for commerce and political alliances (see INDEPENDENCE II—BRAZIL).

Portugal and Atlantic Europe

Throughout much of Portugal's history, northwestern Europe, in particular England and the Low Countries, served as key markets for the country's agricultural products and raw materials, and supplied manufactured goods in return, especially textiles and metalware. The economic importance of the northwestern link was further reflected in the pattern of political and dynastic alliances. Portugal also found long-standing economic partners in France, Germany, and the Baltic countries, but their importance was secondary to that of the English Channel area. France, however, played the role of a key cultural partner. Starting in the late Middle Ages, its universities provided education to generations of Portuguese students, and in the aftermath of the Enlightenment France became a magnet and a stimulating influence for Portuguese intellectuals. In the modern era, many Portuguese political exiles found welcome refuge on French soil (see EDUCATION—BRAZIL; ENLIGHTENMENT—BRAZIL; UNIVERSITIES). After decolonization and the fall of the Estado Novo (Portugal's long-lived fascist dictatorship) in 1974, Portugal's European orientation became even more pronounced in economic and political terms. In 1985 it entered the European Community, and in 2002, with the adoption of the Euro currency, it became a fully integrated member of the European Union (see COLD WAR—PORTUGAL AND THE UNITED STATES; NORTH ATLANTIC TREATY ORGANIZATION).

The basic patterns of commercial exchange between Portugal and various parts of Atlantic Europe were established in the later Middle Ages. Portugal's main exports included wine, fruit, olives and olive oil, salt, cork, fish, honey, wax, hides, and high-quality kermes (purple dyestuff). In exchange, it imported wheat, a wide range of textiles (especially woolens and luxury cloth), unwrought metal, and manufactured metal goods. Portuguese merchants traveled to England, Normandy, Flanders, Brabant, Holland, Germany, and the Baltic. In the fourteenth and fifteenth centuries many northwestern Europeans became accustomed to trading in Portugal, particular the Flemish, Dutch, and English, but also the Basques, Galicians, Bretons, and Germans. England and Flanders competed for primacy in Portuguese markets. Although England had a slight edge in terms of exports to Portugal, the Flemish port city of Bruges was not far behind, and, until it was replaced by Antwerp in 1498–1499, Bruges played a pivotal role in brokering Portuguese commerce with continental Europe.

After the decline of Bruges as the center of international trade, Antwerp was chosen as the new location for the Portuguese royal factory, which mediated the distribution of spices and other products from Asia, Africa, and the Atlantic islands during the peak era of Portugal's overseas expansion. The Portuguese Crown also depended on Antwerp for its purchases of silver and other commodities required to carry on trade in the southern Atlantic, the Indian Ocean, and eventually as far as the China Sea. Finally, Antwerp's importance as a financial market was a prime consideration for the debt-ridden government of Portugal's king, Dom João (King John III) (see MONARCHS OF PORTUGAL). However, in the 1540s Antwerp's advantages began to wane, and the royal factory there was closed in 1549. Lisbon, Seville (the Spanish trade port for American silver), and eventually Amsterdam and London supplanted Antwerp as the key nodes of Portuguese trade and finance (see SILVER).

In the early modern period, Portuguese traditional exports lost none of their importance, although they were overshadowed by exotic overseas commodities. This is particularly true of wine and olive oil (see COLUMBIAN EXCHANGE—AGRICULTURE; WINE). The key role of domestic products, including those of Madeira and the Azores, became very clear after Portugal regained its independence from Habsburg Spain in 1640 (see HABSBURGS). With the rest of Iberia and the Habsburg-controlled Mediterranean largely closed off to Portuguese interests, the country was forced to focus on fostering its own resources, as well as its time-honored Atlantic ties. For both political and economic reasons, England emerged as Portugal's dominant trading partner. The economic ties reached back to the Middle Ages. By contrast, the political ties had to do with Portugal's weakness on the international scene. Refused recognition by both Spain and the papacy, Portugal was used as a pawn by France, and its overseas holdings came under severe attack by the Dutch. England agreed, in exchange for commercial privileges, to protect Portugal's interests and promote the notion of renewed Portuguese sovereignty. Shut out of major peace negotiations, the Peace of Westphalia (1648) and the Peace of the Pyrenees (1657), Portugal found English patronage essential to its political survival (see THIRTY YEARS' WAR). The costly marriage of Charles II of England and Catherine of Bragança further tightened the links between the two countries and brought England important territorial gains overseas (Tangier, Bombay).

The ties with England became even closer in the eighteenth century. The Treaty of Methuen (1703) formalized the already existing relationship: Portugal granted various forms of preference to English textiles and other manufactured goods, and England guaranteed a market for Portuguese wines, regardless of the state of its relations with France, Portugal's main competitor for the English wine market (see METHUEN TREATY). The treaty locked Portugal into its dependence on English manufactured goods. Brazilian gold and diamonds ensured Portugal's solvency in the first half of the eighteenth century, making the relationship quite comfortable. In the second half of the eighteenth century, however, the Marquis of Pombal tried to reduce the country's dependence on Great Britain by promoting Portuguese manufactures and establishing chartered companies to control the Brazilian Atlantic trade. After Napoleon's invasion of Portugal in 1807, the Portuguese Empire became utterly dependent on British military protection, and the Crown was forced to open Brazilian trade to all friendly powers, especially Great Britain (see NAPOLEONIC INVASION AND LUSO-AMERICA). The Anglo-Portuguese Treaty of 1810 put a seal on measures that made Portugal a British protectorate in all but name. British expeditionary forces remained in Portugal for over twenty years, making themselves utterly unpopular across the political spectrum.

The British compelled Portugal to acknowledge Brazil's independence and pressed for an end to slave exports from the African colonies. Portugal was in no position to reject the British alliance, since it needed capital to build up and modernize its economy, crippled by the emancipation of Brazil. The paramount needs in the second half of the nineteenth century included industrialization and the creation of a modern communications and transport system. To achieve these goals Portugal relied not only on British but also on French and German capital. The balance of trade remained unfavorable, and a mounting foreign debt brought the country to the brink of bankruptcy in the 1920s. Colonial disputes, particularly the Ultimatum of 1890, further strained Portugal's relations with Great Britain at the turn of the century. Still, the alliance was strong enough for Portugal to enter World War I in 1917 on the side of the Allies, just in time to experience some of the worst moments in the fields of Flanders (see WORLD WAR I).

Brazil and the United States received Portugal's most valuable export in this era, namely people. Population growth overwhelmed the economic potential of the mother country. After 1880, Portugal exported on average 20,000 people a year to Brazil and many more to the United States (see MIGRATION—TO BRAZIL). The restrictions on immigration imposed by both countries in the 1920s and 1930s created serious difficulties for Portugal, which António Salazar attempted to resolve through the policy of *integralismo,* a programmatic nationalist institutionalism that practically enshrined mass poverty as a national virtue. Fear of Communism led Western powers to accept and support the dictatorial regime that governed Portugal from 1930 to 1974 (see NATIONALISM). Salazar's Portugal, officially neutral in World War II but harboring pro-German sympathies, was in 1949 among the founding countries of the North Atlantic Treaty Organization (NATO) (see WORLD WAR II). In 1967, Lisbon became the headquarters for NATO's Iberian Atlantic Command (IBERLANT), responsible for a vast territory stretching from the coasts of Portugal to the Azores and the Tropic of Cancer. Portugal's role within NATO and its staunch anti-Communist stance helped prolong the life of its colonial empire in Africa and accounted for the thinly veiled dismay with which the United States and other Western powers greeted the Carnation Revolution of 1974, which overthrew the Salazar regime.

Contemporary Portugal has reshaped its economic and political outlook to focus on Europe. Its membership in the European Union brought a considerable increase in prosperity in the last decades of the twentieth century. Many Portuguese emigrants to North America, Australia, and other overseas areas have chosen to return home. Today's Portugal is centrist in domestic policies and follows a moderately pro-U.S. foreign policy. Although it maintains close diplomatic and cultural relations with its former African colonies (the Países Africanos de Língua Oficial Portuguesa [PALOP] countries), its economic interests in the South Atlantic are small compared to its European markets. In this sense, history has come full circle. Portugal is once again firmly attached to Europe, as it indeed was before the beginning of its overseas expansion in the fifteenth century.

Portugal and the Central Atlantic

The Atlantic Ocean south and west of the Straits of Gibraltar was geographically and historically Portugal's gateway to the Mediterranean Sea. During the Reconquista, the gradual retaking of the Iberian Peninsula from the Muslims from the eleventh to the fifteenth centuries, Portugal and Castile hotly contested its waters against Morocco for their strategic, commercial, and fishing value. Despite piracy and privateering on both sides, the Portuguese maintained significant commercial relations with various Moroccan ports, reexporting manufactures from northwestern Europe in exchange for gold, wheat, and other commodities (see ISLAM; MOORS; PIRATES AND PIRACY).

The fifteenth century brought momentous changes. The Portuguese actively pursued explorations in the Atlantic off the shores of northwest Africa (the Maghreb), sought possession of the three major regional archipelagos, and embarked upon a policy of conquest in Morocco. The Canary Islands had been an object of interest to Europeans since the mid-fourteenth century. The Portuguese made several forceful bids to conquer them in the 1420s, 1430s, and 1450s, but were forced to surrender their claim to the islands to Castile in 1479–1480, after King Afonso V's unsuccessful attempt to acquire the Castilian throne.

Portugal was, however, able to claim the two uninhabited archipelagos, Madeira and the Azores, which in the following centuries became an an integral part of Portugal. Rediscovered in 1419, Madeira and Porto Santo were rapidly settled and developed in the course of the fifteenth century. Madeira's passport to prosperity was the production of sugar and wine. Sugar held prominence in the fifteenth and early sixteenth centuries. Wine rose to sustained primacy after Madeira sugar had been eclipsed by the output of São Tomé and then Brazil (see SUGAR). The Azores, discovered between 1428 and 1451, were slower to prosper, but eventually they became an important source of agricultural products, particularly wheat, and a valuable blue dyestuff, woad (see DYES AND DYE-WOOD). The economic importance of both island groups declined somewhat after 1600, but they retained their strategic significance.

In the early modern period, the central Atlantic clung quite credibly to the remnants of its sixteenth-century prosperity, but amid increasing dangers of endemic piracy and privateering. The heightened religious animosity and protonationalist feelings fanned by Portugal's fifteenth- and sixteenth-century aggression and territorial claims in the Maghreb made Portuguese (and Spanish) vessels prime targets for North African (Barbary) pirates (see CATHOLIC CHURCH IN BRAZIL; JESUITS—BRAZIL). Their depredations were aggravated by the activities of English, French, and Dutch vessels intent on preying on the convoys that linked the Iberian Peninsula with the American possessions of both Spain and Portugal. Once Brazil had acquired its independence, the central Atlantic ceased to play a distinct role in Portuguese geopolitics, and Madeira and the Azores became increasingly integrated with metropolitan Portugal.

Portugal and the South Atlantic

The South Atlantic constituted a key dynamic factor in Portuguese history from the late fifteenth to the twentieth centuries. Fifteenth-century explorations opened to Portugal the fringes of this oceanic space, providing the springboard for commerce and ultimately settlement (see CONQUEST II—BRAZIL; CONQUISTADORS; EXPLORERS). From the sixteenth to the early nineteenth centuries, Portugal ended up presiding over a far-flung maritime empire, whose South Atlantic sector helped join together the Atlantic islands, Brazil, and outposts in West Africa and western central Africa. In the nineteenth century, Brazil's independence, at least in theory if not necessarily in practice, cut the empire in half, forcing the former metropolis to focus on the remaining African holdings while clinging to commercial relations with Brazil. For much of the twentieth century, Portugal saw the mirage of exploiting its African colonies as a viable solution to its numerous problems.

Portuguese ships, searching for commercial opportunities and political allies, first ventured south along the coasts of the western Sahara in the 1440s (see SHIPS AND SHIPBUILDING). The nature of the Portuguese presence was defined by the establishment of a permanent trading post off the coast of Mauritania in the mid-1440s and by the opening of seasonal commercial relations with various African societies between the Senegal and Gambia rivers in the 1450s. The Portuguese traded textiles, metal products, and other merchandise for gold, slaves, ivory, drugs and spices, gum arabic, and a variety of other goods. Exploration proceeded rapidly along the shores of West Africa, reaching Sierra Leone by 1460, the Gold Coast by 1470, the estuary of the Congo in 1481, and the Cape of Good Hope in 1487. The discovery and gradual settlement of key islands in the West African Atlantic (the Cape Verde Islands, São Tomé, and Príncipe) in the second half of the fifteenth century greatly enhanced the Portuguese enterprise and aided the establishment of oceanic routes linking Portugal with Brazil and the Indian Ocean.

Although gold was by far the most sought-after item, and the gold-exporting fort of São Jorge da Mina was the focal point of Portuguese claims in West Africa in the fifteenth and sixteenth centuries, slaves quickly became the standard commodity of the Portuguese South Atlantic enterprise (see SLAVE TRADE; SLAVERY I—BRAZIL). Readily available for purchase in many parts of West Africa, they proved a vital source of labor for the plantations and mines of the New World. While continental Portugal, Madeira, and the Azores absorbed a relatively small number of African slaves, the sugar plantations of São Tomé and later Brazil created a voracious demand for the unwilling immigrants.

Slave trade in the Portuguese Atlantic grew exponentially from its beginnings in the fifteenth century to its abolition in the nineteenth (see ABOLITION AND EMANCIPATION). Even before the effective colonization of Brazil, Portuguese slave exports from Africa increased from about 1,000 slaves a year in the 1450s to 4,500 by 1520 (Elbl 1997, 73). A century later, the slave exports rose to 12,000 or 13,000 per year (Lovejoy 1982, 481, Table 3), with the Portuguese still dominating the trade. At the peak of the demand in the early eighteenth century, Brazil received as many as 20,000 slaves each year (Marques 1976, 436). Overall, Brazil absorbed about 40 percent of the approximately 9.5 million slaves transported across the Atlantic before 1807 (Postma 2003, 41, Table 3.3). West Africa supplied a significant percentage of the slaves until the early eighteenth century, but from the 1730s onward its share was quickly eclipsed by western central Africa, particularly Angola. In the course of the eighteenth century, western central Africa supplied 68 percent of the slaves arriving in Brazil, and West Africa supplied 32 percent (Curtin 1969, 207, Table 62). The abolition of the Atlantic slave trade in the first half of the nineteenth century forced Portugal to rethink the economic foundations of its African empire and of the three-hundred-year-old Brazilian-African nexus.

Initially, Brazil had been slow to assume the prominent place it came to occupy in the southern Atlantic, the Portuguese Empire, and the global economy. It was first reached in 1500 by accident, when the second Portuguese fleet to India, led by Pedro Alvares Cabral, sailed far to the west to avoid the equatorial doldrums. For much of the sixteenth century Brazil remained a poor cousin of the Portuguese "tridimensional" maritime empire centered in the Indian Ocean. It was only the growth of sugar production in the late sixteenth and early seventeenth centuries that allowed it to assume a more prominent role (see COLONISTS AND SETTLERS II—BRAZIL). The number of sugar mills increased from 1 in 1533 to 130 in 1585 and 346 in 1629 (Marques 1976, 362). And sugar exports rose from 2,610 metric tons in the 1560s to 14,500 tons in the 1630s and more than 29,000 tons in the 1650s (see ENGENHO) (Ibid.).

The first half of the seventeenth century ushered in a severe political and military crisis in the Portuguese Atlantic. The Dutch, on whom the Portuguese had increasingly come to depend for shipping services, were by 1620 in a position to dominate Brazil's maritime traffic. In the 1630s and 1640s, they proceeded to challenge Portugal in both Brazil and Atlantic Africa (see DEFENSE—COLONIAL BRAZIL; DONATARY CAPTAINCIES). Much of northeast Brazil was lost, as well as the outposts in West and western central Africa, and Dutch entrepreneurs asserted control over both sugar production and the sources of the slave labor. The Dutch were eventually thwarted by Brazilian resistance, English diplomatic pressure, and the decision of the Portuguese government, newly independent from Habsburg Spain, to concentrate on defending its Atlantic holdings at the expense of the Asian ones. In the 1660s, Portugal was stripped of most of its Asian outposts, but regained possession of its core holdings in South America and Africa. This combination was essential to the prosperity of Brazil, whose plantations and mines depended heavily on African slave labor.

In the seventeenth and eighteenth centuries, sugar remained Brazil's leading export, but demand was subject to periods of boom and bust. In 1670, two years after Spain had recognized Portuguese independence, Brazil exported 29,000 metric tons of sugar, but thereafter its sugar industry nearly collapsed in the ripples of Europe's seventeenth-century economic crisis. Output eventually stabilized as a result of the general Atlantic economic recovery, and in 1711 export levels were almost back to the 1670 level (23,200 metric tons). In 1760, shipments reached 36,250 tons, well above seventeenth-century levels. The Brazilian sugar industry nonetheless suffered from Caribbean and Central American competition. In the late eighteenth century, sugar overproduction saturated global demand. Brazilian exports dropped to 21,750 tons in 1776, 9,570 tons in 1809, and as little as 6,670 tons in 1812 (for all these figures, see Marques 1976, 439). In the 1830s, sugar still accounted for 30 percent of Brazil's exports, but the industry faced increasing difficulties. The export of cotton, tobacco, and then coffee and cacao gradually filled the gap left by the decline of sugar (Burns 1970, 140) (see CACAO; COFFEE; COTTON; TOBACCO).

The discovery of rich gold and diamond deposits in its interior dramatically increased both the overall wealth of eighteenth-century Brazil and its labor needs. First tapped in 1699, the alluvial deposits and ore beds of Minas Gerais yielded a gold bonanza, complemented after 1729 by the discovery of diamonds. In 1699, 514 kilograms of gold arrived in Lisbon. In 1701 the volume increased to 2,000 kilograms, in 1703 to 4,406 kilograms, and in 1712 to 14,500. In 1720 gold exports peaked at 25,000 kilograms, settling down to approximately 20,000 kilograms a year in the 1740s and 1750s. In the 1760s, Brazil was still able to ship as much as 14,000 to 16,000 kilograms of gold annually, but in the 1770s and 1780s the volume dropped sharply to around 1,000 kilograms a year (Marques 1976, 389). In 1801 gold still accounted for some 15 percent of Brazilian outbound trade, but by 1816 the "golden century" was definitely over, with gold plummeting to only 0.2 percent of overall exports (Marques 1976, 458) (see GOLD; MINING—GOLD).

Brazil's demography largely reflected the upward trends of the economy. By 1770, population had reached 1.5 million (Marques 1976, 453). Minas Gerais headed the count, with 20.5 percent of the total, followed by Baía (18.5 percent), Pernambuco (15.4 percent), Rio de Janeiro (13.8 percent), and São Paulo (7.5 percent). The rest of Brazil's vast interior accounted for the remaining 25 percent (Marques 1976, 435). Population growth accelerated further after 1770. In 1800, Brazil counted 2.5 million inhabitants, and in 1819 some 3.6 million. More than half of the population consisted of African slaves, but the number of locally born "white" inhabitants also increased dramatically, reaching almost a million in 1819 (Marques 1976, 453) (see NATIVE AMERICANS I–II).

The flight of the Portuguese court from Napoleon's forces to Brazil in 1807 had a notable impact on the development of both Brazilian commerce and political identity. Brazil now became the official center of the Portuguese empire. In 1808 Brazilian ports fully opened to foreign trade, which now could simply bypass the old metropolis. England, Brazil's chief trading partner, benefited greatly from this measure, but so did Brazil itself. The presence of the imperial court fostered the development of infrastructure and various industries, the latter previously hampered by metropolitan protectionist measures. Attempts by the Portuguese cortes (parliament) in 1820–1822 to channel trade with Brazil once again through Lisbon and to return Brazil to the status of a colony helped to bring about the Brazilian declaration of independence.

Although plagued by political instability, nineteenth-century Brazil experienced considerable prosperity, increased exploration and settlement of its interior, and vigorous economic and cultural development (see ARCHITECTURE—BRAZIL; ART AND ARTISTS—BRAZIL; MUSIC AND DANCE I—BRAZIL; POETRY—BRAZIL). The overall demographic trend was sharply expansionary. When Brazil gained independence, it had less than 4 million inhabitants. Fifty years later, its population had doubled, and by 1890 it had tripled. While a sharp population increase indeed characterized most of the Atlantic world, Brazil, like the United States, seemed to have an almost unlimited capacity to attract and absorb immigrants, at least until the eve of the Great Depression.

The transatlantic slave trade continued to play a key role in Brazil's population dynamics in the first half of the nineteenth century. The country received 1,145,000 Africans, largely from Angola and Mozambique, before it officially outlawed slave imports in 1850. While clandestine slave trade continued, much abated, for another decade, Brazil began to rely increasingly on voluntary immigrants from Europe. Immigration grew from approximately 2,000 persons per year in 1850 to more than 55,000 in 1887. In 1888, the year slavery was finally abolished, the number of free migrants more than doubled over the preceding year's level (Burns 1970, 187, Table IV). Until the 1870s, Portugal had provided the majority of Brazil's immigrants, although increasing numbers came from Italy, Germany, and other European countries. In the late nineteenth century, Italians overtook the Portuguese. Many immigrants did not stay, however, eventually relocating to other countries such as the rapidly expanding Argentina, or even returning to Europe. Both the influx of Europeans and the changing sociocultural perceptions of "whiteness" account for the concurrent dramatic change in Brazil's racial demographics. While 38 percent of the population was classified as "white" in 1872, by 1890 the percentage rose to 44 percent, and by 1940 to 63.5 percent (Burns 1970, 266, Table IX). Sometimes referred to as the bleaching of Brazil, the process allowed people of color to become "white" as a token of upward social mobility.

The nineteenth and early twentieth centuries were also an era of economic expansion. Growth continued to rely on agricultural products and raw materials, despite a gradual development of local industries. Coffee replaced sugar as the main export, catering to an unprecedented worldwide boom in the consumption of caffeine and caffeinated beverages. From a mere 18.4 percent of Brazilian exports in the 1820s, coffee rose to 49 percent in the 1850s, and to 64.5 percent in the 1890s (Burns 1970, 140, Table III). Its production nearly doubled in the first half of the twentieth century, despite the crises caused by the two world wars. Sugar declined from 30 percent of exports in the 1820s to only 6 percent at the end of the century, falling even further in the early 1900s. Cotton suffered a similar fate, receding from 20.8 percent to 2.7 percent. The most dynamic export commodity, besides coffee, was rubber (see RUBBER). The industrial demands of the Western economies account for its rise from the last place among major Brazilian exports, with only 0.1 percent, to 15 percent by the end of the nineteenth century. All told, rubber exports tripled between 1880 and 1910, fell by a third in the 1910s, remained steady in the 1920s, but then dropped significantly as a result of the Great Depression and the ultimate acceptance of artificial rubber.

Britain was Brazil's main trading partner in the nineteenth century, but it was eventually overtaken by the United States, who maintained a firm lead throughout the twentieth century. Britain nonetheless continued to play a significant role, as did Germany. France and Portugal maintained and further developed important economic and cultural links with Brazil. The booming demand for Brazil's export commodities in the late nineteenth and early twentieth centuries allowed the country to rely on imports of a broad range of industrial and consumer goods. This reliance left Brazil in a vulnerable position when World War I disrupted peacetime exchange patterns. Brazil's alliance with the United States led it to take the Allies' side in both world wars and to serve them as an important source of raw materials.

Forced to industrialize rapidly after World War I, Brazil experienced serious economic and social difficulties, as well as political instability; its leaders tried to address some of the problems by fostering a climate of nationalism and patriotic zeal. In the second half of the century, Brazil's political history was plagued by military dictatorships and rightist governments, supported during the cold war by the United States. Brazil emerged from this difficult period into the twenty-first century as the leading South American economic power, but it is still considered a developing country rather than a developed one. The social and environmental problems caused by rapid industrialization and by infrastructure development in hitherto unevenly settled areas of the more remote rain forest interior constitute a troublesome legacy for the future.

In the early nineteenth century, Portuguese territories in Atlantic Africa included, in addition to the Cape Verde and Gulf of Guinea islands, only outpost settlements and a relatively narrow strip along the coast of Angola. Yet the loss of Brazil forced Portugal to refocus its attention on these scattered holdings and their uncertain potential. The challenges, both external and internal, were considerable, and the most significant claims were nearly lost early on. Indeed, Brazil initially considered promoting the emancipation of Angola in the wake of its own independence, and it only dropped this ambition in exchange for the recognition of its sovereignty by Portugal.

Slavery and the slave trade played a key role in the economies of all the Portuguese African possessions. Although international pressures to end the Atlantic slave trade induced a series of legislative measures aimed at its suppression, it was only the Brazilian prohibition of African slave imports in 1850 that made a substantial difference (see SLAVE REBELLIONS—BRAZIL). Nonetheless, since the 1830s Portugal had been struggling to develop a new vision for its residual empire, now predominantly African, hoping to shape it into a "new Brazil" while defending it from the colonial ambitions of more powerful Atlantic rivals, in particular England, France, and later Germany. This project meant laying effective claim to the interior of Portuguese Guinea, Angola, and Mozambique, colonizing territory as opposed to imposing tribute on native groups and states, promoting "legitimate" trade and resource-based economies on the African mainland, and attempting to stimulate metropolitan emigration to Africa while preserving the loyalty and cooperation of African creole elites. Yet, though their exploration of the African interior was very successful and quite epic in scope, the Portuguese lacked the capital and human resources to follow it up in the manner later employed by other Atlantic colonial powers. The buildup of transportation infrastructure in Angola and Mozambique, for instance, was largely financed by foreign capital and carried out by foreign firms. A widespread reliance on forced labor, a brutal practice akin to slavery, left Portugal open to severe criticism on both the international and local fronts.

For Portugal, the African empire was a matter of pride rather than economic interest. The cost of maintaining the African claims was overwhelming, far outweighing revenues. Throughout the second half of the nineteenth century and well into the 1920s, Portugal engaged in seemingly endless wars of conquest in the interior, punitive campaigns aimed at suppressing and discouraging rebellions, and frequent hostilities against intruding colonial competitors. Angola's debts alone accounted for 20 percent of the Portuguese national debt in the 1910s and 1920s, and helped to bring Portugal so close to bankruptcy that the debtor powers, particularly England and France, considered partitioning Portugal's colonies should the mother country default. Yet, costly as the African presence was, maintaining it was an ideological imperative for most of Portugal's political leaders. In the 1880s, a Portugal stubbornly defending "its own" amidst the scramble for Africa laid a formal claim to much of southern central Africa, carving out as part of the famous "Rose-Coloured Map" (*Mapa cor de rosa,* drawn in 1886 at the orders of Portuguese foreign minister Henrique Barros Gomes and made public in 1887) a large belt of territory connecting the Atlantic with the Indian Ocean. In response, Great Britain presented its long-term protégé in 1890 with a humiliating ultimatum demanding that Portugal surrender, among other areas, the mineral-rich future Zambia and Zimbabwe (the former British Rhodesia). Portugal was obliged to concede, but the resulting deep resentment made it even more tenacious of its African dreams.

After 1930, António Salazar and his Estado Novo elevated the African empire to further ideological prominence. The policy of *luso-tropicalism* conceptualized Portuguese Africa not only as the beneficiary of a "civilizing mission," but as an integral part of a greater Portugal. The Salazar regime imposed a strictly centralized governance in the African colonies, limiting the local autonomy of influential creole and regional elites. The regime promoted increased metropolitan immigration to Africa, a policy that came to fruition in the 1950s amid the growing economic prosperity of the African colonies, particularly Angola. The influx of settlers from the mother country further upset the existing balance of local power relations and fueled the discontent prompted by increased exploitation and the political repression exercised by the PIDE, Salazar's secret police. In 1961, Angolan nationalists started an armed insurgency that marked the beginning of fourteen years of colonial warfare, which sapped the strength of the Estado Novo and fueled opposition among the new generation of Portuguese army officers, who eventually overthrew the dictatorship in 1974.

The restoration of democracy in Portugal ended the colonial wars, but not armed conflict in former Portuguese Africa. The new republics of Guinea Bissau and Cape Verde, São Tomé, Angola, and Mozambique emerged on the international scene at a time when local issues were seen and acted upon through the polarized overlay of cold war paradigms. Fear that the new countries would become committed clients of the Soviet Union led the United States and other Western powers to arm, support, and nurse opposition and splinter movements, often defined ethnically or regionally rather than ideologically, but strong enough to forestall the emergence of centralized leftist governments. The result was a series of decades-long postcolonial conflicts that are abating only gradually, despite the overt end of the cold war.

References

Birmingham, David. *Portugal and Africa*. Basingstoke, UK: Macmillan; New York: St. Martin's, 1999.

———. *A Concise History of Portugal*. 2nd ed. Cambridge: Cambridge University Press, 2003.

Burns, E. Bradford. *A History of Brazil*. New York and London: Columbia University Press, 1970.

Clarence-Smith, Gervase. *The Third Portuguese Empire*. Manchester: Manchester University Press, 1985.

Curtin, Philip D. *The Atlantic Slave Trade: A Census*. Madison and London: University of Wisconsin Press, 1969.

Curto, José C., and Paul E. Lovejoy, eds. *Enslaving Connections: Changing Cultures of Africa and Brazil during the Era of Slavery*. Amherst, NY: Humanity, 2004.

Elbl, Ivana. "The Volume of the Early Atlantic Slave Trade, 1450–1521." *Journal of African History*, vol. 38, no. 1 (1997): 31–75.

Fausto, Boris. *A Concise History of Brazil*. Translated by Arthur Brakel. Cambridge and New York: Cambridge University Press, 1999.

Lang, James. *Portuguese Brazil: The King's Plantation*. New York: Academic, 1979.

Levine, Robert M. *The History of Brazil*. Westport, CT, and London: Greenwood, 1999.

Lloyd-Jones, Stewart, and António Costa Pinto, eds. *The Last Empire: Thirty Years of Portuguese Decolonization*. Bristol, UK, and Portland, OR: Intellect, 2003.

Lovejoy, Paul E. "The Volume of the Atlantic Slave Trade: A Synthesis." *Journal of African History*, vol. 23, no. 4 (1982): 473–501.

Marques, A. H. de Oliveira. *History of Portugal.* 2nd ed. New York: Columbia University Press, 1976.

Miller, Joseph Calder. *Way of Death: Merchant Capitalism and the Angolan Slave Trade, 1730–1830.* Madison: University of Wisconsin Press, 1988.

Postma, Johannes. *The Atlantic Slave Trade.* Westport, CT: Greenwood, 2003.

Shaw, L. M. E. *The Anglo-Portuguese Alliance and the English Merchants in Portugal, 1654–1810.* Brookfield, VT: Ashgate, 1998.

Sideri, Sandro. *Trade and Power: Informal Colonialism in Anglo-Portuguese Relations.* Rotterdam: Rotterdam University Press, 1970.

Skidmore, Thomas E. *Brazil: Five Centuries of Change.* New York: Oxford University Press, 1999.

Smith, Joseph, and Francisco L. Teixeira Vinhosa. *History of Brazil, 1500–2000: Politics, Economy, Society, Diplomacy.* London and New York: Longman, 2002.

Thornton, John. *Africa and Africans in the Making of the Atlantic World, 1400–1800.* 2nd expanded ed. Cambridge: Cambridge University Press, 1998.

Vieira, Alberto, ed. *Slaves with or without Sugar.* Funchal, Portugal: Atlantic History Study Centre, Regional Tourist and Culture Office, 1996.

Wheeler, Douglas. *The Empire Time Forgot: Writing a History of Portuguese Overseas Empire, 1808–1975.* Lisbon: Edições Universidade Fernando Pessoa, 1998.

SPAIN AND THE UNITED STATES

José Ángel Carreño

The American Revolution initiated the relationship between Spain and the United States. Since then, relations between the two countries have been difficult at times, as, for example, during the war of 1898 or during the initial upset caused in Washington by General Francisco Franco's regime (see AMERICAN REVOLUTION; SPANISH-AMERICAN WAR; COLD WAR—SPAIN AND THE AMERICAS). Today, however, the countries are important allies within the North Atlantic Treaty Organization (NATO) framework (see NORTH ATLANTIC TREATY ORGANIZATION).

The relationship between the two countries can only be fully understood if one considers the full historical background. Long before the United States gained its independence, Spain had already explored a great part of the territories destined to form the United States and had even occupied some of them (see BORDERLANDS; CALIFORNIA; EXPLORERS; FLORIDA; MISSIONS). That lasting presence and Spanish immigration during the nineteenth and twentieth centuries account for Spain's enduring influence in the United States. The first object of Spanish interest was La Florida, understood during the early colonial period as a land north of the Gulf of Mexico whose limits were undefined; in fact, its boundaries were still unclear more than a century later when English colonists settled in Carolina. Nevertheless, La Florida drew Spain's attention to the southeast of what is now the United States from the earliest times.

In 1513, Juan Ponce de León became the first Spaniard to explore La Florida; however, it was not until 1521 that he returned to colonize the region. Although Ponce de León met his death in the attempt, by then Spaniards were already acquainted with the entire northern coast of the Gulf of Mexico (see CONQUEST VI—SOUTHEASTERN NORTH AMERICA; NATIVE AMERICANS VIII—SOUTHEASTERN NORTH AMERICA).

Over the following years explorations across the North American southeast continued. Lucas Vázquez de Ayllón attempted to colonize those lands, but he died during the adventure (in 1526), having attempted to conquer and settle the Carolinas. Esteban Gómez in his search for a strait that connected the Atlantic and Pacific Oceans (1524–1525) surveyed the coast from Cape Hatteras up to Maine. Pánfilo de Narváez led another expedition (1527–1528) and also died in the area. However, a few survivors from his expedition went over a part of Florida, reached Mobile Bay, crossed the Mississippi River, and entered Texas. Álvar Núñez Cabeza de Vaca and other survivors arrived in northwestern Mexico in 1536 after an eight-year journey, during which perhaps they crossed a part of New Mexico and Arizona. Hernando de Soto's 1539 expedition was intended to settle Spaniards permanently in the southeast. In spite of de Soto's death in 1542, his attempt allowed Spain to explore regions of Florida, Georgia, North and South Carolina, Alabama, Mississippi, Tennessee, Arkansas, Louisiana, and Texas, as well as the Mississippi River. However, after so many efforts (and so little reward), the Spanish king Charles I was never able to see his subjects established on that part of the continent.

Expeditions organized to explore what is now the U.S. Southwest met with similar results, and no permanent Spanish settlements. Nevertheless, they provided important geographical knowledge. Vásquez de Coronado's explorations (1540–1542) apparently reached Upper California west of the Colorado River. His men went through part of Arizona, where they discovered the Grand Canyon, New Mexico, Texas, Oklahoma, and Kansas, and reached into what is now Nebraska. At the same time, Hernando de Alarcón navigated the Colorado River upwards from its outlet. Bartolomé Ferrelo, sailing along the Pacific coast, discovered Cape Mendocino, California (1543).

In spite of all the early explorations, when Spanish king Philip II began his reign (1556–1598), none of those regions had been settled permanently. However, the occupation of Florida came soon, after Pedro Menéndez de Avilés expelled French Calvinists and founded the city of San Agustín (1565) (see COLONISTS AND SETTLERS VI—SOUTHEASTERN NORTH AMERICA). From that moment Spanish influence and presence spread not only in Florida but also over Alabama, Georgia, the Carolinas, and Tennessee; Spanish vessels even explored the Chesapeake Bay, and Spanish missionaries attempted to convert Indians in Virginia, all before the sixteenth century ended. In the 1590s Juan de Oñate began the colonization of New Mexico, where Pedro de Peralta founded the city of Santa Fe at the beginning of the next century (see BORDERLANDS; CATHOLIC CHURCH IN SPANISH AMERICA).

During the seventeenth century, Spain further consolidated its presence in North America. In 1603 Sebastián Vizcaíno explored the Pacific Ocean up to the coast of Oregon. By the end of the century the Spanish had established military, civil, and missionary posts in several points of Upper Pimería—Mexican Sonora and southern Arizona, New Mexico, and Texas. Advance toward East Texas was stopped but at the same time encouraged by the threat of a growing French presence at the mouth of the Mississippi (La Salle, 1682) and the short-lived French colony in Matagorda Bay (1684–1685). La Salle's arrival at the Mississippi River was the origin of French Louisiana and the effective cause of the Spanish occupation of Pensacola.

European diplomacy and wars substantially affected North America during the eighteenth century. Wars against England led to attacks on Spanish Florida, with the destruction of some of the area's missions. Spain also waged war against France (1719–1721), during which East Texas was invaded, a Spanish post at Nebraska was attacked, and Pensacola was conquered by the French. Peace brought about the restoration of the status quo prior to the war. Spain then undertook the expansion into East Texas, for which San Antonio (1718) served as the base.

The French and Indian War (1754–1756) and the Seven Years' War (1756–1763) led to important territorial changes in North America (see SEVEN YEARS' WAR). By virtue of the Family Compact (1761), Spain became France's ally and declared war on Great Britain (1762). A resounding British victory led to the Peace of Paris (1763), which forced Spain to cede Florida (with San Agustín and Pensacola Bay), as well as all Spanish possessions east of the Mississippi, to the English. The victorious English also received French East Louisiana. On the other hand, France compensated Spain's losses by giving up West Louisiana and New Orleans (see LOUISIANA PURCHASE).

By that time, burgeoning British and Russian interest in the Pacific coast forced the Spanish government to occupy Upper California. Overall, twenty Franciscan missions and several civil and military posts were founded in California between 1769 and 1821. The Spanish navy also surveyed much of the Pacific coast, reaching as far north as 61 degrees north latitude, as far as Alaska. During the second half of the eighteenth century, Spaniards also reached Nevada and crossed into Colorado and Utah.

The occasion for Spain to avenge the humiliating defeat suffered in 1762 came with the American Revolution. The United States asked for Spanish support, in return for which U.S. envoys offered Spain the possibility of recovering lost possessions on the Gulf coast. Initially, Spain refused to enter the conflict directly; however, it did provide military supplies and important economic backing. In June 1779, Spain officially joined France and the U.S. patriots in the ongoing war against the English. Under the terms of the Peace of Versailles (1783), Spain once again governed Florida.

Once war was over and U.S. independence assured, a vast territory from the Allegheny to the Mississippi and from Canada to the Gulf coast was at issue; this time, however, the conflict was between the United States and Spain. Negotiations took several years, but eventually Spain and the United States signed Pinckney's Treaty (on October 27, 1795), according to which the western border of the United States was fixed at the Mississippi and the southwestern one was to run from the Mississippi at 31 degrees north latitude, following a line westward to the Chattahoochee, Flint, and Saint Mary's rivers and then to the latter's outlet into the ocean. Navigation of the Mississippi would be free for both Spanish and U.S. merchants.

At the opening of the nineteenth century, Spain agreed with Napoleon Bonaparte to return Louisiana to French control (1800–1801); however, the transfer was delayed until a European general peace was reached, which happened at Amiens (1802). A year later,

Bonaparte sold the former Spanish Louisiana (which had stretched from Louisiana to Missouri and had established some posts on disputed lands of Mississippi, Tennessee, and Alabama), to the United States (see LOUISIANA PURCHASE). Several disputes between Spain and the United States erupted over sovereignty in Texas and in the Pacific Northwest. These disputes were not resolved until the 1819 Adams-Onís Treaty, which resolved boundary issues across the continent. Under the terms of the treaty, Spain ceded East and West Florida to the United States. The limits were established along the Sabine and Red rivers, whose flow was to be followed up to 100 degrees west longitude, and then a line was to be drawn due north to the Arkansas River and from 42 degrees north latitude to the Pacific Ocean. The remaining Spanish territories from Texas to California were lost to Spain when Mexico became independent (1821).

Other events that dominated Spanish-U.S. relations during the nineteenth century were the early recognition of young Spanish American republics by the United States, Spanish neutrality during the American Civil War (1861–1865), and the U.S. recognition of the first Spanish republic. But perhaps the most important aspect of nineteenth-century Spanish-U.S. relations centered on the island of Cuba. Throughout the nineteenth century, the United States maintained a keen interest in Spanish Cuba, with which they had established close economic ties. Some Americans, as well as some Cubans, desired the annexation of the island by the United States. When war erupted between Spain and Cuban nationalists, the United States declared war on Spain (1898) (see USS MAINE). As a result of the Peace of Paris (December 10, 1898) Spain relinquished its sovereignty over Cuba and ceded Puerto Rico, the Philippines, and Guam to the United States.

Twentieth-century Spain was marked by the Spanish Civil War (1936–1939), during which the United States declared neutrality. When the war ended, the U.S. government initially recognized Francisco Franco's Spain; however, Franco's close relationship with Fascist Italy and Nazi Germany led Washington to oppose Spain's admission to the United Nations (UN) and to back a UN resolution fostering diplomatic isolation; Spain was also excluded from the Marshall Plan, which helped Europe rebuild after the war (see WORLD WAR I; WORLD WAR II). With the start of the cold war, however, the United States recognized the importance of Spain as an ally and therefore voted at the United Nations in 1950 to end Spanish isolation; three years later the United States signed an agreement with Spain on military and economic assistance (1953) and then supported Spain's entrance into the United Nations (1955).

After Franco's death, Washington warmly welcomed the new Spanish democracy, expressing that welcome by signing a treaty with Spain in 1976 and by encouraging King Juan Carlos I's visit to the United States (1976), his first official trip outside Spain. Spain was admitted to NATO (1982), and an official alliance between Spain and the United States was negotiated that same year. As a result of this alliance, the United States has been able to count on Spain's support on a number of occasions, including the first Gulf War (1991), the Afghanistan campaign, and, until Spain's 2004 national election, the Iraq war.

References

Bemis, Samuel F. *Pinckney's Treaty: America's Advantage from Europe's Distress, 1783–1800.* New Haven: Yale University, 1960.

Chipman, Donald E. *Texas en la época colonial.* Madrid: Editorial Mapfre, 1992.

Cutter, Donald. *España en Nuevo México.* Madrid: Editorial Mapfre, 1992.

Hilton, Sylvia L. *La Alta California española.* Madrid: Editorial Mapfre, 1992.

Engstrand, Iris H. W. *Arizona hispánica.* Madrid: Editorial Mapfre, 1992.

Pereira, Juan Carlos, ed. *La política exterior de España (1800–2003).* Barcelona: Ariel, 2003.

IBERIA AND CANADA

Antonio Cazorla-Sanchez

The relationship between the Iberian Peninsula and Canada began with the arrival of the first Portuguese navigators in the early sixteenth century. In 1501, Gaspar Corte Real explored the northeast coast of Newfoundland and the coast of Labrador (which incidentally means "farmer" in Portuguese). In the following years, Portuguese and Spanish (mostly Basque) fishermen began to appear, as reports spread of the rich banks of cod off Newfoundland. In order to process the fish, Iberian fishermen established small processing factories along the coast, in villages and towns that still bear Portuguese or Spanish names. These seasonal trips continued over the next four hundred years until the late 1970s, when Canada claimed exclusive rights over most of the Great Banks waters (see TURBOT FISH WAR). Relics in churches and tombstones in cemeteries offer grim reminders of the hardships that these men endured.

The significant presence of Iberians, mostly Portuguese, in continental Canada is a relatively recent phenomenon. Transoceanic migration for Iberians in the nineteenth and early twentieth centuries concentrated almost exclusively in Latin America (Brazil for the Portuguese and Argentina for the Spaniards) (see MIGRATION—FROM IBERIA TO THE NEW WORLD). However, a shift to the north began shortly after World War II, when the Canadian and Portuguese governments signed labor contract agreements to supply railway construction and agricultural workers (see WORLD WAR II). In the 1950s, almost 20,000 Portuguese workers arrived in Canada, mostly from the Azores islands, which were overpopulated and extremely poor. As the Portuguese dictatorship of Oliveira Salazar (1926–1974) failed to significantly increase living standards, emigration toward Europe and the Americas increased in the 1960s. By the 1990s, over 300,000 people of Portuguese heritage lived in Canada, most in Ontario (particularly Toronto) but also in Montreal (Quebec). In both cities, Portuguese Canadians have developed a rich community life. This population originally had very low levels of education, reflecting the hard-

47

ship and poverty they left behind. This lack of professional qualifications meant that most immigrants joined the lower ranks of the workforce. This situation has been addressed by both Canadian educational authorities and Portuguese community leaders in the last two decades.

Like the Portuguese, Spaniards were among the first Europeans to reach Canada's east coast in the sixteenth century. The west coast was explored in the eighteenth century by sailors navigating from Mexico and California (see BORDERLANDS; CONQUISTADORS; EXPLORERS). There, they briefly established a number of small, short-lived forts, and, as in the eastern part of Canada, only the names of those navigators remain as a reminder of their presence. The first Spanish immigrants (roughly 2,000 in number) to Canada appeared on the eve of World War I in the huge metalwork factories of Hamilton, Ontario (see WORLD WAR I). With the onset of the Depression, immigration fell to a trickle, with only a few hundred Spaniards arriving during the interwar period. Only in the late 1950s did Spanish immigration to Canada increase; however, the overall numbers were relatively small when compared with the Portuguese or other southern Europeans, such as the Italians and the Greeks. For example, during the peak years of 1966 to 1968, the total number of Spanish immigrants reached only 4,000. Most of them settled first in Montreal, and then later in Toronto. By the end of the twentieth century, Spanish communities in both cities were by far the largest in the country (some 30,000 in Toronto and around 18,000 in Montreal). In socioeconomic terms, most of these people can be described as lower-middle class, with a high proportion of retirees among them. After 1977, Spanish immigration to Canada declined dramatically.

Although most of the immigrants to Canada came because of economic reasons, small groups of Spanish political refugees arrived in the early 1940s. In the anti-Communist context of the prewar period and the cold war, these individuals were received with suspicion, and some even saw their applications for immigration rejected. Support for Franco's regime was strong, especially in Catholic Quebec, where the dictator was praised by both religious and civil authorities for having saved Spain from atheism and chaos. In Conservative, mostly Protestant English Canada, Franco's government (1936–1975), like Salazar's in Portugal, represented, at least until World War II, an authoritarian deterrent to Communism (see COLD WAR—SPAIN AND THE AMERICAS; COMMUNISM). Considering the environment, it is not surprising that Canadians who volunteered in the Mackenzie-Papineau Battalion of the International Brigades to fight Fascism in the Spanish Civil War (1936–1939) returned home, often to be persecuted and questioned by Canadian authorities. The first Canadian monument erected to their memory was in 1994 (in Toronto), while in other democratic countries (such as France, Italy, and the United Kingdom), monuments to Spanish Civil War veterans had been erected decades earlier.

Relationships between the governments of the Iberian Peninsula and Canada have not been a priority for either side. Iberians have always been more interested in Europe and Latin America than in Canada, and Canadians have been more interested in their relations with the United States, the United Kingdom, and now Asia than in their relations with Spain or Portugal. This lack of priority is reflected in the paucity of intellectual and cultural exchanges, and in the weak presence of Iberian studies in Canadian universities and Canadian studies in Iberian universities. For most Canadians, the Iberian Peninsula is an attractive, if slightly remote, holiday destination, while for most Iberians the image of Canada is linked to its vast and overwhelming landscape and open spaces.

References

Álvarez Junco, José, and Adrian Shubert, eds. *Spanish History since 1808.* London: Arnold, 2000.

Costa Pinto, Antonio, ed. *Modern Portugal.* Palo Alto, CA: Society for the Promotion of Science and Scholarship, 1998.

Shubert, Adrian, and Antonio Cazorla. "Spaniards." In *The Peoples of Canada: An Encyclopaedia for the Country,* edited by Paul Magosci. Toronto: University of Toronto Press, 1999.

Teixeira, Carlos, and Victor M. P. Da Rosa, eds. *The Portuguese in Canada: From the Sea to the City.* Toronto: University of Toronto Press, 2000.

A

ABOLITION AND EMANCIPATION

Abolition, and later emancipation, was one of the first truly global movements, and therefore it must be understood in its global context. In the nineteenth century, Iberian rulers and their colonial partners came reluctantly to abandon the Atlantic slave trade and still more reluctantly to emancipate the slaves held in Iberian nations in the Americas. Spanish and Portuguese colonists, like their British and French counterparts in the New World, had considerable incentives to resist ending slavery. From the early sixteenth century until the end of the nineteenth, the use of African and native-born slaves of African descent to harvest and process sugar, mine gold, build ships, and do much of the manual work of the colonies was common throughout Spanish and Portuguese America. Brazil, in particular, was built upon the labor of African slaves; over three and a half million people were brought to labor in sugar fields, mines, and coffee plantations during the course of the trade. The trade itself, along with the labor of slaves in the Americas, returned handsome profits to Iberian merchants, planters, and the Crown. In addition, an elaborate philosophical and religious defense of slavery silenced any humanitarian qualms Iberians had regarding the practice of slavery.

Opposition to the Atlantic slave trade began in Britain in the 1750s among Quakers, who first forced their members to give up slaves, then, along with the Methodists, petitioned Parliament to improve conditions on slave ships. Portuguese reformers achieved similar victories on the peninsula; in 1761 and 1773, the kingdom freed enslaved blacks in Portugal and prevented the importation of slaves thereafter. The movement to ban the Atlantic slave trade emerged most fully in Britain, and that kingdom used its diplomatic and economic power to force other nations to abandon the trade. Portugal, with its heavy dependence on the trade and products of Brazil, had no indigenous interest in abolition in 1807 when British commissioners began to press Portugal to join the global ban on slave trading. In 1817, Portugal reluctantly agreed to an addendum, penned by the British to the Congress of Vienna, that restricted its slave trade to territories south of the equator. This agreement also gave the British the right to detain and search ships outside this range suspected of carrying slaves. British pressure compelled Spain to abolish its trade completely by 1820, although an extensive illegal trade continued to Cuba and Puerto Rico, along with the still legal Portuguese trade to Brazil. Under severe economic and military pressure from the British, including the threat of a blockade of their ports, the Brazilian Chamber of Deputies passed legislation outlawing the trade in 1850. Forty years of international pressure accomplished its goal, but passage of abolition did little to advance emancipation. Over the next two decades, the two million slaves in Brazil and the several hundred thousand in Cuba and Puerto Rico continued to function much as they had before 1850.

As much as the movement for abolition of the trade was by nature an international affair, the energy and effort behind emancipation were a domestic one in Ibero-America. The surprising conclusion of the American Civil War, the emancipation of Russian serfs, and the freeing of slaves in the Portuguese, French, and Danish empires in the early 1860s all put new pressure on Brazil to consider emancipation and gave succor to the few abolitionists working in the country. Leading statesmen considered the issue in the 1860s, but the authority wielded by plantation owners in the still mostly rural nation stymied change. The failure to achieve reform within the government mobilized Brazilian abolitionists, who opened printing presses, convened meetings, and agitated more aggressively for immediate emancipation. Proponents of emancipation marshaled moral and religious arguments against slavery to convert the undecided in Brazil and help preserve the nation's good standing among modern Western commu-

nities. Like most converts to free labor worldwide, Brazilian abolitionists promised more efficient workplaces. In response, the legislature passed a Free Birth bill in 1871. The legislation freed newborn slaves but gave masters the ability to retain their labor until they reached twenty-one years of age, unless the master preferred to relinquish the child to the state at the age of eight.

Although this measure ensured the eventual demise of the formal institution of slavery, it gave masters time to construct new systems of control over their workers. Coffee-producing regions in particular remained strongly committed to slavery throughout the 1870s. In response to the intransigence of large plantation owners, abolitionists preached the necessity of full and immediate emancipation. Using mostly legal and peaceful methods, abolitionists converted a majority of Brazilians to their perspective on slavery by the mid-1880s. At this point, the abolition movement became a popular movement, with huge public meetings and wide support in the national government. Also in this period, slaves fled plantations in larger numbers, with some regional governments abetting their actions. In 1888, the state abolished slavery completely.

As in Brazil, Cuban slaveholders continued to reap profits well into the 1860s. In 1868, Cuba exported 40 percent of the sugar on the global market, using 173,000 slaves on 1,500 sugar estates throughout the country (Scott 1985, 3). Challenging an economically successful institution was not the only problem faced by Spanish and Spanish American reformers. Throughout Spanish America, the confluence of anti-slavery and anticolonial movements produced unexpected outcomes. The rebellions of 1868 in Cuba and Puerto Rico put pressure on Spain, because leaders of the independence movements advocated emancipation over the objections of many colonial elites, who owned slaves. Spanish officials sought to undercut the authority of colonial elites by pushing abolition and unintentionally bolstered the aims of the independence movement.

Puerto Rican and Spanish liberals and republicans had founded the Spanish Abolitionist Society in Madrid in 1865. Members seized on new privileges in the 1869 constitution to vigorously push emancipation in the colonies. In response, Spain passed the Moret law in 1870, which initiated a gradual emancipation of Cuba's 370,000 slaves (Scott 1985, 71–72). Despite the resistance of slaveholders, the Spanish Abolitionist Society and Puerto Rican reformers succeeded in pushing through a bill for immediate abolition in Puerto Rico in 1873. Even with the effect of the Moret law and the loss of slaves as the result of an extended rebellion in the eastern provinces, 200,000 slaves remained on sugar plantations in Cuba (Scott 1985, 86). In 1880, Spain passed a new emancipation law (called the *patronato*), which freed specific numbers of slaves each year, but kept laborers wedded to their owners through apprenticeship and corporal punishment. By 1886, only 26,000 people remained enslaved, at which point Spain abolished the gradual process of the patronato and ended slavery.

Abolition in Brazil was a more calculated and prolonged affair than in Cuba or Puerto Rico, where the contingencies of the anticolonial political and military events shaped the outcome. Nevertheless, in both places, plantation owners retained significant control over workers, even after they were emancipated. Brazil replaced slavery with a heavily coercive system of free labor that kept many former slaves in conditions of poverty and perpetual work. Cuba did much the same, using vagrancy laws and other techniques to bind laborers to their plantations. Just as participation in the slave trade exacerbated systems of hierarchy throughout the Atlantic world, in the Iberian world even abolition movements did little to generate equality among all peoples.

Aaron Sheehan-Dean

References
Baronov, David. *The Abolition of Slavery in Brazil: The "Liberation" of Africans through the Emancipation of Capital.* Westport, CT: Greenwood Press, 2000.

Blackburn, Robin. *The Overthrow of Colonial Slavery, 1776–1848.* New York: Verso, 1988.

Conrad, Robert Edgar. *The Destruction of Brazilian Slavery, 1850–1888.* Berkeley and Los Angeles: University of California Press, 1972.

Corwin, Arthur F. *Spain and the Abolition of Slavery in Cuba, 1817–1886.* Austin: University of Texas Press, 1967.

Lombardi, John V. *The Decline and Abolition of Negro Slavery in Venezuela, 1820–1854.* Westport, CT: Greenwood, 1971.

Scott, Rebecca Jarvis. *Slave Emancipation in Cuba: The Transition to Free Labor, 1860–1899.* Princeton, NJ: Princeton University Press, 1985.

Toplin, Brent. *The Abolition of Slavery in Brazil.* New York: Atheneum, 1972.

See also: Asiento; Atlantic Economy; Bourbon Reforms; Coffee; Conquest and the Debate over Justice; Enlightenment—Brazil; Enlightenment—Spanish America; Mining—Gold; Mining—Mercury; Mining—Silver; Race; Slave Rebellions—Brazil; Slave Rebellions—Caribbean; Slave Rebellions—Spanish America; Slavery I–IV; Slave Trade; Sugar.

ADMINISTRATION—COLONIAL SPANISH AMERICA

Throughout the colonial period, Spain's American dominions were linked to the mother country by a complex and hierarchical bureaucracy. Although the structure and main characteristics of this system had already taken shape during the early conquest era, changes and modifications occurred throughout the colonial period. Despite their Castilian origins, institutions were adjusted to the social and geographic conditions encountered in the New World. The key functions of the administrative system comprised representing the sovereignty of the Spanish Crown over its American territories and subjects, tax collecting, the maintenance of public order, and all major aspects of government, including justice, legislation, and law enforcement, all guided by a paternalistic notion of kingship and underpinned by Roman law. Under the Habsburg dynasty (sixteenth and seventeenth centuries), administration tended to be relatively decentralized, a trend reversed under Bourbon rule (eighteenth century). Although the bureaucratic machinery that tied the colonies to the metropolis came to an end with Spanish American independence (1810–1826), its impact outlasted its demise by providing the institutional structure inherited by the newly born republics.

The main institutions that governed colonial Spanish America had their origins in Spain and developed during the wars of the Reconquest, fought against the Muslim kingdoms in the Iberian Peninsula. The Catholic monarchs, Isabella of Castile and Ferdinand of Aragon, introduced a set of centralizing administrative reforms, encroaching on the power of the nobility, the Church, and local authorities. As the conquest of America was carried out by Castile, Spanish America became subject to the Castilian state, and its institutions were based on a Castilian model.

The Council of Castile represented the cornerstone of this administrative reform; it was a supreme court charged with the supervision of local government and law enforcement, and with legislative and advisory powers. It provided the main mechanism to articulate royal power vis-à-vis the high nobility, which had emerged out of the leading warrior class of the Reconquest, but was now practically stripped of its traditional voice in government. Appointed by the Crown, its members were recruited from the lesser nobility and university-trained jurists, thus providing the substance for a professional bureaucratic organization based on the notion of royal justice. Four *chancillerías* provided the backbone of the judicial system as appellate courts of civil and criminal law, subordinate to the Council of Castile. As early as the fourteenth century, the Castilian Crown began its assault on the privileges of municipal authorities by establishing the *corregidor,* the Crown's representative official to preside over the municipal council, which was constituted of locally elected *regidores.* In areas under ecclesiastical or noble jurisdiction, municipal authority remained governed by the local *alcalde,* untouched by the Crown's centralizing momentum since they provided a way to counterbalance the power of church and nobility. Despite these administrative intrusions, local autonomy survived to a great degree in the Habsburg era in both Spain and Spanish America. Only in the eighteenth century was a renewed centralizing thrust under way.

The discovery and conquest of America brought a vast and distant territory under Spanish rule. Set across the Atlantic and inhabited by a myriad of indigenous societies, the New World required a special administrative response. Many a Spanish conqueror was rewarded with an *encomienda,* a grant of rights to collect taxes and enjoy the labor of conquered indigenous communities. Still, institutionalization of a royal bureaucracy already had begun during the early years and followed each new conquest; the Crown aimed to prevent the rise of a local Spanish aristocracy of *encomenderos,* supervise relations with the indigenous population, and collect its share of the wealth obtained.

Established in 1524 as an offspring of the Council of Castile, the Council of the Indies was entrusted with the administration of all imperial affairs. It was in charge of legislation, and the appointment and supervision of officials. As an appellate court, it was the highest judicial authority for American affairs. Subject directly to the Crown, the council resided in Spain and consisted of a president, four councilors, and several other officials, usually university trained or churchmen.

Jurisdictionally, the American territories were divided into the two viceroyalties of New Spain and Peru, each headed by a viceroy and his staff, subordinate directly to the Council of the Indies. Theoretically the king's alter ego on American soil, the viceroy was the highest executive official in his territory. With few exceptions, all viceroys were Spanish-born, serving their term in the Americas as a stepping-stone to higher bureaucratic positions in Spain. Subordinate to the viceroy, the *audiencia* was an appellate court and an advisory council for the viceroy. Smaller in size than, yet similar in structure to, the Castilian chancelleries, the larger audiencias of Lima and Mexico City consisted of eight *oidores* (civil judges), four *alcaldes de crimen* (criminal judges), and two *fiscales* (crown attorneys). As the uppermost authorities in the Indies, viceroys and audiencias were charged with fiscal, civil, and public administration; the maintenance of order; the provision of justice and welfare; and the supervision of lower-ranking officials. As interpreters of imperial law emanating from the Council of the Indies, viceroys and audiencias practically held some legislative power. In the more remote areas, audiencias usually had more independence from the viceroy and were presided over by a local official of that territory.

Each audiencia's jurisdiction was further divided into a mosaic of local administrative units governed by an official usually appointed by the audiencia. These officials, titled *corregidores, alcaldes mayores,* or *gobernadores,* presided over the municipal council (*cabildo* or *ayuntamiento*), which varied in size and structure, but was largely made up of regidores, locally elected citizens. The corregidor and the cabildo, as well as any of their variations, were charged with current administration of judicial and civil affairs, taxation, and maintenance of public order in their jurisdiction, which usually extended to the countryside surrounding the town that was their seat.

Trade between Spain and Spanish America tended to be highly monopolistic and heavily regulated. Established in 1503, the Casa de Contratación (House of Trade) of Seville was charged with the supervision and regulation of all traffic of goods and people between Spain and Spanish America. Trade across the Atlantic was carried out by the *flota* (convoy) system, and was restricted to Seville in Spain and a few ports on the two routes to New Spain and Peru. Within Spanish America, economic activity was equally regulated by a variety of taxes and restrictive policies administered by the royal bureaucracy.

The bureaucratic imperial apparatus tended to be larger, better organized, and more effective in Mexico and Peru. Peripheral areas received much less administrative supervision. On the northern and southern frontiers, military outposts and missions administered relations with hostile nomadic Indians. Though public office was restricted to Spanish men only, participation in the administration tended to be more lenient toward the racially mixed at lower levels and in peripheral areas. Sedentary indigenous communities usually elected their own cabildo, supervised by a Spanish official. Within those communities, indigenous administrative practices could persist, many times unaltered by Spanish rule. In theory, Spanish American subjects were divided into a Republic of Spaniards and a Republic of Indians, with the king designated as the protector of the Indians to prevent their abuse by Spanish people. Yet in practice, as a result of widespread racial mixture, a caste system was elaborated to define a multitude of racial groups and ascribe the legal rights and prohibitions for each, though it was not equally observed everywhere.

In the second half of the eighteenth century and in response to changing conditions in the New World and Europe, the Crown initiated a set of reforms to reorganize the imperial administration and its own relations with the colonies. The reforms, which came to be known as the Bourbon reforms (named after the new ruling dynasty), were intended to increase royal revenues, especially through more efficient taxation, to reassert the Crown's authority, and to safeguard its American sovereignty against competing European powers. Most of the reforms were implemented during the rule of Charles III in both Spain and Spanish America, and were inspired by the French administrative model and the political philosophy of enlightened absolutism. Cabinet ministries gradually took over most of the responsibilities of the Council of the Indies, which now functioned only as an appellate court.

Jurisdictional reordering took place, most notably with the establishment of two new viceroyalties, one in New Granada and the other in Río de la Plata, as well as the creation of the captaincies-general of Chile and Venezuela. New audiencias were established in response to economic and geopolitical changes in the region. The Crown increased the previously thin military presence on American soil significantly to deter internal disturbances and external threats. The bureaucratic system was further reformed by introducing the intendancy system. Intendants, salaried officials under the direct control of the Crown, replaced the local corregidores and the inefficient system of tax farming. At the higher level, the Crown appointed more Spanish-born bureaucrats than before, whom it considered more capable and loyal, thus displacing American-born Spaniards, or Creoles, from positions of power previously gained through the sale of office.

The Decree of Free Trade of 1778 abolished the flota system and opened trade to several ports in Spain and Spanish America; however, following mercantilist precepts, it was still confined to the Spanish Empire, prohibiting exchange with foreigners. After moving to Cádiz in 1717, the Casa de Contratación was eventually abolished in 1790. The Bourbon reforms accomplished many of their goals, yet a growing tax burden, tighter regulations, and displacement of Creoles from power created unprecedented local discontent, which together with the political chaos in Spain in the early nineteenth century facilitated the collapse of the royal administration and brought about Spanish American independence.

Hillel Eyal

References

Bakewell, Peter. *A History of Latin America.* Malden and Oxford: Blackwell, 1997.

Elliott, J. H. *Spain and Its World, 1500–1700.* New Haven, CT: Yale University Press, 1989.

Haring, C. H. *The Spanish Empire in America.* New York: Oxford University Press, 1947.

Lockhart, James, and Stuart B. Schwartz. *Early Latin America: A History of Colonial Spanish America and Brazil.* Cambridge: Cambridge University Press, 1983.

See also: Alcabala; Altepetl; Atlantic Economy; Audiencias; Bourbon Reforms; Cabildo; Cah; Casa de Contratación; Colonists and Settlers I, III–VI; Congregaciones; Conquest I, III–VII; Corregidor/ Corregimiento; Council of Castile; Council of the Indies; Creoles; Defense— Colonial Spanish America; Encomienda; Enlightenment—Spanish America; Fleet System; Habsburgs; Intendants/Intendancy System; Laws—Colonial Latin America; Missions; Monarchs of Spain; Monopolies; Native Americans I, III–VIII; República de Indios; Trade—Spain/Spanish America; Viceroyalties; Visita.

ALCABALA

Alcabala was the sales tax collected by the Spanish Crown throughout its American colonies as well as in Spain itself. It was perhaps originally a Hispano-Moorish tax, but in 1342 Alfonso XI persuaded the Castilian *cortes* (parliament) to make it a royal duty. Although Queen Isabella considered imposing it on the colonists as early as 1503, the monarchy did not succeed in applying it to the American colonies until the late sixteenth century. Mexico became subject to the alcabala in 1574 and Peru in 1591. Regions newly conquered or settled usually received a temporary exemption. In fact, the royal *capitulación* (agreement or compact between the monarchy and another party) authorizing Francisco Pizarro to undertake the exploration and conquest of Peru also granted the territory a one-hundred-year exemption from the alcabala, although the Crown rescinded the exemption before it expired.

The colonial treasury initially collected the alcabala at a rate of 2 percent, although not all commercial transactions and goods were liable to it. For example, the indigenous population was generally exempted from it when marketing its goods, as was generally the case with basic necessities such as grain and bread sold in public markets. The Crown also excused miners' gold and silver (which paid other taxes), books, paintings, horses, dowries, inheritances, weapons, plunder taken in wars, medicines, and nonprofit ecclesiastical goods. On most other goods, the Crown exacted the alcabala on the first and succeeding sales.

Alcabala rates rose over the years but were not uniform throughout the empire. In 1632, during the Thirty Years' War, Philip IV's chief minister, the Count-Duke of Olivares, raised the alcabala to 4 percent as part of the Union of Arms in an attempt to spread the military costs of the war over all of Spain's kingdoms and alleviate the burden on Castile. Three years later Mexicans suffered another increase, to 6 percent, because the government needed funds to pay for the new Windward Fleet (Armada de Barlovento), created to protect Spanish shipping in the Caribbean. The Crown sometimes made temporary increases in the alcabala to offset the cost of its wars. In the late 1770s, the Peruvian alcabala rose permanently to 6 percent. Peripheral areas of the empire, such as Caracas and Cuba, continued to pay the lower rate.

Imposition of the alcabala and rate increases sometimes provoked serious unrest. Residents of Quito rose in the early 1590s when Philip II extended the alcabala to the Viceroyalty of Peru. Its increase to 6 percent in the late 1770s provoked violent outbursts in the Viceroyalty of New Granada (1780–1781) and in Arequipa of southern Peru (1780). Nonetheless, American rates typically remained below those in Castile, where the alcabala reached as high as 10 percent.

Collection of the alcabala was problematic. The royal treasury lacked sufficient officials to oversee daily commercial transactions, and it consequently tended to negotiate contracts with other institutions and with private individuals to collect the alcabala. City governments (*cabildos*) and merchant guilds (*consulados*) often agreed to pay the tariff, gathering a fixed annual sum to pay the treasury. Sometimes the Crown farmed the alcabala out to individual collectors. During the eighteenth century, the imperial bureaucracy expanded, making personnel available for customs houses, which assumed responsibility for the alcabala. Late colonial commercial expansion, the higher rate, and more efficient collection made the alcabala more valuable to the Crown. By the end of the eighteenth century, it generated 2.5 million pesos per year in Mexico and about a quarter of that in Peru (TePaske 1996, 44).

Kendall Brown

References

Haring, Clarence H. *The Spanish Empire in America.* New York: Harcourt Brace Jovanovich, 1975.

TePaske, John Jay. "Alcabalas." Pp. 44 in *Encyclopedia of Latin American History and Culture.* Vol. 1, edited by Barbara A. Tenenbaum. New York: Charles Scribner's Sons, 1996.

Ucendo, José Ignacio Andrés. "Castile's Tax System in the Seventeenth Century." *Journal of European Economic History* 30, no. 3 (2001): 597–617.

See also: Administration—Colonial Spanish America; Atlantic Economy; Bourbon Reforms; Cabildo; Capitulations of Santa Fe; Casa de Contratación; Conquistadors; Contraband; Council of Castile; Council of the Indies; Credit—Colonial Latin America; Mexico; Monopolies; Peru; Rebellions—Colonial Latin America; Trade—Spain/Spanish America; Viceroyalties.

ALCOHOL

Alcoholic beverages represented one of the most important aspects of the Columbian Exchange, the process of cultural and biological interaction that characterized the discovery and conquest of the American continent by Europeans. In addition to serving as crucial elements in the transatlantic economy, beverages, and the several methods of preparing and consuming them, served as icons of social distinction and tools for the construction of distinct ethnic identities.

When they first contacted Native Americans, the Spanish and Portuguese found a great diversity of methods of preparation and use of alcoholic beverages; for indigenous societies in the Americas, alcohol played an important role in their general diet as well as their political, social, and religious ceremonies. Iberians had, in the consumption of wine, one of the main symbols of their way of life, and they systematically compared this beverage with the ones prepared by the natives, generally considering the latter as "barbaric" or "dirty" and trying, whenever possible, to repress or control their use or even to replace local beverages with wine.

Many tribal societies prepared fermented drinks from fruits, and beer from maize, manioc, and agave. In some instances, Native Americans used production techniques, such as mastication and insalivation, considered nauseating by Europeans. Some of these beverages, such as the *cauim* of Brazilian Tupinambá, or the *chicha* of Amazonian peoples, were fundamental to cannibalistic rituals or as ceremonial and nutritional support to warriors in campaigns. The importance of such beverages made the struggle against their production and consumption one of the primary means of establishing European domination over these societies.

Among the so-called high cultures of Central America and the Andes, the Spanish also found beverages that were fundamental to the economy and religion. In Mexico, the *pulque,* prepared from the fermented juices of the *maguey* cactus, was associated with the worship of several gods (such as the mother-goddess Mayáhuel). Pulque was consumed in rituals of human sacrifice; it was also an important tribute payment demanded of dominated tribes. The Aztec state tried to repress the use of pulque by peasants and other commoners and reserve it for the exclusive use of the religious and warrior elite; however, the prohibition was not always successful.

After the Spanish conquest (aside from the effort of the Catholic Church to eradicate pulque consumption, which it viewed as a tool for idolatry), restrictions on alcohol consumption were lifted. Soon, however, public drunkenness represented a great problem for colonial authorities, causing a series of mutinies and riots among the poorer population. Pulque remained the most consumed beverage in Mexico. In the eighteenth century there were large farms dedicated to its production, and the drink represented (through the taxes generated from its trade) an important source of income to the colonial state, at times reaching half the revenue generated from Mexico's silver mines. Furthermore, the Spanish also used pulque as a means of reaching other indigenous peoples: in 1786, the viceroy of Mexico, Bernardo de Gálvez, proposed that pulque be offered to the Apaches (who did not know alcoholic beverages) as a way to attract them to coming under Spanish dominion.

In the Andes, the Spanish became acquainted with chicha, a maize-based beer. The Inca sovereigns had large production units of this beverage, staffed by specialized artisans. Like the Aztecs, the Inca state attempted to limit the use of chicha by commoners, but after the conquest, widespread drunkenness in the Andes posed a problem to Spanish conquerors, especially when chicha became a symbol of anticolonial rebellions such as the Taqui Ongoy revolt of the 1560s. One of the actions taken during the repression of this rebellion was the struggle against the intoxication caused by the chicha, which was seen as an open door to the spread of idolatry. In other regions, such as Chile, the Spanish also tried to repress the native alcohol consumption. In 1568, the Chapter of Santiago created a body of *alguaciles* (police officers) who specialized in the repression of native beverage consumption, breaking containers and arresting drunken people.

Despite Spanish efforts, pulque and chicha persisted as popular drinks in their areas of origin. However, Spanish settlers were also successful in introducing their own beverage, wine. In the fifteenth and sixteenth centuries, Spain and Portugal were Europe's leading wine producers, establishing an important wine industry within the Iberian Peninsula and on the Atlantic islands of the Canaries and Madeira. After the conquest of America, a new and expansive trade opened for Iberian wines, yet Spain and Portugal were never capable of satisfying American demand, either because of insufficient production or because of high prices. Throughout the colonial period, European wine was consumed almost exclusively by the elite.

Grapevines and the wine industry were introduced experimentally during the first decades of colonization. In Brazil, the experiment failed because of inappropriate climate and soil, as well as resistance from European producers reluctant to lose market share. In Spanish America, it was soon clear to the Crown and the settlers that the enormous demand should be supplied by local production. As early as 1524, Hernando Cortés called out for the settlers to cultivate vineyards, although Mexico did not have an appropriate climate for this culture.

The best results were accomplished in South America. Wine production started in Peru in the 1530s, in Chile in the 1540s, and in Argentina in 1557. Jesuits were among the largest producers, and were re-sponsible for the introduction of the *misión* (or *criolla*) grape, the most cultivated variety in the colonial Americas. The Peruvian haciendas (farms), located in the fertile valleys of the west coast, produced enough wine to satisfy the high demand from Lima and Potosí, as well as markets in Mexico and even the Philippines, where Peruvian wine was traded for Chinese spices and other goods.

The great success of American wine encouraged European producers to lobby the Crown for the prohibition of its trade. In 1595, King Philip II disallowed the cultivation of new vineyards in the Americas; however, this decree was never totally respected. Actually, vineyards spread to new areas such as California, which had, at the end of the eighteenth century, a small production from Franciscan missions, especially San Gabriel (presently in Los Angeles), but also in Santa Bárbara and San José.

Besides the success of South American wine, the crucial event in the history of alcoholic beverages in America was the establishment of the industry of distilled beverages. In the eighteenth century, most of the wine produced in South America was used in the preparation of several types of brandy, which became highly popular and commercially successful. In Peru, for example, *pisco* became the national drink. Sugarcane-based liquors were even more important. After the creation of the first sugar factories in 1513 (Santo Domingo) and 1533 (São Vicente, Brazil), the path was open for the creation of fermented beverages from sugarcane juice and molasses, known as *guarapo* (in the Caribbean) and *garapa* (in Brazil); these beverages were largely consumed by Indian and African slaves, and poor free men, who could not afford imported wine. From the sixteenth to the seventeenth centuries, these beverages started to be used in the production of the distilled liquors that would become the most important beverages in the Atlantic world: the Caribbean *ron* (rum) and the Brazilian *cachaça*.

Besides the advantage of having copious amounts of prime matter (originated naturally in the sugar-making process) and the inexhaustible workforce of the slaves, the dissemination of sugarcane liquors was favored by the readiness of Native Americans and African slave traders in accepting them, which made both the rum and the cachaça valuable tools in the expansion of colonial power. From Brazil to Florida, settlers used these beverages to attract Indians to their sphere of influence; in 1743, for example, the Calusas of southern Florida stated to Jesuits that, without rum, they did not wish to be Christians.

In Africa, American liquors (more potent and resistant to maritime journeys) simply dislodged European wines and liquors, and were included in the "triangular trade" between the Caribbean, the English colonies in North America, and Europe. Both the Spanish and the Portuguese Crowns tried to prohibit the production and trade of rum and cachaça. These restrictions were the result of pressure exerted on the Spanish and Portuguese monarchies from their own producers; however, in spite of Crown regulations, the prohibitions were impossible to execute. By the eighteenth century, both Iberian governments recognized the futility of such efforts, as well as the potential for profit. Therefore, restrictions were discontinued, and royal taxes were imposed on the beverages.

João Azevedo Fernandes

References

Curto, José C. *Enslaving Spirits: The Portuguese-Brazilian Alcohol Trade at Luanda and Its Hinterland, c. 1550–1830.* Leiden: Brill, 2004.

Cushner, Nicholas P. *Lords of the Land: Sugar, Wine, and Jesuit Estates of Coastal Peru, 1600–1767.* Albany: State University of New York Press, 1980.

Kicza, John E. "The Pulque Trade of Late Colonial Mexico City." *The Americas* 37, no. 2 (1980): 193–221.

Mancall, Peter C. *Deadly Medicine: Indians and Alcohol in Early America.* Ithaca and London: Cornell University Press, 1995.

Phillips, Rod. *A Short History of Wine.* London: Penguin, 2000.

Rice, Prudence M. "Wine and Brandy Production in Colonial Peru: A Historical and Archaeological Investigation." *Journal of Interdisciplinary History* 27 (1977): 455–479.

———. "Peru's Colonial Wine Industry and Its European Background." *Antiquity* 70 (1996): 790–794.

See also: Atlantic Economy; Bourbon Reforms; Cannibalism; Catholic Church in Spanish America; Columbian Exchange—Agriculture; Contraband; Hacienda; Human Sacrifice; Idolatry, Extirpation of; Jesuits—Iberia and America; Jurema; Maize; Missions; Monopolies; Native Americans I–VIII; Potosí; Religious Orders; Slavery I–IV; Slave Trade; Sugar; Wine.

ALTEPETL

The *altepetl* was the most important geopolitical entity of pre-Columbian central Mexico. The term signifies a city-state. The word itself is a diphrase, that is, two independent words that are joined or juxtaposed to make a third word. In this case, *altepetl* consists of the words *atl,* meaning "water," and *tepetl,* meaning "hill." They can appear either juxtaposed with the definite article *in,* meaning "the" (*in atl in tepetl),* or combined to form a single word *(altepetl).* In Nahuatl (the Aztec language), there is no difference between the singular and plural forms of the word.

The jurisdiction of the altepetl included both the immediate area of the city and outlying communities, often not connected geographically with the city. This extended jurisdiction caused considerable confusion among Spaniards, as they attempted to understand preexisting jurisdictions. Internally, the city-state frequently had four, six, or eight major subdivisions, known as *calpolli* or *tlaxilacalli* (often translated as "districts"). Each of these minor subdivisions had its own ruler or governor, *teuctli.* The process whereby the local ruler was selected varied greatly through central Mexico, with some being hereditary rulers, others chosen by rotation from among a group of leading families. Each calpolli carried a distinct name. At its founding, Tenochtitlan (modern Mexico City) had four calpolli: Moyotlan, Teopan, Tzaqualco, and Cuepopan.

Though the altepetl was important, especially with regard to relations with other altepetl, the lives of most Nahua (the people popularly called Aztecs) were governed within the smaller calpolli or tlaxilacalli. The units, or wards, provided for local schooling for boys and girls, public sanitation, and allocation of arable land for agriculture; they maintained the local religious establishments and temples and paid taxes to the larger altepetl. The wards also provided soldiers and officers for military service.

The altepetl was governed by a hereditary ruler called the *tlatoani,* meaning "he who customarily speaks," or simply "speaker." The most important city-states, such as Tenochtitlan, were ruled by a supreme ruler, a *huey tlatoani* (superior speaker). The leading nobles of the city elected the tlatoani from an extended ruling family. Hence sons did not always succeed fathers, but often nephews succeeded uncles, or brothers followed one another. In some altepetl the rulership passed from one calpolli to another in a rotational order recognized by the polity.

The altepetl managed the relations between the wards, organized the markets and commerce both within and outside of the city, and engaged in political relationships with other altepetl. The most famous example of external political relations among altepetl is the creation of the Triple Alliance. In the late fifteenth century the altepetl of Tenochtitlan, Tlacopan (modern Tacuba), and Texcoco allied themselves into an empire. The combined troops of the alliance then proceeded to extend the influence of the empire over all of the altepetl of the Valley of Mexico, throughout most of the central highlands, and all the way to the Gulf coast in the Isthmus of Tehuantepec.

John F. Schwaller

References

Lockhart, James. *The Nahuas after the Conquest.* Stanford, CA: Stanford University Press, 1992.

Schroeder, Susan. *Chimalpahin and the Kingdom of Chalco.* Tucson: University of Arizona Press, 1991.

See also: Administration—Colonial Spanish America; Cabildo; Cah; Colonists and Settlers IV—Mexico and Central America; Conquest V—Mexico; Mexico; Native Americans IV—Mesoamerica.

AMAZON

Foreign peoples are no novelty in the Amazon. For millennia, multiple migrations, invasions, wars, expulsions, alliances, and accommodations have linked and divided Amazonia's diverse inhabitants. Spanish and Portuguese entry into the Amazon Basin in 1500 represented a continuation of long-standing struggles over territorial access and possession; however, it also brought important changes. Iberians introduced Christianity, slavery, empire, and the market economy into local societies. Iberian colonization of the Amazon reconfigured boundaries already drawn by Amazonian natives, redirected flows of human movement, and reorganized peoples into pockets of villages, farms, ranches, and cities, far from their ancestral lands and ruled by a king they never saw.

Greater Amazonia encompasses the regions surrounding the Amazon, starting in northeastern Peru where the Marañón and Ucayali rivers join to form the Amazon River. The world's largest river in volume, the Amazon runs eastward from its source 18,000 feet above sea level in the Andes, joined from the north and south by over 200 tributaries. From its point of origin, it flows downstream into the confluence at the Solimões and Negro rivers (the upper Amazon). Beyond the mouth of the Madeira River, the Amazon River is embedded in a valley created by the highlands of Guiana to the north and of Brazil to the south (the middle Amazon). Farther downstream, the lower Amazon flows through the modern state of Pará, Brazil. The river and its offshoots provide 25,000 miles of navigable water of singular importance for nearby inhabitants. The Amazon Basin has two defining features. An intricate system of mighty rivers and tributaries is covered by a thick canopy of tall trees; sunlight barely penetrates the dense foliage. By contrast, savannas, such as the Llanos de Mojos in eastern Bolivia, the Rio Branco Basin in

Explorer with Indian in the Amazon jungle, ca. 1900. (Library of Congress)

northern Brazil and the interior of northeastern and western central Brazil, and other forests and high grasslands surround the tropical wetlands. This range of terrain and climate accounts for the Amazon's diversity in flora, fauna, and human cultures.

The Tutishcainyos, among the first known migrants into the upper Amazon Basin, settled northwest of Lake Yarinacocha in Peru around 2000–1600 BC. But archaeological and linguistic evidence suggests that Greater Amazonia was inhabited as early as 3000 BC, and that waves of invaders, refugees, and migrants moved in and out of the basin. In the lower Orinoco of the Rio Negro Basin, around 800 BC, for example, the Saladeros were driven out to the coast of Venezuela, and later to the Antilles, by the Barrancas of the middle Amazon, who maintained their new territorial claim for over 1,000 years. Among late pre-

Columbian migrants are the Cocamas and Omaguas, whose chiefdom was carefully described by early modern Spanish explorers. Collectively, and despite each considering itself distinct from its neighbors, Amazonian peoples seem to have shared overlapping cultures. Until the recorded arrival of Europeans in 1500, the history of the Amazon owed much to the cultural, economic, and demographic activities of peoples who formed large settled populations; practiced intensive root-crop cultivation (such as the manioc); looked for food primarily in rivers, lakes, and oceans and secondarily in hunting birds and animals; enjoyed beer feasting; utilized the bow and arrow; and developed skills in basketry, pottery, and face-painting. Native communities encountered by the first whites observed the same practices and customs.

Although the Spaniard Vicente Yáñez Pinzón first navigated parts of the basin in early 1500, it is likely that previous unreported shipwrecked travelers, deserters, or sailors blown off course had set foot in the Amazon and met with local inhabitants. But except for Spanish Francisco de Orellana's descent of the river in 1541–1542, the rest of Amazonia remained unknown to Europeans for another century. Despite the diversity of riverine animal and plant life, the fertility of the floodplains, and the wealth of inhabitants such as the Omaguas, the Amazon remained relatively undisturbed by non-Indians. European seamen complained about the forbidding coasts at the mouth of the river, the impenetrable forests and swamps to the north, high winds and strong currents that propelled ships into dangerous reefs and shallows in the Caribbean, and bad points of anchorage. Once into the river's mainstream, how-

ever, the first Spanish explorers penetrated as far upstream as the Negro, Madeira, and Tapajós rivers, encountering many riverine settlements. In the upper Amazon, Arawak-speaking groups dominated, surrounded by less populous Jivaro-Tukano and Pano language communities. In the lower Amazon, Tupi-speaking societies outnumbered neighbors of Carib and Ge languages, especially along the river's southern shore. These societies, like their predecessors, had developed sophisticated watercraft technologies and navigational capabilities to tap into the complex and vast river systems for food, raw materials for manufacturing goods, trade, military and political partnerships, exogamous marriages with other tribes, and exploration of unknown regions and their fauna and flora.

Early Ibero-Indian relations can be described in terms of intermittent contact, trade, and entries and retreats from the late fifteenth century until the first half of the seventeenth century. During this period, Indians desiring to trade for Old World exotica developed a trade jargon with Iberian merchants trekking the coast and sailing upstream. On expeditions into Amazonia, lost Europeans wandered into native villages to request directions, provisions, a resting place, or other forms of assistance. Some of these stragglers were absorbed into local communities as adopted tribesmen, husbands, or wives (as in the case of the two women encountered by Orellana's expedition in 1541–1542). Surrounded as they were by unfamiliar land and peoples, they lived by local customs, spoke native languages, and ate, dressed, hunted, and passed their time according to native traditions.

For those at home in the Old World in the early modern period, Amazonia loomed in the imagination as a fantastic and exotic paradise. Amazon warrior women and one-eyed forest creatures were thought to lurk in the shadows of the dense tropical foliage. Sightings of El Dorado, the king so prosperous that he covered himself in gold dust, or of the mythical land of La Canela (Cinnamon Land), overgrown with the spice that inspired Columbus's voyages and the Portuguese rounding of the African continent, ignited the imaginations of Europeans eager to strike it rich. Spin-off myths, such as the dazzling kingdom of Gran Moxo, located somewhere between Cuzco and Charcas, instigated entries into the upper Amazon. Early Iberian encounters with native Amazonians may have been unremarkable, curious, financially lucrative, emotional, aggressive, or even defensive, but for the most part, Amazonian inhabitants and cultures continued as they had for hundreds of years; Iberian colonization remained so only in name, little more than titles etched onto Spanish and Portuguese maps of northern South America.

Political reasons also contributed to the limited Ibero-Indian interactions during the first century after Spanish discovery of the basin. Both European powers were expending their energies elsewhere. Throughout the sixteenth century, Spain was busy exploring the Caribbean and Central America, and overrunning Aztec rulers from central Mexico and Incan emperors from the Andes. Portugal was occupied with trade and sea routes to East and South Asia, and domestic conflicts also demanded attention. With so little energy remaining to invest elsewhere, Iberia found the attempts it did make to settle the Amazon disastrous. The first known effort was initiated in 1531 by the Spaniard Diego de Ordaz. Difficult shoals and currents made landing impossible, and one ship wrecked. Survivors intermarried with natives, and Ordaz's other ship, still afloat after the harrowing experiences, returned to Spain. A similar experience was repeated by the Portuguese Aires da Cunha, the Portuguese nobleman who had been granted the lands comprising the captaincy of Maranhão. Of the 900 who embarked on his ten ships, a few survivors attempted to establish a colony. Escalating conflicts resulted in Potiguar and Tupinambá Indians thwarting settlement efforts, and many would-be colonists returned to Portugal in 1538. Three more abortive tries between 1530 and 1560 ended the first wave of Luso-Iberian colonization of Amazonia.

Starting from the mid-seventeenth century, however, sustained contact led to the establishment of nascent Iberian institutions. Missionaries wanting to convert natives to Christianity and socialize them to European ways lived among the Indians and actively sought to change Amazonian traditions, resulting in "mission cultures," which blended elements of local and Iberian ways of thinking and acting. Enslavers, called *bandeirantes,* making brief but devastating forays often pushed Ibero-Indian relations beyond reconciliation; otherwise, natives allied themselves with bandeirantes to enslave enemy tribes. News of fertile land led to Portuguese investment in sugar cultivation, and settlements were founded, each one a bit farther north than the other, until the 1616 establishment of Portuguese Amazonia's seat of government in Belém. With a continuing influx of Iberians moving into Amazonian lands and interacting with local communities, the Indian population was devastated by culture shock, demoralization caused by social disintegration, collapse of birth rates, battles, massacres, overwork, enslavement, and lack of immunity to Old World diseases. Although Iberians who settled in the basin continued to depend heavily on local peoples, these most recent of invaders dramatically altered the natural and human landscape of Greater Amazonia. Cultures, technologies, and flora and fauna embedded since prehistory have been replaced by inhabitants whose cultures reflect a blending of Indian and Iberian ways.

M. Kittiya Lee

References

Block, David. *Mission Culture on the Upper Amazon: Native Tradition, Jesuit Enterprise and Secular Policy in Moxos, 1660–1880.* Lincoln: University of Nebraska Press, 1994.

Bruhns, Karen Olsen, ed. *Ancient South America.* Cambridge World Archaeology series. New York: Cambridge University Press, 1994.

Lathrap, Donald W. *The Upper Amazon.* London: Thames and Hudson, 1970.

Sweet, David. "A Rich Realm of Nature Destroyed: The Middle Amazon Valley, 1640–1750." Ph.D. dissertation, University of Wisconsin–Madison, 1974.

See also: Brazil; Catholic Church in Brazil; Colonists and Settlers II—Brazil; Columbian Exchange—Disease; Conquest II—Brazil; Donatary Captaincies; El Dorado; Independence II—Brazil; Jesuits—Brazil; Migration—From Iberia to the New World; Missions; Native Americans I—Amazon; Slavery I—Brazil; Sugar.

AMERICAN REVOLUTION

The outbreak of the war for independence fought by British colonies in North America presented Spain with several vexing problems. Despite a commitment to France through the 1761 Family Compact and his anxiety to regain possession of both Gibraltar, which Britain had seized in 1704, and Florida, which Britain gained control of in the 1763 Treaty of Paris, King Charles III hesitated to act. However attractive the prospects for restitution and revenge, Charles feared the emergence of an independent American republic that would stretch over the Allegheny Mountains into the Mississippi Valley and into lands that Spain claimed for itself. Territories on the Spanish colonial fringe might be usurped by the new nation. An open commitment to the American rebels also presented Charles with the possibility of two rebellions. At home, the British might encourage Spaniards to revolt against the fragile government, and abroad, if republicanism triumphed in North America, it would become more difficult for the Spanish Crown to deny the same rights to its subjects in the Americas. Given these factors, Charles III hoped that the British and the American rebels would battle themselves into exhaustion, resulting in the preservation of the Spanish Crown and its empire. The minister of state, José Moñino y Redondo, Conde de Floridablanca, supported the king's hesitancy.

Spain's reluctance to become openly involved in the American war did not allow it to escape French pressure. The French foreign minister, Comte de Vergennes, and businessman-author Pierre Augustin Caron de Beaumarchais convinced King Louis XVI to secretly provide the American rebels with needed shipments of munitions, money, and supplies, which was done through the fictitious Roderique Hortalez e Compagnie. The French government also permitted American privateers to use its ports to attack British shipping. Vergennes implored the Spanish court to do the same, particularly after the

American victory at Saratoga in October 1777, at which point he offered Spain the possibility of regaining Gibraltar, Florida, and Minorca, as well as securing its western territories in North America. Still, the Spanish resisted.

In 1777, the Americans sent three commissioners, Silas Deane, Benjamin Franklin, and Arthur Lee, to Europe to seek assistance. While Deane and Franklin gained recognition for their successful labors in Holland and France, respectively, Lee's mission to Spain did not. In February 1777 Lee arrived in Spain; however, he was directed to wait in the town of Victoria, away from Madrid. There he met secretly with outgoing minister of state Jerónimo Grimaldi and Spanish businessman Diego de Gardoqui. The American learned that Gardoqui's company had been secretly supplying Massachusetts since 1775 and that supplies were awaiting the rebels in Havana, Cuba, and New Orleans. The gunpowder, clothing, and other material that Spain provided were produced in France and Mexico at Madrid's expense. The precise amount of Spain's material assistance has never been determined. Grimaldi also informed Lee that Spain would request Holland to extend credits and provide shipping to the American cause. But the Crown's fear that open assistance would prompt a British military response prevented Lee from entering Madrid and meeting directly with King Charles III. In March 1777, Lee returned to Paris.

With the February 6, 1778, Treaty of Alliance, France bound itself to the independence of the United States, without the promise of special privileges or additional territory in the Western Hemisphere. At the time, Vergennes did not press Spain over its obligation to assist France under the terms of the 1761 Family Compact. But as the conflict in North America continued, Vergennes became more and more anxious for Spanish participation. He offered Spain Minorca, Florida, a share in the Newfoundland fisheries, ejection of the English from Honduras, even the reconquest of Jamaica; still, Spanish prime minister Floridablanca refused the offer. Instead, Floridablanca increasingly fixated upon Gibraltar, determined that Spain should regain possession of the citadel that guarded the entrance to the Mediterranean and provided security for Spain's southern coast. He was willing to partner with whichever belligerent would satisfy that objective. From the British, Floridablanca wanted Gibraltar as the price for Spanish neutrality.

However, Floridablanca understood that he could not go to war for territory alone; he needed to take the high ground. He therefore offered to mediate the British-American conflict, but on terms that Britain could only reject. In early April 1779, Floridablanca informed the British that, in return for Gibraltar, there must be an indefinite suspension of armed conflict between them and the French, to be broken only on a year's notice, and that, within a year, there must be mutual disarmament on the European continent and in America, Africa, and Asia. This disarmament was to be accompanied by Spanish-sponsored mediation of the conflict between Britain and the American colonies and their French allies. The issues of American independence and boundaries were circumvented. In reality, the British troops would remain in place during the mediation. Although France received a copy of the proposal, only Great Britain was obligated to comply.

As the British considered the Spanish proposal, Floridablanca reached a separate agreement with the French on April 12, 1779, in the secret Treaty of Harangues. According to this convention, Spain pledged to aid France in its war with Britain in return for a French pledge not to make peace with Britain until Spain recovered Gibraltar. France also honored Spain's determination not to become an ally of the United States and not to recognize American independence. Spain also hoped to regain possession of Florida, which had fallen under British control in 1763. Thus, American independence became tied to the French promise to help Spain recover Gibraltar, and possibly Florida. Not until April 1780 did American diplomats in Europe learn of the French commitment.

As Floridablanca expected, the British rejected his mediation offer, and on June 21, 1779, Spain declared war on Britain. Spain's involvement in the American war brought into play two important issues: (1) the rights of navigation on the Mississippi River and (2) the western and southern boundaries of the United States. According to the 1763 Treaty of Paris, British subjects had gained the right to use the Mississippi River for commerce. Until the outbreak of war in 1776, Spain only occasionally interfered with this traffic. That same 1763 treaty granted the British control over Florida, which, after the outbreak of the American war, the Americans began to cast a longing eye on. Spain feared American extension into not only this territory, but also into the Mississippi River valley and beyond.

Floridablanca determined to prevent any American use of the river for territorial

expansion. Thus, John Jay found a hostile audience when he arrived in Madrid in January 1780 to negotiate Spanish recognition of American independence, a $5 million loan, a treaty of amity and commerce, and the Americans' free use of the Mississippi River and right of deposit at a port on the Gulf of Mexico. In September 1780, Floridablanca offered to recognize U.S. independence, provided it surrender its navigation rights on the Mississippi River and recognize the 31st parallel as Florida's northern border. Although Jay discredited the proposed treaty, recognizing that Floridablanca was willing to accept only a weak independent United States, incapable of western expansion and dependent upon Spanish and French protection, the U.S. Continental Congress, desperate for money, accepted the proposal. When Floridablanca refused to negotiate specific details, the treaty hung in limbo. There matters stood when Jay departed Madrid for Paris in April 1782.

Throughout the conflict, Spain continued to provide financial support to the American cause, although not openly. In 1781, Spain also failed in an attempt to seize Minorca and in 1782 turned its blockade of Gibraltar into a siege.

In the meantime, the American war for independence became a European war against Great Britain. In 1780, Russia's Catherine II instigated the League of Armed Neutrality, which resulted in the arming of European merchant ships to resist belligerent attacks, primarily British. In 1781, the Austrian and Russian governments proffered mediation, but to no avail. The financial and human costs of the war eventually prompted the British and the French to seek a way out of the war. In Britain in 1782, the Rockingham ministry replaced that of Lord North, and peace negotiations began in earnest.

The 1783 Treaty of Paris guaranteed the United States its independence, with a southern boundary at the 31st parallel, the northern border of Spanish Florida, and a western boundary at the Mississippi River, with both Spain and the United States enjoying the right of its navigation. Spain received East and West Florida and Minorca, and Britain surrendered its claims to Honduras, save its logging rights. During the peace negotiations, Britain broke the Spanish siege of Gibraltar, resulting in Britain's retention of this important post at the entrance to the Mediterranean Sea.

Although Spain made an important contribution to the independence of the United States, the Spanish never recovered the money advanced to the revolutionary cause. And before the eighteenth century ended, the Mississippi River became an object of diplomatic controversy. Over the long term, Floridablanca's anticipation of U.S. expansion south into Florida and westward into the trans-Mississippi territory became a reality.

Thomas M. Leonard

References

Bemis, Samuel Flagg. *Diplomacy of the American Revolution.* Bloomington: Indiana University Press, 1957.

Chávez, Thomas E. *Spain and the Independence of the United States.* Albuquerque: University of New Mexico Press, 2002.

Dull, Jonathan R. *A Diplomatic History of the American Revolution.* New Haven, CT: Yale University Press, 1985.

See also: Belize; Borderlands; Bourbon Reforms; Colonists and Settlers VI—Southeastern North America; Conquest VI—Southeastern North America; Enlightenment—Spanish America; Florida; Monarchs of Spain; Paris, Treaty of (1763); Pirates and Piracy.

AMIENS, PEACE OF

This treaty of March 27, 1802, brought to an end a long and bitter war (1793–1802), during which Great Britain led a coalition against revolutionary France and its European allies. Over the course of the war, Spain fought on both sides, initially as a British ally against France, and then in 1796, Spain allied with France against the British. The conflict was not limited to the European theater; British blockades of the Spanish port of Cádiz prevented American silver from reaching Spain. As a result, Spain was forced to allow its American colonies to trade with neutral powers, including the United States.

Spain declared war on France in March 1793, after the revolutionary government executed King Louis XVI. As a result of the struggle, Spain had to give up its part of Hispaniola, Santo Domingo, to France by virtue of the Peace of Basle (July 22, 1795). This treaty was followed by that of San Ildefonso (August 18, 1796), under which a new French-Spanish alliance was forged to defend the European and colonial interests of both countries. Under the terms of that treaty, Spain granted French citizens a log-cutting concession in its American colonies, a concession previously accorded to the British. Not surprisingly, the French-Spanish alliance made Spain an enemy of Great Britain. On March 31, 1797, the Batavian republic (the Netherlands) reached an agreement with Spain in order to count on Spanish military assistance to defend the Dutch South American colony of Surinam. Soon afterwards the Batavians agreed to the treaty of San Ildefonso (June 1797).

The treaty of Amiens was agreed upon by Great Britain on the one side and the Spanish, French, and Dutch allies on the

British and French diplomats signing the Treaty of Amiens, which temporarily ended hostilities among England, France, and Spain in 1802. (Bettmann/Corbis)

at Amiens, though French-Portuguese limits in Guiana were.

The Peace of Amiens should be thought of merely as a brief truce achieved before war erupted again, a new conflict into which Spain and its colonies entered in 1804.

José Ángel Carreño

References
Bakewell, Peter. *A History of Latin America.* Oxford: Blackwell Publishers, 1997.
McFarlane, Anthony. *El Reino Unido y América: La época colonial.* Madrid: Editorial Mapfre, 1992.
Navarro García, Luis. *Hispanoamérica en el siglo XVIII.* Sevilla: Universidad de Sevilla, 1991.

See also: Bourbon Reforms; Madrid, Treaty of (1750); Trinidad and Tobago; Turbot Fish War.

other. Under the terms of the peace, Great Britain agreed to return the colonies and territories, with the exception of Trinidad, that it had taken from the three allies.

Another American feature of the treaty was the accord on the long-disputed issue of the Newfoundland fisheries, as well as those of the Gulf of Saint Lawrence. Signers agreed to return to the status quo before the war, which meant that Spain had no recognized titles in the area. Therefore, Spain was once more deprived of a right it had claimed for almost a century.

The treaty made no reference to Spanish-Portuguese hostilities in South America. During a brief conflict between the two countries in 1801, Spain had conquered some peninsular Portuguese lands, and Portugal had conquered Spanish territories in the Río de la Plata region. The disposition of these territories was not settled

ARCHITECTURE—BRAZIL

Broadly speaking, over the past five hundred years, Brazilian architecture has been strongly influenced by European tastes and traditions; however, it should be noted that it often has broken from European orthodoxy. After Pedro Alvarez Cabral's "discovery" of Brazil in 1500, Portugal expanded its colonial possessions, first along the Atlantic coast and then toward the interior, eventually reaching the Amazon rainforest. With the exception of São Paulo and Minas Gerais, Brazil's architectural and urban growth from the sixteenth to the nineteenth centuries was concentrated along the coast, in towns such as Olinda, Recife, Salvador, and Rio de Janeiro. The Portuguese conquest and colonization differed from the Spanish conquest of Mesoamerica and the Andes. For one thing, no indigenous group in Brazil had attained the material or cultural sohistication of the Aztecs, Mayas, or Incas, and the stone-building materials so common in Mesoamerican and Andean architecture were not characteristic of pre-Columbian architecture in Brazil. Furthermore, Brazil's early colonists were less concerned with the reproduction of Portuguese political institutions and urban designs than with the extraction of the region's natural wealth: the brazilwood *(pau brasil)* and sugarcane, followed later by coffee, cocoa, and rubber. It was not until the discovery of gold and diamond mines in the eighteenth century that Brazil's colonists began to pay real attention to urban development and building construction. The slow growth that characterized much of the colonial period changed dramatically with the arrival of Portugal's king, Dom João (King John VI), and his court. Escaping from Napoleon's armies, Dom João settled in Rio de Janeiro from 1808 to 1821. Upon his return to Portugal in 1822, his son, Dom Pedro (Peter I), proclaimed Brazil's independence and declared the country an empire, which lasted until the establishment of the Republic of Brazil in 1889. Brazil's architecture followed this historical process with stylistic transformations. During the colonial period, mannerist and baroque styles prevailed. Neoclassicism dominated during the empire, followed by the eclectic historicism of the architecture of the Old Republic (1889–1930). The Revolution of Getúlio Vargas (1930) brought the Estado Novo (the term for this period of Vargas's dictatorship) (1937–1945), which has given its name to a regionalist interpretation of European modernism that continued through most of the twentieth century.

Buildings from the late sixteenth century through the beginning of the seventeenth century are scarce, due to the pre-carious nature of the construction materials. The church of Nossa Senhora da Graça in Olinda (1580) and the convent of São Bento in Rio de Janeiro by Francisco Frias de Mesquita (1617) remain. Religious orders such as the Jesuits, Franciscans, Dominicans, and Carmelites all invested in the construction of churches and monasteries. The presence of the Jesuits in the south of Brazil in the eighteenth century resulted in the erection of many missions. For two centuries, until the capital transferred to Rio de Janeiro, São Salvador da Bahia constituted the center of colonial architecture. In São Salvador, Vignola's severe Counter-Reformation style, reflected in the cathedral of São Salvador (1657), coexisted with the exuberant baroque, timidly represented in the church façade of the convent of São Francisco (1708), and present in all its fullness in both the exterior and interior of the Ordem Terceira de São Francisco (1702). Contrasting with the characteristically mixed stylistic features of this architecture, the basilica of Nossa Senhora da Conceição da Praia (1739), built entirely from imported stone from Portugal, exhibits Renaissance orthodoxy. A typical eighteenth-century church contained a central nave surrounded by perimeter galleries, one or two towers in the façade, and baroque ornamentation in the gables. One recalls the Recife churches of the Matriz de Santo Antônio and Nossa Senhora do Monte do Carmo, as well as the convent of São Bento in Olinda.

The influence of the Italians Francesco Borromini and Guarino Guarini (Guarini designed the church of the Divina Providência in Lisbon, 1653), who arrived in Brazil in the eighteenth century after the discovery of gold and diamond mines, can be seen in churches in Rio de Janeiro and in Minas Gerais. This influence appears not only in the floral decorations of the façades and in the use of curved shapes, but also in the elliptical plans and in the façades: both Nossa Senhora da Glória do Outeiro (1714) in Rio de Janeiro and Nossa Senhora do Rosario dos Negros in Ouro Prêto show spatial configurations similar to São Pedro dos Clérigosin Oporto (1732). The climax of Brazilian baroque architecture coincides with the works of the architect and sculptor Antonio Francisco Lisboa, called Aleijadinho (the little cripple), who designed a series of churches and sculptural groups that break from orthodox European rules. The use of the so-called *Pedra Sabão* (soapstone), soft and malleable, gave Aleijadinho sculptural freedom for creative decorations in façades and in a sculptural group of prophets in the sanctuary of Bom Jesus de Matosinhos in Congonhas do Campo (1758–1771). Baroque influences, both Italian and German, appear in Aleijadinho's main churches: São Francisco de Assis in Ouro Prêto (1770) and São Francisco de Assis in São João del Rei (1774).

During the reconstruction of Lisbon after the devastating fire and earthquake of 1755, the Marquis of Pombal abandoned baroque ornamental excess and instead supported neoclassicism as a renovating language because of its association with the cultural transformations of illuminism. The new trend arrived in Brazil with the court of Dom João (King John VI), who in 1816 invited a group of French artists to Rio de Janeiro to create the Academy of Fine Arts and to encourage painting, sculpture, and architecture. The founding artists included Félix Émile Taunay, Jean Baptiste Debrét, Joaquim Lebreton, and the archi-

tect Grandjean de Montigny. It was Montigny who built the Chamber of Commerce headquarters in 1819, a fine example of orthodox neoclassicism that served as a model for other buildings. In the capital city, luxurious mansions such as the residence of the Count of Itamaraty (1851), as well as several public buildings, applied this ascetic language. Examples include the Casa da Moeda (1858), the hospital of Santa Casa da Misericordia (1840), and the Hospício de Alienados Don Pedro II (1842), which later became the headquarters of the University of Brazil. This neoclassical influence moved to other areas as well: in Recife, the Frenchman Louis Léger Vauthier built the Santa Isabel Theater (1846).

By the end of the nineteenth century, successive republican governments had worked on modernizing Rio de Janeiro, assimilating the model established by Georges-Eugène Haussmann in Paris for a capital city. This approach was also applied to other cities with burgeoning economic development: São Paulo was the center of the coffee trade, and Belo Horizonte replaced Ouro Prêto as the new capital of Minas Gerais. In 1903, Rio de Janeiro's mayor, Francisco Pereira Passos (1836–1913), began construction on the Avenida Central, which became the fundamental axis of Rio's social life. Along this important avenue, offices, banks, hotels, residences, and public buildings designed with historical language emerged: buildings included the Teatro Municipal by Francisco de Oliveira Passos (1904), the Museu de Belas Artes by Adolfo Morales de los Rios (1906), the Biblioteca National by Héctor Pépin (1905), the Palácio Monroe by Francisco Marcelino de Souza

Church of Nossa Senhora da Graça, Olinda, Brazil. (Gustavo Fadel/iStockPhoto.com)

Aguiar (1906), and the Câmara dos Vereadores (Palácio Pedro Ernesto) by Francisque Couchet and Arquímedes Memoria, from the office of Heitor de Mello (1920). Similar work arose in São Paulo, with the construction of the Escola Politécnica (1895) and the Teatro Municipal (1911), both by Francisco de Paula Ramos de Azevedo. In Belo Horizonte, a group of public buildings was erected around the Praça da Liberdade, and in Porto Alegre, Theo Wiederspahn designed the headquarters of the Correios e Telégrafo (1910) and the delegation of the Tesouro National (1914).

Modern Art Week in San Pablo (1922) highlighted the reaction of vanguard artists against academic historicism. The arrival in Brazil of the Russian architect Gregori Warchavchik (1896–1972), together with

his first rationalist works in São Paulo, paved the way for the modern movement in architecture, nurtured by the lectures delivered by Le Corbusier at the 1929 meetings of the Society of Architects in Rio de Janeiro. The revolution of Getúlio Vargas in 1930 called into question the significance of the architectural symbols of the Old Republic and resulted in the search for a new linguistic representation to reflect the modernization of the state. At the time, a renovation movement took place in the School of Fine Arts, under the direction of Lucio Costa, who became the undisputed leader of the Brazilian modern architectural movement. Costa then directed the team that designed the paradigm-setting plan for the building that became the Ministério da Educação e Saúde (MES, 1936), and he also prepared the *Plano Pi-*

loto (Master Plan) for Brasília, the new capital city, inaugurated in 1960. Oscar Niemeyer (1907), who worked in Costa's office and collaborated with Le Corbusier on the MES project, stands out as the mastermind of the new plastic forms that came to identify Brazilian architecture throughout the world: one recalls the group of buildings in Pampulha (1942), Belo Horizonte; the exhibition facilities in Ibirapuera Park (1954) in São Paulo; and the public buildings of Brasília (1957).

In the early 1950s, the architectural renovation movement gained momentum through the contributions of a group of professionals from Rio de Janeiro and São Paulo, architects such as Jorge Machado Moreira, Affonso Eduardo Reidy, Sérgio Bernardes, João Vilanova Artigas, Rino Levi, and Henrique Mindlin. These architects forged the foundation of a regional modern vocabulary that has influenced successive generations of Latin American architects.

Roberto Segre

References

Bazin, Germain. *A arquitetura religiosa barroca no Brasil.* Rio de Janeiro: Editora Record, 1983.

Bruand, Yves. *Arquitetura contemporânea no Brasil.* São Paulo: Editora Perspectiva, 1999.

Cavalcanti, Lauro. *When Brazil Was Modern: A Guide to Architecture, 1928–1960.* New York: Princeton University Press, 2003.

Da Souza Hue, Jorge. *A View of Brazilian Colonial Architecture.* Rio de Janeiro: Editora AGIR, 1999.

Underwood, David. *Oscar Niemeyer and the Architecture of Brazil.* New York: Rizzoli, 1994.

See also: Architecture—Colonial Spanish America; Architecture—Modern Spanish America; Art and Artists—Brazil; Brazil; Catholic Church in Brazil; Colonists and Settlers II—Brazil; Dyes and Dyewood; Enlightenment—Brazil.

ARCHITECTURE—COLONIAL SPANISH AMERICA

The Spanish discovery, conquest, and colonization of the Americas initiated an intense constructive enterprise for cities and buildings. Assuming traditional stylistic categories, the development of the architecture occurred in four fundamental stages: primitive, baroque, ultrabaroque, and neoclassical. The Antilles constituted the background for the earliest transfer of Hispanic models to the new colonial possessions. In 1502 Nicolás de Ovando founded the city of Santo Domingo on the island of Hispaniola. The city was built based on a semiregular layout that foreshadowed the later regulatory scheme imposed during the reign of Philip II. Following the 1573 promulgation of the *Leyes de Indias* (Laws of the Indies), Spanish cities in the Americas incorporated the main symbols of political, religious, military, and economic power; in Santo Domingo, this scheme was reflected in the construction of the Alcázar, the Palace of Diego Colón, which was defined by its solid stone walls and introverted character (a design that was later imitated in Hernando Cortés's palace in Cuernavaca, Mexico). It can also be seen in Santo Domingo's fortress and its cathedral. The presence of the bishop, Alejandro Geraldi, who had a Renaissance humanist background, promoted architectural syncretism; for example, the nave of the church was inspired by the cathedral in Seville, with its classic façade doorway. Despite its grandeur, however, the aesthetic refinement of Santo Domingo's Catedral Primada de América (the first cathedral in the Americas) was not repeated elsewhere in the Caribbean, or in the recently conquered territory of New Spain (Mexico).

The Crown's main concern in the sixteenth century was to defend its new settlements from Dutch and English attacks and to indoctrinate the indigenous people who inhabited the region. For that reason the Crown invested tremendous resources in the creation of an ambitious defensive system to protect its ports and the galleons of the Spanish fleet. As far as architectural design is concerned, they repeated classic models of the Renaissance, reflected in the castle de La Fuerza (1558) in Havana. Later, Juan Bautista Antonelli, an Italian military engineer who served Philip II, adapted his building designs to take advantage of the local topography and the strategic particularities of each place; this approach is reflected in the fortresses of Havana, San Juan de Puerto Rico, Cartagena de Indias, and Veracruz. The largest fortress in the Americas was La Cabaña in Havana (1763), built after the English invasion of the city during the reign of Charles III; it was based on the designs of the French engineer Vauban.

The emergence of monastery-fortress buildings characterizes the primitive stage of Spanish American architecture. Their originality rests in the military character of the buildings, constructed with solid stone walls and battlement enclosures. One particularity was the creation of an open space to gather the Indians together in order to indoctrinate them; this space served as an open chapel where mass was held. Given the unusual features of the original Iberian models, it could be said that a mixture of influences and styles distinguished them. In almost all early colonial churches, compact and solid naves prevailed, while the façades and doorways were decorated with elements of Islamic influences (*mudéjar* and *plataresco* traditions), which can be seen in the monasteries of Acolman, Huejotzingo, and Cuitzco in central Mexico. The monks occupied the cells around the medieval cloisters, while Renaissance spatial quality appeared in the ceremonial squares that sheltered the religious rituals of the natives.

Between the foundation of Santo Domingo in 1502 and Buenos Aires in 1580, more than 300 settlements arose in the Caribbean, Central America, and on the continent. And although Spanish traditions favored a regular grid layout, settlers in the Americas also were influenced by their personal experiences in Iberian medieval towns; some even adapted to the new reality found in America. These variations help to explain the diversity of city plans throughout Spanish America. For example, consider the "superimposed" cities such as Mexico City and Cuzco; the irregular urban structure of Guanajuato and Tasco; the semiregular grid pattern found in Havana, Cartagena de Indias, and Quito; and the regular orthodox grid pattern reflected in Puebla, Lima, Córdoba, and Buenos Aires. In all cases, the urban grid was configured by means of a compact system of homogeneous blocks. The blocks were defined by an introverted housing scheme with an interior patio. A structural grid of rectilinear streets of the same width culminated in the *plaza mayor* (main square), a square with a rectangular plan; the main square contained the church, the town council, the governor's palace, and the customs house (the Alcázar). The symbolic center of Hispanic power, the plaza mayor constituted the main public space of urban social life. On rare occasions, such as in the city of Havana, separate squares were constructed for each function: the religious in the Plaza de la Catedral, the military and administrative in the Plaza de Armas, and the commercial center in the Plaza Vieja.

Colonial architecture in Spanish America during the seventeenth and eighteenth centuries received many influences from the Iberian Peninsula. However, these influences were not uniform across the Americas. Regional diversity in civic and religious architecture can be explained by several factors: (1) the presence in some areas of prestigious Spanish architects, and the realization of the projects by military engineers or local religious persons with building expertise; (2) the distinct symbolic representations required in different capital cities; (3) the adoption of diverse European models, such as the regulatory scheme of Giacomo Barozzi da Vignola in the churches built by the Jesuit order; (4) the nature and availability of local construction materials and the quality of the indigenous artisans; and (5) the unequal distribution of resources that distinguished territories with large quantities of gold and silver, such as Mexico, Colombia, and Peru, from those regions with a more precarious economy, such as Argentina, Venezuela, the Antilles, and Central America.

Direct Spanish influences were felt in the first large cathedrals and monasteries, built mainly by Iberian architects. Francisco Becerra, planner of the cathedral of Puebla (1575) in Mexico and those of Lima and Cuzco (1584) in Peru, was particularly influential. The cathedral of Mexico (1563), designed by Claudio de Arciniega, is similar to Juan de Herrera's cathedral of Valladolid; likewise, the cathedral of Guadalajara (1571) is similar to the one in Granada, designed by Diego de Siloé. These buildings are characterized by their mixture of stylistic elements: the vol-

umetric heaviness comes from the medieval and Renaissance inheritance, while the façades have baroque, mannerist, or mudéjar decorations. This blending is manifested in San Francisco's monastery in Quito (1537), while the late Jesuit cathedral of Havana (1748) is an exceptional case of formal purism, inspired by the influence exercised by Italian architect Francesco Borromini.

The ultrabaroque that identifies churches built in the eighteenth century is characterized by the crammed decoration in the façades and in the interiors, based on the influence of indigenous iconography and carried out with the participation of local artisans. Lorenzo Rodríguez designed the *sagrario* (sacred chapel) of the cathedral of Mexico (1750). Diego Durán designed the church of Santa Prisca in Taxco (1748); in Puebla, the profuse ornamentation of Rosario's chapel stands out in the church of Santo Domingo (1690). While the façade of the Jesuit church of Tepozotlán (1762) is a gigantic altarpiece sculpted in stone, the small church of San Francisco Acatepec is original for the colorful lining of its tiles. This exuberance spread in Central America, represented in the church of La Merced in Antigua, in Guatemala, and in the Andean region as well. However, it does not appear in Venezuela or Argentina. Instead, the cathedrals of Caracas and of Córdoba (designed in 1729 by Father Andrés Bianchi) show an assimilated treatment of the simplicity of the classic Renaissance layouts favored by the Jesuits; this style also appears in the Jesuit missions of Paraguay, Brazil, and Argentina. Another popular approach appears in Peru and in the Bolivian highlands, in the vicinity of Arequipa and Lake Titicaca, where one finds the popular buildings of the Sanctuary of Copacabana and the church of Totora in Bolivia, or the churches of Juli and Pomata in Peru.

Prior to the Latin American independence movements, during the reign of King Charles III (1759–1788), the sobriety of the neoclassical style was imposed in Spain. Neoclassical style also appeared in Spanish America, especially in the new public buildings. In Mexico City, Manuel Tolsá designed the monumental Palacio de la Minería (1780), while José Gutiérrez and Manuel Gómez Ibarra built the austere Hospicio Cabañas in Guadalajara. In Chile, Joaquín Toesca constructed the historical Casa de la Moneda (1784), and then transformed it into a presidential palace. Finally, Havana, Cuba, and San Juan, Puerto Rico, contain a group of neoclassical buildings that transcend the architectural dimension to assume the urban scale of the city. These monuments define Havana's Plaza de Armas, the Palacio de los Capitanes Generales (1776), the Palacio del Segundo Cabo (1770) (which still maintain baroque ornamental elements), and El Templete (1828). In San Juan, Puerto Rico, in the eighteenth and nineteenth centuries, the Spanish government carried out enormous investments, building the Cuartel de Ballajá, the Hospital de la Concepción, the Asilo de Beneficiencia, and the Antiguo Manicomio, all ascetic constructions built in neoclassical style.

Roberto Segre

References

Bayón, Damián Carlos, and Murillo Marx. *History of South American Art and Architecture: Spanish South America and Brazil.* New York: Rizzoli, 1992.

Early, James. *The Colonial Architecture of Mexico.* Dallas: Southern Methodist University Press, 2001.

Gutiérrez, Ramón. *Arquitectura y urbanismo en Iberoamérica.* Madrid: Ediciones Cátedra, 1983.

Gutiérrez, Ramón, and Rodrigo Gutiérrez Visuales. *Historia del arte iberoamericano.* Barcelona: Lunwerg Editores, 2000.

Gosner, Pamela. *Caribbean Baroque: Historic Architecture of the Spanish Antilles.* Pueblo, CO: Passeggiata Press, 1996.

See also: Architecture—Brazil; Architecture—Modern Spanish America; Art and Artists—Colonial Spanish America; Catholic Church in Spanish America; Cities; Colonists and Settlers I–VI; Conquest I–VII; Culture; Defense—Colonial Spanish America; Fleet System; Jesuits—Brazil; Jesuits—Paraguay; Maps; Missions; Pirates and Piracy; Religious Orders.

ARCHITECTURE—MODERN SPANISH AMERICA

Iberian influences in Spanish American architecture changed dramatically after the nineteenth-century independence movements. Following independence, many of the new Latin American republics turned to England and France for new technical and cultural influences. Twentieth-century Spanish American architecture developed along three fundamental axes: the European, the North American, and the search for regional architectural identity. In the 1920s, neocolonial and art deco styles, both antecedents of functionalism, challenged the prevailing academic tradition. Neocolonialism corresponded to the effort to recover colonial roots and represent them in a modern style; the aim was to adapt modern architecture to the local cultural traditions of each country, reflecting each region's unique character. Continental professionals and theoreticians defended the style; among those of note are the Argentines Ángel Guido and Martin Noel, Peruvians Héctor Velarde and Emilio

The Nacional hotel in Havana, Cuba, reflects North American influences on Cuban and Puerto Rican architecture. (Stephen Ferry/Liaison)

Harth-terré, the Mexican Federico Mariscal and the Cubans Evelio Govantes and Félix Cobarrocas (all born between 1880 and 1900). At the same time in the United States, specifically during the 1920s, Rexford Newcomb and Addison Mizner adopted Hispanic ornamental components in the new architecture of California and Florida. The construction of municipal buildings, hotels, and residences in San Francisco, Los Angeles, and Miami influenced Cuban and Puerto Rican architecture; for example, the Nacional hotel in Havana, designed in 1930 by McKim, Mead and White, is similar to the Hotel Biltmore in Coral Gables, built six years earlier by Schultze and Weaver. The Tower Roosevelt, which dominates the campus of the University of Puerto Rico, was designed in 1936 by Rafael Carmoega and Bill Schimmelpfenning, and bears a striking resemblance to the Giralda in Seville, Spain.

Art deco style spread quickly following the International Exposition of Decorative Arts in Paris (1925); its rapid assimilation can be seen in the skyscrapers of New York and later in the Miami Beach neighborhood. Its influence was felt throughout the Americas. In his 1929 book *The History of the Skyscraper,* Mexican architect Manuel Mujica associated the particular design of the skyscraper with the Mayan and Aztec pyramids, establishing their "Pan American" originality. Among the more significant art deco works, it is important to mention the Bacardí offices in Havana, built in 1930 by Esteban Rodríguez Castells, Santo Domingo's Lighthouse of Columbus by J. L. Gleave (1931–1992), the building Ermita by Juan Segura in Mexico (1930), and in Buenos Aires La

Equitativa del Plata, designed in 1929 by Alejandro Virasoro.

European rationalism was disseminated in South America by Le Corbusier, who in 1929 traveled to Argentina, Uruguay, and Brazil to deliver a series of lectures; Le Corbusier's comments exerted a strong influence over the younger generation of Latin American architects. Between 1930 and 1940, a definitive rupture with the academy occurred, manifested in the application of new constructive technologies with steel and reinforced concrete and the implementation of functional representations with a renewed social content: houses, offices, industries, hospitals, schools, and sport centers. In Mexico, the social initiatives of the revolutionary government, starting from 1910, facilitated the assimilation of rational images, applied to the buildings constructed in the 1930s. It is worth mentioning the workers' housing in the neighborhood of Balbina, designed by Juan Legarreta (1932), and the Technical-Industrial School by Juan O'-Gorman (1933) and the National Institute of Cardiology by José Villagrán García (1937). Rigorously modern works, both public and private, were carried out in Cuba by Max Borges (home of Santiago Claret, 1941) and Mario Romañach (home of José Noval Cueto, 1949) in Havana; Leo and Pou Ricar (School Salomé Henriquez Ureña, 1943) in Santo Domingo; Enrique Seoane (Wilson Building, 1946) in Lima, Peru; Bruno Violi and Leopoldo Rotter (University City, 1941) in Bogotá, Colombia; Roberto Dávila (Club Cap Ducal in Viña del Mar, 1936) and Sergio Larraín (building Santa Lucía, 1934) in Santiago, Chile; Antonio Vilar (headquarters of the Argentinean Automobile Club, 1942), Vladimiro Acosta (Figueroa Alcorta Apart-

ments, 1942), and Alberto Prebisch (Gran Rex Cinema, 1937) in Buenos Aires; and lastly, Julio Vilamajó (School of Engineering, 1936) in Montevideo, Uruguay. North American influence was reflected in the state buildings that were constructed in the central areas of the capital cities, using the modern monumental design characteristic of the New Deal government of President Roosevelt. One notable exception was the original Kavanagh apartments tower in Buenos Aires (1933), designed by Sánchez, Lagos and de la Torre, whose configuration of vertically articulated flat volumes recalls New York's Rockefeller Center.

The years between the end of World War II and the 1960s witnessed the most brilliant period in modern Latin American architecture. Reaction against rationalism and the cosmopolitan approach of the international style coming from the United States privileged the search for an architectural language closely linked with the cultural roots, climatic conditions, and material and technological resources unique to each region. External influences came from the original solutions of Brazilian architects such as Lucio Costa, Oscar Niemeyer, and Affonso Reidy, among others. The regionalist inheritance of Frank Lloyd Wright, the adaptation of Richard Neutra's sense of place, and the expressive freedom of European brutalism identified with the late works of Le Corbusier (such as the Residential Unit of Marseilles from 1946, and the church of Ronchamp and the civic center of Chandigarh, both built in 1950). The countries of the Antilles produced a unique architecture that closely related functional requirements with an adaptation to the climate, using local materials.

During the second half of the twentieth century, aesthetic experiences occurred as architects began to search for designs that truly reflected national identity. For example, in San Juan, Puerto Rico, in 1949, Osvaldo Toro and Miguel Ferrer designed the first "tropical" model for the Hilton Hotel chain; likewise, Heinrich Klumb, one of Neutra's pupils, carried out diverse works on the campus of the University of Puerto Rico at Rio Piedras. Among his works, the Center of Students (1962) stands out for its transparency, horizontality, and the use of elements for protection from the sun. In the Dominican Republic, Rafael Calventi designed the headquarters for the Central Bank (1972), with a refined texture and a proportionate "sun-breakers" system that protected the building's façade from the sun. In Cuba during the 1950s, the formal and spatial explorations of some architects, such as Eugenio Batista, Antonio Quintana, Frank Martínez, Mario Romañach, Aquiles Capablanca, Henry Gutiérrez, and others, continued until the early 1960s, when the effects of the revolution began to be seen in the work of Ricardo Porro, Vittorio Garatti, and Roberto Gottardi. In the National School of Art (1961–1963) of Havana, original constructions of vaults and brick domes are immersed in plants that reflect the power of nature in the tropics.

In Mexico, the formal simplicity of pre-Columbian architecture, combined with chromatic surfaces and the shady interior patios inherited from Mexico's colonial past, served as an important antecedent present most notably in Luis Barragán's influential works; Barragán's influence can be seen in Ricardo Legorreta's design for the Hotel Camino Real in Mexico City (1968). The ascetic textures of the stone of Aztec monuments are present in the volumes of reinforced concrete in the

works of Abraham Zabludovsky and Teodoro González de León. And Mexican architects' search for local cultural roots is clearly reflected on the campus of the Autonomous National University of Mexico (1947–1952).

In Venezuela, Carlos Raúl Villanueva (1900–1975) was the pivotal figure within the modern movement: the campus of the Central University of Venezuela (1952), with the presence of artistic works in buildings and public spaces, reaches a synthesis between cosmopolitan and local traditions; other important works include Tomás José Sanabria's design of the Central Bank of Venezuela (1960), as well as the residences by architect Fruto Vivas. In Colombia, the poetics of brick and the sharpening of their aesthetic potential can be seen in Rogelio Salmona's Torres del Parque (1965).

In the Southern Cone, the scarce presence of indigenous populations strengthened an architecture that was conditioned by external influences and the persistence of a sober and ascetic language. In Santiago, Chile, Corbusier's brutalism was assimilated in the residential complex Portales (1959), which was carried out by a team directed by Fernando Castle Velasco. In Uruguay, Mario Payssé Reyes's residences and Eladio Dieste's church of Atlántida (1958) developed the aesthetic and structural possibilities of brick. In Argentina, the renovation of the rationalistic language began with Juan Kurchan and Jorge Ferrari Hardoy in the apartment building of Virrey del Pino in Buenos Aires (1943); it continued through the purity and technological virtuosity of Amancio Williams in his Casa del Puente (Bridge House) (1945) in Mar del Plata. The work of architect Clorindo Testa represents the culmination of the maturation process of

Argentine architecture, with its free plastic interpretation of the brutalist style, achieved in the robust headquarters of the Bank of London and America of the South (1960), and in the unusual configuration of the National Library (1963), which was designed with Francisco Bullrich and Alicia Gazaniga. These works constitute clear manifestations of the creativity of modern Latin American architecture.

Roberto Segre

References

Bullrich, Francisco. *New Directions in Latin American Architecture.* New York: Braziller, 1969.

Fraser, Valerie. *Building the New World: Studies in the Modern Architecture of Latin America, 1930–1960.* New York, London: Verso, 2000.

Quantrill, Malcolm, ed. *Latin American Architecture: Six Voices.* College Station: Texas A&M University Press, 2000.

Segre, Roberto. *Latin America on Its Architecture.* New York: Holmes and Meier, 1981.

———. *América Latina fin de milenio. Raíces y perspectivas de su arquitectura.* Havana: Editorial Arte y Literatura, 1999.

See Also: Architecture—Brazil; Architecture—Colonial Spanish America; Cities; Culture; Mexican Revolution; Nationalism; Native Americans I–VIII; Syncretism; World War II.

ARGENTINA

The Spanish expeditions to conquer and colonize Argentine territory traveled three different routes, and the conquistadors were mainly interested in finding gold and silver. One of the expeditions, conducted by Pedro de Mendoza, arrived directly from Spain through the South Atlantic Ocean; in 1536 Mendoza founded the Puerto de Nuestra Señora de los Buenos Ayres. His expedition not only had precious metal as a target but also was a colonization effort; Mendoza introduced cattle and horses. However, Indians attacked and destroyed the settlement, which was abandoned in 1541; the inhabitants were transferred to Asunción (Paraguay) by order of Governor Domingo de Irala. At the same time, Asunción became a center for further expeditions to the west and the south. Juan de Garay founded Santa Fe in 1573 and finally the city of Buenos Aires in 1580, which was named the Ciudad de la Santísima Trinidad y Puerto de Santa María de los Buenos Ayres.

Two other groups of Spanish conquistadors came from Santiago (Chile) and Potosí (Bolivia). Under orders from Chile's governor, Garcia Hurtado de Mendoza, the group from Santiago occupied the eastern side of the Andes in 1561, where settlers began to exploit mines on both sides of the mountains. The entire region, known as Cuyo, remained under Chile's jurisdiction until 1776, when the Viceroyalty of the Río de la Plata assumed authority over the region.

An expedition from Cuzco (Bolivia) to the Río de la Plata in 1542, conducted by Diego de Rojas, failed to establish any permanent Spanish settlement. Another conquistador, Juan Nuñez de Prado, led a new expedition in 1549 from Potosí to the Tucumán region, where a Spanish settlement was established. However, Chile's governor claimed the area, and in 1563 another conquistador, Francisco de Aguirre, came from Santiago, captured Nuñez del Prado, and sent him to Chile to be prosecuted. Finally, a royal decree established Tucumán's government in 1563 and thus ended the jurisdictional conflict. By 1617, another royal decree created the government of Buenos

Aires, also named the government of the Río de la Plata.

By the beginning of the seventeenth century, Argentina was divided into four districts: Tucumán, Paraguay, Buenos Aires, and Cuyo. Chile's *audiencia* (royal court) held jurisdiction over Cuyo, while the Audiencia of La Plata de los Charcas had authority over the other three. This political status continued until 1776, when the newly established Viceroyalty of the Río de la Plata assumed jurisdiction over the four districts, as well as the territory that makes up modern Bolivia.

As a consequence of Napoleon's invasion of Spain and Ferdinand VII's imprisonment, on May 22, 1810, officers within the Creole militia issued a call for a *cabildo abierto* (special open meeting of the municipal council) to discuss the crisis in Spain. Representatives at the cabildo formed a new government, which swore loyalty to King Ferdinand VII and thus made no attempt to formulate a new constitution; however, after this meeting Spain never again regained its authority over Buenos Aires. Over the following two years, the United Provinces of the Río de la Plata searched for a political alternative, including a negotiated settlement with Charles IV. No agreement was reached, and the Declaration of Independence in 1816 and the adoption of a republican political system solved the political dilemma. However, the threat of a Spanish invasion to recover the Río de la Plata's colonies remained until 1818.

Although politics played a central role in the creation of the modern state of Argentina, another force helped to shape Argentina's national formation: the Jesuits. From the last quarter of the sixteenth century until their expulsion in 1767, the Jesuits established a series of missions throughout the territory. In northeastern Argentina, Paraguay, Uruguay, and the eastern parts of Bolivia, Peru, and Ecuador, Jesuits established Indian mission settlements. After their expulsion, in 1767, conflict erupted between Río de la Plata's viceroyalty and Brazil; the conflict continued into the early decades of the nineteenth century. It was not until Uruguay's independence in 1830 that the conflict came to an end.

By then, the boundaries of the new nation (following Paraguay's independence in 1811 and Bolivia's independence in 1826) had been established. However, another three decades passed before the region consolidated politically. Between 1827 and 1853, no single state existed; instead, the region was divided into fourteen provinces. Conflicts between provincial leaders were common, but after 1835 Juan Manuel de Rosas, the governor of the province of Buenos Aires, emerged as the region's most powerful political figure. Rosas was overthrown in 1852 and thirteen provinces, excluding Buenos Aires, approved a new constitution. Finally, in 1860, the province of Buenos Aires joined the confederation, and the Argentine republic was born. In 1866, fifty years after it declared independence, Spain officially recognized Argentina.

Despite various internal struggles and two bitter wars, one against the Indian population and the other against Paraguay, Argentina's political system maintained its stability until 1930. Between 1880 and 1930 the economy grew at a dramatic rate. European immigration brought an increased labor force, and the invention of the cold-storage chamber facilitated trade. Railways, harbors, tramways, subways, electric power, domestic gas, telephones, radio stations, and transoceanic communi-

Crowd in Buenos Aires rallies for Juan Perón's campaign speech, March 1954. (Bettmann/Corbis)

cations helped put Argentina among the seven big economies by 1930.

On September 6, 1930, however, a military coup overthrew the constitutional government; the upheaval affected the political, economic, and social spheres of national life. After a couple of years, a new civil constitutional government assumed control; however, the Radical party that had ruled before the 1930 coup was still outlawed. This political structure, named the Concordancia, remained in power until 1943, when a new coup occurred, led by a group of young army officers, among them Juan Perón, imbued with a nationalistic ideology and supported by the Catholic Church. At times, the armed forces and the Church sympathized with

Germany and Italy; by contrast, many people and democratic parties identified with Allied ideals.

Another factor came into play when the Spanish Civil War and World War II drove a new wave of immigration from Spain and later from Italy. Until the mid-1950s, Argentina was a country with large numbers of immigrants. At the same time, however, the political situation under Juan Perón's rule (1946–1955) forced many educated middle- and upper-class people to emigrate. And emigration has been a cyclical but steady process since then.

Perón and his Peronist party were inspired by Mussolini's Fascism, nationalist ideology, and demagogic oratory. Reforms in the labor laws, borrowed from either

Argentine socialist leader Alfredo Palacios or Mussolini's *Carta di Lavoro* (Labor Statement), were enforced. In particular, the labor market was ruled by collective agreements between labor union leaders and employer unions, so that salaries rose yearly and pushed up prices. Foreign companies had been controlling such crucial things as railways, telephones, power, and harbors, and they were now expropriated; other companies, mainly German- and Italian-owned, were confiscated as "enemy property" (Argentina's declaration of war took place in April 1945).

While the state-owned sector quickly expanded its importance, the food shortage in Europe heavily supported Perón's economic policy until 1950, raising Argentine exports and improving income distribution as well as providing higher standards of living. The relationship between Argentina and Spain was extremely important in Perón's foreign policy. After World War II, Franco's government remained isolated from the victorious Allies. Perón, however, established friendly relations with Spain; his wife, Eva Duarte, visited Spain in 1949 and gave Franco financial support to purchase Argentine food in order to cover Spain's shortage.

Argentina's economic success did not last. By 1951–1952, the economy had fallen into crisis, with widespread food shortages and rationing. Press censorship and expropriation, as well as the persecution of political opponents, became daily matters. Eva Perón, who was very influential among Argentina's poor, died in 1952; and in 1954 a controversy erupted between Perón and the Catholic Church, which finally led to Perón's overthrow in 1955 by military coup.

The military government ruled the country until 1958, when a new constitutional government, with Arturo Frondizi as president, assumed power. Under Frondizi's government, a new wave of economic prosperity arrived in Argentina. However, some economic problems, such as inflation and balance-of-payment deficits, remained unsolved. Another military coup followed in 1962, but democracy was restored a year later in 1963. Nevertheless, the economic situation worsened, and a new military coup ended civilian rule in 1966. A new economic policy slowed the rate of inflation, but the political situation remained unstable.

Since Peronists were outlawed, Perón, who was living in Madrid, financed subversive groups, such as the Montoneros, to defeat the military government. Finally, the military government called a general election, and Perón returned to Argentina at the end of 1973; still he was prohibited from becoming a candidate. However, his followers won the election, and the new civilian government revoked the prohibition, dismissed the results, and called an election again in order to let Perón and his third wife, Maria Estela Martínez (nicknamed Isabelita), become president and vice-president respectively.

Immediately Perón expelled the leftist Peronists, and the Montoneros became an urban guerrilla force, mainly after Perón's death in 1974. Lopez Rega, a powerful adviser of Mrs. Perón, organized a paramilitary group, the triple alliance, or AAA, to fight the Montoneros soon afterwards. Additionally, another leftist group, the Leo Trotsky–inspired Revolutionary Army of the People, arrived on the scene as a rural guerrilla force. The general violence led the armed forces to overthrow Mrs. Perón, who was sent into exile in Madrid.

The new military government was known as the Proceso, and it ruled over Argentina until 1983. During those years, thousands of "disappeared," dead, and exiled people became victims of what was known as Argentina's Dirty War. This persecution drove many Argentine refugees out of the country, mainly to Madrid. While the economic situation was prosperous, the Proceso was tolerated; by 1980–1981, however, Argentina's economic woes were added to its political problems. In order to maintain its authority, the military government initiated on April 2, 1982, what is generally referred to as the Falklands War, from the British name for the Malvinas Islands, in order to assert an old claim of sovereignty over the islands.

After seventy-two days of fighting, the armed forces were defeated, and once again the government was handed to civilian rule. A hyperinflation was the consequence of President Alfonsín's economic policy and he handed power to Carlos Menem, who won the presidential election in 1989. Under Menem, Argentina followed a free-market economic policy, and a new wave of prosperity followed; however, high rates of unemployment sparked problems in the last years of Menem's rule. The crisis exploded under his successor, Fernando De la Rua, who was forced to resign in 2001 after popular protests. During Menem's rule, for the first time in modern Argentine history, Spaniards invested heavily in the country, in areas such as communication, airlines, and oil. But the recently elected government is now facing serious social, political, and economic problems. Interestingly, an increasing level of Spanish economic influence in Argentina hints at a rebuilding of ties between the two regions.

Héctor Noejovich

References

Cortés Conde, Roberto, and Ezequiel Gallo. *La formación de la Argentina moderna.* Buenos Aires: Paidos, 1967.

Díaz Alejandro, Carlos Federico. *Argentine Republic.* New Haven, CT: Yale University Press, 1970.

Erro, Davide G. *Resolving the Argentine Paradox: Politics and Development, 1966–1992.* Boulder, CO: Lynne Rienner, 1993.

Ferns, Henry Stanley. *Britain and Argentina in the Nineteenth Century.* Oxford: Clarendon, 1960.

Halperin Donghi, Tulio. *Politics, Economics and Society in the Revolutionary Period.* Cambridge: Cambridge University Press, 1975.

James, Daniel. *Resistance and Integration: Peronism and the Argentine Working Class, 1946–1976.* Cambridge: Cambridge University Press, 1994.

Platt, D. C. M., and Guido di Tella. *Argentina, Australia y Canadá.* New York: St. Martin's, 1985.

Rock, David. *Argentina, 1516–1987: From Spanish Colonization to Alfonsín.* Berkeley and Los Angeles: University of California Press, 1987.

Romero, Luis Alberto. *A History of Argentina in the Twentieth Century.* State College: Pennsylvania State University Press, 2003.

See also: Administration—Colonial Spanish America; Audiencias; Bolivia; Bourbon Reforms; Brazil; Caudillos; Colonists and Settlers V—Southern Cone; Communism; Conquest VII—Southern Cone; Democracy; Explorers; Football; Guerrillas; Independence I—Argentina; Jesuits—Expulsion; Jesuits—Iberia and America; Malvinas/Falkland Islands; Missions; Nationalism; Paraguay; Paraguayan War; Populism; Potosí; Spanish Civil War and Latin America; Uruguay; Viceroyalties; World War I; World War II.

ARMIES—COLONIAL BRAZIL

Portuguese history and geography favored maritime over land-based innovations in warfare, and this tempered the transatlantic influences that its armies in colonial Brazil experienced. The first *terços* (large infantry battalions that massed gunfire) of Portuguese troops arrived in Salvador, Bahia, in the mid-sixteenth century. The use of the term "terço" reveals that early colonial Portuguese units imitated, at least in name, the famous *tercio* infantry of the Spanish army that then dominated much of Europe. These forces were complemented by *ordenanças,* local militia units that required the organization of all free male settlers from age eighteen to sixty, save for nobility and clergy. In the first century of colonization, the ordenanças were the predominant intermediate political structure that linked local governance to colonial administration. However, land forces in Brazil were poorly trained, armed, and supplied, and when they were paid, the pay was niggardly and tardy. Soldiers and officers soon adapted their strategies to the enemies they usually confronted: Indians and maroons, for which terço tactics were none too effective in the Atlantic rainforest.

Spanish influence over the Portuguese Empire diminished when their confederation (1580–1640) ended and the Bragança royal family reasserted Portugal's independence. It was Portugal's war to liberate itself from Spain that saw the formation of a permanent Portuguese army. Meanwhile, in Brazil, Portuguese colonials had their hands full with Dutch invaders, who occupied sugar-rich Pernambuco from 1630 to 1654. These wars brought about the formation of new terços in Brazil, which included the famous racially segregated forces of black troops, led by their black commander Henrique Dias, and a terço of the colonial's indigenous allies, led by Chief Felippe Camarão. These units helped to establish a tradition of racially segregated brown and black militia units, which continued in Brazil into the 1830s. The so-called slow war to expel the Dutch involved combining guerrilla-style indigenous strategies with European tactics adapted to the geographic conditions and capabilities of Portuguese colonial forces.

After the Dutch withdrew, Portuguese colonization focused on the exploration and conquest of the interior. Contemporaries dubbed the series of struggles involved the War of the Barbarians, and it was concurrent with the battles to eradicate the famous Palmares confederation of maroon communities. Locally organized bands, *bandeiras,* bore the brunt of these wars, under their company commanders and ordenança flags. Bandeiras included mostly armed whites, *mestiços* (mestizos), and Indians who were outfitted by local prospectors who hoped to profit, mostly from Indian slaving or the capture of maroons. The *bandeirantes* from the captaincy of São Paulo became the most famous, but they had their counterparts in other regions. Bandeirantes extended Portuguese control into the vast interior, and they discovered the mineral wealth that accelerated the settlement of the backlands in the early 1700s. Crown officials also contracted bandeirantes to fight specific campaigns, as when Domingos Jorge Velho destroyed Palmares in the 1690s. The Jesuit Missions District (namely, the borderland region of modern Brazil, Argentina, and Paraguay that Spain ceded to the Jesuits in order to facilitate the conversion of local Indians to Christianity), which sought to protect Indians from bandeirante depredations, became vulnerable after 1750, when the Treaty of Madrid ceded part of the Missions territory to Portugal. The armed resistance of Indians and some of their Jesuit leaders did not save the mission towns, and it eventually led to the expulsion of the Jesuits from Portuguese territories in 1759.

As a hedge against Spain's power, Portugal came to pursue closer ties with England, and this relationship ultimately fostered steps to modernize Portuguese military forces. Late in the Seven Years' War (1756–1763), Portugal allied itself with Britain and Prussia against Spain and France. The Prussian officer Count Wilhelm de Schaumbourg Lippe reorganized Portuguese forces in Europe and promulgated Portugal's first army legal code, which remained the basis of military law in Brazil until the end of the nineteenth century. Spain and Portugal mobilized land forces in South America, and they clashed in the territory disputed between the two empires near the mouth of the Río de la Plata. Later, French military success provided a new "Latin" model army to emulate, but Brazil's relative geographic isolation meant that the Portuguese Crown, planters, and merchants had little incentive to make the expenditures necessary to imitate the new methods of northern European militarism. Besides, the social-leveling rhetoric that supported military conscription in Revolutionary France, which helped ultimately to give rise to Haitian independence in 1804, seemed dangerous and unnecessary in slaveholding Brazil.

In the colonial Portuguese world, enlisted soldiers had a picaresque reputation that followed them into the twentieth century. The Crown commonly used penal exile as a punishment for civil and religious crimes, in order to rid the kingdom of troublesome and dangerous subjects and to strategically relocate them in sparsely populated colonial territories. When caravels disgorged the first armed force of 600 men in 1549, it included 200 regular soldiers and 400 penal exiles (*degredados*). Portugal's population was much smaller than that of its European rivals, and this factor encouraged Crown authorities to use capital punishment sparingly and penal exile liberally. The *degredo* became a pioneer penal transportation system that other empires subsequently imitated. As core areas of Brazil became more settled, local authorities sent penal exiles to frontier areas. In the eighteenth century, Maranhão and the Sacramento Colony (located in present-day Uruguay) became preferred locations to send penal exiles. In colonial times, *soldado,* "private," became a euphemism for a penal exile and slang for an unmarried man. These usages marked the traditional exemption from coercive military recruitment for married men, who had to provide for their families, and the common use of penal exiles in colonial battalions.

Only a small minority of officers had formal military education in Brazil's more stable late-colonial army. A military academy was founded in Rio de Janeiro shortly after the Bragança court relocated there in 1808 to escape Napoleon's invasion of Portugal; however, enrollments remained relatively low. By the early nineteenth century, most army officers were Brazilian-born, and many had climbed up from the noncommissioned ranks; the sons of nobles and military officers could enter under the privileged status of cadet. Most served out their careers in garrisons near their birthplace, and many kept a hand in agriculture or business to supplement their income. Thus, most provincial officers were con-

nected more to their family and community interests than to a sense of hierarchical
corporate loyalty to the high command in
Rio de Janeiro. The court's relocation
brought with it high-ranking Portuguese
officers and some enlisted men, but there is
little evidence to support traditional asser-
tions that rivalries between Portuguese-
and Brazilian-born officers and troops
played a role in stimulating the movement
for Brazilian independence in 1822. After
independence, these tensions became
much more palpable, to the point that the
Brazilian army became a repository of luso-
phobia. During the struggle for independence, most officers and enlisted men,
whether Portuguese- or Brazilian-born,
opted to support the move toward independence led by Prince Pedro I, but forces
in Bahia and provinces farther to the north
saw brief fighting before Brazil's independence was assured.

Peter Beattie

References

Coates, Timothy J. *Convicts and Orphans:
Forced and State-Sponsored Colonizers in
the Portuguese Empire, 1550–1755.*
Stanford, CA: University of Stanford
Press, 2001.

Kraay, Hendrik. *Race, State, and Armed Forces
in Independence-Era Brazil: Bahia,
1790s–1840s.* Stanford, CA: Stanford
University Press, 2001.

Puntoni, Pedro. "A arte da guerra no Brasil:
Tecnologia e estratégia na expansão da
fronteira da América portuguesa
(1550–1700)." Pp. 43–66 in *A nova
história military brasileira,* edited by Celso
Castro, Vitor Izecksohn, and Hendrik
Kraay. Rio: Fundação Getúlio Vargas,
2004.

Silva, Katalina Vanderlei. *O miserável soldo
ea boa ordem da sociedade colonial—
Militarização e marginalidade na capitania
de Pernambuco nos séculos XVII e XVIII.*
Recife: Fundação de Cultura Cidade do
Recife, 2001.

See also: Armies—Colonial Spanish
America; Bandeirantes; Brazil;
Catholic Church in Brazil;
Cimarrones; Conquest II—Brazil;
Crime; Defense—Colonial Brazil;
Donatary Captaincies; Haitian
Revolution; Independence II—Brazil;
Jesuits—Brazil; Jesuits—Expulsion;
Madrid, Treaty of; Monarchs of
Portugal; Napoleonic Invasion and
Luso-America; Native Americans II—
Brazil; Rebellions—Colonial Latin
America; Seven Years' War; Slave
Rebellions—Brazil; Sugar.

ARMIES—COLONIAL SPANISH AMERICA

Following the sixteenth-century conquest
of the great indigenous civilizations of the
Americas, throughout Spanish America
there were fewer demands for organized
military forces. In most instances, locally
raised militias were sufficient to control the
urban and rural populations. Small companies of professional soldiers guarded the
viceroys in Mexico City and Lima, supported by militia units of merchants, shopkeepers, and guildsmen who maintained
public order. In Mexico City, an urban
proletarian uprising in 1692 led to the organization of the Urban Regiment of Commerce, manned and financed by the merchant guild (*consulado*). The exceptions to
this general picture were the frontier regions and major ports.

In northern New Spain and in southern South America (including Chile and La
Plata), migratory indigenous groups resisted Spanish control tenaciously and employed effective hit-and-run tactics to attack
settlements and to interdict commerce.

The establishment of missions and presidios, guarded by companies of mounted frontier soldiers, served to protect Spanish settlements if not to pacify fully the migratory tribes. Where the Indians adopted the horse, they became more than a match for the frontier garrisons. The development of strategic coastal fortifications at Havana, Veracruz, Panama, Cartagena, and other ports required garrisons of trained artillerymen, supported by local militias. Although the military forces sometimes failed to defend against foreign raiders and buccaneer attacks, until the eighteenth century Spain's enemies were unable to organize and sustain amphibious invasion forces that might threaten the major American possessions. In Brazil, following the expulsion of the Dutch invaders, tough frontiersmen pushed westward with only limited support from organized Portuguese military forces.

The wars of the eighteenth century illustrated a developing British capacity to launch major attacks and even invasions of Spanish American territories on both the Atlantic and the Pacific coasts. Spain responded to the attack led by Admiral Edward Vernon against Cartagena by dispatching a peninsular regular infantry battalion and other reinforcements. In the Seven Years' War (1756–1763), the British invasion and temporary occupation of strategically important Havana (1762) made evident a more general danger that produced many significant changes. Beginning with the island of Cuba and then extending to New Spain, Peru, New Granada, and La Plata, King Charles III adopted proposals designed to raise military forces capable of defending the Spanish American provinces. Although some

Spanish military authorities expressed grave reservations about arming the potentially untrustworthy *americanos,* reality dictated that there was no other alternative. Moreover, in tropical zones and where there were sufficient recruits, the regime recruited *pardo* and *moreno* (mulatto and free black) militia units.

Although many army commanders from the 1760s forward continued to recommend the dispatch of peninsular regiments to serve in the Americas, the ruinous costs and destruction of the units by yellow fever (*vómito negro*), malaria, and desertion forced the imperial authorities to find new solutions. The military reform plans depended upon a limited program to rotate peninsular battalions; furthermore, it called for the recruitment of small leadership armies of regular infantry, dragoon, and cavalry regiments permanently assigned to the American provinces, called *cuerpos fixos* (units that could not be transferred to another province) and the enlistment of a much larger number of provincial militia regiments, battalions, and companies. To develop an adequate level of training and to ensure the loyalty of Creole officers and soldiers, the peninsular army authorities assigned cadres of training officers, noncommissioned officers, and soldiers to each provincial regiment or battalion. Often, army commissions were sold to prestige-hungry members of the Creole elite to raise funds to purchase uniforms, arms, and equipment. Wealthy miners, merchants, and *hacendados* (owners of large landed estates) who were aspirants to the posts of regimental colonel and lieutenant colonel donated enormous sums, and in the 1790s even an infantry captaincy was worth 9,000 pesos. However, to guard against separatist ideas or financial irregularities, the offices of *sargento major* (major) and the adjutants responsible for regimental management and the treasury were reserved for peninsular Spaniards. In each provincial infantry, dragoon, or cavalry regiment there were at least some professional European Spanish army captains, lieutenants, sergeants, corporals, and a few veteran soldiers who handled training, discipline, and administration.

Though few provincial militia units operated at full strength, infantry regiments enlisted 845 troops divided into two battalions of fusileers, led by a grenadier company; the cavalry and dragoon regiments enlisted 367 soldiers. The city and town councils nominated three respectable persons for officer commissions with the military authorities selecting the winning candidate, who received a royal commission. The Crown authorized the use of *sorteos,* "lotteries," to select militiamen from district cities and towns from a pool of eligible single men, or married men who did not have large families to support. During wartime mobilizations, the provincial militia officers and soldiers were granted the *fuero militar,* the privilege of having their judicial cases heard by courts-martial, rather than by the judges and tribunals of the ordinary royal jurisdiction.

Although some historians have argued that the fuero militar and other distinctions granted to the colonial armies caused later praetorian traditions and militarism, the Spanish imperial regime exercised care to keep colonial armies under tight control. There was no official desire to extend martial privileges to militia officers or soldiers, as that might weaken the ordinary royal jurisdiction, or to move them into a separate

privileged caste. Nevertheless, during the wars of the late eighteenth century and first decade of the nineteenth century, Spain no longer was able to rotate regular army units for duty in the Americas, and Creole officers occupied some posts formerly reserved for European Spanish officers.

Colonial armies in Spanish America performed a variety of duties during times of peace and war. Although service in coastal garrisons and fortresses was highly unpopular owing to the high mortality caused by tropical diseases, provincial militiamen also reinforced urban police forces and served at cantonments assembled to intercept invasion threats. In New Spain for example, militiamen from all over the country gained their first experiences with large-scale operations that assembled units from different jurisdictions. In Peru, provincial troops served during the Túpac Amaru uprising (1780–1783) in New Granada to help suppress the Comunero Revolt (1781), and elsewhere in Spanish America in many episodes of popular tumult and in the invasion scares of the late colonial epoch. Beginning in 1810, many of these officers and soldiers fought in the wars, revolutions, and counterinsurgency operations of the independence period. In New Spain and Peru, regular army and provincial militia officers who fought on the royalist side later made the transitions necessary to play important roles in their new independent nations.

Christon I. Archer

References

Archer, Christon I. *The Army in Bourbon Mexico, 1760–1810.* Albuquerque: University of New Mexico Press, 1977.

Hoffman, Paul E. *The Spanish Crown and the Defense of the Caribbean, 1535–1585: Precedent, Patrimonialism, and Royal Parsimony.* Baton Rouge: Louisiana State University Press, 1980.

Kuethe, Alan J. *Military Reform and Society in New Granada, 1773–1808.* Gainesville: University of Florida Press, 1978.

McAlister, Lyle N. *The "Fuero Militar" in New Spain, 1764–1800.* Gainesville: University of Florida Press, 1957.

Vinson, Ben, III. *Bearing Arms for His Majesty: The Free-Colored Militia in Colonial Mexico.* Stanford, CA: Stanford University Press, 2001.

See also: Armies—Colonial Brazil; Bourbon Reforms; Comuneros—New Granada; Conquest I–VII; Conquistadors; Contraband; Creoles; Defense—Colonial Spanish America; Hacienda; Horses; Independence I–VI; Missions; Pirates and Piracy; Race; Rebellions—Colonial Latin America; Seven Years' War; Slavery I–IV; Túpac Amaru Revolt; Viceroyalties; Weapons.

ARMIES—MODERN LATIN AMERICA

The armies that fought to liberate Latin American colonies from Spain and Portugal played fundamental roles in shaping the nation-states of Latin America. Liberation armies and the wars they fought were as diverse as the terrain and the peoples of Latin America, but the militaries that sprang from Iberian traditions played almost uniformly significant roles in shaping the trajectories of the nations they helped to create.

In most of Spanish America, the wars of independence were long, bloody, costly, and disruptive affairs. The instability and widespread military mobilizations weakened but did not debilitate coercive labor institutions like slavery; they also provided new avenues of social mobility to humble men with military talents, even those with African and indigenous ancestry. Many of the political leaders who emerged after independence came to prominence based on their army service. Naval military traditions in Latin America, with the possible exception of the geographically unique nation of Chile, were relatively weak, and armies continued to be the most influential branch of the armed forces. Spanish America fragmented into many pieces that largely corresponded to subunits of colonial administration; however, fledgling national armies were often not capable of maintaining the peace, unity, and stability of their territories in the decades following independence. Indeed, they sometimes contributed to disorder by deposing elected governments themselves. In most of Spanish America this resulted in political fragmentation and insecurity, and in this environment, people turned to local strong men, or caudillos, who commanded their own loyal armies. Caudillos combined military prowess with populist political skills, and conflicts among them sometimes led to the overthrow of central governments and the imposition of dictatorial rule. It was not until the 1870s that national armies in Spanish America began seriously to challenge the power and authority of irregular caudillo armies and militias.

In contrast, Portugal's military weakness, combined with Great Britain's eagerness to recognize an independent Brazilian state and fears of slave rebellion, ensured that the war for independence was a short-lived series of minor, regionally confined conflicts. Most colonial troops, officers, and civilians in Brazil supported the crown prince Pedro when he declared independence, and his royal blood helped smooth the way for a less tumultuous transition to national governance in the form of a constitutional monarchy. For much of the nineteenth century, the army's leadership remained mostly loyal to the monarchy, if not to individual monarchs. Army troops, for example, played a crucial role in the protests that pushed Pedro I to abdicate his throne in favor of his young son in 1831. The liberal regency that ruled in Pedro II's name cut the size of the army's ranks in half and replaced the racially based militia units inherited from colonial times with a quintessential republican institution: a national guard. So many local political bosses sought out the rank of a national guard officer that *coronelismo* (colonelism) became the term for the most basic unit of political organization in Brazil.

A series of regional rebellions in the 1830s and 1840s, some with separatist goals, challenged the central government's authority. Most members of the army fought successfully to defeat each of these insurgencies. In contrast to the situation in Spanish America, Brazilian insurgents never succeeded in overthrowing the central government, and imperial political leaders scorned the caudillo dictators of Spanish America. Indeed, when Brazil, with Argentine and Uruguayan allies, went to war against the Paraguayan dictator Francisco Solano López (1864–1870), part of the rationale for war included ridding the continent of barbaric caudillos. Ironically, it was army officers alienated from the empire's civilian leadership who overthrew Pedro II's government in 1889 and promulgated a republic. Henceforth, the Brazilian army and the armies of Spanish America shared more common traits and trends than distinctions.

The national armies that came to prominence in Latin America in the last third of the nineteenth century sought to modernize their institutions, and they mostly looked to the best armies of Europe for guidance, namely Germany and France.

The maturation of Europe's industrial economies meant that Latin American governments found willing lenders to finance the sale of expensive new technologies. Repeating rifles, railroads, and telegraphs gave national armies an edge over mounted caudillo forces that still depended on lances. These technologies also sewed together the regional patchwork of caudillo-dominated *patria chicas* (little fatherlands) into a more manageable national administrative and commercial framework. The breech-loading rifle reduced the training time necessary for infantry and facilitated the adoption of conscription and a reserve system, ending a tradition of pressing refractory men and boys into service and instilling a more inclusive sense of nationalism among the populace.

Improvements in training and the status of soldiering made Latin American armies more effective and less menacing to the larger public. They strengthened the hands of central governments, enabling them to provide the order that was seen as necessary to economic progress. More uniform officer education and rules of promotion created greater coherence and nationalist identification among officers, but even though these reforms strengthened loyalty to the institution, political factions within the officer corps continued to be common and at times destabilized the chain of command. Military reforms led many Latin Americans to associate their national army with modernization, social leveling, and the disinterested defense of national interests and traditions, particularly when compared to the oligarchs who dominated agro-export commerce and the organs of government. Military officers in particular claimed for their institutions a special role in defending the "nation," a role that was used to rationalize their periodic intervention into the civilian sphere of politics.

Most military officers in larger Latin American nations supported political intervention to stimulate homegrown industrialization capable of supplying the military with the wherewithal to fight the total wars they studied in professional journals. In truth, Latin American armies have been more commonly engaged in the suppression of internal insurgents than in the waging of conventional wars against foreign powers. The Great Depression and World War II provided the conditions for the development of state-led and military-supported industrialization projects in many Latin American nations. A growing wariness of foreign control over vital commodities and infrastructure, which might compromise national autonomy and defense, became predominant among civilians and military officers on both the left and right ends of the political spectrum in the mid-twentieth century. This nationalist impulse often conflicted with the deepening relationship between the militaries of Latin America and that of the United States, after the Allies' victory in World War II catapulted American military influence into a hegemonic position in the region.

U.S. Communist-containment policy concentrated on Europe and Asia, until the 1959 Cuban Revolution brought about the implosion of the Cuban army under the dictator Fulgencio Batista. Fidel Castro's rise to power and subsequent executions of military officers from Batista's regime brought about an increasing militarization of relations between the United States and the other Latin American nations. Most military officers looked at the events in Cuba as an object lesson, showing what might happen to them if Communist insurgents came to power in their countries. Many middle-class students, on the other hand, saw in Cuba and the liberation of other colonial territories in Asia and Africa signs of a leftist world revolution that would be hastened through armed struggle.

President John F. Kennedy announced a Marshal Plan for Latin America, but in truth the funding for development funneled through the Alliance for Progress and the Peace Corps was dwarfed by U.S. military funding to the region. Counterinsurgency training of Latin American officers in U.S. military institutions like the University of the Americas sought to indoctrinate Latin American officers with an anti-Communist ideology and train them to fight insurgents. Washington policymakers began to express fears that the democracies that had spread across much of Latin America after World War II would not be capable of suppressing Communist insurgents. Beginning with Brazil in 1964, military coups deposed elected governments and ultimately replaced them with autocratic military regimes allied with civilian technocrats in the 1960s, 1970s, and 1980s. The United States quickly recognized most of these anti-Communist regimes, which had deposed democratically elected leaders who were the legitimate representatives of their nations.

These authoritarian military regimes became determined to hold the reins of political power long enough to squelch leftist insurgent movements and to accelerate economic development. The first of these goals was pursued with a no-holds-barred zeal that included the suspension of most civil rights, torture, and assassination. In some nations, thousands of suspected leftists were "disappeared," and military officers justified these atrocities in the name of national security. While these autocratic military regimes were in many cases ruthlessly efficient at stemming subversion, they proved much less adept at engineering sustained economic growth. During the so-called lost decade of the 1980s, when Latin American state-led economic growth sputtered under the weight of crushing international debts, the authoritarian military regimes lost their legitimacy and returned power to elected civilian leaders. In the minds of many Latin Americans, the corruption and excesses of authoritarian military regimes tarnished the once-positive image of the armies of Latin America.

Since the 1980s, most officers have returned to the barracks, content to leave politics in the hands of civilian elected officials. Army influence on politics has been subdued, and the military share of national budgets reduced. In Argentina, the system of conscription was abrogated, in part because of the way the generals fought the Malvinas War, or Falklands War, with Great Britain in 1982 by deploying raw draftees rather than the army's crack troops. The role of the military in mostly democratic and free-market Latin American nations is still a subject of debate. Some have pushed to have the army more involved in interdicting the illegal drug trade and narco-gangsterism. Since the tragedies of 9/11, moreover, some policy watch groups have observed a renewed tendency on the part of Washington to militarize U.S. relations with Latin America to counter possible new insurgencies and acts of terror mounted by Islamic fundamentalists. The militaries of Latin America continue to be among the strongest of national institutions and will likely continue to play a vital role in their nations in the twenty-first century. Iberian martial traditions played a significant role in molding Latin American militaries from the colonial period through the nineteenth century, but different national experiences and influences from other North Atlantic armed forces also shaped the powerful and sometimes brutal roles Latin American militaries came to play in the twentieth century.

Peter Beattie

References

Beattie, Peter M. *The Tribute of Blood: Army, Honor, Race, and Nation in Brazil, 1864–1945.* Durham, NC: Duke University Press, 2001.

Gill, Lesley. *The School of the Americas: Military Training and Political Violence in the Americas.* Durham, NC, and London: Duke University Press, 2004.

Loveman, Brian. *For La Patria: Politics and the Armed Forces in Latin America.* Wilmington, DE: SR Books, 1999.

McCann, Frank D. *Soldiers of the Patria: A History of the Brazilian Army, 1889–1937.* Stanford, CA: Stanford University Press, 2004.

See also: Armies—Colonial Brazil; Armies—Colonial Spanish America; Caudillos; Cold War—Portugal and the United States; Cold War—Spain and the Americas; Communism; Cuban Revolution; Defense—Colonial Brazil; Defense—Colonial Spanish America; Drugs; Independence I–VI; Islam; Liberalism; Malvinas/Falkland Islands; Paraguayan War; Terrorism; World War I; World War II.

ART AND ARTISTS—BRAZIL

Owing to the diversity of Brazilian society, the term *art* includes a variety of material cultures and expressive traditions. These traditions include indigenous pottery, textiles, and body art produced by Brazil's numerous and distinct native cultures. They also include plastic and ritual arts that derive from Africa, colonial religious icons and decoration, and the secular beaux arts traditions. The intersection of these traditions has produced the uniqueness of Brazilian art. Luso-American relations affect Brazilian art in relation to two basic phenomena, one most active in the colonial period, the other in the postcolonial period: (1) the unique, syncretist aesthetics engendered by cultural contact; and (2) the conscious artistic engagement with Brazil's ethnic and cultural heterogeneity in the various attempts to define a national aesthetic.

Efforts to convert Brazil's indigenous populations generated the bulk of colonial Luso-Brazilian art. The first missionaries arrived in 1549, and they quickly established a network of churches, monasteries, and colleges in principal northern cities. The decorations and liturgical objects that furnished these structures, such as carved wood retables, pulpits, altars, architectural ornamentation, painted ceilings and panels, and religious statuary, were archaic by continental standards, reflecting not only the primitive conditions in the colonies, but also the weakness of sixteenth-century Portuguese art. Portuguese aesthetics suffered under the combined onuses of foreign rule (during the period when Portugal and Spain were united under Habsburg rule, 1580–1640) and Counter-Reformation monastic reorganization that eliminated institutional training of sculptors and painters. Early Luso-Brazilian art reflects the Portuguese "plain style," in which interiors elaborately decorated with carved and gilded wood and *azulejos* (glazed tiles) compensate for the absence of sculpture and paintings. Sober, geometrically structured statuary reflected the loss of classical proportions and techniques.

Although little seventeenth-century colonial art survived the Dutch occupation of northeastern Brazil (1630–1654), contemporaneous objects in the south suggest the emergence of the aesthetic syncretism that distinguishes Luso-Brazilian art. Although sculpture imported from Portugal or produced locally by Portuguese carvers was prevalent into the eighteenth century, the emergence of a local artisan class corresponded to an increased expressiveness. In São Paulo, a hub for terra-cotta imagery, anonymous artists employed indigenous pottery techniques for icons known as *imagens de bandeirantes* (images of *bandeirantes,* a term that literally means "backwoodsman" but is used to describe the people of the São Paulo interior). Few seventeenth-century sculptors signed their works, exceptions being Agostinho de Piedade who executed four reliquary busts for the church of São Bento, Salvador (1625–1642), and his Brazilian-born pupil Agostinho de Jesus. Although austere compared to the later baroque, their sculptures project unprecedented grace and humanism. The simple retables in southern churches, such as the chapel of São Miguel near São Paulo (1622) and São Lourenço dos Indios, Niterói (ca. 1627), exemplify the mannerist style that adorned early structures. Their design is balanced and ordered, with straight columns and symmetrical floral motifs adapted from European pattern books, as well as Brazilian symbols such as pineapples, guavas, lilies, and cashews. These exotic details returned to the metropole to contribute to Portugal's eclectic "Atlantic baroque" style.

Though the restoration of the Portuguese monarchy in 1640 and the defeat of the Dutch at Guararapes, Brazil, in 1649 provided fertile ground for the optimism and excess of the baroque, Lusitanian artists lacked the skills, resources, and traditions to create true baroque works of art immediately. Late seventeenth- and early eighteenth-century art exhibits a gradual assimilation of the decorative exuberance and heightened emotionalism of the baroque. Retables designed to inspire faith while boasting the power of the Catholic Church subverted classical stability with vigorous curves and twisted columns, while "gold-lined" chapels vaunted the profits of colonial plunder. The gilded, Renaissance-style altar of the Cathedral of Salvador, Bahia (rebuilt 1672), anticipates these transformations, seen in full splendor at the church of São Francisco de Assis, Salvador (completed in 1708), and the Golden Chapel of the convent of São Francisco de Assis da Penitência, Recife. Painting played an increasingly important decorative and pedagogic role with the onset of the baroque. While early painting merely decorated coffers with geometric motifs or exhibited panels with awkward figures copied from period engravings, later proto-baroque developments integrated two-dimensional representations within a more holistic architectural and sculptural environment. In the São Bento Monastery in Rio de Janeiro (1633–1641), for instance, Dutch baroque-style paintings by Ricardo do Pilar (ca. 1630–1702) complement ornate wood carvings by Domingos da Conceição da Silva. Conceição's dramatic realism and dynamic compositions signaled the maturation of Luso-Brazilian sculpture, a tendency further refined by Valentim "Mestre Valentim" da Fonseca e Silva and Francisco "A Cabra" (the mestizo) das Chagas, among others. The quantity and quality of sculpture rose significantly at the end of the eighteenth century, particularly in Bahia and Pernambuco, where local schools consolidated distinct regional styles, often representing religious figures as local ethnic types.

The Brito style and trompe l'oeil ceiling painting marked the culmination of the Brazilian baroque. Introduced at the chapel of the Venerável Ordem Terceira da Penitência, Rio, by sculptors Manuel de Brito and Francisco Xavier de Brito, the style comprised elaborate motifs, which integrated angels and putti with abundant vegetation and mystical sunbursts. The unity of architecture, sculpture, and painting and the emotionally engaging illusionistic ceiling paintings by Caetano da Costa Coelho indicate the influence of Italian Jesuit painter Andre Pozzo's treatise, *Perspectiva pictorum et architectorum* (1693–1700). A later generation of painters, often trained in Lisbon and Rome, such as José Joaquim da Rocha, José Teófilo de Jesús, and Antônio Joaquím Franco Velasco, perfected the genre, producing spectacular imagery with a total unity of visual effect, replicated by local painters throughout Brazil. The Brito style and ceiling painting achieved their finest expression in Minas Gerais, where the discovery of gold and diamonds provided ample resources for the material indulgences that define the high baroque, and the skills and sensibilities of national artists facilitated the requisite aesthetic excesses. The Britos' ornately carved altar at the church of Nossa Senhora do Pilar, Ouro Prêtohitherto (1746–1751), and Manoel da Costa Ataíde's spectacular painting of a floating celestial kingdom at the church of São Francisco (completed ca. 1771) introduced baroque tendencies that quickly spread through the prosperous region. Expressive and whimsical figures by Antônio Francisco "O Aleijadinho" (the little cripple) Lisboa represent the apogee of baroque sculpture. Exemplary of his genius are life-sized, carved images of the Passion of Christ (1796–1799) and the twelve soapstone sculptures of the prophets (1800–1803) at the church of Bom Jesus de Matozinhos, Congonhas do Campo.

In 1808 the Portuguese court escaped Napoleon's encroaching troops by fleeing to Brazil, an event that, paradoxically, weakened Ibero-American influences in Brazilian art. Finding Rio's cultural accommodations inadequate for the seat of empire, they set about establishing an official culture based not on Portuguese tradition, but on the French models that, at the time, epitomized courtly elegance. In a gesture ripe with irony, Portugal's King Dom João IV (King John IV) enlisted the aid of a group of Bonapartist refugees, known as the French Artistic Mission. Led by painter Jean-Baptiste Debret, a former student of French neoclassicist Jacques Louis David, the mission, in 1826, founded the Imperial Academy of Fine Arts in Rio de Janeiro, an exact replica of the French academy, which perpetuated Francophile aesthetics into the twentieth century. Secular themes and naturalist tendencies displaced the religious, baroque traditions associated with colonialism and neoclassicism, and became the official style of the Kingdom of Brazil. In 1872 court painter Pedro Américo de Melo (1843–1905), who studied with Napoleon portraitist Jean Auguste Dominique Ingres, immortalized Dom Pedro II, the first emperor of the independent Kingdom of Brazil, as a tropical sun king, wearing a royal mantle trimmed with coffee, cacao, and pineapple motifs and the feathered collar of an Indian cacique. With the founding of the Republic of Brazil in 1889, historic military battles and mythical Indianist themes increasingly preoccupied academic artists, an interest stimulated by the political context and the rise of romanticism in Europe. Brazilian artists monumentalized the tragic protagonists of popular epic poems. Likewise, the nativist/romantic spirit provoked an interest in plein air, or open air, painting, anticipated by Manuel de Araújo Porto Alegre and German painter Georg Grimm and resumed by João Batista Castagneto and Antônio Diego Da Silva Parreiras.

The influence of French realism, particularly in the work of José Ferraz de Almeida Jr., marked the beginning of Brazil's transition to modernism. Echoing the Barbizon school's response to European industrialization, which produced romantic images of the hardworking French peasant, Almeida Jr. depicted daily life in Brazil's rural interior, emphasizing the local adaptation of authentic *caboclo* (Portuguese and Indian mixed-race) culture. His protomodern imagery preserved traditions threatened by rapid social and economic changes at the end of the nineteenth century, while rejecting the Indianist fantasies associated with the increasingly moribund Old Republic. With the rise of industrialization and urbanization, artists pursued new means more appropriate to their modern environment. While artists such as Eliseu Visconti and Henrique Alvim Correia adopted symbolist techniques to express a sense of cultural modernity, others such as Artur Timóteo da Costa, Rodolfo Amoedo, and Lucílio de Albuquerque undertook urban themes with more traditional means.

Encounters with European modernism in the early twentieth century fostered a growing resentment toward the national academy, derided for upholding the anachronistic, oligarchic tastes of a bygone agricultural era. Calls for aesthetic renewal peaked in 1922 with the Week of Modern Art in São Paulo, which introduced avant-garde tendencies and inspired cultural nationalism. The controversial exhibit included expressionist painter Anita Malfatti, whose works were shown in what many consider to be the country's first modern art exhibition, in 1917, symbolist draftsman Emiliano di Cavalcanti, art nouveau sculptor Victor Brecheret, impressionistic painter Zina Aita, brothers Vincente and Joaquim do Rêgo Monteiro, and Swiss painter John Graz.

Although the 1920s "heroic age" of Brazilian modernism reflected the nativist themes and stable "return to order" forms of interwar French art, the emergent avant-garde challenged the Francophile tastes of the Republican oligarchy by turning to the popular culture of Brazil's Afro-Brazilian *favelas* (shantytowns) and the long-disparaged Portuguese baroque as sources for an authentically Brazilian aesthetic. In 1924 painter Tarsila do Amaral, with her husband, the poet Oswald de Andrade, and French surrealist Blaise Cendrars, embarked on a "rediscovery of Brazil," touring rural villages, including Ouro Prêto, and attending Carnival in Rio. Representative of modernist currents at the time, Amaral, who had studied with painter Fernand Léger in Paris, adopted the simplified forms and vivid colors of popular art, mediating them through cubism to produce a syncretist modernist expression. In 1928 she began a series of surrealist-inspired works of fantastical, "primitive" iconography that inspired the *antrofagista* movement. Demonstrating a precocious awareness of Brazil's postcolonial condition, antrofagistas parodied tropes of the "primitive," advocating the cannibalistic "devouring" of foreign influences as a means toward national self-expression. Other artists, such as Ismael Neri, Antônio Gomide, and Cicero Cícero, likewise modified cubism, primitivism, and surrealism to explore regional and personal themes.

With the Depression and the populist-nationalist Revolution of 1930, modernism became explicitly political. Artists such as Cândido Portinari, Quirino Campofiorito, Eugênio Sigaud, and Osvaldo Goeldi, influenced by postrevolutionary Mexican painting and graphics, allegorized the nation in images of sturdy, mixed-race workers, while the expressionist Lithuanian immigrant Lasar Segall depicted the marginalization of Brazil's Afro-Brazilian underclass. In São Paulo in 1932, surrealist provocateur Flavio de Carvalho founded the radical Club of Modern Art, which supported revolutionary ideologies and aesthetics through conferences and exhibitions; and in Rio de Janeiro, students of idiosyncratic modernist Alberto Guignard battled the hegemony of the academy with avant-garde iconoclasm.

World War II put an end to the nationalist ideologies of the avant-garde. Economic prosperity and rapid development in the 1950s inspired geometric abstraction, known as concrete art. Concrete artists rendered rational forms with machine precision, using industrial materials and employing the science of optics and gestalt psychology. The founding of the São Paulo Biennial in 1951 furthered Brazil's sense of artistic internationalism by putting the local and foreign avant-

Coffee Plantation, *1935, by Candido Portinari (1903–1962). Museo Nacional Bellas Artes, Rio de Janeiro, Brazil. (Art Resource)*

garde on equal footing. Artists suspicious of the blanket optimism expressed by concrete aesthetics pursued alternatives more sensitive to the contradictions of modernity and Brazilian underdevelopment. While *Tachisme* (or lyrical abstraction, an antirationalist tendency that privileges expressive impulses over form) artists Antônio Bandeira, Flávio Shiró Tanaka, and Iberê Camargo expressed the existential angst of the nuclear age through intensely individual gestural abstraction, the neoconcrete movement (founded in 1959) modified the geometric idiom. Deeply influenced by phenomenology, artists undermined concrete art's reliance on vision and scientific objectivity, demanding the harmonization of sensory experiences and human subjectivity. Lygia Clark and Hélio Oiticica redefined the role of artist and spectator through interactive, tactile-visual works that demanded participation. In the late 1960s artists abandoned the object altogether, creating ephemeral, performance-based works. Echoing the nationalist vision of heroic modernism, Oiticica looked to the favelas as the soul of Brazil, working with local communities in projects that negotiated popular traditions such as samba and Carnival and avant-garde strategies such as performance and installation.

Under the military dictatorship (1964–1985) the "dematerialization" of the object associated with Euro-American conceptual art became a potent tool for evading government censorship. Anonymous projects imbued readymades of the kind pioneered by the French dadaist Marcel Duchamp with political urgency. For instance, Cildo Meireles created "insertions," stamping subversive messages on Coke bottles and money and returning them to circulation; Antônio Manuel created a print version of his closed exhibition; and Artur Barrio deposited "bloody bundles" in public places, exposing the anxiety of political violence obscured by a veneer of authoritarian normalcy. Other artists responded to social conditions through strategies that resonated with current international tendencies, such as Antonio Dias's visceral pop art cartoon images of a world gone mad with violence and greed, Anna Bella Geiger's enigmatic rearticulation of advertising and lesson primers that echoed mainstream conceptual proposals, and Mira Schendel's obsessive production of deeply introspective and poignantly fragile rice-paper graffiti.

The return to democracy in 1985 generated a flourishing of artistic production by a younger generation of artists inspired by novel expressive freedom and unprecedented opportunities, and by the wave of artists returning from exile, who brought with them a broad spectrum of conceptual, technical, and aesthetic resources. Much of the art of the "Generation of 80" demonstrates an engagement with Brazilian history and art history as a way to parody tropes of identity and reveal complex dimensions of culture and society. For instance, Leda Catunda created domesticated reinterpretations of geometric abstraction made of discarded clothing; Rochelle Costi made neobaroque prints of rotting food; Mônica Nador conceived and managed the collective decoration of lived spaces in works that harken to Oiticica's participatory projects; and José Leonilson created autobiographical embroideries that com-

bined the exteriority of pop art and the interiority of Mira Schendel. Organized around the theme of anthropophagy, the Twenty-Fourth São Paulo Biennial (1998) addressed such appropriations as a central unifying feature of Brazilian art. The extraordinary level of innovation that allowed Brazilian art to flourish despite authoritarianism established a legacy of creativity and experimentation that distinguishes Brazil as one of the most progressive avant-garde cultures in the world. Beyond the ubiquity of Brazilian artists in international artistic circuits—Tunga, Jac Leirner, Waltercio Caldas, Vik Muniz, Miguel Rio Branco, Ernesto Neto, Adriana Varejão, Daniel Senise, and Regina Silveira—foreign cultural institutions have begun to recognize the caliber of Brazilian modernism, as indicated by the Guggenheim Museum's blockbuster "Brazil: Body and Soul," and by "Brasil, 1920–1950: De la antropofagia a Brasília," organized by the Institut Valencià d'Art Modern (IVAM) in Valencia; "The Experimental Exercise of Freedom" at the Los Angeles Museum of Contemporary Art; and the Houston Museum's "Inverted Utopias."

Contemporary networks for the promotion and exhibition of Portuguese and Brazilian art are, above all, internationalist, as they are for all modern artists. Although the 2000 quincentennial celebrations of the Portuguese arrival in Brazil rekindled Luso-Brazilian cultural exchange, the comparative strength of the Spanish art market and of its cultural institutions, as well as annual large-scale international events like the Feria Internacional de Arte Contemporania (ARCO), have drawn Brazilian art and artists closer into the Spanish orbit.

Edith Wolfe

References

Bayón, Damián, and Murillo Marx. *History of South American Colonial Art and Architecture: Spanish South America and Brazil.* New York: Rizzoli, 1992.

Brasil, 1920–1950: De la antropofagia a Brasilia. Valencia: IVAM Centre Julio González; Generalitat Valenciana, Conselleria de Cultura i Educació, 2000. Includes English translation.

Brasil+500: Mostra do redescobrimento São Paulo, 14 vols. São Paulo: Fundação Bienal de São Paulo, Associação Brasil 500 Años Artes Visuais, 2000. Includes English translation.

Herkenhoff, Paulo, et al. *The Journal of Decorative and Propaganda Arts: Brazil Theme Issue.* Miami: Wolfson Foundation of Decorative and Propaganda Arts, 1995.

Lemos, Carlos Alberto Cerqueira. *The Art of Brazil.* New York: Harper and Row, 1983.

Sullivan, Edward J., ed. *Brazil: Body and Soul.* New York: Guggenheim Museum, 2001.

Zanini, Walter, ed. *História geral da arte no Brasil,* 2 vols. São Paulo: Instituto Walter Moreira Salles Fundação Djalma Guimarães, 1983.

See also: Architecture—Brazil; Art and Artists—Colonial Spanish America; Art and Artists—Modern Spanish America; Brazil; Cacao; Caciques; Catholic Church in Brazil; Coffee; Colonists and Settlers II—Brazil; Conquest II—Brazil; Education—Brazil; Enlightenment—Brazil; Fin de Siècle; Independence II—Brazil; Migration—To Brazil; Music and Dance I—Brazil; Napoleonic Invasion and Luso-America; Nationalism; Native Americans I–II; Poetry—Brazil; Slavery I—Brazil; Syncretism; World War II.

ART AND ARTISTS— COLONIAL SPANISH AMERICA

Collectively, artists from colonial Spanish America produced a substantial body of work, incorporating European, pre-Columbian, and Asian artistic traditions. During the conquest, many artifacts associated with indigenous religious beliefs were destroyed, while precious-metals objects often were melted down. Though Spanish colonialism halted the production of native-made objects that were considered idolatrous, some pre-Columbian artistic traditions continued, though not unaffected by the incorporation of European visual culture. Throughout the colonial period, European artists and their works made their way to the Americas and introduced current European styles of painting, sculpture, and architecture. Simultaneously, as the Spanish-Asian trade route traversed New Spain, certain Asian objects influenced colonial artists. Metropolitan styles and genres produced in urban centers like Mexico City and Cuzco provided artists in peripheral and frontier regions of Spanish America a standard upon which they based their own works, though not without variation. Consequently, popular styles, distinct from their metropolitan counterparts, emerged and flourished in peripheral regions. The sum of these influences and historical developments in the colonial context resulted in a dynamic production of art and the creation of several artistic genres unique to Spanish America.

The richest accounts of native arts at the time of contact are to be found among the chronicles of Spanish conquistadors. The Spanish extirpation of idolatry in the early colonial period included the destruction of objects that were associated with pre-Columbian religious beliefs and rituals. This destruction began during the conquest and is documented in several primary accounts written by conquistadors. For example, in the Inca capital of Cuzco, the conquistador Diego Cieza de León writes that the sacred temple of the Incas, the Coricancha, was covered with a band of gold on its exterior, while the interior housed countless golden objects. Upon seeing the material riches of this temple, the Spaniards were quick to dismantle it.

In another example, upon seeing a horrific sculpted figure of an Aztec deity in the Templo Mayor in Tenochtitlan (the principal religious edifice of the Aztec capital), Hernando Cortés cast it out and replaced it with a European sculpture of the Virgin Mary. This symbolic gesture of the Christian victory over native peoples and beliefs was repeated throughout the conquest and the early colonial period. In many cases, Christian churches were built upon the remains of sacred native sites and buildings. The church of Santo Domingo in Cuzco, built upon the foundation walls of the Coricancha, is a notable example.

A new hybrid art, called Indo-Christian by modern scholars, emerged in New Spain with the missionizing effort of the mendicant orders. Franciscans, Dominicans, and Augustinians were the first to begin evangelization efforts, and they quickly utilized native manpower and artistic talent to erect and decorate churches and their adjacent convents in native communities. Native artists carved elaborate church façades and crosses made of stone, and painted murals inside church and convent walls. Broadly speaking, they incorporated Christian themes into their native styles of sculpture and painting, and at times intertwined native themes into their mural programs. By the end of the sixteenth century, however, Indo-Christian art was replaced with fashionable European styles.

Other native arts useful to the Spanish enjoyed continued production in the colonial period. For example, feather costumes and mosaics produced in the pre-Hispanic period continued, though not unchanged, in the colonial period. In one of the earliest examples of hybrid colonial art, native feather artists in New Spain produced mosaics of religious subject matter and liturgical accoutrements such as bishops' miters.

The native-made manuscripts of Mesoamerica were also valued by the Spanish and served their need to gain knowledge of native languages, religious beliefs, and systems of tribute. In pre-Hispanic times, manuscripts were a vital component of native social, religious, and economic life. Artist-scribes belonged to an elite class and trained in special schools to interpret and produce documents that retold history, recorded tribute, depicted the Mesoamerican calendar, assisted in divination rituals, and mapped the social and spatial relations between native communities. Among the various peoples of native America, Mesoamericans were the only ones who produced manuscripts. And although they did not have a written alphabet comparable to that of Europeans (the closest thing was a system of hieroglyphs developed by the Maya), their system of "reading" images was precise and reliable.

A new genre of manuscript was introduced by the Spanish shortly after the conquest and taught to natives. The cultural encyclopedia incorporated a myriad of cultural, religious, social, and economic information about native society. These hybrid documents incorporated native pictorial styles with European visual components such as text, modeling of figures, perspective, and the incorporation of landscape. While lay Spaniards in governmental positions consulted these manuscripts to learn more about preconquest history and tribute patterns, friars consulted them to gain insight into native religion, language, and social practices. Manuscripts were also of great use to natives and were used as evidence in lawsuits involving land disputes, tribute disputes, and the abuse of natives by Spaniards. The labor put into manuscript production in the colonial period was often divided between a native artist who painted the images and a scribe (not always native) who annotated the images with Spanish or native glosses. Over time, textual manuscripts replaced pictorial ones, as some native languages began a process of alphabetization and textual systemization.

In Peru, two of the most notable native art survivals include *queros* (wooden and stone cups used for ritual drinking by elite natives) and *unkus* (tunics). Though earlier Peruvian and South American civilizations had produced representative art, Incan art was abstract. European influences introduced Peruvian artists to figural art in the colonial period, and some pre-Hispanic art forms that survived the conquest, such as queros, incorporated representative pictorial components such as human and animal forms. Spaniards utilized these native art forms to symbolize their association with native rulers, who, in turn, used them to demonstrate their own elite status and important Incan heritage, though often they were not in fact of Incan heritage.

Shortly after the conquest, an influx of European artists into colonial Spanish America replaced hybrid native-made art. In the sixteenth century, European artists established schools that specialized in popular styles of painting from Spain, Flanders, and Italy. European painters made their way to the Americas in hopes of es-

Ritual drinking vessel (quero), *with Inca-Spanish colonial decoration. An Inca dignitary is preceded by two musicians: a European trumpet player and an African drummer, both wearing cloaks and feathered hats. Wood and polychrome painted, ca. 1650, Inca, Peru. British Museum, London. (Werner Forman/Art Resource)*

tablishing successful careers in an artistic environment considered less competitive than that of Europe. These artists and subsequent generations complied with the precepts of the Council of Trent (1545–1563) in producing their work. Tridentine initiatives indicated that religious art should be didactic and clearly presented, and should inspire the viewer to piety. Much of the religious art produced in colonial Spanish America conformed to these precepts.

In 1575, at the age of twenty-seven, the Italian painter and Jesuit Bernardo Bitti arrived in Peru and established himself as the progenitor of painting in Peru, Ecuador, and Bolivia. Basing his paintings on the works of Italian masters like Rafael, Vasari, Zucchi, the Zuccari brothers, and the Spanish master Luís de Morales, Bitti popularized the style then in fashion in Italy, mannerism. Characterized by graceful lines, disproportionate figures, unrealistic scale, and acidic colors, Bitti's style influenced generations of Peruvian artists. Likewise, the painters Mateo Pérez de Alesio and Angelino Medoro, both of whom trained in Rome, disseminated the mannerist style in Peru as well as present-day Colombia and Ecuador.

Each of these artists trained native pupils, who by the early seventeenth century distinguished themselves stylistically from their Spanish colleagues and masters. This disassociation culminated in 1688, when many native artists, due to their alleged mistreatment by their Spanish and mestizo colleagues, broke from the painters' guild and established their own school, called the Cuzco school by modern scholars. Located in the old Inca capital of Cuzco, this group of native painters continued producing religious art; however, it abandoned current tastes in European painting and embraced a more decorative and ornamental style. Figures became flattened and two-dimensional, and they were stamped with intricate gold-leaf designs in a technique called *brocateado*. The Cuzco school was highly prolific, surviving well into the eighteenth century, and is the style of painting most associated with Peruvian visual culture.

In sixteenth-century New Spain, the painters Simon Pereyns, Andrés de la Concha, and Baltasár de Echave Orio were highly influential. De la Concha, from Andalusia, brought Italian mannerism to New Spain, as Bitti had to Peru. Pereyns, a Fleming, and Echave Orio, a Basque, painted in the Flemish style, then popular in the Spanish court in Madrid. In New Spain, Echave Orio and one of his pupils, Luís Juárez, founded two dynasties of painters who, over the course of three cen-

turies, were responsible for decorating urban churches and cathedrals with massive religious paintings. The descendants of both men, however, distinguished themselves from their progenitors by incorporating in their paintings new European styles as they arose.

Artists of seventeenth-century New Spain, such as Baltasár de Echave Ibía (Echave Orio's son), popularized the so-called prosaic style, characterized by small-scale paintings with religious subject matter, less dramatic and grand than paintings of the sixteenth century. By the end of the seventeenth century, tenebrism (a style of painting distinguished by its high contrast of light and dark) was in fashion and used by many artists in New Spain, including Baltasár de Echave Rioja (Echave Orio's grandson). In addition, prints of famous works by Flemish masters like Peter Paul Rubens influenced the style of several of New Spain's painters. In particular, the works of Cristóbal de Villalpando and Juan Correa, two of the most influential artists of baroque New Spain, incorporated complex themes and dramatic depictions in much the same way as Rubens had. Villalpando and Correa are considered to be the principal artists of the baroque style in New Spain. In general, the baroque is characterized by complex themes, full-figured bodies, dramatic depictions of subject matter, rich colors, sharp contrast of light and dark, and an overall sumptuous or exuberant appearance.

In addition to the various European styles of painting present in Spanish America, Asian goods that filtered into New Spain changed the face of the region's visual culture. Items such as painted ceramics, ivory sculptures, and textiles were prized throughout Spanish America. Also, a group of Japanese artists made their residence in New Spain in the early seventeenth century, where they painted objects based on Japanese art forms. They probably introduced *biombos* (Japanese-style screenfolds) in New Spain, as the earliest examples date from this period. The biombo tradition continued well into the eighteenth century and became part of the artistic repertoire of New Spain's artists. This hybrid art form combined the traditional Japanese screenfold form with European-derived historical and allegorical painting.

Another Asian-American hybrid art form is *nacar,* a combination of painting and mother-of-pearl mosaic. Inspired by Japanese decorative arts inlaid with mother-of-pearl designs, nacar took root in seventeenth-century New Spain and was produced well into the eighteenth century. Images of saints and historical events such as the conquest appeared in large and small scales, and they were highly prized objects.

Chinese ceramics that incorporated intricate blue designs painted on a white base were also of great value in New Spain. Their popularity was in part responsible for the establishment of ceramic workshops based in the city of Puebla that specialized in this style of blue-on-white ceramics. Talavera ceramics, as they are known today, like their Chinese prototypes, were highly sought-after items, though more affordable than imported Chinese ceramics. Talavera ceramics could be found in wealthy and middle-class domiciles as well as convents and palaces throughout New Spain.

Biombos, nacar, and Talavera ceramics, however, were not the only art forms exclusive to colonial Spanish America. Two genres of painting came into being in the eighteenth century, neither of which has

counterparts outside of Spanish America. Casta paintings consist of a series of usually sixteen canvases that portray the various racial types specific to the Americas. Each painting depicts an interracial couple with their offspring, and includes text that indicates the racial designation of each figure. In many casta paintings botanical and man-made items specific to the Americas are also depicted and labeled. For example, a casta painting might depict a Spanish man, native wife, and their mestizo children standing beside an outdoor market stand with textiles and produce exclusive to the Americas.

The social climate in eighteenth-century New Spain was such that the viceregal government and elite Spaniards were alarmed at the growing racial diversity of the populace. A complex racial hierarchy was devised in a vain attempt to order society by lineage, social class, and physiognomy. In addition, scientific systems of order such as Linnaeus's taxonomy were appropriated to categorize the social and racial makeup of the Americas. Many series of casta paintings, reflecting this taxonomy, were produced by artists in New Spain and, to a lesser degree, in Peru.

Another genre of painting that came to fruition in the eighteenth century is referred to as *monjas coronadas,* "crowned nuns." This genre consists of portraits that depict actual nuns recently professed (a subgenre exclusive to New Spain), convent founders, prioresses, those celebrating a milestone anniversary of their religious vows, and recently deceased nuns who led exemplary lives. In most examples, a nun is dressed in her religious habit and bedecked with a floral crown, a floral bouquet, a candle, and an effigy of the Christ child. Below her image, an inscription identifies her and lists other biographical facts, which usually include the name of her parents, the convent to which she belonged, her age at profession, and in some cases, the date of her death.

After the Bourbon reforms of the mid-eighteenth century, which sought, in part, to regulate and reorder religious life, monjas coronadas portraits increased substantially in number. Parents and godparents commissioned artists to execute portraits of their daughters and goddaughters recently professed in order to keep a visual reminder of these newly cloistered women. Convents, on the other hand, commissioned portraits of their founders, prioresses, and the recently deceased, and hung them in places of honor inside the convent.

While urban artists developed genres exclusive to the Americas, artists in peripheral regions of colonial Spanish America developed distinctive styles of painting and sculpture. The colonial art of present-day New Mexico, the northernmost occupied region of Spanish America, is one of the most notable examples of this. By the late eighteenth century, artists and carpenters in New Mexico joined together to furnish churches with large-scale *retablos* (altarpieces) and *bultos* (religious sculptures). In addition, they produced smaller-scale retablos painted on pine panels and bultos for individuals and their households.

Because New Mexico had no formal art schools in the colonial period, most New Mexican–born artists were largely autodidactic, although within workshops, apprentices learned from their masters. Sources for their subject matter included engraved prints in religious books, imported academic paintings, sculptures from central and northern Mexico, and extant New Mexican works. The materials artists used, for the most part, were indigenous to the land. Their painting style is characterized by flat fields of bright colors outlined in black, two-dimensional compositions, while their sculptures are linear, ill-proportioned, and static. Both paintings and sculpture, however, portray a quiet expressive religious fervor distinct from the metropolitan art of colonial Spanish America. Nevertheless, urban styles continued well into the nineteenth century. While some art forms, such as casta paintings, ceased completely, others, such as feather work, Talavera ceramics, and religious art, have continued beyond the independence movements, though not unchanged, to the present day.

James M. Córdova

References

Boone, Elizabeth Hill, and Tom Cummins, eds. *Native Traditions in the Postconquest World: A Symposium at Dumbarton Oaks, 2nd through 4th October 1992.* Washington, DC: Dumbarton Oaks, 1998.

Burke, Marcus. *Treasures of Mexican Colonial Painting: The Davenport Museum of Art Collection.* Santa Fe: Museum of New Mexico Press, 1998.

Cummins, Thomas B. F. *Toasts with the Incas: Andean Abstraction and Colonial Images on Quero Vessels.* Ann Arbor: University of Michigan Press, 2002.

Fane, Diana, ed. *Converging Cultures: Art and Identity in Colonial Spanish America.* New York: Harry N. Abrams, 1996.

Howard, Kathleen, and John P. O'Neill, eds. *Mexico: Splendors of Thirty Centuries.* New York: The Metropolitan Museum of Art, 1990.

Pierce, Donna, Rogelio Ruíz Gomar, and Clara Bargellini, eds. *Painting a New World: Mexican Art and Life, 1521–1821.* Denver: Frederick and Jan Mayer Center for Pre-Columbian and Spanish Colonial Art, Denver Art Museum, 2004.

Reyes Valerio, Constantino. *Arte indocristiano.* México, D.F.: Instituto Nacional de Antropología e Historia, 2000.

See also: Architecture—Brazil; Architecture—Colonial Spanish America; Art and Artists—Brazil; Art and Artists—Modern Spanish America; Bourbon Reforms; Cah; Catholic Church in Spanish America; Chroniclers; Clergy—Secular, in Colonial Spanish America; Codices; Council of Trent; Encomienda; Fiction—Spanish America; Idolatry, Extirpation of; Independence I–VI; Music and Dance I–V; Native Americans I–VIII; Popular Festivals; Religious Orders.

ART AND ARTISTS—
MODERN SPANISH AMERICA

Modern art connotes a broad spectrum of aesthetics that have in common a rejection of tradition in favor of innovative themes and experimental formal strategies. Ibero-American relations manifest in modern art in two principal ways: (1) in a continued dialogue between the Spanish and Spanish American avant-garde; and (2) in efforts to establish a sense of cultural identity based in the legacy of Spanish colonialism. Although Latin American art broadly parallels developments in mainstream Euro-American modernism—that is, modernism, social realism, surrealism, concretism, informalism, conceptualism, and postmodernism—the character of these movements in Spanish America is fundamentally unique. Owing to the emergence and institutionalization of modernism in Latin America during a period of intense nationalism between World Wars I and II, modern art has a tradition of political engagement, functioning alternately as a mouthpiece for progressive state policies and as a way of challenging cultural norms and political repression.

Although modern art appeared in Latin America for largely the same reasons as in Europe, it was delayed in the American context. Into the twentieth century, the ruling oligarchies that rose to power with independence held a monopoly on political power and cultural capital. To eradicate the legacy of Spanish colonialism, republican elites adopted French ideological and artistic models, rebuilding national capitals in the image of Paris and establishing national academies of fine art steeped in conservative Beaux Arts traditions. By the turn of the century, dissent threatened to undermine oligarchic political and aesthetic hegemony. In 1909 students of the National School of Fine Arts in Caracas protested archaic prohibitions against nude models, leaving the academy to form the Circle of Fine Arts (1912). In 1911 students at Mexico's Academy of San Carlos went on strike for pedagogic reform; influenced by the nativism of Gerardo "Dr. Atl" Murillo, they refused to draw from Greek statuary, founding plein air, or open air, schools that valorized local landscapes and ordinary people. In Chile modernism infiltrated the School of Fine Arts. In 1913 a group of students labeled the Generation of Thirteen shocked the academy with an exhibition of vividly colored, impressionistic paintings influenced by Spanish professor Fernando Alvarez de Sotomayor.

By and large, modern art developed outside official institutions. Industrialization created an urban elite that rejected oligarchic values and looked to Europe for modern alternatives. Spanish influence on Latin American modernism is most evident in turn-of-the-century symbolist currents that paralleled literary *modernismo*. Marco Tobón Mejía's (Colombia) decadent nudes and Julio Ruelas's (Mexico) hybrid beasts echo Spanish modernists Joaquín Sorolla and Ignacio Zuloaga, as does the work of

Andrés Santa María (Colombia), who studied under Spanish symbolist Santiago Rusiñol. In the 1910s Joaquín Torres García (Uruguay) and Rafael Pérez Barradas (Uruguay) participated in the Spanish *ultraista* movement; Barradas cultivated an aesthetic of motion and vibration, while Torres García absorbed elements for his eclectic universal constructivism. Following studies in Madrid and Barcelona, Armando Reverón (Venezuela) created light-saturated tropical landscapes, and expressionist painters Francisco Goítia (Mexico) and José Clemente Orozco (Mexico) adopted the intense drama and somber palette of Spanish romanticist Francisco de Goya. For the most part, however, the centrality of Paris overshadowed artistic relations with Spain; variations on cubism and postimpressionism dominated Latin American modernism until World War II.

The Mexican Renaissance of the 1920s and 1930s consolidated an autonomous Latin American vanguard, while establishing an enduring tradition of politicized aesthetics. Following the 1910 revolution, the Mexican government embarked on an ambitious program of mural decoration for public buildings. Led by Orozco, Diego Rivera, and David Alfaro Siqueiros, artists celebrated Mexico's indigenous origins in their interpretations of the official ideology of *mestizaje,* which valued the historical antecedents of its population in contributions to the formation of a new Mexican nationality. This ideology appropriated motifs from pre-Columbian art and popular painting, and reconsidered Spanish baroque traditions that had been subjugated to Francophile tastes. Nativist impulses spread through Latin America in the 1930s and 1940s. Reinforced by Europe's fascination with the "primitive," Latin American modernists emphasized non-European origins in romantic images of timeless Indians and mixed-race types, exemplified by Pedro Figari's crude renderings of rural Uruguayan *candmobles* (Afro-Uruguayan folk dances), Francisco Narváez's (Venezuela) images of humble campesinos, and images of Cuban *guajiro* (white Cuban peasants) farmers and cane-cutters by Victor Manuel.

In Andean countries, *indigenismo* (indigenism) represented a regional variation of social realism, conflating ethnic identity and class struggle. Despite its often insurgent tone, indigenism was gradually institutionalized within the academic system. As director of the National School of Fine Arts in Lima, José Sabogal (Peru) encouraged students to adopt the simplifications of popular art, producing a vibrant indigenist school. Similarly Celio Guzmán de Rojas Ñusta (Bolivia), director of the National Academy of Fine Arts in La Paz, revived popular traditions and colonial influences in Bolivian modernism. After Siqueiros visited Ecuador in 1943, a radical indigenist school emerged in Guayaquil, led by Eduardo Kingman and Oswaldo Guayasamín. In countries with smaller indigenous populations and less sympathetic governments, radicalized artists modified themes and means. Antonio Berni (Argentina) represented the plight of immigrant labor on enormous burlap "portable murals." Carlos González (Uruguay) depicted peasant hardship in inexpensive woodblock cuts that circulated easily and invoked the premodern conditions of his subjects.

Satisfying demands for public, democratic art, graphic arts boomed in the 1930s and 1940s, often produced in collectives such as Mexico's Taller de Gráfica

The Agrarian Revolution of Emiliano Zapata. *From* Porfirianism to the Revolution (Dal Porfirismo a la Revolucion), *by David Alfaro Siqueiros (1896–1974), 1964. (Schalkwijk/Art Resource)*

Popular (Popular Graphics Workshop), founded in 1937, and Argentina's Artistas del Pueblo (Artists of the People) in the working-class Boedo district. Mexican artists helped establish workshops in Puerto Rico and Guatemala. These precedents established a tradition of public art and collective collaboration that continued in the murals of the Chilean Ramona Para Brigades during the Pinochet dictatorship (1973–1990), the publications of *El Dibujazo* in Uruguay in the 1960s, the poster collectives of revolutionary Cuba, the FSLN (Sandinista National Liberation Front) mural projects in Nicaragua, the multimedia *Tucumán Arde* (Tucumán Is Burning) project in Argentina in 1968, and the Los Grupos (The Groups) in Mexico in the 1980s.

Though Paris remained the principal destination for Latin American and European modernists alike, the outbreak of the Spanish Civil War (1936–1939) rekindled relations between Spanish and Latin American artists, forging an Ibero-American surrealist community that bridged the Atlantic. Although surrealism originated in Paris, Spanish artists Salvador Dalí, Juan Miró, and Pablo Picasso were influential participants. When French poet André Breton designated Latin America the "Surrealist continent par exellence" (Breton 1972, 141), a wave of avant-garde tourists flooded the region, lured by promises of the macabre and the fantastic. Simultaneously, Latin Americans, among them Siqueiros and Wifredo Lam (Cuba), departed for Spain to enlist in the Republican army. While Siqueiros returned to paint his radical denunciation of Fascism in *The Portrait of the Bourgeoisie* (1937) for the Electricians' Union building in Mexico City, Lam's experience elicited introspective investigations of Cuba's collective unconscious, inspired by the "primitivist" surrealism of Picasso, with whom Lam studied following the war. In Cuba, Lam's eerie interpretations of Santería and Afro-Cuban traditions in general helped inspire a local surrealist movement that included Carlos Enríquez and Mario Carreño.

The Republican defeat in 1939 intensified modernist activity in Latin America when Mexican president Lázaro Cárdenas offered asylum to Spanish exiles. Spanish socialist realists Luis Seoane, Josep Renau, and Antonio Rodríguez Luna and surrealists María de los Remedios Varo and filmmaker Luis Buñuel joined a Pan American surrealist cohort, including Frida Kahlo (Mexico), Manuel Álvarez Bravo (Mexico), César Moro (Peru), and Carlos Mérida (Guatemala).

World War II stymied Ibero-American relations in the arts. While censorship and government control in Franco's Spain silenced avant-garde dialogue, the rise of abstraction dealt a crushing blow to the aesthetic of mestizaje. Weary of the nationalism of indigenismo and the emotion of surrealism, artists embraced the political neutrality of nonrepresentational aesthetics. In Argentina in the 1940s, the Madí group and the Asociación Arte Concreto Invención (Concrete Invention Art Association) introduced concrete art to the region, in a geometric-based abstraction that assimilated the lessons of Russian constructivism, neoplasticism, and Torres García's universal constructivism. Artists experimented with shaped canvases, cutouts, and articulated sculptures that stressed invention and intellectualism over emotion and intuition. The popularity of rationalist aesthetics grew with the industrial development of the 1950s and 1960s. Arte Generativo (Generative Art) in Argentina and Grupo Rectángulo (Rectangle Group) in Chile, led by Ramón Vergara, produced hard-edged abstraction, often incorporating new technology and industrial materials. Kinetic and op artists approached art as science, investigating the properties of color and motion, as exemplified in the work of Julio Le Parc, Rogelio Polesello, and Venezuelans Jesús Rafael Soto, Alejandro Otero, and Carlos Cruz-Diez.

Alternate tendencies in postwar abstraction addressed the alienation of the atomic age through *informalismo* (informalism). Expressive impulses and emotive gestures characterize the genre, exemplified by Spanish exponents Antoni Tàpies and Antonio Saura and Latin Americans José Antonio Fernández Muro (Argentina), José Balmes (Chile), Lilia Carillo (Mexico), and Francisco Hung (Venezuela). Although the style originated in France, it proved particularly popular in Spain, where it provided a degree of artistic liberation under conditions of authoritarianism. In 1951, attempting to improve Spain's image abroad, Franco invited Latin American artists to study and exhibit in Spain. The artists who accepted, largely from Andean countries, produced regional variations that incorporated pre-Columbian references, as in the work of Enrique Tábara (Ecuador), Fernando de Szyszlo (Peru), Alejandro

Obregón (Colombia), and María Luisa Pacheco (Bolivia). Meanwhile, "neofiguration" recuperated the human figure within expressionist abstraction. In Mexico in the 1960s, José Luis Cuevas and the artists of Nueva Presencia (New Presence) repudiated the heroism of muralism with intimate, existential drawings that verged on the grotesque. Likewise in Argentina, the Otra Figuración (Another Figuration) group rejected "official" ideals of beauty and Peronist socialist realism with their self-declared "anti-aesthetic."

Alberto Greco (Argentina) exemplifies the progression from informalism to anti-art to the ultimate dematerialization of the object in the 1970s. Greco split his time between Madrid, working with the informalists, and Buenos Aires, participating with Otra Figuración. In 1964 he abandoned traditional media entirely in his "Vivo Dito" series of performative projects that designated real people as art with a frame, signature, or gesture. Preference for idea over object anticipated conceptual art, which exploded in Latin America in the 1970s. With the rise of right-wing military dictatorships, artists turned to ephemeral, anonymous, and collective projects to evade government censorship and the cooptation of art into a corrupt system. In Argentina in the early 1970s, *arte de los medios* (mass-media art) employed mass communication to reveal the media's potential for manipulation. The Chilean group CADA (Art Action Collective) undertook acts of civil disobedience and artistic subversion to protest the absence of civil liberties.

Exponents of "mail art" Eugenio Dittborn (Chile) and Felipe Ehrenberg (Mexico, 1943), allowed art to circulate despite government restrictions, and activist initiatives recuperated the public sphere: Victor Grippo (Argentina) constructed a rural oven and distributed bread in downtown Buenos Aires; Lotty Rosenfeld (Chile) transformed a mile of highway divider lines into crosses; and the Peruvian collective Paréntesis (Parenthesis) used the detritus of modern society and symbols recuperated from disenfranchised popular classes. In addition to public projects, by the 1980s performance, body art, installation, and a wide variety of nontraditional and conceptual aesthetics penetrated the artistic and institutional framework of Latin America.

The gradual return to democracy and reopening of Latin American society in the 1980s and 1990s led to an immense expansion of the aesthetic field. The vast proliferation of styles and means coincided with the emergence of postmodernist aesthetics and identity politics that diversified international avant-garde modernism. It has been proposed that in Latin America postmodernity arrived before modernity (García Canclini 1995). Latin American artists have long employed the appropriation, mixing of styles and genres, and embrace of popular culture that loosely defined Euro-American postmodernism to address the heterogeneity of postcolonial society. In recent years, Latin American modern artists have resumed explorations of the meaning of Ibero-American identity through often ironic meditations on shared historic and art-historic origins, and by addressing a myriad of coexisting and competing identities and issues that challenge the universalizing master narratives of the nation, such as gender and sexuality, displacement, migration and exile, transnationalism, and globalization.

Edith Wolfe

References

Barnitz, Jacqueline. *Twentieth-Century Art of Latin America.* Austin: University of Texas Press, 2001.

Breton, André. *Frida Kahlo de Rivera* (1938). Reprinted in *Surrealism and Painting.* Translated by S. W. Taylor. New York: Harper and Row, 1972.

García Canclini, Néstor. *Hybrid Cultures: Strategies for Entering and Leaving Modernity.* Minneapolis: University of Minnesota Press, 1995.

Mosquera, Gerardo. *Beyond the Fantastic: Contemporary Art Criticism from Latin America.* Cambridge, MA: MIT Press, 1996.

Ramirez, Mari Carmen, and Hector Olea. *Inverted Utopias: Avant-Garde Art in Latin America.* New Haven, CT: Yale University Press, 2004.

Rasmussen, Waldo, ed. *Latin American Artists of the Twentieth Century.* New York: Museum of Modern Art, 1992.

Sullivan, Edward J., ed. *Latin American Art in the Twentieth Century.* London: Phaidon, 1996.

Traba, Marta. *Art of Latin America, 1900–1980.* Baltimore: Johns Hopkins University Press, 1994.

See also: Architecture—Modern Spanish America; Art and Artists—Brazil; Art and Artists—Colonial Spanish America; Culture; Democracy; Fiction—Spanish America; Fin de Siècle; Independence I, III–VI; Literary Relations—Spain and the Americas; Mestizaje; Music and Dance II–V; Poetry—Modern Spanish America; Spanish Civil War and Latin America; World War I; World War II.

ARTISANS

Since pre-Columbian times, artisans have played a central role in Latin America as producers of manufactured goods. The establishment of a colonial society in the 1500s and the introduction of guilds and *cofradías* (religious brotherhoods) brought major changes for artisans. Initially domi-nated by Europeans, both institutions were adopted by Indian, black, mestizo, and mulatto artisans, for whom trades offered opportunities of social mobility within a hierarchical society. Following the creation of modern nation-states in the early 1800s, artisans in many regions were drawn into national politics, first as supporters of pro-tectionist caudillos, and subsequently as opponents of liberal free trade. By the 1850s, artisans embraced liberal notions of citizenship, established new forms of asso-ciation (mutual aid societies), and eventu-ally reached out to other workers and con-tributed to the development of modern working-class identities. While labor unions overshadowed artisan organizations in twentieth-century politics, artisans re-mained active and organized in different ways to produce for national and, increas-ingly, for global markets.

We have limited knowledge of pre-Hispanic artisan organizations. Yet the so-phistication of pre-Columbian textiles, ce-ramics, masonry, and numerous other objects suggests a high level of specializa-tion among artisans in many regions. Ex-perts consider pre-Columbian Andean tex-tiles from such cultures as Paracas and Nazca among the finest ever woven in the world. Some evidence suggests the exis-tence in the Andes of specialized commu-nities (*ayllus,* extended kinship groups) of silversmiths and potters. Artisans may even have enjoyed special privileges: the Inca, for example, exempted certain groups of artisans from military service.

The Spanish and Portuguese conquests brought substantial changes to the trades through the introduction of new technolo-gies and institutions. Artisans were among the largest social group that arrived with the early settlers, and though European artisans began to dominate the trades (particularly the most prestigious ones such as silversmithing), Indian, black, and mestizo artisans were quickly integrated into the production process; Europeans alone could not keep up with the growing colonial demand. Within the social and racial hierarchies of colonial society, the trades soon became a prime vehicle for social mobility for mestizos, Indians, and blacks. In some cases, black and Indian master artisans even presided over Spanish apprentices.

During the colonial period, two new institutions came to be associated with the world of the trades, the guild and the cofradía. Guilds, which in theory regulated production and set quality standards, actually remained quite weak throughout the colonial period, in comparison to their medieval European predecessors. Though they were often highly visible in public celebrations, guilds did not succeed in imposing their examinations on all artisans, many of whom operated outside the guild system. A more vibrant artisan institution was the cofradía, or religious brotherhood. Cofradías were associated with the cult of a saint and offered their members financial assistance during times of illness and paid for burial services. Some cofradías and their saints came to be associated with specific trades, for example, San Eloy for silversmiths, San Homobono for tailors, and San Crispín and San Crispiniano for shoemakers. Many cofradías and guilds had clear racial affiliations.

Inspired by the Enlightenment, the late eighteenth-century Bourbon reforms brought changes to the trades. The writings of Spanish enlightened reformers challenged long-standing prejudices against manual labor in the Hispanic world, and presented labor as the cornerstone of eco-

nomic prosperity. While some Spanish reformers attacked the guild, ironically the Bourbon reforms strengthened guilds in some parts of Spanish America by reorganizing them to increase state control and tax artisans more effectively. As a result, the guild survived into the nineteenth century, although in a somewhat different form, as an institution that served fiscal purposes and also helped with recruitment for state militias.

Following the nineteenth-century wars of independence, artisans emerged as visible political actors. They first gained national visibility in the context of caudillo politics, as caudillos turned to urban artisans to build a political base. In exchange for artisan support, caudillos implemented protectionist policies to shelter national goods from foreign competition. Artisans supported Juan Manuel de Rosas in Argentina, Agustín Gamarra in Peru, and Manuel Belzú in Bolivia, and artisans often participated in urban militias. Caudillos also offered some artisans a form of state patronage through contracts for the production of military provisions ranging from uniforms to saddles. In some cases, artisans worked in government foundries to produce weapons.

During the 1840s and 1850s, as economic liberalism gained ground throughout Latin America, artisans emerged to become vocal opponents of free trade. In Bogotá, as early as 1847, the Sociedad de Artesanos challenged a law lowering tariffs in Colombia. In Peru, the guilds sent artisan leader José María García to address Congress in 1849; García condemned free trade and called for tariffs to protect national artisans. As liberalism gained popularity, some artisans turned to more violent forms of protest. In 1858, in Lima's port city of Callao, artisans, led primarily by carpenters, threw a shipment of imported door and window frames into the Pacific Ocean. However, by the 1850s artisans had lost the battle over trade policy.

Despite their defeat on the economic front, artisans continued their political activity and took advantage of new opportunities for participation within the liberal polity. Artisans founded new associations called mutual aid societies, which gave members renewed respectability as liberal citizens conforming to modern forms of association. Mutual aid societies did away with the colonial racial categories and hierarchies. Meetings were publicly announced, and internal elections for positions were open to all members. The mutual aid society also replicated the functions of the older cofradía by providing assistance during illness and serving as a burial fund for its members at the time of death, and by celebrating the the day of its patron saint.

Despite injunctions in their rules against political activity, these societies clearly played a political role. In Lima, the Sociedad de Artesanos de Auxilios Mútuos was instrumental in gaining the artisan support that in 1872 helped elect the Partido Civil's Manuel Pardo, Peru's first civilian president. Mutual aid societies appeared throughout the continent in Chile, Ecuador, and Bolivia, and in Mexico and other countries. Liberals considered artisans as a symbolically important constituency: liberal political discourse emphasized the centrality of work to national prosperity, and given their connection to the world of labor, artisans emerged as idealized independent citizens. In Chile, Francisco Bilbao and a number of Chilean liberals mobilized artisans in 1850 through the Sociedad de la Igualdad (Society of Equality), leading to an armed insurrection against the government.

During the late 1800s, artisans contributed to defining a new working-class identity. Artisans interpreted liberalism in their own way, embracing some aspects of the liberal project and rejecting others. In particular, artisans challenged the liberal view of politics as made up only of individual political actors and continued to identify as a distinct social sector and eventually as a working class. Typesetters played an important role in the process of extending an artisan identity to broader segments of workers, who now read their own artisan and worker newspapers, such as *El Artesano* (1873) and *El Obrero* (1875) in Lima. Peru's first syndicalist confederation was the Confederación de Artesanos Unión Universal (1878).

During the transition to the twentieth century, in the context of incipient industrialization, syndicalism became the most prominent form of worker organization, and artisan mutual aid societies became less visible. Workers in the textile industry, in shipping, and from other industries began to unionize and make greater demands on governments, such as the struggles for the eight-hour workday. The eventual creation of government-run social security systems during the mid-1900s rendered the social functions of mutual aid societies obsolete. In rare cases, artisan mutual aid societies survived these changes; for example, Lima's Sociedad Fraternal de Artesanos continues to operate as an old mutual aid society.

The growth of the labor movement during the twentieth century did not do away with artisan organizations. Artisans continued to play a prominent role in production and to organize in different ways, ranging from national organizations such as Ecuador's National Confederation of Professional Artisans of Ecuador (founded in 1949) to local cooperatives such as the women's weaving cooperative Tsobol Antzetik in Chiapas, Mexico. In countries with long traditions of indigenous craftsmanship (Peru, Mexico, Guatemala), there has been a resurgence of artisan production for national and global tourist markets. In the context of globalization, twenty-first-century artisans face new challenges to market their goods and retain the strength of their local organizations.

Iñigo García-Bryce

References

García-Bryce, Iñigo. *Crafting the Republic: Lima's Artisans and Nation Building in Peru, 1821–1879.* Albuquerque: University of New Mexico Press, 2004.

Grimes, Kimberly M., and B. Lynne Milgram, eds. *Artisans and Cooperatives: Developing Alternative Trade for the Global Economy.* Tucson: University of Arizona Press, 2000.

Johnson, Lyman. "The Silversmiths of Buenos Aires: A Case Study in the Failure of Corporate Social Organization," *Journal of Latin American Studies* 8, no. 2 (1976): 181–213.

Samayoa Guevara, Héctor Humberto. *Los gremios de artesanos en la ciudad de Guatemala.* Guatemala: Editorial Universitaria, 1962.

Sowell, David. *The Early Colombian Labor Movement.* Philadelphia: Temple University Press, 1992.

See also: Alcabala; Art and Artists—Brazil; Art and Artists—Colonial Spanish America; Art and Artists—Modern Spanish America; Atlantic Economy; Ayllu; Bourbon Reforms; Caudillos; Colonists and Settlers I–VI; Confraternities; Conquest I–VII; Enlightenment—Brazil; Enlightenment—Spanish America; Fin de Siècle; Guatemala; Independence I–VI; Liberalism; Mexico; Native Americans I–VIII; Peru; Race; Saints and Saintliness; Slavery I–IV; Women—Modern Spanish America.

ASIENTO

The *asiento* was a contract for a monopoly on the introduction of African slaves into Spain's colonial realms in the Americas, by which the Spanish Crown endeavored to facilitate, control, and derive profit from slave trading by private commercial interests. Individuals or companies, generally non-Spanish, received monopoly rights for a fixed period over the delivery of a stipulated number of enslaved Africans to designated Spanish American ports in return for making predetermined annual payments to the Crown. Foreigners found the contracts attractive, since they provided legal cover for infringement upon the general monopoly on trade with Spain's American colonies enjoyed by merchants from Seville and, later, Cádiz. Portuguese, Genoese, Dutch, French, and English interests held the asiento at various points between 1595 and the mid-eighteenth century, after which global conflict and a series of economic reforms, culminating in the extension of internal free trading privileges to all corners of Spain's American empire in 1789, combined to produce the system's demise.

Beginning in 1518, the administrations of King Charles I (Holy Roman Emperor Charles V) and Philip II sought to establish the transatlantic slave trade on a solid and reliable footing by experimenting with a diverse array of licensing arrangements with German, Genoese, and Portuguese merchants. The Crown eventually granted a full-blown, nine-year monopoly over the trade, generally seen as the first true asiento, to Pedro Gomes Reynel in 1595. Over the next several decades a succession of Portuguese *asentistas* and their Genoese financiers pushed slave imports into mainland Spanish America to an all-time high. Some 270,000 Africans are estimated to have survived the journey across the Atlantic to Spain's American territories between 1595 and 1640, the vast majority ending up in New Spain, Peru, and other mainland destinations. This massive and unprecedented transoceanic movement of enslaved laborers probably owed more to the involvement of asentistas in contraband trading than to their fulfillment of contractual obligations. In fact, it is most properly attributed to the general expansion of trading opportunities experienced by Portuguese merchants during the Spanish Crown's sixty-year reign over Portugal and its commercial networks between 1580 and 1640.

The loss of Portugal led to Spain's temporary abandonment of the asiento system, but it was revived in 1662, as the Crown sought once again to spur legal importation and at the same time curb the growing threat posed to royal revenues by Dutch, French, and English smugglers. Commercial interests representing Spain's increasingly powerful northern European rivals were not to be denied access to the Spanish American slave trade, and they soon gained control of the asiento, either unofficially through Genoese, Portuguese, and other third parties or, as the Crown bowed to the new realities of international politics, more formally. The slave-supply monopoly began to assume the character of a full-fledged treaty provision, illustrated in a ten-year contract with the Royal French Guinea Company in 1701 and, even more strikingly, a thirty-year concession to the English under the terms of the Treaty of Utrecht in 1713. The smuggling opportunities afforded by the latter agreement were exploited to the hilt by the South Sea Company, albeit with several interruptions, until the renewal of major Spanish-English hostilities in 1739 led to its final abrogation. Thereafter, the Spanish Crown employed limited versions of the asiento for another half-century as part of a relatively unsuccessful strategy to reduce contraband trade and keep foreign interests at bay.

Paul Lokken

References

Eltis, David. "The Volume and Structure of the Transatlantic Slave Trade: A Reassessment." *William and Mary Quarterly,* 3rd series, 58, no. 1 (January 2001): 17–46.

Mellafe, Rolando. *Negro Slavery in Latin America.* Translated by J. W. S. Judge. Berkeley and Los Angeles: University of California Press, 1975.

Rout, Leslie B., Jr. *The African Experience in Spanish America: 1502 to the Present Day.* Cambridge: Cambridge University Press, 1976.

Vila Vilar, Enriqueta. *Hispanoamérica y el comercio de esclavos: Los asientos portugueses.* Seville: Escuela de Estudios Hispanoamericanos, 1977.

See also: Atlantic Economy; Bourbon Reforms; Contraband; Monopolies; Pirates and Piracy; Slavery I–IV; Slave Trade; Trade—Spain/Spanish America; Utrecht, Treaty of.

ATLANTIC ECONOMY

The discovery of the New World and its conquest and colonization by Spain and Portugal led to the emergence of an economic system that encompassed the Atlantic Basin and extended ties to other regions of the globe. The isolation of the Americas quickly faded, and the Western Hemisphere soon became crucial to the world economy. European expansion transformed American economic activity, focusing on the production of goods in demand outside the Americas and forcing indigenous labor into activities that served European demand.

The Atlantic economy, of course, existed prior to 1492 and the epic discovery in that year by Christopher Columbus. Scandinavians and Basques plied the North Atlantic, drawn in part by its rich fisheries. The west coast of Africa beckoned the Portuguese, who probed farther and farther south, searching for gold, slaves, and other goods. Their motives were often economic, although not always in a modern capitalistic sense: Prince Henry the Navigator, who sponsored many of the early Portuguese expeditions along the African littoral, wanted riches to launch a great crusade against the Muslims of North Africa. During the 1400s the Portuguese set up fortified trading posts along the west coast of Africa, trading for gold, ivory, slaves, and even spices brought into the area by Muslim merchants. Before the Great Enterprise of 1492, Columbus himself navigated the Atlantic waters from Iceland to Africa. Portugal settled the Azores and Madeira, while Spain had completed the conquest of the Canary Islands by the late 1400s. Imported sugarcane flourished on the Canaries and Madeira, and several Portuguese islands became renowned for their viticulture.

Except for the royal financing of the first Columbus voyage, the early Iberian expeditions to the New World were privately funded expeditions, whether for trading or for exploration and conquest. Columbus aimed to reach East Asia and establish commercial relations there. He had convinced himself that somewhere near Cathay lay a region rich in gold, which he equated with the biblical land of Ophir. He hoped to obtain gold from the Far East to underwrite the final crusade to liberate Jerusalem from the Muslims and usher in the End of Times. This, of course, was the opposite of the trade that eventually developed, whereby Europe exported precious metals largely obtained in the Americas to East Asia in exchange for spices, silks, and other trade goods. Queen Isabella of Castile, who backed the first voyage, saw it as a royal trading expedition that, if successful, would provide commercial profits to the monarchy. She and Columbus envisioned the establishment of Spanish trading posts in East Asia; certainly they did not imagine the conquest of China. Likewise, Pedro Álvarez Cabral, who claimed Brazil for Portugal in 1500 when his fleet was reportedly blown westward from Africa, was sailing to India, as the second expedition around Africa along the route pioneered by Vasco da Gama.

Neither the Spanish nor the Portuguese Crown was capable of monopolizing the emerging Atlantic economy, and consequently they turned to private initiative to exploit the new colonies. Merchant capital underwrote many of the early ventures, giving the Atlantic economy a mercantilist orientation. Iberian and other European merchants still hoped to trade goods for the precious commodities of the Far East, especially for the spices of Indonesia and the silks and porcelain of China. However, once conquest and settlement of the Americas got underway, the mercantilist ventures as originally conceived had to develop in other ways for the Atlantic economy to flourish as part of the larger global economic system. The islanders of the Caribbean, the Mayas of the Yucatán Peninsula, and Brazil's Tupi-Guaranís lacked trade goods that the Spanish and Portuguese could easily turn to commercial profit. The Iberians soon bartered for or plundered the indigenous inhabitants' small stocks of gold and then had to devise other means of tapping the region's economic potential. The same held true for Mexico and Peru, where Hernando Cortés and Francisco Pizarro and their men found much larger stockpiles of gold and silver to plunder, but indigenous economic activity offered little else that the Europeans could turn to commercial advantage.

The solution in Spanish America was to establish new economic activities largely carried out through slavery or forms of coerced labor that extracted profits through tributary impositions on the indigenous population. The economic system could sustain such tributary exactions over the long term, but only by impoverishing much of the population. Columbus divided the islanders into *encomiendas* (grants of tribute that the Spaniards could collect in labor or kind) on Hispaniola and thus provided workers for gold mining. The early fleets brought with them horses, cattle, and pigs, and livestock soon proliferated. In 1502 Nicolás de Ovando arrived as governor. He increased gold output, but more importantly for the long term, Ovando brought with him sugarcane from the Canaries. The conquest of Cuba in 1511 repeated the economic model of Hispaniola: plunder followed by gold mining and agriculture with forced labor. On the Brazilian coast, a different pattern emerged: the Portuguese set up factories where they traded goods for brazilwood, a reddish dyewood coveted by European textile manufacturers. The indigenous population cut the brazilwood and brought it to the Portuguese, often by floating it down rivers to the coast. Such barter arrangements eventually gave way to the enslave-ment of the Indians, particularly with the introduction of sugarcane and the establishment of the first plantations.

The new Spanish and Portuguese nation-states supported the development of Atlantic mercantilism by providing political and military muscle to protect colonial economic investments and commercial routes and to ensure tributary exactions from the local population. The governments usually associated mercantilism with bullionism, the belief that true wealth lay in precious metals, for which there seemed to be a demand everywhere. Spain and Portugal consequently tried to stimulate and protect international and colonial trade that brought gold and silver in exchange. They also forbade the export of bullion, although the ban was often violated. The monarchies provided the political infrastructure for ruling colonies around the Atlantic Basin and garnered profits from the economic enterprises stimulated by mercantilist activity, both by taxing production and by imposing trade tariffs.

The Iberian nations found fabulous treasures of gold and silver in their American colonies that far exceeded the amount extracted in the initial pillaging of the indigenous population. Gold flowed across the Atlantic from Colombia, Mexico, and especially from Brazil, beginning in the 1690s. It was American silver, however, that enriched Spain. American bullion production between 1500 and 1650 may have increased European gold stocks by 5 percent and its silver supply by at least 50 percent. This not only stimulated economic life throughout the Atlantic region, but also provided the most important medium of exchange for Europeans to trade with China and made the Iberian empire crucial to the world economy. The massive influx of silver into Spain from Peru and Mexico touched off waves of inflation, which rippled through Europe and became known as the Price Revolution. The 1500–1650 bullion output was remarkable because of its size relative to preexisting European stocks. The next century and a half witnessed even greater production. Brazilian gold flooded into Portugal and then passed to that nation's chief trading partner, Great Britain. Although the great Andean silver mines at Potosí were increasingly played out by the 1700s, bonanzas at several Mexican camps during the eighteenth century yielded a great age of silver. The resulting increase in bullion helped monetize the world economy at the time England and the Low Countries entered the path of industrialization. In the Caribbean, pirates and smugglers competed with legitimate Spanish merchants for a share of the treasure, as it made its way from the mines to Europe.

Both Spain and Portugal imposed mercantilist regulations to restrict access to their colonial markets and to monopolize colonial production. To protect and regulate Spanish transatlantic shipping, Queen Isabella established the House of Trade (Casa de Contratación) in 1503, with its headquarters in Seville. It registered cargoes and passengers traveling to and from Spanish America, and thus allowed Seville to control colonial trade until the eighteenth century, when the board shifted its headquarters to Cádiz. The Consulado (Merchant Guild) of Seville dominated trade with the colonies. *Consulados* in Mexico and Lima similarly regulated colonial commerce. The guilds helped the Crown enforce mercantilist regulations, while at the same time protecting the merchants' interests against national and foreign competition. This situation also meant that Spaniards showed less interest in the development of peripheral areas that lacked gold and silver but that had rich agricultural potential, such as the Río de la Plata and Chile.

Both Spain and Portugal attempted to protect and regulate their shipping in the Atlantic. By 1526, Spanish merchant vessels were required to travel in fleets, and over the following decades the pattern developed of dispatching an annual convoy to Mexico (the *flota*) and another to Panama for Peru (the *galeones*). The flota provided goods for the Caribbean and held a great fair at Veracruz, from which Mexican merchants bought merchandise to supply that viceroyalty. Sold at a fair in Panama, goods from the galeones were hauled over the isthmus and then reembarked for Lima, whence they were distributed throughout Spanish South America. Originally merchants in Lima also supplied markets as far away as Asunción and Buenos Aires. The system was cumbersome, but it proved effective in protecting shipping from Spain's enemies, the most famous exception being the 1628 capture of the entire treasure fleet by a squadron of the Dutch West Indies Company commanded by Piet Heyn. Whereas Spanish fleets sailed directly to the Caribbean via the Canaries, Portuguese convoys linked the metropolis with the Atlantic islands, Africa, Brazil, and the trading factories in East Asia.

Such control and regulation benefited the Crown and the monopolist merchants who enjoyed political favor, but the mercantilist policies impeded economic development, both in the Iberian Peninsula and in the colonies. Spain's obsession with mining meant that labor and capital resources were concentrated in that sector of the economy, giving short shrift to other forms of colonial output. Some colonies had the potential for producing large quantities of sugar, tobacco, cacao, hides, and textile dyes (cochineal and indigo). But they had to compete with the mining industry for labor and capital. The latter was scarce, as much of the bullion was drained out of the colonies to Europe. Besides merchants, the Catholic Church was often the chief lending institution in the colonies. Furthermore, in its attempt to extract profit from the colonial economies, Spain prohibited most intracolonial commerce. Mexico and Peru could not trade with each other, for example, in part because the Crown feared that instead of flowing to Spain, Peruvian silver would pass via New Spain to the Far East on the Manila Galleons. The Crown restricted trade between Spanish America and Asia to two annual galleons sailing between the Philippines and Acapulco. If colonists were to buy Asian goods, Spain insisted that they purchase them from Spanish suppliers, rather than obtaining them directly from the Philippines.

The tonnage of Spanish trade with the Americas grew until the early 1600s, but then declined, in part because the colonies were able to produce for themselves many basic items that had previously been imported. Furthermore, Spanish spending on wars in Europe in a futile attempt to reassert Catholic and Habsburg hegemony weakened Spain's economic hold over the colonies. It lacked the maritime resources to send annual fleets. As the period between the dispatch of the flota and galeones stretched to two or three or even four years, foreign smugglers stepped in to supply American consumers with goods.

Mercantilist thinking also held that Spain and Portugal should provide the manufactures consumed by the colonies. But neither was able to do so consistently. The inflation caused by New World bullion imports made Spanish and Portuguese labor expensive, and thus Iberian manufacturers had difficulty competing with industry from elsewhere. Furthermore, Spanish and Portuguese cultures seemed predisposed against the scientific and technological requirements of industrial entrepreneurship. The Consulado of Seville grew wealthy by importing foreign manufactures and then reexporting them to the colonies, and the Crown tolerated such violations of mercantilist principles because it was well paid by the consulado for permitting the exceptions. Consequently, much of the gold and silver that arrived from the Americas went immediately to pay foreign commercial and industrial interests. Genoese merchants had great influence in Seville in the early 1500s, and Dutch, French, and English suppliers later gained footholds. Portugal's dependence on British manufactures was notorious, codified in the Treaty of Methuen, by which British goods received favored status in the Portuguese Empire and Portuguese wines gained easy access to English markets.

Backed by royal political power, the mercantilist drive for commercial profits transformed societies throughout the Atlantic world. When disease, gold mining, and sugar planting wiped out Caribbean villages, the Spanish enslaved residents of neighboring islands. In Brazil, the pressure of the emerging sugar economy could not rely for long on the comparatively sparse indigenous population, which largely died off or retreated inland. The Portuguese consequently turned to their African outposts for labor and sent a great wave of human chattels across the Atlantic. Before the Portuguese, Dutch, and British slavers were through, they had forcibly uprooted millions of Africans to grow sugar and tobacco, mine for gold and diamonds, produce artisanal goods, and perform other labors that helped keep the Atlantic economy humming. As sugar plantations proliferated in Brazil and the Caribbean, enslavement burgeoned, but many Africans also ended up working in American tobacco and cotton fields and in Brazil's gold mines. Altogether it is estimated that the Atlantic slave trade took more than 9.5 million humans out of Africa to provide labor for the Atlantic economy. Of these, more than 60 percent were enslaved during the eighteenth century. Brazil was the chief destination, receiving 3.6 million Africans (Curtin 1969, 268).

Of course, the Atlantic economy did not rely solely on African slavery for labor. The American silver that flooded into Europe came from mines often located in remote mountainous areas of Mexico and the Andes, to which Spaniards had to relocate workers through coercion or economic incentives. The infamous Andean *mita* system of rotating forced labor devastated provinces subject to it. Many workers taken out of their villages to toil at the Potosí silver mines or the Huancavelica mercury mines never returned home, all too frequently because they had died. Many others fled to escape serving in the mita, thereby depopulating the provinces. The economy's dependence on indigenous labor suffered a clear setback when the inevitable but inadvertent introduction of Old World diseases devastated the Americas. Perhaps 90 percent of the indigenous population died from smallpox, typhus, measles, and other epidemics, plus the abuse and disruption caused by the conquest and colonization. The drop in labor handicapped the economy and may have contributed to a prolonged malaise during the mid-1600s. Only in the eighteenth century did Mexico and Peru begin to recover demographically.

During the 1600s, the British, French, and Dutch managed to occupy some Caribbean islands, where they established sugar plantations, setting the stage for intensified competition within the Atlantic economy after 1700. The Dutch, for example, gained expertise in sugar production when they temporarily occupied parts of northeastern Brazil from 1629 to 1654 (they also seized Portuguese outposts in Africa and became serious rivals in the slave trade). When finally driven out of Brazil, the Dutch moved to the West Indies, where they and later the French and British offered stiff competition to the Brazilians, whose technology failed to keep pace and whose transportation costs to Europe were higher. Brazil never recovered its dominant position in the Atlantic sugar industry.

For nearly two centuries Brazil's contribution to the Atlantic economy was chiefly agricultural. In the late 1690s, however, discovery of major gold deposits in Minas Gerais rocked the foundations of the Portuguese imperial economy. A massive gold rush drained slaves into Minas Gerais and away from the stagnant sugar regions, where planters could not compete with the inflated prices gold miners were willing to pay for chattels. Discovery of diamonds in the 1720s only added to agriculture's woes. The Portuguese Crown became so concerned, in fact, that it tried to limit migration to Minas Gerais. It believed that agriculture was a more stable and enduring economic activity than the boom-and-bust cycles of mining. The mines did constitute an important internal market for the ranching and farming production and thus helped integrate Brazil economically. Brazilian gold, diamonds, and sugar, along with Portuguese wines, were all critical to the Portuguese economy, as they were the chief goods that permitted Portugal to obtain British manufactures.

In the face of mounting competition from their European rivals, both Spain and Portugal attempted to reform their imperial economies in the eighteenth century. The English gained an economic foothold in Spanish America in 1713 when the Peace of Utrecht granted them the right to sell a limited number of slaves and a shipload of merchandise to the Spanish colonies. Merchantmen from Britain's mainland colonies became frequent visitors to the Caribbean, including the Spanish colonies, as they sailed in the triangular trade that linked New England, Africa, and the sugar islands. The new Spanish Bourbon dynasty carried out a series of reforms to make imperial commerce more profitable. It abolished the traditional fleet system and its constraints on the flow of merchandise across the Atlantic. Their governments needed more revenues to strengthen imperial defenses.

This need became especially clear to the Spaniards when the British seized Havana in 1762 during the French and Indian War. Although it was returned to Spain by the Treaty of Paris (1763), Charles III and his advisers recognized that the empire's weak navy and colonial defenses left it dangerously exposed to British expansionism.

He consequently increased fiscal pressure on the colonies and tried to promote economic growth to pay for improvements to imperial defenses. During his reign (1759–1788), the monarchy liberalized intra-imperial commerce by permitting all Spanish ports to trade directly with the American colonies and authorized trade between the colonies themselves. The government also tried to promote manufacturing in Spain to supply the colonies, but much of the merchandise continued to be goods of foreign origin that Spanish merchants reexported to American consumers. Under the leadership of the Marquis of Pombal, Portugal also tried to make its imperial economy more profitable. As in Spain, this process involved breaking the power of the merchant elites who had profited from the traditional economic policies, including Portugal's dependence on Britain for manufactured goods.

Political and economic factors conspired to undercut the reformist policies. The death of José I of Portugal removed Pombal from power, and ministers of the new monarch, Maria I, reverted to traditional policies. With a weak industrial base, Spain could not supply its colonies. In the late 1790s, Spain found itself allied with Revolutionary France against Great Britain, whose navy effectively cut the Spaniards off from the colonies. From that point onward, Spain was never able to reassert any type of commercial control over its empire. Matters grew even worse with the Napoleonic invasion and occupation of the Iberian Peninsula, which touched off the movement for Latin American independence. Brazil gained its independence peacefully but became an economic colony of the British. Pro-independence sentiment was especially strong in some of the economically peripheral areas of Spanish America, such as Argentina, Chile, and Venezuela. Prolonged, destructive wars were necessary before liberation came to the old viceregal centers of Mexico and Peru, and several decades passed before they recovered economically. Meanwhile, what influence Spain and Portugal still had over the Atlantic economy disappeared with their loss of political control, to be replaced by the power of the industrial nations of the North Atlantic.

Kendall W. Brown

References

Bakewell, Peter. *A History of Latin America.* Malden, MA: Blackwell, 1997.

Braudel, Fernand. *Capitalism and Material Life, 1400–1800.* New York: Harper and Row, 1967.

Curtin, Philip. *The African Slave Trade: A Census.* Madison: University of Wisconsin Press, 1969.

Fisher, John Robert. *The Economic Aspects of Spanish Imperialism in America, 1492–1810.* Liverpool: Liverpool University Press, 1997.

Furtado, Celso. *The Economic Growth of Brazil: A Survey from Colonial to Modern Times.* Berkeley and Los Angeles: University of California Press, 1963.

Garner, Richard L. *Economic Growth and Change in Bourbon Mexico.* Gainesville: University of Florida Press, 1993.

Klein, Herbert S. *The Atlantic Slave Trade.* Cambridge: Cambridge University Press, 1999.

Miller, Joseph C. *The Way of Death: Merchant Capitalism and the Angolan Slave Trade, 1730–1830.* Madison: University of Wisconsin Press, 1988.

Prado, Caio Jr. *The Colonial Background of Modern Brazil.* Berkeley and Los Angeles: University of California Press, 1967.

Stein, Stanley J., and Barbara H. Stein. *Silver, Trade, and War: Spain and America in the Making of Early Modern Europe.* Baltimore: Johns Hopkins University Press, 2000.

Weaver, Frederick Stirton. *Latin America in the World Economy: Mercantile Colonialism to Global Capitalism.* Boulder, CO: Westview, 2000.

See also: Artisans; Bourbon Reforms; Casa de Contratación; Columbian Exchange— Agriculture; Columbian Exchange— Disease; Columbian Exchange— Livestock; Contraband; Cotton; Defense—Colonial Brazil; Defense— Colonial Spanish America; Dependency Theory; Dyes and Dyewood; Encomienda; Fleet System; Gold; Independence I–VI; Methuen Treaty; Mining—Gold; Mining—Mercury; Mining—Silver; Mita; Napoleonic Invasion and Luso-America; Napoleonic Invasion and Spanish America; Native Americans I–VIII; Paris, Treaty of (1763); Pirates and Piracy; Potosí; Silver; Slavery I—Brazil; Slave Trade; Sugar; Thirty Years' War; Tobacco; Trade— Spain/Spanish America; Utrecht, Treaty of; Viceroyalties; Wine.

AUDIENCIAS

Audiencias were the most important governing bodies in the colonial administration of the Spanish Empire. They were modeled on the two law courts of the Kingdom of Castile at Valladolid and Granada. In the New World, however, audiencias were much more than law courts and had extensive administrative, political, and military functions. An audiencia was always paired with the chief administrative officer of a major region—whether viceroy, captain-general, or governor—in order to advise, control, and replace him in his absence. Audiencias were added as the Spanish Empire expanded, and suppressed as areas lost importance.

The first audiencia in the New World was established in Santo Domingo in 1511, to act as a counterbalance to the claims of Christopher Columbus's son Diego, who had just been appointed viceroy. A second audiencia came next in Mexico City in

1528 to take over after Hernando Cortés's conquest. With the conquest of Peru and New Granada, audiencias followed in Lima and Santafé de Bogotá in 1544 and 1549 respectively. Other audiencias appeared in Guadalajara, Manila, Central America, Charcas (Bolivia), Cuzco (Peru), Santiago (Chile), Buenos Aires, Quito (Ecuador), and Caracas (Venezuela). Audiencia boundaries anticipated the formation of the modern Hispanic nations of Argentina, Chile, Bolivia, Peru, Ecuador, Colombia, Venezuela, Panama, Mexico, and the Philippines, as well as the hoped-for but never successful unitary states of Central America and the Caribbean.

Members of the audiencia were the president; four to eight *oidores* (judges) and a *fiscal* (crown attorney) who protected royal interests, outlined the main legal issues, and participated in all deliberations; plus lesser officers. The president of the audiencia was the chief administrative officer of the region, either the viceroy, captain-general, or governor. He had no vote in judicial cases; only oidores did. The fiscal had no vote in cases involving the Crown but could break a tie in other matters. Audiencias heard both criminal and civil cases, but after 1542 only civil decisions worth more than 10,000 pesos could be appealed to Spain.

Audiencias had extensive administrative and legislative functions, and their oidores individually sat on a wide variety of administrative bodies that regulated colonial life. Ecclesiastical matters, urban and provincial life, tax issues, native affairs, mining, ranching, agriculture, commercial disputes, and probate all fell under their purview. Oidores might be sent on a long tour of a distant province, a *visita*, to carry out a census of the native population, as-

sign tribute quotas, and fix and distribute labor assignments. They might survey the needs of a mining district or a port area and make on-the-spot laws to resolve the problems encountered. They would then report back to the audiencia in written form as to what had been done, and their action would have legal standing unless the audiencia decided otherwise.

Audiencia oidores served unlimited terms until recalled or promoted. They might serve all their lives in one audiencia, rising from junior to senior oidor, be promoted to the prestigious audiencia in Mexico City or Lima, and in rare instances even be returned to Spain to serve on the Council of the Indies. As career bureaucrats trained as lawyers at the university, they brought to the table professional values and an esprit de corps that were the mainstay of Spanish colonial administration.

Maurice P. Brungardt

References

Haring, C. H. *The Spanish Empire in America.* New York: Harcourt, Brace and World, 1947.

Lockhart, James, and Stuart B. Schwartz. *Early Latin America: A History of Colonial Spanish America and Brazil.* Cambridge: Cambridge University Press, 1983.

Phelan, John Leddy. *The Kingdom of Quito in the Seventeenth Century: Bureaucratic Politics in the Spanish Empire.* Madison: University of Wisconsin Press, 1968.

See also: Administration—Colonial Spanish America; Cities; Laws—Colonial Latin America; Mexico; Mining—Silver; Mita; Ordenanza del Patronazgo; Peru; Viceroyalties; Visita.

AYLLU

The *ayllu* is the basic social unit in Andean America. It is best described as an extended kinship unit, including parents, children, grandparents, and uncles and aunts. Ayllu members traditionally traced descent from a common "mythical" source, usually a place of symbolic significance, such as a mountain peak, an unusual stone outcropping, a spring, a cave, or a lake. Rarely are animals seen as the origin of the ayllu. The nature of ayllu organization, governed by the principles of reciprocity and redistribution, helps ayllu members overcome the challenges of the climatic and geographic variations of the central and southern Andes. In the vertical world of the Andes, the ayllu unit is largely self-sufficient; ayllu members engage in productive activities that range from puna grassland herding of llamas and alpacas to the raising of middle-elevation crops such as corn, potatoes, and quinoa, or lower-elevation products such as tomatoes, chile peppers, coca, and fruits.

Land is held in common, although actual cultivation is controlled by individuals; in case of death community needs take precedence in the new land distribution. Members of the ayllu cooperate for major projects, such as the construction of residences or rethatching of roofs, the maintenance of irrigation channels, and public religious ceremonies. Ayllu elders are respected and have significant authority over relationships within and outside the group. After the Spanish conquest of the Andes, the role of the ayllu gradually weakened; however, the speed of disintegration seems to have accelerated in the twentieth century, with modernization and increasing migration from rural areas to large urban centers. More modern Catholic religious and social relationships such as godparentage and confraternity affiliation have assumed some of the functions of the traditional ayllu, as have memberships in local or regional associations in large urban centers. Yet in parts of the Andes, the ayllu continues to have relevance in many isolated rural highland communities.

Noble Cook

References

Murra, John V. *The Economic Organization of the Inka State.* Greenwich, CT: JAI Press, 1980.

Rostworowski de Diez Canseco, Maria. *History of the Inca Realm.* New York: Cambridge University Press, 1999.

Zuidema, R. Tom. *Inca Civilization in Cuzco.* Austin: University of Texas Press, 1990.

See also: Colonists and Settlers I—Andes; Confraternities; Congregaciones; Conquest I—Andes; Kuraca; Native Americans V—Central and Southern Andes; Quipu; Yanancona.

B

BANANAS

This large perennial seed plant extensively cultivated for its fruit is one of the world's most important foods, thanks to its pleasing flavor, nutritional value, and yearlong availability. Classified as the genus *Musa* of the family Musaceae, banana plants flourish throughout the tropics. There are hundreds of varieties of banana, but only a few are commercially valuable exports. The most familiar fruit is the yellow-skinned sweet and pulpy raw banana of international trade. The plantain, also a part of the banana family, is consumed cooked. Unlike wild varieties, cultivated bananas are produced without pollination and have evolved sterility.

Banana plants are actually enormous herbs. What looks like the trunk of the plants consists of tightly bound overlapping leafstalks. The fruit, which contains a sizable amount of starch and sugar, has substantial value as a foodstuff. Bananas are high in carbohydrates and generate more calories per pound than any other fresh fruit. Rich in potassium, they also provide relatively large quantities of vitamins A, B, and C.

Bananas are native to Southeast Asia, where they have been cultivated for over 4,000 years. About 2,000 years ago, humans carried bananas west into Africa. By AD 1000, the banana plant was known to the Mediterranean world. Europeans transported banana plants from the Canary Islands to the Indies soon after Christopher Columbus's first Atlantic crossing. Banana cultivation spread from Hispaniola to other Caribbean islands and the mainland to become a staple food crop in much of Latin America. Due to its perishable nature, the banana was consumed domestically and traded locally.

The Caribbean region gave birth to the corporations that dominate the banana industry. In the nineteenth century, the banana was introduced to markets in the United States, which has remained the world's largest consumer, aided by refrigeration technologies and faster transportation systems that made possible an international market for the fruit. The United Fruit Company was the first big international name in the banana export industry. In 1870, the merchant seaman Captain Lorenzo Dow Baker started importing bananas from Jamaica for sale in the United States. He gradually purchased more and larger schooners, along with Jamaican banana plantations. In 1885, Baker and fellow

Massachusetts entrepreneur Andrew W. Preston established the Boston Fruit Company.

Four years later, the United Fruit Company was formed, after Minor C. Keith, a U.S. businessman and Central American railroad builder, merged his various holdings with the Boston Fruit Company. Preston served as president of United Fruit Company until his death in 1924. Baker became a managing director of the company's Jamaican division. In 1929, United Fruit merged with Samuel Zemurray's Cuyamel Fruit Company. The mergers united extensive cultivation, transportation, and distribution resources with vast landholdings in several Latin American and Caribbean countries. Zemurray, a Russian immigrant to the United States, served as United Fruit Company's managing director in charge of operations from 1932 to 1938 and president from 1938 to 1951. Over the years, United Fruit has changed its name to AMK, United Brands, and, in the early 1990s, Chiquita Brands, Inc.

In 1899, Vaccaro Brothers and Company, three Sicilian-American orange growers and a son-in-law, began importing bananas to New Orleans. By World War I, they had become the largest investors and exporters in Honduras, and second only to United Fruit in the international banana trade. The Vaccaros established the public Standard Fruit and Steamship Company in 1925. James Dole's Hawaiian Pineapple Company, founded in the 1850s by the Harvard-educated Bostonian, later merged with the firm Castle and Cooke, which acquired Standard Fruit in 1968. In 1991, Castle and Cooke changed its name back to Dole Food Company.

Sizable landholdings, combined with the control of railroads, harbors, and communications, helped make U.S. banana corporations both influential and controversial. The term *banana republic* emerged as these corporations became involved in Central American politics to secure favorable conditions from governments in order to expand production. By 1948, United Fruit controlled three-quarters of the world trade in bananas. This monopoly caused the U.S. government to force the company to sell its operations in some production regions, reducing its domination of the banana industry.

The modern labor movement in the Central American plantations began in Honduras in May 1954, when approximately 12,000 workers went on strike for sixty-seven days at the Tela Railroad Company, a subsidiary of United Fruit. During the 1953–1958 presidential term of José Figueres Ferrer, the Costa Rican government negotiated the increased remission of United Fruit Company profits to the national government from 15 to 42 percent. Other banana-exporting nations subsequently pursued similar agreements.

In 1952, Ecuador became the world's largest banana producer, a position it held at the close of the twentieth century, followed by Brazil. Central America, northern South America, and the West Indies are also major growers. In the 1990s, the European Union enforced a quota system for banana imports, giving preference to those produced in their former colonies in the Caribbean, Africa, and the Pacific. The Latin American growers faced tariffs and no quota in their exports to Europe. The United States protested the European Union policy at the World Trade Organization, which found the policy unlawful and sided with the United States. The European Union argued that without the policy, the banana export industry of its former colonies would collapse. In 2000, the United States retaliated by imposing heavy tariffs on luxury goods imported from Europe. The following year, the European Union and the United States settled their differences, promising expanded access to the European market for Latin American bananas.

Five large companies dominate world trade in bananas in the early twenty-first century. Two-thirds of the trade is controlled by Chiquita, Dole, and the Del Monte Company, which entered the international banana business in 1968. The fourth largest banana exporter is the Ecuadorian company Noboa. In fifth place is the Irish-based company Fyffes, which is the second-largest distributor in the European Union market. The companies cultivate areas in the producing countries but also buy from contract growers, who may be locally owned companies or small-scale family farmers. Vertical integration extends along the production chain, as the multinationals operate shipping and distributing companies in the major markets of North America, Europe, and Japan.

David M. Carletta

References

Dosal, Paul J. *Doing Business with the Dictators: A Political History of United Fruit in Guatemala, 1899–1944.* Wilmington, DE: Scholarly Resources, 1993.

Karnes, Thomas L. *Tropical Enterprise: The Standard Fruit and Steamship Company in Latin America.* Baton Rouge: Louisiana State University Press, 1978.

Langley, Lester D., and Thomas Schoonover. *The Banana Men: American Mercenaries and Entrepreneurs in Central America, 1880–1930.* Lexington: University of Kentucky Press, 1995.

McCann, Thomas P. *An American Company: The Tragedy of United Fruit.* New York: Crown, 1976.

Stewart, Watt. *Keith and Costa Rica: A Biographical Study of Minor Cooper Keith.* Albuquerque: University of New Mexico Press, 1964.

See also: Atlantic Economy; Cacao; Coffee; Columbian Exchange—Agriculture; Costa Rica; Cotton; Dyes and Dyewood; Food; Guatemala; Henequen; Honduras; Maize; Sugar; Tobacco; Trade—Spain/Spanish America; Wine.

BANDEIRANTES

Bandeirantes were armed bands of colonists who set out from the coastal settlements of Brazil during the colonial period in search of gold and slaves in the unexplored interior. From the Portuguese word for flag, *bandeiras,* or commercially motivated expeditions whose members were known as bandeirantes, most often originated in São Paulo. Heterogeneous groups of armed men set off for periods of months or years, traveling across vast stretches of the South American interior by foot or canoe, in an epic quest for riches, be they in the form of gold or Indian slaves to feed the demand exerted by coastal sugar plantations.

Bandeiras typically included individuals of different ethnic origins, including Afro-Brazilians (both enslaved and free), mulattoes, and *mamelucos* (mixed Indian and Portuguese). Their journeys accelerated the processes of miscegenation and cultural exchange that provided the roots for Brazilian national identity in the twentieth century. Because of his mixed ethnic heritage and close identification with the land, the figure of the bandeirante who roamed the vast Brazilian interior proved attractive to later nationalists.

Mobility was a key characteristic of the bandeirante, leading some scholars to label bandeirantes as *pathfinders* instead of simply *colonists* or *pioneers.* Bandeirantes acted in various capacities: as slavers, prospectors, and militiamen. Though private investors typically organized and funded the bandeiras, at times the state played that role. For example, in the 1690s a bandeira under the leadership of Domingos Jorge Velho launched a final, successful effort to destroy Palmares, the famous runaway slave community (*quilombo*).

In the early colonial period, ongoing disputes between bandeirantes and Jesuits characterized life in the mission region surrounding present-day Paraguay. While the missionaries sought to "civilize" the Indians, the bandeirantes sought to capture them and sell them as slaves on coastal plantations. In response to the slaving raids, the Jesuits fortified their missions and received Crown permission to arm their indigenous residents. Thenceforth Indians living within the missions were generally safe from the slavers, though bandeirantes continued to launch raids against various native groups.

Early on, the bandeirantes discovered modest amounts of alluvial gold to the south of São Paulo, leading to the foundation of numerous new settlements throughout the seventeenth century, when the bandeirantes were at their height. The discovery of extensive deposits of mineral wealth, most notably gold, in the captaincy of Minas Gerais in the 1690s justified the pathfinders' ongoing quest. The core mining areas were settled quickly, as prospectors rushed in and the Crown sought to extend its power in Minas Gerais.

On the heels of the bandeirantes came settlers who extended economic activities in the newly accessible territories and founded permanent settlements. Beyond their direct financial contribution in terms of prospecting and slaving, the bandeirantes' explorations opened new lands to exploitation. Immense wealth flowed to Lisbon as a direct result of the bandeirantes' actions. The opening of the Brazilian interior brought tremendous economic rewards to Portugal, which used its new wealth to purchase manufactured goods from the English.

From that point the bandeirantes pushed farther westward and northward into Goiás and the Amazon region. The bandeirantes' activities directly contributed to the Portuguese Crown's acquisition in 1750 of lands lying far to the west of the boundary drawn between Spanish and Portuguese dominions by the 1494 Treaty of Tordesillas. The Treaty of Madrid voided the line of Tordesillas and instead demarcated the borders of the Spanish and Portuguese Empires in South America according to the principle of *uti possidentis,* which bases land ownership upon occupation or use rather than historical claim.

As they made their way through the Brazilian interior, the bandeirantes spread the Portuguese language and incorporated African and indigenous cultural traditions, contributing to the emergence of a new, truly American way of life. As a hybrid product of the Portuguese colonizers, indigenous Brazilians, and women and men of African descent, free and enslaved, the bandeirantes typified the kind of racial and cultural mixing that historian Gilberto Freyre identifies as the foundation of Brazilian national identity. In the interior, away from the interference of colonial authorities, the bandeirantes adapted to the land and changed the people living in the interior, while helping extend the boundaries of the Portuguese Empire. To many indigenous people in the interior, the bandeirantes represented their first direct contact with Europeans and Africans. The effects of these initial meetings were devastating, as disease, enslavement, and war contributed to the devastating depopulation of Brazil's indigenous populations.

By the late eighteenth century, the era of the bandeiras had come to an end. Planters utilized African rather than Indian slaves, and the Iberian powers had more or less settled their borders. The Brazilian interior remained largely unsettled and inaccessible until the middle of the twentieth century, when a generation of Brazilians took up where the bandeirantes had left off, seeking to exploit the interior's boundless economic potential. The legacy of the bandeirantes was in their extension of the borders of Portuguese America, discovering new sources of wealth and establishing routes of communication and transportation, as rudimentary as they were. Brazilian scholar Clodomir Vianna Moog compares bandeirantes with North American pioneers and concludes that the economic activities of the former were extractive rather than productive, and thus the bandeirantes failed to create sustainable settlements in the lands they claimed.

Beyond their material contribution, the bandeirantes' image survives. The figure of the bandeirante is a thoroughly American type that has inspired many a romantic paean from twentieth-century nationalists. Since São Paulo provided the staging ground for many of the bandeiras, the phenomenon is closely associated with the state, and the bandeirantes' popular image is central to contemporary constructions of national identity.

Emily Story

References

Morse, Richard M., ed. *The Bandeirantes: The Historical Role of the Brazilian Pathfinders.* New York: Knopf, 1965.

Vianna Moog, Clodomir. *Bandeirantes e pioneiros: Paralelo entre duas culturas.* 19th ed. Rio de Janeiro: Graphia, 2000.

See also: Amazon; Armies—Colonial Brazil; Bandits and Banditry; Brazil; Cimarrones; Colonists and Settlers II—Brazil; Columbian Exchange—Disease; Conquest II—Brazil; Defense—Colonial Brazil; Donatary Captaincies; Engenho; Jesuits—Brazil; Madrid, Treaty of (1750); Missions; Mulatto; Native Americans I–II; Palenque; Poetry—Brazil; Race; Slave Rebellions—Brazil; Slavery I—Brazil; Sugar; Tordesillas, Treaty of (1494); Women—Brazil.

BANDITS AND BANDITRY

Banditry has a long history on the Iberian Peninsula and in Latin America. Some bandits were social or political rebels, but few were actual Robin Hoods. Nevertheless, in both regions, many bandits achieved legendary status and are regarded as national heroes in popular culture. The prevalence of banditry in Iberia and Latin America, and the popularity of some bandits, have much to do with historical links between these regions, as well as similar socioeconomic structures and elements of a shared culture.

Banditry in Iberia dates back to at least the Roman Empire. However, it became far more widespread in Spain than Portugal after the sixteenth century. The Spanish region most notorious for banditry was Andalusia, where bandits enjoyed a golden age in the late eighteenth century. The most renowned brigand was Diego Corrientes (1757–1781), whose career lasted three years before he was captured and executed. Ballads about Corrientes credit him with defending unfortunate peasants against oppressive landlords.

Andalusia was also famous for women bandits, known as *serranas,* "mountain women," like the nineteenth-century heroines Torralba of Lucena and María Márquez Zafra (known as La Marichambo, a colloquial term that suggests her masculine qualities) who, according to legends, turned to outlawry to avenge the loss of their honor.

Banditry is most typical in societies with a predominantly rural and peasant population, and seems to rise at moments of intense social and economic crisis. Chronic banditry persisted in Spain until the early twentieth century, in the context of political upheaval and economic stagnation. It declined thereafter, but surged periodically as Spanish anarchists resisted Francisco Franco's regime after the Spanish Civil War. Their political banditry continued into the 1960s, and it resembles campaigns now waged by some Basque separatists.

Spanish bandits have fascinated both writers and artists. Bandits were painted by Spain's Francisco Goya and other European artists. Georges Bizet adapted his opera *Carmen* from the 1845 novel by Prosper Mérimée; in both works the character of Don José is based on the Andalusian outlaw José María. Meanwhile, Diego Corrientes appeared as a minor figure in *Astucia* (1865), a Mexican novel about smugglers and bandits written by Luis Gonzaga Inclán. Today, Corrientes remains the most celebrated figure; countless versions of his legend have appeared in the Spanish press, theater, songs, novels, poetry, and cinema, including the 1936 classic *Diego Corrientes,* by director Ignacio Iquino.

Banditry arrived in Latin America with the Spanish and the Portuguese. In colonial Brazil, banditry is usually associated with the *bandeirantes,* frontiersmen on slaving expeditions who raided indigenous settlements and missionary communities, or with raids by fugitive African slaves living in sanctuaries in the interior. Brazil's most famous bandits were *cangaceiros* (bandits) of the northeastern *sertão* (backland): Antônio Silvino and Virgulino Ferreira da Silva. Both were linked to local elites involved in power struggles, but each enjoyed a reputation as a popular hero.

In the Spanish colonies, banditry was sometimes associated with smuggling, and was most common along highways that linked silver and gold mining centers to coastal ports. New Spain, Peru, Colombia, and Panama were among the regions most afflicted. Banditry peaked in New Spain in 1710 before it was crushed by the Acordada, a new agency that received extraordinary powers to apprehend outlaws. The Acordada was exempt from judicial review procedures and had no restraints on jurisdiction or the number of agents appointed. Its success prompted other viceroyalties to introduce the Acordada and to enlarge its functions to include policing contraband and alcohol.

The many nineteenth-century wars of independence and their aftermath brought a resurgence of Latin American banditry. Existing bandit gangs offered mercenary services to royalist or patriot forces, often switching to the winning side. Cuban bandits plagued Spanish officials into the late nineteenth century, as outlawry and insurgency intertwined between the Ten Years' War (1868–1878) and the Cuban War of Independence (1895). This kind of partic-

Immortalized in songs and poems, Virgolino Ferreira da Silva, better known as Lampião, remains synonymous with his 23-year reign of terror in the arid hinterland of Brazil's impoverished northeast. Maria Bonita, Lampião's companion, is also shown standing alongside him. He earned the nickname Lampião, which translates as "Lantern," for his uncanny ability to light a path in the dark with lightning-fast shots from his rifle. Enduring fascination with Lampião has turned the bandit into a pop culture hero. (Reuters/Corbis)

ipation by bandits also happened during Latin America's many nineteenth-century civil wars. In Mexico during the War of the Reform (1858–1861) and the French Intervention (1862–1867), both liberal and conservative armies recruited bandits, known as the *plateados* (the silvered ones).

Latin America's bandits also captured the imagination of nineteenth-century Latin American and foreign observers. The rural and urban poor lionized their bandit heroes in forms of popular culture such as the *corrido,* a type of epic ballad that evolved from the Spanish *romance.* Some intellectuals also romanticized them, as did Argentina's José Fernández in his poem *El Gaucho Martín Fierro* (1879). Most writers, however, saw bandits as dangerous and backwards, as did Argentine Domingo Sarmiento (*Civilization and Barbarism,* 1845) or Frances Calderón de la Barca, the wife of Spain's first ambassador to Mexico, who discussed banditry in her *Life in Mexico* (1843). Mexican novelist Manuel Payno expressed this view in *Los bandidos de Río Frío* (1891), which he published in Spain while serving as consul in Barcelona.

Mexican bandit Pancho Villa is perhaps Latin America's most famous outlaw, and is today regarded by many as a hero of the Mexican Revolution (1910–1920). During the revolution, Villa expelled Spaniards from Chihuahua and appropriated their estates. Like Corrientes' in Spain, Villa's legend is widespread in Mexican culture.

As in Spain, banditry has declined in twentieth-century Latin America; however, it has not disappeared. Improved communication and transportation, as well as more effective policing, have reduced the scope for banditry, but it has persisted in areas plagued by economic, social, and political crises. Banditry became endemic in Colombia during and after the *Violencia,* a period of political warfare between liberals and conservatives that began in the late 1940s and still persists in many parts of the country.

Something of the aura of banditry has also appeared in popular attitudes toward the underworld of narco-trafficking. In Mexico and elsewhere, musical groups like the Tigres del Norte have popularized the so-called narco-corrido, which celebrates modern drug lords, just as bandit corridos once did outlaw heroes.

Chris Frazer

References

Hobsbawm, Eric. *Bandits.* New York: Pantheon, 1981.

Katz, Friedrich. *The Life and Times of Pancho Villa.* Stanford, CA: Stanford University Press, 1998.

Quiros, Constancio Bernaldo de. *El bandolerismo en España y México.* México: Editorial Juridica Mexicana, 1959.

Slatta, Richard, ed. *Bandidos: The Varieties of Latin American Banditry.* New York: Greenwood, 1987.

See also: Bandeirantes; Bourbon Reforms; Colombia; Contraband; Cuba; Fiction—Spanish America; Independence I–VI; Mexican Revolution; Mexico; Spanish Civil War and Latin America.

BANKS AND BANKING

Banks are establishments that safeguard, lend, exchange, or issue money, and commercial banks, investment banks, and central banks provide a wide range of services within these parameters. The development of such institutions in Latin America was severely hampered by the lack of such institutions in Spain—the late development of financial institutions in Latin America can be seen as a consequence of the lack of formal financial institutions in the mother country. Portuguese traders financed their trade through a variety of incipient credit transactions, but it was not until the early nineteenth century that the first formal lending institutions were created in Latin America.

Colonial Latin American witnessed the creation of a series of institutions that performed banking functions, which sometimes called themselves banks. However, these institutions were loosely organized as private investment groups. In fact, most of the lending in colonial Latin America was done by the Catholic Church or local merchant-traders. The nineteenth-century banks distinguished themselves from earlier institutions by the fact that they had official licenses to operate from the state. Commercial banking in Latin America in the nineteenth century developed under the aegis of European (mainly English, German, and French) merchant bankers. For example, the first Latin American banks were founded in Brazil in 1821 and Argentina in 1822, and these banks were funded by foreign investors.

The first official bank in Latin America was the first Banco do Brasil, established in 1808 on the initiative of the recently arrived Portuguese regent. Although local banks were the result of local initiative, foreign banks and bankers played an important role in the development of banking in Latin America in the second half of the nineteenth century. Foreign banks' involvement in Latin America was closely related to the growth of foreign trade and investment, the main instruments of the export-led economic development of the nineteenth century. British banks, following the steps of British merchants and paving the way for British investors, led the way with the establishment of both the London Buenos Ayres and River Plate Bank in 1862, and the London and Brazilian Bank in the same year. Their example was followed by other European banks, which settled in areas that were crucial to their trading interests.

More significant for Latin American bank development was the creation of the second Banco do Brasil in 1851, established by the Brazilian financier and industrialist Baron of Mauá. The bank merged in 1853 with the Banco Commercial de Rio de Janeiro to form the first large-scale institution of commercial credit in Latin America, followed by the foundation in 1854 of the Banco de la Provincia de Buenos Aires in Argentina. In Mexico, the first private banks were formed during the time of Emperor Maximilian's reign (1864–1867), but it was not until a commercial code outlined specific bank charter regulations in 1884 under President Porfirio Díaz that banks became an important part of the financial system. The Banco Nacional de Mexico, or Banamex, was the largest and most important bank of late nineteenth-century Mexico. Banamex had almost exclusive note-issuance privileges, managed the government's budget, and was in charge of servicing the government's domestic and foreign debt. Thus it behaved

much as central banks do today, but it was a private bank, with a large number of European banks holding important proportions of Banamex shares. Regional banking also expanded during this period, although it was rather slow compared to regional banking development in other parts of the world. While regional banks flourished in Great Britain, France, and the United States, regional banking in Mexico was more in line with the trends in regional banking in Spain. Even with bank charters, Latin American governments exercised little control over foreign and local banks. Banks applied for a charter or operating license, and thereafter operated independently, like any other business. The restriction of note-issuance privileges (that is, the right to print money) and the introduction of reserve ratios and controls of banking legislation were characteristics of twentieth-century banking.

Note-issuing privileges were gradually stripped from private banks as governments increasingly participated in discussions about monetary policy and at times were instrumental in the creation of monetary policy. Today, only central banks issue money, and they have become the sole managers of the banknote supply. These institutions were created throughout Latin America in the 1920s. In the aftermath of turn-of-the-century currency depreciations caused by the increasing indebtedness of Latin American governments, the notion of establishing central banks to serve as overseers of the system, clearinghouses, and monetary policy directors was championed by Edwin Kemmerer. Kemmerer was a U.S. economics professor from Princeton who traveled to Colombia, Chile, Ecuador, Bolivia, and Peru in the 1920s and 1930s to aid in the establishment of independent central banks. Sir Otto Niemeyer of the Bank of England was equally important in the creation of the Argentine Central Bank in 1935. Kemmerer and Niemeyer reflect both the continuing importance of foreign influence and experience in the development of the Latin American banking system, as well as the concern of the international markets for creating stable financial systems in Latin America.

The Mexican Central Bank, the Banco de Mexico, was created in 1925 after the destruction of the Porfirian bank system during the Mexican Revolution (1910–1917). The Mexican Central Bank was created to oversee the financial system and to preserve the soundness of the country's fiscal policy. The accompanying banking legislation gradually transformed Mexico's Central Bank into the axis around which the country's financial system turned.

Modern banking in this sense in Brazil also dates to the early twentieth century, where it was instituted in response to the institutional shocks caused by the end of the centralized empire in 1889. The new Brazilian republic experienced a series of bank failures in 1900 and 1901 that, like the Mexican Revolution, left the country with no organized banking system. The creation of the Banco do Brasil and Brazil's adherence to the gold standard after 1905 were the first steps in Brazil's modern banking history. The Banco do Brasil functioned as a central bank to the government and was also the only national commercial bank for the private sector. New banking legislation and the strength of the Banco do Brasil paved the way for stability and growth in the regional banking system, which became increasingly responsive to the needs of the growing economy, while the federal government used the banking system through the Banco do Brasil to implement monetary policy and reallocate financial resources throughout the public sector. The Banco de la Republica Oriental del Uruguay played a similarly dual role, as a large commercial bank with central bank functions. It was not until 1965 that the public- and private-sector activities of the Banco do Brasil were formally separated, resulting in the creation of the Banco Central do Brasil; in 1967, Uruguay followed suit and created the Banco Central del Uruguay.

Latin American governments became increasingly involved in encouraging specific economic activities, especially because for most of these long-term development projects, private commercial support was hard to find. Peru established the Banco Agrario in 1931, the Banco Industrial in 1936, and the Banco Minero in 1941, created to support agricultural, industrial, and mining projects respectively. The Venezuelan government followed the same strategy and set up the Banco Agricola y Agropecuario in 1928, the Banco Industrial in 1937, and the Banco Obrero, which financed low-income housing, in 1941; the Colombian Caja de Credito Agrario, Industrial y Minero was founded in 1931. In Mexico and Brazil, state-run corporations were created to finance long-term domestic development. Nacional Financiera (Nafinsa) was created in Mexico in 1934 and the Banco Nacional de Desenvolvimiento Economico (BNDE) in Brazil in 1952. Both institutions raise funds internationally and domestically to provide long-term funds for domestic development projects, especially in infrastructure.

The greatest challenge to the stability of Latin American banks was the debt crisis of the 1980s. Central banks oversaw commercial banks to ensure their solvency and liquidity by establishing minimum capital requirements, capital-to-deposit ratios, and limits on credit expansion. These controls, however, failed tragically in the early 1980s. The debt crisis was the result of Latin America's inability to maintain full service on its foreign debt, which had grown to dangerously high levels during the 1970s. Both Mexico and Venezuela, as major petroleum exporters, benefited from rising international oil prices during the 1970s. The oil income made these countries very favorable credit risks, and this attractiveness, coupled with a worldwide slump in interest rates, led to increasing rates of foreign indebtedness. Foreign banks offered credit at very low interest rates, and both countries relied on future oil income to service and pay back any amount of indebtedness. Brazil's military government followed a similar logic, and increased its foreign indebtedness in the wake of better-than-average economic growth during the 1970s. Even in Latin American countries that did not produce oil, foreign bankers still offered loans, as the success of the oil-producing economies spread throughout the region. As Latin American countries opened to foreign markets (under a widespread policy known throughout Latin America as "import-substitution industrialization"), foreign private and institutional lenders warmed to the new opportunities presented by the region. Latin American governments and banks were all too eager to borrow from foreign banks. Between 1970 and 1980, the region's total foreign debt increased by more than 1,000 percent.

The end of the 1970s brought about a world recession, which gradually eroded demand for Latin America's main export goods. At the same time, interest rates rose

in the United States and Western Europe, as governments sought to curb inflationary pressures and make other difficult adjustments. As interest rates rose, floating interest rate debt service increased, and as currencies depreciated, Latin America faced an increasingly high debt bill, with fewer resources with which to pay it. In September 1982, Mexico declared a moratorium on its foreign debt, and nationalized its crippled banking system soon thereafter. The debt crisis highlighted one of the main weaknesses of the Latin American banking system: its overreliance on external funds and low levels of domestic savings. While nationalizations such as Mexico's remained exceptional, throughout most of the 1980s, governments shaped the restructuring of their banking system through policies implemented by the central banks. However, political changes led to increasing support among Latin American governments for independent central banks and increasing foreign ownership of domestic banks. This shift was bolstered by the need to avoid another round of overexposure problems and help strengthen the banking system after the crises that rocked Latin America in the mid-1990s and the ripple effect of the Asian debt crisis in the late 1990s. Today, Mexico's, Brazil's, and Argentina's central banks no longer are extensions of the government's budgetary and monetary policy and have become independent institutions, while most of the largest commercial banks and financial groups have merged with or increased the shareholder participation of U.S., Canadian, and European banks. However, with the exception of Banco Santander's purchase of large shares of Latin American banks, Spain's role in banking in Latin America is relatively small.

Juliette Levy

References

Bulmer-Thomas, Victor. *The Economic History of Latin America since Independence.* Cambridge: Cambridge University Press, 1994.

Coatsworth, John H., and Alan M. Taylor, eds. *Latin America and the World Economy since 1800.* Cambridge: Harvard University, David Rockefeller Center for Latin American Studies, 1998.

Ludlow, Leonor, and Carlos Marichal, eds. *Banca y poder en Mexico, 1800–1925.* Mexico: Grijalbo, 1986.

Triner, Gail D. *Banking and Economic Development: Brazil, 1889–1930.* New York: Palgrave, 2000.

See also: Atlantic Economy; Caribbean Community and Common Market; Catholic Church in Brazil; Catholic Church in Spanish America; Credit— Colonial Latin America; Independence II—Brazil; Mexican Revolution; North American Free Trade Agreement; Oil; Trade—Spain/Spanish America.

BEATAS

Beatas were celibate women dedicated to a religious life who did not belong to a monastic order. They were a relatively common feature of late medieval and early modern Spanish and Spanish American society, but the Catholic Church began to question their religious status by the late sixteenth century.

As a group, beatas are difficult to characterize. They often donned a religious habit even though they had not taken monastic vows. Some lived alone, either in their own homes or in those of their patrons; others resided in communities, *beaterios.* Some engaged primarily in charitable activities, such as teaching young girls or ministering to the ill, elderly, or abandoned; others devoted themselves largely to prayer and contemplation. Beatas ranged across the economic spectrum. Many came from poor families who could not afford the substantial dowries that convents regularly demanded upon profession as a nun. These beatas either labored or begged for their livelihood. On the other hand, some possessed enough wealth to found beaterios and fund works of charity. Because beatas did not swear solemn vows, they could pursue a religious life either temporarily or permanently.

On occasion, certain beatas acquired reputations for exceptional holiness and gathered followings of devotees. These exceptional beatas often gained renown on account of the visions and other mystical states they experienced. Others gained adherents because of their remarkable asceticism or heroic acts of charity. María de Toledo, a fifteenth-century beata chosen as the subject of a hagiography, practiced both charity and contemplation at different points in her life. She began her charitable activities, work in hospitals and prisons, and distribution of food to the poor after her husband died. She later lived as a hermit and practiced severe self-mortification. During the latter phase of her life, she was known to have visions, and reportedly predicted the fall of Muslim Granada to Ferdinand and Isabella. A handful of beatas earned such fame that they became candidates for canonization, for example Juana de la Cruz, a sixteenth-century beata from Spain. Many of these notable beatas used their positions to preach sermons or advocate reforms of public religious life. María de Toledo, for instance, played an instrumental part in persuading Ferdinand and Isabella to establish the Spanish Inquisition.

The influence some beatas exercised transgressed established gender roles and could prompt the Church to question a beata's religious orthodoxy and undermine her status. Although most beatas confided in male confessors, a priest's supervision could not necessarily forestall an investigation by the Inquisition. Because beatas wielded religious authority but were not subject to the discipline of the cloister, their status was always insecure.

After the Council of Trent (1545–1563) decreed enclosure for all nuns, the position of beatas became more precarious. Inquisition cases against beatas, usually for false visions or excessive religious enthusiasm, increased over the late sixteenth and early seventeenth centuries as the Church sought to disperse communities of beatas or transform beaterios into convents. The Church's campaign against beatas was largely successful by the end of the seventeenth century, as beaterios, and presumably beatas as well, decreased in number.

Brian R. Larkin

References

Muñoz Fernández, Angela. *Beatas y santas neocastellanas: Ambivalencias de la religion y políticas correctoras del poder (ss. XIV–XVI).* Madrid: Comunidad de Madrid, 1994.

Perry, Mary Elizabeth. *Gender and Disorder in Early Modern Seville.* Princeton, NJ: Princeton University Press, 1990.

See also: Catholic Church in Spanish America; Clergy—Secular, in Colonial Spanish America; Council of Trent; Inquisition—Spanish America; Papacy; Religious Orders; Women—Colonial Spanish America.

BELIZE

Located on the Caribbean coast, with Mexico to the north and Guatemala to the west and south, Belize is the only former British colony in Central America. Once known as British Honduras, the nation became independent in 1981. The Spaniards who ar-

rived in the late sixteenth century found Mayas inhabiting the region. Mayan communities granted in *encomienda* (a grant of rights to collect taxes and enjoy the labor of conquered indigenous communities) to the few Spanish settlers were forced to pay tribute, but Spain's authority remained weak due to resistance, rebellion, and flight.

The British presence in Belize began with the buccaneers' use of the Bay of Honduras as a base for attacking Spanish shipping. The abundance of logwood trees, used to produce textile dyes, prompted interest in a permanent settlement, which was abandoned and resettled many times, as British baymen came under repeated attack from Spanish authorities. In addition to logwood, baymen sought mahogany, which was used to build ships and furniture and continued to be the area's primary export until surpassed by sugar in the mid-twentieth century. In the 1720s, baymen began importing African slaves, who outnumbered their masters by the end of the century. The Spanish and English entered into various treaties granting logging rights to the baymen while acknowledging Spanish sovereignty.

Britain was hesitant to set up formal government in the settlement for fear of provoking Spain. By 1738, baymen were governing themselves through annually elected magistrates. Rear Admiral Sir William Burnaby, commander in chief of Jamaica, codified the settlement's laws in 1765. The first British superintendent of the settlement, Colonel Marcus Despard, was sent from Jamaica to take up his post in 1786. That same year, when the British evacuated settlements at Roatán and the Mosquito Coast, over 2,000 new settlers and their slaves moved to Belize. The Garifunas, descendants of Caribs and Africans who escaped slavery, were forcibly resettled in the Bay Islands (now Islas de la Bahía, Honduras) after their deportation from Saint Vincent in 1796. The Garifunas then migrated to the Central American Caribbean coast, including present-day southern Belize.

In 1798, Arturo O'Neil, captain-general of Yucatán, was defeated in Spain's final military attempt to remove the bay-men at the battle of Saint George's Cay. Belize benefited from increased British trade with the newly independent nations that emerged from colonial Spanish America after 1821. Slaves were emancipated in the 1830s, but many freedmen soon found themselves in debt peonage. By the 1850s, thousands of Maya and mestizo refugees from the Caste War in Yucatán (1846–1848) had migrated to Belize.

The 1859 Anglo-Guatemalan Treaty defined the boundaries of Belize and called for the building of a road from Guatemala City to the Caribbean coast. In 1862, the settlement was designated as a crown colony, which was officially administered through Jamaica until 1884. A year after the designation, Britain and Guatemala negotiated responsibilities regarding the road's construction, but Guatemala failed to ratify the agreement within the specified time. The road was never constructed, leading to enduring claims by Guatemala that the unfulfilled treaty signified that it had never ceded the land of Belize inherited from Spain after independence.

In 1871, the crown colony governmental system was introduced, whereby colonial administrators were appointed by the British Crown. Land ownership remained dominated by a few wealthy families affiliated with metropolitan corporations. By 1880, the colony's largest landholder was the Belize Estate and Produce Company. Between 1880 and 1930, the export of chicle, a sapodilla tree extract used to make chewing gum, provided further economic growth. The Great Depression of the 1930s brought widespread labor unrest, which developed into a nationalist movement. Elections in the colony resumed in 1936 under a severely restricted franchise. Nevertheless, elected officials increasingly influenced administration. The General Workers' Union was registered in 1943. The union supported the nationalist movement, which gained strength after the formation of Belize's first political party, the People's United Party, and the expansion of the franchise to all literate adults in 1954.

After internal independence was granted in 1963, Guatemala suspended diplomatic relations with Britain in protest. Ten years later, British Honduras was officially renamed Belize. The ongoing dispute with Guatemala delayed formal independence as a member of the Commonwealth of Nations until 1981. George Cadle Price, one of the founders of the People's United Party, was elected the country's first prime minister in a parliamentary democracy based on the Westminster system. Guatemala did not reopen diplomatic relations with Britain until 1987. The influx during the 1980s of an estimated 30,000 Central American war refugees and settlers into a population of 200,000 profoundly changed Belizean society. By 1991, the nation's Spanish speakers were a majority. The withdrawal of the United Kingdom's garrison in 1994 had marked economic effects in Belize, where tourism has become a major source of revenue, capitalizing on rich archaeological sites and the world's second longest barrier reef.

David M. Carletta

Belize's Prime Minister George Price (L) accepts Constitutional Instruments for Belize from Prince Michael, Duke of Kent, on Independence Day for the world's newest nation in Central America, September 1981. (Bettmann/Corbis)

References

Bolland, O. Nigel, *The Formation of a Colonial Society: Belize, from Conquest to Crown Colony.* Baltimore: Johns Hopkins University Press, 1977.

Dobson, Narda. *A History of Belize.* London: Longman Caribbean, 1973.

Krohn, Lita Hunter, ed. *Readings in Belizean History.* 2nd ed. Belize City: Belizean Studies, St. John's College, 1987.

Merrill, Tim. *Guyana and Belize: Country Studies.* 2nd ed. Washington, DC: Federal Research Division, Library of Congress, 1993.

See also: Caste War of Yucatán; Dyes and Dyewood; Encomienda; Guatemala; Native Americans IV—Mesoamerica; Pirates and Piracy; Sugar; Travel and Tourism.

BIGAMY, TRANSATLANTIC

Bigamy—the crime of marrying one person while legally married to another—evolved from the Catholic notion that marriage created a permanent and indissoluble union. During the colonial period, the Church accepted neither long absences of a spouse, adultery, nor a quarrelsome or troublesome spouse as grounds for terminating marriage.

Trials of accused bigamists took place in either secular or episcopal courts, as marrying twice contravened not only canon law but also the laws of civil society. Some bigamists defended themselves by arguing that they had been coerced into their first marriage. Lack of consent was a key defense in bigamy trials, as Spanish Catholicism (after the Council of Trent, 1547–1563) placed a high priority on the individual's right to choose a spouse without interference. Punishment for bigamy included fines, prison sentences, a hundred or more lashes, temporary exile or banishment from the area, and galley sentences for men. Women and men were also ordered to have no association with their second spouse and/or to take up residence with their first spouse.

Population movement, often over long distances, during the colonial period contributed to the number of bigamous relationships that came to trial. Spanish men regularly traveled far from their home regions, where a combination of high population densities and predominance of marginal land limited their opportunities. Some crossed the ocean to escape debt, the law, and the constraints of an unwanted marriage, as well as to seek brighter prospects and fortune. In the colonies, such as Mexico, the contingent and mobile nature of some types of employment, including those engaged as muleteers, shepherds, seamen, soldiers, and even artisans, required or facilitated men's movement.

Temporary absences could turn into permanent ones, and second marriages often followed after a new life had been established. Although many male bigamists initially entered into sexual relations with women with no intent on marrying, community members, clerics, and officials often pressured the couple to marry. The decree issued by Charles I that all *encomenderos* (Spanish men who had received *encomienda* grants) live in unions of marriage led some to remarry in the colonies. Some bigamists willingly remarried to fill the requirements of respectability and to be judged as law-abiding Christians. Marriage offered a way to integrate their new families into the social and religious world of the parish, as well as to ensure personal and familial honor.

For the women in Spain who remained behind under the watchful eye of friends and family, the temporary sojourns of their husbands often turned into permanent disappearances. Some wives, desperate and angry after waiting an average of fifteen to twenty years, remarried. A rumor of a husband's death was another reason, but long distances sometimes meant that news was not accurate or made written certified proof of death, which was needed for an official declaration, difficult. Women accused of bigamy were often those who had married without proof of a husband's death, or perhaps had forged the necessary documents. In Mexico, abandonment and *la mala vida* (literally, "the bad life"), which referred to abuse, overwork, and lack of support, led women to leave their spouses and later remarry.

Susanne Eineigel

References

Altman, Ida. "Emigrants and Society: An Approach to the Background of Colonial Spanish America." *Comparative Studies in Society and History* 30, no. 1 (January 1988): 170–190.

Boyer, Richard. *Lives of the Bigamists: Marriage, Family, and Community in Colonial Mexico.* Albuquerque: University of New Mexico Press, 1995.

Cook, Alexandra Parma, and Noble David Cook. *Good Faith and Truthful Ignorance: A Case of Transatlantic Bigamy.* Durham, NC: Duke University Press, 1991.

Poska, Allyson M. "When Bigamy Is the Charge: Gallegan Women and the Holy Office." Pp. 189–205 in *Women in the Inquisition: Spain and the New World,* edited by Mary E. Giles. Baltimore: Johns Hopkins University Press, 1999.

Seed, Patricia. *To Love, Honor, and Obey in Colonial Mexico: Conflicts over Marriage Choice, 1574–1821.* Stanford, CA: Stanford University Press, 1988.

See also: Catholic Church in Spanish America; Council of Trent; Encomienda; Family—Colonial Brazil; Family—Colonial Spanish America; Inquisition—Luso-America; Inquisition—Spanish America; Laws—Colonial Latin America; Marriage; Prostitution; Women—Brazil; Women—Colonial Spanish America.

BOLIVIA

At once a place of cultural richness and substantial natural resources, Bolivia, one of South America's two landlocked nations, remains one of the poorest and least developed countries in the Western Hemisphere. Its current population of just over 8 million people suffers from one of Latin America's lowest life expectancy rates (61 for males and 66 for females), highest infant mortality rates (60.4/1,000), and highest percentage of citizens living in poverty. Indeed, over 70 percent of Bolivians live at or below the poverty level, a fact that becomes even more shocking considering the relatively high rate of poverty (35 percent) for Latin America as a whole (Goodwin 2004, 67–70).

Bolivia's story, however, is not one of perpetual hardship and steady sorrow. It was the birthplace of one of the world's most sophisticated and fascinating prehistoric dynasties (the Inca). And early in its colonial history, King Charles V bestowed the title of Imperial City on Potosí, Bolivia's most famous mining city. Potosí was the nerve center of Spain's dominion in the New World for at least a fragment of the colonial period, and the silver extracted from Bolivian mines provided for the Habsburg and Bourbon kings an enormous source of revenue, which they used to, among other things, beautify, develop, and enrich Spain and its vast empire.

How then did this land of plenty become so poverty-stricken? How can a place that counts among its natural resources tin, natural gas, petroleum, zinc, tungsten, silver, iron, lead, gold, and hydropower be so indubitably poor? Why are Bolivians, as a whole, malnourished when the country's soil and climate enable the potentially abundant growth of soybeans, corn, sugarcane, coffee, rice, potatoes, and a wide array of tropical fruits and vegetables? The answer to these questions is complicated and controversial. But by most accounts, Bolivia's long and difficult colonial past (orchestrated by the Spanish monarchy and its royal authorities in the New World), combined with the vagaries of its national history, replete as it is with lost wars, extreme social inequality, racial unrest, and political instability, has much to do with the country's current predicament.

European colonialism began in Bolivia with the arrival of the Spaniards in the 1530s. Long home to Native American groups (mainly Aymara speakers) who were restless subjects of the mighty, imperialistic Incas (rulers of much of the Central Andean highlands from roughly 1200 to the 1530s), the territories south and east of Lake Titicaca were not particularly attractive to the Spanish newcomers until the discovery of rich silver veins in Potosí in the mid-1540s. Most of the colonial mining centers, including the Imperial City, were located in the windswept *altiplano* (high plateau), a dry tableland that runs south from Lake Titicaca between the great Andean mountain ranges. At an average of over 12,000 feet in elevation, this inhospitable, rugged ecological zone became, by 1600, one of the world's

strongest human magnets, attracting enterprising Spanish colonists and their subjugated (Indian) and enslaved (African)
laborers.

To recognize the growing political and
commercial importance of the region,
Philip II officially created the Audiencia
(High Court) of Charcas by issue of a royal
decree dated June 12, 1559. This territory,
which was also called Upper Peru, came to
encompass most of the territory of modern
Bolivia. Chuquisaca (the name of which
was changed by the Spaniards to La Plata,
after independence renamed Sucre in hom-
age to the famous liberator Antonio José de
Sucre) and Potosí were the important administrative and mining centers in the
south. Santa Cruz de la Sierra became the
frontier staging center for military and missionary expeditions in the east. The cen-
trally located Cochabamba Valley and its
surrounding area grew from a collection of
small farms into the primary granary of Potosí. And La Paz, with its ecologically diverse provinces and dense indigenous populations, dominated the northern sector of
Upper Peru.

As happened elsewhere in the Americas, Indians under Spanish rule in Upper
Peru died from European diseases and suffered from the colonists' exploitation of
their labor. But the relative density of the
pre-Columbian population in the region
ensured Spaniards a fairly steady workforce
throughout most of the colonial period.
The *encomienda,* which granted labor
rights and locally produced goods to "de-
serving" Spaniards, survived in most parts
of Upper Peru until the implementation of
Viceroy Francisco de Toledo's reforms of
the 1570s, which transferred direct control
over Indian populations to the Crown. The

most consequential of the Toledan reforms,
in terms of its effect on Upper Peru's social
structure, was undoubtedly the *mita,*
which required all able-bodied men from
specific districts to work for six-month periods, once every seven years, at Potosí (or
another mine) or on Spanish-owned farms
and ranches. These rotational draft laborers
(called *mitayos*) might also be required to
work on public work projects for the
Crown or in the service of Spanish-owned
businesses.

To be sure, the mita system's labor requirements posed a serious threat to Native
American social structure in Upper Peru
throughout the colonial period. Some Mitayos never returned home from their work
assignments because of death or flight. Native American women sometimes uprooted
their families from their ancestral homelands to become wage laborers themselves
in the mining districts and their supporting
cities. Indian children, as young as seven or
eight, sometimes went to work in the un-
derground mines to help themselves and
their families survive.

As the colonial period wore on, Native
Americans throughout Upper Peru began
to resist the draft labor system (called *repartimiento* in New Spain) in creative ways.
Many abandoned their native villages and
became members of a floating, and ever-
expanding, migrant labor force not subject
to the onerous demands of the mita. These
forasteros, as they were called, may have had
few rights and limited access to land, but
they were also not bound to pay tribute
taxes to the Crown until the eighteenth
century. Still other Native Americans
(called *yanaconas*) attached themselves to
local large landowners (*hacendados*), becoming in effect indentured servants who,

in exchange for their labor on the estates, obtained usufruct land use and, more importantly, protection from the Crown's labor and tribute tax obligations. By the end of the colonial period, forasteros and yanaconas in Upper Peru well outnumbered Indians (called *originarios* or *tributarios*) who maintained their traditional connections to their ancestral homelands.

Bolivian society from the 1530s to the early 1800s (and indeed beyond) is a case study of socioeconomic and racial polarization. Even during the silver-mining depression, which lasted from 1650 to 1750, most whites living in Upper Peru enjoyed a significantly better and certainly longer life than their darker-skinned workers. Nevertheless, the depression had a profound effect on Upper Peruvian society on the whole, as Spaniards (and their capital) moved out of the mining districts, and as the economy in the secondary markets, namely La Plata and Cochabamba, constricted.

In the late 1750s, 1760s, and 1770s, however, the silver-mining industry in Potosí and throughout many altiplano provinces (especially Oruro) experienced a momentary, yet portentous, revival. This boom was significant for a number of reasons, not the least of which had to do with the renewed and extensive exploitation of Indian labor in the mines. But in terms of the region's late colonial and early republican history, this economic recovery was accompanied by a major shift of focus, politically and commercially, away from Peru and toward Argentina. In fact, as part of the Bourbon reforms implemented in the latter half of the eighteenth century, the Audiencia of Charcas was transferred to the jurisdiction of the Viceroyalty of the Río de La Plata, based in the viceregal capital of Buenos Aires.

This legal, administrative change had less impact on the average Upper Peruvian than other Bourbon reforms that targeted, among other things, more efficient tax collection and increased production. Logically, those paying most of the taxes (namely originarios and, by this time, forasteros) and those doing most of the work (the same) were those most unhappy with the new laws. The fact that the Andean region in general, and the altiplano specifically, experienced a surge of local rebellions after the 1750s is not surprising. Between 1750 and the outbreak of the famous Túpac Amaru and Túpac Catari rebellions in 1781 (which spanned an area roughly from the Cuzco region in the north to Oruro in the south), colonial officials recorded no fewer than ninety-six popular insurrections.

While the Amaru and Catari movements, in Lower and Upper Peru, respectively, ultimately failed to achieve their leaders' main goal of self-rule, the reverberations of the revolts were felt years later when, in the first decade of the nineteenth century, Latin America's wars for independence from Spain began. Racial fears and distrust, coupled with distinct memories of the violence and bloodshed of the early 1780s (over 100,000 people were killed, mostly Native Americans), united most whites in Upper Peru to resist opening the door to political change, even while revolutionaries like José de San Martín and Simón Bolívar were liberating most of the rest of South America in the 1810s and early 1820s. Indeed, it was not until Upper Peru stood alone as the only mainland territory still part of the Spanish Empire that the region's Creole elite recognized the inevitable and went over to the patriot cause to defeat the royalists at the last battle (Tumusla, April 1, 1825) in the Latin American wars for independence. Just over four months later, on August 6, 1825, Upper Peru (now Bolivia, named of course after the Great Liberator, Simón Bolívar) achieved independence from Spain and thus the country's difficult transition from colony to republic and modern nation began.

Bolivia's national history is best understood as a series of struggles, experiments, and setbacks, interspersed with moments of prosperity and hope. Since 1825, Bolivia has alternately been ruled by caudillos, elected presidents, and, in the twentieth century, military dictators. Each government (there have been about eighty changes of government and sixteen different functional constitutions since independence) has had to deal with profound economic problems, social discord, and pressure from external forces, which at times has threatened Bolivia's national integrity.

One of the primary obstacles to economic growth and stability stems from the country's loss of its coastline and adjoining rich nitrate fields to Chile in the War of the Pacific (1870–1883). In fact, over time Bolivia has lost about half of its original national territory (and thus access to valuable natural resources like rubber, petroleum, and natural gas) as a result of lost wars with neighboring countries (Brazil, 1903; Paraguay, 1932–1935). In the twentieth century, Bolivia was one of the world's leading producers of tin, but recent labor disagreements, market instability, the relatively high cost of shipment to the coast, and the declining quality of the mined ore have led to emphasis on agricultural exports like soybeans, coffee, and cotton.

The 1952 revolution led by the reformer Victor Paz Estensorro and his middle-class Movimiento Nacional Revolucionario (MNR) party sparked a dramatic transformation in Bolivia, which resulted in the redistribution of land to peasants, the universal right to vote, and the nationalization of Bolivian mines. Paz Estensorro's populist demands for government-led development gained widespread acclaim in progressive political circles, but he was never able to overcome the historical legacy in Bolivia, which seems to favor military-based rule. Indeed, the MNR was overthrown by army generals in 1964, but Paz Estensorro returned to the presidency in the mid-1980s and championed neoliberal reforms to diminish the effect of Bolivia's hyperinflation, caused in part by the excessive borrowing of previous governments.

One especially controversial feature of Bolivia's historical development in the twentieth century centers on the nation's production and export of coca. Long considered a sacred plant, coca, which is used in countless social, religious, and domestic rituals among the nation's peasantry, today has become a symbol for many Bolivians of their heritage, independence, and national honor. Indeed, foreign-led efforts headed by the United States to eradicate the coca plant have provoked widespread social and political opposition movements. In any case, coca remains an important part of the national economy, with, according to some estimates, roughly 400,000 Bolivians engaged in some aspect of its production, harvest, transportation, and export.

Bolivia is, by international standards, a rural country, with over half its residents living outside the major urban areas of La Paz, Santa Cruz, Cochabamba, and Sucre.

View of dense crowd gathering to greet President Victor Paz Estensorro during inauguration ceremonies for the new Cochabamba–Santa Cruz highway. Cochabamba, Bolivia, October 1, 1954. (Time Life Pictures/Getty Images)

The major languages spoken are Spanish, Quechua, and Aymara, and about 95 percent of Bolivians consider themselves to be Roman Catholic. Ethnically, Bolivia remains one of the most indigenous of all nations in Latin America, with whites of European ancestry constituting only 15 percent of the total population. This ethnic minority, however, continues to control most of the nation's businesses and political parties, and thus in some respects Bolivia has not been able to shed the colonial pattern of European domination.

Caleb P. S. Finegan

References

Abercrombie, Thomas. *Pathways of Memory and Power: Ethnography and History among an Andean People.* Madison: University of Wisconsin Press, 1998.

Arnade, Charles. *The Emergence of the Republic of Bolivia.* New York: Russell and Russell, 1970.

Arzáns de Orsúa y Vela, Bartolomé. *Tales of Potosí.* Edited, with an introduction, by R. C. Padden; translated by Francis M. López-Morillas. Providence, RI: Brown University Press, 1975.

Cole, Jeffrey. *The Potosí Mita, 1573–1700: Compulsory Indian Labor in the Andes.* Stanford, CA: Stanford University Press, 1985.

Cornblit, Oscar. *Power and Violence in the Colonial City: Oruro from the Mining Renaissance to the Rebellion of Túpac Amaru.* Cambridge: Cambridge University Press, 1995.

Goodwin, Paul Jr. *Global Studies: Latin America.* 11th ed. Dubuque, IA: McGraw-Hill/Dushkin, 2004.

Grindle, Merilee, and Pilar Domingo, eds. *Proclaiming Revolution: Bolivia in Comparative Perspective.* London: Institute of Latin American Studies, 2003.

Klein, Herbert S. *A Concise History of Bolivia.* Cambridge: Cambridge University Press, 2003.

Larson, Brooke. *Cochabamba, 1550–1900: Colonialism and Agrarian Transformation in Bolivia.* Durham, NC: Duke University Press, 1998.

See also: Atlantic Economy; Audiencias; Ayllu; Bourbon Reforms; Catholic Church in Spanish America; Chaco War; Coca; Coffee; Colonists and Settlers I—Andes; Columbian Exchange—Disease; Conquest I— Andes; Cotton; Drugs; Encomienda; Habsburgs; Hacienda; Independence I—Argentina; Independence VI—Peru; Mining—Silver; Mita; Monarchs of Spain; Native Americans V—Central and Southern Andes; Peru; Potosí; Repartimiento; Rubber; Túpac Amaru Revolt; Yanancona.

BORDERLANDS

The term *Borderlands* is used to define a historical region colonized by Spain that embraces areas that are today parts of northern Mexico and the American Southwest. The identification of the Mexican and the U.S. states that comprise the Borderlands varies, but generally includes the following: in Mexico, Baja California, Sinaloa, Sonora, Durango, Chihuahua, Coahuila, Nuevo León, and Tamaulipas; in the United States, California, Arizona, New Mexico, and Texas. Some scholars include Florida, although the Spanish colonization of Florida followed a different trajectory, with closer ties to the Caribbean than to Mexico. The term has also come to be used to refer to the theory that the history of this region is different from the history of Mexico and the United States, that it is a hybrid history. Historian Herbert E. Bolton defined the concept in the early twentieth century and spawned an academic subfield in Borderlands history.

The Borderlands constituted the northern frontier of Mexico at the end of the colonial period, though of course the frontier, in the sense of the region at the edge of the settled area, shifted during the history of colonial Mexico. The first frontier can be called the near northern frontier, a region that developed after about 1550, following the discovery of silver at Zacatecas in 1548. Zacatecas was located beyond the area populated by sedentary natives, and the nomadic hunter-gatherers, collectively called the Chichimecs, began to raid the supply trains moving from central Mexico to Zacatecas. What followed was a war that lasted for forty years, until the Spanish developed a strategy to pacify the Chichimec bands. The far northern frontier is what today is conventionally referred to as the Borderlands.

Within the far northern frontier of colonial Mexico, there were several different types of frontiers. For example, Durango and Chihuahua were first colonized after the discovery of mineral deposits in the second half of the sixteenth century. What followed was the foundation of missions, haciendas, and farms that supplied the mining centers. Mines also played an important role in the colonization of Sinaloa, and particularly Sonora. Other areas of the Borderlands were strictly mission frontiers, such as Baja California, California, and Texas. And although these regions had different types of settlements, including towns and military garrisons known as presidios, the dominant colonial institution was the mission.

The mission was a multifaceted colonial institution. On the one hand, it was a center for religious conversion. It was also an experiment in social engineering designed to create stable communities of natives who would provide labor for Spanish entrepreneurs and pay tribute (a head tax) to the Crown. The mission was also seen as a cost-effective way to incorporate natives into the new colonial world, and through the control of land, water, and labor, it contributed to the region's economic development. Missions were the dominant institution in Baja California, California, and Texas, but mission frontiers did not attract many settlers. One of the Spanish Crown's motivations for colonizing frontier regions was a concern over the establishment of competing colonies at strategic points near Spanish territory. In 1565, following the establishment of a colony of French Protestants near the Saint Johns River, the Spanish established Saint Augustine in Florida. A short-lived French colony on the coast of Texas in the mid-1680s prompted the Spanish move to colonize Texas in 1690. And in 1769, José de Gálvez organized an expedition to colonize California following reports of increased Russian activity in Alaska and James Cook's expedition in Polynesia.

It was still the mission, however, that was the quintessential Borderlands institution. Born of the crucible of the Chichimec War (1550–1590), it found a basis in policies developed in central Mexico. The Spaniards encountered sedentary peoples in central Mexico, and adapted existing institutions, including the payment of tribute and the provision of labor, for their own needs. The native peoples on the northern frontier were nomadic hunter-gatherers, semisedentary farmers who practiced seasonal transhumance, or sedentary residents of tribal states. They did not live in hierarchical state systems. The missionaries attempted to congregate the natives and convert them into sedentary agriculturalists. This program met with mixed results.

For example, in Nueva Vizcaya (modern Chihuahua and Durango), Jesuit and Franciscan missionaries attempted to congregate the native populations, but had to compete for Indian laborers with mining entrepreneurs, ranchers, hacienda owners, and farmers. Many natives left the missions seasonally or for longer periods of time, and some natives perceived the missionaries, particularly the Jesuits, as being precursors of Spanish exploitation. There were several major revolts against Spanish rule, and some fled into mountain valleys outside Spanish reach. Franciscan missionaries in Texas were frustrated in their efforts to congregate native peoples, who did not always cooperate. The Karankawas, hunter-gatherers who inhabited the Texas Gulf coast, practiced seasonal migration between permanent village sites, and generally they did not abandon their way of life. The missionaries complained about what they called the fickle nature of the native peoples as well as a lack of support from Spanish military officials who would not or could not retrieve fugitives from the missions. At the other extreme were the Franciscan missions of California, where the missionaries congregated thousands of natives. In 1820, roughly 21,000 natives lived in twenty missions, an average of more than 1,000 per mission. The California missions also produced large crops, as well as large numbers of cattle, sheep and goats, and horses.

One consequence of the congregation of natives in the missions was the drastic population decline caused by periodic epidemics of highly contagious crowd diseases such as smallpox and measles, chronic maladies including venereal disease, and generally unhealthy living conditions. Some epidemics killed more than 10 percent of the mission population. The one exception to the general population decline was in New Mexico, where the native population recovered and grew, beginning in the late eighteenth century. Children born in the missions often did not survive to adulthood, and in some instances 80 to 90 percent died before reaching age ten. Life expectancy in the missions was low, much lower than in contemporary European populations. Moreover, many mission populations showed evidence of gender and age imbalances, with higher mortality rates among women and children.

The end of the eighteenth century, with the advent of Enlightenment ideas, witnessed a growing skepticism about the efficacy of the mission as an institution on the frontier. Moreover, the decline of the native populations living on the missions made it difficult to justify further funding of the mission system. The government ordered the closure of some missions because of declining native populations. For example, in the 1790s local officials closed San Antonio de Valero mission in the San Antonio, Texas, area, as well as six missions located in the La Junta de los Ríos region of northern Chihuahua and Texas. However, missions continued to operate into the 1820s and 1830s, until 1833, when liberal politicians in Mexico City passed a secularization law.

The mission was an important frontier institution, but there were also other settlement types, including the presidio, or military garrison, and the settler community, or pueblo. In the late seventeenth and eighteenth centuries, the Spanish government funded the establishment of presidios across the northern frontier to protect missions and other settlements from raids by hostile natives. But soldiers were poorly trained and equipped, and corruption was rampant. In 1727 and again in 1766, the Spanish government sent teams to inspect the presidios, with an eye to cutting costs in a variety of ways, including cutting salaries, and to relocating garrisons to more strategic sites to enhance defense. Presidios were located in different political jurisdictions, and often there was little coordination between jurisdictions, which limited the effectiveness of campaigns against hostile native groups. Reform instituted in the 1770s attempted to overcome the difficul-

ties. The creation of the *Provincias Internas* (Internal Provinces), a superjurisdiction on the northern frontier, created a single chain of command that facilitated more coordinated military commands.

The Spanish equated civilization with town life, and promoted settlement by nonnative settlers in order to populate the Borderlands. Spanish officials encouraged retired soldiers to settle around the presidios and also promoted settlement at the garrisons, with the expectation that settler militias could replace the presidios. There were also farming hamlets, ranches and haciendas, and mining camps, and the missions themselves became centers of settlement. Mining camps proved to be unstable communities, particularly when miners exploited placer deposits. Placers are deposits of gold or silver nuggets or flakes carried there by streams and rivers, and mixed in with sand and gravel. The discovery of placers initiated boom-and-bust cycles: an initial rush of people to exploit the gold or silver was followed by an exodus, once the miners exhausted the deposits. The La Cieneguilla mining district in northern Sonora is an example of the boom-and-bust cycle. A military patrol discovered the placers at La Cieneguilla, an unpopulated site, in early 1771. Within a year 5,000 people lived in the mining district, and 7,000 after two years. By 1778, seven years following the initial discovery of the placers, only 775 people remained, most having moved on to newly discovered mineral deposits.

Most areas in the Borderlands were linked directly or indirectly to the economy of central Mexico. Durango, Chihuahua, Sinaloa, and Sonora had important mines, which in turn stimulated the

A French map of North America in 1656, showing the colonial holdings of Spain and France. California is shown as an island, as it was then supposed. This map was made by Nicolas Sanson d'Abbeville, member of a mapmaking family and cartographer to the king. (Corbis)

development of ranches, farms, and haciendas to supply the mines. Saltillo in Coahuila was a wheat-producing region that supplied markets along the northern frontier, including Texas. Nueva León produced livestock, including sheep, consumed locally and also driven to central Mexico (Jackson 1998, 93).

The Borderlands remained a sparsely populated frontier, despite efforts by royal officials to promote settlement in the region. For example, in 1800 only 3,600 nonnative settlers lived in Texas (Jackson 1998, 127). This small population size became an issue for the newly independent Mexico government after 1821, particularly with the expansion of the United States to the border of Texas following the Louisiana Purchase in 1803. The United States had come to believe in the "manifest destiny" of the United States to ex-

tend from the Atlantic Ocean across the continent to the Pacific Ocean. Moreover, with political instability in Mexico following independence, U.S. political leaders feared that other countries such as Great Britain or France would seize prime pieces of Mexican real estate, particularly California. In 1821, Mexico initiated the *empresario* system in Texas, a system that allowed non-Mexicans to claim large land grants in exchange for bringing settlers to Texas. The program was also open to Mexican citizens, but it was primarily Anglo-Americans who took advantage of the offer. Between 1821 and 1830, 10,000 Anglo-Americans settled in Texas under the empresario program, at which time the Mexican government suspended further grants. Over the next six years, another 20,000 Anglo-Americans migrated to Texas illegally. Although designed to populate a sparsely settled area to prevent the loss of Texas to the United States, the empresario program brought Anglo-Americans into Texas who eventually supported the revolt, in 1835–1836, that resulted in Texan independence. In the 1820s, different Mexican governments passed colonization laws to promote settlement of the frontier. In California, following the secularization of the missions beginning in 1833, local politicians used the colonization laws to carve up the lands of the ex-missions in grants to friends, relatives, and associates, who also used the herds of the ex-missions to stock their newly acquired properties.

Eventually, Mexico lost the northern tier of the frontier to the United States. As discussed, Anglo-Americans in Texas initiated a revolution in 1835 and 1836 that resulted in independence, since the government of Andrew Jackson decided not to annex Texas at the conclusion of hostilities with Mexico in 1836. Although this war was cloaked in the rhetoric of the American Revolution, the underlying causes of the Texas revolution included the desire to practice slavery without any hindrance from the Mexican government, as well as land speculation by companies chartered in the United States. A decade later, in 1846, the United States, under the leadership of President James K. Polk, provoked a war with Mexico, based on a spurious claim of sovereignty over the Rio Grande Valley of Texas. Weakened by internal turmoil, Mexico was no match for invasion from the United States, and in 1848 Mexico signed the Treaty of Guadalupe Hidalgo, which gave up approximately half of Mexico's national territory, including claims to Texas, New Mexico, Arizona, California, Nevada,

and Utah. The United States paid Mexico $20 million, although half went to pay claims against the Mexican government by citizens of the United States.

The Spanish colonization of the Borderlands left a mark on the development of the region. This included place-names, laws, and patterns of land tenure that persist to this day. There was also a demographic imprint of settlement, reinforced with subsequent patterns of migration.

Robert H. Jackson

References

Deeds, Susan. *Defiance and Deference in Mexico's Colonial North.* Austin: University of Texas Press, 2003.

De la Teja, Jesus Frank. *San Antonio de Bexar: A Community on New Spain's Northern Frontier.* Albuquerque: University of New Mexico Press, 1995.

Gerhard, Peter. *The Northern Frontier of New Spain.* Princeton, NJ: Princeton University Press, 1982.

Jackson, Robert H. *Indian Population Decline: The Missions of Northwestern New Spain, 1687–1840.* Albuquerque: University of New Mexico Press, 1994.

———. *Race, Caste and Status: Indians in Colonial Spanish America.* Albuquerque: University of New Mexico Press, 1999.

———. *From Savages to Subjects: Missions in the History of the American Southwest.* Armonk, NY: M. E. Sharpe, 2000.

———, ed. *New Views of Borderlands History.* Albuquerque: University of New Mexico Press, 1998.

Jackson, Robert H., with Ed Castillo. *Indians, Franciscans, and Spanish Colonization: The Impact of the Mission System on California Indians.* Albuquerque: University of New Mexico Press, 1995.

Moorhead, Max. *The Presidio: Bastion of the Borderlands.* Norman: University of Oklahoma Press, 1975.

Wade, Maria. *The Native Americans of the Texas Edwards Plateau, 1582–1799.* Austin: University of Texas Press, 2003.

Weber, David. *The Spanish Frontier in North America.* New Haven, CT: Yale University Press, 1992.

BOURBON REFORMS

The Bourbon reforms were a series of reforms undertaken by the Bourbon monarchs of Spain in the eighteenth century. Set within the context of the French Enlightenment and its emphasis on reason, the reforms sought to bring Spain and its colonies into the modern world and enable the Spanish to meet the burgeoning challenge of the French and the English on the international stage. When the Bourbon dynasty came to the Spanish throne at the beginning of the eighteenth century, the new rulers sought to give new direction to Spain's floundering imperial system. While all of the Bourbon monarchs—Philip V (1700–1746), Ferdinand VI (1746–1759), and Charles III (1759–1788)—contributed to this ideal, it is Charles III who is generally held up as the example of the reforming monarch. The innovations in Spanish colonial policy were reflected in commercial, administrative, and military reforms.

The broader context of the Enlightenment involved European struggles for empires and the commerce that made those empires so valuable. These factors and the political ideals of enlightened absolutism influenced Charles III as he sought to strengthen Spain's hold over its colonies. The Spanish monarch sought to secure that relationship for two very specific reasons: One was the need to respond to foreign threats to Spain's empire, as other European powers challenged Spain's hegemony in the Americas. For example, during the Seven Years' War, Havana was captured by the British. This was a cruel blow to Spain's naval supremacy in its own waters and created a situation that could not be tolerated. The other underlying rationale for the reforms had to do with Spain's mounting deficits and the ever-growing cost of maintaining the imperial system's integrity.

As king of Naples, Charles III had focused on the problem of low agricultural production, which resulted in periodic famines in that region. With the help of his first minister, Bernardo Tanucci, Charles III implemented an effective program of land reform and redistribution, as the government took over land from nobles who held vast estates and divided it among landless peasants and small farmers. These reforms, while initially highly successful, unfortunately did not outlast the Tanucci administration, and Naples' nobility quickly reacquired the land after the minister's death.

In Spain, Charles III and his ministers worked to create a miniature industrial revolution; the king recognized the need for Spain to compete with the English in the manufacturing sector. To this end, Charles III sought to alter the Spaniards' peculiar abhorrence for manual labor. He established state-owned textile mills, inviting foreign technical experts to Spain to train Spaniards in the latest technologies. He furthered the development of agriculture by curbing the privileges of the Mesta, the stockbreeders' corporation, and he resettled regions of the country that had been abandoned. Charles III also tried to foster shipbuilding and transport and communication. Yet despite these efforts, the Crown never challenged the existing social order and the enormous wealth and privilege of the nobility.

The Bourbon reforms in the Americas were implemented to rationalize the colonial system, to strengthen the colonies' links to the metropolis, and to undermine the many abuses that had developed within the system. The reforms aimed to maximize colonial production and the transatlantic trade with Spain, as well as to cut off the enormous contraband trade by making legal trade more profitable than smuggling. Those were the commercial reforms, and naturally they sought to increase the amount of money that would end up in Spain by increasing Spain's trade with its colonies. Spain's first Bourbon monarch, Philip V, had attempted to reduce smuggling and to revive the fleet system *(flota),* which had fallen into much decay. During the sixteenth century, the Spanish sought to maintain their monopoly on trade with the colonies by adhering to a strict schedule of sailings for the merchant fleets. The fleets sailed twice each year and this allowed the Spanish to control who and what was transshipped, and to protect the shipping against marauders. However, in 1713 at the Treaty of Utrecht, the English had struck a tremendous blow to the Spanish trade monopoly when the *asiento,* a contract that gave the exclusive right to transport slaves to Spanish America, was granted to the South Sea Company. Aside from that right, the company was also allowed to send one shipload of merchandise each year to the fair at Portobelo where the

ships from the second fleet unloaded their goods for transshipment across the Ithmus of Panama to be reloaded and shipped down the Pacific coast to Peru. Naturally the English took this opportunity to smuggle as much contraband as they could into the Spanish colonies. The Spanish had sought to reduce smuggling in the Caribbean by a system of *guardacostas,* or coast guard vessels, but the attacks these ships made on the English became a great source of tension between the two countries and eventually led to the outbreak of war in 1739. The challenge presented to the Spanish monarchy by contraband trading was never overcome and the guardacostas eventually were replaced by register ships (individual ships that were licensed to trade in the colonies), though the Consulado (Merchant Guild) of Cádiz still maintained its monopoly. Over the course of the eighteenth century that monopoly was gradually eroded until free trade was finally allowed in 1778.

The first crack in the monopoly held by the Cádiz merchants was the creation of the Caracas Company, which was to trade on the Venezuelan coast and in return would drive away both English and Dutch interlopers. This measure was quite effective; shipments of cacao to Spain doubled, and exports of tobacco, cotton dyewoods, and indigo also increased. Other companies were created in the hopes of bringing trade to peripheral areas of the empire; however, these companies were usually undercapitalized and generally failed. After the Seven Years' War (1756–1763), however, Cádiz's trading monopoly was gradually eliminated. During the second half of the eighteenth century, the Spanish Crown reluctantly acknowledged its inability to control trade, and, gradually, various ports in the Americas were thrown open to free trade. The decree of free trade was issued by Charles III in 1778 but it was only in 1789 that all American ports could legally trade between Spanish ports and other American provinces. Beyond this, the bewildering constellation of taxes and duties was also simplified with an ad valorem duty of 6 or 7 percent. The removal of restrictions on trade greatly advanced the development of Buenos Aires and the Río de la Plata region in the South Atlantic.

In the end, though, the commercial reforms were only as successful as the Spaniards' ability to control international shipping lanes. During the latter part of the eighteenth century, Spain could not prevent foreign traders from breaking its hold on trade with the colonies. Beyond this, Spain's own industrial output was incapable of supplying the markets in the colonies so foreign goods filled the gaps between supply and demand. Ultimately, then, although Spain's colonial trade increased substantially during the Bourbon reform period, in the end the commercial reforms were not that successful. This failure was reflected in the need to throw colonial trade open to commerce with neutral powers like the United States during periods of war in 1797–1799 and again in 1805–1809.

Along with trade, the Spanish government sought to increase the efficiency of its tax collection, both of taxes on trade and taxes imposed on the colonists, such as the *alcabala* (sales tax). The implementation, or rather the enforcement, of the collection of these taxes led to serious doubts among some of the colonists about the value of maintaining their relationship with the metropolis: major rebellions such as the Comuneros Revolt in New Granada saw people from various sectors of society, rich and poor, Indian, Spaniard, and mestizo, join together to challenge the implementation of sales taxes on tobacco and other items of importance to daily subsistence. While ultimately unsuccessful in its goal of eliminating Crown monopolies on consumer goods such as tobacco and spirits, rebellions such as this one signalled a disturbing level of dissatisfaction in the colonies.

Aside from these fiscal reforms, the Bourbon monarchy also sought to revamp the entire colonial administration. It sought to do away with the most obvious contradictions and abuses that fostered discontent and potential rebellion among subaltern groups. For example, the office of *corregidor* (royal governor of a district; *corregidor de indios* governed indigenous towns) was eliminated, and these officials were replaced with *subdelegados* (district officials—representatives of the Crown), because the *repartimientos* (labor draft—conscription of indigenous labor for use by Spaniards; *repartimientos de mercancías* were the forced purchases of goods sold to indigenous people by the corregidor) imposed by the corregidores were so hated and lent themselves so well to widespread abuses. Subdelegados were supposed to be honest colonial officials, with at least a minimum education. Through the reorganization of the royal administration at local levels the Crown sought to revitalize its presence in the colonies and strengthen its hold on regional populations.

On a grander level, other administrative reforms included the formation of two new viceroyalties, that of New Granada in 1739 and that of the Río de la Plata in

1776. The decision to create the Viceroyalty of New Granada reflected the rapid population growth in Colombia's central highlands, as well as the vulnerability of Spain's long South American coastline to foreign attack. The creation of the Viceroyalty of Río de la Plata reflected the shifting patterns of influence in trade and international relations as Buenos Aires and the South Atlantic came into their own. In addition to the creation of the new viceroyalties, between 1782 and 1790 the intendant system was transferred to Spanish America. The Crown hoped to increase administrative efficiency and royal revenues through the use of intendants, provincial governors who ruled from the capitals of their provinces. These officials were expected to relieve the viceroys of some of their burdens, especially in financial matters. They were supposed to further economic development by promoting the cultivation of new crops, the improvement of mining, and the building of infrastructure such as roads and bridges.

Furthermore, Spain's Bourbon monarchs sought to reform the local high courts, the *audiencias,* and create a career bureaucracy that would serve only the Crown's interests. It has been argued that the replacement of local dignitaries by foreign officials in these courts did help to extend the monarchy's power in the colonies; however, this increased power came at a price. Some historians claim that the reform of the colonial bureaucracy helped to create a sense of disenchantment within the Creole elite in the colonies and aided in the development of Creole nationalism that would eventually lead to independence.

Another area of reform was the strengthening of military defenses, especially the empire's land and sea defenses. The disasters of the Seven Years' War and the loss of Havana and Manila in 1762 led to a serious reconsideration of the role of naval defenses. Fortifications of important ports were strengthened, and colonial armies, or militias, were created. Again the results of these reforms were ambiguous. Some historians have argued that they enhanced the colonial defensive capacities in some cases, while producing very mixed results overall.

The Bourbon monarchs and their reforming ministers also challenged the authority and economic power of the Church, a challenge most clearly seen in the Crown's actions against the Jesuit order. The expulsion of the Jesuits from Spanish America in 1767 and their eventual dissolution as an order aimed to undermine Jesuit political and economic power in the Americas. The perception that undergirded these reforms was that the Jesuit order was far too economically and politically independent of the Crown, and its power had to be curbed if royal absolutism was to flourish in the colonial setting. The final solution to this problem was the expulsion of the order and the expropriation of Jesuit properties and wealth in 1767.

The Bourbon reforms have been the subject of much study as historians have sought to determine the nature of their effects, both in Spain and its colonial empire. In these studies historians have attempted to determine whether or not the reforms achieved their intended goals and how innovative they were. Some historians argue that the reforms were implemented only after events in the colonies had moved ahead and that they were reactive rather than innovative. Generally, though, since the Spanish colonies experienced independence revolutions in the early nineteenth century the Bourbon reforms are often examined in order to determine whether or not they stimulated or put off the development of nationalist sentiments within the colonies. Notwithstanding the interpretations of these reforms and their effects, historians of Latin America recognize their importance in shaping the history of the Spanish colonies in the eighteenth and nineteenth centuries.

Renée Soulodre–La France

References

Archer, Christon I., ed. *The Wars of Independence in Spanish America.* Wilmington: Scholarly Resources, 2000.

Bakewell, Peter. *A History of Latin America.* Oxford: Blackwell, 1997.

Barbier, Jacques. *Reform and Politics in Bourbon Chile, 1755–1796.* Ottawa: University of Ottawa Press, 1980.

Brading, D. A. *Miners and Merchants in Bourbon Mexico, 1763–1810.* Cambridge: Cambridge University Press, 1971.

Lynch, John. *Bourbon Spain, 1700–1808.* Oxford: Blackwell, 1989.

McFarlane, Anthony. *Colombia before Independence: Economy, Society and Politics under Bourbon Rule.* Cambridge: Cambridge University Press, 1993.

See also: Administration—Colonial Spanish America; Alcabala; Armies—Colonial Spanish America; Asiento; Atlantic Economy; Cacao; Caracas Company; Colombia; Comuneros—New Granada; Contraband; Corregidor/Corregimiento; Defense—Colonial Spanish America; Dyes and Dyewood; Enlightenment—Spanish America; Fleet System; Intendants/ Intendancy System; Jesuits—Expulsion; Monopolies; Native Americans I, III–VIII; Peru; Rebellions—Colonial Latin America; Science and Scientists—Colonial Spanish America; Seven Years' War; Ships and Shipbuilding; Tobacco; Trade—Spain/Spanish America; Túpac Amaru Revolt; Utrecht, Treaty of; Viceroyalties.

BRAZIL

Brazil's colonial and early national trajectory was unique in the Western Hemisphere. Since Portugal's mercantile interests were mostly located in Asia and Africa, Brazil did not receive the same attention granted to colonial America by the Spanish authorities. Initially exploration and exploitation were left to private initiative; royal control of the colony did not start until the second half of the sixteenth century. During the seventeenth century, Portugal intensified its grip over Brazil to take advantage of sugar production and mineral resources. Metropolitan centralization reached its highest point with the Marquis of Pombal's reforms during the second half of the eighteenth century. The 1808 arrival of the Portuguese court in Brazil marked a turning point in Brazil and Portugal. These events set in motion processes that eventually led to Brazil's independence in 1822. Despite formal separation from Portugal, Pedro I maintained links with the metropolis not definitely severed until 1831, when he abdicated in favor of his six-year-old son. His death brought to an end any dreams of reuniting Portugal and Brazil under one ruler and initiated a new era in the relations between both countries.

In 1500, Pedro Alvares Cabral reached the coasts of Brazil and landed near present-day Bahia. The area was called Land of the Holy Cross, but the name was changed to Brazil as a result of the red dyewood that grew in the region *(pau brasil)*. In accordance with the Treaty of Tordesillas (1494), Cabral claimed the area for Portugal and continued his journey around Africa to reach India, his original destination. Initially, Brazil generated little interest in Portugal. Unlike Spain's, Portugal's commer-

An engraving of Portuguese navigator and explorer Pedro Alvares Cabral (1467–1526) landing at Terra da Vera Cruz, Brazil, and coming ashore to claim it for Portugal, 1500. (Kean Collection/Getty Images)

cial empire was not centered on the New World. King Manuel's resources were concentrated in the spices, slaves, and gold that could be obtained from Asia and Africa. Brazil came in third, with its scattered Indian population and brazilwood. The Crown established a monopoly over the plant's exploitation. Among their obligations, merchants were expected to explore and defend the coastal areas against foreigners and surrender a percentage of the profits to the Crown. Each contractor established points of exchange along the coast where Indians bartered the logs for European trinkets. Brazil was inhabited by semisedentary Tupi-speaking peoples. These groups practiced slash-and-burn agriculture, hunting, and gathering for subsistence. Since tree felling was a traditional male activity, initially the relationship with the Portuguese was not disruptive for the community. During the early 1510s, however, increasing needs for labor and foodstuffs led settlers to raid native villages in search of Indian slaves.

News of Cabral's landing and the profits from the brazilwood trade attracted Spanish and French vessels to the area. Portugal's king, Dom João (King John III), used a strategy of combining diplomacy and coastal patrols, but it failed to eliminate the threat. Therefore, Portuguese authorities resorted to a new scheme: the captaincy system. From 1533 to 1535, the

Brazilian coast was divided into twelve hereditary captaincies, strips of territory that ranged from 30 to 100 leagues in width and extended inland until the line marked by Tordesillas. The Crown granted those areas to donees (*donatarios*) with broad privileges and powers, such as the right to found towns, appoint officers, distribute land, administer criminal and civil justice, promote colonization, and collect taxes. The captaincy system opened the way toward more stable settlement in Brazil. However, with the exception of São Vicente and Pernambuco, captaincies failed due to mismanagement, lack of resources, and Indian attacks.

In 1532, Martim Alfonso de Sousa founded the town of São Vicente on the coast southwest of present-day Santos. The donee was granted rights to the dyewood trade, but the prosperity of the captaincy came from sugar production. By 1548 the area had six sugar mills worked by thousands of Indian slaves. Duarte Albuquerque Coelho arrived in Pernambuco in 1535. Initially, the region was exclusively devoted to dyewood trade, but Coelho used his connections and resources to promote sugar production. By midcentury, Pernambuco had become the most prosperous region of Brazil, with fifty sugar mills that shipped an annual average of forty to fifty vessels loaded with sugar to Portugal.

Confronted with the failure of the captaincy system, Dom João (King John III) moved to take more direct control over the region. In 1549, the Crown appointed Tomé de Sousa as Brazil's first governor-general. The establishment of Brazil's capital in the town of Salvador and the appointment of royal officers inaugurated a new era in Brazilian colonial history, a

change that was consolidated under Mem de Sá (1558–1572), who furthered colonization, displaced Indian populations, founded Rio de Janeiro (1567), and eliminated the French threat with the destruction of La France Antartique, a colony that had been established in Guanabara Bay in 1555. During the second half of the sixteenth century, the Portuguese authority created the institutional mechanisms necessary to establish a centralized system of colonial rule. The highest royal authority was a governor-general (viceroy after 1720) who resided in Salvador (until the capital was transferred to Rio de Janeiro in 1763) and exercised executive, administrative, military, commercial, and fiscal powers. The governor reported directly to the king and the Overseas Council, created in 1642 in Lisbon to formulate policies and regulate Brazilian affairs. Crown-appointed treasurers supervised Portugal's financial interests, leased royal monopolies on commodities, and watched over the tax collection bidding system. A high court of appeals was established in Salvador in 1609 and represented the supreme authority in judicial matters, from which individuals could appeal only to Lisbon.

The first religious order to arrive in the area was the Society of Jesus in 1549; the Jesuits were followed by Franciscans, Augustinians, and Carmelites. The Jesuits, who had no vow of poverty, turned their attention to agriculture and cattle raising, thus becoming the wealthiest and most commercially active order in Brazil. Jesuit colleges were established in most coastal towns. The order assumed a position against Indian slavers that resulted in countless conflicts between the religious entity and settlers. Disputes among royal officers, mostly caused by jurisdictional problems, ill-defined mandates, and difficulties in communication with Portugal, characterized this period as well. Foreign threats added another destabilizing component to Brazil's early colonial history. Besides French attempts in the area, the Dutch occupied the coast of Bahia in 1624 and Pernambuco between 1630 and 1654. The Dutch West India Company stimulated the sugar industry by improving credit mechanisms and promoting investments in new milling technologies. The progressive rule of Governor Johan Mauritus of Nassau could not, however, compete with nationalist sentiments among the Portuguese population, and the Dutch were forced out of Pernambuco in 1654.

Sugarcane, milling technology, and expertise had been introduced from Madeira Island to Brazil during the early 1500s. The sugar industry rapidly attained considerable importance and became the most important economic activity in the colony. In a few years, Brazil became the largest sugar producer in the Atlantic world. In 1590 there were thirty-six mills in Bahia and sixty-six in Pernambuco. A decade later, sugar exports amounted to approximately 30 million pounds. News of Brazil's prosperity attracted Portuguese settlers to the colony. Even though a large number of these migrants were of low status (released convicts among them), others came with trades and set up businesses, such as the Jewish émigrés who established congregations in Pernambuco and Bahia, until expelled during the first half of the seventeenth century.

Portuguese settlers were unable to meet the needs of the labor-intensive sugar industry. Moreover, in stark contrast to the situation in Spanish America, Portuguese authorities failed to create a base of Indian labor. A diminishing labor force, due to death, disease, flight, and resistance, encouraged the importation of slaves from Africa. The Africans who traveled to Brazil came from many parts of West Africa and western central Africa. African slavery lasted for almost four centuries. Throughout this period, Brazil received an estimated 3.5 million slaves. Slaves performed all tasks in both urban and rural areas. They were the field hands on plantations, worked in cattle ranching, and mined for gold and diamonds. As domestic servants, they were occupied as cooks, housekeepers, seamstresses, washers, and wet nurses. In the cities, slaves worked as retailers or served as beasts of burden, moving loads on their heads and carrying their masters on sedan chairs. Skilled slaves were employed as masons, carpenters, and silversmiths, among other trades. Slaves endured strenuous working conditions, intolerable living conditions, systematic abuse, and exploitation on a daily basis.

By 1600, Africans had replaced Indians as slaves, and the sugar industry had become the most prosperous economic activity in the area. Nevertheless, despite a promising start, the second half of the seventeenth century was characterized by an economic slowdown. Throughout the seventeenth century, groups of adventurers known as *bandeirantes* (each group followed a *bandeira,* the Portuguese word for "banner") marched into the interior in search of precious minerals, runaway slaves, and Indians. Inhabitants of São Paulo were the most involved in these undertakings, although expeditions also left from Salvador, Recife, and Belém. The great bandeira of Antonio Raposo Tavares (1648–1652) combined official and private support; it traversed Brazil from São Paulo to Belém and led to the establishment of a Portuguese outpost in Colonia do Sacramento. These movements opened inland areas to trade and settlement, raided and enslaved Indian populations, established alternative means of communication using inland routes rather than the ocean, and found precious metals, which contributed to Brazil's economic prosperity during part of the eighteenth century. The discovery of gold and diamonds in Minas Gerais, Goiás, and Matto Grosso redirected the focus of colonial activity toward central southern Brazil. Population and resources left the coastal towns of the northeast in search of precious metals in the area. Gold production rose steadily until the 1750s, when as a result of inefficient production and lack of technological innovation, metal extraction experienced a significant decline, which led to the economic slowdown that characterized Brazil during the second half of the eighteenth century.

This period marked a significant turning point in the relations between Portugal and Brazil. In similar fashion to Spain's Bourbon reforms, the new prime minister, Sebastião José de Carvalho e Mello, later Marquis of Pombal, instituted a series of reforms intended to increase Portugal's control over the colony. Among other measures, the minister appointed Portuguese officers who reported directly to the metropolis (limiting the power of local officials), moved the capital from Salvador to Rio (reflecting Brazil's economic shift from the northeast to the south), created new monopolistic trading companies (such as the Company of Pernambuco and Paraíba), and reduced the power of religious orders (the Jesuits were expelled from Portuguese territories in 1759). Pombal's reforms set the stage for Brazil's economic growth during the last years of the eighteenth century and early 1800s. However, the reforms also resulted in increasing social tensions between Portuguese and Brazilians, tensions that led to conspiracies and rebellions such as the "Tailors' Revolt" in Bahia in 1798.

Brazilians' dissatisfaction with the reforms served as the backdrop to a series of political events that contributed to Brazil's unique path to independence in the early nineteenth century. In 1807, when Napoleon invaded Portugal, the British army assisted the royal family in escaping to America. For the first time, European monarchs ruled an empire from the colony rather than from the metropolis. The king, Dom João (King John VI), launched a series of highly unusual reforms, which reached a climax in 1815, when Brazil was declared a kingdom of equal standing with Portugal, thus creating a unique situation in the history of America's colonies. In 1820, a liberal uprising in Portugal demanded João's return to Europe. Reluctantly, the king returned, but he left behind his son Pedro as Brazil's regent. Portuguese liberals instituted reforms with the purpose of returning Brazil to its former colonial status. As a response, on September 7, 1822, Pedro declared Brazil's independence and was acclaimed as Emperor Pedro I of Brazil. The emperor's lingering ties with Portugal and his authoritarian behavior, among other reasons, alienated Brazilians. In 1831, Pedro I was forced to abdicate in favor of his six-year-old son and soon set sail for Europe. His death in 1834 brought to an end any dreams of reuniting Portugal and Brazil under one ruler. However, ties between both countries were never completely severed. This became apparent in the second half of the nineteenth century, when Brazil became the destination of choice for almost one-third of those emigrating from Portugal in search of a better future.

Patricia Juarez-Dappe

References

Boxer, Charles. *The Golden Age of Brazil, 1695–1750*. Berkeley and Los Angeles: University of California Press, 1962.

Burns, Bradford. *A History of Brazil*. 3rd ed. New York: Columbia University Press, 1993.

De Abreu, Capistrano. *Chapters of Brazil's Colonial History, 1500–1800*. Translated by Arthur Brakel. New York: Oxford University Press, 1997.

Lockhart, James, and Stuart B. Schwartz. *Early Latin America: A History of Colonial Spanish America and Brazil*. New York: Cambridge University Press, 1983.

Russell-Wood, A. J. R., ed. *From Colony to Nation: Essays on the Independence of Brazil*. Baltimore: Johns Hopkins University Press, 1975.

———. *Society and Government in Colonial Brazil*. Brookfield, VT: Variorum, 1992.

See also: Administration—Colonial Spanish America; Amazon; Architecture—Brazil; Armies—Colonial Brazil; Atlantic Economy; Bandeirantes; Catholic Church in Brazil; Colonists and Settlers II—Brazil; Conquest II—Brazil; Defense—Colonial Brazil; Donatary Captaincies; Dyes and Dyewood; Engenho; Enlightenment—Brazil; Independence II—Brazil; Inquisition—Luso-America; Jesuits—Brazil; Migration—To Brazil; Monarchs of Portugal; Monopolies; Music and Dance I—Brazil; Napoleonic Invasion and Luso-America; Native Americans I—Amazon; Native Americans II—Brazil; Pirates and Piracy; Poetry—Brazil; Science and Scientists—Brazil/Portugal; Slave Rebellions—Brazil; Slavery I—Brazil; Slave Trade; Sugar; Tordesillas, Treaty of; Women—Brazil.

BULLFIGHTING

The bullfight was one of the many institutions Spaniards took with them to their American colonies. As early as 1529, a special ceremonial bullfight was held in Mexico City to mark the anniversary of Hernando Cortés's conquest of Tenochtitlan only eight years before. Bullfights soon formed part of the ceremonies around the entry into the capital of a new viceroy, and continued to be held for this purpose until the end of Spanish rule. In both Mexico City and Lima, bullfights celebrated the accession of new monarchs, royal births and weddings, and the end of war.

After independence, the bullfight served as a focus for nationalism in some parts of the Americas, although not always in the same way. In Cuba, for example, nationalists seeking independence from Spain presented the bullfight as a symbol of backwardness and Spanish colonialism, against which they promoted baseball as an alternative. Spanish authorities responded to the popularity of the U.S. sport by banning it as anti-Spanish in the 1870s and again in the 1890s. For their part, U.S. authorities banned bullfighting almost immediately after taking control of the island, although clandestine corridas took place occasionally.

The situation in Mexico was more complex. At first, the independent state continued the practice of using bullfights to mark important occasions, but over the course of the nineteenth century, elite attitudes changed, and by the 1890s they had turned their attention to other, newer pastimes such as baseball, horse racing, boxing, and cycling. At one point, Mexico's President Porfirio Díaz banned bullfights in the capital, although the prohibition did not last long.

Among the Mexican lower classes, the bullfight remained both popular and a vehicle for nationalism and anti-Spanish sentiment. Visiting Spanish matadors were often given a hard time; on one occasion Luis Mazzantini required a military escort to leave the bullring, and in 1897 another visitor was taunted with cries of *"Cuba Libre!"* ("Free Cuba!") Mexico produced bullfighters too, and one, Ponciano Díaz, became a national hero. He angered his fans when he returned from a tour in Spain having adopted Spanish dress, but he was always careful to keep his moustache. Unlike their clean-shaven Spanish counterparts, Mexican bullfighters wore moustaches to mark their masculinity.

The bullfight was a form of connection between Spain and its former colonies after they won independence in the first decades of the nineteenth century. Starting in the 1840s, Spanish matadors found opportunities in a number of Latin American countries: Mexico, Chile, Ecuador, Venezuela, Peru, Colombia, and Guatemala. For a few established stars, America provided highly lucrative contracts in the Spanish off-season, between October and April. They were also treated as celebrities and lionized by local elites.

For a much larger number, America served as a place to get established or as a haven for those who were over the hill. Particularly after 1890, there were many more aspiring bullfighters in Spain than could make a living there, and a large number went to America. Some remained for only a few years before returning home, while others stayed permanently.

Adrian Shubert

References

Beezeley, William. *Judas at the Jockey Club and Other Episodes of Porfirian Mexico.* Lincoln: University of Nebraska Press, 1987.

Pérez, Louis, Jr. "Between Baseball and Bullfighting: The Quest for Nationality in Cuba, 1868–1898," *Journal of American History,* 81, no. 2 (September 1994): 493–517.

Shubert, Adrian. *Death and Money in the Afternoon: A History of the Spanish Bullfight.* New York: Oxford University Press, 1999.

See also: Columbian Exchange—Livestock; Culture; Football; Horses; Mexico; Popular Festivals; Sports.

C

CABILDO

The *cabildo* was the Spanish municipal council. As one of the many institutions brought by Spaniards to the New World, a cabildo was installed in every Spanish settlement in the Americas. Some Native American communities also established cabildos, with exclusively native council officers. In both the native and the Spanish American cabildo, councilors were drawn from the pool of principal local men (never women), representing the prominent families in the community. However, in other ways the native and the Spanish cabildo differed.

The Spanish American cabildo consisted primarily of officers of the rank of *alcalde* and *regidor*. In addition to serving as councilors, alcaldes acted as judges for minor offenses (the term might thus be translated as "magistrate"). Regidores were the cabildo's junior councilors. In theory (and according to various royal edicts), the cabildo comprised two alcaldes and four regidores, but in practice the number of these officials, especially regidores, varied according to the size and importance of the town; councils could also include fine collectors, constables and guards, inspectors of weights and measures, and other lesser of-

ficials. Early colonial cabildos had sweeping powers and held annual elections, but for most of the colonial period cabildo authority was subordinate to that of regional officers, variously titled *corregidor, alcalde mayor,* and, later, *intendente.* In the typical cabildo, posts were sold, inherited, or granted honorifically by the viceroy or other high official. The prestige of cabildo office declined during colonial times.

Native cabildos also varied in size and in the titles of their officers. There were alcaldes and regidores, but seldom in a 2:4 ratio; for example, Tenochtitlan (which had its own native cabildo, while Mexico City, located on the same site, had a Spanish cabildo) had an 8:12 ratio of these officers in 1600, and Cacalchen, a village in Yucatán, had a 3:6 ratio in 1647. In contrast to Spanish councilors, native officers were ranked below a governor, who was usually a hereditary lord (often still holding the pre-Columbian title of supreme local ruler). Unlike Spanish notaries, native *escribanos* (notaries or scribes) were not only cabildo members, but high-ranking ones, especially in Mesoamerica (roughly Mexico and Guatemala, where there had been a rich pre-Columbian tradition of literacy). The notary might go on to become governor, and in most native cabildos in the Spanish colonies, only notaries received salaries. Below these officers there were constables, majordomos, and a potential plethora of officials holding titles in the local native languages and enjoying roles and responsibilities related to, if not directly perpetuating, pre-Columbian custom.

Native cabildos in most regions maintained annual election rituals, some of them elaborate and festive. This made the election process more public than its Spanish counterpart, but no more democratic; governors played major roles, as did considerations of class, dynastic privilege, factional maneuvering, and systems of rotational representation.

Spanish cabildos kept minutes, called *actas,* of their deliberations and acts of local administration. Some native cabildos also kept such records (in Mesoamerica in native languages), although their responsibilities were more wide-ranging; they included keeping books of wills and land sales; adjudicating local disputes; collecting tribute; providing mail carriers; maintaining roads, public buildings, and the community granary; ensuring the sick, the imprisoned, and the very poor did not starve; and administering community fields and cattle ranches.

Because the cabildo was the institution through which native communities were able to govern themselves during the colonial period, it remained crucial, and ultimately more important to native peoples than the Spanish cabildo was to colonists.

Matthew Restall

References

Gibson, Charles. *Spain in America.* New York: Harper Colophon, 1966.

Haskett, Robert. *Indigenous Rulers: An Ethnohistory of Town Government in Colonial Cuernavaca.* Albuquerque: University of New Mexico Press, 1991.

Restall, Matthew. *The Maya World: Yucatec Culture and Society, 1550–1850.* Stanford, CA: Stanford University Press, 1997.

See also: Administration—Colonial Spanish America; Altepetl; Audiencias; Cah; Codices; Columbian Exchange—Livestock; Native Americans IV—Mesoamerica; Viceroyalties.

CACAO

Cacao (*theobroma cacao,* "the food of the gods") is the fruit of the tropical cacao tree. The beans are covered in a mucilaginous coating, within a pod that grows from the trunk or major lower branches of the tree. These beans, when dried and processed, become chocolate and other minor products. Cacao probably originated in the Amazonian rainforest, but was first planted and cultivated by humans in Mesoamerica.

Consumed only by elites according to some scholars, and also used as coinage, cacao beans were a major tribute item before the Spanish invasion. Chocolate drinks, which at first repelled Spaniards, soon became popular among all classes in colonial Mexico. Most sixteenth-century cacao was imported from Soconusco and the Pacific coasts of Guatemala and El Salvador. These cacaos were of the *criollo* variety, still greatly prized. By the mid-seventeenth century, a large share of the Mexican market had been seized by Venezuelan exporters, and later by more prolific and hardier *forastero,* or "wild" cacaos from coastal Ecuador around Guayaquil.

By this time Spanish settlers had added vanilla, sugar, cloves, and other ingredients to the drink, and had brought it to Europe. Great quantities went from Spanish Caribbean ports to Seville, and Spain became the European pioneer of hot chocolate drinks. Dutch smugglers from Curacao also brought Venezuelan cacaos to the Amsterdam exchange. Its use in Europe gradually spread, and for a while in eighteenth-century elite drinking clubs it challenged tea and coffee. The Portuguese brought forastero cacaos from Brazil to the offshore islands of West Africa, and from there they spread to the mainland, with important consequences for today's world markets.

Joseph Fry in England, soon followed by the rival firms of Cadbury and Rowntree, first made hard chocolate in bars an item of mass consumption. Gradually chocolate as a drink left the field of adult drinks to its rivals coffee and tea. Cocoa, heavily laced with sugar, became a drink for children, and chocolate bars and wrapped candy became the emphasis. Dutch and English entrepreneurs were then surpassed by the Swiss. Henri Nestlé, a chemist, developed powdered milk, and with his partner Daniel Peter, he produced the first milk-chocolate bars. Rodolphe Lindt then invented a process called conching (1879), which produced smoother and more aromatic chocolate. Lindt and Nestlé are corporate giants today. In the United States, Milton Hershey of Pennsylvania became the Henry Ford of chocolate manufacture by discerning the possibilities of economies of scale, uniformity in production, and vertical integration and ownership of supplies such as sugar, milk, and cacao.

Hershey's chocolate for the masses and other large-scale producers led to the expansion of cacao plantations. Cacao is now a world commodity grown in many tropical regions of the world. Venezuela has retained a minor but respectable place as a supplier. Guayaquil was the world's major exporter for most of the nineteenth century, but plant disease in the 1920s, followed by depressed world prices in the 1930s, severely weakened the Ecuadorian industry.

By the 1920s, the Gold Coast, now Ghana, led the world in output, and Africa had passed America in exports. World trade in the product expanded almost 800 percent between 1900 and 1940. Nigeria and Cameroon became competitive exporters, and by the 1990s the Ivory Coast became the world's leading producer, and retains this position today in spite of civil war. New rivals such as Indonesia and especially Malaysia now, in their turn, challenge Africa's dominance. America, via Spain, had added another great foodstuff to worldwide stocks, and the enthusiasm for the food of the gods continues to grow.

Murdo J. MacLeod

References

Coe, Sophie D., and Michael D. Coe. *The True History of Chocolate.* New York: Thames and Hudson, 1996.

Young, Allen M. *The Chocolate Tree: A Natural History of Cacao.* Washington, DC: Smithsonian Institution, 1994.

See also: Atlantic Economy; Bananas; Coca; Coffee; Columbian Exchange—Agriculture; Contraband; Cotton; Food; Henequen; Maize; Native Americans I–VIII; Pirates and Piracy; Sugar; Tobacco; Trade—Spain/Spanish America; Venezuela; Wheat.

CACIQUES

Spaniards called local rulers of the Caribbean *caciques,* a term adopted from the Arawakan word for leader, *kassiquan* (meaning "to have or maintain a house"). The term was later applied to local dynastic rulers (known in Nahuatl as *tlatoque, yva* in Mixtec, and *batabob* in Maya) of *altepetl* (ethnic states) in Mesoamerica. It was also applied to native leaders throughout Spain's colonial possessions in South America, except in Peru where local leaders often were referred to by the Quechua term for ruler, *kuraca*. Caciques proved vital to the establishment and administration of colonial society. Over time the use of the term *cacique* changed to signify a rural boss who wielded coercive and arbitrary power.

Scholars debate the functions of caciques in the contexts of their communities and the colonial order. Under Spanish rule, noble Indian males held official administrative posts, while female *cacicas* were denied formal positions. Some *cacicas* maintained informal power, particularly in Mixtec communities where men and women had traditionally ruled together. In the Mixtec regions, as elsewhere, caciques served as administrators, tax collectors, and brokers between the Spanish and indigenous worlds. In some instances, caciques used their positions to maintain and preserve the integrity of traditional Indian society. Spaniards granted caciques the right to collect tribute and extract labor from commoners, and some actively participated in the Spanish economy. Caciques received privileges, including the right to bear arms and ride horses, and frequently adopted prestigious Spanish surnames and honorific titles.

The fate of caciques remains a subject of academic controversy, in part because of the extent of regional variation. The decline in native populations and the increasing pressures exerted by Spanish rule during the later sixteenth and early seventeenth centuries jeopardized the position of caciques. According to local circumstances, Spaniards might select only one of several rulers as cacique, or else elevate a commoner to cacique status. As tribute levels dropped, the income available to caciques similarly diminished, such that Spaniards might assume the place of caciques, especially in areas with a sizable Spanish population.

In some instances, the establishment of Spanish institutions like *cabildos* (town councils) worked to circumvent cacique authority. Initially caciques held the position of governor *(gobernador)* in the cabildo for life, reflecting continuity with pre-Hispanic traditions. Some historians argue that caciques maintained their position for the duration of the colonial period. Others disagree, suggesting that the relative power and prestige of caciques diminished over time, as social distinctions lessened and caciques encountered increased competition from people of lesser status. By the mid-seventeenth century, caciques only rarely held prominent offices.

After independence, the term *cacique* took on a more general meaning, similar to that of "caudillo." The term found expression in Spain, Spanish America, and in Brazil where it was called *coronelismo*. Scholars argue over the difference between caudillos and caciques. One basic distinction is that while caciques came to be known as regional and local leaders who wielded coercive and arbitrary power, caudillos were local leaders who had successfully imposed their power at the national level, for which they had relied upon the relative weakness in political power and legitimacy of the early nation-states.

Richard Conway

References

Chance, John K. "The Caciques of Tecali: Class and Ethnic Identity in Late Colonial Mexico." *Hispanic American Historical Review* 76, no. 3 (1996): 475–502.

Gibson, Charles. *The Aztecs under Spanish Rule: A History of the Valley of Mexico, 1519–1810.* Stanford, CA: Stanford University Press, 1964.

Haskett, Robert S. *Indigenous Rulers: An Ethnohistory of Town Government in Colonial Cuernavaca.* Albuquerque: University of New Mexico Press, 1991.

Kern, Robert, ed. *The Caciques: Oligarchical Politics and the System of Caciquismo in the Luso-Hispanic World.* Albuquerque: University of New Mexico Press, 1973.

See also: Administration—Colonial Spanish America; Altepetl; Brazil; Cabildo; Cah; Caudillos; Congregaciones; Encomienda; Independence I–VI; Kuraca; Nationalism; Native Americans I–VIII; Race; Repartimiento.

CAH

The *cah* is the Yucatec Maya municipal community. The Yucatec term means "village or town," with *noh cah* ("great cah") meaning "city." From pre-Columbian times to the twentieth century, the cah was the fundamental unit of Maya society, the focal point of Maya identity and organization.

The term *cah* was used in pre-Columbian Yucatán, probably for many centuries, and is semantically related to the verb *cah,* "to reside or live" (the terms were spelled the same by colonial Mayas, but in linguistic orthography the noun is *kàah* and the verb is *kah,* reflecting their slightly different pronunciations). In the Spanish period (1542–1821), there were over two hundred *cahob* (plural of cah) in the colony of Yucatán all classified by the Spaniards as pueblos, as well as scores of other cahob in the unconquered regions of the peninsula. The provincial capital of Mérida was the only settlement in the colony classified as a city by Spaniards and a noh cah by Mayas. Mayas today still use cah to mean "village or town," but the full social implications of the term are only found in more rural communities.

Because regional political activity and identity were suppressed by the Spaniards, the importance of the cah to Maya social and political organization was strengthened in the colonial period. Yucatec Mayas did not refer to themselves as Mayas, but as *cahnalob*—cah members or residents, of a specific, usually named cah. Maya identity was thus based on cah affiliation, as well as family or lineage (the patronym-group, termed *chibal),* although even chibal identity held little meaning outside its cah context.

In a geographical and sociopolitical sense, there were two dimensions to a cah. One was the residential cah, the concentrated core of homes grouped in clusters before the conquest and in blocks in the colonial period, centered on a plaza. The plaza was square or rectangular, delineated by the church (often built by the remains of the pyramid or platform upon which the pre-Columbian temple had stood), by the town hall, and by the homes of the ruling families of the cah. The other dimension was the territorial cah, the sum of all the lands held by the community and its members. More remote lands might lie more than a day's walk from the residential cah, forming a complex cah boundary recorded in maps and writing by the notary of the *cabildo* (the ruling council of the cah). Most lands, forested and agricultural, were owned privately by individual cahnalob; theoretically owners could not sell property to outsiders without permission of the cabildo, but such sales became increasingly common in the last colonial century.

Colonial policies and settlement patterns turned some cahob into suburbs of Mérida and other Spanish towns, while in some cases pairs of cahob were folded into a single complex community, sometimes containing subdivisions. The cah—in its origins, history, colonial florescence, and complex meaning—is equivalent in most ways to the *altepetl* of the Nahuas of central Mexico and the *ñuu* of the Mixtecs of Oaxaca.

Matthew Restall

References

Brown, Denise F. "Yucatec Maya Settling, Settlement, and Spatiality." Ph.D. dissertation, University of California, Riverside, 1993.

Hanks, William F. *Referential Practice: Language and Lived Space among the Maya.* Chicago: University of Chicago Press, 1990.

Restall, Matthew. *The Maya World: Yucatec Culture and Society, 1550–1850.* Stanford, CA: Stanford University Press, 1997.

———. "The Ties That Bind: Social Cohesion and the Yucatec Maya Family," *Journal of Family History* 23, no. 4 (October 1998): 355–381.

———. "The People of the Patio: Ethnohistorical Evidence of Yucatec Maya Royal Courts." Pp. 335–390 in *Royal Courts of the Ancient Maya.* Vol. 2, edited by Takeshi Inomata and Stephen Houston. Boulder, CO: Westview, 2001.

See also: Administration—Colonial Spanish America; Altepetl; Cabildo; Guatemala; Mexico; Native Americans IV—Mesoamerica; Race.

CALIFORNIA

The Spanish first coasted California in 1542, and they continued to do so for the next two hundred years. It was not until 1769, however, that actual colonization occurred. Spain implanted a new society and colonial system in California that transformed the region and has left a continuing legacy. In the eighteenth century, California was an isolated frontier region, but it gained importance following Mexican independence.

The Spanish first arrived in what is today the state of California in 1542, when Juan Rodriguez Cabrillo explored the coast past Cape Mendocino. Cabrillo's expedition was part of the larger Colorado expedition to New Mexico (1540–1542). There were several other expeditions along the California coast, but the Spanish largely ignored the region for some two centuries. One consideration that contributed to Spanish interest in the region was the need for the Manila Galleon, a merchant ship that traveled between Mexico and the Philippines, to replenish supplies before making the long trip along the North American coast to Acapulco. In 1697, following several failed colonization efforts, the Jesuits established the first of a chain of missions in Baja California (Lower California), and by the 1740s were considering the logistics of advancing the mission frontier to Alta California (Upper California).

Two unrelated events hastened the colonization of California in 1769. In the mid-1760s, King Charles III granted José de Gálvez extensive powers to reform Mexico's colonial bureaucracy and its economy. Gálvez ventured to the northern frontier and tried to rationalize colonial policy and particularly the mission system. Gálvez arrived in Baja California in 1768 and initiated the organization of an expedition to occupy California. Two global events gave Gálvez's planned occupation a sense of urgency. The first was the reports of increasing Russian activity in Alaska, and the second was the expedition of James Cook to Polynesia, which suggested that Great Britain, the European country that the Spanish government feared most, was showing greater interest in the Pacific Basin.

Spain accomplished the colonization of California in the most cost-effective way possible. Spain eventually established four military garrisons, or presidios, in California (San Diego, Monterey, San Francisco, Santa Barbara), three towns (San Jose, Los Angeles, Villa de Branciforte), and twenty-one missions administered by the Franciscans of the Apostolic College of San Fernando, located in Mexico City. Under the terms of an agreement reached between royal officials in Mexico City and Friar Junípero Serra, O.F.M., the father-president of the California missions, the Franciscans agreed to supply food and other supplies to the military garrisons at a price set by the governor of California. In exchange, the government granted the Franciscans complete control over the mission temporalities, essentially the mission economy. The Franciscans organized the production of surpluses, and moneys paid for the supplies provided to the military allowed the Franciscans to purchase goods in Mexico. The government benefited because it did not have to pay the high cost of supplying the military from Mexico.

In order to produce surpluses, the Franciscans had to convert the local native population into a disciplined labor force. This endeavor created a more disruptive mission regime, and the missions proved to be unhealthy environments. Mission populations experienced high mortality rates, particularly among young children and women. The mission populations grew as long as the Franciscans brought new re-

Franciscan friar Junípero Serra led the establishment of twenty-one Spanish missions throughout the area of Alta California, then part of the Spanish Empire. (Library of Congress)

cruits to live at the missions, but then declined after about 1825 as the number of new recruits dropped. Mexican liberal reformers who viewed the missions as colonial anachronisms legislated the closure of the missions in 1833. The ultimate beneficiaries of the redistribution of mission wealth were the local politicians, many of whom descended from military families, and who administered the estates of the ex-missions. Moreover, following the secularization of the missions, California governors carved up the former mission lands, and issued over eight hundred land grants to settlers. The natives who had constructed the missions and provided the labor that created mission wealth ended up as laborers for the new lords of the land, who also started their own herds with animals from the estates of the ex-missions.

California became important economically in the first four decades of the nineteenth century with the growth of the so-called hide and tallow trade, the export of cattle hides and tallow used in the manufacture of candles and soap. California hides supplied the New England shoe industry, and foreigners began to settle in California in increasing numbers. This trade was illegal under Spanish and Mexican law, but it flourished as foreign merchants visited the California coast. The catalyst for the growth of foreign trade was warfare—the French Revolutionary and Napoleonic wars in the 1790s and early nineteenth century, and later, after 1810, the outbreak of civil war in Mexico, which led to Mexico's independence in 1821. International war caused volatility in prices for imported essentials, such as wine, spices, and other goods. Wine prices, for example, more than doubled in some years because of the disruption of trade to Spanish America from Spain resulting from the war, and these price increases cut into the budgets the missionaries had for purchasing goods. As the crisis deepened, the missionaries had to purchase less through legal channels, but they were able to purchase goods from foreign merchants. The missions owned thousands of head of cattle, and began culling the herds to supply the growing international demand for hides. Over the next forty years, the trade grew, and California became part of a growing world economy. The discovery of gold in 1848, following the occupation of California by U.S. forces during the Mexican-American War (1846–1848), only acceler-

ated the process. Spanish occupation paved the way for subsequent settlement; however, it also had unwanted consequences, such as the devastation of the native population. California's Indians continue to deal with this legacy.

Robert H. Jackson

References

Castillo, Edward, and Robert H. Jackson. *Indians, Franciscans, and Spanish Colonization: The Impact of the Mission System on California Indians.* Albuquerque: University of New Mexico Press, 1995.

Jackson, Robert H. *Indian Population Decline: The Missions of Northwestern New Spain, 1687–1840.* Albuquerque: University of New Mexico Press, 1994.

See also: Borderlands; Bourbon Reforms; Colonists and Settlers VI—Southeastern North America; Conquest VI—Southeastern North America; Florida; Missions; Napoleonic Invasion and Spanish America; Religious Orders; Wine.

CANNIBALISM

Cannibalism in the Iberian American world was a fundamental category for the understanding of native populations. The veracity and credibility of much Iberian reportage on this issue has rightly been treated with suspicion, since it advanced the colonial agenda of conquest by obscuring or justifying all kinds of punitive violence against native populations. However, anthropophagy was certainly part of the cultural practice of Native American peoples, just as the imagery of cannibalism suffused Christian theology. It is the way these differing traditions of symbolizing and enacting cannibal rituals clashed that does much to explain both Iberian attitudes and native reactions.

In this light, cannibalism may be thought of as one of those cultural practices that allowed Spanish colonial regimes to separate the "good" from the "bad" Amerindian. Most notorious in this regard was the dualistic ethnic typology, originated by Columbus, of Arawaks and Caribs. This apparently objective ethnolinguistic distinction is in fact highly suspect, but it became widespread across the Caribbean region, and in time a component of Amerindian identity itself. Royal decree by Isabella in 1503 also enshrined this scheme in legal statute, allowing the plunder and enslaving of those populations considered Carib.

As missionaries began systematic evangelization, this ready-made distinction became self-fulfilling, since opposition to the missionaries was defined as Carib. In this way the Arawaks, who accepted evangelization, were seen as favorable to colonial development. But this distinction was, and still is, based on more than these competing representations of Amerindian tractability and intractability. The notions of Carib and Arawak refer also to spatial location and ritual proclivity. Consistent with the demonic nature of the colonial imagination of the interior of the continent, the Caribs are pictured as interior bush-dwellers exemplifying the secretive, dangerous, and violent nature of the dark heart of the region. The Arawaks, coastal dwellers and even urbanites, in turn signal the possibility of indigenous redemption, reform, and development. These competing images of the indigenous population could then be made to fit varying political and ethnic circumstances, using linguistics to bolster the idea of a fundamental difference in the cultural ontologies of Arawaks and Caribs. Even though linguistic practices do not actually conform to this scheme, it has remained a passionate debate in contemporary anthropology and archaeology.

Linguistics thus anchor a demonology of the indigenous in the ethnology of the region, through the linguistically inscribed association of *caribes* and *caníbal,* the terms being directly related etymologically in Iberian usages. The discovery of cannibals was therefore in the interest of the Spanish, both economically and politically, given the legal provisions that allowed special violence against them. As a result, the literary and ethnological production of the cannibal has gone hand in hand with the military and political domination of the native population in South America. The violence of conquest in the region referenced cannibalism as part of its justification, and representations of the native population suppressed descriptions of Arawak torture and cannibalism, emphasizing rather the barbarity of the Carib as a means of politically isolating resistance to Iberian colonial rule.

It is therefore important to realize that in other contexts, cannibalism per se simply did not function in this way, as a justification for colonial or national violence against indigenous communities. Indeed, in the Luso-American territory of Brazil, the cannibal designation operated with another kind of dynamic. The French and Portuguese commentaries on the Tupis of coastal Brazil from the sixteenth century also make a distinction between the "good" and "bad" Indian, but do so with reference to the ritualization of the cannibal rite. This resulted from the way in which the encounter with the Tupis provoked theological debate over the nature of the Catholic Eucharist and its doctrine of transubstantiation between French Catholic and Protestant theologians. In this scheme, the elaboration of cannibal ritual, alleged among the allies of the French and denied among the allies of the Portuguese, served to produce political and military distinctions among the native population, since such ritual elaboration was taken as an indication of a relative sophistication in the meaning of cannibalistic practice, as in the Christian Eucharist itself, rather than as a barbarous necessity. French indifference to the cannibalism of Portuguese prisoners of war by their native allies should thus be understood as a way of sustaining these political and military alliances. Ironically, then, the very ritual practice that, to the north, was considered, in any form, a defining characteristic of a recalcitrance and hostility to colonial and national development was tolerated as an analogy of the Christian Eucharist in Brazil. The violence of the cannibal ritual was not problematic, but rather the nature of collective participation in that ritual violence. The participation of women and children implicitly undermined the colonial state's political justifications for its violent modes of control, since these were the supposedly "innocent" heathen who were to be rescued from the savagery of the warrior's cannibalism, along with the cannibal victim.

By the end of the eighteenth century, however, as is evident from the French sources themselves, the "cannibal" had begun to fade away into that mist of nostalgia and remorse for the premodern. The conquest and control of native societies had led to the virtual extermination of most autonomous native polities, leaving only relatively isolated remnants in the deep interior, or the emergent neoteric groups grounded in the social and cultural relations of the colonial world. In either case the spiritual practice of cannibalism, directly connected to the creation of political power in native societies through the way in which it promoted the eminence of chiefs and warriors, was therefore itself in decline. The previous ritual sponsors of such events were now engaged in the politics of incorporation within the burgeoning national societies of the region.

As a result, the potential violence and barbarity of the intractable Indian to the colonial observer became occluded and hidden, a matter of inner orientation and belief, no longer an aspect of public culture. Thus, with the suppression of native warfare, and the loss of autonomy that implied, the uncontrolled and unknowable realm of spiritual and mystical assault through sorcery and magic emerges as the site of demonization. Whereas before the warrior or cannibal-killer was the object of colonial nightmare, in the new world of nineteenth-century progress the infrastructure of native autonomy was absent, and so colonial fears centered on the figure of the skulking assassin, the vengeful and lone killer, realized in the native practices of assault sorcery and dark shamanism.

The meanings and uses of cannibalism were therefore multiple and complex in Latin America, and that complexity has continued to the present day, at least in Brazil, where the *antropofagista* movement adopted the cannibal sign as an authentic and truly Brazilian riposte to the advance of European modernism.

Neil L. Whitehead

References

Conklin, B. *Consuming Grief: Compassionate Cannibalism in an Amazonian Society.* Austin: University of Texas Press, 2001.

Lestringant, F. *Cannibals.* Berkeley and Los Angeles: University of California Press, 1997.

Whitehead, Neil L. "Hans Staden and the Cultural Politics of Cannibalism." *Hispanic American Historical Review* 80, no. 4 (2000): 41–71.

———. "Arawak Linguistic and Cultural Identity through Time: Contact, Colonialism, and Creolization." Pp. 26–51 in *Comparative Arawakan Histories,* edited by F. Santos-Granero and J. Hill. Urbana: University of Illinois Press, 2002.

See also: Amazon; Art and Artists—Brazil; Catholic Church in Brazil; Catholic Church in Spanish America; Diabolism in the New World; Human Sacrifice; Idolatry, Extirpation of; Native Americans I–VIII; Religious Orders; Syncretism; Travel Literature—Brazil; Travel Literature—Colonial Spanish America; Witchcraft.

CAPITULATIONS OF SANTA FE

In the Middle Ages, capitulations consisted of letters of favors or privileges that a king unilaterally conceded persons or institutions. The Capitulations of Santa Fe spelled out the favors that the Catholic Monarchs, Ferdinand and Isabella, offered Christopher Columbus on April 17, 1492, if his projected voyage west to the Indies proved successful. The name "Capitulations of Santa Fe" derives from the place where they were issued in the valley of Granada, Santa Fe. The Catholic Monarchs resided in Santa Fe, and it was there they established a military camp to direct the siege of Granada, the capital of the Islamic Nasrid kingdom, which they entered triumphantly on January 2, 1492.

Although not a formal agreement, the Capitulations of Santa Fe resulted from a process of negotiation. The last conversations between Christopher Columbus and the Catholic Monarchs took place from January to April 1492, and led to the ac-ceptance of the proposal, which had previously been rejected by a committee of experts. Queen Isabella personally took charge of the matter and convoked another learned assembly, which was composed of philosophers, astrologers, sailors, pilots, university graduates, prelates, and magnates, to reexamine the Genovese mariner's plan. These experts considered absurd the distances between Spain and the Indies that Columbus had calculated. Moreover, the monarchs distrusted Columbus's political and economic pretensions. Nevertheless, in the end, a group of influential persons at court convinced the monarchs that they would lose little if the project failed and would gain much if it succeeded. Among the men who persuaded the Crown to grant favor to Columbus were the archbishop of Toledo, Fr. Hernando de Talavera; the notary Luis de Santángel; the instructor of the monarchs' son Prince John, Fr. Diego de Deza; and the chamberlain and trusted servant of King Ferdinand, Juan Cabrero.

The queen, upon agreeing to the project, decided to delay its onset because of the excessive costs incurred in the conquest of Granada. The final negotiations nevertheless went forward, without the personal participation of the monarchs or Columbus. The royal secretary, Juan de Coloma, represented the Crown, while the friar Juan Pérez defended Columbus's interests. Finally, Juan de Coloma was ordered to formulate the accepted capitulations. The favors granted to the famous mariner were as follows: the office of admiral with civil and criminal jurisdiction, the organization of armadas and fleets and economic privileges to be assigned within his jurisdiction, the office of viceroy and governor of the land discovered, prerogatives in naming subordinates, the tenth part of all riches and merchandise obtained in his admiralship, the capacity to intervene in any lawsuits that stemmed from the importation of riches from those latitudes, and the right to contribute a share of one-eighth of the merchandise to any ship that planned to engage in trade with the regions of his discoveries, allowing Columbus to receive one-eighth of the benefits in exchange. All of these concessions were to be his for life and then pass to his heirs in perpetuity. In theory, the Capitulations gave Columbus full jurisdiction over the ocean and the land he was to discover in the Indies, as well as the status of a Spanish nobleman, thus promising to fulfill his tenacious ambitions for nobility, power, honor, dignity, and wealth. The monarchs' concession of such important privileges can be explained by the fact that they doubted that the expedition would be successful or that Columbus would discover such a vast and rich land.

Carlos Alberto González Sánchez

References

Manzano Manzano, Juan. *Cristóbal Colón: Siete años decisivos de su vida.* Madrid: Cultura Hispánica, 1964.

Varela, Consuelo. *Cristóbal Colón: Textos y documentos completos.* Madrid: Alianza, 1982.

See also: Administration—Colonial Spanish America; Conquest III—Caribbean; Conquistadors; Explorers; Laws—Colonial Latin America; Monarchs of Spain.

CARACAS COMPANY

In Spanish, this is Real Compañía Guipuzcoa de Caracas. A monopoly trade firm granted exclusive control over commerce between Spain and Venezuela from 1728 to 1780. It was the first of various companies that contracted with the Spanish Crown as part of the Bourbon monarchs' effort to exert greater control over Spain's American colonies. In return for its commercial privilege, the company agreed to defend the coast, suppress smuggling, supply the province with finished goods and slaves, and spur the diversification and integration of the colony's economy. Venezuela, once a peripheral outpost, had developed by the early eighteenth century a thriving export economy, producing cacao, tobacco, hides, and other products. The Crown sought greater control over this abundance. Venezuelan growers and merchants preferred to trade with Mexico and Curaçao, rather than with Spain. The exchange with New Spain was legal, although regulations were frequently bent or violated. Trade with Curaçao, however, was prohibited. Rampant smuggling helped make the island the Caribbean's premier entrepôt in the eighteenth century. Most of the cacao that reached Spain in the late seventeenth and early eighteenth centuries arrived by way of Willemstad and Amsterdam. The Caracas Company aimed to redirect the province's exports toward Spain and impose greater control over the flow of European imports into the colony.

The company showed considerable initial success. According to contract, at least two merchant ships were to sail to Venezuela yearly. The military response to smuggling included permanent patrols along the Tierra Firme coast. On land the company built ports, storage facilities, interior trading posts, and the infrastructure to join them. The combined commercial and military efforts against smuggling forced a decline in Venezuelan trade with Curaçao. The company's activities also undercut the Mexican trade. Though smuggling was never eliminated and, during times of war, rebounded, the company could boast of successful reductions in export leakages and a significant expansion of Venezuela's direct trade with Spain.

In Venezuela, the company's reception was mixed. Many appreciated the consistent demand for cacao and other products and the infrastructural improvements. More lands came under cultivation, and new entrepreneurs entered the transatlantic economy. Others were less enthusiastic about the loss of autonomy that came with the company's success. The Caracas elite, which dominated the trade with New Spain, correctly perceived the company's activities as part of a wider effort to reduce their economic and political power. Growers and traders who made their living trading with the Dutch were exasperated, and many colonial subjects in Caracas and the province's interior resented the growing political and economic influence of the Basque immigrants who came with the company's presence.

The cumulative impact of these complaints and challenges in Venezuela, combined with the late eighteenth-century move toward free trade within the Spanish imperial system, undermined the company's standing with the Crown. By the 1780s it had fallen out of favor. Its monopoly privilege was revoked in 1780, and in 1785 the company was liquidated, with investors' remaining stock transferred to the newly created Philippine Company.

Jeremy Cohen

References

Aizpurua, Ramón. *Curazao y la costa de Caracas: Introducción al estudio del contrabando de la Provincia de Venezuela en tiempos de la Compañía Guipuzcoana, 1730–1780*. Fuentes para la Historia Colonial de Venezuela, number 222. Caracas: Biblioteca de la Academia Nacional de la Historia, 1993.

Ferry, Robert J. *The Colonial Elite of Caracas: Formation and Crisis, 1567–1767*. Berkeley and Los Angeles: University of California Press, 1989.

Hussey, Roland Dennis. *The Caracas Company: A Study in the History of Spanish Monopolistic Trade*. Cambridge: Harvard University Press, 1934.

Méndez Salcedo, Ildefonso. *La Real Compañía Guipuzcoana de Caracas: Una relación biblio-hemerográfica comentada*. Caracas: Fundación Polar, 1997.

See also: Atlantic Economy; Bourbon Reforms; Cacao; Contraband; Food; Monopolies; Pirates and Piracy; Slave Trade; Tobacco; Trade—Spain/Spanish America; Venezuela.

CARIBBEAN COMMUNITY AND COMMON MARKET (CARICOM)

The Caribbean Community and Common Market (CARICOM) was established in 1973 by the Treaty of Chaguaramas, which was signed by the governments of Barbados, Jamaica, Guyana, and Trinidad and Tobago. The eight other territories of the Caribbean (Antigua, British Honduras, Dominica, Grenada, Saint Lucia, Montserrat, Saint Kitts/Nevis/Anguilla, and Saint Vincent) became full members in 1974. Several states subsequently joined. The Bahamas joined the Community (but not the Common Market) in 1983, Suriname in 1995. Haiti became a full member in 2002. In the interim, members established the Commonwealth Caribbean Regional

U.S. Secretary of State Colin Powell (center) poses with foreign ministers from Caribbean islands, members of CARICOM, after their meeting at the State Department, March 26, 2001. (Reuters/Corbis)

Secretariat, based in Georgetown, Guyana (1968), and the Caribbean Development Bank, based in Bridgetown (1969).

The establishment of CARICOM was the result of a long-standing desire on the part of Caribbean leaders to attain a higher level of economic cooperation and integration to advance the collective interests of the region. CARICOM, as an organization primarily of the British legacy in the Caribbean Basin, complemented efforts in the Hispanic Caribbean to achieve comparable collaboration in trade relations. It was also based on economic rather than political goals. The more politically oriented West Indies Federation, which had a brief existence between 1958 and 1962, was more the result of the objectives of the British Colonial office to promote the independence of its Caribbean colonies than the goal of Caribbean leaders. The Federation's only members were Jamaica, Trinidad, the Windward and Leeward Islands, and Barbados. The subsequent decision of Jamaican leaders to leave the Federation made it no longer viable. Jamaica held half the population. The failure of the Federation did not end the desire for economic collaboration, with the result that in 1965 regional leaders from Antigua, Barbados, Trinidad and Tobago, and Guyana agreed to establish CARIFTA, the Caribbean Free Trade Association. Between 1965 and the early 1970s, Jamaica, Belize, Montserrat, Dominica, Grenada, and Saint Kitts/Nevis/Anguilla joined as well.

The trend toward globalization and the establishment of other more powerful trading blocs, in particular the North American Free Trade Agreement and the European Union, increased the importance of CARICOM to the economic well-being of the Caribbean. At the eighth ministerial meeting in 1987, members agreed to replace the Common Market with the CARICOM Single Market and Economy (CSME) to make the region more competitive in the global marketplace.

There has been no effort to achieve political integration among CARICOM members, but there has been a successful initiative to promote regular consultation among parliamentarians from member states. To that end members have established the Assembly of Caribbean Community Parliamentarians, which has held several sessions, in 1996, 1999, and 2000. In 1999, as further institutionalization of relations, the Community established the Caribbean Court of Justice.

Caribbean leaders have recognized that they share many common challenges, not only economic but also social and political. CARICOM documents underline common concerns about organized crime, especially associated with international narcotics trafficking, and the threat of AIDS/HIV to their populations. Member countries have also sought to develop a common approach to foreign policy issues. In keeping with the desire to address social and political as well as economic challenges, in 1997 Caribbean leaders signed the Charter of Civil Society to promote respect for fundamental civil rights in the region.

Stephen J. Randall

References

Payne, Anthony. *The Politics of the Caribbean Community, 1961–1979: Regional Integration among New States.* Manchester, UK: Manchester University Press, 1980.

Randall, Stephen J., and Graeme S. Mount. *The Caribbean Basin: An International History.* London: Routledge, 1998.

See also: Atlantic Economy; Guyana; Human Rights; North American Free Trade Association; Oil; Trinidad and Tobago.

CASA DE CONTRATACIÓN

The House of Trade was created by Queen Isabella in 1503 to oversee commerce between Spain and its New World colonies. Ten years earlier, when Columbus returned from his first voyage, Queen Isabella appointed her chaplain, Juan Rodríguez de Fonseca, to oversee the provisioning of his return trip with goods so that the monarchy could profit from the trade. Rodríguez de Fonseca continued to supervise trade with the Caribbean until January 20, 1503, when the Crown issued the decree that established the Casa de Contratación, a measure perhaps taken at the chaplain's suggestion.

The Casa was the first institution created specifically to deal with American matters. Housed briefly in Seville's Atarazanas (arsenal), it was soon transferred to the city's Alcázar, a royal palace and fortress. Three main officials supervised its operations: a treasurer, who received and secured jewels and bullion sent to the Crown from the colonies; a comptroller, who kept the books related to the Casa's broad responsibilities; and a factor, who inspected and provisioned shipping.

The Casa's chief function was the supervision of commerce. It acquired and stored merchandise to be shipped to the colonies, provided naval stores for transatlantic shipping, and handled goods received from America. The House of Trade registered cargoes of departing and incoming vessels. Thus, its location in Seville gave the city a monopoly over colonial commerce. As the institution authorized to issue passports, it registered passengers and controlled travel to and from the New World. Its cargo and passenger lists are rich sources of economic and social data concerning life in colonial Spanish America. In addition, the House of Trade provided charts and other navigational aids to ships plying the American routes, resolved commercial disputes, oversaw the inspection of ships, and received moneys sent to the Crown from America. The goods of Spaniards who died in the New World were sold and the money remitted to the House of Trade, which then distributed it to the heirs in Spain. The Casa's fiscal responsibilities included collection of the *almojarifazgo,* a maritime tax, as well as the *avería,* a tax to pay for defense of Spanish shipping.

In 1524 Charles V created the Council of the Indies, and it assumed some of the broader duties previously carried out by the Casa de Contratación. The latter focused its activities more strictly on commerce. In 1532 the Crown authorized it to issue the licenses required for importing slaves into the empire. Once the Consulado (Merchant Guild) of Seville was established in 1543, it worked with the House of Trade. For example, the Consulado helped organize the fleets to the New World and supervised the loading and unloading of ships. It also helped the Casa collect the maritime taxes. The relationship between the Casa and the Consulado did little, however, to curtail commercial fraud and contraband, which became a mounting problem in the 1600s.

By the late seventeenth century, Cádiz had largely replaced Seville as the port for the American trade, but the Casa de Contratación only moved there in 1717. The House of Trade then conducted its operations from Cádiz until 1790, when it was abolished, as part of the liberalization of intra-imperial trade.

Kendall W. Brown

References

Fisher, John. *The Economic Aspects of Spanish Imperialism in American, 1492–1810.* Liverpool: University of Liverpool Press, 1997.

Haring, Clarence Henry. *Trade and Navigation between Spain and the Indies.* Cambridge: Harvard University Press, 1918.

See also: Administration—Colonial Spanish America; Alcabala; Atlantic Economy; Council of the Indies; Laws—Colonial Latin America; Liberalism; Migration—From Iberia to the New World; Monarchs of Spain; Monopolies; Trade—Spain/Spanish America.

CASTE WAR OF YUCATÁN

Mexico freed itself from Spain in 1821, but the social and mental disentangling from a distant mother country proved far more complicated. This point emerges clearly in the case of Yucatán and its prolonged peasant rebellion known as the Caste War. This conflict erupted in 1847 when political instability and sudden socioeconomic changes destabilized the old colonial order, causing long-subordinated Mayan peasants to rise up against property owners and the state. It continued until the federal army's occupation of southeastern areas of the peninsula in 1901. Although matters of internal politics and resources dominated the Caste War, the Spanish presence always hovered in the background. Embroiled in their own internal reforms, Spanish statesmen had only minimal awareness of events in a backwater Mexican province. But at an individual level, Spaniards had much to do with Yucatec affairs. The Iberian imprint came early here, for the descendants of the original conquistadors settled permanently in Yucatán, bringing their language, customs, folklore, and a host of recurring surnames: Alcocer, Canto, Castillo, Escalante, Pacheco, Peraza, and Quijano, among others. Ties dwindled over the centuries as Creole nationalism replaced colonialist allegiances. A brief anti-Spanish hysteria followed independence, but by 1847 Spain had relinquished its dreams of a Mexican reconquest, and numerous Spaniards remained as permanent residents. Recent arrivals, including the politically important Barbachano family, usually had three motives for operating in the peninsula: family or institutional connections, retail activities, and the slave trade. At the same time, the Bourbon reforms of the eighteenth century had brought a small but influential body of Iberian military officers to Mexico. These men represented some of the few individuals not trained in the Church, and they functioned as conduits of Enlightenment ideas. They (or their children) served as military leaders in the pre-1850 years. The greatest institutional tie remained the Catholic Church, which preserved a strongly Iberian character well into mid-century. The last European-born bishop, Agustín Estévez y Ugarte, had come to Yucatán in 1797, and had brought with him a coterie of priests from the provinces of Granada and Málaga.

The second motive, legitimate commercial activities, cast Spaniards in the same role that the Chinese have often played in Southeast Asia: that of ubiquitous merchant and moneylender. Numerous Spanish entrepreneurs took part in Yucatán's economic life. By the 1830s, Spain's bourgeoisie had a strongly mercantile nature; the American trade remained dynamic, above all with the booming sugar-slave complex on Cuba, and it was a short hop to retail interests on the Yucatán Peninsula. The 1850s witnessed the birth

of business corporations, limited partnerships usually dedicated to agriculture or commerce, and the surviving articles of incorporation reveal a strong Spanish presence, particularly in urban retail (Yucatecs themselves dominated landholdings). More important, perhaps, was their share in the international arms trade. When Yucatán broke from Mexico in 1840, leaders of the new nation quickly procured arms from Spanish merchants, among others. These arms allowed Yucatán to resist Mexico, but also prepared the way for the disaster to come; once dispersed into the countryside, these arms proved impossible to recall. British merchants in Belize are usually identified as arms suppliers to the Caste War rebels, but the Belizean merchant community was international in nature, and included various Spaniards.

Third, a handful of Iberian entrepreneurs used the Yucatán Peninsula as a platform for the Cuban slave trade. It began in 1848 as a way of getting rid of unwanted Maya prisoners of war; when these ran out, military officers captured and sold Maya refugees found living in the woods, much as colonial Portuguese settlers had done in seventeenth-century Brazil. But the parochial military officers needed middlemen with Cuban connections, and Spaniards emerged to fill the gap. Such intermediaries typically came to the peninsula via Cuba, still a Spanish colony and at that moment with a voracious need for human labor. Spain's involvement in the trade grew at precisely the moment that England's and France's declined, and Spanish investors understood the fortunes to be made by delivering slave labor to the island. Participants included Miguel Pon and Gerardo Tizón, but also the poet José Antonio Zorrillo, author of the classic *Don*

Juan Tenorio and later Spain's poet laureate. These merchants became active middlemen in Yucatán's slave trade to Cuba, and developed a network of suppliers in most of the rural towns. The trade did finally end, but the vengeful Liberals who assumed power in 1867 imposed confiscatory taxes on the Spanish merchants who remained: the latter were wealthy enough to tax, but without the familial ties or nationalist credentials that might have protected them from such extortion.

In the final analysis, the facts regarding Spaniards may have mattered less than the contradictory attitudes that surrounded them. Mexican Hispanics and Creoles had their own mixed opinions about the old country. To many, Spanish colonialism was a dark age, and early national writers preened themselves on having broken away from it. Yet national-era Creoles still valued their Spanish heritage and bloodlines. For Maya peasants, the term *español* meant anyone who spoke Castilian and owned property, and early Caste War leaders complained bitterly of the treatment of Mayas by *españoles* who to us seem no more Iberian than the cornstalks. Here as elsewhere, the term functioned as a catchall for wealthy oppressors, a useful vagary of folk terminology.

After the rise of the dictator Porfirio Díaz in 1876, the political climate quieted remarkably, and Spaniards once more emerged as merchants and entrepreneurs. The anticlericalism of the Liberal reform also subsided, and the Yucatecan church admitted a significant if unstudied number of Spanish priests. Increasingly, however, the Spaniards yielded to Lebanese Christians who came to the Americas at the turn of the century, and who proved every bit as aggressive and enterprising as the old

Castilians had been. Still, the Spanish presence has continued to inform Mexico's culture and commerce, in Yucatán as elsewhere, to the present day.

Terry Rugeley

References

Dumond, Don E. *The Machete and the Cross: Campesino Rebellion in Yucatán.* Lincoln: University of Nebraska Press, 1997.

Gabbert, Wolfgang. *Becoming Maya: Ethnicity and Social Inequality in Yucatán since 1500.* Tuscon: University of Arizona Press, 2004.

Rugeley, Terry. *Yucatán's Maya Peasantry and the Origins of the Caste War, 1800–1847.* Austin: University of Texas Press, 1996.

———. *Of Wonders and Wise Men: Religion and Popular Cultures in Southeast Mexico.* Austin: University of Texas Press, 2000.

———, ed. *Maya Wars: Ethnographic Accounts from Nineteenth-Century Yucatán.* Norman: University of Oklahoma Press, 2001.

Sullivan, Paul. *Xuxub Must Die: The Lost Histories of a Murder on the Yucatan.* Pittsburgh: University of Pittsburgh Press, 2004.

See also: Bandeirantes; Bandits and Banditry; Bourbon Reforms; Catholic Church in Spanish America; Henequen; Independence V—Mexico; Maize; Mexico; Native Americans IV—Mesoamerica; Slave Trade; Slavery II—Caribbean; Slavery III—Spanish America.

CATHOLIC CHURCH IN BRAZIL

The Catholic Church has played an important role in the historical development of Brazil. The Portuguese brought the organizational structure of the church to Brazil, along with their folk and lay devotions and practices. In fact, during the time of exploration, the "church militant," which grew out of the reconquest of the Iberian Peninsula, served as the moral underpinning for the expansion of the Portuguese Empire and the conquest and enslavement of non-European peoples. In colonial Brazil, the church was the structure through which the Portuguese population, as well as large segments of the non-European population, could join in communities, engage in charitable acts, and organize their society. The church was also a powerful financial institution in the colonial period, yet through the *padroado real* (royal patronage), the church also remained dependent on the Portuguese state. Unlike the situation in Spanish-American nations, the padroado real remained in effect after independence and up to the end of the Brazilian empire in 1889, when church and state were officially separated in Brazil. In the 1930s, however, the church regained some of its influence with the Brazilian government. By the 1950s, some parts of the Brazilian Church, especially in the northeast of Brazil, were beginning to define a different role for the church, to address serious social questions of poverty. After Vatican II (1962–1965), important segments of the Brazilian Church became active in Liberation Theology and as activists in speaking out against Brazil's military dictatorship. Today, the Brazilian Catholic Church has elements that still are socially active and others that tend to be more conservative. There is also a new movement known as Charismatic Renewal that is a direct response to Protestant, primarily evangelical, churches that have been spreading rapidly through Brazil in the last thirty years and now challenge the dominance of the Catholic Church in Brazil.

The church should be understood as being made up of three main organizational structures, all of which have played a role in Brazil's history. The diocesan structure of

A grand colonial-era Catholic church in Belém, Brazil. (Wolfgang Kaehler/Corbis)

the church is the part of the church organized into the territorial hierarchies of parishes, dioceses, and archdioceses, which come under the authority of parish priests, bishops, and archbishops respectively. The clergymen who serve in this structure are often called secular clergy. Alongside the diocesan structure are the religious orders, the most prominent in Brazil being the Jesuits, Franciscans, and Dominicans. The priests in these orders are known as religious clergy. The third element in the Catholic Church in Brazil is the lay religious brotherhoods, or confraternities, which serve as the organizations in which laypeople can actively practice their own devotions, engage in charitable acts, and take care of the bodies and souls of the dead. Often these confraternities are the locations for the development of a devout folk, or "popular," Catholicism. All three of these branches have played important roles in the history of Brazil, but their relationships to one another, to the Portuguese and Brazilian states, and to the Catholic Church in Rome have fluctuated throughout the five hundred years of Brazilian history.

Successive Portuguese monarchs justified their explorations and conquests with the concept of the "just war," which developed out of a crusading mentality that saw the conquest and forcible conversion of non-Catholics as a primary responsibility of the church. In fact, the church actively supported the expansion, dividing the newly discovered territories between the Spanish and Portuguese in the Treaty of Tordesillas (1494). Even more important, however, was the series of papal bulls that resulted in the padroado real, a privilege given to the head of the Order of Christ (usually the king of Portugal) that granted the right to control the diocesan church in all new territories. This privilege included the right to name bishops, collect the tithe, and censor letters from Rome. The padroado real, which lasted until the end of the Brazilian empire in 1889, basically made the church a branch of the state. As a result, during the colonial period the diocesan church in the Portuguese colonies was administered by the Mesa de Consciência e Ordens (the Board of Conscience and the Orders) in Lisbon rather than by the Vatican.

The official church in Brazil arrived with the first royal governor, Tomé de Sousa, in 1549. The king chose to send the Jesuits, an order that had only been founded in 1540, to take charge of the conversion of the Native Americans in the American territories. Six Jesuits, including

Father Manuel de Nóbrega, arrived in Brazil to minister to the Indians. The Jesuits began the *aldeia* system, creating villages to bring the Indians out of their "savagery" to learn agriculture, to wear clothes, and to learn Christian doctrine. The Jesuits created aldeias throughout Brazil in the colonial period, but almost always encountered violent resistance from the settlers, who wanted to use Native Americans as slaves, and the diocesan church, which believed that the conversions remained superficial. One of the main defenders of the Indians, and certainly one of the most important Jesuits in the Portuguese Empire and throughout the world in the seventeenth century, was Padre Antonio Vieira, who became a world-renowned scholar and orator.

When the king decided to make Brazil into a crown colony, he erected the first diocese in Brazil in 1551, centered in Salvador Brazil. The first bishop, Dom Pedro Fernandes Sardinha, took a rigid stance against the Jesuits and their Native American charges, and pushed the Jesuits out of the area to a region in the south, where they founded the aldeia of São Paulo de Piratininga, which later became the city of São Paulo. When the king heard of the discord between Sardinha and the Jesuits, he recalled Sardinha to Lisbon. Ironically, Sardinha's vessel shipwrecked on the coast of Brazil, and the bishop was captured and eaten by the very Indians that he so disliked. The conflict between the religious orders and the diocesan church continued throughout the colonial period.

After the first decades of settlement, the diocesan church spread slowly through Brazil, following the main routes of Portuguese expansion. In general, the diocesan church was spread very thin throughout the colonial period and the empire, and remained subsumed under the state bureaucracy. By the end of the empire, in 1889, there was only one archdiocese and eleven dioceses for all of Brazil, and each priest served an average of 4,200 parishioners. Eighty percent of the present-day dioceses in Brazil were formed after the turn of the twentieth century.

The religious orders remained active through the colonial period in missionary work with the Native Americans, especially in the southern mission district and the northern region of Maranhão and Grão Pará. They also engaged in missionary work among recently arrived Africans. The Jesuits were also responsible for education in Brazil, although no schools of higher education were established in Brazil until the nineteenth century. Convents were also established by religious orders, and convent life became an important option for women who wanted an education, who could not or did not wish to marry, and for widows.

It is worth noting that the Inquisition did not have an office in colonial Brazil. Instead, the Inquisition sent ecclesiastical visitors to the colonies to check on the regularity of the practices of the church and the faithful in the colonies. Inquisition cases tended to focus primarily on the widespread practice of concubinage, but the institution also tried cases of heresy, witchcraft, and divination. Punishments tended to be the imposition of fines, imprisonment, or forced labor.

The uneven spread of the diocesan church and the dispersed presence of the Inquisition contributed to the energy with which laypeople organized their own religious expression. Rural plantations often constructed their own chapels and hired their own chaplains to serve the family, retainers, and slaves on the plantations. In towns and cities, confraternities became the most important single church structure in the colony. The laity organized each confraternity around a particular devotion, which might occupy an altar in a large church or, if the confraternity had funds to build, in its own church. Often the organization of lay religious confraternities preceded the arrival of the diocesan church in a new territory; in fact, often the first two confraternities would be those dedicated to the Most Holy Sacrament for the whites and the rosary for the blacks. As regions became more socially complex, different confraternities were founded to represent different groups in society. The confraternities hired their own chaplains, collected alms, celebrated feast days, buried the dead, organized hospitals, raised dowries for their members, and in short engaged in important social and religious obligations. Although confraternities were subject to some oversight by both the diocesan church and local crown officials (who squabbled over jurisdiction), they remained fiercely independent organizations.

In the mid-eighteenth century, the Pombaline reforms attempted to reassert the power of the state over the church, especially over the religious orders and the confraternities, both of which had remained relatively independent from diocesan and state control. In 1759, the Marquis of Pombal, the author of the reforms, expelled the Jesuits from Portugal and Brazil, and seized their substantial properties. Pombal also seized the assets of the Mercedarians and forced other orders to lend money to the government. He evicted the nuncio (papal ambassador) from Portugal and severed relations with the Vatican. For ten years the church in both Portugal and its colonies was completely national. Relations with the Vatican were reestablished in 1770, but the attack on the religious orders weakened the institutional Catholic Church in Brazil.

The reforms also tried to centralize the power of the state over the confraternities. For example, since the beginning of the Brazilian colony, the confraternity statutes had been approved at the local or regional level. After 1765, all confraternity statutes were to be sent to the Mesa de Consciência e Ordens in Lisbon. Other measures included the abolition of the requirements of some confraternities to prove the "purity" of their bloodline, the reduction of the dues of the judges and other board members, and a prohibition against the annual coronation of kings and queens in the black brotherhoods. During this same period, local parish priests also started to demand more control over the confraternities in their parishes.

After Brazil gained its independence in 1822, the new constitution gave the emperor, Dom Pedro I, the right to continue the padroado, and state control of the Brazilian Church moved to Rio de Janeiro. The mood had changed in Rome, however, and throughout the nineteenth century, the Vatican became increasingly interested in unifying doctrine and practice and centralizing power in Rome. The steps toward that end became known as the Ultramontane reforms. The church was responding to the challenge of liberalism, which was spreading throughout Europe and the Americas. Latent conflicts between the Brazilian Catholic Church and the Roman Catholic Church became manifest in the nineteenth century, when

they developed into an international struggle of wills between successive popes and Brazil's emperors.

Although the last emperor of Brazil, Dom Pedro II, held tenaciously to his power over the church, he allowed his bishops to attend the first Vatican Council called by the ultramontanist Pope Pius IX. Seven of the eleven Brazilian bishops attended the conference, and in 1870 they brought back to Brazil an ultramontanist agenda that proposed to free the church from state control and settle it under the wing of the pope in Rome. The growing conflict finally came to a head in an incident known as the Religious Question of 1874, in which two ultramontane bishops barred Masons from participation in certain church activities and forbade Catholics to join the Masons. The Masons appealed to the emperor, who sided with them; he imprisoned and imposed sentences of five years' hard labor on the two bishops. Although the bishops' sentences were eventually reduced, and they were finally pardoned, this conflict symbolized the ongoing tension between the Brazilian government and the Vatican.

When Brazil became a republic in 1889, the new constitution firmly separated church and state. The church, without the institutional support of the state, had to expand its own structure. It expanded the number of dioceses and archdioceses, reformed the seminaries, tried to replace some of the Brazilian popular devotions with more universalistic devotions, and brought in foreign priests to minister to the people. The church also became interested in social conditions, especially in the increasingly squalid living and working conditions of the urban poor. In 1891

Pope Leo XIII promulgated the important papal encyclical Rerum Novarum, which addressed the social question of the working classes, not only in Brazil, but throughout the Americas.

The church expanded steadily, and began to regain its influence in the state after 1930, with the rule of Getúlio Vargas. Cardinal Leme was the main promoter of increased state support for the church, and he successfully lobbied for the recognition of religious marriage and the presence of religious teaching in the schools. He was deeply committed to involving the laity as a means of increasing the influence of the Catholic Church and founded Catholic Action in Brazil in 1935 to fulfill this commitment. In the 1950s, Catholic Action became less involved in increasing the influence of the church and more important as a social movement in Brazil, especially among youth groups, which began to give serious attention to the grave problems in Brazilian society. At the same time, the Brazilian Church, especially the Conference of Brazilian Bishops (CNBB), founded in 1952 by Dom Helder Câmara, moved toward a socially progressive stance even before Vatican II (1962–1965). After the military dictatorship took power in 1964, the church took a public stand in favor of human rights and against the repressive policies of the successive military governments.

Building on this already progressive tradition, Liberation Theology became significant in Brazil after the 1968 Conference of Latin American Bishops in Medellín, Colombia, affirmed that the church should have a "preferential option for the poor." Liberation Theology, which reached its peak in the 1970s and 1980s, advocated a grassroots Christian movement that criticized structural economic inequalities in Brazil. Priests started Christian Base Communities (CEBs) with their parishioners to discuss the Bible and its potentially revolutionary significance for modern times. Priests also got involved with their parishioners in progressive social movements. Since the 1980s, the Catholic Church in Brazil has become more conservative, but many CEBs remain active. The biggest challenge to the church today is the growing influence of the Pentecostal churches in Brazil. In response, the Catholic Church has started its own "Charismatic Renewal" to give people a more active role in church services.

In addition to the religion of the official Catholic Church, folk, or "popular," Catholicism has remained widespread throughout Brazil and continues to be significant for a vast number of Brazilians. Pilgrimages are an example of this popular Catholicism. Over 5 million people make annual pilgrimages to the Basilica of Our Lady of the Blessed Apparition (*Nossa Senhora da Aparecida*), the patron saint of Brazil. On the other hand, 2 million people make pilgrimages each year to the northeastern shrine of Padre Cícero, a nineteenth-century priest who was expelled from the Catholic Church for supporting popular Catholicism. Smaller, less well-known pilgrimages are undertaken every day throughout Brazil. Every city, town, and village has a patron saint who is celebrated enthusiastically on his or her feast day. In some regions traditional confraternities still dominate local religious expressions. Although these folk expressions sometimes come into conflict with the official church, they should be seen as part of the many different ways that Catholicism has been expressed in Brazil, and perhaps more than those other ways they reflect the unique blend of Portuguese, African, and indigenous influences in Catholicism in Brazil.

Elizabeth Kiddy

References

Boxer, C. R. *The Church Militant and Iberian Expansion, 1440–1770.* Baltimore: Johns Hopkins University Press, 1978.

Brandão, Carlos Rodrigues. "Popular Faith in Brazil." In *South and Meso-American Native Spirituality from the Cult of the Feathered Serpent to the Theology of Liberation,* edited by Gary H. Gossen. New York: Crossroad, 1997.

Bruneau, Thomas C. *The Political Transformation of the Brazilian Catholic Church.* London: Cambridge University Press, 1974.

———. *The Church in Brazil: The Politics of Religion.* Austin: University of Texas Press, 1982.

Groot, C. F. G. de. *Brazilian Catholicism and the Ultramontane Reform, 1850–1930.* Amsterdam: CEDLA, 1996.

Hoornaert, Eduardo. *História da igreja no Brasil.* Petrópolis: Editora Vozes, 1977.

Neuhouser, Kevin. "The Radicalization of the Brazilian Catholic Church in Comparative Perspective." *American Sociological Review* 54 (April 1989): 233–244.

Russell-Wood, A. J. R. *Fidalgos and Philanthropists: The Santa Casa da Misericórdia of Bahia, 1550–1755.* Berkeley and Los Angeles: University of California Press, 1968.

See also: Brazil; Catholic Church in Spanish America; Clergy—Secular, in Colonial South America; Colonists and Settlers II—Brazil; Confraternities; Education—Brazil; Enlightenment—Brazil; Family—Colonial Brazil; Inquisition—Luso-America; Jesuits—Brazil; Jesuits—Expulsion; Jesuits—Iberia and America; Liberation Theology; Marriage; Papacy; Protestant Reformation; Religious Orders; Tordesillas, Treaty of; Witchcraft; Women—Brazil.

CATHOLIC CHURCH IN SPANISH AMERICA

Two main features affected the nature of the Catholic Church in Spanish America. One was the close relationship between the church and the Spanish Crown. The second was the main internal division of the church, into the secular and regular clergy. The church and the Crown developed a close relationship because the discovery and conquest of the New World were closely linked to the Reconquest of the Iberian Peninsula by the Christian monarchs. In the latter phases of that effort, the Crown embraced the importance of spreading Christianity as an essential part of regaining lands inhabited by Muslims. This fervor then carried on to the exploration and discovery of the Americas. Yet the church was not a monolithic institution; rather, it was divided internally into smaller constituencies that frequently vied with one another for power and precedence. These two themes, then, form the background for understanding the Catholic Church in Spanish America.

The Muslim presence on the Iberian Peninsula from the eighth century until the late fifteenth century had a direct effect on the development of Spanish institutions. As the process of regaining lands initially taken by the Muslims developed, it took on a crusadelike nature. The last phase of the Reconquest, in the 1490s, served the Catholic Monarchs, Isabella and Ferdinand, in their attempt to unify the fractious elements of the political society. And Christianization of the Muslims became one of the central themes of the last battles.

From the fourteenth century on, the Portuguese had engaged in voyages of exploration down the west coast of Africa. One of the motives for their explorations, beyond the obvious benefits of trade, was to spread Christianity, in return for which the papacy granted certain privileges to the Portuguese Crown. Christopher Columbus arrived on the scene in Spain at just the moment when the last Muslim redoubt of Granada was falling to the Christian monarchs. He had sailed for many years in the Portuguese overseas exploration, and so both of these trends came together in his voyage. On one hand, Columbus sought commercial benefits for Spain; on the other, Spain would ultimately claim possession of the lands he discovered on the basis of having supported the spread of Christianity to hitherto un-Christianized lands.

Upon Columbus's return to Spain in 1493, the Spanish Crown immediately sought two things: a demarcation of the world into two spheres of influence, recognizing the Portuguese claim to trade in Africa, and potentially in India, and grants and privileges from the papacy recognizing Spain's role in the Christianization of the newly found lands. As the extent and nature of Columbus's discoveries became better known, the Crown continually sought further clarification and validation from the papacy. The collection of papal bulls issued during the first few decades of the exploration and conquest of the Americas came to form the basis for rights and privileges the Crown claimed over the Catholic Church in the New World. Those rights and privileges became known as the royal patronage, or *patronato real*.

Because of this right of royal patronage, the Spanish Crown considered itself to be the absolute patron of the church in the New World. In keeping with earlier European traditions, in return for the financial support that the Crown gave to the New World church, it had the right to appoint the individuals who served in the offices of the church. Thus, for having backed the missionary endeavor that accompanied Columbus's voyage and the other expeditions of discovery and conquest, the Spanish kings could appoint the bishops and archbishops, and upper and lower clergy, in the Americas. This range of privileges that the Spanish Crown enjoyed in the New World was lacking in nearly all of Spain's European territories. Also, in return for the commitment to financially support the American church, the popes the Crown granted the right to collect the ecclesiastical tax, the tithe, on all agricultural production in the New World. The Crown in turn granted that privilege to the local bishops and archbishops, reserving one-ninth for itself to cover costs pertaining to the Christianization. Through these rights and privileges, the Spanish Crown came to exercise direct control over the institutional church in the New World.

As mentioned above, however, the church the Spanish Crown controlled was far from being a monolith. One basic division has always been present: the Catholic clergy is divided into two basic groups, the secular clergy and the regular clergy. The regular clergy are those clerics who belong to organized religious orders, such as the Franciscans, Dominicans, and Augustinians. Some of these clerics are priests, and some are simple friars. All take special vows peculiar to the order to which they belong, promising to follow the rule of the order. Each order has a rule, a system of mandates that each cleric must follow. Because of this, members of the religious orders are known as regular clergy, from the Latin word for rule, *regula*. Religious orders have their own internal system of authority, ranging from the local abbot, to the provincial, to the head of the religious order, and ultimately the pope. On the other hand, the common parish priest, who, generally speaking, does not belong to a religious order and who is responsible to the local bishop, is called a secular cleric. The term *secular* comes from the Latin word *saeculum,* signifying the world, since such priests are not cloistered, but live out in the world. Secular clergy operate under the authority of the local bishop or archbishop, who, in the case of Hispanic America in the colonial period, was subject to the Spanish Crown. Consequently, of the two great divisions of the Catholic clergy, one was directly subservient to the Crown, while the other was largely independent of Crown authority.

There was a clearly religious aspect to the conquest of the New World. The leading conquerors all saw spreading Christianity as part of their essential mission, along with extending the Spanish realm, and gaining personal wealth and power. Most major expeditions of conquest in the sixteenth century included members of both the secular and regular clergy. The function of these clerics was primarily to minister to the spiritual needs of the members of the expedition and secondarily to convert the natives.

The Christianizing mission of the conquest expeditions is exemplified by a document called the Requirement, or *Requerimiento.* Theologians and lawyers in Spain debated the basis upon which Spain claimed possession of the Americas. The conclusion was that possession was based upon the papal grants issued to the Spanish Crown, recognizing the spread of the Gospel to new peoples. Additionally, the

scholars considered whether or not it was lawful to make war upon the native peoples of the Americas. They decided that war was lawful only under specific circumstances. Specifically, the native peoples had to be apprised of the Christian religion and the desire of the Spanish Crown to enter into peaceful relations with them. If they willingly accepted these conditions, then war could not be made. However, if they rejected them, and attacked the Spaniards, then a lawful war could be waged against them to bring them into submission. The Requirement was drafted to outline the essential information that was needed by the native peoples in order to make this decision. It was to be read upon engaging a new group of natives, prior to making war. Nonetheless, one can imagine that in actual practice it was hardly an effective tool, since the natives could not understand the document even when it was read to them, since it would be read in Spanish. Nor was it likely that they understood the underlying premises assumed in the document.

Popular religion played an important role in the conquest of the Americas. The expeditions had their priests accompanying them. They carried their holy banners into battle. Hernando Cortés, for example, had a banner with the image of Our Lady of the Remedies emblazoned upon it. Bibles and prayer books appeared frequently in the narratives of the conquest, and tales of miraculous interventions spread. Saint James, the patron of Spain, was seen riding into battle to assist the Spanish. The priests of the expeditions frequently entered native temples and threw down pagan images, erected crosses, and in other ways manifested publicly the triumph of Christianity over pagan gods.

In the wake of the military phase of the conquest, it was necessary to begin the ambitious labor of converting the natives to Christianity. Many of the first missionaries believed that they were living in the end times. They felt that once the Gospel had been preached to the last soul on earth, once Christianity had been spread to the farthest reaches of the globe, Christ would return and usher in the millennium. This belief created a deep sense of urgency among many missionaries.

Few secular clerics were in the New World immediately following the conquests; instead, the great majority of early missionaries were members of religious orders. On the islands of the Caribbean, the religious orders began their missionary efforts during the first wave of settlement following Columbus's voyage. Among the orders active in the islands were the Jeronimites, Dominicans, and Augustinians. The Dominicans, and in particular Fr. Antonio de Montesinos, were harsh critics of the Spanish regime, and in particular of the treatment of the native peoples. In addition to the religious orders, by 1512 the Spanish Crown had sought, and gained, the creation of three dioceses to organize the church in the New World. Similarly, as the Spanish conquered the mainland territories of the Americas over the next few decades, the first missionaries tended to come from the regular clergy, while slightly later, secular priests arrived, followed by the eventual creation of dioceses.

The early missionaries used a wide variety of techniques to Christianize the natives. Each order had its own peculiar methods. The Franciscans had a long tradition of attracting people to the Christian faith through emulating a Christ-like attitude. Their strict observance of poverty and humility, they felt, set them apart from other orders. The Dominicans had originally been created as a preaching order, attracting people to the faith through articulate and emotional arguments. All of the orders, as well as the secular clerics, needed to learn the native languages in order to effectively convert the natives. As a result, some of the first books written, and printed, in the New World were grammars, dictionaries, and other tools to assist the missionaries in learning the native languages. Similarly a wide range of didactic materials was written, and printed, in the native languages to be used in the conversion. Many collections of sermons, statements of the Christian doctrine, catechisms, and confessional guides appeared in the native languages. In the process there was a homogenization of native languages. Rather than learn all of the hundreds of different languages spoken in a given region, the missionaries adopted the use of linguas franca, native languages that enjoyed a wide degree of acceptance. For example, in Mexico, much of the conversion was conducted in the Aztec language, Nahuatl, and in Peru in the Inca language, Quechua. In this manner, the Spanish missionaries continued a pattern of cultural hegemony that predated them.

Since the first missionaries were usually regular clerics who operated far outside of the jurisdiction of any bishop, they enjoyed a large degree of autonomy. Nevertheless, church practice limited the powers of priests, with certain sacraments reserved for bishops, most often confirmation and ordination. Similarly, it was possible that spiritual issues would arise that only a bishop or other qualified person might be able to resolve. The absence of bishops complicated this greatly. As a result the Franciscans requested, and received, a papal letter granting the missionaries the powers of a bishop when they operated in regions located more than two days' ride from a bishop. In fact, this papal letter, traditionally called *Omnimoda,* granted full papal authority to the missionaries. Eventually the other religious orders secured similar papal grants. Once dioceses were erected and bishops appointed, the religious orders came into conflict with the newly installed bishops over the exercise of power. Conflicts occurred between the secular and regular clergy for other reasons as well.

Traditionally in Europe, the secular clergy served in parishes, while the regular clergy carried out specific vocations of teaching, preaching, healing, and the like. All priests who served in parishes and administered the sacraments to the faithful needed to have explicit permission of the bishop of the diocese. In the New World, de facto parishes existed under the control of the regular clergy, and the regulars did not seek permission from local bishops to administer the sacraments. Two events led to the eventual resolution of this conflict. The Council of Trent, convened by the Catholic Church to confront the threat of the Protestant Reformation, granted full control over the diocese to the local bishop and required that religious orders seek episcopal permission to administer the sacraments. Shortly thereafter, the Spanish monarch promulgated a definitive ordinance dealing with the Royal Patronage. It too placed the control over the administration of the sacraments in a diocese explicitly in the hands of the bishop. Moreover, the king reiterated his position of control over the secular clergy, including the appointment not just of bishops and officials of the upper clergy, but even of parish priests. Furthermore, the Crown called for the eventual exclusion of regular clerics from parishes altogether.

The financial bases of the two branches of the clergy differed significantly. The secular clergy, including the bishops and other administrators, were supported through the ecclesiastical tax, the tithe. The tithe was a 10 percent levy on agricultural production. For example, of a crop of one hundred bushels of wheat, a farmer would pay ten to the church. For ten lambs born in a given year, one would go to the church. Members of the secular clergy insisted that the native peoples also pay the tithe, but eventually the Crown overrode that, granting the natives an exemption from the tithe.

The tithe collection could follow any of several patterns. Church officials could collect it directly, selling the goods at auction to convert produce into cash. Sometimes they held back and stored grains, and other nonperishables, in order to sell them when the price increased. The problem with these methods was that it might take months or even years for the produce to be sold, thus potentially creating a cash-flow problem for the church. Frequently, church officials sold the right to collect the tithe to private parties. A person would purchase the right to collect, say, wheat from a given district for a given price. This was known as the rental of the tithe. The rental usually occurred at a public auction, to ensure the best price for the church. The renter paid cash up front for the right to collect the tithe. He then had to collect the tithe he had rented and convert it to cash, hoping to get more than he had originally paid in the auction. The benefit for the church was that it received the cash up front, although the total might be considerably less than if it was collected directly. It could also lead to abuses if tithe renters attempted to collect more than was actually owed by individual farmers and ranchers.

The regular clergy relied on gifts and donations from the faithful for support. The Franciscan and Dominicans, in particular, were known as mendicant orders, since they sustained themselves uniquely through begging. The orders also collected the inheritance of each member. Those who entered a religious order gave up their right to hold personal property. All their property went to the order. Consequently, when a parent of a religious died, the share of the family estate that would have gone to the religious instead went to the order, although this was usually negotiated at the time the person entered the order. As a result of these donations and gifts, the orders frequently received more than they needed for operating expenses in any given year. The excess would be invested in land, either directly through the purchase of land or indirectly through the offering of mortgages on land to private parties. Similarly, the orders frequently received gifts of land, which they could administer directly or rent to others.

With the exception of the Franciscans, all religious orders acquired agricultural real estate. They administered these properties directly and used the production on the estates as a source of income for the order. The Jesuits were especially successful at supporting their order through commercial agriculture. In Mexico, the Jesuits owned cattle ranches and sugar estates; in Peru they also owned vineyards; in Ecuador they ran textile mills as well as large sheep and cattle operations. Whatever products the region could produce for the market economy, the Jesuits invested in them. This pattern was emulated by all the other orders as well, except the Franciscans.

Both the secular clergy and the regular clergy also benefited from the creation of "pious works." A pious work was an endowment from which the interest generated went to support the specific purpose of that pious work. In a pious work the church, either the secular clergy or a religious order, received a principal endowment in one of three forms. The principal could be in the form of cash, usually a minimum of 1,000 pesos, a piece of property, or a lien on a piece of property worth at least 1,000 pesos. In the case of the cash endowment, the church would loan the money to a private person in the form of a mortgage or lien. The interest rate was roughly 7 percent until the early seventeenth century, after which it dropped to 5 percent. In the case of an endowment based on a lien, the interest rate was the same. In the case of an endowment based on property, the church would either rent the property or sell the property and invest the proceeds in a lien or mortgage. The interest on the liens and mortgages, or the rents from the property, created the annual budget for the pious work. The most common pious works were chantries (*capellanias*). In a chantry, the interest generated by the endowment went to pay a priest to say masses for the benefit of the soul of the founder of the chantry and those other persons designated by the founder, in perpetuity. The importance of pious works was that the church relied on the interest generated, not on the repayment of the principal. Consequently, those who owned land could borrow money based on their holdings and only have to service the interest, not repay the principal.

In the seventeenth century, in spite of both royal decrees and the rulings of the Council of Trent, some religious orders still rejected supervision by the local bishop. A particularly difficult situation arose in the diocese of Puebla, Mexico, when the Jesuits refused to seek episcopal licenses for priests who administered the sacraments in public. In retaliation, the bishop then demanded that the order pay the tithe on the production of its numerous estates in the diocese, which the order refused, noting that religious orders were exempted from paying the tithe. The bishop countered that if they defied his authority, they would lose their clerical privileges, including exemption from the tithe. Eventually the standoff was settled. Both parties backed down: the Jesuits eventually did seek episcopal permission to exercise the sacraments, and the bishop granted them exemption from the tithe. Nevertheless, for the Crown this was yet another reminder that in many ways the religious orders existed outside of its realm of control.

The Inquisition was, strictly speaking, not a part of the church structure. Though the role of inquisitor to defend the purity of the faith is a role specifically granted to bishops, the Spanish Crown had received permission to organize and appoint inquisitors, independent from local bishops. After a case that caused great unrest in the sixteenth century, when an Indian noble was burned at the stake for backsliding, the Crown removed native peoples from the jurisdiction of the Inquisition. Though policing the spiritual orthodoxy of the natives no longer fell to the Inquisition, the local bishops could, and did, appoint ecclesiastical judges to police the native peoples. This power was especially used in Peru in the seventeenth century, in what is known as the extirpation of idolatry. The bishops of Peru commissioned priests to carry out investigations of idolatry throughout the realm in several different campaigns. Although the punishments meted out did not rise to the level of severity of the Inquisition, it was a clear case of the colonial state, through the offices of the church, using brute force to bring about cultural change among the natives. There were similar officials in Mexico at the same time, but the campaigns there were not as well organized or as widespread as in the Andes.

In the seventeenth and eighteenth centuries, missionary techniques continued to evolve. The regular clergy still provided most of the impetus for missions to frontier areas. In the north of Mexico, in the Amazon Basin of Peru and Bolivia, and in the Río de la Plata region, the Franciscans and Jesuits were the prime missionary orders. The Franciscans based their missions on Colleges of the Propagation of the Faith. These colleges were based on gifts and donations of the faithful, and were developed to train missionaries to be sent to frontier regions, and also to revive religious fervor in already converted areas. They were particularly effective in the regions that now include Texas and California, as well as in the Peruvian Amazon. The Jesuits continued their use of agricultural estates to support missions in northern Mexico and in the Río de la Plata, to name but two areas. The missions to northern Mexico also relied on the presence of Spanish troops to pacify what were perceived to be warlike natives. This approach was a marked contrast to Franciscan mission techniques in the early period, which sought to attract natives to the faith through humility and poverty.

The change of dynasty in Spain after 1700, from the Habsburgs to the Bourbons, brought about concomitant changes in the relationship of the church and the state. The general pattern was for the Bourbon monarchs to exercise even greater control over the church than before. The process of secularization, whereby the religious orders abandoned parishes in favor of the seculars, was completed in the core areas of Hispanic America. The Crown actively sought to limit the power and influence of the regular clergy. The Bourbon monarchs placed limits on the number of monasteries and convents that could be built, on the number of novices that could enter each order per year, and on the property that an order might own. By the latter half of the eighteenth century, this process peaked. In 1769 the Jesuit order was expelled from the Americas, and their lands and wealth were confiscated by the Crown. At the same time, bishops and archbishops demonstrated their willingness to comply fully with royal wishes, even when they were in direct conflict with papal directives. Eventually, in the early nineteenth century, the Crown took possession of all the mortgages and liens that had been issued to support pious works, a significant portion of all the available capital in the colonies. The Crown replaced the mortgages and liens with royal bonds, but the recall of the principal caused significant economic turmoil. As a result of these and other actions, many clerics, both secular and regular, saw the Crown as a direct threat to the church.

John F. Schwaller

References

Costeloe, Michael P. *Church Wealth in Mexico, 1800–1856.* Cambridge: Cambridge University Press, 1967.

Cuevas, Mariano. *Historia de la iglesia mexicana.* 5 vols. El Paso, TX: Editorial Revista Católica, 1921–1928.

Farriss, Nancy M. *Crown and Clergy in Colonial Mexico.* London: Athlone, 1968.

Griffiths, Nicholas. *The Cross and the Serpent: Religious Repression and Resurgence in Colonial Peru.* Norman: University of Oklahoma Press, 1996.

MacCormack, Sabine. *Religion in the Andes: Vision and Imagination in Early Colonial Peru.* Princeton, NJ: Princeton University Press, 1991.

Schwaller, John F. *Church and Clergy in Sixteenth-Century Mexico.* Albuquerque: University of New Mexico Press, 1987.

Shiels, W. Eugene. *King and Church: The Rise and Fall of the Patronato Real.* Chicago: Loyola University Press, 1961.

Taylor, William B. *Magistrates of the Sacred: Priests and Parishioners in Eighteenth-Century Mexico.* Stanford, CA: Stanford University Press, 1996.

Van Oss, Adriaan C. *Catholic Colonialism: A Parish History of Guatemala, 1524–1821.* Cambridge: Cambridge University Press, 1986.

Vargas Ugarte, Rubén. *Historia de la iglesia en el Perú.* 3 vols. Lima: Imprenta Santa Maria, 1953–1961.

See also: Borderlands; Bourbon Reforms; California; Clergy—Secular, in Colonial Spanish America; Confraternities; Conquest and the Debate over Justice; Council of Trent; Diabolism in the New World; Education—Colonial Spanish America; Franciscan Millennial Kingdom; Habsburgs; Idolatry, Extirpation of; Inquisition—Spanish America; Jesuits—Expulsion; Jesuits—Iberia and America; Monarchs of Spain; New Laws of 1542; Ordenanza del Patronazgo; Papacy; Protestant Reformation; Religious Orders; Requerimiento; Salamanca, School of; Syncretism; Virgin of Guadalupe; War of the Spanish Succession.

CAUDILLOS

As regional leaders who successfully attained national power (often by force), caudillos have held pivotal roles in the histories of several Latin American nations. Historians and social scientists have engaged in debates concerning the characteristics of caudillos, particularly as they tended to be controversial figures, sometimes hailed for protecting national interests, sometimes vilified for their damaging authoritarian rule. Caudillos possessed common characteristics, including a propensity for charismatic leadership, recourse to coercion, and dictatorial practices that circumvented established norms of governance. Caudillos also secured access to and control over economic and political resources, and relied on the support of loyal followers who benefited from systems of patronage.

The term extends back to the Latin word *caput* (meaning "head" or "person"), and old explanations for the rise of caudillos assumed a cultural orientation and continuous tradition of authoritarianism that extended back to Roman times. Recent scholarship has moved away from notions of caudillos as expressions of cultural character and has instead emphasized the importance of historical circumstances in their rise to power. The absence of formal political power and legitimacy facilitated the rise of caudillos, as did weakness in state institutions and political parties, especially in regions far from political centers. Caudillos might also gain power by drawing support from patron-client relationships. A certain generality surrounds the term *caudillo,* as shown in its occasional confusion with the term *cacique.* Contemporary usage sometimes proved vague, with a leader being described as a caudillo because of the way he wielded power in relation to public office, constitutional arrangements, and notions of legitimacy as conferred through institutions.

Following the conquest of Mexico and Peru, Spanish *encomenderos* (individuals who received so-called *encomiendas,* grants of Indian tribute and labor), including Hernando Cortés, are said to have assumed characteristics of caudillos. Similarities to caudillos have also been observed among *hacendados* (owners of large landed estates) in the late colonial period. With independence, caudillos rose in prominence as the colonial system collapsed, assuming power with the help of personal armies.

Social scientists have identified two types of caudillos. With the instability of emerging nation-states between 1800 and 1870, "classic" caudillos assumed power by using force and gaining popular peasant support. Caudillos of this period included Antonio López de Santa Anna (1794–1876) in Mexico, Juan Manuel de Rosas (1793–1877) in Argentina, and José Antonio Pérez (1790–1873) in Venezuela.

Subsequent "modern" caudillos have included the Mexican dictator José de la Cruz Porfirio Díaz (1830–1915), who promoted strong nationalist tendencies and came to power at a time of increased political stability. Modern caudillos encouraged the institutionalization of authoritarian practices based on the state's monopoly on force. Historians debate whether the leaders of the Mexican Revolution displayed the characteristics of caudillos, and a few historians suggest that the postrevolutionary generation of politicians in the 1920s, like some contemporary North American politicians, embodied new forms of *caudi-*

llismo. The postrevolutionary Mexican state, some have asserted, succeeded in completing the process of institutionalizing caudillismo.

Richard Conway

References

Brading, David A., ed. *Caudillo and Peasant in the Mexican Revolution.* New York: Cambridge University Press, 1980.

Hamill, Hugh M. Jr., ed. *Caudillos: Dictators in Spanish America.* Norman: University of Oklahoma Press, 1992.

Lynch, John. *Caudillos in Spanish America, 1800–1850.* Oxford: Clarendon Press, 1992.

Wolf, Eric R., and Edward C. Hansen. "Caudillo Politics: A Structural Analysis." *Comparative Studies in Society and History* 9 (1966–1967): 168–179.

See also: Argentina; Encomienda; Estancia; Guerrillas; Hacienda; Independence I–VI; Mexican Revolution; Mexico; Nationalism; Terrorism; Venezuela.

CENSORSHIP—BRAZIL

Censorship in Brazil can be traced to the earliest years of Portuguese colonial government. Throughout the first 308 years of colonial rule, the Portuguese Crown never allowed a printing press to exist in Brazil. All reading matter was thus either imported from the metropolis or smuggled into the colony.

While such direct control was obvious, indirect control occurred as the result of Portuguese education policies in the colony. Even primary education was severely limited, generally available only to males of the upper and upper-middle classes. As a general rule, African slaves were not taught to read or write the Portuguese language. Indigenous peoples who survived the conquest and subsequent dis-ease increasingly fled into the interior. In effect, only well-born white males enjoyed access to printed matter beyond the ecclesiastical, a fact that inherently limited the diffusion of ideas, especially those that might be construed as a challenge to Portuguese dominance in Brazil.

Ideas were limited not only by controlling access to them, but also by restricting the potential audience to those who had a stake in the existing structure of government. Yet even the sons of privilege and wealth could receive only a secondary education in Brazil. Thus, ideas were further limited by the complete absence of institutions of higher education in the colony.

During the second half of the eighteenth century, ideas of the Enlightenment filtered into Brazil via the University of Coimbra, Portugal's leading institution of higher education, to which the scions of Brazil's leading families were sent to complete their training. Many of these young men went on to postgraduate study in French universities before returning to Brazil. Especially during the last decades of the eighteenth century, Enlightenment ideas began to interest educated Brazilians and inspire them to imitate the example of their peers in the Iberian metropolis. During the time of the reforms instituted by the Marquis of Pombal, educated Portuguese had begun to form private societies for discussion of pertinent economic and political questions of the day. Such groups proliferated both in Portugal and in Brazil. Indeed, the censorship policy of the Portuguese Crown was to some degree vindicated by the fact that from precisely such a group stemmed the most notorious of the late eighteenth-century republican conspiracies against colonial rule, the Inconfidencia Mineira (also known as the Tiradentes conspiracy) in Minas Gerais. Tiradentes, which means "tooth-puller," refers to Joaquim José da Silva Xavier, a part-time dentist and one of the leaders of the conspiracy.

In 1807, facing invasion by the forces of Napoleon, the Bragança court fled Lisbon for Brazil. Establishing his new seat of Portuguese government in Rio, Portuguese king Dom João (King John VI) demonstrated his regal largesse by endowing several new educational and cultural institutions, while also installing the first printing press in Brazil.

With the first printing press came the first imposition of press regulation by the government. Royal censors were appointed to ensure that nothing could be printed that might be construed as opposition to the government, contradiction of the Catholic religion, or contravention of morality. A recurring justification was the government's responsibility to protect citizens from political venom and falsehood that might deceive simple and ignorant people. Such a stance presumed a patriarchal relationship of benevolent protection between government and citizen.

Nonetheless, this direct infusion of European culture proved difficult to reverse. From then on, elite Brazilians and those of the upper-middle professional classes increasingly became accustomed to reading about and discussing the pressing political issues and cultural trends of the day. Naturally, such advantages and habits did not extend to the lower classes, and certainly not to slaves; however, increasing numbers of talented mulattoes were educated and exposed to the latest ideas.

Despite the significant role of the press in urging independence from Portugal, the independence proclaimed by Dom Pedro I in 1822 did little to alter fundamental assumptions of prior state censorship. Indeed, in the first year of the existence of the Empire of Brazil, the Council of State moved to protect the government against the publication of incendiary and subversive doctrines and disorganizing and abhorrent principles. Such doctrines and principles were to be determined at the discretion and convenience of the state.

During the mid-nineteenth century, much press activity consisted of *pasquins*, pamphlets or broadside sheets that satirized government policies and politicians. It could be said that both the government's measures of censorship and its opponents' use of the press were routinely scurrilous. Nonetheless, the institutional press did on occasion rise to a higher level of public debate, notably in its coverage of the struggle over the abolition of slavery, which led directly to the end of the empire and the proclamation of the First Republic.

During the First Republic, the state's positivist orientation, its drive for modernization, and its commitment to "Order and Progress" led to a corresponding growth in the influence of the press, which paralleled processes of increased urbanization and industrialization. Large-scale publishing enterprises were founded. Modern newspapers were established in the major cities. The publishing industry was allowed, indeed encouraged, to progress technologically and professionally. Yet it remained ever subject to direct government intervention and control.

Continued state control of a modern, professional press led to increased resistance to censorship by publishers and editors resentful of the state's restrictions. For nine months in 1924–1925, the government prevented circulation of the Rio de Janeiro daily *Correio da Manha,* which challenged the censorial action in court. Although the court upheld the right of the daily newspaper to circulate freely, it demurred on the right to publish freely. The government prevailed on the issue of prior censorship, even before the ascension to power of an even more state-oriented government in 1930.

During the populist/corporatist Estado Novo proclaimed by Getúlio Vargas in the late 1930s, opposing views on both the right and the left were censored. Vargas went so far as to exile or imprison his leading opponents, Plinio Salgado of the Fascist Integralist Party and Luis Carlos Prestes of the Communist Party. The Vargas dictatorship cracked down on its opposition, while at the same time it offered potential opponents entrée to the regime. In effect, Vargas made potential opponents offers they could seldom refuse. If they went along with his policies and programs, they received state subsidies and other favors, valuable if not essential to their ability to survive and prosper. If they made trouble, their property might be destroyed and they themselves physically threatened, abused, or eliminated.

Intense, direct, coercive state intervention began with the 1930 revolution that first brought Vargas to power. In 1932, the new government instituted an Official Department of Propaganda, the state agency responsible for censorship. Even though the Constitution of 1934 specified the right to freedom of the press, it also prohibited public presentation of anything that might incite violence or subvert the existing political or social order. Official censors tended to interpret broadly the potentially deleterious effects of publications or presentations in other media that came under their purview.

As the Department of Press and Propaganda (DIP) displaced the Official Department of Propaganda, state violation of supposed constitutional guarantees of free speech and free press became increasingly systematic and pervasive. The new censorship agency issued daily orders to newspaper editorial boards concerning news that the DIP considered detrimental to the state. If a newspaper wanted to stay in business, it dutifully followed instructions. At the same time, the DIP planted prefabricated stories favorable to the Vargas regime, the publication of which was considered essential to the reconstruction of the nation.

In order to conduct business or pursue their profession, not only journalistic enterprises but also individual journalists had to be officially registered with the state, which routinely denied registration to media outlets, editors, and writers believed to oppose the regime. At its sole discretion, the state also extended or withheld subsidies to press enterprises, at the same time that it controlled the supply of newsprint. While the Estado Novo took extraordinary measures to control the written word, Vargas himself strove to master the emerging medium of radio in order to communicate directly with the rural masses and the great number of Brazilians who remained illiterate.

When the Vargas dictatorship was deposed by the military in 1946, the new regime, though nominally democratic, retained many of the censorship measures imposed by the Estado Novo. The publication of anything regarded by the government as a challenge to the established social and political order was still prohibited. At

Communist propaganda seized by police in raids following the overthrow of Brazilian leftist president João Goulart. (Time Life Pictures/Getty Images)

the same time, the press had grown accustomed to government control and manipulation, both by force and by the extension or denial of favors. As had many other Brazilian businesses, the major publishers had come to rely on the government for subsidies and credits, which continued only so long as the press hewed to the official line. Still, when a diminished Vargas was returned to power by election in 1951, many major newspapers and magazines opposed him and trumpeted the scandals that led to his political downfall and ultimate suicide.

Sensing his position to be too weak to directly suppress publications that opposed him, Vargas had sought to promote the publication and circulation of his own points of view by having the government-owned Bank of Brazil extend substantial credit to a nationwide chain of pro-Vargas media outlets. By contrast, during the late 1950s, President Juscelino Kubitschek moved to confiscate editions of publications he deemed offensive, and he revoked the television concessions of a media corporation to whose publications he took exception. Similar acts of government suppression of news media occurred regarding the resignation of President Janio Quadros and Vice-President João Goulart's succession to the presidency.

Since at least 1930, whether in its occasional resistance to government censorship or in more prevalent collusion with and capitulation to government interests, Brazil's press has seldom been independent. Moreover, as evidenced by mainstream press opposition to Goulart, the politically influential print media in Brazil have tended toward classic liberalism and elitism, opposing democracy itself when it dared to propose fundamental socioeconomic reforms such as land redistribution. At the same time, the mainstream press's support for the rule of law and observance of constitutional guarantees led it to oppose the 1964–1985 military governments in their institutionalization of repressive measures such as mass arrests, torture, and extrajudicial executions.

In response, the military shut down one of its major critics, confiscated editions of offensive newspapers and magazines, occupied editorial offices, arrested editors and publishers, and continued the long-standing practice of bringing financial pressures to bear on its opponents in the press. Quite apart from the rampant political censorship of the military governments, which attacked both mainstream mass media and alternative publications of miniscule circulation, censorship of cultural productions on moral grounds continued to be legal and socially acceptable, as had long been the case.

Under the military authoritarian governments that ruled Brazil from 1964 through 1985, censorship of all communications media was pervasive, extreme, and systematic, as was political repression in general. In response, literary, musical, and dramatic artists grew increasingly creative in their public expressions of opposition to the regime. A brilliant and moving example of such imaginative opposition was the song "Calice," composed by singer-songwriters Chico Buarque and Gilberto Gil.

Challenging the military dictatorship, this taut and mournful song took its refrain verbatim from Christ's plea to God the Father in the Garden of Gethsemane: "Father, may this chalice pass from my lips . . . this red wine of blood." An inspired play on words, the song assailed repression by availing itself of the similar Portuguese pronunciation of *calice*, meaning "chalice," and *cala-se*, meaning "keep quiet, shut up." Indeed, when Buarque and Gil defied censors and attempted to perform the song publicly at a 1973 music festival in São Paulo, all the microphones on stage were sequentially disconnected, leaving the performers effectively speechless and providing an immediately tangible example of the censorship that Buarque and Gil protested. Buarque was not allowed to perform the song publicly until six years later, when the military authoritarian regime began a transition to democracy.

The constitution of 1988, as amended in 1996, prohibits censorship. Title II (Fundamental Rights and Guarantees), Chapter I, Article 5, Section IV, declares: "The expression of thought is free, and anonymity is forbidden." Section V ensures the right of reply, in proportion to the offense, as well as the right to compensation.

By 2003, with the accession to power of the government of President Luis Inácio Lula da Silva, who selected the previously censored artist Gilberto Gil as his minister of culture, there was hope that censorship in Brazil, one of the more unfortunate gifts of Portugal to the New World, would finally be eradicated.

John Gordon Farrell

References

Johnson, Randal. "Literature, Culture, and Authoritarianism in Brazil, 1930–1945." Wilson Center Working Paper no. 179, 1989.

Marchant, Alexander. "Aspects of the Enlightenment in Brazil." Pp. 95–118 in *Latin America and the Enlightenment*, edited by Arthur P. Whitaker. Ithaca, NY: Cornell University Press, 1961.

Skidmore, Thomas E. *Politics in Brazil, 1930–1964: An Experiment in Democracy.* New York: Oxford University Press, 1967.

———. *The Politics of Military Rule in Brazil, 1964–85.* New York: Oxford University Press, 1988.

———. *Brazil: Five Centuries of Change.* New York: Oxford University Press, 1999.

Smith, Anne-Marie. *A Forced Agreement: Press Acquiescence to Censorship in Brazil.* Pittsburgh: University of Pittsburgh Press, 1997.

See also: Abolition and Emancipation; Art and Artists—Brazil; Brazil; Colonists and Settlers II—Brazil; Communism; Democracy; Education—Brazil; Enlightenment—Brazil; Independence II—Brazil; Monarchs of Portugal; Music and Dance I—Brazil; Napoleonic Invasion and Luso-America; Native Americans II—Brazil; Science and Scientists—Brazil/Portugal; Slavery I—Brazil; Universities.

CENSORSHIP— SPANISH AMERICA

Censorship in Spanish America was at once different from and similar to that experienced in Brazil. It differed in that, from the earliest years of the colonial enterprise, the Spanish Crown not only permitted but actively encouraged higher education in its American colonies, particularly in Mexico and Peru, the seats of colonial power and wealth. Moreover, again unlike Brazil, from the earliest years people in the Spanish colonies had access to the printing press, and therefore to locally produced books, newspapers, pamphlets, leaflets, broadsheets, and other means for the dissemination of ideas, both European and American.

Nonetheless, the Spanish colonies were subject to the same standards and practices of censorship prevalent in contemporary Spain. Since the church functioned as both the guardian of morality and an arm of the government, censorship was applied to the works and ideas of the Protestant Reformation, as well as to works of drama or literature considered excessively salacious. Of course, in an absolute monarchy, direct challenge to the authority of the Crown was never tolerated.

Ample latitude, however, was provided for the exercise of intelligence and the expression of human passions. Works by the great writers and dramatists of the Spanish Golden Age—Miguel de Cervantes, Francisco de Quevedo, Lope de Vega, Pedro Calderón de la Barca, and Tirso de Molina, among others, were avidly read and applauded in the colonies, as well as in the metropolis.

Perhaps the greatest and most poignant failure to allow sufficient freedom of expression in the colonies was the suppression of the work of the brilliant Mexican nun, Sor Juana Inés de la Cruz. Sor Juana was certainly one of the most gifted and able literary minds of the seventeenth century, whether in Iberia or America. Yet she was censored; the censorship of her writings involved patriarchal attitudes toward women, power rivalries between competing viceroys, and an archbishop determined to exert his authority over one of his flock.

The vigilance of the Spanish Inquisition was surely a potent force that encouraged self-censorship among writers. The ecclesiastical instinct for eradication of nonconformist thought waxed and waned but never disappeared entirely during the colonial period. In the Americas, however, the Inquisition (established in Mexico City and Lima in 1569, in Cartagena in 1610) seems to have addressed itself more to issues of suspected heresy among Protestant interlopers and New Christians (converted Jews) than to political ideology.

During the eighteenth century, works of the Enlightenment were officially proscribed yet circulated widely among learned Creoles (*criollos*), those of Spanish blood born in the New World, as well as *peninsulares,* those born in Spain. At the same time, while philosophical works challenging the divine right of kings and promoting individual rights and political liberties did not find favor with the Bourbon monarchs and their New World viceroys, governors-general, and intendants, the Spanish Crown found virtue in those aspects of Enlightened thought that advanced "useful knowledge." Censorship generally no longer dampened scientific inquiry, because the potential economic benefits to be derived were perceived to outweigh the risks.

With the independence movements of the early nineteenth century came the rise of news and literary enterprises promoting republican causes. Though most of the first-generation republican leaders were preoccupied with military matters, many of their liberal successors (finding themselves violently opposed by conservative and autocratic forces) turned to journalism while in exile to advance their point of view. Exemplary in this regard was Domingo Faustino Sarmiento, whose celebrated *Facundo: Civilización y barbarie,* a thinly veiled assault on the caudillo mentality of the Argentine dictator Juan Manuel de Rosas, was originally published in Chile in serial installments. In 1841, Sarmiento himself succinctly crystallized the dilemma of most nineteenth-century Latin American governments regarding censorship: he argued that there could be no liberty or progress without a free press; however, he lamented that with such freedoms, public order could barely be maintained.

Sarmiento and his liberal colleagues held as an article of faith that a vigorous, free press was essential to civilization, the only sure antidote to ever-encroaching barbarism. Yet, even in Chile, the most politically stable of the new Spanish American republics, an intemperate and vociferous free press had fomented unruly assemblies that often turned riotous. Especially when its practitioners indulged in offensive and outrageous allegations against political opponents, the civilizing antidote itself seemed to promote virulent barbarism.

Indeed, the press in nineteenth-century Spanish America was narrowly partisan in its support of particular political parties, interest groups, and individuals. Many press enterprises arose as if out of

nowhere, agitated their point of view, reviled their opponents, and disappeared almost immediately, once the particular issue or election they were concerned with had passed from the scene. Intended to influence a small electorate, few of these "newspapers" enjoyed wide circulation. Their generally poor quality was surpassed only by their lack of balance and fairness.

Given their avowedly and often viciously partisan nature, such publications were all the more likely to disappear if their opponents won political power. The constant battle for control of republican governments, usually pitting liberals against conservatives, was not for the fainthearted, or for those who considered themselves to be above the fray; and one of the main weapons employed by both sides was censorship of opposition media.

As for Church-related censorship of literary or other forms of art deemed "immoral" by the arbiters of decency, the extent to which this was enforced depended largely on which political group was in power. Under liberals, determined to curtail the influence of the Church in public affairs, such censorship would tend to diminish. Under conservative governments, long allied with ecclesiastical interests, it would tend to increase.

Toward the end of the nineteenth century, as the political turbulence of the early republican period gave way to an era of national consolidation, certain of the previously ephemeral press enterprises matured into "modern" newspapers, that is, established organs for the dissemination of news, information, and entertainment. Though they might maintain a quasi-liberal political perspective, editorial policy, and self-image, established newspapers and magazines generally evolved into socially and economically conservative media, an evolution that parallels that of previously liberal political parties into positivist forces for "modernization." Nowhere was this trend more apparent than in Mexico, where a self-consciously progressive *cientifico* such as the historian and public intellectual Justo Sierra dutifully sang the praises of seven-term president-for-life Porfirio Díaz, the personification of a youthful liberal firebrand evolving into a positivist who found "order and progress" far more consequential than liberty or social and economic justice.

In the twentieth century, as press enterprises evolved into potent economic engines, the ability of governments to control their content also adapted, taking on more modern forms. Especially under statist governments, such as those of Argentina under Juan Perón, or Mexico under the Partido Revolucionario Institucional (PRI), withholding essential, imported newsprint or denying lucrative government advertising revenues to politically wayward publications proved an effective means of controlling the content of published articles, photographs, and editorials. Where such logic failed to persuade, governments of both Left and Right were willing to resort to more direct means of censorship, such as denying distribution, harassing reporters, threatening editors, jailing publishers, and expropriating entire enterprises.

Just as governments could and did withhold essential newsprint from opposition publications, so too did they withhold vital imported electronic parts and equipment, such as transmitter power tubes, from recalcitrant radio and television stations. Moreover, as the capitalization costs of radio and television stations generally exceeded those of print media outlets, the government could often control the flow of information and opinion from such outlets by subsidizing, or refusing to subsidize, their operations. Especially in those countries where illiteracy was (and sometimes remains) widespread, control over electronic media was considered crucial to governments, particularly unpopular governments. Among such were the decades-long dictatorships of Alfredo Stroessner in Paraguay and Rafael Trujillo in the Dominican Republic.

Even governments that enjoyed widespread popular support among the masses sometimes considered censorship. By mid-century, Perón in Argentina and Fidel Castro in Cuba had developed an ingenious counterargument to that made by publishers opposing their policies. While the owners of press enterprises insisted on their right to publicly contradict the government, based on their rights to private property and freedom of the press, the populist rulers proclaimed that workers at press enterprises enjoyed a corresponding right, at least as regards freedom of the press. In the early 1960s, employing labor unions at press enterprises as a countervailing force against owners and managers, the Castro government promoted the addition of a disclaimer at the end of articles opposing its policies.

The military authoritarian governments that ruled in most of Spanish America for a generation, from the mid-1960s in Brazil to the early 1990s in Chile, seized power in direct and preemptive response to a perceived threat of Communist domination. Under such unpopular governments, censorship became the norm. Without a doubt, the censorship practiced by these military governments represents the most systematic and violent repression against journalists, writers, artists, filmmakers, dramatists, indeed practitioners of all forms of creative expression, ever practiced in Spanish America. In Brazil, Uruguay, Chile, and Argentina, military authoritarian governments took power in coups d'état against democratically elected governments and proceeded to assassinate or "disappear" many opponents; many more were arrested, detained, imprisoned, tortured, and killed. Not surprisingly, such policies successfully intimidated most of the rest of the opposition. From the late 1960s through the 1980s, civil wars in Guatemala, Nicaragua, and El Salvador led to censorship of news media and violent repression and murders of journalists and others, such as priests and nuns, who publicly opposed government policies.

Under such circumstances, as well as the policies pursued earlier by governments such as those of Díaz, Vargas, Perón, the PRI, and Castro, among others, it is little wonder that journalists, whether reporters, editors, or publishers, began to practice self-censorship, preferring not to risk the wrath of government censors. As ever, a seductive carrot accompanied the threatening stick. A journalist who supported the existing regime not only avoided punishment, but might also be generously rewarded for neither hearing, seeing, nor speaking any evil of its policies.

A relatively recent complement to government-imposed censorship has been that imposed by drug traffickers. Particularly in Mexico and Colombia, organized crime has achieved such wealth and power that any journalist who dares to expose its operations may as well sign his or her own death warrant. Such drug-related violence, often protected by the complicity of police

or government officials, is another compelling argument for journalists to practice self-censorship.

Despite long-standing practices of censorship in Spanish America, as well as more recent threats to freedom of expression, journalists, writers, and artists continue to insist on their right to publish facts and express their opinions publicly, without risk of professional or physical reprisal. In this regard, national and international professional associations and nongovernmental organizations have been supportive. Though dominated by the United States and thus sometimes presumptuous in its pronouncements, the Inter-American Press Association (IAPA) has nonetheless, since 1926, proven invaluable in documenting the record of persecutions suffered by journalists. Rather more evenhanded has been the work of organizations such as the Zurich-based International Press Institute; Index on Censorship; the Committee to Protect Journalists; PEN, the international association of writers; Human Rights Watch; and Amnesty International.

Spanish American governments have ranged from mild to harsh dictatorships, across almost the entire breadth of the political spectrum, from nationalist governments of the Right and the Left, to autocratic dictatorships, to authoritarian military regimes, to Communist rule. All of these variations have relied on both overt and covert censorship to bolster their own administrations and degrade political opponents. Spanish American republics enjoying genuine freedom of expression for mass media have always been exceptions to the rule. Moreover, those in the fortunate minority have repeatedly changed places with those whose media are censored, rendering much of their mutual criticism more than a little hypocritical and justifying the observation that the pot has called the kettle black. Thus, to a degree, the influence of Iberian colonial norms of censorship is still apparent in contemporary Spanish America.

John Gordon Farrell

References

Alisky, Marvin. *Latin American Media: Guidance and Censorship.* Ames: Iowa State University Press, 1981.

Burkholder, Mark A., and Lyman L. Johnson. *Colonial Latin America.* 3rd ed. New York: Oxford University Press, 1998.

Callado, Antonio. *Censorship and Other Problems of Latin American Writers.* Cambridge: Centre of Latin American Studies, University of Cambridge, 1974.

Dubois, Jules. *The Fight for Freedom in Latin America.* Lawrence, KS: William Allen White Foundation, 1960.

Freedom to Write Committee, eds. *Latin America: The Freedom to Write.* New York: PEN American Center, 1980.

Jaksic, Ivan, ed. *The Political Power of the Word: Press and Oratory in Nineteenth-Century Latin America.* London: Institute of Latin American Studies, University of London, 2002.

Ruiz, Teofilo F. *Spanish Society, 1400–1600.* London and New York: Longman/Pearson Education, 2001.

See also: Art and Artists—Colonial Spanish America; Art and Artists—Modern Spanish America; Catholic Church in Spanish America; Caudillos; Censorship—Brazil; Communism; Creoles; Cuba; Cuban Revolution; Education—Colonial Spanish America; Enlightenment—Spanish America; Guerrillas; Human Rights; Independence I–VI; Inquisition—Spanish America; Intendants/Intendancy System; Jesuits—Iberia and America; Jews—Colonial Latin America; Liberalism; Literary Relations—Spain and the Americas; Mexican Revolution; Mexico; Nationalism; Populism; Positivism; Protestant Reformation; Religious Orders; Universities; Viceroyalties; Women—Colonial Spanish America.

CHACO WAR (1932–1935)

The Chaco War, the most important war fought in South America during the twentieth century, was rooted in boundary disputes that dated back to the Spanish colonial era. The war was fought between Bolivia and Paraguay for possession of the Chaco Boreal, a vast but desolate area that both countries had claimed since gaining independence from Spain. Bolivia was also interested in gaining an outlet to the Atlantic Ocean by establishing ports on the Paraguay River. Both sides were ill prepared, and both underestimated the formidable terrain over which they had to wage war. The Paraguayans were able to mobilize faster and soon expanded their army dramatically. Paraguay also found a competent leader in General José Estigarribia, who won the full backing of his government. Bolivia, on the other hand, failed to declare a general mobilization, and the military command and civilian leadership argued over strategy. Nevertheless, Bolivia advanced and quickly captured several small Paraguayan outposts. On September 29, 1932, Estigarribia mounted a counterattack on Fort Boquerón, which drove the Bolivians back. The battle was costly; both sides sustained over 3,000 casualties.

Paraguay's victory resulted in the appointment of General Hans Kundt, the former head of the German military mission to Bolivia, to take command of the Bolivian army. In December 1932, Kundt initiated a general offensive against a string of Paraguayan forts. However, Kundt's yearlong offensive failed to dislodge the Paraguayan defenders. It resulted in heavy casualties, and ultimately led to his being relieved of command. With Bolivia's attack blunted, Estigarribia launched an of-

General Hans Kundt with soldiers of the Bolivian army in the fight against Paraguay for possession of the Chaco border, La Paz, Bolivia, 1933. (Bettmann/Corbis)

fensive, and his forces gradually drove the Bolivians from many of their Chaco forts. By the summer of 1934 the Paraguayan army had driven into Bolivia proper. Estigarribia feared that his forces were overextended and ordered a gradual retreat. Bolivia pursued his army deep into the Chaco, but in December 1934, a reinforced Paraguayan army encircled the Bolivians and took 6,000 prisoners. By early 1935, Paraguay controlled most of the disputed territory; however, Bolivia rallied and finally declared a general mobilization. The war had drained the national treasuries and manpower of both countries, and on June 12, 1935, a cease-fire was signed.

Bolivia and Paraguay signed the Treaty of Buenos Aires in 1938, which formally ended hostilities. Paraguay acquired 75 percent of the disputed territory, while Bolivia was granted access to the Paraguay River for use as an outlet to the Atlantic Ocean. The casualty rate was high; Bolivia lost 57,000 men and Paraguay nearly 36,000.

George Lauderbaugh

References

Ynsfrán, Pablo Max, ed. *José Felix Estigarribia: The Epic of the Chaco.* Austin: University of Texas Press, 1952.

Zook, David H. *The Conduct of the Chaco War.* New Haven, CT: Bookman Associates, 1960.

See also: Armies—Modern Latin America; Bolivia; Paraguay.

CHILDHOOD IN COLONIAL LATIN AMERICA

From 1492 onward, Iberian, African, and indigenous American children helped to shape the nature of society, culture, and economy in the Americas. And while childhood was not often separated from work in Iberia and America, concepts of childhood varied culturally.

In both Iberia and America, children contributed to the growth of agriculture and industry; however, documentation about their lives is scarce for the colonial period. Female and male children of African, indigenous, and Iberian families began to work at an early age, the majority by seven or eight years old. Children labored as field and ranch hands, fishers, miners, spinners, potters, vendors, servants, and laborers in a variety of other occupations. Many Amerindian societies used age to determine when a person began certain occupations. For example, the Inca used a decimal ranking system and believed that children even younger than ten were productive members of their family and community.

The largest Brazilian indigenous group, the Tupis, recognized the paternal line of children and practiced rituals to protect them from illness and danger. Tupi fathers chose children's names to represent strength and success, using names for animals, fish, or trees considered supernaturally powerful. A Tupi child spent its first two years of life strapped into a small hammock (*tipoia*) on its mother's back; Tupi mothers nursed their children for at least as long. Children accompanied mothers in their daily labors, from fieldwork to cooking. Boys and girls were segregated at puberty, and both had their hair cut short. Pubescent boys lived in houses called *baito* where they were initiated into manhood through ritual trials and where they learned the arts of war, hunting, building, and their people's history. The skin of pubescent girls was cut and cured so that scars formed patterns on their bodies. When a girl's hair had grown long and her scars healed, parents presented her to a husband.

African civilizations were characterized by a great diversity of beliefs about and rituals for children. Many groups used rituals to protect children from disease and danger; they honored ancestral spirits to secure them safe and healthy futures, and women usually socialized children. The correct name for a child helped to ward off evil; some children were ritually scarified. Among the Ibo of Niger, children resided with the father's family, and age-rank determined male and female authority inside and outside the home. Polygamy was common in many regions, so families often comprised large extended kin networks. The Atlantic slave trade disrupted many of these networks, but also saw their persistence and transformation across the seas. Slave traders brought several million Africans to the Americas, especially to the Caribbean and Brazil, from the 1500s to the 1800s. Merchants preferred to buy men, since they were supposed to resist disease and toil better than women and children, who were enslaved in smaller numbers. Children were usually separated from their families upon capture or purchase. Once enslaved in the Americas, many

African women were forced to bear the children of their masters; these racially mixed children were called *mulatos* (mulattoes) and were occasionally freed by their masters. Any child born of an enslaved woman inherited her slave status, until nineteenth-century abolition laws abrogated that rule. Enslaved children performed lighter tasks like cleaning and sewing until they were physically ready for agricultural work or, in urban contexts, manufacturing and commerce.

Similar to early modern Africans and indigenous Americans, many Iberians believed in the supernatural and the power of ritual to overcome malevolent forces. Iberians often called upon local patron saints to protect them and their children from evil. Iberian children were baptized eight days after birth and, typically, had three godparents. Early modern Catholic Europeans believed children had been born with original sin, to which they attributed misconduct and immaturity. Children were not considered immoral, but rather amoral; they needed to learn appropriate behavior and ethics. Parents were obligated to provide children with material, religious, physical, and moral education. Considered incapable of reason until the age of seven, children began formal schooling then. The Iberian legal system defined children as wards of their fathers; mothers had limited authority. The doctrine of *patria potestad* (paternal authority) determined family life: children were expected to obey their parents as wives obeyed husbands. Children had to address their parents with respectful titles and ask parents for daily blessing. Older children had authority over their younger siblings, but a father's authority reigned supreme. Puberty did not exist in Iberian legal concepts of childhood. Ac-

cording to civil and canon law, a girl's childhood ended at twelve and a boy's at fourteen; then they could marry, enter the church, and write wills. These dictates applied to any Catholic in the Americas, but race and class barriers still restricted most Amerindians and Africans from access to the property and privilege that many Iberians enjoyed.

Only noble or wealthy Iberian children received any formal education in the colonial period. Basic training in the Catholic catechism formed a part of the dominical education of most commoners across the Americas. The Catholic Church focused considerable evangelical effort on children of all races and languages to educate them in the Christian faith. This dominical education was not written biblical instruction in Sunday school, but rather spoken call and response with a cleric. Basic literacy and advanced studies in the arts and sciences were limited to elite Iberian children. Elite education differed according to gender: boys could advance to study law or theology in universities, while girls studied the Bible, domestic management, and decorative arts, and usually only until the age of twelve, unless they entered a convent. The eighteenth-century Enlightenment introduced new attitudes toward female education, and formal schooling became accessible to more girls.

Infant mortality rates were extremely high in colonial Latin America, but were even higher among indigenous and enslaved African peoples. Malnutrition and disease claimed the lives of many infants. Parents often conceived many children, in part to ensure that their family line would endure, and also to secure their own existence with the promise of their children's future work and income. Despite its likelihood, Latin

Americans did not grow callous about child death. Among Christians, the unbaptized infant dead were considered angels who had escaped life; they were buried at crossroads or near homes, not in cemeteries.

Abandonment was common response to poverty in Latin America. Children were left with relatives and with wealthy or charitable people, or in orphanages established by local churches. These children worked from an early age, either laboring in an adoptive family's home or apprenticing with a craftsman or cleric. The government allowed orphans to work for pay from the age of seven, but placed no limits on the kind of work they performed. Well into the 1800s, families asked orphanages to send children to work in their homes.

In wealthy Iberian families, children were usually reared by nursemaids, who were often African or racially mixed women. Enslaved and freed Africans formed large populations in Brazil, the Caribbean and circum-Caribbean, New Spain, and Peru. Wealthier Iberian women ran households in which their own children lived and played with the nonwhite children of domestic servants and slaves. Iberian men tended to marry much later in life than did Iberian women, who had few alternatives to marriage. Many couples in the Americas never married at all. Men often had relationships and children with women of lower social rank and of a different racial category. Iberian patterns of treatment of illegitimate children differed little from the Old to the New World. A father might recognize the child of an informal union, which conferred some legal and financial protection. Still this so-called *hijo natural* (natural child) did not hold the same social rank as a legitimate child. For example, a "natural" son might work closely with his father as a steward or aide, but he would never gain social or legal equality with any of his legitimate half-siblings.

Stark relationships of power in Iberia and the Americas favored the will and whim of Iberian men. Informal unions and interracial households did stimulate greater social and cultural contact and change over the centuries. It was still important to Iberians in the Americas to maintain clear racial boundaries, since a child's lineage was an important factor in determining his or her social status. Given the prevalence of racial mixture in the colonies, it became difficult to determine what Iberians considered "purity of blood" (*limpieza de sangre*). Despite the theoretical insistence on Iberian supremacy, by the end of the eighteenth century, many traditional hierarchies of racial and social rank had dissolved, and new social orders had coalesced. Latin American children encountered new opportunities for social advancement through education and employment. In the early nineteenth century, as war raged and independent states emerged across the Americas, many aspects of children's lives, from school to work to play, again altered in deep and subtle ways.

Meri L. Clark

References

Cunningham, Hugh, and Pier Paolo Viazzo, eds. *Child Labour in Historical Perspective, 1800–1985: Case Studies from Europe, Japan, and Colombia.* Florence, Italy: UNICEF, 1996.

Hawes, Joseph M., and N. Ray Hiner, eds. *Children in Historical and Comparative Perspective: An International Handbook and Research Guide.* New York: Greenwood, 1991.

Hecht, Tobias, ed. *Minor Omissions: Children in Latin American History and Society.* Madison: University of Wisconsin Press, 2002.

Kuznesof, Elizabeth Anne. "Brazil." Pp. 147–177 in *Children in Historical and Comparative Perspective,* edited by Joseph Hawes and N. Ray Hiner. New York: Greenwood, 1991.

Lavrín, Asunción. "Mexico." Pp. 421–445 in *Children in Historical and Comparative Perspective,* edited by Joseph Hawes and N. Ray Hiner. New York: Greenwood, 1991.

Lipsett-Rivera, Sonya. "Model Children and Models for Children in Early Mexico." Pp. 52–71 in *Minor Omissions: Children in Latin American History and Society,* edited by Tobias Hecht. Madison: University of Wisconsin Press, 2002.

Milanich, Nara. "Historical Perspectives on Illegitimacy and Illegitimates in Latin America." Pp. 72–101 in *Minor Omissions: Children in Latin American History and Society,* edited by Tobias Hecht. Madison: University of Wisconsin Press, 2002.

Muñoz Vila, Cecilia. "The Working Child in Colombia since 1800." Pp. 91–104 in *Child Labour in Historical Perspective, 1800–1985: Case Studies from Europe, Japan, and Colombia,* edited by Hugh Cunningham and Pier Paolo Viazzo. Florence, Italy: UNICEF, 1996.

Pollock, Linda A. *Forgotten Children: Parent-Child Relations from 1500 to 1900.* Cambridge: Cambridge University Press, 1983.

Premo, Bianca. "Minor Offenses: Youth, Crime, and Law in Eighteenth-Century Lima." Pp. 114–138 in *Minor Omissions: Children in Latin American History and Society,* edited by Tobias Hecht. Madison: University of Wisconsin Press, 2002.

See also: Catholic Church in Brazil; Catholic Church in Spanish America; Education—Brazil; Education—Colonial Spanish America; Enlightenment—Brazil; Enlightenment—Spanish America; Family—Colonial Brazil; Family—Colonial Spanish America; Independence I–VI; Marriage; Mulatto; Native Americans I–VIII; Poverty; Race; Religious Orders; Slave Trade; Slavery I–IV; Universities; Women—Brazil; Women—Colonial Spanish America.

CHILE

Iberian-Chilean relations, as in most of Latin America, started with the arrival of the first Spanish conquerors to the area. The levels of complexity then reached by local native societies determined not only their reactions toward the invaders, but also the success of Spanish settlement. Over time, the development of an agrarian capitalism deeply marked the colony's life and determined the formation of distinct social categories. The eighteenth century witnessed the espousing of protonational ideals, eagerly coined by the local elite. Although Chile achieved its political independence from Spain by the early nineteenth century, the extent of Iberian influence over Chilean society can be perceived even today.

Located along the southwestern side of the Andes, Chile was home to several Indian groups in pre-Columbian times. Diaguitas, who distinguished themselves for their clever use of the Atacama Desert's extremely inhospitable ecosystem, populated the northern region. Araucanians, who occupied most of central and southern Chile, were agricultural people who combined cropping with the gathering of wild foods. Composed of three major related groups, the Huilliches, Picunches, and Mapuches, Araucanians took advantage of the fertile valleys of central Chile. A related group, the Pehuenches, controlled passes in the Andean foothills that connected Chile with the Argentine pampas. Onas, Alakalufs, and Yaghans populated Tierra del Fuego, several islands separated by inlets and channels in southern Chile. Gradually killed off by illnesses, these last groups were largely hunter-gatherer societies who relied primarily on fishing for subsistence.

It has been documented that the Inca Empire started its expansion toward the south under the reign of Inca Túpac Yupanqui (ca. 1448–ca. 1482). Archaeological data show that Indians in Chile reacted in different ways to the invasion. Diaguitas offered fierce resistance at first, a fact proved by the many *pukaras* (Indian fortresses) scattered throughout the area. In spite of their initial fight, the Diaguitas eventually accepted Inca rule and became subjects of the empire. The Araucanians, on the contrary, successfully opposed the *Cusqueño* (Cuzco-centered) expansion and made central Chile the southern frontier of the Inca Empire.

The Spanish invasion of Chile followed a similar pattern. In 1535, Diego de Almagro, a veteran of the conquest of the Inca Empire and Francisco Pizarro's former partner, organized his own band and headed south. Tired of fighting for the spoils of the Inca Empire, and no match for the Pizarro brothers, Almagro deemed true a rumor among the Indians and decided to look for gold in Chile. The expedition survived incredible hardships, crossing the Andes and the Atacama Desert. Once certain that no gold mines were within reach, Almagro and his men went back to Cuzco. Only five years later, in 1540, Pedro de Valdivia, one of Francisco Pizarro's best officers and a relative of his, was granted permission to conquer Chile. Valdivia and his men began their march south, following the route inaugurated by Almagro. Upon arriving in the valleys of central Chile, Valdivia founded the city of Santiago del Nuevo Extremo in February 1541. Although he founded several other cities in the following years, the colony did not prosper. Two main problems thwarted the efforts of the Spanish settlers: namely, the lack of gold and the constant hostility of the Araucanian Indians.

Pedro de Valdivia was a well-educated man, and he praised the military abilities of his opponents in several elegant letters addressed to the Spanish king. Another Spaniard who battled the Araucanians is recognized as having written the finest Spanish historical poem, *La Araucana*. Alonso de Ercilla y Zúñiga, a Spanish poet who engaged in the conflict between 1556 and 1563, described the heroic Indian rebellion and gave details about the natives' history. Ercilla divided his epic poem in three parts, which were published in 1569, 1578, and 1589.

The Indian leaders of the revolt have also achieved fame. Lautaro, for instance, later became the symbol of Chilean independence. He was captured at a young age by the Spaniards and spent several years serving Valdivia. In 1553, he managed to escape and returned to his people. Shortly thereafter, Lautaro was appointed the leader of the Indian alliance that organized a rebellion against the Spanish invaders. Through his exposure to Iberian culture, Lautaro had become familiar with Spanish military tactics, and at the battle of Tucapel, in December 1553, he inflicted a severe defeat on the Spaniards. Alerted to the rebellion, Valdivia rushed with reinforcements, only to be ambushed and executed on arrival. Following his victory, Lautaro launched a massive insurrection and in the following months destroyed several recently founded cities and placed Santiago under siege. Betrayed by one of his closest assistants, Lautaro was ambushed in his encampment and killed. The rebellion continued under a new leader, Caupolicán, who, after failing to recapture the city of

Concepción in 1558, was kidnapped, tortured, and killed.

The killing of Caupolicán did not bring the war to an end. Spanish control over territories located to the south of the Bío-Bío River remained feeble for decades. The relative success of the Araucanians against the invaders was due largely to their adaptability and ingenuity in warfare. Horses, in particular, proved to be an asset for the Indians, who soon became expert cavalrymen. Although the "War of Chile" halted the Spanish expansion, the Crown kept the original policy of relying upon the private financing of the conquest, thus encouraging the persistence of seigniorial warfare. The Crown had to reconsider this measure in 1598, when another major Indian uprising started with the execution of the governor, García Oñez de Loyola. Within less than two years, all major Spanish settlements south of the Bío-Bío River were destroyed or abandoned. The tenuous situation forced the Spanish Crown to establish the *situado,* a permanent military subsidy. The situado freed local settlers from contributing to war efforts and became a symbol of the poverty of the colony. With this innovation, conquest and pacification became public affairs and, as professional troops began to arrive, warfare was modernized. The situado had additional effects on the Indians. As Chile became a matter of concern for the Royal Council of the Indies, the Crown issued clearer regulations regarding Indian labor, and soon the legal enslavement of the natives, an issue much debated initially, was approved.

With war efforts in the hands of the Crown, Spanish settlers turned their attention to economic matters. Chile was an isolated colony, located far from important colonial centers; furthermore, it lacked any major gold or silver mines. The combination of these factors prompted the early development of an agrarian economy. This shift set in motion one of the most crucial events in Chilean history: the emergence of large estates. Such landholding patterns prompted the formation of a landowning elite and a semiservile rural population. Major estates had their origins in the land grants (*mercedes de tierras*) that Valdivia had assigned to his most loyal collaborators back in the sixteenth century. By the early seventeenth century, modest-size ranching constituted the backbone of the Chilean economy. The garrisons in the south, as well as an unpretentious trade with the Viceroyalty of Peru and the Potosí mines, created market demands that Chilean settlers were willing to meet. During this period, Chilean products were mostly cattle hides, *charqui* (jerked beef), and tallow. Additionally, Chilean landowners provided Potosí miners with mules.

The earthquake that struck Peru in 1687 had unforeseen consequences for the Chilean economy. Following the damages that resulted from the seismic activity, a plague attacked Peruvian wheat production and created an important market. Chilean landowners rushed to take advantage of the opportunity, and soon their wheat (cheaper and of better quality) permanently controlled the Peruvian market. In addition, the growth of an internal mestizo population created a domestic demand that chose European over native foodstuffs. As a result, land started to be concentrated in fewer hands, and soon large haciendas controlled the countryside. Haciendas proved to be one of the most stable Chilean institutions, and they decisively shaped the country's national psychology.

Changes in labor accompanied the emergence of haciendas. As *encomiendas* (grants of rights to collect taxes and enjoy the labor of conquered indigenous communities) lost their importance and Indian slavery could not meet the new demands for workers, a new labor system began to emerge. Hereditary tenants, who rented small plots in a given hacienda over generations, formed a new distinctively rural social class, the *inquilinos.* As haciendas became social centers, rural life outside these estates grew precarious. By the eighteenth century, a floating population of peons and vagabonds, who turned occasionally to cattle-rustling or banditry, was of great concern to colonial authorities.

At the opposite end of the social spectrum, the Chilean elite shared a noteworthy sense of unity. Previously established power networks used marriage ties to rapidly incorporate into their ranks the Basque population that migrated to Chile during the eighteenth century. It has been documented that many elite families had extended family connections that allowed them to curb even the most progressive eighteenth-century royal officials. Because of its cohesiveness and geographical isolation, the Chilean elite was somewhat insular: the colony did not have newspapers, education was rather rudimentary, and social life was restricted to family celebrations. Catholicism, certainly one of the most powerful influences in Chile, provided most of the occasions for public ceremonies.

The Jesuit order was arguably the most influential representative of Catholicism in colonial Chile. Since its arrival in 1593, the Society of Jesus had managed to acquire many estates and workshops, making them an important player in the local market. The affluence of the Jesuits, combined with their political opinions, resulted in their expulsion from the Spanish Empire in 1767. Even as the expulsion placed many haciendas on sale, the event left a dramatic mark in the memory of the local elite.

The eighteenth century witnessed several royal reforms in the spirit of the Enlightenment that promoted a sense of regionalism among Chilean upper social groups. Most importantly, the Bourbon reforms made it all too clear to the local elite that access to the highest levels of the colonial administration was not to be granted. Complaints against Spain's policies soon multiplied and a handful of local intellectuals began to produce protonational writings denouncing Chile's social and economic problems. These texts shared an optimistic belief in the colony's potential, but they blamed the imperial administration for catering to Spanish interests and thwarting Chile's national progress.

As in the rest of Latin America, Napoleon's dethronement of Ferdinand VII in 1808 triggered important events in Chile. Local elites channeled their concerns about the future of the colony through the *cabildo,* the quintessential Spanish institution of the city council. In September of 1810, the cabildo of Santiago, by far the most important city in the colony, openly voiced the need for an independent junta to govern Chile. The original intentions of safeguarding Chile until Ferdinand VII's return vanished after José Miguel Carrera, a young officer who had returned from Spain, took control of the situation. Shortly thereafter, Bernardo O'Higgins, the illegitimate son of Governor Ambrosio O'Higgins, a competent eighteenth-century administrator, became the leader of the separatists. Spain launched an organized military offensive, and O'Higgins and his troops escaped to Argentina, where José de San Martín, the leader of the movement for independence in Río de la Plata, helped them. With a better equipped army, O'Higgins and San Martín returned to Chile in April 1818, and they inflicted a devastating blow to Spanish troops at the battle of Maipú. Although Spanish resistance continued in the south for a few years, Maipú ensured Chile's political independence from Spain.

Maria N. Marsilli

References

Barbier, Jacques. *Reform and Politics in Bourbon Chile, 1755–1796.* Ottawa: University of Ottawa Press, 1980.

Bauer, Arnold. *Chilean Rural Society from the Spanish Conquest to 1930.* Cambridge: Cambridge University Press, 1975.

Collier, Simon, and William F. Satter. *A History of Chile, 1808–1994.* Cambridge: Cambridge University Press, 1996.

Galdames, Luis. *A History of Chile.* Chapel Hill: University of North Carolina Press, 1941.

Loveman, Brian. *Chile: The Legacy of Hispanic Capitalism.* New York: Oxford University Press, 2001.

See also: Bandits and Banditry; Bourbon Reforms; Cabildo; Colonists and Settlers V—Southern Cone; Conquest I–Andes; Conquest VII–Southern Cone; Conquistadors; Council of the Indies; Encomienda; Enlightenment—Spanish America; Explorers; Hacienda; Independence I–VI; Jesuits—Expulsion; Mestizaje; Poetry—Modern Spanish America; Potosí.

CHRONICLERS (CRONISTAS)

Eyewitnesses to both the Spanish conquest of the Americas and the colonial period, chroniclers (*cronistas,* in Spanish) produced detailed descriptions of Iberian-American relations. Mostly Spaniards, these authors described the geography of the Americas, the military efforts to subdue native peoples, and the effects that the European invasion had on the Indian population. The discovery of the New World initiated an unprecedented interest in geography and history among European witnesses and their audiences. In recording their observations and inquiries, chroniclers also produced valuable ethnographic descriptions of Indian groups in the Americas. Of sundry origins and serving diverse agendas, explorers, conquistadors, royal officials, churchmen, mestizos, and even Indians filled the ranks of this group of writers.

Christopher Columbus was the first chronicler of the New World. In a series of letters addressed to the Spanish monarchs, he offered detailed descriptions of the Caribbean and even established some analogies between the Old World and the New. His son Fernando was also a keen observer and compiled a landscape taxonomy in his *Descripción y cosmografía de España,* published in 1523, and his *Historia del Almirante,* a biography of his father, published in 1538. Given the lack of information about the new continent, the Spanish Crown sought to collect reliable data and sent a royal official with humanistic credentials to complete the task. Gonzalo Fernández de Oviedo spent twenty years in the Americas and many more putting his findings and observations in writing. The bulk of his *Historia general y natural de las Indias,* published from 1535 to 1537, and his *Sumario de la historia natural de las Indias,* published in 1526, are devoted to the history of Spanish exploration and conquest and include important geographic and biotic data. The last sixteenth-century scholar who attempted a general description of the New World was the Jesuit Joseph de Acosta, whose *Historia natural y moral de las Indias* appeared in 1590.

Soldiers who participated in the conquest also left noteworthy testimonies. For instance, Bernal Díaz del Castillo, who witnessed the fall of the Aztec Empire, produced a detailed description of Aztec society and its traditions. His *Historia verdadera de la conquista de Nueva España* (The True History of the Conquest of New Spain) was published in 1632. In the Andes, Pedro Cieza de León, a member of Francisco Pizarro's band, traveled around the Inca Empire carefully observing and documenting its political organization and architectonic achievements. Borrowing from personal interviews with Indians and Spaniards, Cieza de León wrote several celebrated accounts, such as his *Crónica del Perú* (Chronicle of Peru), a comprehensive history of the Inca Empire published in 1553, and his *Descubrimiento y conquista del Perú* (Discovery and Conquest of Peru), a detailed description of the Spanish conquest, published in 1554.

Among texts produced by conquistadors, letters sent by expedition leaders to Spain are of great value. For instance, Hernando Cortés wrote lengthy letters containing detailed descriptions of Aztec civilization. His observations were expanded in 1552 by his biographer, Francisco López de Gómara, in his *Conquista de Mexico* (Conquest of Mexico). In the 1550s, Pedro de Valdivia wrote elegant epistles describing the Araucanian Indians of southern Chile to the Spanish monarch.

Spaniards who became intimate with Indian groups also produced valuable texts. Alvar Núñez Cabeza de Vaca, for instance, entered the annals of colonial Texas as its first historian, ethnologist, and physician-surgeon. He also experienced remarkable personal growth as he accepted the Karankawas Indians on their terms. The royal treasurer of an ill-fated Spanish expedition, Cabeza de Vaca spent several years wandering among the Indian groups of present-day Florida, Texas, and Mexico. He later collected his memories in his *Relación,* an alluring text published in 1555. In Chile, another soldier, Francisco Núñez de Piñeda y Bascuñán, constitutes a similar case. Captured in 1629 by Araucanian Indians, Piñeda y Bascuñán later published his *El cautiverio feliz,* a moving account of his life among the natives. Other Spaniards became acquainted with Indian culture in less dramatic ways. Juan de Betanzos, for example, was rapidly accepted by his wife's kin group after marrying an Inca princess and became a well-known Quechuist (expert in Quechua, the language of the Inca Empire). In 1576, he completed his *Suma y narración de los Incas,* a meticulous history of the Inca elite.

Clergymen also wrote accounts of paramount importance. Fr. Ramón Pané, a poor anchorite of the Order of Saint Jerome, was one of the first witnesses to the European-Indian encounter. Pané described the beliefs in the hereafter, ritual medicine practices, and linguistic distribution of the Taino Indians, who originally populated the Caribbean and rapidly disappeared after the Spanish invasion. His *Relación acerca de las antigüedades de los Indios,* completed around 1498, is the first book written in a European language in the Americas. Also a witness to the Caribbean tragedy, the Dominican Fr. Bartolomé de Las Casas assembled during the 1540s and

1550s his *Historia de las Indias,* a massive corpus of information on the rituals and customs of the Indians; the work aimed to demonstrate the Indians' rational capability. His best-known work, however, is his *Brevísima relación de la destrucción de las Indias* (Brief Account of the Destruction of the Indies), which appeared in 1552. A passionate yet inaccurate description of the abuses suffered by the natives at the hands of the Spaniards, this book earned Las Casas the title "Apostle of the Indians."

In Mexico, Bernardino de Sahagún embodied the ideal missionary priest and scholar. He produced the finest cultural research of the sixteenth century, his Florentine Codex. Fluent in Nahuatl, the language of the Aztec Empire, Sahagún produced detailed accounts of the Aztecs' past and a comprehensive dictionary to be used in Indian catechism. His twelve-volume work was completed in 1579 and constitutes an unparalleled encyclopedia of Aztec culture. Sahagún collected his material thanks to in-depth interviews of indigenous informants that he conducted over decades. Diego de Landa, the second bishop of Yucatán, offers a compelling although intimidating portrait of the churchman-chronicler. In 1562, in response to allegations that the Mayas had organized surreptitious pagan ceremonies, Landa and his fellow Franciscans launched a violent inquiry, during which thousands of Mayans were tortured. He also destroyed numerous Maya hieroglyphic texts, in the conviction that these books had been inspired by the devil. Landa's chronicle, *Relación de las cosas de Yucatán* (Account of the Things of Yucatan), appeared in 1566. In contrast, Fr. Toribio de Benavente, who adopted the Indian name

Portrait of Bartolomé de Las Casas (1474–1566), eighteenth century. (Corbis)

Motolinía (meaning "poverty" in Nahuatl), fervently sided with the Indians and sought to protect them from abuses. His *Historia de los Indios de Nueva España* (History of the Indians of New Spain), published in 1541, ranks among the best sources for understanding Mexican native peoples and their conversion to Catholicism.

Agents of the Catholic Church also shaped important accounts in the Andes. Concerned about religious orthodoxy, members of different religious orders, as well as diocesan priests, wrote various texts on pre-Columbian Indian beliefs. For instance, Pablo José Arriaga, an influential member of the Jesuit order in Peru, became identified with the task of uprooting native religion in the Andes. In 1621, he completed his *Extirpación de la idolatría en el*

A monk forces an Indian to weave. From Felipe Guaman Poma de Ayala's El primer nueva corónica y buen gobierno. *It is the only extant codex from Peru showing sixteenth-century Peruvian life, ca. 1565. (Snark/Art Resource)*

Perú (The Extirpation of Idolatry in Peru), a text crucial for the study of religious survival in the area. Also devoted to the extirpation of "idolatry," Francisco de Avila, the vicar of Huarochirí (a town in central Peru), was an active researcher into the Andean past. He is credited with collecting a meticulous anthology of oral accounts circulating among the Indians of his parish. Completed around 1598, the text is known as *El manuscrito de Huarochirí* and constitutes the most comprehensive primary source on Andean spirituality. Other clergymen produced more general studies. For instance, Bernabé Cobo, a Jesuit scholar with long residence in Peru, was a keen observer of nature and man in the Andes. A priest and missionary, Cobo obtained valuable information from the Indians, and he

used the data to write his *Historia del Nuevo Mundo,* a text published in 1653. Members of other religious orders wrote noteworthy texts as well. Fr. Antonio de la Calancha, an erudite Augustinian monk living in Chuquisaca (present-day Bolivia), wrote his *Corónica moralizada de la orden de N.S.P.S. Agustín en el Perú,* a comprehensive account of the conversion of local native peoples to Catholicism, in the early seventeenth century. Also working in the highlands, the Augustinian Alonso Ramos Gavilán produced in 1612 his *Historia de Nuestra Señora de Copacabana,* a detailed description of the links between the Inca Empire and Lake Titicaca.

Natives also wrote accounts that have been widely used by scholars. The anonymous *Popol Vuh* (Book of the Council), a series of narratives from the Quiché Mayas of Guatemala about the origin of the world and their town and culture, was written toward the middle of the sixteenth century. The text remained buried in an archive and was discovered and translated into Spanish at the beginning of the eighteenth century. Another widely studied Indian manuscript is the *Relación de Santa Cruz Pachacuti,* a text produced by Juan de Santa Cruz Pachacuti Yamqui, an Indian whose community initially fought the Incas but finally submitted to them. Apparently, Santa Cruz Pachacuti wrote his text around 1613 but did not publish it. His work was discovered in the late nineteenth century. Felipe Guaman Poma de Ayala, another Peruvian Indian, completed a lengthy letter addressed to the Spanish monarch around the same date. The text, known as *El primer nueva corónica y buen gobierno,* aimed at informing the king about the wrongdoings of the Spanish administration in the Andes. Consequently, it shed light on numerous aspects of Indian daily life during colonial times. Additionally, the numerous drawings that Guaman Poma used to illustrate his prose constitute one of the most conspicuous features of the manuscript. The letter never reached the king's attention and, like the *Popol Vuh,* remained in an archive until the beginning of the twentieth century. In Mexico, the counterpart of Guaman Poma was probably Fernando de Alba Ixtlilxochitl (1568–1648), the great-grandson of the king of Texcoco. A well-educated member of the colonial Indian nobility, Alba Ixtlilxochitl wrote several texts documenting the Indian past that were not published during his lifetime. His *Historia de la nación Chichimeca* and his *Obras históricas* are his best-known works.

Finally, accounts produced by mestizo writers deserve special attention, for these texts provide an unsurpassed view of the complexity of Iberian-native relations. In this regard, the books produced by Inca Garcilaso de la Vega best reflect the nature of the exchanges that took place between Iberian and native cultures. Son of an Incan princess and a Spanish soldier, Garcilaso spent his childhood years with his mother's relatives, in the company of other mixed-race children. At the age of twenty-one, the young mestizo moved to Spain, never to return to Peru. From there Garcilaso wrote several books that aimed at explaining the complexities of Incan society to European audiences. Arguably his masterpieces are *Comentarios reales de los Incas* (Royal Commentaries of the Incas), published in 1609, and the *Historia general de Perú* (General History of Peru), published in 1617, the first conceived to honor his mother; the second, his father.

Maria N. Marsilli

References

Adorno, Rolena. *Guaman Poma: Writing and Resistance in Colonial Peru.* Austin: University of Texas Press, 2000.

León Portilla, Miguel, and Jorge Klor de Alva. *The Aztec Image of Self and Society: An Introduction to Nahua Culture.* Salt Lake City: University of Utah Press, 1992.

Mignolo, Walter. *The Darker Side of the Renaissance: Literacy, Territoriality, and Colonization.* Ann Arbor: University of Michigan Press, 1995.

Zamora, Margarita. *Language, Authority, and Indigenous History in the* Comentarios Reales de los Incas. New York: Cambridge University Press, 1988.

See also: Clergy—Secular, in Colonial Spanish America; Codices; Conquest and the Debate over Justice; Conquistadors; Family—Colonial Spanish America; Fiction—Spanish America; Languages; Mestizaje; Native Americans I–VIII; Race; Religious Orders.

CIMARRONES

Originally, the Spanish used *cimarrones* (sing. *cimarrón*) to refer to runaway cattle and swine, but later they used it for Indian and African slaves who escaped European control to form free communities in hidden locales. The English adapted the word to *maroons* and the French and Dutch to *marrons.* Cimarrones challenged slavery throughout the Americas, from Florida to Colombia, but they were most prevalent in areas of high slave importation, such as the Caribbean islands and Brazil. Slavery never went uncontested by the enslaved, and slave flight was ubiquitous wherever there was slavery.

As early as 1503 in the mountainous terrain of Hispaniola, African slaves escaped to become cimarrones. These fugitive slaves joined the Taino Indian wars of resistance, and when the last indigenous leader made peace, they fought on. In 1521, Wolof slaves led the first recorded slave revolt in the Americas, and survivors joined the cimarrones in the mountains. Despite escalating fears of slave revolt, the planters of Hispaniola demanded more slaves, and by 1542, Spanish officials estimated the island's black population at 25,000–30,000, the white population at only 1,200, and the maroon population at 2,000–3,000.

A similar demographic profile characterized other Spanish settlements. Puerto Rico held 15,000 blacks and only 500 Spaniards (Memorial of Pedro Menéndez de Avilés 1893, 322) and the captain-general of Cuba claimed that the same racial disparity held true in Cuba, Veracruz (Mexico), Puerto Cavallos (Honduras), Cartagena (Colombia), and Venezuela. Spaniards battled black slaves and cimarrones in Hispaniola (1521); Santa Marta, Colombia (1530); Cuba (1533); Mexico City (1537, 1546); Hispaniola (1545–48); Honduras (1548); and Barquisimeto, Venezuela (1555).

Although the cimarrones generally attempted to be self-sufficient, they also raided plantations and became notorious roadside bandits. They traded with plantation slaves and with Europeans for materials they could not obtain in the wild, subverting all efforts to monitor and control colonial economies. Cimarrones living near the coasts established a lucrative trade with corsairs and pirates. The cimarrones of Panama helped Sir Francis Drake capture a treasure in Spanish silver in 1572. Like Europeans and Amerindians, cimarrones carefully evaluated their positions and acted in what they perceived to be their own best interests. They could and did choose sides, and they could alter the balance of power in critical ways. Some became military allies of one or another European power.

Among the most famous cimarrones were the so-called *zambos* (persons of mixed African and Indian descent) of Esmeraldas, on the coast of Ecuador. A Spanish priest who encountered the Esmeraldas maroons in the sixteenth century reported that they were engaged in timbering, metallurgy, and canoe building. They were also growing plantains, corn, cassava, cacao, tobacco, cotton, rice, and sugarcane, and raising pigs and chickens for their own consumption and for sale to the nearby Indian villages. While the women performed much of the labor associated with agriculture and small-animal husbandry, the men also occupied themselves in hunting and fishing.

Similar findings were reported by Spaniards who attacked a seventeenth-century *palenque* (runaway slave community) outside Veracruz in New Spain (Mexico). Although the cimarrones had only inhabited the site for nine months, the Spaniards found fields planted with cotton, sweet potatoes, chiles, tobacco, squashes, corn, beans, sugarcane, and other vegetables. The residents were also raising chickens, cattle, and horses, and had built impressive fortifications and sixty houses. In the houses the Spaniards found a wide variety of clothing, swords, hatchets, a few arquebuses, some salt, corn, and money. The latter items were probably acquired by trade with, or raids on, nearby haciendas or by robbing travelers along the royal road to Mexico City.

Cimarrón leaders employed various mechanisms to establish and then legitimize authority in their ethnically mixed settlements. These were based on such concepts as political seniority, religious power, military prowess, and corporate or familial connections. Some figures claimed to descend from African royalty and assumed the role of religious leader of the community—the sort of "sacred chieftainship" or "divine kingship" noted in African societies of the time. Others were military leaders, whose bravery in defending their communities earned them the loyalty of adherents and subjects. The cimarrones typically accommodated ethnic and religious differences by sharing leadership roles on the basis of proportional representation, with war captains leading groups of warriors of their own ethnolinguistic group. Attempts to create perpetual chieftainships or dynasties with acknowledged legitimacy were buttressed by origin myths, assumed titles, rituals, and in the case of Ganga Zumba in Brazil, elaborate royal courts and large kinship networks that linked multiple village sites. When necessary and possible, maroons further stabilized their leadership and documented dynastic right through treaty with European powers.

Because cimarrón settlements were an ever-present lure to slaves and undermined slave-based economies, slaveholders expended considerable energy and funds trying to locate and eliminate them. Cimarrones protected themselves with ingenious and effective defense works, laid false trails to deceive the enemy, and established jungle patrols and sentry systems to guard their settlements. They also developed mutual defense systems and alliances among networks of maroon settlements. If discovered, cimarrones usually melted away into the jungles, mountains, and swamps, only to coalesce again and form new encampments. When they had to, the cimarrones fought their attackers. These conflicts could become full-blown wars, as in sixteenth-century Hispaniola, seventeenth-century Brazil, and eighteenth-century Jamaica and Suriname. U.S. military commanders acknowledged that the three Seminole Wars in Florida fought in the nineteenth century were actually wars against the "blacks" who had escaped slavery and lived among the Seminoles.

Marronage became unnecessary as slavery was abolished throughout the Americas, but at least some cimarrón communities survived into the present day in places like Mexico, Colombia, Jamaica, and Suriname. And in Texas, Oklahoma, and Mexico, descendants of the black Seminoles continue to celebrate their ancestors' maroon heritage.

Jane G. Landers

References

Deive, Carlos Estéban. *Los guerrilleros negros: Esclavos fugitivos y cimarrones en Santo Domingo.* Santo Domingo: Fundación Cultural Dominicana, 1989.

Landers, Jane. "*Cimarrón* Ethnicity and Cultural Adaptation in the Spanish Domains of the Circum-Caribbean, 1503–1763." Pp. 30–54 in *Identity in the Shadow of Slavery,* edited by Paul E. Lovejoy. London: Continuum Press, 2000.

———. "Maroon Women in Colonial Spanish America: Case Studies in the Circum-Caribbean from the Sixteenth through the Eighteenth Centuries." Pp. 3–18 in *Beyond Bondage: Free Women of Color in the Americas,* edited by David Barry Gaspar and Darlene Clark Hine. Urbana: University of Illinois Press, 2004.

Memorial of Pedro Menéndez de Avilés, undated (1561–1562). In E. Ruidíaz y Caravia, *La Florida: Su conquista y colonización por Pedro Menéndez de Avilés,* vol. 2. Madrid: Imprenta de los hijos de J.A. García, 1893.

Price, Richard. *Maroon Societies: Rebel Slave Communities in the Americas.* Baltimore: Johns Hopkins University Press, 1992.

Taylor, William B. "The Foundation of Nuestra Señora de Guadalupe de los Morenos de Amapa." *Americas* 26 (1970): 439–446.

CINEMA

The history of Latin American cinema begins as early as the history of film. Only a few months after the Lumière Brothers presented their first public film in December of 1895, their invention was introduced in Mexico City, Buenos Aires, and Rio de Janeiro. Shortly thereafter, a number of Latin American countries were engaged in setting up their own film productions. In general, Argentina, Brazil, and Mexico led the way in terms of the size of their domestic markets; Chile, Colombia, Cuba, Peru, and Venezuela followed with intermediate markets, while countries like Bolivia and Ecuador made up small markets. Political, social, and economic circumstances, together with the state, have played a determining role in the development of Latin American film, as have, at least throughout most of the twentieth century, the politics of the United States and Hollywood's role in asserting its monopoly in the film industry.

Most film histories tend to privilege feature films over documentaries, but this unfortunately does not do justice to film production in Latin America, particularly during the silent era. Although there were a few fiction films such as *El fusilamiento de*

Dorrego (The Shooting of Dorrego, 1908), directed by the Argentine Max Gallo; the Mexican films *Don Juan Tenorio* (1898), *El grito de Dolores* (The Cry of Dolores, 1908), and the docudrama *El automóvil gris* (The Gray Car, 1919); and the Brazilian film *Os estranguladores* (The Stranglers, 1908) by Antonio Leal, which reconstructs a sensationalized crime in Rio, most of the early films produced in Latin America were newsreels and documentaries that concerned local, regional, and national events. Equipment, film stock, and films were imported primarily from France and Italy, the two countries that had the strongest influence in Latin America until the end of World War I, when the United States made a concerted effort to disrupt the European market. By 1928, 90 percent of the films exhibited in Latin America were produced in the United States, and Hollywood controlled the distribution market.

Despite the foreign monopoly on imports, Latin American countries made a significant mark in the production of documentaries that were closely tied to current events. In Mexico, for example, General Porfirio Díaz made ample use of film to promote his particular image of Mexico, with himself at the center. As early as 1896, Bon Bernard and Vayre screened the first scenes of Mexico in *General Díaz Strolling through Chapultepec Park*. During the Porfiriato, a strong partisan view of Mexico predominated; with the outbreak of the Revolution in 1910, however, filmmakers compelled to "sell the news" began to chronicle everything, uncensored by partisanship. Fictional cinema was left behind, as filmmakers spread through the country wherever there were battles and rebellions, wherever treaties were signed, wherever any other activity related to the Revolution took place. The style of the films had a newspaperlike quality, influenced by the newsreel *Revista Nacional.* Among the many films dealing with the Revolution, *La revolución de Veracruz* by Enrique Rosas and *La revolución de Chihuahua* by the Alva brothers stand out. When the fighting calmed down, the municipal government of Mexico City appointed inspectors to regulate the chaos of Mexico's overcrowded cinemas, most of which were unsanitary and unsafe. This attempt quickly gave way to regulations concerned with censoring the films themselves, not with their screenings. Documentaries began to adopt a more propagandistic image of the events recorded, which eventually led to their decline by 1916.

In the same way that Mexico documented its revolution and changes, cities like Buenos Aires and Rio de Janeiro that were undergoing major transformations, with the widening of boulevards and the building of railway systems and elegant houses, carefully chronicled their transformations in their newsreels and documentaries.

The end of the silent era challenged Hollywood's monopoly. Initially it helped boost the national film industry, precisely because of the language barrier. Since dubbing at this stage was impossible, Hollywood tried to make foreign-language versions of its films in an attempt to preserve its audiences abroad. However, the films were too expensive, and audiences had acquired a taste for Hollywood stars and were not interested in watching unknown Spanish replacements on screen, with their different accents and dialects, as was the case among Argentines, Cubans, and Mexicans. Thus Latin Americans pushed their own national production through music and song, musical comedies and melodramas. For example, Carlos Gardel acted in several Argentine films from 1933 to 1935 in which the tango played a major role. Mexico created its *ranchera* comedy, a musical melodrama based on nationalist or folkloric themes, emblematized in the extremely popular film *Allá en Rancho grande* (Out on the Big Ranch, 1936).

As dubbing and subtitling technology improved, Hollywood regained its hold on Latin American markets. This effort was accompanied by Franklin D. Roosevelt's successful Good Neighbor policy of the 1930s, in which film played a significant role. Under this policy, the film regulation body in charge of improving the industry's image and enforcing regulations and a strict moral code, the Hays office, appointed a Latin American expert to advise Hollywood on how to avoid stereotypes. Since the Mexican Revolution, the United States had constructed an image of Mexico, which extended south throughout the continent and was felt to apply to the whole of Latin America, as lying south of a border that separated chaos and order. Mexicans were represented as violent, irresponsible, and treacherous. But now, with World War II looming ahead, the State Department wanted to produce films that carried a message of democracy and friendship below the Rio Grande. The results were two films by Disney that looked at the neighbors of the United States through the eyes of Donald Duck: *Saludos Amigos* (1943) and *The Three Caballeros* (1945). The other icon that appeared at this time was Carmen Miranda, who replaced the stereotype of the violent Latin male with that of the oversexed, featherbrained, fruit basket–carrying female dancer in films like *That Night in Rio* (1941).

The outbreak of World War II had a strong influence on the film industry, both in Latin America and in the United States, and in particular Mexican cinema. Hollywood's exports to Latin America diminished during the war, and U.S. hostility toward Argentina for not supporting the Allies hindered foreign investments. The United States went as far as blocking sales of raw film to Argentina, while it enhanced its investments in Mexico, offering support in terms of processing labs and market distribution. This support combined with Mexico's own national reformist politics under President Avila Camacho, and Mexican cinema entered its golden age.

Mexico's golden age encompassed directors Emilio "El Indio" Fernández and Fernando de Fuentes, cinematographer Gabriel Figueroa, and several brilliant actors, among them Dolores del Río, María Feliz, Pedro Armendáriz, and Cantinflas. Films like *María Candelaria* (1943) and *Enamorada Doña Barbara* (Lady Barbara in Love, 1943) offered an image of Mexico that included courage, an idealized landscape, true Mexican virility in the men, and femininity in the women, a country where a progressive nation could be forged and a nationalist cinema created.

The next important phase in Latin American cinema is what critics have called the New Latin American Cinema, a cinema that makes a clear break with the dominant hegemonic discourses imposed by Hollywood. It is a lucid, critical, neorealist, anti-imperialist, and revolutionary cinema that contests the traditional premises of auteurship and challenges mainstream cinematic production modes and reception. The Cuban Revolution (1959) had a major effect in setting the tone for the instrumental role of film in delivering a political message and molding a collective consciousness. The young directors of this new cinema had a clear political agenda; they not only underscored the need for social engagement and change, they wrote manifestos theorizing and explaining the goals behind their new aesthetic. The Grupo Cine Liberación, headed by the Argentines Octavio Getino and Fernando Solanas, promoted a Third Cinema (rebelling against Hollywood as the first, and the auteur films as the second, type). For them, the Third Cinema was a militant one, as their classic four-and-a-half-hour documentary *La hora de los hornos* (The Hour of the Furnaces, 1968) attests. The other major theoretical formulations during this time are the Cuban concept of Imperfect Cinema advanced by director Julio García Espinosa; the Aesthetics of Hunger developed by Brazilian Cinema Novo director Glauber Rocha, which proposed to make sad, ugly films to expose a reality most middle-class Brazilians ignored; and Bolivian director Jorge Sanjinés's writings on Revolutionary Cinema.

This was an extremely productive decade in Latin American cinema, one that reached its apex in 1967 with the first Latin American film festival, held in Viña del Mar, Chile. There, filmmakers established their first major network in the continent and shared material and ideas. From 1968 to the early 1970s, films by García Espinosa and Tomás Gutiérrez Alea in Cuba, Octavio Getino and Fernando Solanas in Argentina, Jorge Sanjinés and the Ukamau group in Bolivia, Glauber Rocha and Nelson Pereira dos Santos in Brazil, and Miguel Littín and Raúl Ruiz in Chile, among many others, circulated throughout Latin America, promoting a new aesthetic and cinematic practice.

During the 1970s, a wave of military dictatorships swept through the south of the continent: Argentina (1976), Brazil (1968, 1971), Bolivia (1971), Chile (1974), and Uruguay (1973), which had a detrimental effect on film production, while Colombia, Peru, and Venezuela, aided by state funding and economic growth, saw a boost in their national film production, though it did not extend beyond their national borders.

Compared to the 1960s and early 1970s, the films of the 1980s were much more diverse and their aesthetics more diffused. Diversified entertainment industries, such as TV, via deregulated cable and satellite, in addition to widespread economic problems, limited financial support for filmmakers. In some cases, the return of democracy stimulated a series of films in coproduction with Spain and France about exile and the experience of the dictatorships. For example, the film *La historia oficial* (The Official Story, 1986) earned Argentinian director Luis Puenzo an Oscar. The Peruvian Francisco Lombardi stands out for his successful commercial films, such as *Maruja en el infierno* (Maruja in Hell, 1983) and *La boca del lobo* (The Mouth of the Wolf, 1988), both of which focused on social violence, while other directors like Federico García focused on indigenous issues, as in García's film *Kintur Wachana* (Where the Condors Are Born, 1977). Challenging more traditional modes of narration, a series of films appeared that focused on female characters and their perspectives: the Venezuelan films *Macu, la mujer del policía* (Macu, the Policeman's Wife, 1987) by Solveig Hoogesteijn and Fina Torres's *Oriana* (1985); the Cuban films *La mujer transparente* (The Transparent Woman, 1993), a

coproduction of five films woven together under the direction of renowned director Humberto Solás; Daniel Díaz Torres's *Alicia en el pueblo de maravillas* (Alice in Wondertown, 1991); Brazilian director Susana Amaral's *A hora da estrela* (The Hour of the Star, 1985); the Mexican films *Danzón* (1989) by María Novaro and *Novia que te vea* (Like a Bride, 1993) by Guita Schyfter; and the Argentine film *Camila* (1984) by María Luisa Bemberg. These and several others were all commercial successes.

Since the 1990s, Latin America has seen a significant rise in its film production. There is not a clear thematic or technical characteristic. Films like the Argentine *Nueve Reinas* (Nine Queens, 2000) by Fabian Bielinsky, or the Brazilian *Central do Brazil* (Central Station, 1998), by Walter Salles, have had great commercial success offering a less daunting portrayal of society. Although *Central do Brazil* presents life in the northeast, it is far from the kind of sad and ugly film Glauber Rocha had advocated. The Mexican films *Amores perros* (Love's a Bitch, 2000) by Alejandro González Iñarritu, and the stunningly beautiful *Japón* (Japan, 2002) by Carlos Reygadas, have certainly made a mark nationally and abroad for their camera movements and narrative techniques. Other films continue to focus on the hardships of daily life, such as Colombian films like Victor Gaviria's *Rodrigo D: No futuro* (Rodrigo D: No Future, 1989), *La estrategia del caracol* (The Strategy of the Snail, 1994) by Sergio Cabrera, and *La virgen de los Sicarios* (Our Lady of the Assassins, 2000), a Barbet Schroeder film based on Fernando Vallejo's novel and screenplay. Cuban directors have offered a critique of contemporary society through humor in films such as *Fresa y chocolate* (Strawberry and

Still scene from the Brazilian Central do Brazil *(Central Station), 1998, by Walter Salles. (Sony Pictures Classics/Kobal Collection/Prandini)*

Chocolate, 1993) by Gutiérrez Alea and Juan Carlos Tabío.

Among young directors, there is a distinct interest in experimenting with the medium itself, which has led to innovative narrative techniques that incorporate many elements from the documentary, which has also had recent success. Argentine films *Balnearios* (Seaside Resorts, 2002) by Marcelo Llinás, *Los rubios* (The Blonds, 2003) by Albertina Carri, and *Tan de repente* (All of a Sudden, 2002) by Diego Lerman are a few of the films that are reshaping Argentine cinema. *25 Watts* (2001) by Pablo Stoll and Juan Pablo Rebella and Beatriz Flores Silva's *En la p*** vida* (Never in Your F***ing Life, 2001) have done the same for Uruguay.

Even though Latin America has struggled throughout its history with devastating economic crises and political turmoil, as well as lack of private and state funding, recent films reveal a remarkable resourcefulness in overcoming these limitations, as Latin American filmmakers continue to develop a creative cinema that demonstrates it still has a lot to give.

Nina Gerassi-Navarro

References

Bernades, Horacio, Diego Lerer, and Sergio Wolf, eds. *Nuevo cine argentino: Temas, autores y estilos de una renovación.* Argentina: Fipresci, 2002.

Johnson, Randall, and Robert Stam, eds. *Brazilian Cinema.* Austin: University of Texas Press, 1988.

King, John. *Magical Reels: A History of Cinema in Latin America.* London: Verso, 1990.

Mora, Carl J. *Mexican Cinema: Reflections of a Society 1896–1988.* Rev. ed. Berkeley and Los Angeles: University of California Press, 2004.

Schnitman, Jorge A. *Film Industries in Latin America: Dependency and Development.* Norwood, NJ: Ablex, 1984.

Schumann, Peter B. *Historia del cine latinoamericano.* Translated by Oscar Zambrano. Buenos Aires: Legasa, 1987.

See also: Art and Artists—Brazil; Art and Artists—Modern Spanish America; Cuban Revolution; Culture; Mexican Revolution; Music and Dance I–V; Nationalism; Poetry—Brazil; Poetry—Modern Spanish America; Popular Festivals; Sports; Women—Brazil; Women—Modern Spanish America; World War I; World War II.

CITIES

From the earliest periods of colonization in the sixteenth century, life in Latin America has centered on cities. The individuals and groups that initially came to the New World established urban centers as part of the colonial process. To Iberians, civilization meant urbanization, and as Spanish and Portuguese control intensified, cities became the preferred focus of political, economic, social, and cultural activities and interaction. Still, the region as a whole remained fundamentally rural, in terms of settlement patterns as well as the key economic activities of mining and agriculture. Cities continued to mature and grow as Latin America underwent profound changes, first during the Bourbon reforms of the late eighteenth century, later with independence and economic growth in the nineteenth century, and the arrival of industrialization and modernization in the twentieth century. Today, primary urban centers, with populations numbering in the millions, are common in most Latin American nations, and cities continue to play an important role in con-temporary political, economic, and socio-cultural arenas.

The Iberian conquest and colonization of the New World was fundamentally an urban venture. Iberians traditionally placed a high value on living in compact, densely settled urban centers. Cities provided them with the social and cultural contexts they craved and were important in establishing centralized political and economic systems. Spaniards, in particular, were city-minded people, and Spanish settlers placed more emphasis on putting urban ideals into practice than did their Portuguese counter-parts. Nevertheless, in general, when the Spanish and Portuguese arrived in the Americas, their first priority was to establish cities.

Cities in colonial Spanish America were remarkably uniform in their form and structure, illustrating the fact that colonization in the New World was a planned undertaking, directed by the Crown. The establishment of towns and the planning of their sites were codified by Philip II in 1573 in a series of edicts contained in the *Ordenanzas de Descubrimiento y Población.* These guidelines postdate the founding of most of the area's major cities, but they represent what colonists found to be the most successful aspects of town planning and construction. They include advice concerning the selection of sites, detailed information on the physical layout of plazas and streets, and guidelines for the construction of private housing and the location of major administrative and cultural buildings, such as the viceregal palace, town council hall, customhouse, arsenal, hospitals, churches, and various stores. They also included recommendations concerning city services such as water and waste disposal, and measures for dealing with indigenous populations. In terms of the physical layout of cities, the twin concepts of a central plaza and the checkerboard pattern of straight streets oriented toward north, south, east, and west dominated the construction of urban areas. These concepts were initially used in the establishment of Santo Domingo in 1496, and were repeated throughout Spanish America.

By serving as the administrative centers of an empire, cities in the colonial context aided the Spanish in their desire to control local resources. Established for the purpose of colonial exploitation, their political structures often preceded their economic base. The two most important urban centers in colonial Spanish America were Mexico City and Lima, both of them large political and commercial centers. Founded in 1521, Mexico City, the capital of the Viceroyalty of New Spain, was built upon the ruins of the former Azteca capital of Tenochtitlan. Despite Spanish attempts to keep the European and Indian populations physically separated, the living patterns of these two groups quickly merged. Lima, on the other hand, was quite different from Mexico City. Situated on the coast, the capital of the Viceroyalty of Peru remained distant from the large indigenous populations of the Andean highlands. Founded in 1535, Lima attracted a much smaller Indian population and influence, yet maintained its importance, in part because of its access to the Pacific Ocean through the port at Callao.

The twin exploitative activities of mining and agriculture helped to sustain many cities during the colonial period. The mining of precious metals, most notably silver, was the mainstay of such highland cities as Potosí in the Viceroyalty of Peru, and Zacatecas, Guanajuato, and Potosí in Mexico.

However, the nature of mining meant that the populations of these cities were highly transient. Coastal cities focused on oceanic commerce and military defense. They also had large transient populations, which ebbed and flowed according to the rhythms of trade. Cities such as Havana and Santo Domingo in the Caribbean, Veracruz and Acapulco in Mexico, Portobello in Panama, and Cartagena on the South American coast were notable for their large fortifications, soldiers' quarters, supply houses, and commercial buildings.

A third group of cities comprised the highland administrative and agricultural cities founded in parts of Mesoamerica and the Andes with dense Indian populations. Because of an ample supply of labor and a variety of economic activities, these cities were characteristically more stable and thus constituted the heart of colonial Spanish America. Mexico City and Cuzco (Peru) provide two of the earliest examples of this type of settlement. Spanish colonists found it easy to adjust to the temperate climate and geography, and they discovered that the existing Indian settlements were developed enough to support them. Spaniards could easily rely on indigenous groups to supply them with the physical means of survival, while at the same time exploiting Indian labor, not only for the initial building of colonial cities, but also as a means of economic profit.

Beginning with the earliest examples, city planning in colonial Latin America followed the classic grid pattern popular in Spain at the time. Streets were placed on north-south and east-west axes, with the main plaza, known as the *plaza mayor,* at the center. City planners, following the Crown's lead, also adopted the practice of reserving the center part of the city, or the

National Palace from the cathedral, Mexico City, Mexico, ca. 1913. (Library of Congress)

traza, exclusively for Spanish residents. In general, the opulence, wealth, and power of colonial society were situated within the traza, in particular around the plaza mayor, which housed government offices, churches, important economic enterprises, and the homes of society's wealthiest families. Theoretically, this area was off limits to the indigenous population, who were relegated to neighborhoods outside the city center. Moving out from the traza, urban space became less organized, less impressive, and more haphazard, dominated by the modest structures and shelters non-Spanish populations called home.

Initially, the Crown designed the traza to protect Indians from the bad examples and influences of the Spanish, while at the same time insulating the Spanish from the inferior Indian population. While the Spanish minorities in most cities were heavily dependent on the labor of the indigenous majority for the functioning of the colonial economy, the fear of an urban indigenous uprising and the toppling of the colonial system that would inevitably follow strongly influenced city planning at the time. The establishment of a Europeans-only zone was one of the first attempts by Spaniards to enforce separation and physical control. The development of a highly structured racial hierarchy, which placed Spaniards at the top and Indians at the bottom, functioned to preserve Spanish superiority and Indian inferiority, and formed the basis of the colonial regime. It also served as a system of social control that in theory was to provide security and stability in the city. In most cases, however, this spatial division between Spaniards and Indians quickly broke down. As different urban factions, both civil and religious, began to fight over access to Indian labor and tribute, boundaries meant to limit Indian movement were reconfigured. The necessity of indigenous labor for different economic activities in urban centers allowed for the constant movement of Indians in and out of the traza, which led to permanent indigenous settlement there.

The development of cities in colonial Portuguese America presented a marked contrast to the Spanish experience because of the economic and political differences between the two. Unlike the Spanish, who built their urban centers around existing Indian civilizations as a means of exploiting their labor, the Portuguese tended to organize cities based on economic viability. The absence of large indigenous populations in Brazil meant that urban development was limited to the coast. Also, individuals, not the Crown, drove colonization in Brazil. The Portuguese Crown, relatively weak compared to its Spanish counterpart, was unable to plan and sustain large-scale urbanization and settlement projects. In form and structure, cities in Brazil were quite different from those in Spanish America. Rather than exhibiting the uniformity of the checkerboard design, cities such as Recife, Salvador, and Rio de Janeiro were haphazard in the layout of their streets. Though they did contain a central space known as the *rossio,* it was quite unlike the stately plaza mayor that dominated the urban landscape in colonial Spanish American cities. The rossio was a typically unorganized public space that lacked any

special architectural embellishments to set it apart from the rest of the urban landscape.

Besides the important political and economic roles that shaped urban areas, cities also became the centers of social and cultural life, and the variety of cultural preferences illustrated the class divisions that existed. As mentioned earlier, Spanish elites preferred the creature comforts of urban lifestyles, considering life in the city as more refined, cultured, and civilized than its rural counterparts. A variety of intellectual and cultural events dominated city calendars: religious festivals, theatrical and musical performances, poetry readings, intellectual salons, and bullfights, to name a few. Elites were also able to display their wealth through their sumptuous homes, ornate carriages, and opulent clothing and jewels, and they gained a level of social stature through their support of pious works. Plebeian culture in cities stood in marked contrast to the culture of the elite. It was public in nature, focusing on the streets. The lower class, composed of poor Indians, blacks, mestizos, mulattoes, and other racially mixed persons, as well as poor peninsular Spaniards and Creoles (those of Spanish blood born in the New World), embraced a variety of activities. Drinking, gambling, dancing, and gossiping, as well as participation in church celebrations and saint's days, all marked popular culture. It was baroque in its design and form: uninhibited, expressive, and reckless.

While popular culture embraced the insecurity of life for the urban lower classes, it represented to elites the presence of social disorder and chaos. During the eighteenth century, elites began to adopt the Bourbon style of austerity, grandeur, simplicity, and order when it came to cultural expression. Popular pastimes for elites were marked by restraint and composure, and through official legislation and unofficial pressure, elites attempted to force this Bourbon style and aesthetic onto the plebeian classes.

Colonial cities also faced a number of difficulties. A lack of sufficient scientific knowledge and technology meant that sanitation was abysmal, even in the most organized and developed urban centers. Access to potable water was irregular at best. Consequently, disease was a constant feature of urban life, complicated for the poor by a lack of material resources. Crime also plagued the urban landscape, propelled to a certain extent by the vast gulf between the rich and the poor, and the economic uncertainty in which the majority of urban residents lived. These problems only increased in the eighteenth century, as rising populations, with a resulting increase in migration to the cities throughout Latin America, exacerbated an already problematic situation.

The eighteenth century produced other changes that affected life in the cities. In their desire to increase the efficiency, and thus the profits, of their colonial systems, the royal houses of Portugal and Spain embarked on a series of economic, political, and social reforms, known as the Pombaline reforms in Brazil, and the Bourbon reforms in Spanish America. The results of these reforms were varied, but they did increase trade, encourage new investment, open up new areas for colonization, and revitalize a number of stagnant institutions. In many ways the reforms invigorated cities, creating new economic opportunities for urban residents and redefining the importance of the urban setting in

Latin America. Veracruz, Santiago de Chile, and Buenos Aires in particular benefited from the economic changes of the Bourbon/Pombaline era. At the same time, however, increasing levels of wealth were realized at the expense of the urban lower classes, who often reacted violently to the rising economic uncertainty and stress they experienced. For example, the Comuneros Revolt of 1781 in New Granada is indicative of the frustrations that many poor urban residents experienced toward the end of the colonial period.

The civil conflicts that characterized the political history of the majority of Latin American countries during independence and the decades following meant that urban development slowed down dramatically during the first half of the nineteenth century. The spatial structure of cities changed little, while they continued to be plagued with the same physical problems faced during the colonial period. The situation changed during the second half of the century, however, as the realization of political stability and new economic opportunities brought a number of changes. First, urban elites placed a much greater emphasis on accumulating wealth, as the opening of trade with the rest of the world increased economic opportunity. Consequently, class began to displace race as the major determinant of social standing in the cities. Urban elites became wealthier and more diversified, as the roles of merchants, traders, and middlemen of all sorts grew to new prominence.

Second, there were significant demographic changes. Natural rates of population growth began to return, invigorating rural-to-urban migration. As Latin America embraced a larger role in the world economy, immigration from Europe significantly changed the face of the urban populations in Argentina, Uruguay, southern Brazil, Chile, and Cuba. Immigrants constituted a high percentage of the populations of Buenos Aires, Rosario, Santa Fe, La Plata, Montevideo, São Paulo, Santos, Rio de Janeiro, and Havana, in some cases as much as 50 percent. Economically, they took on roles in petty commerce and construction, and promoted numerous small industries and artisan workshops. Immigrants also played key roles in urban politics, introducing new ideas and attitudes about worker's rights, labor organization, and grassroots political movements.

Physically, Latin American cities underwent a profound metamorphosis during the last decades of the nineteenth century. Economic changes brought about by increased trade meant the construction of new railway lines, opening up vast new territory, as well as the refurbishing of port facilities. This development, in turn, motivated the construction of thousands of new cities and towns. With the increasing influence of foreign economic interests, as well as foreign immigrants in Latin America, French and British urban design was introduced to city planning, affecting in particular the opening and design of new avenues, the placement of monuments, the design of parks, and architectural styles. An excellent example of this process is the Paseo de la Reforma in Mexico City. Built in the mid-nineteenth century, it was designed and modeled after the Champs Elysées in Paris to reflect the growing political, economic, social, and cultural sophistication of Mexico City.

Advances in technology meant that many of the physical problems that cities had historically faced, such as inadequate sanitation and lack of potable water, were finally overcome. Electricity brought with it important urban elements such as street lighting and trams that connected city centers to outlying suburbs. However, not all urban challenges were eliminated. The rising wealth of elite groups contrasted with the continued economic insecurity of the lower classes. While elites fashioned palatial homes in emerging suburbs, the working poor continued to live in simple, often crowded conditions. During this time a new type of urban housing emerged: the *conventillo,* as the tenement house was called. As rural and foreign migrants flooded into cities, old colonial structures were subdivided to meet the increasing need for urban housing, introducing the tenement into urban Latin American culture.

Although cities maintained economic and political dominance throughout Latin America during the nineteenth century, it is important to remember that despite this power, the majority of residents in the region continued to live in rural areas. Nevertheless, the development of urban areas established two important trends that dominated urbanization during the twentieth century. First is the primacy of capital cities. Even today, metropolises such as Mexico City, Lima, Buenos Aires, and Santiago de Chile retain economic and political dominance over their respective nations at the expense of other major cities. The second trend is rural-to-urban migration, which has focused on these dominant cities. Lacking resources and adequate training, and affected by frequent regional and national economic crises, rural migrants continue to seek out new opportunities in the cities, just as their colonial counterparts did. Unfortunately, their move to urban areas has outpaced the creation of jobs, thus swelling a floating population of unemployed and underemployed. Urban municipalities, in turn, have been unable to absorb the thousands of new migrants. As a result, slums, shantytowns, and general overcrowding have emerged as one of the markers of the urban environment in Latin America, widening the contrasts between the rich and the poor. In general, the physical and material marginality of the urban poor, exacerbated by a lack of employment, housing, educational opportunities, and urban services, characterizes modern urbanization in Latin America.

Sharon Bailey Glasco

References

Butterworth, Douglas, and John K. Chance. *Latin American Urbanization.* Cambridge: Cambridge University Press, 1981.

Greenfield, Gerald Michael, ed. *Latin American Urbanization: Historical Profiles of Major Cities.* Westport, CT: Greenwood, 1994.

Hardoy, Jorge E., ed. *Urbanization in Latin America: Approaches and Issues.* Garden City, NY: Anchor, 1975.

Hoberman, Louisa Schell, and Susan Migden Socolow, eds. *Cities and Society in Colonial Latin America.* Albuquerque: University of New Mexico Press, 1986.

Joseph, Gilbert M., and Mark D. Szuchman, eds. *I Saw a City Invincible: Urban Portraits of Latin America.* Wilmington, DE: Scholarly Resources, 1996.

Morse, Richard, Michael Conniff, and John Wibel, eds. *The Urban Development of Latin America, 1750–1920.* Stanford, CA: Center for Latin American Studies, 1971.

See also: Administration—Colonial Spanish America; Architecture—Brazil; Architecture—Colonial Spanish America; Architecture—Modern Spanish America; Art and Artists—Brazil; Art and Artists—Colonial Spanish America; Artisans; Atlantic Economy; Bourbon Reforms; Comuneros—New Granada; Culture; Migration—From Iberia to the New World; Race; Trade—Spain/Spanish America; Viceroyalties.

CIVIL WARS (PERU)

These violent struggles between Spanish factions beset Peru in the two decades following the Spanish conquest of the Inca Empire. On November 16, 1532, a band of Spanish adventurers and soldiers under the command of Francisco Pizarro captured Atahualpa, ruler of the Tawantinsuyu (the realm of the Incas), at Cajamarca. During the following months, they executed Atahualpa, moved south to occupy the Inca capital of Cuzco, and installed a puppet ruler, Manco Inca. Yet the issues that led to the civil wars were already at work: animosity between Pizarro and his erstwhile partner, Diego de Almagro, and between their respective supporters; competition between the original conquistadors and Spaniards who arrived later in the hope of sharing in the plunder; and disputes over how much freedom the Spaniards should have to exploit the conquered Andean population.

In 1524 Pizarro and Almagro, for twenty years soldiers of fortune in Central America, entered into a partnership (which also included priest and business manager Hernando de Luque) to undertake the exploration and conquest of lands south of Panama. However, when Pizarro went to Spain (1528–1529) to secure royal authorization for the expedition, he shrewdly secured leadership and many of the rewards for himself. More vigorous and a more dynamic leader than Almagro, Pizarro headed the forces that captured Atahualpa, with Almagro and his men arriving later and thus losing out on the ransom the Inca ruler paid. This outcome left Almagro disgruntled, but he still cooperated with Pizarro when the Spanish occupied the Inca capital of Cuzco. Pizarro informed Almagro that he could explore, conquer, and

Nineteenth-century engraving depicting Spaniards under command of Francisco Pizarro burning the Inca leader Atahualpa at the stake. In reality, the Inca ruler was strangled rather than burned. (Library of Congress)

rule the lands south of Cuzco, whereupon Almagro and his men began an arduous trek through the mountains and deserts of northern Chile (1535–1537). They discovered nothing of value, although ironically the greatest treasure of colonial Peru, the fabulous silver mines of Potosí, were discovered in 1545 within the territory Pizarro assigned to Almagro.

Frustrated and angry, Almagro returned to Cuzco in early 1537 and found the region engulfed by a great indigenous rebellion. Manco Inca, the puppet ruler installed by Pizarro, had slipped away and raised a huge army that threatened to drive the Spanish from Cuzco and the Andes. Almagro defeated an indigenous force at Cuzco and then in April of 1537 claimed the city as his own. At the battle of Abancay, he vanquished another *pizarrista* army coming to fight against Manco's army.

However, he was unable to consolidate his victory, and the Pizarro faction crushed his forces and captured Almagro at the battle of the Salinas in mid-1538. Almagro was executed shortly thereafter, but his death did not end the *pizarrista-almagrista* struggle: on June 26, 1541, vengeful supporters of Almagro broke into Pizarro's residence in Lima and killed him. Thus, less than a decade after embarking on the expedition to conquer Peru, both Pizarro and Almagro had died violently, at the hands of each other's partisans.

Meanwhile, Charles V had become aware of the war raging between his conquistador subjects in Peru and sent Cristobal Vaca de Castro, a judge from the high court of Valladolid, to Peru to restore order. Vaca de Castro arrived in 1541, and a year later, with the assistance of Francisco de Carvajal, a Pizarro stalwart, defeated forces loyal to Diego de Almagro the Younger, the conquistador's mestizo son.

Although the pizarrista-almagrista animosity continued to simmer, other issues now took center stage to plunge Spanish Peru once again into civil war. Chief among these was the issue of the *encomiendas* (grants of indigenous tribute awarded to conquistadors and other meritorious individuals, ostensibly for their service to the Crown, but often for their loyalty to Pizarro or some other Spanish leader). Weak government in the newly established colonies made it nearly impossible for the Crown to regulate those who held encomiendas (*encomenderos*). Amerindians suffered awful abuse, as encomenderos extorted excessive amounts of tribute. Thus, Charles V issued the New Laws of 1542, which prohibited further grants and ordered the reversion to the Crown of all encomiendas upon the death of the original encomendero. In 1544 Viceroy Blasco Núñez Vela arrived with the king's appointment as Peru's first viceroy and with orders to enforce the New Laws. Arrogant and politically obtuse, the viceroy antagonized the conquistadors, who saw his attack on the encomiendas as a threat to their economic power. Tensions ran so high that the judges of the Lima *audiencia* (high court) ordered Núñez Vela's arrest and deportation to Spain. When he escaped from the ship at Tumbez and began to gather forces, Gonzalo Pizarro (Francisco's half brother), who headed the rebellious encomendero faction, captured and executed him in 1546.

The following year Father Pedro de la Gasca arrived, sent to head the Lima audiencia. He announced that the king had relented and would no longer insist on suppression of the encomiendas. Skillfully offering pardons to many of Gonzalo Pizarro's supporters and playing to the interests of those who had not openly sided with the rebellion, Gasca managed to defuse the tumult. He tendered no pardon to Pizarro, however, whose followers abandoned him to the royal executioner during the battle of Jaquijahuana (April 9, 1548).

However, Pizarro's death did not end the civil wars in early colonial Peru. Francisco Hernández Girón, who had supported Viceroy Núñez Vela against Gonzalo Pizarro and was unhappy with the large encomienda granted to him as a reward, organized the final episode of the civil wars. Critical of the government's attempt to limit the amount of tribute that encomenderos could collect and its prohibition on forced indigenous labor, Girón revolted in November 1553. The new uprising centered on Cuzco. Its outcome signaled the growing strength of royal power in the Andes. Despite some initial triumphs, Girón was defeated at the battle of Pucará in October 1554, when many of his supporters deserted him. His attempted flight by sea failed, and viceregal forces captured him and took him to Lima for execution on December 7, 1554.

Although Girón's defeat ended the last major military campaign of the civil wars, the viceroyalty remained awash with adventurers and vagabonds determined to obtain booty and indigenous workers for themselves. Because the encomiendas and plunder had already been distributed, however, the newcomers could only hope to realize their avaricious dreams by finding another Mexico or Peru, or more realistically by taking the encomienda grants of other Spaniards. Viceregal authorities sent expeditions into the Amazon in search of El Dorado and to free Peru of troublemakers, most infamous of whom was the sociopath Lope de Aquirre, who murdered his way to control of Pedro de Ursúa's expedition in 1560–1561. The continued existence of a rump Inca state in the mountains north of Cuzco at Vilcabamba also perturbed political tranquillity, until its destruction by Viceroy Francisco de Toledo in the 1570s. Nonetheless, the civil wars were over, and the Spanish monarchy had begun to consolidate its hold over the Andes.

Kendall W. Brown

References

Hemming, John. *The Conquest of the Incas.* New York: Harcourt Brace Jovanovich, 1968.

Howard, Cecil. *Pizarro and the Conquest of Peru.* New York: American Heritage, 1968.

Varón Gabai, Rafael. *Francisco Pizarro and His Brothers: The Illusion of Power in Sixteenth-Century Peru.* Norman: University of Oklahoma Press, 1997.

See also: Colonists and Settlers I—Andes; Conquest I—Andes; Conquistadors; El Dorado; Encomienda; Laws—Colonial Latin America; Native Americans V—Central and Southern Andes; New Laws of 1542; Peru; Túpac Amaru Revolt; Viceroyalties; Visita.

CLERGY—SECULAR, IN COLONIAL SPANISH AMERICA

The secular, or diocesan, clergy took a secondary role in the Christianization of the New World. The earliest missionaries tended to be from the religious orders (the regular clergy), although there were important early missionaries from the secular clergy. The term *secular clergy* denotes those priests who normally engage in parochial duties and are subject directly to the authority of a bishop. The term *secular* comes from the fact that they live out in the world (*saeculum,* in Latin) and not cloistered away. This contrasts with regular clergy who are members of organized religious orders, take special vows, and live according to a special rule of life (*regula,* in Latin).

The structure of the secular clergy was highly hierarchical. The lowest level consisted of the local parish priests who also served as a local ecclesiastical judge; he held the additional title of *vicario,* indicating that he held judicial powers vicariously from the bishop. All clergy were subject to the authority of the bishop, but one group frequently tried to rival his authority, the cathedral chapter. The chapter was made up of priests appointed to specific offices to provide for the spiritual and administrative needs of the cathedral, the principal church of the diocese. The term *cathedral* comes from the fact that the bishop's throne (*cathedra,* in Latin) is housed there. Under the best of circumstances there were twenty-seven members of the chapter, divided into four ranks. The highest-ranking group was that of the dignitaries. Each of these priests held a special title of office and enjoyed the use of the Spanish honorific, *don.* In descending order the titles were as follows: dean, archdeacon (*arcediano*), precentor (*chantre*), schoolmaster (*maestrescuelas*), treasurer (*tesorero*). Following in order of importance were the ten canons (*canonigos*), six rationeers (*racioneros*), and six half-rationeers (*medio-racioneros*). These last two categories took their names from the fact that members of the chapter received their salaries as specified portions of the ecclesiastical tax, the tithe (*diezmo*).

The bishop governed all of the secular clergy, as well as the spiritual and temporal affairs of the diocese. At times he was assisted in his work by two officials, the provisor and the vicar general. The provisor exercised the power of the "ordinary," the judicial function of the bishop. The vicar general was the administrative assistant to the bishop. As dioceses grew, the number of offices associated with the bishop also increased to include provisors for the natives and other assistants.

The secular clergy fell administratively under the power and authority of the king. Based upon papal bulls from the late fifteenth and early sixteenth centuries, the Spanish Crown claimed the right of patronage over the Church in the New World. The right of patronage included, but was not limited to, the right to appoint ecclesiastical officials. Under the claim of royal patronage, the Spanish Crown appointed archbishops and bishops, members of cathedral chapters, and even local curates. In the case of archbishops and bishops, the names chosen by the monarch had to be conveyed to the papacy for formal approval. For the lower offices, appointment by the monarch sufficed to empower the person to collect the fruits of the office, that is, whatever salary or other income it generated. In order to actually exercise the office, the appointee needed local approval from the bishop or archbishop in the form of canonical institution.

In the latter part of the sixteenth century, Philip II codified the Crown's claims to patronage in the Ordinances of the Royal Patronage (1574). In addition to outlining the procedures referred to earlier, under the new ordinances the king instituted a process through which bishops would fill vacant curacies. The Crown solemnly pledged to be responsible for paying the annual salary of parish priests. This act converted the curacy into a beneficed curacy, that is, a curacy with a guaranteed income. Beneficed curacies carried with them several tangible benefits, not the least of which was the guaranteed income. Additionally, once appointed and formally installed, the beneficed curate held the office for life. Rather than depending simply on the will of the bishop to fill these posts, the Ordinance of the Patronage mandated that candidates for benefices undergo a series of competitive examinations. Local ecclesiastical officials, on the basis of the exams, would then nominate the best-trained cleric for the office and submit his name to the local royal official, usually the viceroy or governor of the province. The appointment to the benefice came from the royal official back to the bishop, who would then canonically institute the person into the office. In the case of vacancies, bishops could still appoint curates on a temporary basis, until competitive exams could be scheduled to fill the office permanently.

The secular clergy depended on several sources of revenue. The most important of these was the tithe, a 10 percent tax on agricultural production. While in the Old World the tithe applied to nearly all products, in the New it was limited to agricultural products. Native peoples were eventually exempted from paying the tithe, since they were required to pay a head tax to the Crown, the fruits of which in part went to pay local curates. The collection of the tithe was the responsibility of the cathedral chapter. Since the chapter officials' income depended directly on the tithe, they tended to be enthusiastic in its collection. Tithe collection took two forms. The chapter, and its employees, could collect the tax directly from those who owed it. This process was not a simple one; it involved dealing in agricultural products and then selling them for the best price possible. The possibility for loss was significant. The other method of tithe collection was to rent it to private collectors. The private collectors would bid to collect a certain part of the tithe, say, yearling calves. The collector with the highest bid then gained the right to collect the tithe. The collector then hoped that the tithe collected would result in more money than he had originally bid. The chapter had to be content with whatever the winning bid was.

The promulgation of the Ordinance of the Patronage also mandated that the religious orders eventually were to give up the parishes they had developed in favor of the secular clergy, a process known as secularization. In fact, this process took about two centuries to accomplish. The purpose of the secularization was to better control the New World Church. Because of the grants of patronage, the Crown exercised a great deal of control over the secular clergy, but had little authority over the regulars. By diminishing their role in the parishes, the Crown could, in effect, diminish their influence overall. The secularization meant a splitting of the spheres of activity between the secular and the regular clergy. The regular clergy became more closely associated with missionary activity in the frontier regions; the secular clergy, with the organized urban and village churches.

Pious works were an important source of income for many clerics. Pious works consisted of funds invested with the church, the income of which went to pay for certain spiritual benefits, such as masses. These pious works could also be instituted on the basis of property, the rents of which formed the income for the spiritual benefits. Similarly, many religious sodalities came to have property and investments, the profits from which went to further the ends of the sodality. In general, the secular hierarchy, and in particular the parish priests, benefited directly and indirectly from these funds. The clergy could exercise an important influence in the investment of these funds, normally based solely in mortgages on real property. Similarly they enjoyed the income by saying the masses or officiating at the ceremonies designated as the spiritual benefit.

With the increasing secularization, secular clerics became more ubiquitous in the hinterland. In many areas, the only contact native peoples had with Spanish authority was through the local curate. The judicial, moral, and spiritual authority of these "magistrates of the sacred" represented the power and authority of the monarch himself. They came to exercise significant social and economic control over the hinterland. Secularization also brought about limitations on the regular clergy, and an overall increase in royal control over the Church.

While the Crown particularly targeted the regular clergy in increasing its control over the Church (for example, expelling the Jesuit order in 1769), the secular clergy also suffered increased scrutiny. In 1802 the Crown took over the loans that the Church held to support its various pious works. In return, the government issued bonds to the Church to pay the interest needed for the ongoing works. This had a serious detrimental effect on the economy and on the lives of many clerics who received salaries from these works. Then, in 1812, the Crown suspended the *fuero eclesiástico,* the right of a cleric to have most routine legal cases heard by the ecclesiastical courts. These and other actions created uncertainty within the clergy. At the same time, some clerics were beginning to explore Enlightenment ideas as they slowly entered the Hispanic world. As a result, a few priests became convinced of the need to break ties with Spain and reassert local control over local institutions.

Miguel Hidalgo launched an attempt to overthrow the Spanish viceregal government of New Spain in 1810. While he was ultimately unsuccessful, he did stimulate further discontent against the Spanish Crown. Another priest, José María Morelos, took up the mantle of independence upon the arrest and execution of Hidalgo. Other secular priests took leadership roles in independence movements throughout the Americas. In fact, when independence came to Mexico, it was under the banner of "Freedom, Equality, and Religion." Secular clerics took an active role in the wars of independence in other countries of the region. The Church also regained its position of power and authority throughout the Hispanic Americas with the arrival of independence. In fact, the secular clergy came to exercise great power under the national governments. National governments signed concordats with the Vatican establishing the Catholic Church as the national church and passing some formerly royal prerogatives to new governments.

The Church became allied with conservative political movements in Latin America. An opposition grew up, espousing liberal ideals based on Enlightenment thinking, calling for the separation of church and state. The alliance of the Church and secular clergy with the conservative forces involved the clergy directly in the political events of the Latin American republics.

John F. Schwaller

References

Schwaller, John F. *The Origins of Church Wealth in Mexico.* Albuquerque: University of New Mexico Press, 1985.

———. *The Church and Clergy in Sixteenth-Century Mexico.* Albuquerque: University of New Mexico Press, 1987.

Taylor, William B. *Magistrates of the Sacred.* Stanford, CA: Stanford University Press, 1996.

Van Oss, Adriaan C. *Catholic Colonialism.* Cambridge: Cambridge University Press, 1986.

See also: Beatas; Cannibalism; Catholic Church in Brazil; Catholic Church in Spanish America; Confraternities; Conquest and the Debate over Justice; Diabolism in the New World; Idolatry, Extirpation of; Inquisition—Spanish America; Jesuits—Iberia and America; Laws—Colonial Latin America; Ordenanza del Patronazgo; Religious Orders; Witchcraft.

CLOTHING IN COLONIAL SPANISH AMERICA

"Clothes make the man" goes a popular aphorism; but clothes also defined the social relations of the many peoples who were part of the conquest and colonization of the Americas. Consequently they were an important part of Iberian-American relations. The way people dressed provided clues as to their identity in terms of race and class. These linkages were at times enforced by sumptuary laws or other kinds of regulations. In addition, people believed that character and morality were revealed by an individual's choice of dress. Finally, cloth and the clothing that resulted were central parts of the pre-Hispanic and the colonial economy, serving as a form of wealth, at times as a currency, and finally as a form of credit.

When Christopher Columbus first set eyes upon the native people of the Caribbean, one of his strongest impressions was of their nudity. He wrote, "It seemed to me that they were a people very deficient in everything. They all go naked as their mothers bore them, and the women also" (Columbus 1989, 23–24). Indeed the Caribs and Arawaks of the region did not cover their bodies with cloth as much as they did with a kind of pigment that protected their skin from the sun. They did wear clothes, which in the case of the leaders were sometimes studded with gold nuggets; but generally, to Spanish eyes, they were singularly exposed. In fact they excelled at weaving, and the name of the skirts worn by women who were married (*naguas*) was adopted by the Spaniards and used throughout the Americas to describe petticoats, although the word became *enaguas*. Columbus, like other Europeans, made cultural assumptions about the natives of the Caribbean based on their clothes or lack of them. He took for granted that they were uncivilized and indeed even doubted if they spoke any language or had any religion. In the same way, the attitudes of the Spanish when they first saw other indigenous peoples such as the Mayas, the Aztecs, and the Incas were conditioned by the fact that these people had ideas about clothes that were similar to their own.

Indigenous urban civilizations such as the Mayas, the Aztecs, and the Incas all believed that dress should be a covering for more than just the genitalia and used it to cover most of the body. They also believed that clothes should reflect the people who wore them, and therefore their costumes usually indicated their place of origin and in some cases their social status, age, occu-

pation, or military standing. These messages could be conveyed not only by the style of clothing but also by the patterns or designs contained within the weaving.

The Aztecs had strict sumptuary laws, which clearly distinguished the aristocracy from other classes and rewarded men who excelled in military endeavors. Aztec law prohibited plebeians from wearing cotton clothes, which were reserved for the upper classes. The clothes of the rich were not only made of cotton but also fringed with rabbit fur and elaborately decorated with feather work, an Aztec specialty. Commoners were not allowed to use jewelry unless the emperor gave them nose plugs or earrings because of their military prowess. In fact, none of the clothes or items of jewelry that denoted military achievements could be purchased, nor were they available in the many Aztec markets. It was only the emperor who could obtain these articles, and he used them to reward bravery among his soldiers. Many Aztec plebeians, although their clothes were perforce made from the coarser maguey, yucca, or palm fiber, had clothes decorated with elaborate designs, and thus they did not accept the kind of drabness that Aztec sumptuary law seemed to dictate.

Aztec clothes also differentiated people by gender and age. Men of all classes wore a loincloth called *maxtlatl*. It was associated with manhood and only worn after the age of thirteen. Men also wore hip-clothes—squares of material folded into a triangle and tied usually on the right side. For men, however, the most important item of clothing and the one that most denoted their status was their cloak, or *tilmatli*. The cloak's length also symbolized military achievements. Commoner men were not allowed to wear long cloaks, with the exception of warriors wounded in the legs.

Aztec women wore the *cueitl,* a kind of skirt that was wrapped around their waist and went down to the middle of their calves. The other basic garment for women was the *huipil,* a kind of shirt that went down to a little below the hips or reached the upper thighs. Women showed their morality by the lack of ornamentation in their appearance. Not only would they avoid overly showy clothes, but also proper women refrained from using flamboyant accessories such as feathers for their head or coloring like indigo for their hair or cochineal for their teeth, lest they be mistaken for prostitutes.

The Aztecs felt superior to other neighboring indigenous peoples who did not wear the loincloth. They also thought neighboring peoples such as the Otomís, who wore such things as feathers in their hair, demonstrated their lack of culture and morality by their appearance.

In the Andean region, the Incas and other peoples defined their ethnic affiliation by their clothes. The patterns of weaving, the style of clothing, and especially the headdresses all indicated the place from which they came. This usage of headdresses to indicate place of origin might be a precursor of the way that Andean native peoples now use hats as a marker for their local identity. Within Inca society, wealth and social status were denoted by the use of extremely fine cloth as well as jewelry. When people attended important social events, the luxury of their clothes was a way of positioning themselves in society and trying to ascend the social ladder. Impressive clothes included shirts decorated with silver or gold and caps topped with feathers and silver. These more impressive items

Aymara woman dressed in an embroidered Inca costume at the Carnival parade of Oruro, Bolivia, February 1982. (Gian Berto Vanni/Corbis)

were often used to reward loyal followers. The Inca lord gave such clothes to the local headmen, the *kurakas,* who in turn could recompense members of their own communities. Cloth itself was also an important item within rituals and was often a gift during the major festivals of the Inca religious calendar. All rites of passage entailed the giving of cloth, and people received new clothing at puberty and at marriage.

The clothing of Andean people might be elaborate in its ornamentation and the fineness of the weaving, but structurally it was quite simple. It was made with simple straight panels of cloth. The panels that men used were shorter and narrower than those used by women. Men used one panel for a kind of breechclout and another to form a sleeveless shirt. This was their basic costume. Women pinned the cloths in order to wrap them around their bodies.

Within the Andean region, spinning wool and weaving were extremely important activities. For young women, the passage to adulthood was marked by their assumption of responsibility for caring for herds of llama, alpaca, and vicuña and learning to spin and weave. Cloth was an important item for tribute, and the Inca lord made sure that his subjects could provide cloth for themselves and for the state warehouses by ensuring that all his subjects had herds of animals. There were also specialists who wove the fine cloth called *cumbi*. Women who had joined the *aqlla*, a religious organization, wove fine cloth for the state. But men also wove this fine cloth, although in this case for the mummified remains of previous Inca lords. These mummy bundles were dressed in the finest cumbi and brought out for ceremonial occasions.

In both the Inca and the Aztec Empires, cloth was an important tribute item. The peoples who were subject to these regimes provided cloth, which in turn was frequently used as a currency and stored in royal warehouses for future needs. The weaving technology used in the Americas was quite simple, consisting of the drop spindle and the backstrap loom (a backstrap loom is a very simple technology that consists of a portable device that is attached to a tree, a door, or whatever is available and has a strap that goes around the weaver's back—thus giving it its name; thus, weaving was portable and could be combined with other activities such as watching over children and selling in the marketplace). These tools limited the width of the cloth panel produced to about

thirty-two inches and meant that production was not abundant. Twenty years after contact, the Spanish had brought their weaving technology to America: treadle looms, carding boards, spinning wheels, rotary wheels, and other innovations. These machines were usually used in workshops known as *obrajes*. The obrajes were concentrated in areas where there was a market for the cloth, mostly in Mexico and Peru, and also where there was waterpower. Obrajes were found in the Valley of Mexico, the Bajío, Puebla-Tlaxcala, the Ecuadorian and Colombian highlands, and near Cuzco. The Spanish also introduced many animals into the landscape, but sheep had the most impact in terms of cloth because they provided a new source of raw material for weaving. The founding of these obrajes and the adoption of wool into typical clothing meant the spread of sheep and the use of local producers to spin wool.

Generally in Mexico the indigenous people made their own clothing. For men, this consisted of breeches and a shirt of cotton with a wool *sarape* (in English usually "serape") if the climate warranted it. For women, normal dress consisted of a skirt, a huipil, or long blouse, and a *quechquemitl*, or triangular shawl. The style and material reflected region and ethnicity.

The clothing and the ideas about clothes that the Spanish brought with them to the Americas were a product of their background. Some of their beliefs were actually similar to those of the Aztecs and the Incas. For example, the Spanish believed that clothes could convey many messages about the wearer. The colors used in clothing were highly symbolic. Brighter colors were reserved for the wealthy and powerful, but color and texture were also emblematic of individual qualities. Widows, for example, demonstrated their grief but also their seriousness by wearing rough sackcloth in white, black, or gray. At the same time, it was important to demonstrate the gravity of the occasion by avoiding ostentation and by only allowing the people closest to the deceased to wear mourning clothes. The color of clothes could also convey a very different message. In early modern Seville, for example, prostitutes had to wear yellow, a stricture that led respectable but mischievous young women to wear yellow to seem daring. Clothes could define a person as respectable, could place them within the social hierarchy, and, in effect, became a kind of extension of the person's identity. At the same time, the humiliation or punishment of a person could be effected through clothes. Women could be shamed by the cutting of their skirts, which seems to have been an official punishment, a kind of ritual humiliation by the legal authorities that was imitated by common folk.

Just as in the Americas, clothing in Spain was an important commodity. It was part of a woman's dowry, and parents also usually gave gifts of clothes at the time of marriage. To mark the new union, bridegrooms frequently gave new garments to their wives. At death, clothes had to be accounted for, and many wills mentioned the division of clothes among the family of the deceased. Widows were usually allowed to keep any clothes that they used, but they had to return their jewels to their husband's family unless they were part of their own patrimony.

Indigenous peoples altered their dress to a greater or lesser degree as they came into contact with the Spanish or Portuguese, especially with missionary brothers, to conform to standards of morality imported from Europe. The importation of metal shears to cut fabric made it easier to produce different styles of clothing. Missionaries encouraged the wearing of trousers by men, and eventually many men adopted a style of shirt with sleeves and buttons. The dress for women in the Americas was generally more acceptable to the friars, but the tendency was for their skirts to become longer and for them to adopt head coverings.

Both church and state tried to ensure that all subjects wore clothes appropriate to their station. Therefore, the dress of indigenous people appeared indigenous, even if in many instances indigenous people's costumes were altered because of moral concerns (covering enough) or the availability of new products. But dressing appropriately also meant sumptuary laws that did not allow people of the lower classes to wear luxurious clothes. People of African ancestry were often singled out for wearing silk or other expensive cloths and also for their use of jewelry.

Clothes revealed a lot about rank in colonial Mexico. Indigenous women continued to wear the huipil, which marked their ethnicity. Creole ladies and those born in Spain used the mantilla (a lace head scarf elegantly draped over the hair), while poorer women, particularly indigenous or mestiza women, used a type of shawl called the rebozo. The type of cloth—silk, satin, and velvet as opposed to the more common and less valued cotton—meant that a person's wealth and status were obvious to contemporary observers. At the same time the style of dress also indicated status; wealthier women wore a type of petticoat called the enaguas under their skirts or dresses. Poorer women by contrast wore the enaguas on its own as a skirt.

Clothes were among the most common possessions that people could pawn. Furthermore, items of clothing were an important form of credit for the poor. People could also pawn clothing at *pulquerías* (taverns specializing in pulque), leading to the accusation that men pawned their wives' clothing (causing nudity) in order to drink. However, women were the most common clients of the pawnshop, and they seem to have managed the household credit situation as well as the clothing situation. Women also might invest in clothing as a hedge against future bad times; they could always get some ready cash for these goods. Cloth was the most common item pawned at the turn of the nineteenth century in Mexico City. Thieves often targeted clothes because of their value. The way to dispose of stolen clothes was mostly through the pawnshops, but also at times through various small businesses.

Except at the highest echelons of society and in the wealthiest classes, people did not change their dress often. When people reported a crime and described the assailant or criminal, they went into much more detail about what the person was wearing than other physical characteristics, because it was highly likely that the accused would not be able to change clothes. Thus a description listing color and type of hat as well as color and style of clothes was considered accurate enough to help the authorities find the individual. Fashion did not change quickly, and therefore people kept their clothes for many years and even bequeathed them to their descendants. In fact clothes of the deceased are mentioned in many wills of the period.

Clothes were closely connected to both personal identity and social position. The way people dressed in colonial Latin America placed them within their ethnic or racial group, and also defined their morality, their profession, even their ranking within a guild or other group. Every item of clothing provided messages through the color, texture, type of cloth, cut, headdress, style, and jewelry. Because clothes were essentially malleable markers, people could adopt the dress of another group in order to pass as members of that group. Such passing was not always complete because other defining features could give them away. Still, the fact that Indians or mulattoes could adopt certain items of the dress of the upper classes was of great concern to the members of the colonial elite because it put into question the whole social order. At the same time, no one worried when members of the indigenous upper classes adopted European dress, because they were part of the ruling elite, even though not part of the Spanish elite.

People who defied categories in general provoked anxiety. When young men, following the fashions of the day, wore clothes perceived to be too feminine, moral authorities worried about the blurring of the gender lines. At the same time, there were a few documented cases of women who wore male dress, an offense that was very serious. However, such fashion crimes were rare, and most colonial Latin Americans accepted their place in society and dressed accordingly.

Clothes were an essential part of people's perceptions of each other, but also they were a means to define one's place in society and one's character. Before the Spanish conquest, sumptuary laws enforced a strict separation of upper and lower classes within both Aztec and Inca societies. But apart from rules from above, people sought to differentiate themselves, and their dress concealed many messages. The Spanish brought new ideas about morality and dress but they also invoked class differences as well as racial differences in the types of clothing that they imposed.

Sonya Lipsett-Rivera

References

Anawalt, Patricia Rieff. *Indian Clothing before Cortés: Mesoamerican Costumes from the Codices.* Norman: University of Oklahoma Press, 1981.

Bauer, Arnold J. *Goods, Power, History: Latin America's Material Culture.* Cambridge: Cambridge University Press, 2001.

Clendinnen, Inge. *Aztecs: An Interpretation.* Cambridge: Cambridge University Press, 1991.

Columbus, Christopher. *The Journal of Christopher Columbus: His Own Account of the Extraordinary Voyage to Discover the New World.* Translated by Cecil Jane. New York: Bonanza, 1989.

Dillard, Heath. *Daughters of the Reconquest: Women in Castilian Society, 1100–1300.* Cambridge: Cambridge University Press, 1984.

François, Marie. "Prendas and Pulperías: The Fabric of the Neighborhood Credit Business in Mexico City, 1780s–1830s." *Estudios de Historia Novohispana* 20 (1999): 67–106.

Gauderman, Kimberley. *Women's Lives in Colonial Quito: Gender, Law, and Economy in Spanish America.* Austin: University of Texas Press, 2003.

Salvucci, Richard J. *Textiles and Capitalism in Mexico: An Economic History of the Obrajes, 1539–1840.* Princeton, NJ: Princeton University Press, 1987.

Sauer, Carl. *The Early Spanish Main.* Berkeley and Los Angeles: University of California Press, 1966.

Spalding, Karen. *Huarochirí: An Andean Society under Inca and Spanish Rule.* Stanford, CA: Stanford University Press, 1984.

Stern, Steve. *Peru's Indian Peoples and the Challenge of Conquest: Huamanga to 1640.* Madison: University of Wisconsin Press, 1982.

See also: Alcohol; Atlantic Economy; Caciques; Catholic Church in Spanish America; Columbian Exchange—Livestock; Credit—Colonial Latin America; Creoles; Culture; Kuraca; Mestizaje; Missions; Mita; Mulatto; Native Americans I–VIII; Obraje; Popular Festivals; Poverty; Prostitution; Race; Slavery I–IV; Women—Brazil; Women—Colonial Spanish America; Women—Modern Spanish America.

COCA

A shrub native to the Andes, coca (*Erythroxylum novogranatense*) produces a mildly stimulant leaf that is chewed or taken as tea. Chemical processing isolates coca's cocaine alkaloid to produce cocaine. Domesticated between 5000 and 2000 BC, coca became, and remains today, an important cultural item. The Incas valued coca's stimulant qualities and the power gained by distributing a coveted crop to other ethnic groups. Native Andeans employed coca as an offering in a wide range of communal and individual rituals. The conquering Spanish both condemned coca as an obstacle to Christianization and praised coca as a valuable commodity. In the 1800s and 1900s, leaders in Andean republics created a negative stereotype of native peoples as coca users. Coca continues to create controversy, as growers and traditional users defend their culture and a source of income against U.S.-backed efforts to end the international traffic in cocaine by destroying coca fields.

Four varieties of coca exist, each adapted to a specific ecological niche and favored over other crops in that zone. The Incas, the Spanish, and people today grow the most valuable varieties in the *yungas,* two narrow subtropical bands that stretch the length of the Andes (between 500 and 2,000 meters above sea level in the eastern foothills and 300–2,300 meters in the west). Coca's location ensured that, through vertical exchange or through direct control of lands at various elevations, many Native Andean communities enjoyed access to the crop. Coca sustains workers at high elevations, transforms dietary carbohydrates into glucose, and functions as a "vehicle of reciprocity" among people and between people and deities.

Incas associated coca with ritualized authority and manipulated ethnic groups' access to it. Spanish colonizers appropriated coca fields and shifted distribution away from kinship and political channels to mercantile circuits. Mass recruitment of workers for the mines created a market for coca. Growers and merchants built fortunes with the profits. However, many missionaries and ecclesiastical authorities condemned coca's association with pre-Hispanic religion and ongoing local ritual practice. Other clergymen argued that mine owners provided coca to laborers instead of adequate wages, food, and water. Crown and Church dependence on coca and silver revenue prevented resolution. Each region's authorities decided whether to prohibit coca or promote it. Many communities' access to coca survived.

Until cocaine's popularity, coca leaf remained a marker of native Andeans' ethnicity and a medicinal oddity (serving, for example, as Coca-Cola's special ingredient). Cocaine was first produced in laboratories in the mid-1800s, recognized as a valuable medicine by 1900, and condemned as an addictive narcotic in the 1950s. In the 1970s, international demand for illegal cocaine led to increased coca cultivation in Peru, Bolivia, and Colombia (the major refiner and distributor). There were no viable cash crop alternatives, and coca's boom absorbed seasonal and permanent migrants unable to find work in rural areas, cities, or mines. In the 1980s, Latin America's severe economic crisis accelerated this trend, and armed revolutionaries moved into Peru's and Colombia's coca-growing lowlands. A parallel economy now exists based on coca and cocaine, and generates as much as half of the nations' foreign exchange.

Leo J. Garofalo

References

Allen, Catherine J. *The Hold Life Has: Coca and Cultural Identity in an Andean Community.* Washington, DC: Smithsonian Institution Press, 1988.

Gade, Daniel W. "Valleys of Mystery on the Peruvian Jungle Margin and the Inca Coca Connection." Pp. 137–156 in *Nature and Culture in the Andes.* Madison: University of Wisconsin Press, 1999.

Gagliano, Joseph A. *Coca Prohibition in Peru: The Historical Debates.* Tucson: University of Arizona Press, 1994.

Pacini, Deborah, and Christine Franquemont, eds. *Coca and Cocaine: Effects on People and Policy in Latin America.* Cambridge, MA: Cultural Survival, 1986.

See also: Alcohol; Bolivia; Cacao; Catholic Church in Spanish America; Coffee; Colombia; Columbian Exchange—Agriculture; Drugs; Ecuador; Food; Henequen; Idolatry, Extirpation of; Maize; Medicine; Mining—Silver; Mita; Native Americans V, VI; Peru; Potato; Potosí; Wheat; Wine.

CODICES

Mesoamerican pictorial writings, known as codices, constitute a rich record of indigenous societies from pre-Columbian times until the colonial period. The term is the plural of the Latin word *codex,* meaning "ancient manuscript." Codices provide de-

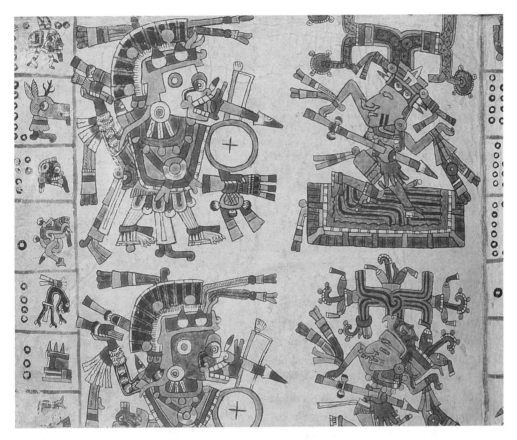

Detail of the Codex Cospi, *an Aztec divinatory calendar, showing the planet Venus, Tlauixcalpantecuhtli, attacking warriors. Year symbols are on the left of the image. (Werner Forman/Corbis)*

tailed information on subjects such as history, genealogy, royal dynasties, geographical descriptions, astronomy, cosmology, and religion.

Before the Spanish conquest and the introduction of European paper, indigenous peoples made codices from deerskins, bark, or fibers from cotton and maguey (known as *amate*). Indians produced various types of codices, including *tiras,* consisting of long strips that were either rolled or folded like screens. *Lienzos* (cotton canvases) and *mapas* (on paper) were codices consisting of single sheets of cloth. Writing on codices ranged from direct pictorial representations and ideograms to the use of

phonetic referents. Some Maya codices also employed a kind of alphabet. Codices made after the conquest demonstrate the adoption of the Roman alphabet as well as Renaissance artistic conventions like the use of perspective.

The earliest codices date from around AD 300, but similarities to glyphs at archaeological sites suggest the possibility of an earlier origin. Although debate surrounds the provenance of certain codices, scholars commonly locate most of them in the cultural regions of Maya, Mixtec, and Puebla-Tlaxcala. The *Borgia* and *Vatican* codices from the Puebla-Tlaxcala region reveal the importance to Nahuas of calendar systems and cosmology, and they contain representations of gods, religious practices, and rituals. In the Mixtec region, which art historians further subdivide into coastal and highland areas, the *Nuttall* and *Bodley* codices present historical narratives, myths, and genealogies associated with dynastic kingdoms. Codices made of unfolding sections or screens, like the *Dresden* and *Paris* codices, detail Maya concepts of astronomy and mathematics, as well as the 260-day ritual calendar. The *Madrid Codex* functioned as a book of divination for the Maya.

Following the conquest, Spaniards like the Franciscan friar Diego de Landa (1524–1579) in the Yucatán Peninsula destroyed the majority of codices for their association with idolatry. Those deemed free of idolatrous representations survived, as did those successfully hidden by Indians. Spaniards encouraged Indians to write codices for insights into newly conquered territories. The *Codex Mendoza,* commissioned by the Spanish viceroy Antonio de Mendoza, shows tribute collection arrangements of the old Aztec Empire, as well as offering a history of Tenochtitlan and a portrayal of Nahua daily life.

The manufacture of codices in the colonial era continued under the auspices of Spanish ecclesiastical authorities. The friar Bernardino de Sahagún gathered native scribes to assist in making the *Florentine Codex,* which presented Nahua natural history and religious and social life in twelve folio books that contain hundreds of indigenous drawings. Other colonial codices, such as the *Codex Kingsborough,* served in legal cases brought by Indians. Litigation concerning land ownership involved the use of codices such as those be- longing to the Techialoyan group from the seventeenth century, which some scholars consider related to another genre of documents known as primordial titles. Codices also include the corpus of annals, Nahua municipal, or *altepetl* (ethnic state), histories, exemplified in the writings of Domingo de San Antón Muñón Chimalpahin.

Richard Conway

References

Berdan, Frances F., and Patricia Rieff Anawalt. *The Codex Mendoza.* 4 vols. Berkeley and Los Angeles: University of California Press, 1992.

Boone, Elizabeth Hill. *Stories in Red and Black: Pictorial Histories of the Aztecs and Mixtecs.* Austin: University of Texas Press, 2000.

Robertson, Donald. *Mexican Manuscript Painting of the Early Colonial Period: The Metropolitan Schools.* New Haven, CT: Yale University Press, 1959.

Wauchope, Robert, Howard Cline, Charles Gibson, and H. B. Nicholson, eds. *Handbook of Middle American Indians.* Vol. 14, *Guide to Ethnohistorical Sources.* Austin: University of Texas Press, 1975.

See also: Altepetl, Cabildo; Cah; Catholic Church in Spanish America; Chroniclers; Clergy—Secular, in Colonial Spanish America; Languages; Native Americans IV—Mesoamerica.

COFFEE

Since leaving the lands of Ethiopia and Arabia five hundred years ago, coffee has traveled enormous distances for purposes of trade, and for some three and a half centuries it has formed a part of urban European life. In the seventeenth century, during the rise of modern capitalism, coffee was renowned as a nonintoxicating, stimulating, and somewhat exotic beverage. Fast becoming an essential element in modern sociability, it animated the conversations of aristocrats, politicians, intellectuals, and businessmen who met in local coffeehouses.

In the world commodities market of the twentieth century, only oil came to acquire higher value than coffee. In Latin America, coffee is the export product with the highest value, the most labor-intensive production methods, and the largest extent of land under cultivation. Coffee is a key factor for understanding the agrarian and political history of many Caribbean and Central and South American countries, but it should not be forgotten that it also forms part of the principal list of luxury goods of industrial and postindustrial countries.

The geography of the production of this tropical shrub, classified by Carolus Linnaeus as belonging to the Rubiacea family in 1752, followed the path of European colonial expansion during the eighteenth and nineteenth centuries. In fact, the coffee trade came to play an important part in the world power structure created by the dominant imperial nations. Until the last third of the nineteenth century, the most important coffee ports were Le Havre and Amsterdam, and if London did not figure among them, it was due mainly to the fact that coffee never managed to replace tea in British habits.

In the eighteenth century, the agents of Dutch colonialism opened coffee cultivation to trade by taking plants to Ceylon (Sri Lanka), and to the islands of Java and Sumatra in Indonesia. Meanwhile, the French introduced the shrub into Saint Domingue (Haiti), which was, in late eighteenth-century coffee-producing terms, the equivalent of the São Paulo region in the twentieth century; next in line came Cuba, Venezuela, and Puerto Rico. With the French Revolution, the abolitionist policies of the French National Convention, the Haitian rising of 1791, and the Napoleonic wars, Haiti lost its supremacy as market leader to the Dutch East Asian colonies, and Amsterdam became the hub of the coffee trade.

It was also the Dutch who introduced coffee to Latin America. The first coffee plantation was established in Suriname in 1714, and cultivation spread imperceptibly west to Venezuela and southward to Brazil. Due on one hand to the devastation of the Asiatic plantations after 1850, and on the other to favorable local social and political conditions and the excellent properties of the soil, the Paraiba Valley near Rio de Janeiro (followed years later by the northern part of São Paulo and the southern part of Minas Gerais) became the center of coffee production. From that moment, Brazil, and Latin America as a whole, won the leadership in coffee production, although after World War II, Africa greatly increased its coffee production, as did Asia in the latter part of the century.

After 1830, coffee drinking began to descend the rungs of the social ladder; by the mid-nineteenth century it had become an object of popular consumption in many countries and was regarded by both middle and working classes as an essential part of breakfast and a popular drink at other times of day. In other words, coffee became a part of daily life in the burgeoning new industrial societies. The preference for coffee became evident during the U.S. Civil War, and a few years later in continental Europe. From then on, it was the demand in North America that set the standard.

By then, Asia was already being replaced by postcolonial Latin America, with Brazil in the lead and Venezuela and Costa Rica following a long way behind. The shift in the geographical pattern of production was also reflected in politics and business. The greater flexibility and aggressive style of U.S. businesses led to the predominance of U.S. capitalism, as it moved to organize the biggest and most powerful multinational corporations to control stocks in the centers of production. U.S. businesses also set out to control the exportation, transportation and importation, processing, packaging, and distribution of coffee. And New York became the undisputed center of the world coffee market, a position it still holds today. It was there that transnational enterprises like the American Coffee Company, a subsidiary of the Atlantic and Pacific Tea Company, or years later the W. R. Grace Company, became established. These companies began to dictate consumer tastes, and may be regarded as the forerunners of the large twentieth-century processing and marketing consortia, such as Nestlé and General Foods.

Nevertheless, unlike the mining enclaves, the Cuban sugar refineries, or the banana plantations of Central America and Colombia, U.S. capitalists did not invest directly in coffee production; as a result, political control of the product remained in the hands of the national upper classes, linked, of course, to international capitalist interests. This structure explains why in twentieth-century Brazil, Colombia, and Central America popular nationalist feelings and movements did not derive part of their strength from repudiation of their countries' main export product, as did those in Cuba, Chile, Mexico, Peru, and Venezuela, to take a few examples, where production of sugar, petroleum, copper, and bananas was in the hands of U.S. or British companies.

Historically, the most cultivated coffee bean is the *Coffea arabica typica,* of which several varieties exist, such as Bourbon, Maragogype, and recently Caturra, which are known in the international market as mild coffees (the names vary somewhat among cultivators in Latin America and the Caribbean). The common arabica coffee plant has a productive life of thirty years, coming into full commercial production between the fifth and sixth years, and reaching the peak of productive output between the seventh and fifteenth years before beginning a gradual decline. Another important type of coffee is Canephora, of which the Robusta is a variety, which yields a more acidic bean with a higher level of caffeine than that of the mild coffees.

Like many other plants, coffee was not untouched by the Green Revolution of the 1960s. The normal botanical cycle was shortened, bringing the shrub into production in the third year; however, by the tenth year the bush is worn out. Also, as a result of cultivation taking place in full sun without shade-providing trees, and given the hillside environments on which it is often grown, the soil is soon exhausted or the vegetable layer lost by erosion. The environmental cost of this high productivity is excessive, though public policies tend not to take it into consideration.

Like wine, tea, or chocolate, coffee is not a staple food product; and like rubber and cacao trees and banana and tea plants, the coffee shrub grows only in tropical zones, in contrast to cotton, tobacco, hides, timbers, and sugar, raw materials that can also be produced in subtropical or temperate zones. These two characteristics, the fact that coffee is a luxury good (notwithstanding its popularity) and its restriction to certain regions of production, help to explain the volatile and speculative nature of the coffee trade, as well as the extraordinary geographical movements of production throughout the last two centuries. Coffee is also subject to a climatic cycle, which cuts across the economic cycle.

Once it reaches a certain level of popular consumption, coffee is a commodity with low demand elasticity. In other words, huge and sustained price rises are needed for consumers to feel obliged to give up the habit of drinking it. On the cultivators' side, the supply is similarly inelastic. For coffee growers to abandon their plantations, prices must fall considerably and stay low for long periods.

From the mid-nineteenth century on, the major factor that caused price variations was frost in Brazil, which killed the high-growing plants. Since world supply was concentrated in Brazil from roughly 1850 until the mid-twentieth century, the effect of such frosts was to reduce supplies and raise consumer prices, a pattern that encouraged producers in Brazil and other parts of the world to extend their plantations. Since a period of five to six years had to pass between planting and the first commercial harvest, five years after a Brazilian frost saw a phase of overproduction at the world level, with a consequent fall in prices, which discouraged producers.

Although coffee is closely linked to an image and an ideology of "free trade" (and it is quite clear that market forces did mold the situation of coffee production during the nineteenth century, at least after 1830), the fact that the upper classes of São Paulo controlled world supplies led to a paradoxical situation: the political regulation of the market. This situation began modestly enough in 1902 through a prohibition on new plantations. The prohibition was the result of the so-called coffee cycle: the high prices of the 1880s and much of the 1890s encouraged the extension of coffee planting not only in Brazil but into other countries, such as Colombia and El Salvador. When, in 1896, high levels of overproduction were reached, prices began to fall, until the market value became catastrophically low at the beginning of the new century. It was at that moment that São Paulo growers and merchants failed to take note of two important facts: first, that a unilateral reduction of supply would imply a subsidy to competitors, some of whom were peasant producers in Central America and Colombia, and second, they needed to deal with the problem of quality, since their competitors' mild coffees were obtaining considerable appeal in the centers of consumption.

The big São Paulo coffee growers and exporters succeeded in having the government finance stocks, from successive crop retentions, in order to raise world prices. Under this scheme, the government bought the entire harvest and retained a part, which it put into granaries, thus regulating the supply and raising the price. This new model of interventionist policies started in 1905 and was refined yearly, until by 1930 it had become a complex Brazilian state policy in defense of coffee. With the help of this umbrella, Colombia and Central America became important world producers and the first in mild coffees.

After 1928, due to the world crisis, the situation in Brazil deteriorated; 70 million sacks, the equivalent of the entire world's harvests for two years, were destroyed. In 1939, the European market, which represented nearly half of world consumption, closed. The United States, with an eye on maintaining hemispheric stability and fearing a potential expansion of Nazism and other pro-Fascist forces, was anxious to avoid the destabilization of countries that depended to a high degree on coffee. It therefore decided to finance the surplus production that Europe could not absorb, through an Inter-American Quota Agreement (1940) that guaranteed profitable coffee prices for Latin American countries. Despite efforts to reestablish the free market after World War II, and with Europe still economically ruined, it was considered prudent to maintain the inter-American agreement, at least until the enormous demand of the first half of the 1950s caused prices to rise again, stimulating producers around the world. It was only in 1956, when the United States was still the principal world consumer and its multinational companies were trying to impose the new culture of instant coffee (invented by Nestlé in 1939, just before World War II began), that prices dropped, as competition from African producers began to be felt.

The political and macroeconomic stability of Brazil, Colombia, and Central America still depended on the prices and quantities of coffee, traded mainly on the New York Stock Exchange. It was fortunate for the region that the cold war raised its head in the form of Castro's Cuba with its attempt to "export" revolution. Without the Cuban Revolution it would have been unthinkable for the U.S. Congress to approve the United States joining the International Coffee Organization, which stabilized, by means of successive international agreements, the income of coffee producers at a higher level than those dictated by market forces. In 1989, the rescission by the United States of the agreement's stronger clauses put an end to a long era of political control over what had been Latin America's principal export product throughout the twentieth century.

The social history of coffee expresses the relationship of humanity and the land and also the social relations of work and power. In many Latin American countries, coffee was a frontier crop, at least in the initial phases of settlement. Many areas of Brazil, Colombia, Guatemala, Costa Rica, and southern Mexico were colonized thanks to coffee. In the Caribbean islands, exploited under the French and Spanish colonial regimes, coffee showed considerable compatibility with slavery, a phenomenon apparent also in the first decisive stages in the Rio de Janeiro region after 1850. The history of coffee growing in Brazil is, however, particularly interesting, since (following the abolition of slavery in 1888) the *fazendeiros* (estate owners) of São Paulo, Rio de Janeiro, and Minas Gerais preferred to support strategies for recruiting European labor in peculiar sharecropping systems. In Costa Rica and Colombia, on the other hand, big landowners were unable, in the long run, to exercise any kind of control over labor, which, given the characteristics of the cultivation, maintenance, and harvesting of coffee, reproduced the pattern of the small-scale family farm.

The peasant rationale for this kind of family enterprise lay in its capacity not only to absorb and put to work all the available family labor, fitting it to the needs of the annual cycle, but also to cultivate, alongside coffee, subsistence crops that would guarantee family livelihood independently of the level of coffee prices. This is why the upper classes in Colombia were willing to shower blessings on the small farmer, exemplified in the mythical figure of Juan Valdez adopted many years later as a logo by Colombia's National Coffee-Producers' Federation, during the coffee depression of the 1930s. These blessings came on top of the subsidy given to the farmers after the destruction of the harvests in Brazil.

Nevertheless, during the second half of the twentieth century, and particularly since the 1970s, the Green Revolution (which introduced more productive varieties and new methods of planting and crop management, making production more capital-intensive) has to some extent pushed aside small cultivators, who have tended to become itinerant wage earners.

Even so, the world coffee crisis, accentuated by the abandonment of political market regulation systems in 1989, offers no clear signals for capitalist coffee cultivation in Latin America. The market is now highly concentrated and controlled by multinational chains of processors and traders. This means that, even though profits have dropped for producers since 1990, supermarket prices for instant or vacuum-packed roasted or ground coffee have risen sharply. The fall in prices for producers was due in part to a combination of a relatively modest increase in demand combined with a dramatic increase in production during the 1990s, in part thanks to new technologies for controlling destructive pests, but even more due to the expansion of planting in Brazil, Indonesia, Vietnam, and Mexico.

Coffee continues to be in high demand, and an enormous number of families earn their living directly as producers. Some others obtain share dividends or wages, thanks to the feverish activity of cultivation, maintenance, harvesting, processing, transportation, packaging, and distribution of coffee throughout the world.

Marco Palacios

References

Font, Mauricio A. *Coffee, Contention, and Change in the Making of Modern Brazil.* Cambridge, MA: Blackwell, 1990.

Gervase, William, Clarence Smith, and Steven Topik, eds. *The Global Coffee Economy in Africa, Asia and Latin America, 1500–1989.* Cambridge and New York: Cambridge University Press, 2003.

Holloway, Thomas H. *Immigrants on the Land: Coffee and Society in São Paulo, 1886–1934.* Chapel Hill: University of North Carolina Press, 1980.

Paige, Jeffrey M. *Coffee and Power: Revolution and the Rise of Democracy in Central America.* Cambridge, MA: Harvard University Press, 1997.

Palacios, Marco. *Coffee in Colombia, 1850–1970: An Economic, Social, and Political History.* Cambridge and New York: Cambridge University Press, 1980.

Roseberry, William, Lowell Gudmundson, and Mario Samper Kutschbach, eds. *Coffee, Society and Power in Latin America.* Baltimore: Johns Hopkins University Press, 1995.

Stein, Stanley J. *Vassouras, a Brazilian Coffee County, 1850–1900: The Roles of Planter and Slave in a Plantation Society.* Princeton, NJ: Princeton University Press, 1957.

See also: Alcohol; Atlantic Economy; Bananas; Brazil; Cacao; Colombia; Columbian Exchange—Agriculture; Costa Rica; Cotton; Dyes and Dyewood; Guatemala; Henequen; Oil; Sugar; Tobacco; Trade—Spain/Spanish America; Wine.

COLD WAR—PORTUGAL AND THE UNITED STATES

During the cold war, Portugal's main interaction with the Americas consisted of its interaction with the United States. The authoritarian regime of Oliveira Salazar in Portugal, established in the early 1930s, was greatly helped by the emergence of the cold war. Portugal maintained neutrality during World War II, but the Allied triumph over the Axis powers gave hopes to Salazar's democratic opposition that international pressure would lead to the end of his regime. These hopes, however, were frustrated. Under Salazar, the Portuguese government had anticipated the postwar world since late 1943, when, without abandoning its official neutrality, Portugal signed an agreement with the United Kingdom, providing the British with certain naval and air facilities on the Portuguese islands of the Azores.

The United States was also interested in acquiring facilities in the Azores and began separate negotiations with the Portuguese. These negotiations were conducted by George Kennan, chargé d'affaires in Portugal, and by Ambassador Henry Norweb. Portugal resisted the first approaches, but eventually Salazar recognized that a gradual entry into the U.S. sphere of influence would be crucial, both for the maintenance of his regime and for Portugal's colonial possessions in Africa and Asia. Particularly important was the situation in East Timor, which had been occupied by the Japanese since early 1942. When Portugal asked to participate in the campaign for the liberation of East Timor, Ambassador Norweb replied to Salazar that the best help Portugal could give would be to authorize the construction of a second airfield in the Azores for U.S. use. Salazar acquiesced.

The Portuguese-U.S. agreement was signed on November 28, 1944. The United States accepted Portugal's participation in operations in the Pacific and in the restoration of East Timor to Portuguese sovereignty. In return, Portugal authorized the construction and use of an air base on the island of Santa Maria, for the purpose of facilitating the movement of U.S. forces to the theater of war in the Pacific. The agreement marked a significant change in terms of Portuguese foreign policy. Portugal's traditional association with the British was now accompanied by an alliance with the United States. With the change, Portugal not only recovered East Timor but also received a formal promise by the United Kingdom and the United States to respect Portuguese sovereignty over its colonial empire.

During World War II, U.S. military planners had conceived a vast system of U.S. military bases for the postwar period. The Azores played a prominent role in these plans, and its strategic importance was reinforced with the emergence of the cold war. A few months after the war, when the 1944 agreement expired, Portugal and the United States engaged in negotiations for the signature of a new agreement. The Portuguese government required stronger political assurances from the United States. Facing Salazar's reluctance and the new international context created by the emergence of the cold war, in late 1946 the United States offered Portugal assurances that any threat to the territorial security of Portugal would constitute a threat to the security of the Atlantic. If any Portuguese territory were threatened, the United States would be required to use force against any aggressor in the maintenance of peace.

A new agreement was signed on February 2, 1948, granting transit facilities for U.S. aircraft through Lajes do Pico in the Azores for a period of three years without payment of any tax or rental. The preamble to the agreement explained the "manifest utility to the government of the United States . . . in continuing the transit through Lajes," given its "international responsibilities." It also mentioned the "advantages which those facilities will achieve for the security of Europe and for the reestablishment and consolidation of world peace" (*United States Treaties and Other International Agreements* 1951, Vol. 2, Part 2, pp. 2266–2271).

The Marshall Plan also favored the integration of Portugal in the U.S. sphere of influence in the early cold war period. Portugal accepted the invitation to participate in the European Recovery Program, although it declined, initially, any type of economic and financial aid. Salazar feared the hegemonic intentions of the United States in Europe and believed that financial aid through the Marshall Plan was merely an instrument of this design. In 1948, however, facing serious financial and economic difficulties, the Portuguese government accepted the financial aid of the European Recovery Program.

Equally important was Portuguese participation in NATO. Portugal was invited by the Western powers to participate in the Atlantic alliance mainly because of the strategic value of the Azores. The Azores and the U.S. base were in fact the main reason why Portugal, a colonial and nondemocratic nation, was a founding member of NATO. In the early 1950s, the secretary general of NATO defined the Azores as the most im-

portant contribution that Portugal could make to NATO defense. The U.S. government believed that under the umbrella of NATO they would finally convince a reluctant Salazar to accept U.S. presence in the territory on a long-term basis. In 1951, Portugal and the United States signed the two major agreements that regulated not only the use of the Azores facilities but also the political and military relations between the two countries over the next two decades. The Mutual Defense Assistance Agreement was similar to the agreements signed between the United States and other members of NATO, under the Mutual Defense Assistance Act of 1949. The other agreement, related to the Azores, granted the United States "in case of war in which they are involved during the life of the North Atlantic Treaty . . . the use of facilities in the Azores" (ibid., Vol. 2, Part 1, pp. 438–452). Both governments also agreed to build new installations and improve preexisting facilities on the Azores. The presence of U.S. forces in the Azores in time of peace was authorized for a period of five years.

The 1951 agreements also set the tone for the cordiality of U.S.-Portuguese relations during the first years of the Eisenhower administration. By 1954, however, the first signs of trouble began to emerge. The problems were above all related to Portuguese colonialism. Portugal resisted the wave of decolonization in the postwar years, but it began to feel strong pressure from India regarding its territories of Goa, Damão, and Diu. Portugal always refused to negotiate, and, in the summer of 1954, the Indian government seized the Portuguese enclaves of Dadra and Nagar Aveli on Damão. After these events, the Portuguese government tried to obtain a formal declaration from the United States condemning the Indian government's actions, but the Department of State refused to issue such a statement. Portugal resented the U.S. attitude, and the resulting coolness was a major obstacle to the negotiations for the renewal of the Azores agreement that began in 1955.

The crisis in Portuguese-U.S. relations experienced an important transition during the presidency of John Fitzgerald Kennedy. The Kennedy administration, in its early years, defined and adopted a new policy for Africa, a policy that directly affected the U.S. position toward Portuguese colonialism. According to the new principles that guided Kennedy's policy toward Africa, the United States moved to abandon its ambiguous attitude toward European colonialism and instead actively supported self-determination and independence for the colonial peoples of Africa. This new African policy brought great distress to the Portuguese government, which considered the maintenance of its colonial possessions in Africa and Asia an essential factor for the survival of the regime and also of Portugal's sovereignty. U.S. and Portuguese aims finally clashed during the first months of 1961. In early February, the Portuguese faced an armed revolt in Angola, which by March 15 had erupted into a full-scale war. Facing this new situation, the U.S. government informed Portugal of the new policy of the United States and recommended urgent adoption of political, economic, and social reforms in all Portuguese territories in Africa. In March 1961, the situation in Angola was brought to debate in the United Nations Security Council, and for the first time the United States sided with the Soviet Union and several African countries, voting favorably on a defeated resolu-

tion condemning Portuguese colonialism. Not surprisingly, the action provoked a serious crisis in U.S.-Portuguese relations.

The crisis gradually dissipated throughout 1962 and 1963, and the Kennedy administration's strong stance was replaced by a more complacent attitude toward Portuguese policy in Africa. U.S. policymakers recognized the strategic importance of the Azores base and therefore turned a blind eye to human rights violations in Angola. The Azores caused a major "retreat" from the policies adopted by the Kennedy administration.

During the presidency of Lyndon B. Johnson, the behavior of the United States regarding Portuguese colonialism continued to follow the trend started in 1962 and 1963. Gradually, the United States ceased to exert any significant pressure on the Portuguese government to accept the principle of self-determination; by the end of this period, silence had become the rule as far as Portuguese colonialism was concerned. Portuguese Africa had virtually become a nonissue within the administration, completely absorbed and submerged by other problems such as the involvement in Vietnam. In late 1968, Salazar was replaced by Marcello Caetano, and in early 1969 Richard Nixon succeeded Johnson in the White House. These changes in the governments of both countries marked the beginning of a new phase of cooperation in the relations between Portugal and the United States.

After the Portuguese transition to democracy, initiated by the military coup of April 1974, relations between Portugal and the United States tended to normalize, despite the fears expressed by U.S. policymakers that Portugal might shift dangerously to the left. However, a democratic, pluralistic

Demonstration in Lisbon supporting the Portuguese government's policies in the nation's overseas African provinces (Angola, Mozambique, and Guinea), August 30, 1963. On August 29, the U.S. presidential envoy under Secretary of State George W. Ball arrived for discussions with Prime Minister Antonio Oliveira Salazar on problems causing friction between Portugal and the United States, including the U.S. stand on Portugal's Lajes Air Base in the Azores. (Bettmann/Corbis)

regime emerged after the transition period, and in 1979 both countries signed a new extension of the Azores agreement.

Luís Nuno Rodrigues

References

Rodrigues, Luís N. *Kennedy-Salazar: A crise de uma aliança. As relações luso-americanas entre 1961 e 1963*. Lisbon: Editorial Noticias, 2002.

———. "About-Face: The United States and Portuguese Colonialism in 1961," *E-Journal of Portuguese History* 2, no. 1 (Summer 2004).

———. "'Today's Terrorist Is Tomorrow's Statesman': The United States and Angolan Nationalism in the Early 1960s," *Portuguese Journal of Social Science* 3, no. 2 (2004): 115–140.

Rollo, Fernanda. *Portugal e o Plano Marshall: Da rejeição à solicitação da ajuda financeira norte-americana (1947–1952)*. Lisbon: Editorial Estampa, 1994.

Telo, Antonio. *Os Açores e o controlo do Atlântico (1898/1948)*. Lisbon: Edições Asa, 1993.

———. *Portugal e a NATO: O reencontro da tradição atlântica*. Lisbon: Edições Cosmos, 1996.

United States Treaties and Other International Agreements. 2 vols, 1951.

See also: Brazil; Cold War—Spain and the Americas; Communism; Cuban Revolution; Guerrillas; North Atlantic Treaty Organization; World War I; World War II.

COLD WAR—SPAIN AND THE AMERICAS

After World War II, the United States and the Soviet Union emerged as the two primary world powers. Allies during the war, these two historic antagonists espoused opposed economic systems and competed to expand their spheres of influence. The cold war was the name given to the confrontation between them, which lasted through 1991, when the Soviet Union collapsed. It is termed a cold war because there was no open and direct military confrontation between the two powers, in spite of the fact that both sides amassed extraordinary arsenals, including weapons of mass destruction. For other geographic regions, however, especially in Latin America and Asia, the confrontation between the two northern powers was very much a hot war. Avoiding direct military confrontations that could too easily have escalated into a nuclear holocaust, the two powers instead fought each other for global influence in a series of proxy wars elsewhere.

The Western Hemisphere was considered the backyard of the United States, firmly within its sphere of political, economic, and cultural influence. From 1933 to 1945, the reigning U.S. foreign policy in Latin America was Franklin D. Roosevelt's

Good Neighbor policy, a policy of nonintervention that was designed to prevent revolutions and promote mutual defense, trade, and development between the United States and the region. As the outlines of the new cold war conflict emerged, the Good Neighbor policy gave way to policies designed to prevent, at all costs, Communist revolutions in the Western Hemisphere. Foreign policy not only included overt financial, political, and diplomatic pressures, but increasingly included covert military operations designed to destabilize regimes that were deemed potential socialist or Communist threats.

In Spain, the cold war presented an opportunity for the Francisco Franco regime. After World War II, Spain had lost considerable influence with the Allies because of its Fascist and Nazi sympathies. With the cold war, however, Spain was able to escape this isolation by aligning itself with the Western powers; Franco's staunch anti-Communism also softened Western critiques of his authoritarian regime. For Spain, its cold war relations with the Americas can be divided into two phases: before and after the death of Franco in 1975. The key characteristic of Spain's foreign policy until 1975 was ensuring the domestic stability of the Franco regime. The Eisenhower administration, seeking to establish a military presence on the Iberian Peninsula, entered into a military alliance with Franco in 1953 and later aided the incorporation of Spain into the United Nations in 1955.

The first U.S. cold war intervention in Latin America was the overthrow of the democratically elected Guatemalan government of Jacobo Arbenz in 1954. Arbenz had instituted various social programs, including an agrarian reform law that ad-versely affected the small landowning oligarchy and international agricultural concerns. Additionally, Arbenz was considered a Communist sympathizer who refused to purge Communists from his government and who steered the country to vote against the United States in its regional diplomatic anti-Communist initiatives. In 1954, the U.S. Central Intelligence Agency (CIA) aided a small invasion force of disgruntled military men, which overthrew Arbenz in just two weeks. The Guatemalan operation was considered by the CIA and the U.S. government to have been a great success; they had achieved their goal of replacing a government sympathetic to Communism in their backyard with a military dictatorship that fully supported U.S. anti-Communist efforts, all while maintaining plausible deniability of U.S. involvement.

In Havana, on New Year's Day in 1959, a small group of revolutionary students forced the Cuban dictator Fulgencio Batista into exile and began a radical revolutionary experiment. Although essentially nationalist in character, the Cuban Revolution quickly radicalized into a more orthodox socialist revolution. The United States was determined not to allow a small island just miles away from Florida to become "Communist." Using the same template that had proven so successful in Guatemala, the CIA trained a small force of Cuban dissidents to invade and topple the Cuban regime. On April 17, 1961, this dissident force landed at the Bay of Pigs. Unlike Guatemala, however, the Bay of Pigs was a total military failure and became a foreign policy debacle for President Kennedy, who had authorized a plan he had inherited from the Eisenhower administration.

Cuba struggled economically, in part because of a U.S. embargo on its primary product, sugar; furthermore, Cubans found it difficult to secure the oil they needed. With their traditional trading partner unavailable, the Cubans entered into the Soviet sphere of influence. In October of 1962, Kennedy publicly announced that the Soviet Union was building secret missile bases in Cuba. Kennedy demanded that the Soviets remove their bases and ordered a naval blockade of the island to prevent Soviet ships from docking. The Soviet premier, Nikita Khrushchev, authorized the launching of nuclear weapons against the United States if Cuba were invaded. After seven terrifying days, the Soviets acceded to Kennedy's demands and retreated. The Cuban Missile Crisis was perhaps the closest the cold war came to an open confrontation between the two superpowers.

In 1961, Kennedy initiated the Alliance for Progress, a policy aimed at preventing revolutionary regimes in the region by promoting multilateral programs to combat poverty and social inequality. By the late 1960s, however, the United States had reduced its commitments to Latin America, as more of its attention was diverted to Southeast Asia, and the promise of the Alliance for Progress as a means of reducing the impetus for socialist revolutions began to wane. In Chile, the socialist Popular Unity candidate, Salvador Allende, was democratically elected to the presidency in 1970. The government began an agrarian reform and nationalization of the economy, including the critically important copper industry. The Nixon administration increased its aid to opposition sectors of Chilean society and blocked multilateral foreign aid. For the next three years, Chilean society became increasingly polarized, and its economy was crippled.

On September 11, 1973, right-wing military officers launched a successful coup against Allende. The military dictatorship that followed, led by General Augusto Pinochet, brutally repressed any opposition sector it defined as Communist and instituted a neoliberal economic policy.

In November of 1975, Franco died, and Spain entered a transition period to democracy. Diplomatic relations with socialist countries, including the Soviet Union, were normalized in 1977. Spain's Latin American foreign policy increasingly stressed cooperation and advocated for human rights. By 1976, much of Latin America was ruled by right-wing military dictatorships, including the Southern Cone, Brazil, and most of Central America. These regimes were in general friendly to U.S. political and economic interests and became, to different degrees, notorious abusers of human and civil rights.

In 1979, in Nicaragua, a guerilla insurgency (the Sandinistas) succeeded in overthrowing the dictator Anastasio Somoza, whose family had been helped into power in the 1930s by the United States. The success of the Sandinistas was a shock to the ruling elites of neighboring countries, including Guatemala and El Salvador, who were also waging war against leftist insurgencies. On January 31, 1980, a group of armed men took over the Spanish embassy in Guatemala City to protest military atrocities. While the Spanish ambassador tried to negotiate with the occupiers, Guatemalan security forces attacked the embassy, and thirty-seven people died in a fire, trapped inside. Spain broke off relations with the Guatemalan regime. Days later, groups took hostages and occupied Spanish embassies in El Salvador and in Peru. This "crisis in the embassies" led

Spain to consider what role it should play in the democratization of Latin America and led to some instability within Spain itself, as right-wing groups questioned foreign policy objectives since Franco's death.

Spain joined NATO in 1982, as part of a larger strategy of alignment with European interests. During the 1980s, the Reagan administration began covertly funding Nicaraguan dissidents to destabilize the Nicaraguan Sandinista regime; these Contras waged a guerilla war for years that slowly sapped the political and economic will of the country. The Sandinistas lost elections in 1990, but remained a powerful opposition party. The Reagan administration also embarked on ambitious new federal spending on defense, causing massive budget deficits and rekindling cold war rhetoric. In the Soviet Union, Mikhail Gorbachev rose to power and instituted a series of political reforms that eventually led to an attempted coup by antireformist elements in 1991. Even though the coup failed, Gorbachev lost power, as regional Soviet leaders capitalized on surging nationalist sentiment. By the end of the year, Gorbachev resigned as leader of a Soviet Union that had politically disintegrated. The cold war was over.

In the post–cold war world, Spain has played an important role in Latin America's reconciliation with its recent military past and its legacy of human rights abuses. Baltasar Garzón, a Spanish judge, has been working since the mid-1990s on various cases against military officers in Chile, Argentina, and other countries for assassinations and human rights violations committed during the military dictatorships. In 1998, Garzón signed an order for the arrest of Chile's Augusto Pinochet alleging genocide; Pinochet was arrested in London but was eventually allowed to return to Chile because of his advanced age and poor health.

Myrna Wallace Fuentes

References

Allison, Graham T., and Philip Zelikow. *Essence of Decision: Explaining the Cuban Missile Crisis.* 2nd ed. New York: Addison Wesley, 1999.

Blight, James G., and Peter Kornbluh. *Politics of Illusion: The Bay of Pigs Invasion Reexamined.* Studies in Cuban History. Boulder, CO: Lynne Rienner, 1997.

Gleijeses, Piero. *Shattered Hope: The Guatemalan Revolution and the United States, 1944–1954.* Princeton, NJ: Princeton University Press, 1991.

Grandin, Greg. *The Last Colonial Massacre: Latin America in the Cold War.* Chicago: University of Chicago Press, 2004.

Kornbluh, Peter. *Nicaragua: The Price of Intervention: Reagan's Wars against the Sandinistas.* Washington, DC: Institute for Policy Studies, 1987.

———. *The Pinochet File: A Declassified Dossier on Atrocity and Accountability.* A National Security Archive Book. New York: New Press, 2003.

See also: Cold War—Portugal and the United States; Communism; Cuba; Cuban Revolution; Guerrillas; Human Rights; Monroe Doctrine; Nationalism; North Atlantic Treaty Organization; Pinochet Case; United Fruit Company; World War II.

COLOMBIA

Colombia first experienced Iberian influence during the Spanish conquest. In the first stage of the conquest, Spaniards (1499–1508) explored the Caribbean coast and seized indigenes as slaves for use in Hispaniola. With the founding of Spanish bases in Darien (1510), Santa Marta (1529), and Cartagena (1533), another phase of rapine began, consisting of demands for gold and food from local Indians. This phase continued as Spaniards penetrated the interior and conquered the Muiscas in the eastern highlands (1536–1538). Seizure of the relatively dense, sedentary Muisca population led to the distribution of *encomiendas* (grants of rights to collect taxes and enjoy the labor of conquered indigenous communities) among the initial conquistadors, along with more regularized demands for labor and supplies of food. Nonetheless, excursions in search of ready treasure continued well into the sixteenth century.

The arrival of Spaniards brought a relatively rapid decline of the indigenous population, in part because of demands upon Indian labor, but also because of the introduction of European diseases, against which the indigenes lacked biological protection. Indigenous population decline was particularly devastating in gold mines (exploited from 1550) and along transportation routes.

Decimation of the Indian population in gold-mining regions induced Spanish entrepreneurs increasingly to rely on African slave labor, particularly in mines west of the Magdalena River (1580–1620). In these years, at least 22,000 African slaves were imported legally, not counting those brought by contraband. However, declining gold production after 1620 reduced demand for African slaves until 1680, at which point increased gold extraction from the Chocó region, and later elsewhere in the west, revived the slave trade, particularly around 1696–1743.

Spanish treatment of the Indians and the rapid decline of the indigenous population prompted debates in Spain during much of the sixteenth century, a process of self-questioning unique in the history of European expansion. Spanish authorities consoled themselves that they were bringing to the New World the light of Christianity, and thereby eternal salvation to its subjugated inhabitants. However, in New Granada, as much of present-day Colombia was known during the colonial period, the conversion of the indigenous population was pursued much less energetically than had occurred earlier in New Spain. The evangelization of indigenes in the most settled area, the eastern highlands, was impeded by the resistance of Spanish clergy to learning indigenous tongues and by the relatively small number of friars. Perhaps also in the early decades, Hispanic clergy were reluctant to venture far from the small islands of European culture in such Spanish communities as Tunja and Santafé de Bogotá.

In these small Hispanic nuclei, Spaniards quickly moved to replicate features of their Iberian culture. The Indian huts of *bahareque* (branches sealed with mud) in which the conquistadors first dwelled gave way to houses constructed in a Spanish mode, with walls of *tapia pisada* (pressed earth) and tile roofs. Houses had Mediterranean-style patios, even in the cold climates of Tunja and Santafé de Bogotá. As elsewhere in Spanish America, cities generally were organized on a grid plan, centering on a plaza presided over by the principal church, at first constructed of wood, later of stone. In the early 1540s, Spanish women began to arrive, as did such familiar Iberian foods as wheat, barley, chickpeas, green beans, and other garden plants. Within a few decades, aspects of Hispanic and indigenous material cultures had become entwined. Sheep, pigs, and chickens entered the Indians' domestic economy, while Spaniards grew indigenous maize and potatoes as well as European crops.

The indigenous population of the eastern highlands remained widely dispersed in small communities until the beginning of the seventeenth century, when Spanish administrators sought to concentrate them into larger communities, organized in the standard Hispanic American grid plan, with a church dominating a central plaza. This concentration was designed to facilitate religious conversion, tax collection, and more intensive use of indigenous labor. It also opened land formerly farmed by indigenes to appropriation by Spanish landowners. This concentration process represented a stronger assertion of control over the indigenous population.

A more aggressive approach to indoctrination of the indigenous population and control of more extended territory was manifest throughout the seventeenth century, in Augustinian missions in Urabá, Franciscan missions in the Chocó, and missions in the eastern plains established by Augustinians, Franciscans, Dominicans, and Jesuits. Jesuits, notably Alonso de Sandoval and Pedro Claver, also strenuously pursued the evangelization of African slaves in and around the port of Cartagena in the first half of the seventeenth century.

Clerical energies also brought the further development of urban culture, through the initiation of educational institutions in the principal cities of the seventeenth century. The Jesuits, arriving in 1604, soon established *colegios* in Cartagena, Santafé de Bogotá, Tunja, Pamplona, Popayán, Honda, and Mompós. Subsequently a Dominican friar, Cristobal de Torres, archbishop of Santafé after 1634, established there the Colegio de Nuestra Señora del Rosario (1653). The moral authority of the Church, the substantial wealth it accumulated from pious donations, and its control and operation of educational institutions, hospitals, and orphanages together made it the most powerful institution in the colonial era.

The Colegio del Rosario and the Jesuit colegio of San Bartolomé in Santafé became the two most important institutions of higher education in the colonial period. Both attracted students from distant provinces. Early in the eighteenth century, these institutions still served mainly to train priests. During the eighteenth century, however, both were increasingly educating Creole lawyers, who aspired to positions in colonial administration. When Napoleon's arrest of the Spanish monarchs in 1808 initiated the independence process in Spanish America, Creole lawyers, many graduates of el Rosario and San Bartolomé, led the way in articulating rationales for New Granada's independence. The connections these lawyers established while studying in Santafé also furthered independence by providing important links between Santafé and the provinces.

During the independence process, Creole advocates alleged that Spain had kept them in ignorance. New Granada truly was behind in science, but this was because Spain itself was backward, not because of some repressive Spanish design. Indeed, Spanish administrators in the 1760s, and particularly in the 1780s, sponsored the introduction to New Granada of aspects of the scientific Enlightenment. A Spanish priest, José Celestino Mutis, who came in 1761 as a physician to a viceroy, introduced Copernican astronomy at the Colegio del Rosario, sparking a decades-long debate with staunch adherents of the Ptolemaic system. Archbishop-Viceroy Antonio Caballero y Góngora sponsored Mutis's proposal for a natural history survey in New

Granada in 1782. And in 1783 Caballero y Góngora championed instruction in natural sciences of practical application to the economy. The currents of the scientific Enlightenment encouraged by Spanish administrators provided part of the underpinning for incipient Creole nationalism in the years after 1780. A corps of Creoles, recruited by Mutis into his Botanical Expedition, roamed the country in search of plants and other natural resources, thereby coming to learn in a palpable way about their country and imagine its potential.

The Spanish Bourbon reforms of the eighteenth century, it has been argued persuasively, were motivated by Spanish concern to regain control of their effectively autonomous American possessions. But the Bourbon reforms also aimed at mobilizing the forces of the Spanish Empire as a whole, in Spain as well as in Spanish America. Having been battered by the British in a series of wars, the Spanish Bourbons sought to rebuild Spain's military strength, which required more financial resources, which in turn required a more productive economy, more efficient administration, and more effective collection of revenues. As in the case of the Botanical Expedition, some of these reforms fostered conditions that later encouraged some Creoles to seek independence from Spain. The freer trade system implanted in the 1780s stirred hopes for profits among Creole merchants, which were dashed when British wartime blockades choked off maritime trade. And increased tax exactions, accompanied by Spanish administrative arrogance, provoked sporadic protests, of which the most significant was the Comunero (communal) rebellion of 1781.

The Comunero rebellion was not a direct precursor of independence. It was largely a tax rebellion, in which the rebels professed complete loyalty to the Spanish Crown. But the 1781 rebellion was connected indirectly to the later independence movement. The memory of the Comunero upheaval played a role in expressions of dissidence in the 1790s, and memories of both 1781 and the 1790s were in play in 1809–1810.

Scholars have emphasized the role of Spanish legal doctrines, particularly those associated with Francisco Suárez (1548–1617), in providing ideological underpinning for the Comuneros of 1781. Some historians have argued that Suárez's writings, or other traditional Spanish legal ideas, rather than French Enlightenment sources, also informed the ideas of early leaders of Colombian independence. In reality, at different times Colombian leaders displayed Spanish or foreign Enlightenment ideas, choosing one or the other tactically, depending upon the context. Spanish doctrines shaped their arguments until they were fully committed to independence. French Enlightenment rhetoric and English American constitutional notions came to the fore once they were committed to a complete break with Spain.

In the independence process, the Roman Catholic Church lost some financial resources, and the number of clergy diminished. Nonetheless, the Church remained the strongest and most influential institution, and conservatives in particular looked to it as the key to social order. Until the 1850s, however, for most conservatives, allegiance to the Church did not necessarily mean sympathy for Spain. Juan García del Río (1794–1856), an advocate of conservative political solutions in the 1820s, was allergic to French Enlightenment ideas, but he also condemned the backwardness of Spain. Mariano Ospina Rodríguez (1805–1885), a founder of the Conservative Party, took an equally negative view of the Spanish colonial period. José Eusebio Caro (1817–1853), another founding member of the Conservative Party, was influenced variously by nineteenth-century French authors—the liberal individualist economist Claude Frédéric Bastiat, as well as the utopian "socialist," Comte de Saint-Simon and the reformist Catholic priest Félicité Robert de Lamennais. Like both Saint-Simon and Auguste Comte, the founder of positivism, J. E. Caro believed science would resolve social problems. J. E. Caro and Ospina looked to the example of the United States in technical development and economic enterprise. Of this generation, José Manuel Groot (1800–1878) and Sergio Arboleda (1822–1888) were among the few notable authors who were perceptibly sympathetic to Spanish traditions. Arboleda shared the providentialist ideas of the Spanish aristocrat Juan Donoso Cortés (1809–1853).

Around 1850, renewed interest in Spain and Spanish authors became evident among conservative writers. *La Civilización* (Bogotá, 1849–1851) printed writings of the ultraconservative Spanish priest Jaime Balmes (1810–1848). Balmes provided the initial philosophical formation for the son of J. E. Caro, Miguel Antonio Caro (1843–1909), introducing him to the medieval scholastic philosopher Thomas Aquinas, the seventeenth-century French philosopher René Descartes, and Joseph de Maistre, an advocate of papal absolutism. All of these were important influences in the writings of M. A. Caro. The younger Caro, like de Maistre and Donoso Cortés, asserted that authority came from God and strongly supported the doctrine of papal infallibility. He also subscribed to Pope Pius IX's Syllabus of Errors, which rejected religious tolerance and freedom of religion, as well as progress, liberalism, and modern civilization. M. A. Caro identified with Spanish culture much more than his father's generation. But the Church and papal authority were more at the center of his belief than Spanish tradition.

The Regeneration (1885–1903), presided over by the former liberal Rafael Núñez and M. A. Caro, established a centralized regime, which restored to the Church privileges and influence similar to those it had enjoyed in the colonial period. During the Regeneration and the subsequent period of continuing Conservative dominance (1903–1930), the ranks of the clergy were bolstered by religious support from Spain, France, and Germany. Colombian bishops of moderate inclinations preferred French orders; intransigent antiliberal bishops favored Spanish orders. Some Conservative administrations of 1910–1930 were in a traditional, pro-clerical mode, but during the 1920s, in the context of a coffee boom, an orientation to business and finance became dominant, and the United States became the focus of Colombian elite attention. During the Spanish Civil War (1936–1939), however, Spain was at the center of political controversy, with leading Colombian Conservatives supporting Franco, while salient Liberals backed the Republicans. Since that time, Conservative elites have been increasingly oriented to capitalist development, a theme for which, until recently, Spain did not serve as a relevant model.

Frank Safford

References

Bushnell, David. *The Making of Modern Colombia: A Nation in Spite of Itself.* Berkeley and Los Angeles: University of California Press, 1993.

Gómez Hoyos, Rafael. *La revolución granadina de 1810: Ideario de una generación y de una época, 1781–1821.* 2 vols. Bogotá: Editorial Temis, 1962.

Jaramillo Uribe, Jaime. *El pensamiento colombiano en el siglo XIX.* Bogotá: Editorial Temis, 1964.

Phelan, John Leddy. *The People and the King: The Comunero Revolution in Colombia, 1781.* Madison: University of Wisconsin Press, 1978.

Safford, Frank, and Marco Palacios. *Colombia: Fragmented Land, Divided Society.* New York: Oxford University Press, 2002.

See also: Architecture—Colonial Spanish America; Bourbon Reforms; Catholic Church in Spanish America; Cities; Coffee; Colonists and Settlers I—Andes; Columbian Exchange—Disease; Comuneros—New Granada; Congregaciones; Conquest I—Andes; Contraband; Creoles; Defense—Colonial Spanish America; Education—Colonial Spanish America; El Dorado; Encomienda; Enlightenment—Spanish America; Hospitals; Independence IV—Colombia, Ecuador, and Venezuela; Jesuits—Iberia and America; Mining—Gold; Napoleonic Invasion and Spanish America; Native Americans VI—Northern Andes; Papacy; Rebellions—Colonial Latin America; Religious Orders; Science and Scientists—Colonial Spanish America; Slavery III—Spanish America; Spanish Civil War and Latin America.

COLONISTS AND SETTLERS I—ANDES

Once the initial travails of conquest were over, European settlement in the Andes came easily. A sophisticated infrastructure was already in place, especially in the Inca heartland. The Incas had constructed an astonishing road system that ran from Quito to present-day Santiago, with transverse link roads knitting the whole system together. This system provided the essential communications network from port to hinterland throughout the three centuries of colonial rule. The major axis of colonial prosperity was the "royal road" *(camino real)* that joined Lima, Potosí, Buenos Aires, and intermediate centers, and which followed the Inca road system for much of its distance. Similarly, irrigation canals (many still in use) also linked ecological zones, bringing highland waters to the arid coast, greatly enhancing productive capacity. The large cities of Cuzco, Chan Chan, and Huánuco Pampa were complemented by settlements at regular intervals along the coast and in the sierra. Settlement nucleation was already well advanced by the time the Spaniards set foot on Andean soil. The eastern tropical lowlands of the hostile "Antis" were mainly uncolonized; Incan presence there was signalled only by a few fortresses that were sometimes ritual complexes: Choquequirao and Machu Picchu are the best-known examples.

Incan settlement patterns had deep roots, most obviously in the case of the Moche, Chimu, Tiahuanaco, and Huari foundations. Yet settlement initiatives long predated the growth of autochthonous states and imperial expansion in the Andes. The so-called archipelago system that conjoined the three ecological niches of coast, highlands, and tropical lowlands depended on communities establishing either temporary or permanent settlements, with a view to capturing products in short supply in the home area. The success of these *mitmaqkuna* settlements depended on the forbearance of already existing communities;

however, these communities usually had a reciprocal interest in establishing their own far-flung settlements, and for the same ends. This small-scale settlement tradition was the embryo of later Incan settlement endeavors. Successive Inca emperors implemented large schemes that involved the translocation of whole populations from one end of their empire to the other. These forced marches were arranged with military precision and under military control. They facilitated imperial reorganization and, above all, served to secure newly conquered polities. This was social engineering on a massive scale; for example, under the Inca ruler Huayna Capac, the Cochabamba region was emptied of its original inhabitants who were replaced with a cognate population from the north. Manpower was highly controlled under the Incas, with corvée labor deployed in agriculture and public works. A highly organized labor force that was tightly controlled at local, regional, and imperial levels presented early Spaniards with a marvelous opportunity. Early settlers were looking for riches—the great fortunes of the Andes derived from agriculture and silver mining—and these were dependent on a large, well-organized labor force, either free or heavily subsidized. Previous Andean overlords, and the Incas especially, had done the European newcomers a great favor. However, almost four decades separated Columbus's first voyage across the Atlantic and the arrival of Spanish conquistadors in the Andean region.

Rumors of a golden civilization far to the south had reached Hispaniola and Cuba by 1520, and impelled a group of restless or disaffected conquistadors to chance their luck and modest fortunes. Accordingly, the first pathfinder expeditions from Panama under Francisco Pizarro made landfall on the Quito coast (1524–1525) and northern Peru (1526–1527). The invasion proper commenced in 1531, encountering the good fortune of civil war between competing Inca half brothers Atahualpa and Huascar. Exploiting this internecine strife, and with the assistance of disaffected client states such as the Cañaris and Chachapoyas in the north and the Huancas of the central sierra, Pizarro marched on Cuzco. With the defeat of Manco Inca, settlement began in earnest.

That the Spaniards came not just for booty but to colonize was immediately apparent when, in 1531, Pizarro founded the city of San Miguel de Piura. Within a few years most of the major cities of the Andes were founded: Trujillo, near the ancient city of Chan Chan, was settled by Diego de Almagro in 1534, though its foundation dates from 1535. Jauja, the first capital of Spanish Peru, was settled in 1533, then formally founded in 1534, the same year that the capital was moved to Lima, the City of Kings. City foundations sometimes had a ritual quality: the Inca capital, with its estimated population of 40,000 inhabitants, was founded as a Spanish city on March 23, 1534. Two other Inca cities, Cajamarca and Tumbes, however, apparently never received formal Spanish foundations; instead, they were just taken over and settled as they were, forming part of the first *encomiendas* (a form of grant discussed later). The key colonial cities of Arequipa and Huamanga (modern Ayacucho) were also founded early (1534 and 1569 respectively), but Huancavelica, the only center for the production of the mercury crucial for the smelting of silver, was not founded until 1569, shortly after the discovery of its abundant mercury lodes.

Urban settlements were redoubts in which Spaniards felt secure; they were the principal conduit of colonialism. Here conquistadors could finally lay down their arms, to profit from land distributions *(solares)* and settle as notable stakeholder-residents *(vecinos)*; even those of modest provenance might become town councillors. Honor was won on campaign, but displayed in an urban milieu.

The Quito region was conquered early by the *pizarrista* captain Sebastián de Benalcázar in 1534, whence expeditions penetrated into the interior and the Bogotá region. The port of Guayaquil was formally founded in 1537, but Cuenca, an existing Incan town, received its foundation only in 1557. Pizarro was slow to initiate the conquest and settlement of Charcas or Upper Peru (largely coterminous with modern Bolivia, northern Argentina, and northern Chile), because Manco Inca's army remained undefeated until late 1536. Thereafter, conquest and settlement moved rapidly but thinly. In 1540, La Plata (Chuquisaca) became the first city in Charcas; however, it was the discovery of the fabulously silver-rich mines at Potosí that spurred European settlement in Upper Peru. Potosí became the fulcrum of the axis of the Spanish South American internal market, and its silver became the principal raison d'être of the export market. The nodal commercial city of La Paz was founded in 1549, followed in 1571 by Cochabamba, which became a principal granary and later emerged as a center for cheap textiles. The mining economy of Upper Peru (Potosí, Porco, Oruro) was the principal motor of this trading axis, soon joined by the Lower Peruvian mines of Huancavelica, Cerro de Pasco, and Hualgayoc, and the gold mines of the Quito and Bogotá regions. The entire internal market, beyond subsistence activities, was geared to the production of silver, with grain production, textiles, sugar, *aguardiente* (sugarcane rum), yerba maté, and mules supplied to feed the demand generated by mining and miners.

Although silver production reached astonishing levels by 1600, the early decades of colonialism were chiefly characterized by what has been called the booty economy. Emblematic of this phase was the encomienda, a grant of Indians to an individual *encomendero* who received tribute in kind or cash and obligatory labor service in return for evangelization and, ostensibly, protection; all indications are that the postconquest tribute Indians had to pay was vastly greater than under Inca rule. Coeval with indigenous population decline, however, went a burgeoning increase in Spanish immigration to the Andes: between 1506 and 1600, roughly 250,000 Spanish immigrants came to the New World.

This second wave represented the beginnings of orderly Spanish settlement in the Andean kingdoms, but it began when there was little left to plunder. These immigrants came not to toil as smallholders or to sell their labor, but rather to become rich. In lieu of gold booty they wanted Indians, or rather, free or heavily subsidized Indian labor. Such labor supply was inelastic under the encomienda system, because encomenderos could determine who received labor, how much, and when manpower would be available. By 1630 this gave way almost entirely to a *corregimiento* system, which consisted of a network of provincial governors, *corregidores,* who operated a labor distribution (*repartimiento*) system connected to tributary arrangements. In order to pay tribute and the often exorbitant parish or sacramental fees demanded by parish clergy, an Indian needed to work on private haciendas and *estancias* (farms) or in domestic service to obtain cash, usually at the nominal per diem rate of two *reales* (eight reales equaled one peso). Forced labor on public works or in mines (*mita de minas*) further burdened indigenous communities. Thus was labor secured for all settlers.

This free or subsidized labor was the linchpin of colonialism, the sine qua non for successful European settlement in the Andes. Nevertheless, cheap or forced Indian labor was not the only response to the sixteenth-century demographic disaster. The available figures are generally unreliable, and estimates vary greatly, but it is widely accepted that the precontact population of Peru was between 6 and 12 million, and that the native population had declined to some 750,000 by 1600; it is only after the 1720s that a slow recovery is perceptible. Epidemics such as smallpox and measles, against which native Andeans had no immunity, were the root cause. The Quito region lost at least three-quarters of its Indians by 1600, after which the numbers recovered, only to stagnate in the eighteenth century; that region alone suffered five major epidemics, in 1524–1527, 1531–1533, 1546, 1558–1560, and 1585–1591. The trend in Charcas/Bolivia was similar to that in Peru: highland decline in both territories was much lower than the unrivaled population catastrophe in Peru's coastal valleys, and it stabilized earlier.

An early attempt at enslaving Indians was soon forbidden under the New Laws of 1542. The next logical step was to import African slaves to work in the mines, but the experiment failed: Africans could not withstand the rigors of hard labor in high-elevation mines such as Potosí. However, African slave labor did provide the mainstays of the coastal sugar and cotton haciendas, and the city of Lima teemed with African slave and free domestic servants: indeed, these constituted more than half the population of mid-seventeenth-century Lima; thereafter they diminished in numbers, if not in palpable presence.

Notwithstanding the appeal of mining fortunes, a settler society is first and foremost about land. Settlers came for land and cheap labor to work it. Land distributions to Spaniards implied the alienation or abandonment of indigenous lands, a process that was facilitated by the forced nucleation of settlements in the 1570s, the state sale of ostensibly untenanted land tracts, and the creation of a community land system in the 1590s. In effect, the precipitous, disease-driven decline of indigenous groups exacerbated the impact of the many modes of land usurpation of indigenous lands by venal colonial officials and their settler allies. This process of indigenous land alienation occurred pari passu with the emergence of a colonial land market regime, embracing haciendas, estancias, small but prime urban grants (*solares, mercedes*), and multiple forms of rental property, all of which threatened indigenous community and traditional common grazing territory.

The complex social stratification evident in Inca society was made even more complex by Spanish social categories broadly pertaining to class, race, and estate. Moreover, miscegenation led to the creation of a complicated racial index. In practice, such multiple social gradations were pared down to a few categories: peninsular Spaniard (born in Spain), Creole Spaniard (born in the New World), Indian, mestizo, mulatto, "free black," and slave. However, these categories were fluid, varying according to region and chronological juncture, and their definitions were sometimes capricious. For example, an "Indian" in colonial Peru was defined as whoever paid tribute, with the corollary that whoever was exempt from tribute was therefore not *indio,* irrespective of phenotype, dress, language, or community ascription.

Wealth in the upper tiers of society could sometimes confer enough prestige to erase racial discrimination. At the pinnacle of settler society was a cluster of noble titles, such as *condes, marqueses,* and *mayorazgos,* supplemented by a few immigrant *hidalgos,* military officers, and peninsular corregidores, whose kinship networks were highly endogenous. Nevertheless, whether of Creole or Indian descent, nobles were by definition few. Many Creoles of means staffed the bureaucracy and the courts; they invested in urban and rural real property, accumulated dowries, and founded pious endowments. Though their natural habitat was the city, their kind was spread throughout the larger towns of the region or on small rural holdings. In both town and country there was some social mobility, albeit gradual and infrequent.

Below this middling sort was a large group of Creoles and mestizos who teetered on the brink of poverty. They emerge from the historical shadows as petitioners and petty place seekers, assistants to notaries, minor bureaucrats, and small-scale merchants; their number included the better sort of artisan and the penurious *hacendado* (estate owner), a grandiose term that might also embrace subsistence farmers *(chacareros).* This group was never far from sinking into the urban proletariat

(populacho), which was often barely distinguishable from the *cholada* and mainly deracinated *indiada*—transient muleteers *(arrieros),* traders, itinerant artisans, or smallholders of the urban fringe. There were numerous indigenous communities, based on the *ayllu,* a mainly endogenous extended kin group settled on inalienable Crown land, and a plethora of private indigenous smallholdings that abutted the urban core. On the whole, however, indigenous society was located primarily in the provinces.

Women were deeply enmeshed in all areas of economic life, despite legal provisions that ostensibly circumscribed their freedom of action. Such restrictions often bore more heavily on elite Hispanic women than they did on their indigenous or mixed-race counterparts. The exceptions to this rule were female slaves, whose conditions ranged from poor to appalling. Yet here, too, ways were found to navigate legal prohibitions to one's own advantage: domestic, especially urban, slaves often enjoyed a fair measure of de facto liberty, at least in comparison to their counterparts on rural haciendas and coastal plantations, where conditions of life were often dire.

Among elite Hispanic women, there were wealthy matriarchs, often widows, who ruled over extended families whose various and interlocking economic activities usually guaranteed the family's long-term prosperity. There were also the nuns, both rich and poor; elite status derived largely from the size of a nun's dowry and the strength of her family's social connections. Less well endowed and less socially and racially exclusive were the quasi-religious institutions (called *beaterios*) for women (called *beatas*) who devoted themselves to a religious life without taking vows, and the *casas de recogimiento*—in equal parts school, refuge, retreat, and remand center—which provided alternatives to a nun's life, although sometimes charging dowries. These institutions provided an enclosed female space that allowed women refuge from a life of dependent spinsterhood or from the pervasive harshness of colonial urban life. Lower-class women were fully integrated into economic life, prominent as vendors of produce and craftware in marketplaces, dabbling in regional trade networks, working as domestic servants, and, in the case of indigenous women, involved in a wide range of gender-specific agricultural tasks.

Spanish settlement in the Andes was complete by 1600. The structures and patterns of colonial economy, society, religious observance, and cultural life were set in place by that date; of course, the evangelization of the indigenous world and the borrowed Hispanic baroque culture were still developing. There was never more than a small military presence in the Andes, and the Church, organized as religious orders and in dioceses and numerous rural parishes, was the main guarantor of the *pax colonial* away from the principal towns. The threat to Spanish settlement always came from below, from the overwhelmingly indigenous majority whose forced and subsidized labor underwrote Spain's entire settlement project in the Andes. When the Spanish colonial project ended in 1825, it was the American Spaniards, the Creoles, who were the beneficiaries; their indigenous compatriots entered into a new phase of exploitation by settlers and their descendants—"same horse, different rider."

David Cahill

References

Early, Edwin, ed. *The History Atlas of South America: From the Inca Empire to Today's Rich Diversity.* New York: Macmillan, 1998.

Gibson, Charles. *Spain in America.* New York: Harper and Row, 1966.

Hemming, John. *The Conquest of the Incas.* London: Macmillan, 1970.

Klarén, Peter Flindell. *Peru: Society and Nationhood in the Andes.* New York and Oxford: Oxford University Press, 2000.

Klein, Herbert S. *A Concise History of Bolivia.* Cambridge: Cambridge University Press, 2003.

Lane, Kris. *Quito 1599: City and Colony in Transition.* Albuquerque: University of New Mexico Press, 2002.

Lockhart, James. *Spanish Peru, 1532–1560.* 2nd ed. Madison: University of Wisconsin Press, 1994.

See also: Atlantic Economy; Ayllu; Beatas; Catholic Church in Spanish America; Civil Wars; Colombia; Colonists and Settlers II–VI; Columbian Exchange—Disease; Conquest I—Andes; Conquistadors; Corregidor/Corregimiento; Ecuador; El Dorado; Encomienda; Estancia; Family—Colonial Spanish America; Hacienda; Independence VI—Peru; Marriage; Mestizaje; Migration—From Iberia to the New World; Mining—Silver; Mita; Native Americans V, VII; New Laws of 1542; Peru; Potosí; Race; Slavery III—Spanish America; Transportation—Colonial; Túpac Amaru Revolt; Women—Colonial Spanish America.

COLONISTS AND SETTLERS II—BRAZIL

Over the first few decades of the sixteenth century, Portugal modeled its colony in Brazil on the vast trading outposts it had established in Asia and Africa. With a population of roughly 1 million inhabitants (compared to the 7 million people who lived in Spain), Portugal could ill afford to authorize the emigration of large numbers of colonists to Brazil. Instead, many of Brazil's early colonists were criminals, banished to the New World as punishment for their crimes. Perhaps the first of them was a man by the name of Afonso Ribeiro, who had been convicted of murder and banished to India. However, Pedro Álvares Cabral, who commanded the fleet, decided to leave Ribeiro in Brazil, along with another convicted criminal. The two men were later rescued by the expedition of Gonçalo Coelho, in 1501–1502. By then, Ribeiro and his companion had acquired knowledge of the Tupi language and provided valuable information to the Portuguese about the local Indian culture.

Many of Brazil's early colonists shared similar experiences, having been banished to Brazil to serve their sentences or shipwrecked. Some of these individuals, however, gained widespread fame for the services they provided to the Portuguese during the sixteenth century. Such was the case of João Ramalho, who was born in Vizeu, in northern Portugal; Ramalho had lived in Brazil since 1512. It is unknown if he was shipwrecked or banished, but it is certain that he became a distinguished member of the Tupiniquim Indians, renowned as a great warrior and an expert in their language. Martim Afonso de Souza met him when he founded the village of São Vicente in 1532 and witnessed Ramalho's Indian habits. Ramalho had many Indian wives, one of them named Bartyra, a daughter of the most important Tupiniquim chief, named Tibiriçá. João Ramalho promoted an alliance between Martim Afonso and Tibiriçá, and played an important role in the Portuguese settlements in São Paulo and São Vicente.

Diogo Álvares Correia was another of the early colonial shipwreck survivors. He was born in Minho, Portugal, but lived in Bahia, Brazil, for almost thirty years, where he died in 1557. Known as Caramuru, "the son of thunder" in the Tupi language, he joined the Tupinambá Indians. Like Ramalho, he too became a great warrior and married Paraguaçu, a daughter of one of the most powerful native leaders in Bahia. Transformed into an Indian chief, Caramuru traded brazilwood with French merchants and later with the Portuguese; in the 1530s, he provided important services to the lord of the Bahia captaincy, Francisco Pereira Coutinho, and later to the first governor-general, Tomé de Sousa. Caramuru also played an important role in facilitating the Portuguese settlement of Bahia and also in helping the Jesuits in their early missions during the 1550s, even though he was also an Indian slave dealer.

The rather mysterious but fascinating Bachelor of Cananéia is another example of Brazil's early settlers who deserves mention; he was banished to Brazil around 1502. The Bachelor of Cananéia emerged as the apparent leader of shipwreck survivors and the banished; he established close relations with several of Brazil's Indian groups, especially the Carijós in the south of Brazil, in the modern state of Santa Catarina. The Bachelor gained vast knowledge of the area; he knew very well the so-called *sierra de la plata* (silver mountain) in Peru, and he provided valuable information to Martim Afonso de Sousa, including important geographic details about the routes of the Iguaçu and Paraná rivers.

The experiences of João Ramalho, Caramuru, and the Bachelor of Cananéia offer examples of the first group of Portuguese settlers in Brazil; many served as important cultural intermediaries between the Portuguese and the native people, thus preparing the field for the later Portuguese colonial system. Nevertheless, their actions have been described as a process of accidental colonialism, because they were not a function of a preconceived design plan to colonize Brazil.

During the sixteenth and the seventeenth centuries, several documents from the Portuguese Holy Office provide information about many people who were banished to Brazil, condemned as heretics; it is well documented that New Christians, as Jews who converted to Christianity, probably in order to avoid being expelled from Portugal, were called, played a central role in the settlement of the sugar-producing captaincies of Pernambuco and Bahia. Several merchants, slaveholders, and sugar mill owners were in fact Portuguese New Christians. An important example can be found in the Antunes family. Heitor Antunes and his wife, Ana Rodrigues, arrived in Brazil in 1557, traveling aboard the same ship as Brazil's third governor-general, Mem de Sá. Heitor Antunes established an important sugar mill in the Matoin region, and he served the new governor well in several matters. In return for his services, Antunes received the important title of Knight of the King. Most of the daughters of Heitor and Ana Rodrigues married Old Christians, some of them of noble origin. This experience offers an example of the mixed marriages that characterized Brazil's early colonial history, connecting New and Old Christians. The example also illustrates New Christian marriage strategies, perhaps driven by the desire to hide or dilute the Jewish blood in the family. In this case,

however, the outcome turned tragic in 1591, when the first Holy Office inspector, Heitor Furtado de Mendonça, arrived in Bahia. Heitor Antunes was already dead at the time, but Ana Rodrigues, who was around eighty years old, was denounced for Jewish beliefs and rites. She was arrested and dispatched to Lisbon, where she died in prison in 1593. Years later, in 1604, she was condemned as a heretic, her body exhumed, and her bones burned. Ana Rodrigues has the unfortunate distinction of being the first Brazilian woman condemned to the flames of the Inquisition.

Another famous case was that of Branca Dias, a New Christian woman who ran away to Pernambuco in the middle of the sixteenth century. She was the wife of another New Christian, Diogo Fernandes, a sugar mill owner in the Camaragipe region; Fernandes was also known as a secret rabbi. Although she was already deceased when the Inquisition's first official visitor arrived, she was denounced for her Judaism.

Brazil was also the refuge or the place of banishment of witches, bigamists, and sodomites. Portuguese Inquisition papers offer several examples of individuals who were sent to Brazil as punishment for their actions, individuals such as Maria-Ardelhe-o rabo, a witch who lived in Bahia. To take another example, Isabel Antônia and Francisca Luiz were exiled to Bahia as punishment for allegedly being lesbians. Many priests were also sent to Brazil after being accused of sodomy in Portugal or the Atlantic islands. One of those priests, Frutuoso Álvares, a churchman in Matoim, confessed to more than one hundred acts of sodomy.

Nevertheless, it must be stressed that banishment worked not only as an act of punishment; it also served the purposes of a policy aimed at increasing the settlement of Brazil. However, it is also important to note that from 1534 to 1536, Portugal's king Dom João (King John III) divided Brazil into fifteen separate captaincies, granted to twelve donees. These donatary captaincies were large, averaging roughly fifteen leagues in length. Individuals who received such grants were given authority to tax, make administrative appointments, impose laws, and issue land grants, known as *sesmarias*. In return for these privileges, each donee was expected to provide military service if the king required it and to protect the territory on the king's behalf.

Most of Brazil's early settlers were men, especially if one considers the large numbers of male slaves introduced to work Brazil's burgeoning sugar plantations. There were regions, however, especially the captaincy of Pernambuco, that attracted entire families. Couples with children who had received sesmarias were quite common in Pernambuco during the government of Duarte Coelho, the first lord of the captaincy. A similar process occurred during the 1550s in Bahia, though on a much smaller scale than in Pernambuco.

Nevertheless, in most of the captaincies, the settlement pattern was dominated by young males; such patterns can be seen in São Vicente, Porto Seguro, and Espirito Santo, as well as in many other regions. Perhaps the most obvious case of male migration patterns in colonial Brazil occurred in the eighteenth century in Minas Gerais, where the discovery of gold and diamonds attracted large numbers of treasure seekers. Waves of migrants, mostly males, arrived from different parts of Brazil and Portugal, hoping to profit from the region's tremendous mineral wealth.

In addition to the Portuguese, other Europeans played a role in the settlement of Brazil. Many Spaniards resided in Brazil during the sixteenth century, especially during the period of the Iberian union of the Spanish and Portuguese Crowns (1580–1640). The French had settled in Ganabara Bay in the 1550s, led by Nicolau Durand de Villegaignon; some of his men joined the Indian women of the Tamoio. The French also settled in Maranhão, in northern Brazil, at the beginning of the seventeenth century. However, their numbers were never high, and consequently the French played only a small role in Brazil's colonial settlement. On the other hand, the Dutch were far more important, especially in the mid-seventeenth century, in places such as Pernambuco, Paraíba, and Itamaracá.

In spite of the foreign presence, the settlement of colonial Brazil was conducted mainly by the Portuguese, their descendants, African slaves, and *mamelucos,* the sons and daughters of Portuguese and the Indian women. Without the mamelucos, the settlement of Brazil would have been restricted to the coast. From the sixteenth century onwards, mamelucos were responsible for the spread of colonialism into the hinterland. Typical mamelucos were the so-called *bandeirantes,* men who spoke Indian languages and acted as cultural intermediaries between the Portuguese and the natives. At the same time, one must recognize the importance of African slaves in the colonization of Brazil. Over the course of the colonial period, roughly 3.5 million slaves entered Brazil, vastly outnumbering Brazil's Indian population. Africans introduced new staples into the Brazilian diet, such as red peppers, black beans, and okra; they influenced local practices in metallurgy, weaving, and pottery making, and their religious practices, music, and folklore helped shape the course of Brazilian history.

Finally, one cannot forget that the Indians were in fact the first settlers of Brazil. Capistrano de Abreu, the great twentieth-century Brazilian historian, has correctly noted that the first settlers of Brazil were the Indians, who considered both the Portuguese and the Africans as foreigners.

Ronaldo Vainfas

References

Abreu, Capistrano de. *Chapters of Brazil Colonial History, 1500–1800.* New York: Oxford University Press, 1997.

Boxer, Charles. *The Dutch in Brazil, 1624–1654.* London: Oxford University Press, 1957.

Burns, E. Bradford. *A History of Brazil.* 2nd ed. New York: Columbia University Press, 1980.

Freyre, Gilberto. T*he Masters and the Slaves (A Study in the Development of Brazilian Civilization).* New York: Knopf, 1947.

Johnson, Harold. B. "The Donatary Captaincy in Perspective: Portuguese Background of the Settlement of Brazil." *Hispanic American Historical Review* 52, no. 2 (1972): 203–214.

Schwartz, Stuart. *Sugar Plantations in the Formation of Brazilian Society: Bahia, 1550–1835.* Cambridge: Cambridge University Press, 1985.

Skidmore, Thomas E. *Brazil: Five Centuries of Change.* New York: Oxford University Press, 1999.

See also: Bandeirantes; Bigamy, Transatlantic; Brazil; Colonists and Settlers I, III–VI; Conquest II—Brazil; Donatary Captaincies; Dyes and Dyewood; Engenho; Family—Colonial Brazil; Gold; Independence II—Brazil; Inquisition—Luso-America; Jesuits—Brazil; Jews—Colonial Latin America; Marriage; Mining—Gold; Monarchs of Portugal; Music and Dance I—Brazil; Native Americans I–II; Slave Rebellions—Brazil; Slavery I—Brazil; Sugar; Women—Brazil.

COLONISTS AND SETTLERS III—CARIBBEAN

The 1492 arrival of the *Niña, Pinta,* and *Santa María* in Caribbean waters marked an important milestone in recorded human history. Celebrated by some as the fortuitous extension of enlightened Western culture and vilified by others as the wanton destruction of ancient civilizations, the European "discovery" of the Indies has had an enduring impact on the course of Iberian-American relations. Although Christopher Columbus ostensibly set out to find a western route to Asia, improvements in navigational and cartographic techniques, the defeat of the last Muslim stronghold in Granada (the culmination of the project of reconquering the peninsula from the Muslims, a project known as the *Reconquista,* "Reconquest"), and the recent Spanish conquest and colonization of the Canary Islands preceded his enterprise. Before sailing, Columbus successfully negotiated a deal, ratified in the *Capitulaciones de Santa Fé,* granting him the title of Admiral and Viceroy and a percentage of any future profits in the event his voyage proved successful.

Regardless of the specific factors behind Columbus's transatlantic journey—gaining new adherents to the Catholic faith, the rise of capitalism, scientific breakthroughs, and European imperial aspirations—Iberians did bring along an assortment of pathogens, animals, plants, and worldviews largely unknown in other parts of the planet. As the initial contact point between the New and Old Worlds, the Antilles was the first American area to experience the full weight of Iberian overseas expansion. And the ensuing post-Columbian encounter had far-reaching biological, social, religious, economic, and

The ships of Christopher Columbus, the Niña, Pinta, *and* Santa Maria. *(Library of Congress)*

political consequences for the colonists and settlers of this region.

The *peninsulares,* as those born in Spain came to be called in the New World, who followed on the heels of Columbus in the early 1500s were mostly males of modest social backgrounds who moved around from place to place hoping to *hacer la América,* that is, to strike it rich in the Indies. This powerful stimulus swayed ambitious colonists to reconnoiter the breadth and length of the Caribbean and surrounding shorelines in search of the elusive El Dorado. Along the Lesser Antilles, the first explorers made contact with a seafaring, mobile people whom local informants knew as Caribs, a derivative of Kalina, Kalinago, and Galibi, as the natives called themselves. The Europeans mistook their practice of retaining the bones of dead relatives and alleged ritual sacrifices of enemy captives for outright cannibalism. When the Caribs tried to repel the intruders, the Spaniards retal-

iated by launching slave-raiding expeditions, camouflaged as defensive military operations, against their strongholds in the eastern Caribbean and on the "wild coast" of South America.

With the exception of occasional stops to weather storms, repair ships, gather supplies, and capture Carib "savages," the bulk of the initial Iberian expansion in the Caribbean region centered on Hispaniola, Cuba, and Puerto Rico. These are among the largest islands in the archipelago, and they were the most densely populated at that time. They were home to the Tainos, who seemingly shared the islands with several smaller groups, such as the Ciboneyes, Guanabateyes, and Mayaris. The sedentary, agriculturally oriented Tainos lived in villages ruled by caciques, or chiefs, and had occupied the islands for at least a half-century prior to the arrival of the Europeans.

At first, the Spaniards and Tainos remained on friendly terms, as each attempted to understand the other's intentions, strengths, and weaknesses. But relations quickly soured when the Spaniards began dividing up the natives among themselves via *repartimientos* and *encomiendas,* forcing them to toil in the riverbeds, mines, pearl fisheries, and agricultural estates. With the holy war precedent of the Reconquista still fresh in their minds, Iberians also outlawed Taino religious ceremonies and imposed Roman Catholicism as the official faith. Worse still, epidemics of smallpox, measles, and influenza, against which the Amerindians lacked immunity, ravaged entire communities. With no natural predators to stand in their way, Iberian livestock multiplied quickly, encroaching on land that the Tainos had been using for their *conucos,* "gardening plots." Subsequently, vast tracts of lands previously devoted to subsistence crops, such as yucca and corn, became carpeted with newly imported, commercially valuable sugarcane.

The Tainos put up a stiff resistance to the European colonization of their homelands, but they were unable to defeat the equally resolved but combat-tested Spanish soldiers aided by horses, attack dogs, and sophisticated weaponry. Warfare, servitude, diseases, and the devastation of their ecological base of survival exacted a heavy toll on the Amerindian population. Faced with this demographic catastrophe and determined to improve their lot at all costs, Europeans resorted to importing "sturdier" captive Africans. The colonists not only denied Africans their humanity, but very often lacked the additional resources or will to properly look after the physical, spiritual, and emotional well-being of their *dotaciones,* "slave crews." Oppressive living and working conditions induced Africans

to poison masters, refuse to work, commit suicide, rebel, or run away. Some of the escapees built ties with surviving Tainos, Caribs, sympathetic free coloreds, and other "masterless" fugitives on the fringes of colonial society, creating the foundation for the formation of independent rebel communities known as *palenques.*

Internal dissension within the Spanish ranks fueled by class cleavages between the *pueblo llano* (commoners) and the *gente de calidad* (literally, the "people of quality," the white, aristocratic elite) generated much friction in early settler society. Personal feuds, graft, petitions, and frivolous suits frequently overloaded the colonial bureaucracy. The rapid exhaustion of placer deposits and the near extinction of the Amerindian workforce devastated the region's economy. As currency became scarce, wages plunged, and the cost of food, clothing, tools, rentals, and slaves rose dramatically, colonists saw their prospects for social advancement fade. By the middle of the sixteenth century, record numbers of Spaniards had abandoned the islands to try their luck in the mineral enclaves of Mesoamerica and the Andean highlands.

Because the Spanish Crown concentrated almost exclusively on the mineral enclaves of Mexico and Peru, Iberian hegemony in the Caribbean eroded throughout the seventeenth and eighteenth centuries. The Bahamas, Jamaica, the western portion of Hispaniola, and the Lesser Antilles all fell to European rivals. In the absence of legal commercial channels with Spain, vast quantities of provisions and draft animals from the Hispanic Caribbean found their way clandestinely to British, Dutch, French, and Danish interlopers. While strategically vital for imperial defense, Puerto Rico became dependent on the *situado mexicano,* an annual subsidy from the treasury of New Spain. Sparsely settled, vulnerable to foreign encroachments, and disconnected from the imperial economy, most of what remained of the Hispanic Caribbean stood outside the plantation system prior to the nineteenth century.

The Bourbon dynasty, and especially the reign of Charles III (1759–1788), sought to reestablish Spanish royal authority in the Hispanic Caribbean with a string of military, political, agrarian, and economic reforms. Defenses were revamped, dispersed settlers congregated into towns, the African slave trade resumed, free immigration was encouraged, commercial ties with Spain strengthened, and lands were converted into producers of cash crops. These measures brought the peripheral colonies back into the Spanish imperial fold and simultaneously renewed social tensions in the region. Communities of *cimarrones* (Indian and African slaves who escaped to form free communities; known in English as "maroons") multiplied in eastern Cuba and the western portion of Hispaniola. To put a stop to this development, Spain signed slave restitution agreements with France, Denmark, and Holland. The Crown also instituted mandatory military service for all males between the ages of sixteen and sixty and cracked down on the idle, vagrants, deserters, cimarrones, and illegal traders.

Spanish immigration into the Hispanic Caribbean picked up considerably in the second half of the eighteenth century, but most of it apparently consisted primarily of stowaways, adventurers, sailors, and soldiers. Politically safe non-Hispanic immigrants possessing resources, marketing ties, and technological know-how partially made up for the dearth of Spanish colonists. A significant weak link in the Spanish American imperial system, Trinidad was the first Hispanic Caribbean colony to profit from the liberalization of immigration restrictions against foreigners. Spain sought to revitalize Trinidad's economy by luring farmers and skilled workers from the French and Danish Caribbean with offers of free land and the right to import slaves. The 1783 *Cédula de Población* (population decree) brought these concessions together into a comprehensive immigration plan. Unfortunately for Spain, England seized Trinidad in 1797, just as its economy was beginning to show signs of growth.

The Haitian Revolution (1791–1804), which led to the establishment of the second independent nation in the New World, was a major turning point in Iberian American relations. The collapse of Saint Domingue put a major dent in the world supply of sugar and coffee, affording Spain an ideal opportunity to realize its long-sought goal of building the Hispanic Caribbean into a thriving plantation emporium. The Spanish Crown sheltered thousands of Dominguan émigrés, many of whom were farmers and skilled workers familiar with turning tropical staples into profits. Ironically, some 6,000 were later expelled from Cuba in retaliation for the Napoleonic invasion of Spain. Those who had taken refuge in Santo Domingo retreated to Puerto Rico after Haitian rebels repeatedly occupied the Spanish side of Hispaniola between 1801 and 1844. Fear of Haitianization, unconfirmed reports of antislavery infiltrators, and rumors that blacks planned to exterminate all whites reached phobic proportions across the archipelago. Port administrators and regional military commanders in the Spanish, British, Dutch, and Danish Caribbean had firm orders to keep "contaminated" Africans and free blacks from landing in their territories.

Racial tensions in the Hispanic Caribbean intensified and took center stage during the last century of Iberian colonial rule. The bloody aftermath of the Haitian Revolution made Creoles (those of Spanish blood born in the New World) painfully aware of just how vulnerable they were. The realization that free coloreds and slaves together equaled or surpassed the white population in Cuba and Puerto Rico for much of the nineteenth century was a constant source of anxiety. Mounting slave insurgency and flight in both islands made this uneasiness all the more acute. Moreover, chattel slavery was officially abolished in Santo Domingo in 1844 and in the non-Hispanic Caribbean between 1834 and 1848. With good reason, the planter elite in Cuba and Puerto Rico now felt increasingly threatened by slaves and subordinate free nonwhites at home, and besieged by internal and external abolitionist pressures. Iberian administrators in Spain and the Caribbean also had to contend with the possible collaboration among slaves, *pardos* (slave of mixed ancestry), abolitionists, and pro-independence activists.

The legal and surreptitious importation of African slaves continued in Cuba and Puerto Rico through the 1850s. Additional purchases of *negros ladinos,* or creole slaves, were transacted in the non-Hispanic Caribbean. In both cases, supplies proved insufficient to meet the local demand for labor in the sugar plantations. Spanish authorities in Puerto Rico tried to address the "labor shortage" by using antivagrancy statutes to force peasants and the unemployed, now labeled *jornaleros,* to toil on plantations. The various ordinances culminated in the implementation of the 1849

libreta system, which remained in effect until 1869. A number of other strategies to procure alternative sources of labor introduced during this period brought indigenous Yucatecan and Chinese coolie contract workers to the Cuban sugar estates. Schemes for increasing the proportion of whites became one of the salient features of the immigration proposals put forth in the closing years of Iberian colonial rule in the Hispanic Caribbean. Most came in reaction to slave unrest and the need to settle zones susceptible to cimarrón (maroon) raids or exposed to enemy attacks. In Cuba, white migrant *colonias* were established in Matanzas, Trinidad, Bayamo, Fernandina de Jagua, Sagua, Nuevitas, Cienfuegos, Guantánamo, Santo Domingo, Mariel, and the Isla de Pinos. Although none were set up in Puerto Rico, Galicians, Asturians, and Viscayans were frequently mentioned as potential colonists. The *Cédula de Gracias* (1815–1830), a royal decree designed to attract foreigners with capital, agricultural implements, slaves, and plantation-applicable skills by offering them tax exemptions, free land, and the prospects of obtaining Spanish citizenship, was slanted in favor of white settlers. Article nine, borrowed directly from Trinidad's *Cédula de Población,* granted white colonists four and two-sevenths *fanegas* of land. Free black and mulatto settlers and heads of family obtained one-half the amount of land allotted to whites. Planters in both Cuba and Puerto Rico also recruited Canary Islanders, but many of the *isleños* (islanders) objected to doing the jobs traditionally associated with slave labor. Some signed up to come to the Hispanic Caribbean, only to board other ships to take them to South America. Since slavery existed in Cuba and Puerto Rico until the late nineteenth century, potential European immigrants skipped both islands altogether and headed for greener pastures in the United States, Venezuela, Brazil, Uruguay, and Argentina.

Jorge L. Chinea

References

Chinea, Jorge L. *Race and Labor in the Hispanic Caribbean: The West Indian Immigrant Worker Experience in Puerto Rico, 1800–1850*. Gainesville: University Press of Florida, 2005.

Knight, Franklin W. *The Caribbean: The Genesis of a Fragmented Nationalism*. New York: Oxford University Press, 1990.

Martínez Fernández, Luis. *Torn between Empires: Economy, Society and Patterns of Political Thought in the Hispanic Caribbean, 1840–1878*. Athens: University of Georgia Press, 1994.

Moreno Fraginals, Manuel, Frank Moya, and Stanley I. Engerman, eds. *Between Slavery and Free Labor: The Spanish-Speaking Caribbean in the Nineteenth Century*. Baltimore: Johns Hopkins University Press, 1985.

Newson, Linda A. *Aboriginal and Spanish Colonial Trinidad: A Study in Culture Contact*. London: Academic Press, 1976.

Ortiz, Altagracia. *Eighteenth-Century Reforms in the Caribbean: Miguel de Muesas, Governor of Puerto Rico, 1769–76*. Rutherford, NJ: Fairleigh Dickinson University Press, 1983.

Williams, Eric. *From Columbus to Castro: The History of the Caribbean*. New York: Harper and Row, 1970.

See also: Bourbon Reforms; Cannibalism; Capitulations of Santa Fe; Catholic Church in Spanish America; Cimarrones; Columbian Exchange—Disease; Columbian Exchange—Livestock; Conquest and the Debate over Justice; Conquest III—Caribbean; Conquistadors; Contraband; Cuba; Defense—Colonial Spanish America; El Dorado; Encomienda; Explorers; Haitian Revolution; Hispaniola; Migration—From Iberia to the New World; Native Americans III—Caribbean; Palenque; Puerto Rico; Race; Repartimiento; Slave Rebellions—Caribbean; Slavery II—Caribbean; Trinidad and Tobago.

COLONISTS AND SETTLERS IV—MEXICO AND CENTRAL AMERICA

Spanish conquest and colonization took place in Mesoamerica (Mexico and Central America) during the first decades of the sixteenth century. The Spanish quickly set about establishing government and finding an economic base to support permanent European settlements. Mexico's conquest was an outgrowth of the colonization of Cuba in the 1510s. Northern Central America was explored and conquered from Mexico in the 1520s. Southern Central America was explored and conquered in the 1520s from the colony founded in Panama in the early 1500s. It took until the end of the 1530s to subjugate the Native Americans in Guatemala, while Costa Rica was not settled until the 1560s. By that time, the discovery of silver deposits in Zacatecas had pushed settlement to the north and northwest of Mexico City.

Early government in Mexico and Central America was by the conquistador leaders, but the establishment of royal administrations soon followed. The Viceroyalty of New Spain was established in 1535 to govern the newly conquered territories on the mainland and in Central America. The Kingdom of Guatemala, encompassing the modern countries of Belize, Guatemala, El Salvador, Honduras, Nicaragua, and Costa Rica, as well as the Mexican state of Chiapas, evolved as an administrative entity theoretically subordinate to the Viceroyalty of New Spain but in practice autonomous.

After 1521 most settlers favored New Spain over the Caribbean colonies. The new immigrants came to Mexico and Central America from the various Spanish kingdoms; a few came from other European countries; and after 1567 even a few

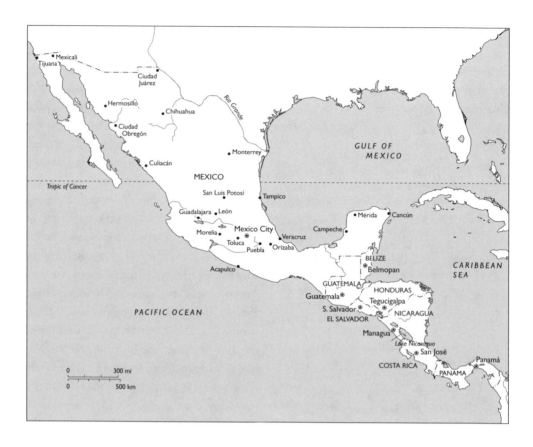

Filipinos settled in New Spain. African slaves arrived with the earliest expeditions.

Population estimates vary for the early colonial period (to about 1650) in Mexico and Central America, but scholars agree on several basic points. The Spanish population was never very large in number. Indigenous populations suffered catastrophic losses in the first century after contact; their numbers reached a low point in the early to mid-seventeenth century before they began to recover. The main cause for the devastating population loss was the introduction of epidemic diseases such as smallpox, measles, chicken pox, and influenza, against which Native Americans had little or no resistance. African slave populations were small in Mexico and Central America, due to the kinds of economic activities that predominated. In the

first century of colonization, relatively few Spanish women settled in Mesoamerica. This led to racial mixing, through both marriage and consensual unions. The *castas* (mixed-race groups) grew steadily in numbers from first contact onward.

A number of sources cite a figure of about 1.75 million for Mexico's population in 1650. Of this population, about 75 percent were Indians, 11 percent Europeans (most of them American-born Creoles), and 13 percent castas, fairly evenly split between mestizos (persons of Indian European heritage) and mulattoes (persons of African European heritage). The 35,000 blacks present in Mexico in 1650 made up only 2 percent of the total, and this figure declined by the end of the colonial period. In 1650 Central America had a population of around 650,000, about 83 percent indigenous, 8 percent European and Creole, 3 percent black, and 6 percent castas, two-thirds of whom were mestizos.

Colonial society was legally divided by racial categories. Spaniards and their descendants dominated society, both legally and socially. They were encouraged to marry within their own group, and they placed great value on being "Old Christians," with *limpieza de sangre* (literally, "cleanness of blood"; that is, blood without Jewish or Muslim "impurity"). Native Americans and Africans (free or slave) were legally restricted and exploited subordinate groups. In an effort to protect them from corrupting influences, Indians were by law ordered to live in their own self-regulated towns without Spaniards. Spaniards lived in separate self-governing towns with neighborhoods set aside for the other racial groups. In practice, however, this segregation policy could not be enforced effectively.

Secondary and higher education, guild membership, positions in the royal bureaucracy, and the professions were closed to non-Europeans and women. Castas, that is, mestizos, mulattoes, and *zambos* (persons of Indian-African heritage), who were denigrated by assumptions about the inferiority of racially mixed persons (as well as tainted with the stigma of illegitimacy), suffered the same restrictions legally as free blacks and Indians, but could sometimes better their position by "passing" as Spanish.

Women of all races and economic standings experienced further limitations based on gender. For peninsular and Creole women of the elite class, family honor dictated marriage to an acceptable (Spanish) partner or entrance into a cloistered convent. Educational opportunities were limited; women could not attend the univer-

sity. The wives and daughters of middle-class artisans and shopkeepers frequently worked alongside their fathers and brothers, increasing productivity and the family income; however, these women could not join guilds or become master craftsmen themselves. Married women were not independent before the law—they could not make contracts, dispose of property, or bring lawsuits independently of their husbands. Only widows had independent legal status and control of their property. A double standard applied in the application of the Church's strict code of sexual behavior to men and women.

Mulatas, mestizas, free black women, *Indias,* and other poor women were forced by economic necessity to pursue a variety of productive activities. For free black and casta women, marriage was possible but not common, and convent life did not provide an alternative; for most of the colonial period only white women could become fully professed nuns in convents. Consensual unions predominated among the poor and often left women alone to provide for themselves and their children.

Conversion of the large native populations to Christianity was a priority for the church and state in Mesoamerica. The first clerics arrived with the conquistadors, and missionary work began quickly afterward. The first Franciscan missionaries arrived in Mexico in 1523 and in Central America the following year. The Dominicans, Augustinians, Mercedarians, and Jesuits soon followed. Small numbers of regular clergy were able to baptize large numbers of eager Indian converts, although the amazing estimates of converts, provided by the missionaries themselves (9 million in the first twenty years in Mexico alone), should be viewed with some caution. Early missionary work centered on heavily populated Indian towns, but as indigenous populations drastically declined, the Church began to congregate dispersed Indians into communities to make it easier to teach them proper Christian and civilized conduct. This process began as early as the late 1530s in Central America.

Settlers who came to Mesoamerica expected to acquire wealth quickly. They frequently accomplished this in Mexico, with its dense Indian populations and rich silver deposits with lucrative supporting businesses; however, the rapid accumulation of wealth proved more elusive in Central America. In the immediate postconquest period, Hernando Cortés distributed most of the Indians of the Aztec heartland in *encomiendas* (grants of Indian tribute) to guarantee the Spaniards a living. This institution was subject to many abuses, and the Crown attempted to phase it out with the New Laws of 1542. However, it took into the seventeenth century to do so, despite drastic population decline, and new encomiendas continued to be awarded at the end of the sixteenth century on New Spain's northern frontier. In theory, all encomiendas went to Spaniards, but in practice sometimes they were held by other Europeans, mestizos, and even prominent Indian families such as the descendants of the Aztec emperor Moctezuma II. With the great silver strikes of the 1540s and after, Mexico developed a prosperous mining economy with extensive support industries.

The quick wealth the conquerors and early settlers sought in Central America proved difficult to find, and in frustration a number of them signed on to expeditions to South America in the 1530s. Like Cortés before them in Mexico, the conquerors of Central America awarded encomiendas to their subordinates as rewards for services, but the conquistadors and colonists wanted Indian labor for moneymaking enterprises more than their tribute payments in kind. This need for labor led to abuses of the encomienda amounting to forced labor. Only after 1550 was the Crown able to crack down on the worst abuses visited upon the Indians. Before 1550, the economic mainstays of Central America were the Indian slave trade and some silver and gold mining, both centered in Honduras and Nicaragua. Central American Indians, some legally enslaved in "just wars" and many illegally rounded up and branded as slaves, were sold to buyers in the Antilles, Peru, and Mexico. Mining took place mostly in Honduras (silver) and Nicaragua (placer gold) but was of little importance compared to the mining in Mexico. After 1550 the Indian slave trade became less profitable, and agriculture, for both cash crops and foodstuffs, became the base of the colonial economy in the Kingdom of Guatemala.

The limited number of Spanish immigrants and the settlers' cultural prejudice against manual labor dictated that Indian labor would be exploited; but the Indians' reluctance to work for the Europeans and the constantly dwindling indigenous population in the first century after settlement made labor a constant problem. The encomienda was introduced in both Mexico and Central America as a way to guarantee incomes for selected settlers without having to force the Indians to work for the Spaniards, but many Spaniards converted the in-kind tribute payment into personal service (labor) to use in enterprises such as mining, construction, transportation, and agriculture. This abuse was difficult to eliminate, especially in Central America. When the Crown began to phase out encomiendas in the second half of the sixteenth century, the *repartimiento* (a forced wage-labor institution) was introduced to allot scarce Indian labor resources equitably among Spaniards. Abuses also plagued this institution. Black slaves were imported to help ease the labor shortage, but were expensive and were never present in large numbers. They were used in plantation agriculture and mining, and as household servants of the wealthy. As the mixed-race groups grew in number, they, along with free blacks and poor Spaniards, formed a free wage-labor pool.

Spaniards who settled in Mexico and Central America intended to establish Iberian customs and traditions in the Indies. Often before complete pacification had taken place, the colonists moved to recreate an urban European environment. Spaniards were used to living in villages, towns, and cities. In Mexico and Central America, the Spanish incorporated self-governing towns and built the churches, residences, shops, and public buildings. The characteristic New World city had an urban core laid out in a grid pattern around a *plaza mayor* (central plaza). This pattern can be seen today in the colonial centers of Mexico City, Guatemala City, and Santa Fe, New Mexico. Although some early Central American settlements employed New World building techniques such as adobe brick and mud-covered reed walls with thatched roofs, the material goods and artisans (skilled craftsmen) necessary to build European-style buildings and furnishings were quickly assembled. Expensive luxury items were imported from Europe. Everyday items like tools, shoes, cutlery, and furniture were manufac-

tured in Mexico and Central America by European and Creole artisans, often aided by indigenous or casta assistants. Churches and public buildings in the sixteenth century were generally built by Indian labor, and indigenous artists were utilized in their decoration, but under the supervision of Spanish or Creole architects, builders, and artists.

Spanish settlers transplanted their intellectual life in the early period of colonization in New Spain. The first printing shop opened in Mexico City in the 1530s. Mexico produced over 100 works in the first forty years of printing, mostly religious texts for use in missionary work. In 1553 the Royal and Pontifical University of Mexico opened, offering a curriculum based on the University of Salamanca. The first printing press was operating in Santiago de Guatemala by 1660. The University of San Carlos, first requested by Bishop Francisco de Marroquín in the 1550s, was founded in 1676.

Europeans even transplanted their cuisine and grew the foodstuffs necessary to prepare it. The colonists recognized that Native American foods were sustaining, nutritious, and even tasty (the Spaniards took almost immediately to chocolate), but from the 1520s the temperate zones of Mesoamerica produced a variety of Iberian fruits, vegetables, and most importantly wheat to make the bread that was the staple of the Spanish diet. The settlers raised pigs, chickens, cows, goats, and sheep for food, as well as horses, oxen, and mules for labor and transportation. Nevertheless, Europeans never completely succeeded in their attempt to create a "New Spain" in America. Native Americans and African slaves clung to their traditional foodways and material culture, and over time a colonial society and culture combining European, Amerindian, and African elements emerged.

Victoria H. Cummins

References

Gerhard, Peter. *A Guide to the Historical Geography of New Spain.* Rev. ed. Norman: University of Oklahoma Press, 1993.

Jones, Oakah L. *Guatemala in the Spanish Colonial Period.* Norman: University of Oklahoma Press, 1994.

Knight, Alan. *Mexico: The Colonial Era.* New York: Cambridge University Press, 2002.

Lockhart, James. *The Nahuas after the Conquest: A Social and Cultural History of the Indians of Central Mexico, Sixteenth through Eighteenth Centuries.* Stanford, CA: Stanford University Press, 1992.

MacLeod, Murdo J. *Spanish Central America: A Socioeconomic History, 1520–1720.* Reprint. Berkeley and Los Angeles: University of California Press, 1984.

Meyer, Michael C., and William H. Beezley, eds. *The Oxford History of Mexico.* New York: Oxford University Press, 2000.

Sherman, William L. *Forced Native Labor in Sixteenth-Century Central America.* Lincoln: University of Nebraska Press, 1979.

See also: Administration—Colonial Spanish America; Architecture—Colonial Spanish America; Beatas; Belize; Catholic Church in Spanish America; Cities; Colonists and Settlers I–III, V–VI; Columbian Exchange—Agriculture; Columbian Exchange—Disease; Columbian Exchange—Livestock; Congregaciones; Conquest IV–V; Conquistadors; Costa Rica; Creoles; Education—Colonial Spanish America; El Salvador; Encomienda; Food; Guatemala; Honduras; Independence III, V; Jews—Colonial Latin America; Laws—Colonial Latin America; Marriage; Mestizaje; Mexico; Migration—From Iberia to the New World; Mining—Gold; Mining—Silver; Native Americans IV—Mesoamerica; New Laws of 1542; Nicaragua; Panama; Prostitution; Race; Religious Orders; Repartimiento; República de Indios; Slavery I–IV; Universities; Viceroyalties; Women—Colonial Spanish America.

COLONISTS AND SETTLERS V—SOUTHERN CONE

The southern region of South America, the "Southern Cone," comprises what are today the states of Argentina, Chile, and Uruguay, with Paraguay sometimes included. Essential to understanding Iberian settlement of the Southern Cone is the fact that the entire area existed on the periphery of Iberian power in the Americas, which centered on Mexico and Peru, as well as the coastal regions of Brazil.

Amerigo Vespucci mapped the northeastern coastline of the Southern Cone for Spain in 1502. In 1516, Juan Díaz de Solís landed briefly in what is now Argentina. In 1519, Ferdinand Magellan anchored in the bay of what is now Montevideo, Uruguay, and sailed past the entire region, on through the straits that today bear his name.

Iberian settlement of the Southern Cone began with Pedro de Mendoza's 1536 expedition. However, it is likely that Portuguese explorers in southern Brazil had made coastal forays prior to Mendoza's landing on the shores of the broad estuary into which flowed two large, navigable rivers, the Paraná and the Uruguay. Mendoza's expedition was in part an attempt to ward off Portuguese intrusion into what was Spanish territory under the Treaty of Tordesillas.

Mendoza's attempt to colonize the land near what is today the city of Buenos Aires proved ill-fated. He found no precious metals to exploit. The nomadic indigenous inhabitants, the Querandí Indians, grew hostile, and members of the disillusioned expedition nearly starved. Most of the remnant, including the unfortunate Mendoza, who died at sea, chose to return to Spain in 1537.

In 1541, a small band of die-hard survivors of the Mendoza expedition withdrew from their original settlement and made their way up the Paraná River to the site of what is now Asunción, Paraguay. There, the semisedentary indigenous Guaranís were more receptive to their presence. Not for another forty years would Iberians again venture south beyond the mouth of the Paraná. In 1580, under Juan de Garay, they succeeded in establishing a permanent Spanish presence there and named the port "Santa Maria de los Buenos Ayres" (now Buenos Aires), in honor of a patron saint of mariners.

For nearly two hundred years, the town remained an unimpressive outpost on the periphery of Spanish power. During this time, it served mainly as a convenient warehouse and distribution center for contraband moving to and from the silver mines in Upper Peru, today Bolivia. Legitimate trade flowed through Lima and followed the Pacific coast to what is today Panama, then across the isthmus to the Caribbean ports where Spanish fleets called twice a year. Over time, however, Buenos Aires, adjacent to abundant grasslands, began to function as a valued source of horses, mules, and oxen for the mines, located some two months of travel to the northwest.

For two centuries these mines were the main economic engine for much of the Southern Cone. Most of the region, south of an east-west line from Buenos Aires to the town of Mendoza in the foothills of the Andes, south of the Bío-Bío River in Chile, was a wild and dangerous land effectively empty of Iberian settlement well into the nineteenth century. South of this line, secure Iberian settlement proved impossible to achieve. In Argentina, marauding Pampa Indians dissuaded would-be settlers. In Chile, Araucanian (Mapuche) Indians proved an intrepid and courageous foe. Indeed, the geographically conical aspect of the Southern Cone was largely chimerical for the first three hundred years of Iberian presence in the region, since those who valued their lives seldom ventured very far to the south. Only with the advent of industrial technologies—railroads, the telegraph, repeating rifles—did Iberians manage to eradicate the Indian threat within the cone.

Still, in the north, along the river up to Paraguay and the trail from Buenos Aires

to Potosí, new cities emerged. Among these were Santa Fe, Rosario, Entre Rios, and Corrientes in the east, settled from Buenos Aires; Córdoba, Tucumán, and Salta to the west and north were settled from the mining district of what is today Bolivia. Several of these cities, notably Córdoba, outstripped the backwater of Buenos Aires in providing the amenities of Spanish colonial existence. Meanwhile, Buenos Aires languished in relative cultural and economic stagnation, from which it did not emerge until the Bourbon reforms of the mid-eighteenth century.

In 1776, the Bourbon Crown chose to designate La Plata (today Argentina, Uruguay, Paraguay, and Bolivia) as a new viceroyalty, with its capital city at Buenos Aires, by then an easier journey from Seville and Cádiz than was Lima. This tended to undermine the importance of Peru and greatly increase the importance of the port of Buenos Aires. With a rising merchant class in the capital city creating wealth based on the export of silver, hides, and salted beef and the import of manufactured and luxury goods, Buenos Aires grew in size and influence. So rapidly did its economic and political importance increase that it soon elicited the jealousy of provincial capitals. Such rivalries proved to be a political and economic problem in Argentina well into the nineteenth century.

Spaniards came to Paraguay in 1541, when Domingo Martinez de Irala led the survivors of Mendoza's expedition into the territory and founded the city of Asunción near a fort built there by Juan de Salazar y Espinosa. In contrast to their methods in Mexico and Peru, Spaniards survived in Paraguay less by conquering than by assimilating the culture of the indigenous Guaranís. According to Guaraní tradition, alliances were sealed through the granting of women in marriage, a custom the Spaniards were more than willing to accept. In Paraguay, as the Spaniards found themselves dependent on the indigenous people, the process of mestizaje proceeded less violently and more in a spirit of mutual benefit and accommodation than in other regions of Spanish America.

In 1580, the second attempt by Spaniards to establish a settlement at Buenos Aires coincided roughly with the arrival of Jesuits in Paraguay and what is now northern Argentina. As the focus of Spanish settlement shifted south, Jesuit priests and brothers began to establish missions throughout Paraguay and adjacent territories. These *reducciones* (reductions) sought to concentrate indigenous peoples, chief among them the Guaraní, and thus facilitate not only their protection and conversion to Christianity, but also the institution of advanced techniques of agriculture.

Paraguayan Jesuit enterprises, including the vast estate of Paraguarí, proved remarkably successful both spiritually and economically. One result was the large-scale production of yerba maté, the stimulating tea of the Guaraní, which proved a valuable and increasingly popular commodity for trade with other sectors of the Southern Cone. Even after the expulsion of the Jesuits in 1767, the Guaraní, thanks to their peripheral location relative to other areas of Spanish settlement, managed not only to survive but also to prosper, maintaining linguistic and cultural influence on comtemporary Paraguayan society.

Chile, geographically isolated from the rest of the Southern Cone, was settled separately from Argentina, Uruguay, and Paraguay. Until the wars of independence, Chile pertained administratively to the Spanish Viceroyalty of Peru. The main area of Spanish settlement in Chile, the fertile central valley, was cut off from the major Spanish city in South America, Lima, by deserts that stretched more than a thousand miles. It was blocked from Buenos Aires and La Plata by the imposing peaks of the Andes, more than 7,000 meters high.

Spaniards first came to Chile in 1535, on an expedition led by Diego de Almagro, partner and chief rival of the Pizarro brothers, self-proclaimed lords of Peru. Almagro and his followers advanced south from Cuzco, crossing with great difficulty through Andean mountain passes to enter what is now Chile at Copiapó, and then advanced as far south as the Maule River. In 1537, Almagro returned to Peru by way of the coastal deserts, there to challenge the authority of the Pizarros in an internecine confrontation that Almagro lost.

Pedro de Valdivia, Pizarro's chief lieutenant, then struck out to the south, along the trail blazed by Almagro, to extend Spanish dominion and to seek his own fame and fortune. With some 1,000 Peruvian Indians and about 150 Spaniards, Valdivia reached the verdant valleys and forests of central Chile by 1541. Over the course of the ensuing decade, he founded the settlements of Santiago, La Serena, Concepción, Valdivia, and Villarica.

During his conquests, Valdivia captured an Araucanian boy, Lautauro. Grown to manhood, Lautauro, having studied the ways of the Spaniards while in captivity, escaped and led his people against the invaders. The Araucanian leader seized Valdivia in battle and killed him on December 25, 1553.

The Araucanians then went on the offensive, destroying Spanish settlements and driving the Spaniards north, toward Santiago; yet the Spaniards were not easily deterred. Valdivia's successor, Francisco de Villagra, took up the challenge, and in 1557, Lautauro fell in battle. The tide turned in favor of the Spaniards, and the Araucanians withdrew into their mountainous and forested strongholds.

Spanish settlers managed to rebuild the settlements destroyed by the Araucanians and prosper in the central valley, north of the Bío-Bío River. Yet they were never entirely at ease along their southern frontier, fending off military forays by indigenous peoples well into the nineteenth century.

Uruguay was settled both from La Plata (Argentina) by Spaniards and from southern Brazil by Portuguese. The fertility of the grasslands proved attractive to both branches of the Iberian family. For almost three hundred years, there existed conflict over who would control and exploit the land called the Cisplatine Province by Brazilians, the Banda Oriental (Eastern Shore) by Argentines, and now known as Uruguay.

In 1516, the Spanish navigator Juan de Solís reached the shores of what is today Uruguay, only to be killed by indigenous peoples, probably the local Churruas. Spanish interest in the Banda Oriental further flagged when Mendoza's expedition failed in its first attempt to establish Buenos Aires across the estuary of the erroneously named Río de la Plata. Not until Buenos Aires was successfully reestablished in 1580 did the Spaniards begin to look into the possibility of colonizing the area.

In 1603, Hernando Arias de Saavedra, Spanish governor of Río de la Plata, ignored the absence of precious metals in Uruguay, choosing instead to focus his economic vision on its well-watered grasslands. He introduced cattle onto the lush plains, and the herds soon multiplied and flourished.

In 1624, at Soriano, the Spanish established their first permanent settlement on the eastern shore of the La Plata estuary, and the indigenous Churruas were soon decimated by European disease. In an attempt to rival the Spanish, Portuguese settlers from Brazil briefly established a settlement at Colonia, opposite Buenos Aires, in 1680, then built and occupied a fort on the present-day site of Montevideo in 1717, until the Spanish drove them out in 1724.

Under Spanish rule, Montevideo, its natural harbor offering shelter to the Spanish fleet, began to rival the port at Buenos Aires, where cargo could only be off-loaded some distance from the shore. Even when Buenos Aires was designated capital city of the new Viceroyalty of La Plata in 1776, Montevideo maintained the right to trade directly with Spain.

All the while, the Portuguese in Brazil and their British patrons continued to cast an envious eye on Uruguay, which the British occupied during 1807, the same year they were defeated by the Buenos Aires militia. Portuguese settlers from Brazil occupied the region in 1812. From 1821 to 1828, Brazil annexed the territory. Not until 1828, with the agreed establishment of Uruguay as an independent buffer state between Argentina and Brazil, was the issue of Uruguayan governance decided.

John Gordon Farrell

References

Burkholder, Mark A., and Lyman L. Johnson. *Colonial Latin America.* Oxford: Oxford University Press, 1998.

Dominguez, Luis L., ed. *The Conquest of the River Plate (1535–1555),* comprising "Voyage of Ulrich Schmidt to the Rivers La Plata and Paraguai" and "The Commentaries of Alvar Nuñez Cabeza de Vaca." London: Hakluyt Society, 1891.

Lockhart, James, and Enrique Otte. *Letters and People of the Spanish Indies.* Cambridge: Cambridge University Press, 1976.

Lockhart, James, and Stuart B. Schwartz. *Early Latin America: A History of Colonial Spanish America and Brazil.* Cambridge: Cambridge University Press, 1983.

Pocock, H. R. S. *The Conquest of Chile.* New York: Stein and Day, 1967.

Vernon, Ida Stevenson Weldon. *Pedro de Valdivia, Conquistador of Chile.* Austin: University of Texas Press, 1946.

See also: Argentina; Atlantic Economy; Bourbon Reforms; Brazil; Chile; Cities; Columbian Exchange—Disease; Congregaciones; Conquest VII—Southern Cone; Contraband; Explorers; Fleet System; Independence I—Argentina; Jesuits—Expulsion; Jesuits—Paraguay; Mestizaje; Missions; Native Americans V—Central and Southern Andes; Paraguay; Potosí; Religious Orders; Silver; Tordesillas, Treaty of; Trade—Spain/Spanish America; Viceroyalties; Women—Colonial Spanish America.

COLONISTS AND SETTLERS VI—SOUTHEASTERN NORTH AMERICA

Although Spain attempted several times to establish colonies in southeastern North America between 1521 and 1564, none were successful until the establishment of Saint Augustine on Florida's Atlantic coast in 1565. Except for a brief twenty-year interval (1763–1783), Spain maintained that beachhead as the anchor of its American empire's northeastern borderland, *La Florida,* for the next 256 years. Spain's vision of colonization was an urban vision that equated civilization, conversion, and control with rational urban living. In Spanish Florida, this vision forced African, Indian, and Spanish worlds to overlap and provided ample opportunities for Euro-pean- and American-born Spaniards (*peninsulares* and *criollos*), mixed-bloods (mestizos and mulattoes), Africans, and Indians to interact and create dynamic, multiethnic, multicultural communities.

As the conquest of New Spain proceeded during the first half of the sixteenth century, the establishment of a permanent Spanish presence in La Florida became increasingly important. Formal settlement attempts were made by Juan Ponce de León (1521), Lucas Vásquez de Ayllón (1526), and Tristán de Luna y Arellano and Ángel de Villafañe (1559–1561). All of them were unsuccessful, and by the early 1560s the Crown was ready to abandon the seemingly hopeless quest for a permanent colony in La Florida. Almost simultaneously, however, developments in the Caribbean provided the catalyst for a more vigorous and successful Spanish colonization effort. During the 1550s and 1560s, the Spanish Crown lost ground in the Caribbean and South Atlantic to the French, who also established two footholds in La Florida: the first under Jean Ribault at Port Royal on the South Carolina coast (1562) and the second under René de Laudonnière at Fort Caroline on Saint John's River in Florida (1564–1565).

French settlement in the Southeast quickly revived Iberian interest in La Florida and led to the first successful Spanish colonial venture in the region under Pedro Menéndez de Avilés. He arrived on the Florida coast in late August 1565 and within seven weeks had destroyed French Fort Caroline, captured and executed most of the shipwrecked escapees, and begun building the first permanent settlement and military outpost at Saint Augustine. Within months he launched a second colony at Santa Elena on the South Carolina coast and set up the first North American Indian mission, Nombre de Dios, just outside Saint Augustine. Over the next two years, he fortified the Atlantic coast and aided the Jesuits in setting up missions. Most of these gains proved short-lived, however, as the outlying garrisons and missions had been withdrawn by the time Menéndez left Florida for good in 1572. Even Santa Elena was permanently abandoned in 1587, leaving Saint Augustine as the only Spanish town in the province until 1720.

Despite these and other setbacks, including a brief period of British occupation (1763–1783), Spain retained sovereignty over La Florida until 1821. Although the colony never fulfilled its aspirations for self-sufficiency or profit, it remained a strategically vital colonial outpost guarding the empire's sea lanes, cementing its claims to the southeastern part of North America, and serving as a buffer against England's colonies farther north. Spanish colonists recruited from throughout Spanish America and the Iberian Peninsula came to La Florida in increasing numbers during these years. At no time, however, did the Spanish population approach that of the indigenous inhabitants, and Spanish control over La Florida owed much to the non-Spanish and mixed-ethnic residents of the colony. Essentially a military outpost, the settler population, both African and Spanish, remained predominantly male, and interracial relationships were common since Spanish colonial households rapidly incorporated native and African women through intermarriage, concubinage, and servitude.

Indians were ubiquitous in the Spanish colonial Southeast. Although the region lacked the large-scale extractive ventures that elsewhere led to extensive use of native labor and the *encomienda* system, importa-

tion of native slaves from throughout Spanish America and the extraction of labor tribute from local populations resulted in a significant Indian presence in and around Spanish rancheros, towns, and missions. In Saint Augustine and throughout Spanish Florida, Indians performed vital services for the support of the colony, planting and harvesting food, constructing buildings and roads, trading fish and other wares in Spanish markets, and cooking and cleaning in Spanish houses. They prayed in Spanish churches, raised children in Spanish homes, and sought asylum from English slave raiders in Spanish missions. In the process, they helped create a new and diverse Spanish American society in La Florida.

Africans, free and enslaved, also played significant roles in Spain's exploration and settlement of the Southeast. By 1565, the Crown considered black labor indispensable to the successful colonization of La Florida and granted Menéndez permission to import 500 slaves to help establish the new settlement. Though he never filled the contract, by the 1580s royal slaves imported from Havana were repairing the fort, sawing timber, erecting public structures, and clearing land for planting. Throughout the colonial period, slaves provided food through hunting, fishing, and trapping and were among the artisans, domestics, sailors, and soldiers who maintained and guarded the colony. Since Spanish law allowed for self-purchase by slaves as well as manumission, sizable numbers achieved freedom, and Saint Augustine became home to a significant free black community during the seventeenth century. By 1683, a free black and mulatto militia established by the Spanish governor regularly harassed the new English colony of Carolina to the north and provided reserves for La Florida's badly understaffed military.

Another key element of Spanish colonial society in La Florida consisted of runaway slaves, or *cimarrones*. Forced African migration to the New World often resulted in rebellion expressed as self-theft, particularly since runaways frequently found refuge among local Indians, intermarrying and allying with them against the Spanish. After 1685, escaped Carolina slaves changed the dynamic somewhat as they began to seek refuge in Saint Augustine. Seeing political and strategic advantages in the situation, the Spanish sheltered them, instructing and baptizing them in the Catholic faith; in 1693 Charles II officially granted them freedom. In 1738, these British runaways, who had demonstrated their loyalty and value to the Spanish countless times, were granted their own town just north of Saint Augustine, Gracia Real de Santa Teresa de Mose. Until 1763, Mose and its roughly one hundred free black inhabitants continued to provide La Florida with valuable skills and information as well as military service.

At the close of the Seven Years' War in 1763, Spain temporarily lost control of La Florida to the British as part of the peace settlement. During the next twenty years, British colonists and other Europeans occupied the region, as nearly 4,000 Spaniards, slaves, and free blacks took refuge elsewhere in Spanish America or returned to Europe. Several British schemes to promote colonization of Florida were attempted, the most successful of which brought 1,400 Mediterranean settlers, mostly Catholic Minorcans, to a plantation south of Saint Augustine to cultivate indigo. Although "New Smyrna" failed as an independent economic enterprise, the bulk of the surviv-

ing colonists (500–600) took refuge in Saint Augustine and remained there. Florida also became a haven for Loyalists during the American Revolution, and by 1783 over 13,000 refugees (8,000 of them black) had settled in east Florida, most of them in and around Saint Augustine. When Spain reclaimed its colony at the close of the Revolution, most of the British and American settlers left, but the majority of the Minorcans and many free blacks remained, forming the nucleus around which the subsequent community of returning *Floridanos* was built. The second Spanish occupation lasted only until 1821, when it succumbed to increasing American pressure on its border, and Florida became a permanent part of the United States.

Nancy L. Hagedorn

References

Cook, Jeannine, ed. *Columbus and the Land of Ayllón: The Exploration and Settlement of the Southeast.* Darien, GA: Lower Altamaha Historical Society–Ayllón, 1992.

Deagan, Kathleen. *Spanish St. Augustine: The Archaeology of a Colonial Creole Community.* New York: Academic, 1983.

Fretwell, Jacqueline K., and Susan R. Parker, eds. *Clash between Cultures: Spanish East Florida, 1784–1821.* St. Augustine, FL: St. Augustine Historical Society, 1988.

Landers, Jane. *Black Society in Spanish Florida.* Urbana: University of Illinois Press, 1999.

Thomas, David Hurst, ed. *Columbian Consequences.* Vol. 2, *Archaeological and Historical Perspectives on the Spanish Borderlands East.* Washington, DC: Smithsonian Institution, 1990.

See also: American Revolution; Asiento; Borderlands; California; Catholic Church in Spanish America; Cimarrones; Cities; Columbian Exchange—Disease; Conquest VI—Southeastern North America; Defense—Colonial Spanish America; Encomienda; Explorers; Florida; Missions; Native Americans VIII—Southeastern North America; Palenque; Seven Years' War; Slavery IV—Borderlands.

COLUMBIAN EXCHANGE—AGRICULTURE

Columbus's arrival in the Americas in 1492 heralded the beginning of an exchange of crops and agricultural practices that was to fundamentally alter the livelihoods and diets of people throughout the world. Crops that were domesticated in one part of the world have since become major staples in other regions. Initially the exchange was between Europe and the Americas, but with the development of the slave trade, the exchange extended to Africa, and later Asian crops appeared with the increasing Dutch and English presence in the Americas. The introduction of new crops was often accompanied by the arrival of new agricultural implements and changes to agricultural practices.

The Spanish and Portuguese, like all colonizers, attempted to replicate their culture in their colonies as well as develop agricultural production for export. Europeans favored the production of wheat bread, wine, and oil, and sugar fetched high prices in Europe. All ships involved in early exploratory expeditions were required by the Spanish Crown to carry seeds, plants, and fruit stones to establish the cultivation of European crops. Those taken by Columbus on his second voyage included wheat, chickpeas, vines, melons, onions, and radishes, as well as a variety of other garden vegetables, herbs, and fruits. Among the most successful fruits introduced in the early colonial period were oranges, lemons, and limes. However, the establishment of such crops in the Americas was not a simple process.

Many European crops were not suited to the environmental conditions of much of Latin America. Wheat and barley could be grown in the temperate climate of the highlands of Mexico and the Andes, but could not be cultivated in lowland tropical regions. Some crops represented a fundamental change to the system of agricultural production. The cereals and, to some extent, sugar required dedicated fields and specialized equipment or animals for their cultivation or processing. Finally, agriculture was already well developed in most parts of Latin America, with advanced forms of irrigation and terracing having a long history in the Andes and highlands of Central America. Maize, beans, and squashes were the main crops cultivated in Mexico and Central America, while in the more temperate Andes the staples were potatoes and quinoa and in the tropical lowlands manioc and sweet potatoes. Like the Spanish, the Indians preferred the foods with which they were familiar. These were often more productive than European crops and had some cultural meaning. Indians were therefore slow to adopt many plants introduced from the Old World, and in colonial times their staple crops remained essentially the same as those they had cultivated in pre-Columbian times. However, they did adopt those plants that added something new to their diet, such as onions and garlic, or those that could be grown alongside indigenous plants in household gardens. They also cultivated small patches of sugarcane, which they used as a cheap and effective substitute for honey or syrup from the maguey plant.

Given the general reluctance of the Indians to adopt Old World crops, the Spanish initially tried to encourage their production by requiring Indians to pay them as tribute. This was particularly the case with wheat. However, they were often not suited to the local environmental conditions, and the Indians often lacked the plows and oxen necessary to cultivate them. Hence, the Spanish assumed control of production, establishing haciendas where they employed Indian labor in their cultivation. Nevertheless, Spaniards often became resigned to eating maize rather than wheat bread.

Other important ingredients of Old World diets were wine and olive oil, the former being essential for the Catholic mass. In 1519 the Board of Trade in Spain was ordered to ensure that each ship sailing to the New World carried vines for the establishment of vineyards. Vines did not do particularly well in Mexico, but by the mid-sixteenth century wine was being produced in Peru and Chile. Toward the end of the century, however, the Spanish Crown became concerned about competition with its domestic industry and in the seventeenth century banned further plantings and the export of wine to regions that could easily be supplied from Spain. These bans were not very effective, however, and the wine industry flourished in Chile and northern Argentina. Similarly, olive trees grew well in the Peruvian coastal valleys and were later subject to similar ineffective bans.

The Spanish and Portuguese were also interested in establishing the production of sugar, but for export to Europe rather than for local consumption. Originally a Southeast Asian domesticate, sugarcane was carried to the Iberian Peninsula by the Moors. In Iberia, however, it was produced on only a small scale and it remained a luxury item. It was introduced to Hispaniola on Columbus's second voyage, and by the 1530s thirty-four sugar mills were in operation. Slightly later the Portuguese, who had developed sugar production in Madeira, introduced sugarcane to Brazil, where it was being produced for export by the 1520s. Sugar became the mainstay of the economies of Brazil and many Caribbean islands. It created labor demands that were met initially by the transatlantic slave trade and later by indentured Asian labor, both of which radically transformed the racial composition of those regions. In Brazil sugar and slavery were so closely linked that it was said, "No slaves, no sugar, no Brazil."

European diets also benefited from the export of indigenous American crops, whose production remained largely in native hands. Cacao was used by the Aztec elite to make drinking chocolate, the name being derived from the Nahuatl term *chocolatl*. It was taken back to Spain by Hernando Cortés in 1528 and soon became a much desired beverage in Europe. In Mexico it had been mixed with ground spices and seeds such as chiles, annatto, and vanilla, but this kind of mixture proved too bitter for the European palate, which, although it accepted vanilla, preferred other ingredients such as honey or cloves. Meanwhile cochineal and indigo dyes produced by Indians in southern Mexico and Central America were much sought after by the textile industry. Of more dubious value was tobacco. Columbus observed tobacco smoking in Hispaniola in 1492, and small-scale commercial production began there in the 1530s and in Brazil in the 1540s. Initially it was used for medicinal purposes as much as for pleasure.

As the African slave trade developed, plants from Africa began to arrive in the

Americas. Many of these, such as yams, millet, sorghum, okra, aubergine, the congo bean, and ackee, were cultivated mainly by slaves or free Africans, often on small plots on the fringes of haciendas or in the hills. On the other hand, rice, bananas, and plantains spread widely, particularly in lowland tropical regions. Plants from Arabia, Asia, and the Pacific were last to appear in the New World. Some of them, such as the mango, were probably introduced from West Africa, which had received them from Arab traders. Others, such as coffee, which are now important to many Latin American economies, and the breadfruit did not appear until the eighteenth century when they were introduced from English, French, and Dutch colonies in the Caribbean and the Guianas.

The Columbian Exchange also involved the introduction of new methods of farming and the tools that went with them to the New World. In the Old World, cereals were sown by broadcasting, whereas in the New World seeds were generally planted individually. Many Old World crops, notably the cereals and to some extent sugar, required specially prepared fields, whereas in the New World crops were often grown together in swiddens or simple gardens. By far the most important implements introduced from the Old World were iron tools, which included axes, hoes, and knives. In pre-Columbian times the Indians had used mainly wooden or stone tools. Metal tools were more durable and greatly facilitated forest clearance and the cultivation of heavy soils. Metal tools were highly sought after, and they soon became important items in native trade networks.

In pre-Columbian times, Andeans had developed the foot plow, which was more

like a spade, but the Spanish introduced the plow drawn by draft animals. The main type of plow introduced to the New World was the Mediterranean scratch plow, which was the type commonly used in Andalusia and Extremadura, where most Spanish colonists came from. The adoption of the plow required an investment in both draft animals and labor to care for them, and it altered the basic agricultural system. For that reason, it was employed primarily on Spanish haciendas, though Indians in Mexico made some use of it in valley bottoms and on gentle slopes. The Spanish also introduced Arabic techniques of irrigation, notably canal and reservoir irrigation, though these forms of irrigation were similar to those that had been previously developed in the New World. Despite the greater knowledge of irrigation techniques during the colonial period, the extent of irrigated land declined as population losses undermined effective management systems. This was also true of terracing and other intensive forms of cultivation such as raised and drained fields.

In terms of the basic staples, European and African crops made little headway against well-established indigenous crops in the New World. However, American foods, notably potatoes, maize, and manioc, transformed the diets of much of the Old World. In pre-Columbian times, over 200 varieties of potatoes were grown in the Andes, where they were often stored in a freeze-dried form known as *chuñu*. The potato was not suited to the Mediterranean climate, but by the end of the sixteenth century it was being cultivated in northern Spain, whence it was introduced to Ireland, where it thrived in the cool, wet climate. At first the spread of the potato to the rest of Europe was slow; it was considered unhealthy and a food of the lower classes. Eventually its productivity in cold climates and its nutritional advantages were recognized, and during the eighteenth century its cultivation expanded rapidly, particularly in Germany, Poland, and Russia. Here it soon became the main staple underpinning population growth and industrialization in those regions.

The other major crops to become food staples outside the Americas were maize and manioc. Maize spread virtually worldwide, and its impact was perhaps greater outside Europe. Columbus himself introduced maize to Spain, but it made little headway against wheat. In the eighteenth century, however, it spread to the cooler mountains of the Balkans, where it became an important staple. Maize and manioc from Brazil arrived in Africa much earlier in the sixteenth century. Their commercial production was stimulated in part by the need to provide provisions to support the slave trade. They became essential components of West and Central African diets, in some cases supplanting the traditional crops, millet, sorghum, and yams. In China, maize and sweet potatoes were both being cultivated by the mid-sixteenth century, maize probably having been introduced over the Burmese border. Sweet potatoes spread more rapidly than maize, since they did not compete with rice.

The spread of crops from the Americas was not limited to the major staples but covered a wide range of vegetables and fruits. Most important was the tomato, originally an Andean domesticate, but whose name derives from its Aztec name, *tomatl.* The early history of the tomato in Europe is obscure, but it appeared in Italy in the sixteenth century where it was given the name "golden apple," *pomi d'oro.* It soon became an essential ingredient of the Italian diet, which was carried back to Argentina by Italian immigrants in the nineteenth century. Other American vegetables and fruits to make an impact on Old World agriculture included many types of beans, peppers, pumpkin, pineapple, guava, papaya, avocado, and peanuts.

Linda A. Newson

References

Bauer, Arnold J. *Goods, Power, History: Latin America's Material Culture.* Cambridge: Cambridge University Press, 2001.

Crosby, Alfred W. *The Columbian Exchange: Biological and Cultural Consequences of 1492.* Westport, CT: Greenwood, 1972.

Foster, George M. *Conquest and Culture: America's Spanish Heritage.* Chicago: Quadrangle, 1960.

Galloway, Jock H. *The Sugar Cane Industry: A Historical Geography from Its Origins to 1914.* Cambridge: Cambridge University Press, 1989.

Kiple, Kenneth F., and Kriemhild C. Ornelas, eds. *The Cambridge World History of Food.* 2 vols. Cambridge: Cambridge University Press, 2000.

Langer, William. "American Foods and Europe's Population Growth, 1750–1850." *Journal of Social History* 8, no. 2 (Winter 1975): 51–66.

Super, John C. *Food, Conquest, and the Colonization in Sixteenth-Century Spanish America.* Albuquerque: University of New Mexico Press, 1988.

Viola, Herman J., and Carolyn Margolis. *Seeds of Change.* Washington, DC: Smithsonian Institution, 1991.

See also: Atlantic Economy; Bananas; Cacao; Casa de Contratación; Coffee; Columbian Exchange—Disease; Columbian Exchange—Livestock; Cotton; Engenho; Food; Hacienda; Henequen; Maize; Migration—From Iberia to the New World; Moors; Potato; Slavery I–IV; Slave Trade; Sugar; Tobacco; United Fruit Company; Wheat; Wine.

COLUMBIAN EXCHANGE—DISEASE

Alfred W. Crosby advanced the concept of the Columbian Exchange in a provocative collection of essays that examined the biological and cultural consequences of European transatlantic passage. Ecological, not ideological, considerations were Crosby's primary concern. The pursuit and impact of empire, therefore, were examined not by looking at the actions and deeds of men; instead, Crosby observed how the transfer of plants, animals, and disease radically altered life in the Old World and the New in the aftermath of the first Columbus landfall. If the shipment of plants and animals back and forth across the Atlantic may be considered an exchange of more or less equal proportions, this is decidedly not the case with disease. With the notable exception of syphilis, the origins and diffusion of which are still contested, no New World diseases had remotely the same devastating repercussions on the Old World as the diseases of the Old World had on the New. The concept of the Columbian Exchange has considerable merit, but with respect to disease transfer, the exchange was catastrophically unequal, more a cul-de-sac of destruction than a two-way street.

Sadly, the destruction in question pertains to human lives, in all probability the greatest loss of life in history. Scholars will never know precisely how many died in the New World in the wake of European intrusion, but it is now possible, even in the midst of ongoing controversy about the numbers involved, to identify which factor out of a tragic and potent mix proved the most destructive. That factor is disease. Whether the scene of disaster is the Mexican northwest or the Chilean south, European expansion unleashed on Native American peoples abrupt and unprecedented collapse by exposing their immune systems to hitherto unknown forms of sickness. Disease and depopulation go hand in hand in any attempt to comprehend the meaning of Iberia in America.

Of course, the impact of colonial rule was not uniform throughout the New World. Some Indian groups fared much better than others in the face of European expansion. The Taino of Hispaniola, for example, have vanished, as have scores of native peoples in Brazil, where fewer than 350,000 Indians make up a mere 1.5 percent of the national population. On the other hand, between 5 and 6 million Mayas constitute roughly half of Guatemala's national population, still speaking more than twenty different languages and asserting their rights as never before. Many factors besides disease must be taken into account when explaining patterns of survival or demise. The key to grasping the scale and rapidity of Native American depopulation, however, lies in the role played by Old World disease, particularly in the decades immediately following contact. Europeans fell sick and died from illness too, just as countless Indians perished by fire and sword or from trauma and exploitation, deaths more attributable to politics, economics, and religion than to genetics and germs. But disease ranks first, in the dynamics of the Columbian Exchange, in understanding why colonialism took root so early and so profoundly, at the expense of native welfare throughout the Americas.

This entry focuses on the role disease played in depopulating four regions of Spanish America: Hispaniola (the Caribbean island shared by Haiti and the Dominican Republic), central Mexico, Guatemala, and the central Andes of Bolivia, Ecuador, and especially Peru. The period subjected to scrutiny runs from the time of initial contact to the early seventeenth century. That period is of crucial importance because its temporal span is one in which diseases that in the beginning were "visiting people" (Greek *epidemos*) eventually became endemic, diseases that stayed among or "in people" (Greek *endemos*). The four case studies illustrate problems that researchers encounter with data, chronology, impact, and identification. A final reflection situates the disease factor in a comparative explanatory context.

In terms of contact demography, no scenario provokes such intense argument, or such wide disagreement, as Hispaniola. Massimo Livi-Bacci (2003) presented estimates by seventeen scholars of native population size in 1492, estimates that range from a low of 60,000 to a high of 8 million. Given that researchers consult essentially the same sources, the range of estimates is staggering. David Henige (1978, 237) was skeptical if not scornful of such an undertaking, declaring that "it is futile to offer any numerical estimates at all on the basis of the evidence now before us." Others have disagreed, evaluating sources for new interpretations and fresh insight.

Numbers matter. However, in the case of Hispaniola, whatever estimate one contemplates is but a prelude to extinction. Criticized for promoting a low estimate "in order to defend the enterprises of Columbus," Angel Rosenblat (1976, 45) observed that "it scarcely seems that explaining the extinction of 100,000 instead of 3,000,000 implies a glorification of colonization." Regardless of the numbers involved, by 1519 Hispaniola and neighboring islands had been reduced to what Carl Sauer (1966,

294) described as "a sorry shell." What could have caused such sudden, irreversible depopulation?

Until recently, the disease factor could not be invoked with confidence because most researchers believed that the first major outbreak of Old World sickness to strike Hispaniola did so in December 1518. Sauer (1966, 204) called that outbreak "the first epidemic of merit." More categorically, Henige (1986, 19) asserted that his perusal of sources reveals "no serious or epidemic incidence of infectious disease in Hispaniola before late 1518." Sherburne F. Cook and Woodrow Borah (1971, Vol. 1, 409–410), however, argue for a much earlier introduction of disease. "From the first voyage [of Columbus] on," they write, "there was disease among the Spaniards," a circumstance that made it "most unlikely that the sick would have been kept so isolated that the natives would not have picked up any disease of epidemic possibility." Their contention now has the support of two independent analyses. Francisco Guerra (1988) interprets the evidence to diagnose influenza, introduced following the return of Columbus to Hispaniola on his second voyage in 1493. Noble David Cook (2002), basing his argument on documentation authenticated by noted Columbus specialists Consuelo Varela and Juan Gil, links the return of the admiral in 1493 with smallpox. The search for answers continues.

With Hispaniola and other Caribbean islands gutted within a generation, ambitious Spaniards wanted nothing more to do with the ruin that they and their actions had precipitated. Wealth lay on the mainland to the west, toward which sailed an expedition led by Hernando Cortés. In its wake was smallpox.

Upon landing on the Mexican coast of Veracruz on Good Friday, 1519, Cortés and his forces soon became aware that they had entered a world organized and inhabited very differently from the Antilles they had been so determined to leave. Known today as Mesoamerica (a term used to define a far-flung area including central and southern Mexico, Guatemala, Belize, El Salvador, the westernmost parts of Honduras and Nicaragua, and the Nicoya Peninsula of Costa Rica), Cortés landed in a region that was home to scores of cultures not only capable of meeting basic needs, but also advanced and articulate in astronomy, mathematics and the measurement of time, plant domestication, environmental management, and written and pictographic communication. Towns and cities were architectural as well as functional marvels, none more so than the Aztec (Mexica) capital of Tenochtitlan.

Spaniards entered Tenochtitlan on November 8, 1519, but the great city did not fall into their hands until August 13, 1521. In the time between Cortés's initial entry into Tenochtitlan and the city's fall almost two years later, an event occurred that directly influenced the outcome of the military confrontation. Just as the Aztecs could not have been defeated without the collaboration, under Spanish command, of warriors furnished by the city-state of Tlaxcala and other peoples opposed to the rule of Tenochtitlan, so also is capitulation impossible to imagine without the havoc wrought by an outbreak of smallpox. Because of the Aztec ability to record their own version of events, a native text gathered by the Franciscan friar Bernardino de Sahagún (1978, 64) provides us with graphic commentary:

> At about the time that the Spaniards had fled from Mexico, before they had once again risen against us, there came a great sickness, a pestilence, the smallpox. It started in the month of Tepeilhuitl and spread over the people with great destruction of men.
>
> It caused great misery. Some people it covered with pustules, everywhere—the face, the head, the breast. Many indeed perished from it. They could not walk; they could only lie at home in their beds, unable to move, to raise themselves, to stretch out on their sides, or lie face down, or upon their backs. If they stirred they cried out with great pain. Like a covering over them were the pustules. Indeed many people died of them. But many just died of hunger. There were so many deaths that there was often no one to care for the sick; they could not be attended [to]. . .
>
> The pestilence lasted through sixty day signs before it diminished. When it was realized that it was beginning to end, it was going toward Chalco. The pestilence became prevalent in the month of Teotleco; it was diminishing in Panquetzaliztli. The brave Mexican warriors were indeed weakened by it.
>
> It was after all this had happened that the Spaniards came back.

While scholars generally agree that the pestilence described in the above passage was smallpox, disagreement persists as to how many perished because of it and, as in the case of Hispaniola, how many were alive to begin with. Estimates of the precontact population for central Mexico range from 1 million to 25 million, the latter calculated by Cook and Borah (1971, Vol. 1, viii) as the first in a sequence of seven that charts native depopulation between 1518 and 1605, during which time, they claim, that Indian numbers fell precipitously. Cook and Borah (1979, Vol. 3, 102) concluded that by 1620–1625 "the Indian population of central Mexico, under the impact of factors unleashed by the coming of the Europeans, fell to a low of approximately 3 percent of its size at the time the Europeans first landed on the shores of Veracruz." Whether or not one accepts the findings of Cook and Borah, the fact remains that their research has served as a catalyst for further inquiry.

Attributing demographic collapse in the century following conquest to the disease factor leads logically to a discussion of particular epidemic episodes. The convergence of opinion that identifies the first major bout of sickness as smallpox does not extend to the second outbreak (1531–1532), nor to subsequent outbreaks between 1538 and the early seventeenth century. Hanns J. Prem (1992) evaluated both Aztec and Spanish sources before venturing an opinion as to what possible diseases match the symptoms and characteristics described. He concluded that the manner in which a disease is presently thought to behave may not correspond to its manifestation in the past; and that only the earliest epidemics, few in number but lethal in impact, involved one specific pathogen, the greater probability being that later outbreaks of sickness involved compound epidemics. Prem suggested that, though one principal agent may be singled out, its predominance does not preclude other forms of sickness. The incidence of measles and typhus in thirty-year intervals in sixteenth-century Mexico is striking.

Equally striking is the rate of increase of introduced livestock, an upward trajectory that is the inverse of aboriginal attrition and another key dynamic of the Columbian Exchange. As Indians disappeared, herds of cattle, sheep, and goats became a prominent feature of the Mexican landscape; and by the early seventeenth century, Old World animals became roughly nine times more numerous than native inhabitants.

As in Mexico, the existence of native texts for Guatemala affords us some idea of how disease and depopulation appeared through Indian eyes. The first great outbreak of sickness is recorded in the *Annals of the Cakchiquels* (Recinos and Goetz 1953, 115–116) as having occurred between August 1519 and October 1520, four or five years before the wars of conquest waged by Pedro de Alvarado:

> It happened that during the twenty-fifth year [1520] the plague began, oh, my sons! First they became ill of a cough, they suffered from nosebleeds and illness of the bladder. It was truly terrible, the number of dead there were in that period . . .
>
> Little by little heavy shadows and black night enveloped our fathers and grandfathers and us also, oh, my sons! It was in truth terrible, the number of dead among the people. The people could not in any way control the sickness . . .
>
> Great was the stench of the dead. After our fathers and grandfathers succumbed, half of the people fled to the fields. The dogs and the vultures devoured the bodies. The mortality was terrible. Your grandfathers died, and with them died the son of the king and his brothers and kinsmen. So it was that we became orphans, oh, my sons! So we became when we were young. All of us were thus. We were born to die!

While it is fortunate that such a poignant account is available for consultation, difficulties abound, for opinion is divided as to what particular disease, or diseases, the passage refers to. Dozens of researchers have scrutinized the description and proposed a diagnosis. The balance of commentary favors smallpox, but not unanimously so, for alternative designations suggest influenza, measles, pulmonary plague, and exanthematic typhus.

Identification, then, is problematical. Decidedly not, however, is the clear reference to the high mortality, social disruption, fear, and panic that this sickness set in motion. In terms of origin and chronology, Prem (1992) correlated the Guatemalan outbreak with the smallpox that lashed central Mexico in 1520 and 1521, but this connection fails to account for the appearance of the disease in 1519. However, the problem is resolved if the source of infection is sought in the Yucatán, where smallpox made an earlier American landfall (Cook and Lovell 1992, 218–219) than the commonly accepted date of 1518. Even if the Cakchiquels were the sole diligent recorders of the sickness, its entry into a "virgin soil" environment must also have affected neighboring Maya communities in Guatemala. In a memorable turn of phrase, Murdo MacLeod (1973, 40–41) referred to the disease outbreaks that preceded Alvarado's intrusion as "the shock troops of the conquest." These "shock troops" were the harbingers of bitter times to come in Maya territory; as many as eight disease outbreaks between 1519 and 1632 constituted widespread, even pandemic, episodes, with another twenty-five recorded incidences relating to more local, epidemic flare-ups (Lovell 1992). A contact population of perhaps 2 million Mayas may have fallen by 1625 to around 128,000, a mirror image of the central Mexican scenario (Lovell and Lutz 1995, 7).

In terms of cultural development, comparisons are inevitably made between Mesoamerica and Tawantinsuyu, the name by which the Incas referred to their Andean empire, which stretched from southern Colombia through Ecuador, Peru, and Bolivia to northern Chile and northwestern Argentina. These two vast realms held the most attraction for materially minded Spaniards, for their resources were varied and abundant. We know more about Mesoamerica than about Tawantinsuyu because the former, at the time of contact, had long-established and sophisticated traditions of writing, which the latter lacked. This lack is particularly crucial when it comes to documenting the swath cut by disease, for few native texts exist to illuminate the principal Spanish sources, though advances in interpreting the Andean communication device known as the *quipu* are being made, and in time may yield pertinent results.

The evidence at hand indicates that, as in Guatemala, sickness preceded the physical presence of Spaniards by several years, diffusing ahead of them to weaken opposition and sow turmoil. An outbreak of what may have been hemorrhagic smallpox, whereby a strain of the disease infects the blood, causing a rash on the skin similar to that produced by measles, entered the Ecuadorian Andes in 1524. There it caused heavy mortality. Among its victims was the Inca ruler Huayna Capac, who was then in Quito to consolidate Inca power over northern territories recently brought to heel. The epidemic also took the life of Huayna Capac's designated heir, igniting a bitter civil war between the brothers Atahualpa and Huascar, rival contenders for the Inca throne. By the time Francisco Pizarro followed up his coastal reconnaissance of the late 1520s with a full-fledged campaign in the 1530s, the chaos that sickness and internal feuding had brought to Tawantinsuyu facilitated the Spanish conquest, a fact that the invaders themselves acknowledged.

After the initial outbreak of smallpox, more than twenty different disease episodes are recorded between 1530 and 1635, six of them pandemic. The cumulative effect, as in central Mexico, was to decrease native population by the early seventeenth century to a fraction of its contact size. Noble David Cook (1981) examined the fate of "Indian Peru" between 1520 and 1620, subjecting to critical scrutiny six different methods by which means estimates can be made of contact population size. The most novel of Cook's procedures was his deployment of disease mortality models, whereby death rates known to have been experienced during certain epidemics were applied to the Peruvian disease chronology. Working from a documented base of 671,505 in 1620, he estimated contact population size to be a maximum of 8,090,421 and a minimum of 3,243,985. Cook's reasoning was episode-specific: 30 to 50 percent mortality during the first outbreak of smallpox; 25 to 30 percent mortality during the first outbreak of measles; and 30 to 60 percent mortality when smallpox and measles erupted together, as they did in the calamitous epidemic of 1585–1591, along with mumps, influenza, and typhus. His model overlooks many influential variables such as differential immunity, age-specific mortality, and physiological adaptation; however, it offers a grounded basis for calculation, provided that disease identification has been established with some degree of confidence. Cook championed an estimate of 9 million for the contact population of Peru and 14 million for Tawantinsuyu as a whole. Disease, he reckoned, almost completely wiped out Indians living along the Pacific coast, but not their counterparts in the Andes, where the heirs of the Incas are very much alive today.

Discussions of contact population size and the reasons behind postconquest demographic collapse continue to engage an international community of scholars whose research interests are related to the operation of the Columbian Exchange. A considerable historiography now exists, ranging from classic contributions by Henry F. Dobyns (1966) and William M. Denevan (1976) to more recent additions by Noble David Cook (1998) and Suzanne Austin Alchon (2003). Debate about the issues involved still rages, best represented by the adversarial position adopted by Henige (1998). Where do we stand at present in dealing with the disease factor?

It would be a mistake to think that balanced recognition prevails, for this is manifestly not the case. The disease factor is distorted or downplayed for all sorts of reasons. Juan Friede (1967, 341), for instance, asserted that "when there were epidemics in Spanish America, these were neither general nor of identical consequences throughout the regions affected." While we may concede Friede the latter point, he seems unusually blinkered on the former. His work is overly influenced, perhaps, by the particular situation he examines. For Friede, there exist "numberless documents which definitely attribute Indian population loss to excessive work, malnutrition, flight, segregation of the sexes, ill-treatment, cruelty, conscription for expeditions, enslavement, and [the labor draft known as] the *mita*." Livi-Bacci (2003) takes a similar approach.

At the same time, however, other scholars invoke the disease factor all too readily, almost exclusively, the primary thrust of Alchon's (2003) critique of the literature. The trait is particularly evident among Spanish researchers, whose emphasis on epidemiology and biological inequality only serves to dilute that which cannot be denied: Indians suffered dreadfully from barbarous heavy-handedness on the part of conquering Spaniards and their descendants. Thus while we may concur with Elías Zamora (1985, 131) that disease must be considered "the fundamental cause" of native depopulation, we must express strong reservation at its being designated the "almost single" cause of Indian demise. Guerra (1986, 58) also oversimplified the matter, stating with more than a shrug of resignation that "the American Indian was victimized by sickness, not Spaniards." Historical autopsy should not be performed that surgically, least of all on the millions of Native Americans who died a conquered death, by whatever means, as a consequence of the Columbian Exchange.

W. George Lovell

References

Alchon, Suzanne Austin. *A Pest in the Land: New World Epidemics in a Global Perspective.* Albuquerque: University of New Mexico Press, 2003.

Cook, Noble David. *Demographic Collapse: Indian Peru, 1520–1620.* Cambridge: Cambridge University Press, 1981.

———. *Born to Die: Disease and New World Conquest, 1492–1650.* Cambridge: Cambridge University Press, 1998.

———. "Sickness, Starvation, and Death in Early Hispaniola." *Journal of Interdisciplinary History* 32 (2002): 349–386.

Cook, Noble David, and W. George Lovell, eds. *"Secret Judgments of God": Old World Disease in Colonial Spanish America.* Norman: University of Oklahoma Press, 1992.

Cook, Sherburne F., and Woodrow Borah. *Essays in Population History.* Vols. 1 and 3. Berkeley and Los Angeles: University of California Press, 1971 and 1979.

Crosby, Alfred W. *The Columbian Exchange: Biological and Cultural Consequence of 1492.* Westport, CT: Greenwood, 1972.

Denevan, William M., ed. *The Native Population of the Americas in 1492.* Madison: University of Wisconsin Press, 1976.

Dobyns, Henry F. "Estimating Aboriginal American Populations: An Appraisal of Techniques with a New Hemispheric Estimate." *Current Anthropology* 7 (1966): 395–449.

Friede, Juan. "Demographic Changes in the Mining Community of Muzo after the Plague of 1620." *Hispanic American Historical Review* 47 (1967): 338–359.

Guerra, Francisco. "El efecto demográfico de las epidemias trás el descubrimiento de América." *Revista de Indias* 46 (1986): 41–58.

———. "The Earliest American Epidemic: The Influenza of 1493." *Social Science History* 12 (1988): 305–325.

Henige, David. "On the Contact Population of Hispaniola: History as Higher Mathematics." *Hispanic American Historical Review* 58 (1978): 217–237.

———. "When Did Smallpox Reach the New World (and Why Does It Matter?)." Pp. 11–26 in *Africans in Bondage: Studies in Slavery and the Slave Trade,* edited by Paul E. Lovejoy. Madison: University of Wisconsin Press, 1986.

———. *Numbers from Nowhere: The American Indian Contact Population Debate.* Norman: University of Oklahoma Press, 1998.

Livi-Bacci, Massimo. "Return to Hispaniola: Reassessing a Demographic Catastrophe." *Hispanic American Historical Review* 83 (2003): 3–52.

Lovell, W. George. "Disease and Depopulation in Early Colonial Guatemala." Pp. 49–83 in *"Secret Judgments of God": Old World Disease in Colonial Spanish America,* edited by Noble David Cook and W. George Lovell. Norman: University of Oklahoma Press, 1992.

Lovell, W. George, and Christopher H. Lutz. *Demography and Empire: A Guide to the Population History of Spanish Central America, 1500–1821.* Boulder, CO: Westview, 1995.

MacLeod, Murdo J. *Spanish Central America: A Socioeconomic History, 1620–1720.* Berkeley and Los Angeles: University of California Press, 1973.

Prem, Hanns J. "Disease Outbreaks in Central Mexico during the Sixteenth Century." Pp. 20–48 in *"Secret Judgments of God": Old World Disease in Colonial Spanish America,* edited by Noble David Cook and W. George Lovell. Norman: University of Oklahoma Press, 1992.

Recinos, Adrián, and Delia Goetz, eds. and trans. *The Annals of the Cakchiquels.* Norman: University of Oklahoma Press, 1953.

Rosenblat, Angel. "The Population of Hispaniola at the Time of Columbus." Pp. 43–66 in *The Native Population of the Americas in 1492,* edited by William M. Denevan. Madison: University of Wisconsin Press, 1976.

Sahagún, Bernardino de. *The War of Conquest: How It Was Waged Here in Mexico.* Edited and translated by Arthur J. O. Anderson and Charles E. Dibble. Salt Lake City: University of Utah Press, 1978.

Sauer, Carl O. *The Early Spanish Main.* Berkeley and Los Angeles: University of California Press, 1966.

Zamora, Elías. *Los mayas de las tierras altas en el siglo XVI: Tradición y cambio en Guatemala.* Sevilla: Diputación Provincial de Sevilla, 1985.

See also: Codices; Colonists and Settlers I–VI; Columbian Exchange—Agriculture; Columbian Exchange—Livestock; Congregaciones; Conquest and the Debate over Justice; Conquest I–VII; Mexico; Migration—From Iberia to the New World; Mita; Native Americans I–VIII; Peru.

COLUMBIAN EXCHANGE— LIVESTOCK

Christopher Columbus's second voyage to the Americas in 1493–1494 initiated a profound transformation in the Americas and the world. Outfitted to establish a European colony and Spanish control over the newly claimed territories, Columbus's ships carried a wide variety of Old World grains, grasses, vegetables, and livestock. The transfer of these seemingly mundane articles to the Americas and the reciprocal flow of American plants and animals to Europe, Africa, and Asia over the following decades and centuries initiated what has been called the Columbian Exchange. Within decades, common European livestock such as pigs, horses, cattle, sheep, goats, donkeys, mules, and chickens had become an integral part of the American scene, as had large dogs, domestic cats, bees, and rats. Before the arrival of Europeans, the region had known none of these animals, but by the end of the sixteenth century, the colonial economy and society depended on them.

At the same time, some animals traveled from the Americas to the New World, becoming a part of the local diet, though mostly as exotics. These included turkeys, some varieties of ducks, and small dogs and guinea pigs as pets. There were also some later introductions of North American beaver into Europe, with disastrous ecological results. Recently, llamas from the Andes have become an artisanal livestock industry in parts of North America, Europe, and Australia. However, the exchange and its impact were decidedly one-way: from Europe and Africa to the Americas.

Unlike most Native Americans, Spaniards and Portuguese came from cultures that relied on domesticated animals for virtually all daily routines. Since none of the animals necessary for Iberian survival existed in the Americas, it was logical for explorers and settlers to import what they perceived as indispensable into their new environments. To the amazement of the early immigrants, the introduced livestock flourished beyond all expectations, although ecological conditions determined which prospered best in any one region.

At the same time, native peoples were affected dramatically by the arrival of Europeans, suffering precipitous declines in population over the course of the sixteenth century due to the introduction of Old World diseases and overwork. This decline was exacerbated as Iberian swine, sheep, and cattle ranged freely over abandoned agricultural lands, weakening the alimentary and social base of aboriginal communities. The Spanish Crown sought to protect indigenous lands and peoples from being overrun completely, although royal decrees had mixed results and often Indian communities themselves adopted livestock. In addition, Iberian immigrants and enslaved Africans entered the Americas in increasing numbers, supported by this expanding source of food, clothing, and draft labor.

Incomplete records indicate that Columbus set sail in 1493 with eight pigs, twenty-five horses (see the Horses entry), three mules, and an unknown quantity of cattle, sheep, goats, and chickens. Other expeditions followed over the next few years with many more livestock. The pigs were typical Iberian swine, small, long-legged, with a narrow snout to aid in foraging. Finding ideal ecological conditions in the Americas, these self-sufficient, prolific animals soon overran many of the areas they inhabited. Early Spanish expeditions often travelled with herds of hogs to feed the troops, and thousands became feral. Native peoples soon adopted the pig into their own economies, often due to tribute obligations, although their croplands also had to be protected from the voracious omnivores. By the end of the six-teenth century, an organized swine industry raised pigs for meat, lard, soap, and hides. A half-century later, some 30,000 pigs were consumed annually in Mexico City alone, and by the end of the colonial period in California the Franciscan missions allegedly raised over 300,000 swine.

The breed of pig in Iberoamerica changed little over the colonial era and into the independence period until the introduction of specialized breeds developed during the Industrial Revolution. Today, most pigs in Latin America are produced on large hog farms for urban markets, though descendants of the original Iberian breed are found in poorer communities and among native peoples. The pig played a major role in the transplanting of Iberian culture to the Americas, and today is an essential element in the Latin American diet.

Sheep were also a vital part of the Columbian Exchange. Wool, sheep's milk, and mutton defined much of the Iberian economy of the late fifteenth century, and were fundamental in transforming the Americas. The animals adapted easily to their new environment, and aided by Crown land grants for sheep raising, *obrajes* (wool workshops) developed, especially in New Spain (Mexico) and Peru, to supply local need and for export. And despite population decline, a ready supply of indigenous labor guaranteed early success of these industries.

The environmental impact was severe in some regions, as sheep participated in what has been called "ungulate irruptions." These animal populations expanded rapidly in the first century of Iberian occupation, often at the expense of native agriculturalists, but soon declined as a result of overpopulation and accompanying environmental degradation. While early observations suggest as many as 6 to 8 million head in New Spain alone in the early seventeenth century, by the middle of that century sheep numbers had declined dramatically, often requiring new importations. The number of sheep did not stabilize until the eighteenth century.

As native communities adopted sheep, the animals became an essential element of local economies, establishing roots in the temperate zones of Mexico, the mountains of the Andes, and eventually on the plains of the Pampas of Argentina and Uruguay, where a major export industry of wool, sheepskins, mutton, and tallow developed in the early nineteenth century. By the early twentieth century, sheep raising had expanded into Patagonia (Argentina and Chile), where it remains to this day. The breed of sheep imported by the Spaniards was the merino, which developed into a generic creole (*criollo*) breed in the Americas, though losing much of the fine wool quality carried by its ancestor. By the late nineteenth century, new breeds were imported from Europe, and at the end of that century even some Australian sheep were being raised in Argentina. The sheep industry declined over the twentieth century but has had a significant impact on several regional and national economies and is still an important part of local animal husbandry and wool production, especially in the Andes.

Cattle, though initially transported in smaller quantities than pigs or sheep, were also a key aspect of Iberian culture transferred to the Americas. The animals flourished on the islands, particularly Hispaniola, and large herds developed, encouraged by the Spanish Crown through land grants. By the late sixteenth century, cattle were found throughout Spanish and Portuguese America, and by 1620 New Spain hosted up to two million head. Many throughout the colonies became feral, particularly in the La Plata region (Argentina). They fed the immigrant Iberian population with meat and milk, and their hides supplied local consumption and eventually a profitable export business. Tallow was extracted for candles, manure fertilized sugar and tobacco fields, and draft animals were an integral part of mining and plantation economies until the advent of machinery in the nineteenth century. At the same time, bullfighting was imported from Spain, most notably to Mexico City. Some scholars speculate that over the course of the colonial period cattle produced more income for the colonies than did mining.

The ranching industry expanded significantly during the nineteenth century, as the Industrial Revolution demanded raw materials, including hides and beef, the latter especially after the invention of refrigerated shipping in the late century. Mexican ranching supplied the United States; Argentine, Uruguayan, and Brazilian cattle sustained Europe; and Venezuelan and Colombian animals fed expanding local markets. Several countries relied heavily upon cattle to sustain their national economies, a situation that in some cases has continued to the present.

The breeds imported into the Americas were primarily from southern Iberia. Small and carrying relatively little meat, these animals were also extremely hardy and adaptable to local American conditions, whether semiarid, humid temperate, or tropical. As with sheep and horses, they came to be referred to as creole, though local ecological adaptations often led to the development of specialized characteristics.

These creole cattle were the ancestors of the famed longhorn of Texas. The creole suffered significant challenges in the late nineteenth and early twentieth centuries from breeds developed during the Industrial Revolution in Europe. Hereford, Shorthorn, and Holstein became the breeds of choice, as the Latin American cattle industry was "rationalized" to serve urban industrial economies at home and abroad. Indian humped cattle, zebu, were introduced in the late nineteenth century to tropical and semitropical regions, particularly Brazil, and today dominate in those environments throughout Latin America. The modern science of animal husbandry has expanded rapidly in Latin America, and cattle breeding is a lucrative business for ranchers throughout the region. Creole cattle are now preserved as part of the national heritage in several nations, but with the exception of the poorest regions, they have ceded their place after five centuries of indispensable labor.

Donkeys, also known as burros, and mules played important roles in the economies of Latin America from early settlement to the twentieth century, and helped to link both economies and cultures across vast expanses of territory. The Spanish Crown encouraged the importation of donkeys, in part to replace the declining population of human bearers and workers. Donkeys were used in agriculture, mining, and long- and short-distance transport. Adapting easily to the benign environments of much of the Americas, donkey populations expanded quickly, in several areas becoming feral and causing the same kind of problems for native peoples and their ecosystems as pigs and sheep. Once they were established, Iberian settlers soon bred them to mares to produce mules, which became an integral part of virtually all colonial economies.

Over the course of the colonial period and into the twentieth century, mules were bred for use in silver mining, sugar milling, and mule trains, as well as to pull plows and thresh wheat. In many regions, mules were preferred over horses or cattle, as steeds or to transport loads. This was particularly the case in the mountainous regions of Peru, where these surefooted animals outperformed others and were much hardier than horses. Northern Argentina and the Brazilian region of São Paulo became the prime areas for mule breeding, helping to integrate the interior into the dominant mining and sugar economies of these colonies. Annual or semiannual mule fairs commonly traded as many as 60,000 to 100,000 animals at a time. With the arrival of the railroad in the mid-nineteenth century, mule breeding declined, and by the early twentieth century rail and road transport had caused the industry to virtually disappear. Today, mules are found primarily in the poorer regions of the continent.

Other important livestock of the Columbian Exchange were goats and chickens. Goats, originating in southern Spain and Portugal as well as Africa, through the slave trade, did well in the Americas, proliferating wherever they were introduced, frequently with a deleterious impact on local ecosystems. Some native peoples took to raising goats early, since they required relatively little care and were reliable sources of meat and hides; by the seventeenth century goat milk and cheese had become an important part of many native people's diets. Sailors and pirates often released goats (as well as pigs and sheep) on islands as future supplies of meat and milk, which over time caused extensive environmental harm. Feral goats frequently destroyed the habitats of native species, causing some to become extinct. As part of the farm economy, goats were most useful in arid and semiarid regions, and became an essential part of the impoverished economies of northern Mexico and the northeast of Brazil, where they are still important.

Chickens accompanied the earliest explorers and settlers to the Americas and quickly became the most easily accessible source of animal protein for Iberians and aboriginals. Native peoples, in some cases familiar with semidomesticated turkeys and waterfowl, adopted the chicken early and have maintained it as an essential part of their diet to today. These fowl were also imported for entertainment, as cockfighting was a popular sport among Iberians and many African cultures. Though most chickens came from southern Iberia, in the tropical Americas a common farm bird is the guinea fowl, originally from Africa. Today, chicken and eggs are consumed by all classes in Latin America, and industrial poultry farms are found in major urban centers.

Though not usually considered livestock, dogs, cats, honeybees, and rats were other importations that contributed significantly to the Columbian Exchange. Little is known about cats, except for some anecdotal references to feral cats in colonial cities and their use in controlling rats; the canine contribution, however, was enormous. Although small dogs were native to the Americas, European dogs, especially mastiffs and greyhounds, were constant companions of the early conquerors. Their utility as war dogs contributed to the battlefield successes of the Spaniards and Portuguese, and after the conquests they were used in hunting game, for chasing down

runaway slaves, and to subdue resistant native peoples. As more dogs were imported, especially to guard early Spanish and Portuguese forts and plantations, they interbred with local dogs, and many went feral, becoming a scourge of the newly established livestock economies. Over the centuries, Iberian dogs flourished alongside their human companions as sentinels and in sheepherding, while in recent decades they have been crossbred with imported breeds for work or show, creating some uniquely Latin American breeds.

In a region of the world in which rats did not exist until the arrival of Europeans, they are now ubiquitous. The black rat accompanied the first expeditions and established itself immediately, while the brown rat immigrated to Latin America in the late eighteenth century, partially displacing the black rat over the next century. Little is written on the impact of the rat, although observers over the centuries constantly complained about their extensive numbers in ports and cities.

Honeybees probably came to the Americas in the early seventeenth century. Native bees existed in the Americas, but none that produced honey in the quantities of the European species. By the eighteenth century, the honeybee had spread so far and wide that native peoples in North America referred to it as the "English fly," portending European arrival. By the twentieth century, well-developed beekeeping industries based on the European honeybee had been established in many parts of the Americas. In the middle of that century, Brazilian beekeepers intent on increasing honey production imported larger African bees to breed with the established honeybee population. Some of these bees escaped into the wild and proliferated rapidly throughout South America. By the end of the century, swarms had arrived in the southern United States, causing unjustified alarm based on exaggerated reports of their aggressiveness. This most recent case is representative of the impact and continuous character of the Columbian Exchange, as the cultures and the ecosystems of the Americas have been modified dramatically, largely due to the animals that accompanied the new settlers.

Robert W. Wilcox

References

Crosby, Alfred W., Jr. *The Columbian Exchange: Biological and Cultural Consequences of 1492.* Westport, CT: Greenwood, 1972.

Denhardt, Robert M. *The Horse of the Americas.* Rev. ed. Norman: University of Oklahoma Press, 1975.

Laguna Sanz, Eduardo. *El Ganado español, un descubrimiento para América.* Madrid: Ministerio de Agricultura, Pesca y Alimentación, 1991.

Melville, Elinor G. K. *A Plague of Sheep: Environmental Consequences of the Conquest of Mexico.* New York: Cambridge University Press, 1994.

Río Moreno, Justo L. del. "El cerdo: Historia de un elemento esencial de la cultura castellana en la conquista y colonización de América (siglo XVI)." *Anuario de estudios americanos* 53, no. 1 (1996): 13–35.

Rouse, John E. *The Criollo: Spanish Cattle in the Americas.* Norman: University of Oklahoma Press, 1977.

Varner, John Grier, and Jeannette Johnson Varner. *Dogs of the Conquest.* Norman: University of Oklahoma Press, 1983.

See also: Atlantic Economy; Borderlands; Bullfighting; California; Cimarrones; Colonists and Settlers I–VI; Columbian Exchange—Agriculture; Columbian Exchange—Disease; Conquest I–VII; Contraband; Defense—Colonial Brazil; Defense—Colonial Spanish America; Engenho; Food; Hacienda; Horses; Mining—Gold; Mining—Silver; Missions; Native Americans I–VIII; Obraje; Pirates and Piracy; Sports; Trade—Spain/Spanish America; Weapons; Wheat.

Columbian Exposition of Chicago (1893)

Staged in Chicago to commemorate the four-hundredth anniversary of Christopher Columbus's first landing in the West Indies, the six-month world's fair opened in May 1893 and hosted 27 million visitors. The governments of Haiti, Spain, Brazil, Colombia, Venezuela, Costa Rica, and Guatemala sponsored national pavilions, while numerous private groups contributed goods to the various buildings dedicated to industry, mining, agriculture, ethnology, and anthropology. Mexico planned a large pavilion for the 1893 exhibition, but the economic (silver) crisis of the 1890s forced the organizers to lower their level of participation.

For many Latin American governments, the fair presented an occasion to display to the world a national image of modernity, cosmopolitanism, and progress. It generated debates within each country over how best to present the nation's resources, peoples, and history. The fair also offered an opportunity to stimulate commercial and investment activity. This hope coincided with increasing world interest in Latin America's commercial potential for investment in railroads and natural resource extraction, as well as for new markets for U.S. surplus production. In their respective countries after the fair, Latin American officials reported medals the nation had been awarded as a means of boosting productivity and craftsmanship at home.

Fair organizers did not ostracize Latin American countries as they did Asian and African countries. Latin American nations were given space outside the Midway, the amusement section of the fair, to which nonwhite and non-Western cultures were relegated. Nevertheless, some indigenous cultures from Latin America were represented in ethnological villages constructed by Western anthropologists and relegated to the Midway. Ecuador produced an illustrated tourist guide for visitors that included idealized studio photographs of posed Indians. In the ethnology building, numerous Mexican antiquities were exhibited, along with pictures of ruins, models of popular types (*tipos populares*), cloth woven by indigenous peoples, and Indian skulls.

At the Republic of Haiti pavilion, artifacts celebrated the nineteenth anniversary of Haitian independence. The pavilion contained paintings, portraits, busts, and mementos of independence leader Toussaint L'Ouverture. Frederick Douglass, the former slave turned author and statesman, who had served for a time as minister to Haiti, attended the fair as a representative for the Haitian pavilion. At the pavilion dedication ceremonies, Douglass lectured on the history of the Western Hemisphere's first black republic and condemned American policies toward Haiti.

Latin American and Spanish women contributed to the Woman's Pavilion at the personal invitation of the pavilion's Board of Lady Managers. Female organizers decided early to devote attention to the figure of Queen Isabella of Castile, since they believed she had enabled Columbus to make his voyage. During the fair's ceremonies, female participants unveiled a statue of the former Castilian queen. For the Spanish exhibit itself, Queen Cristina of Spain personally directed the work on Spain's contribution, which included souvenirs of Queen Isabella. Among Latin American countries, Cuba, Brazil, and Guatemala sent officially funded exhibits, while individual contributors from Peru, Colombia,

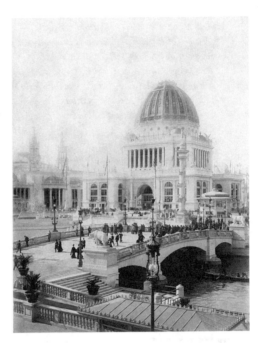

World's Columbian Exposition, Chicago, 1893.
(Library of Congress)

Chile, and Ecuador funded private exhibits. In Mexico, Carmen Romero Rubio, wife of President Porfirio Díaz, personally chose items to send to the Woman's Pavilion and sponsored an anthology of poetry of Mexican female writers edited by the Mexican educator and author José María Vigil.

Susanne Eineigel

References

Muratorio, Blanca. "Images of Indians in the Construction of Ecuadorian Identity at the End of the Nineteenth Century." In *Latin American Popular Culture: An Introduction*, edited by William H. Beezley and Linda A. Curcio-Nagy. Wilmington, DE: Scholarly Resources, 2000.

Pérez de Mendiola, Marina. "The Universal Exposition Seville 1991: Presence and Absence, Remembrance and Forgetting." In *Bridging the Atlantic: Toward a Reassessment of Iberian and Latin American Cultural Ties,* edited by Marina Pérez de Mendiola. New York: State University of New York Press, 1996.

Rydell, Robert W. *All the World's a Fair: Visions of Empire at American International Expositions, 1876–1916.* Chicago: University of Chicago Press, 1984.

Tenorio Trillo, Mauricio. *Mexico at the World's Fairs: Crafting a Modern Nation.* Los Angeles: University of California Press, 1996.

Weimann, Jeanne Madeline. *The Fair Women: The Story of the Woman's Building. World's Columbian Exposition Chicago 1893.* Chicago: Academy Chicago, 1981.

See also: Fin de Siècle; Knights of Columbus; Mexico; Monarchs of Spain; Universal Expositions in Spain; Women—Modern Spanish America.

COMISSÁRIOS

These clerical officials of the Inquisition were subordinate directly to the inquisitors. In regions where there were no tribunals of the Inquisition, *comissários* represented the highest inquisitional authority, to whom all other inquisitional officials reported. Comissários personally oversaw all inquisitional activities and inquisitional officials. They received denunciations and performed investigations of accused heretics and background investigations for candidates for inquisitional office, such as those for the *familiares* (lay officials). They also questioned witnesses in inquisitional cases, published the Edicts of Faith (which listed the crimes against the faith that all Catholics should denounce), controlled the entrance of books into the various ports, and oversaw the confiscation of property and the behavior of inquisitional officials. Under no circumstances could they delegate these responsibilities without direct authorization from the Inquisition. The comissários operated under strict limitations and could not legitimately engage in any inquisitional activity without specific instructions from the Inquisition.

The comissários underwent a rigorous background investigation to ensure that they had pure blood (*limpieza de sangre;* that is, no Moorish or Jewish blood) and a good public reputation. They had to be ecclesiastics of recognized prudence and virtue. Preference was given to secular clerics who had university degrees and to those who possessed a benefice (an ecclesiastical office with an attached salary).

The tribunal of Lima, Peru, limited the number of comissários in 1569. In Portugal and Brazil, comissários were technically limited to one in each of the most important towns and ports after 1613. These limits were seldom enforced. The Spanish American Inquisitions also experienced difficulty finding sufficient numbers of clerics with pure blood to hold the office.

There were at least 2,561 comissários in the Portuguese Empire (Wadsworth 2002, 52–59). Most of them tended to concentrate in the high-population centers, but they were also scattered throughout the countryside. Brazil had around 200 comissários between 1613 and 1821, with the highest concentration in the captaincies of Pernambuco and Bahia. Together with the network of familiares, they permitted the Inquisition to extend its reach far beyond the confines of the tribunals.

The numbers of comissários in the Spanish Empire expanded rapidly in the sixteenth century, but then declined in the eighteenth century. The opposite was true in the Portuguese Empire, where the number of comissários remained low until the eighteenth century, after which the numbers increased rapidly, coinciding with the rise in the number of familiares during the same period.

Complaints of abuse of authority by comissários were frequent. False comissários also appeared, as men sought to profit from the power and authority of the office. The quality of the comissários was often in question, as bishops and inquisitors complained that they were unsavory characters who sought the appointment to escape the jurisdiction of ecclesiastical leaders and gain power and influence in local affairs. Others, such as the ex-Jesuit Joaquim Marques de Araújo in Pernambuco, Brazil, energetically pursued the inquisitional agenda. Without these officials, the inquisitors could not have carried out their duties in the countryside and in the colonies.

James E. Wadsworth

References

Alberro, Solange. *Inquisición y sociedade en México, 1571–1700.* Mexico City: Fondo de Cultura Económica, 1988.

Bethencourt, Francisco. *História das Inquisições: Portugal, Espanha, e Itália.* Lisbon: Temas e Debates, 1996.

Kamen, Henry. *The Spanish Inquisition: A Historical Revision.* London: Weidenfeld and Nicolson, 1997.

Lea, Henry Charles Lea. *A History of the Inquisition of Spain.* 4 vols. New York: Macmillan, 1922.

Wadsworth, James E. "Agents of Orthodoxy: Inquisitional Power and Prestige in Colonial Pernambuco, Brazil." Ph.D. dissertation, University of Arizona, 2002.

See also: Brazil; Catholic Church in Brazil; Catholic Church in Spanish America; Clergy—Secular, in Colonial Spanish America; Donatary Captaincies; Familiares; Idolatry, Extirpation of; Inquisition—Luso-America; Inquisition—Spanish America; Jesuits—Iberia and America; Race; Religious Orders.

COMMUNISM

Communist parties have had an influential and complex role in both Spanish and Latin American history. Although the influence of Communist parties is pervasive throughout Europe and Latin America, there have never been particularly remarkable relationships between or among Spanish and Latin American Communists. The history of Communism is usually examined on a case-by-case basis (as institutional studies of the various individual Communist parties); there are few comprehensive analyses of the international aspect of Communism in Latin America, and none that specifically deal with Latin American Communism and Spanish Communism. The Communist parties of Spain and Latin America are not systematically linked, but they are linked by a common ideology. The history of Communism in Spain, however, is more firmly rooted in Europe. In Latin America, Marxism-Leninism was arguably the most important political ideology of the twentieth century, but most historians agree that this influence was not a result of Soviet internationalism. So the link both among Latin American Communists and between Latin American and Spanish Communists is more generally ideological, rather than historical or political.

The Communist Party of Spain (PCE) was founded in late 1921. In January 1936, the PCE joined with the Socialist Party (PSOE) and the Republican Union Party to form an electoral coalition called the Popular Front. Soon after, many of the rightist parties of Spain formed their own coalition, called the National Front. A contingent of Spanish army officers (including Francisco Franco) plotted the overthrow of the Popular Front government. This conspiracy eventually resulted in the outbreak of the Spanish Civil War in July of 1936. After the beginning of the civil war, the influence of the Communist Party within the

Popular Front grew. More importantly, the civil war internationalized the cause of Spanish Communism, bringing in the support of Communists and other progressives from all over the world, including the leadership of the Third Communist International (the Comintern). The Popular Front was defeated by Franco and his Nationalist Army in March of 1939. Most of the leaders of the Communist Party were forced into exile. Many Spanish Communists took refuge in Mexico and in other parts of Latin America and the Caribbean.

Social radicalism became an important ideological force in much of Latin America during the end of the nineteenth century and the first few decades of the twentieth century. The increased influence of these radical ideologies was spurred on by waves of European working-class immigrants, the expansion of an export-based economy with the accompanying social and economic dislocation, and the formation of an urban working class in some countries. When urban working-class and middle-class activists began to challenge the political stronghold of traditional landed elites, they were often influenced and organized around radical European ideas of that era (e.g., Socialism, anarchism, anarcho-syndicalism, and Communism). Although these ideas existed in almost every country in Latin America by 1900, the most notable cases were in Argentina, Chile, and Brazil.

Argentina's working-class radicalism emerged with several well-known newspapers, political parties, and trade unions well before 1900. Argentina had representatives to the Second International before World War I. After the Russian Revolution in 1917, pro-Soviet dissidents from the Argentine Socialist Party formed the International Socialist Party, which became the Communist Party in 1920 when they joined the Comintern.

Chile's Democratic Party was committed to a socialist agenda when it was initially formed in 1887. As the party moved toward the right, leftist dissidents formed their own Socialist Labor Party in 1912. By 1919, they began to conform with the agenda of the Comintern, and renamed themselves the Communist Party in 1921. They were the only major leftist party in Chile until the Chilean Socialist Party emerged in the 1930s. While Chilean Socialists and Communists often allied with other radicals to create Popular Front coalitions, Chilean leftists were generally not inclined toward Soviet-line Communism. This made the Chilean Communist Party a relatively minor player in these coalitions.

Immigrants also brought radical European ideas to Brazil at the end of the nineteenth century. Several intellectual publications and newspapers espoused Marxist and other radical views well before the turn of the twentieth century. Brazilians convened a Socialist Congress in 1892, and a Brazilian Socialist Party was formed in 1895, although anarchism was still the more influential philosophical trend among working-class Brazilians into the twentieth century. Rivalry between the anarchists and Socialists intensified during World War I. A faction from the Brazilian Socialist Party broke away (over the failure of the Socialist Party to support Lenin and the Bolshevik revolution in Russia) and formed the Brazilian Communist Party in 1922. The Brazilian Communist Party was modeled on the Argentine Communist Party.

José Carlos Mariátegui of Peru is perhaps the best-known Marxist *pensador* (thinker) from Latin America. Like Chile, Argentina, and Brazil, Peru also had a series of nineteenth-century radical publications influenced by European ideas, such as anarchism and socialism. In 1884, there was a small anarcho-syndicalist union of artisans in Peru as well. But this early radicalism was soon overshadowed by the emergence of Peruvian *indigenismo,* an attempt to combine Marxist ideals with the reality of Peru's large indigenous peasant underclass. Indigenismo is mostly associated with Mariátegui, but as an ideological framework, it was influential all over Latin America. It was perhaps the first attempt to explain and analyze Latin American social reality as unique (from Europe and North America). Mariátegui was one of the founders of the Peruvian Socialist Party in 1928. Mariátegui and the Socialists were openly supportive of the Soviet Revolution, but Mariátegui believed that Peru's path to socialism would necessarily follow a different route. Although he thought of himself as both a Marxist and a Socialist, he never allied his Socialist Party with the Comintern. When he died in 1930, his Socialist Party, under pressure from the Comintern, changed its named to the Communist Party of Peru.

Although Mexico was influenced by European radicalism, and had Marxist-oriented journalism and at least one anarcho-syndicalist political party—the Partido-Liberal Mexicano (PLM) created by the Flores Magon brothers in 1906— early Mexican radicalism was completely dominated by the events of the Mexican Revolution. The Mexican Communist Party was officially created in 1918 by three non-Mexicans. They were the first Communist party in Latin America to join the Comintern. Mexican Communists were active in the organization of miners, campesinos, and schoolteachers through-out the seven decades of the Mexican revolutionary regime. Although the Mexican Communists were at various times persecuted by the Mexican revolutionary party, and although they were often at odds with other leftist parties and movements, they continued to play a role in Mexican politics throughout the twentieth century. Moreover, for much of the mid-twentieth century, Mexico was a magnet for exiled and disaffected Communists from Europe and the rest of Latin America. The most notable Communist refugee in Mexico, Leon Trotsky, was assassinated by a Stalinist KGB agent in Mexico City in 1940.

The whole face of Latin American Communism changed dramatically with the Cuban Revolution of 1959. Although Castro and his 26th of July Movement were not formally aligned with the Cuban Communist Party, many members of the movement were Communists, including Fidel's brother, Raul. After Fidel Castro declared himself a Marxist-Leninist in 1961, both the organizational and ideological nature of Latin American Communism shifted. Castro did not launch the new Cuban Communist Party until its first party congress in 1976, but the new model of Cuban Communism was immediately influential in the early 1960s. The triumph of a new brand of Cuban Communism ended once and for all the haranguing over what kind of relationship Latin American Communist parties should have with the Soviet Union. After 1959, few Latin American Communists remained committed to a Soviet-style revolution. Cuba's success made it possible for dozens of new intensely nationalist revolutionary movements to emerge. These new guerrilla organizations were nominally committed to Communist revolution, but they were suddenly free to go ahead with insurgent projects without having to concern themselves with the approval of the Soviet Union.

The Cuban strategy of *foquismo* emphasized the idea that guerrilla warfare could be successful in the rest of Latin America with a relatively small amount of preparation or organization. The reality of a large and marginalized peasant class, which was excluded from national life economically, socially, and geographically, was believed to be the real key to revolutionary victory. Although the *foquista* strategy proved disastrous in the rest of Latin America, rural-based Communist insurgencies regrouped and continued to press (with guerrilla armies) for radical social transformation in most of Latin America. Guatemala, El Salvador, Nicaragua, Colombia, and Peru had particularly notable experiences with Communist-led insurgent movements. The Sandinista National Liberation Front (FSLN) overthrew the dictatorship of Anastasio Somoza in Nicaragua in 1979, in what appeared to be the second successful Marxist-inspired revolution in Latin America. The collapse of the Soviet Union and the electoral defeat of the Sandinistas in 1990 eventually dashed the hopes of many Latin American Communists and other leftists.

In the early 1990s, with the collapse of the Soviet Union and the end of the cold war, both Latin American militaries and guerrilla movements had strong incentives to negotiate peace. Although Communist-led insurgencies remained active in Colombia and Peru, the traditional loyalty to Marxism-Leninism had begun to ring hollow, and it is now rarely mentioned by the only viable Communist insurgency left—the Rebel Armed Forces of Colombia (FARC). Although nominally Communist, the FARC has taken to emphasizing what is called Bolivarianism as their new ideology. Bolivarianism is a Pan-American ideal that emphasizes a common Latin American cultural and political identity united in solidarity against North American imperialism. Although the Cuban Communist Party continues in power, traditional Communism has largely become a fringe radical movement in Latin America. Communist parties have been replaced by more diverse communities of labor organizers, human rights activists, ethnic-based movements, and popular groups who oppose the diverse effects of neoliberalism and globalization. New social movements in Latin America are structurally transnational and much more global in their orientation. Ironically, the collapse of Communism has allowed the workers of the world to unite more effectively than they could in the twentieth century.

Rachel A. May

References

Caballero, Manuel. *Latin America and the Comintern, 1919–1943.* 2nd ed. New York: Cambridge University Press, 2002.

Castaneda, Jorge G. *Utopia Unarmed: The Latin American Left after the Cold War.* New York: Knopf, 1993.

Liss, Sheldon B. *Marxist Thought in Latin America.* Berkeley and Los Angeles: University of California Press, 1984.

See also: Argentina; Brazil; Chile; Cold War—Portugal and the United States; Cold War—Spain and the Americas; Colombia; Cuba; Cuban Revolution; Fin de Siècle; Guerrillas; Human Rights; Liberalism; Mexican Revolution; Migration—From Iberia to the New World; Nationalism; Nicaragua; Organization of American States; Populism; Positivism; Spanish Civil War and Latin America; World War I; World War II.

COMUNEROS—NEW GRANADA

In 1781, peasants and members of the lower class initiated a violent rebellion in the captaincy-general of New Granada, located in modern Venezuela and Colombia. Forming communes, whence the name *Comuneros,* the rebels were influenced by both material and ideological factors. Utilizing the ideology of the traditional Spanish comuneros, who defended their traditional privileges through revolutionary means, New Granada's Comuneros posed a threat to Spain's hegemony in the region. The rebellion was sparked by an increase in local taxes as well as a sense, prevalent in the late eighteenth century, that the Bourbon reforms initiated under Spain's King Charles III brought an increased and unwelcome presence of the Spanish Crown into the lives of New Granada's inhabitants.

The most important reforms Charles initiated were military, political, and economic. The military reforms involved the strengthening of the military while also increasing the *fueros,* or privileges of the military caste. In political terms, Charles introduced the intendancy (*intendencia*) system in the New World. Utilized in Spain, the intendancy system imported a new crop of Spanish bureaucrats into the New World. Moreover, Charles reorganized the local municipal system so that power was extricated from the local bureaucrats, mostly Creoles (those born in the New World whose parents were of Spanish descent), and offered to peninsular Spaniards. Economically, the Bourbon reforms continued to create commercial monopolies for the Crown and established a neomercantilist philosophy.

The Crown found it necessary to fund the restructuring of the new colonial system utilizing Spaniards, specifically Juan Francisco Gutiérrez de Piñeres, the visitor-general. Gutiérrez was charged with implementing the Bourbon reforms through increasing the *alcabala,* a sales tax, to 4 percent and reorganizing the price of tobacco and spirit monopolies. The reforms outraged many Creole politicians, who refused to pay the taxes. Thus, the burden of paying the new taxes fell on a poor population, most importantly New Granada's small-scale farmers.

The result of the reforms was a social rebellion in March 1781 in the cities of Socorro and San Gil. The Creole leadership that had refused to pay the imposed taxes attacked government warehouses and drove out the Spanish authorities. The rebellion spilled over into Andean Venezuela. At its peak, the rebels had a force of over 20,000 men. Essentially, the goal of the rebellion was economic, and to a large degree the upheaval was conservative in nature. Many rebels joined the movement to protest the modernity of the reforms. The rebels called for a return to a golden age, an era in which traditional political arrangements were in force in the New World as well as in Spain. Armed with seemingly conservative values, the insurrection transcended class and ethnic lines. As the rebellion became increasingly a challenge to the policies of the Bourbon monarchy and its policies of modernization and innovation, the Spanish imperial system entered into a phase of weakness. It has been suggested that the Comunero rebellion was a precursor to future insurrections of the late eighteenth century as well as the independence movements of the early nineteenth century.

Jaime Ramón Olivares

References

Lynch, John. *Bourbon Spain, 1700–1808.* Oxford: Blackwell, 1989.

McFarlane, Anthony. "Civil Disorders and Popular Protests in Late Colonial New Granada." *Hispanic American Historical Review* 64, no. 1 (1984): 17–54.

Phelan, John Leddy. *The People and the King: The Comunero Revolution in Colombia, 1781.* Madison: University of Wisconsin Press, 1978.

See also: Alcabala; Alcohol; Bourbon Reforms; Cabildo; Colombia; Corregidor/ Corregimiento; Defense—Colonial Spanish America; Independence IV— Colombia, Ecuador, and Venezuela; Intendants/Intendancy System; Monopolies; Rebellions—Colonial Latin America; Tobacco; Venezuela.

CONFRATERNITIES (COFRADÍAS)

Confraternities (*cofradías* in Spanish, *irmandades* in Portuguese) are charitable corporate organizations run by the laity and organized around a specific Catholic devotion. They first appeared in Europe in the thirteenth century as organizations primarily concerned with fulfilling charitable acts. By the time of the voyages of exploration, confraternities had become the way that laypeople organized their society, took care of the bodies and souls of the dead, engaged in charitable acts, and expressed their devotion through lavish feast day celebrations. Members of the organizations elected their own boards of directors, hired their own chaplains, and when they could, built their own churches. In this way confraternities remained relatively independent of the diocesan church structure through the colonial period.

Confraternities served as one of the organizing principles of society that the Portuguese and Spanish brought over to the Americas. In many cases, the first Spanish and Portuguese settlers opened branches of confraternities in the colonies in order to ensure their salvation and a proper burial. As society in the Americas became more complex, different social groups began their own confraternities. Among the Europeans and their descendants, confraternities were often divided along lines of wealth and status, and there were also many confraternities of Africans, Native Americans, and their descendants.

In Spanish America, the religious orders promoted confraternities as a major part of their strategy for converting the indigenous population to Christianity. Numerically, the strategy was a success throughout the Americas, and from Mexico to Peru, in both rural and urban regions, Indians became active participants in confraternities. By 1585 there were 300 Native American confraternities in Mexico City, and there were 60 in Lima by 1619. This success was matched in the countryside, where in some villages 100 percent of the indigenous community participated in the local confraternity. Whatever the original purpose, confraternities were popular among the Native Americans because of the similarities to traditional patterns of social organization, and the practices within the indigenous brotherhoods tended to be a mixture of elements from Christianity and traditional indigenous beliefs. These syncretist practices can still be found in indigenous communities throughout Spanish Latin America.

Confraternities also played an important role in the lives of Africans in Latin

America, and especially in Brazil. In the early years religious orders started confraternities for recently arrived African slaves, but by the end of the colonial period, Africans and their descendants were opening their own confraternities. The confraternities became places where Africans and their descendants could rebuild corporate identities by mixing elements of their African cultures into Catholicism. Often Africans from many different backgrounds would unite into a single confraternity, but in some of the major urban ports the black confraternities divided along ethnic lines. In some regions, Afro-Brazilian confraternities have survived until today, and in others, practices that developed in the colonial confraternities can be seen in popular festivals, such as Carnival and Congados, the feast day celebrations dedicated to Our Lady of the Rosary.

In the nineteenth century, confraternities came under pressure from both the liberal states of Latin America and the Catholic Church, which had undergone Romanization in response to the liberal ideas spreading throughout Europe. Both challenged the independence of the confraternities and sought to stamp out "folk" practices that had flourished in them. Nonetheless, the impact of the confraternity system is felt throughout the region in devotional practices that echo both the social organization of the Euro-American confraternities and the syncretist practices in indigenous and Afro–Latin American organizations.

Elizabeth Kiddy

References

Meyers, Albert, and Diane Hopkins, eds. *Manipulating the Saints: Religious Brotherhoods and Social Integration in Postconquest Latin America.* Hamburg: Wayasbah, 1988.

Russell-Wood, A. J. R. *Fidalgos and Philanthropists: The Santa Casa da Misericórdia of Bahia, 1550–1755.* Berkeley and Los Angeles: University of California Press, 1968.

Webster, Susan Verdi. "Research on Confraternities in the Colonial Americas." *Confraternitas* 9, no. 1 (Spring 1998): 13–24.

See also: Catholic Church in Brazil; Catholic Church in Spanish America; Clergy—Secular, in Colonial Spanish America; Jesuits—Iberia and America; Native Americans I–VII; Religious Orders; Slavery I—Brazil; Syncretism; Virgin of Guadalupe.

CONGREGACIONES

Also called *reducciones, congregaciones* were forced settlements of Amerindians in European-style towns. The concentration of people into villages was a policy designed to make it easier for the Spanish to control Amerindians politically and economically, and to assist in the efforts to convert Amerindians to Christianity. The first American experiment in creating such settlements came on the island of Hispaniola in the early sixteenth century. There and elsewhere, one of the principal reasons for the need to establish new towns was the sharp reduction in the size of the native population following contact between the peoples of the Old and New Worlds. But in some regions of the Americas where the urban tradition was weak or nonexistent, people whose settlement pattern was a dispersed one also needed to be concentrated into centers. By the time of King Philip II's reign (1556–1598), well developed ordinances guided the process. In the minds of the bureaucrats in the Council of the Indies who helped to establish the guidelines, all was intended for the "good government" of the natives. The land site was to be surveyed with an eye toward an adequate water supply, level land for town construction, and proximity to agricultural fields. The new towns were laid out in a regular grid pattern, centering on a public plaza, bordered by the church, the *cabildo* (municipal council) building, and the house of the *corregidor*. Provision was made for election of town officials, local magistrates (*alcaldes*), the sheriff, and the jailor. The streets were laid out in a uniform width.

The process of congregación was perhaps most completely established in the Andes, where the Spanish viceroy Francisco de Toledo (1569–1581) forced the Amerindians to destroy their old hamlets and build new towns. The disruption to traditional economic and social relationships was enormous, and many resisted the process unsuccessfully. The increased population densities of the towns actually had the unintended consequence of further reducing population size, because the spread of sicknesses, especially epidemic diseases, is directly related to the density of settlement. The disastrous Andean epidemics of 1588–1591, some of the most deadly of the sixteenth century, are clearly linked to these changes. In some regions the congregaciones did not persist, as people returned to their ancestral homes as soon as officials lost interest in maintaining the system. But in other regions, in spite of resistance to the process, and the ecological modifications associated with the moves, many of these largely sixteenth-century settlements continue to the present.

Noble Cook

References

Cook, Noble David. *Demographic Collapse: Indian Peru, 1520–1620.* Cambridge: Cambridge University Press, 1981.

Gibson, Charles. *The Aztecs under Spanish Rule.* Stanford, CA: Stanford University Press, 1964.

Spalding, Karen. *Huarochirí: An Andean Society under Inca and Spanish Rule.* Stanford, CA: Stanford University Press, 1984.

See also: Administration—Colonial Spanish America; Cabildo; Caciques; Catholic Church in Spanish America; Cities; Colonists and Settlers I—Andes; Columbian Exchange—Disease; Corregidor/Corregimiento; Encomienda; Native Americans I–VIII; Visita.

CONQUEST AND THE DEBATE OVER JUSTICE

The discoveries of Columbus enmeshed Spaniards in a decades-long debate over their justification for making war against the Amerindians, occupying their lands, and forcing them to work for the invading Spanish. Bulls issued by Pope Alexander VI in 1493 granted to Castile title to the lands that Columbus had discovered, and charged the monarchy with Christianizing the people living there. In later years, as the Spaniards spread through the Caribbean and the American mainland (see map on the following page), they believed that the lands belonged, through papal donation, to the Spanish king.

While almost no Spaniard questioned Iberian sovereignty over the Americas, important philosophical and religious questions arose as to how the Europeans should deal with the inhabitants of the newly discovered regions. Columbus's log of his first voyage shows that he was puzzled by the islanders whom he encountered. They were gentle, intelligent, and generous, but they went about completely naked, lacked metal tools and weapons, and seemed suited for

servitude. In fact, on a later voyage Columbus enslaved some islanders for sale in Spain. He distributed islanders in what were called *encomiendas,* thereby requiring them to provide labor and other tribute to the Spaniards. In exchange, the Indians were to receive protection and religious instruction. Although Queen Isabella declared the islanders her vassals, some Spaniards wondered whether they were humans at all or whether they had souls. Thus, Spaniards had to define the Amerindians' humanity. Meanwhile, Spanish-indigenous relations were unfolding in a context of unfettered conquest, occupation, and abuse. Despite the Crown's humanitarian inclinations, it too was determined to profit from the colonies.

Assuming their own political, social, religious, and cultural standards to be universal norms, Spaniards carried Greco-Roman and Christian cultural expectations to the Americas and imposed them on the peoples there. The resulting categorizations and judgments served political and economic decisions and justified religious policies.

Despite some attempts to limit exploitation of the islanders, abuse continued relatively unabated for nearly two decades following the discovery. In 1510, however, a group of Dominicans arrived on Hispaniola and soon challenged the colonists on their treatment of the Indians. In late 1511 Friar Antonio de Montesinos preached a courageous sermon proclaiming that the Spaniards were in mortal sin for their abusive practices. The resulting controversy was partially responsible for King Ferdinand convoking a group of theologians, lawyers, and philosophers the following year to discuss the treatment of the Indians. The outcome was the Laws of Burgos, which placed some limitations on the settlers but allowed them to demand as much as nine months' labor per year from adult male Indians. In 1513 the Crown issued the Requirement *(Requerimiento),* to be read to the Indians before making war on them. It informed them that, through the papal donation, the Americas belonged to the Spanish monarchy and that they must submit to its sovereignty in order to avoid war. Those who resisted might suffer attack and enslavement. The Requirement also invited but did not force them to become Christians.

But the controversies continued among theologians and political theorists regarding Spanish justification for taking indigenous lands and enslaving the inhabitants or forcing them to work for the Spaniards. In 1535 Vasco de Quiroga, the Franciscan bishop of Michoacán, argued in his treatise "Información en derecho" that because the Amerindians had failed to establish an authentic civil society (as defined by Europeans), the lands of the New World were unoccupied and available to peoples capable of creating such a society and government. The thrust of his argument was taken up by Juan Ginés de Sepúlveda, who contended that Amerindians were so primitive and barbaric as to be what Aristotle and Aquinas classified as natural slaves. Thus, they were unfit for self-rule but suited to servitude.

Meanwhile, in 1537 Pope Paul III, in *Sublimis Deus,* confirmed the Indians' basic humanity, which meant they were capable of becoming Christians. He also forbade their enslavement and the seizure of their property and lands.

Theologians at the University of Salamanca accepted the monarchy's sovereignty but challenged Spain's right to American lands and labor. Foremost was Francisco de Vitoria, the founder of international law. In *De Indis,* he denied that through their actions the Amerindians had forfeited their natural right to their own lands and labor. He concluded that Spaniards had the right to evangelize in the New World, although not to coerce conversions, and that if the Amerindians tried to prevent such preaching, the Spaniards could justly make war against them and overthrow their rulers. Noting the Amerindians' childlike characteristics, Vitoria suggested that the Spaniards might be justified in holding them temporarily in tutelage. His student Melchor Cano rejected such tutelage if it meant that the Spaniards first had to conquer the Amerindians to impose it. He only allowed his countrymen the right to enter indigenous lands to evangelize or to defend innocent peoples, but this gave them no right to take or occupy the lands or to extort labor.

Charles V convened a committee in 1550 at Valladolid, with the diverse sides represented. It included the Dominican Bartolomé de Las Casas, the great champion of indigenous rights who had persuaded the emperor to issue the New Laws of 1542 to eliminate the encomiendas (although colonial resistance forced the Crown to back down). Arguing against Sepúlveda's position, Las Casas held that though the Spanish monarchy might be sovereign, Spaniards had no right to land or labor in the Americas. Indeed they might rule only if invited to do so by the Amerindians. Las Casas asserted that except for missionaries and a few soldiers to protect them, Spaniards should withdraw from the Americas entirely. Some colonists feared that as a matter of conscience Charles V might abandon the Americas altogether, but in the end the Valladolid conference produced no conclusive policies regarding Spanish occupation of the New World and the treatment of its inhabitants.

Such debates tempered but did not reverse Spanish actions. After the death of Las Casas in 1566, the cause of indigenous rights lost its greatest champion. By the seventeenth century, legalists such as Juan de Solórzano y Pereyra asserted that regardless of the legal and moral justifications for or against the conquests, the fact remained that the Spanish monarchy, honestly convinced that it held sovereignty over the New World, had occupied the Americas. With the passage of time such possession had given Spain title to the lands inhabited by the Amerindians.

Kendall W. Brown

References

Hanke, Lewis. *The Spanish Struggle for Justice in the Conquest of America.* Boston: Little, Brown, 1965.

————. *All Mankind Is One: A Study of the Disputation between Bartolomé de Las Casas and Juan Ginés de Sepúlveda in 1550 on the Intellectual and Religious Capacity of the American.* De Kalb: Northern Illinois University Press, 1974.

Pagden, Anthony. *The Fall of Natural Man: The American Indian and the Origins of Comparative Ethnology.* Cambridge: Cambridge University Press, 1982.

————. *Spanish Imperialism and the Political Imagination: Studies in European and Spanish-American Social and Political Theory, 1513–1830.* New Haven, CT: Yale University Press, 1990.

Wagner, Henry Raup, and Helen Rand Parish. *The Life and Writings of Bartolomé de las Casas.* Albuquerque: University of New Mexico Press, 1967.

See also: Clergy—Secular, in Coloinial Spanish America; Colonists and Settlers I–VI; Conquest I–VII; Conquistadors; Defensor de Indios; Encomienda; Jesuits—Iberia and America; Laws—Colonial Latin America; Laws of Burgos; Monarchs of Spain; New Laws of 1542; Papacy; Religious Orders; Requerimiento; Salamanca, School of; Tordesillas, Treaty of.

CONQUEST I—ANDES

From 1524 to 1527 Francisco Pizarro led expeditions south from Panama to explore the northwestern coast of South America, and then, in 1530, the Spaniards launched the successful conquest of the Andean region. In 1532 they captured the Inca ruler Atahualpa, and the following year they occupied the city of Cuzco. Quito fell to Spanish forces under Sebastián de Benalcázar in 1534. A massive Andean rebellion from 1535 to 1537 failed to drive the Spaniards from Peru, although the neo-Inca state of Vilcabamba managed to survive until 1572, when Túpac Amaru, its last ruler, was captured and executed.

In 1522, Pascual de Andagoya mounted the first Spanish expedition to investigate reports of the "Birú" people somewhere south of Panama. He then sold his ships to three veterans of the Spanish exploration and conquest of Central America: Francisco Pizarro, Diego de Almagro, and Hernando de Luque. Pizarro and Almagro's first expedition took them only halfway along the west coast of modern Colombia. Despite great suffering, they returned sufficiently encouraged to establish a formal partnership with Luque on March 10, 1526. A second expedition (1526–1527) was planned, during which the Spaniards crossed the equator and made contact with Inca traders. Pizarro and a few comrades doggedly pushed on to the Inca city of Tumbez, south of Guayaquil Bay. Following their return to Panama, the partners decided to send Pizarro to Spain to secure royal authorization for an expedition of exploration and conquest. On July 26, 1529, Pizarro obtained the contract (*capitulación*), which named him governor of Peru, a stipulation that rankled Almagro when he learned about it. Pizarro recruited his brothers and other men from his hometown of Trujillo before returning to Panama.

In late December 1530, Pizarro again sailed south from Panama, at the head of less than 200 men. Almagro was to follow with reinforcements. Pizarro's force, reinforced by Hernando de Soto and his men, moved slowly, only reaching Tumbez in May 1532. They discovered much of the city in ruins, destroyed by civil war. The great Sapa Inca Huayna Capac and his heir had died unexpectedly several years earlier, perhaps from the first smallpox epidemic that devastated mainland South America. Huayna Capac's death (and that of his heir) sparked a dynastic dispute between two of his sons, Huascar and Atahualpa, and their supporting factions. Atahualpa gained the upper hand in the war, and his army captured Huascar. The resulting animosity created bitter divisions, which the Spaniards were able to exploit.

Leaving a small detachment on the coast, Pizarro and a force of 62 men on horseback and 106 on foot pushed up into the mountains toward Cajamarca to meet Atahualpa and his army. Having talked tactics with Hernando Cortés in Spain, Pizarro knew how the Spaniards had seized the Aztec ruler Moctezuma in Mexico; he probably hoped to follow Cortés's example and capture the Inca ruler Atahualpa. The Inca ruler, on the other hand, seemed little concerned with the Spaniards, but sent them ceramic fortresses and plucked fowls as intimidating messages. As commander of tens of thousands of Andean warriors, he was confident the small band of Spaniards posed little threat. The Spaniards reached Cajamarca in mid-November 1532 and occupied it, whereupon Pizarro sent a squadron under his brother Hernando and Hernando de Soto to greet the Inca ruler, who was encamped at thermal baths nearby. Atahualpa agreed to come to Cajamarca the following day to meet with Pizarro.

Accompanied by several thousand ceremonially armed guards, Atahualpa entered Cajamarca on the afternoon of November 16. The contingent was too large to fit in the central plaza, where Pizarro sent out Father Vicente de Valverde to meet with the Sapa Inca. Valverde explained the *Requerimiento*, which informed the Inca that the Christian God, through the pope, had granted sovereignty over the Andes to the Spanish monarchs; and that he, Atahualpa, must submit to Pizarro, their emissary. When Atahualpa angrily rejected Valverde's bizarre demand, the Spaniards stormed into the plaza from surrounding buildings where they had been hiding. They slaughtered the bodyguards and took Atahualpa prisoner. In a futile attempt to free himself, Atahualpa offered to fill a room with gold and twice with silver. Pizarro greedily agreed, but after llama teams carried in the treasure, he refused to release his prisoner. Meanwhile, fearing the Spaniards would liberate Huascar and make him ruler of Tawantinsuyu (the Inca realm), Atahualpa ordered the execution of his brother. Thus, rather than trying to unite the Andean population against the invaders, Atahualpa strengthened the animosity of the Huascar faction against himself.

Meanwhile, small Spanish parties, assisted by Huascar's faction, began to reconnoiter southward. Hernando Pizarro led a party to the central coast, where they plundered the great religious shrine of Pachacamac. Hernando de Soto and a few others went to Cuzco, the capital of Tawantinsuyu. Back at Cajamarca, Pizarro gathered the treasure provided by Atahualpa and readied it for distribution among the men. The Spaniards melted down the gold and silver objects to make ingots. They carefully set aside the royal fifth for King Charles I (Holy Roman Emperor Charles V) and then divided the remainder among themselves. Francisco Pizarro received the greatest share, more than 600 pounds of gold and almost 1,300 pounds of silver. Horsemen received more than foot soldiers, and Almagro's men, who had not been present at Cajamarca for the capture of Atahualpa, did not receive part of the ransom, much to their resentment. At this point, Pizarro decided, given the support of Huascar's people, that he no longer needed his royal captive. False reports that Atahualpa had ordered one of his generals to raise an army and attack the Spaniards made Pizarro so anxious that he decided to eliminate the Sapa Inca. Following a quick, irregular trial, the Spanish condemned Atahualpa to die by fire at the stake. Father Valverde promised Atahualpa that if he converted to Christianity, the Spaniards would strangle rather than burn him. He consequently accepted baptism, probably to preserve his body, as the Incas worshiped the mummified remains of dead rulers. Despite the conquistadors' attempts to justify the execution, King Charles I remained unimpressed by the rationale for the regicide.

Soon after Atahualpa's execution on July 26, 1533, Pizarro installed a puppet ruler, Tupac Huallpa, and then moved his forces toward Cuzco. As the expedition approached Jauja, it finally confronted serious resistance. An army led by Yucra-Huallpa tried to block the Spanish march but lacked tactics for combating the Spaniards' cavalry. The horsemen gave the conquistadors tremendous mobility, and the cavalry devastated indigenous forces in open areas. After the massacre at Jauja, Pizarro bivouacked his forces there for a couple of weeks, during which time Tupac Huallpa unexpectedly died. Anxious to reach Cuzco, Pizarro left the slower-moving parts of his expedition at Jauja, converting the city into the first Spanish capital of Peru. He ordered treasurer Alonso Riquelme to command the rearguard and to watch over the booty, while the horsemen pushed ahead. Drawing near Cuzco, a lead party under Hernando de Soto reached the Apurimac River and found the suspension bridge had been destroyed. They forded the river unopposed, but their recklessness and Andean tactical adaptability caused a near disaster for the Spaniards. At Vilcaconga, on November 8, 1533, with de Soto's party tired and separated from each other as they climbed a ridge, General Quisquis attacked. The Indians rolled rocks down on the Spaniards, and with the horses' maneuverability limited by the terrain, managed to engage the Spaniards on more equal footing. Only nightfall and the arrival of Spanish reinforcements the following morning saved de Soto and his men.

A week later, on November 15, Pizarro's force entered Cuzco and occupied the Inca capital. The following month, the Spanish conferred the royal fringe on Manco Inca, another of Huayna Capac's sons, who seemed eager to cooperate with the conquistadors. Indeed, during the following two years, the Spaniards managed to consolidate their hold over the Andes with relatively little overt opposition. In June 1534 Sebastián Benalcázar took Quito, the stronghold of Atahualpa's power. Recognizing that he needed a city on the coast to facilitate communication and trade with Panama, on January 6, 1535, Pizarro founded the City of Kings where the Rimac River flowed into the Pacific near Pachacamac. The new settlement became the capital of Peru and eventually was better known as Lima. In mid-1535 Pizarro and Almagro managed to paper over their resentments and decided that Almagro should lead a new expedition to explore and conquer the region south of Cuzco. He and his supporters departed for Chile in July 1535 and wandered for two fruitless years, much of it in the arid wastelands of the Atacama Desert. Meanwhile, Pizarro rewarded his men with *encomien-*

das, grants of indigenous labor and tribute; the Spaniards took indigenous women as mistresses and occasionally as wives. Colonial society began to emerge.

As the oppressive nature of that society became more and more obvious, Manco Inca rebelled. He secretly ordered a huge army, perhaps as many as 100,000 strong, to assemble near Cuzco. The siege of the Inca capital began on May 6, 1536, with the Spaniards and their indigenous allies, commanded by Hernando Pizarro, fighting desperately to hold the city. Waves of Spanish adventurers arrived from Panama, attracted by the stories of fortunes to be won in the Andes. Francisco Pizarro sent them as reinforcements to Cuzco, but hundreds of recruits were killed in ambushes on the way. In mid-1536 a rebel force under Quizo Yupanqui destroyed a Spanish relief expedition. Even Lima came briefly under attack. The Incas vowed to drive all Christians from Tawantinsuyu, and the fighting was horrific. Both sides mutilated prisoners, and the Spaniards intentionally killed the warriors' wives who accompanied Manco's armies to provide the fighters with logistical support. Manco believed his vast numbers would win a war of attrition, yet he failed to capture Cuzco despite besieging it for nearly a year. Although the Incas adapted somewhat to the challenge of Spanish steel and horses, Manco and his warriors remained a stone-age army in terms of their weaponry. They also waged war according to the religious and agricultural calendar, interrupting the campaign to celebrate rituals and even disbanding their forces and allowing the warriors to return to their fields at planting and harvesting times.

In early 1537, with his army's strength waning, Manco withdrew northward to

Vilcabamba, a tacit recognition that the attempt to drive the Spaniards from Peru had failed. At roughly the same time, Almagro's force returned from Chile. It had found no reward for the hardships it endured. Bitter against Pizarro, Almagro opened negotiations with Manco in the hope of forming an alliance to take Peru from his old partner. However, Manco refused to trust either Spanish faction and left the Pizarrists and Almagrists to fight. Almagro seized Cuzco but was then defeated at the battle of the Salt Pits (April 26, 1538) and executed by Hernando Pizarro. Three years later, in 1541, Almagrists broke into Francisco Pizarro's home in Lima and assassinated him. Meanwhile, Manco established a neo-Inca state in Vilcabamba, which managed to survive until 1572, when its last ruler, Túpac Amaru, was captured and executed. That brutal act ended Inca rule in the Andes, but any real possibility of reviving Tawantinsuyu had died when Manco lifted the siege of Cuzco in 1537.

Kendall W. Brown

References

Cieza de León, Pedro de. *The Discovery and Conquest of Peru: Chronicles of the New World Encounter.* Translated by Alexandra Parma Cook and Noble David Cook. Durham, NC: Duke University Press, 1998.

Guilmartin, John F. "The Cutting Edge: An Analysis of the Spanish Invasion and Overthrow of the Inca Empire, 1532–1539." Pp. 40–69 in *Transatlantic Encounters: Europeans and Andeans in the Sixteenth Century,* edited by Kenneth J. Andrien and Rolena Adorno. Berkeley and Los Angeles: University of California Press, 1991.

Hemming, John. *The Conquest of the Incas.* New York: Harcourt, 1970.

Pizarro, Pedro. *Relation of the Discovery and Conquest of the Kingdoms of Peru.* Translated by Philip Ainsworth Means. New York: Krause Reprint, 1969.

Prescott, William H. *History of the Conquest of Peru.* New York: Dutton, 1968.

Varón Gabai, Rafael. *Francisco Pizarro and His Brothers: The Illusion of Power in Sixteenth-Century Peru.* Translated by Javier Flores Espinoza. Norman: University of Oklahoma Press, 1997.

Zárate, Agustín de. *A History of the Discovery and Conquest of Peru, Books I–IV.* Translated by Thomas Nicholas. London: Penguin, 1933.

See also: Bolivia; Catholic Church in Spanish America; Chile; Civil Wars—Peru; Colonists and Settlers I—Andes; Columbian Exchange—Disease; Conquest II–VII; Conquistadors; Diabolism in the New World; El Dorado; Ecuador; Encomienda; Idolatry, Extirpation of; Mining—Silver; Mita; Native Americans V—Central and Southern Andes; Panama; Peru; Potosí; Requerimiento; Yanancona.

CONQUEST II—BRAZIL

Historians often characterize the early years of Portuguese expansion to South America as a period of "discovery and colonization," rarely employing the term *conquest.* After all, nothing in Brazil resembled the spectacular collapses of the Aztec Triple Alliance or the Inca Empire of Tawantinsuyu, two events that set the measure for this term. But this contrast can be misleading, because the Portuguese struggle for control over indigenous land, labor, and souls shared many of the same characteristics present in the conquest of nonimperial societies throughout the territories that were to become Spanish America. Dispersed and discontinuous, spanning decades and even centuries, the subordination of indigenous peoples to colonial rule constitutes an important chapter in Brazilian history, one that has commanded surprisingly little attention from historians.

A growing awareness of indigenous rights and history has reshaped the vocabulary used to describe Portuguese-Indian relations; terms such as *invasion, conquest,* and *decimation* constitute important catchwords among activists. But the term *conquest* has deeper roots and was meaningful from other perspectives already in colonial times. Beginning in the sixteenth century, the Portuguese Crown referred to its overseas possessions as "conquests." In their narratives, Jesuit missionaries often referred to their activities as a "spiritual conquest." And private colonists, in their petitions for royal favors and privileges, on many occasions described their exploits as the "conquest of heathen peoples." Early historical accounts from the seventeenth and eighteenth centuries include long descriptions of countless battles between Europeans and Indians. According to Sebastião da Rocha Pita, an eighteenth-century historian, the vast expanses that the king had granted to the colonists in leagues had to be won inch by inch in bloody confrontations with native peoples.

Subordination by force of arms was a key feature in colonial narratives of conquest, but Portuguese-Indian relations entailed a far more intricate web of exchange, alliance, warfare, slavery, and conversion. Following Cabral's initial landfall in 1500, Portuguese, French, and Spanish traders maintained sporadic contacts with coastal Tupi-Guaraní speakers, although a handful of European castaways, exiled criminals, and interpreters settled among the Indians for more protracted periods. In the 1530s, alarmed by a growing French presence along the coast, the Portuguese Crown decided to promote settlement through the distribution of fifteen hereditary captain-cies to private proprietors. Few captaincies developed on any significant scale before the second half of the sixteenth century, either because of their proprietors' indifference or because the settlers failed to guarantee alliances with local Tupi polities. Pernambuco and São Vicente constituted the two main exceptions, as the Portuguese established strong pacts with powerful Tupi groups in these captaincies. As in Spanish America, where alliances played a critical role in the dynamics of conquest, Portuguese-Tupi pacts in coastal Brazil contributed to the military defeat and political subordination of enemy Tupi-Guaraní and Ge-speaking peoples. At the same time, the deployment of indigenous warriors against enemy groups became an important strategy for supplying slaves to sugar mills, which developed precociously in these two captaincies during the 1540s and 1550s.

In 1549, the establishment of royal government in Salvador and the arrival of the first Jesuit missionaries introduced important new elements that reshaped the conditions for subjecting indigenous peoples to colonial control. While private slaving expeditions continued to thrive on many fronts well into the eighteenth century, protective legislation and the emergence of missions began to place constraints on such initiatives by the 1550s. During Mem de Sá's term as governor (1558–1572), the Portuguese consolidated the conquest of coastal Tupi peoples from Pernambuco to São Vicente. The Portuguese unleashed three forces (albeit one unwittingly) in their onslaught: soldiers recruited among the allies, the Jesuit "Soldiers of Christ," and a microscopic army of deadly pathogens. Although the Crown and the Jesuits took a stand against Indian slavery, the governor and his successors pursued an aggressive policy of subordinating indigenous peoples to direct colonial control, permitting the enslavement of "rebellious" groups subject to the prosecution of just wars, while forcing many others to resettle in *aldeias* (mission villages) within the colonial sphere.

Designed as Christian communities under the strict control of Jesuit and, to a lesser degree, Franciscan missionaries, these mission villages provided an alternative to the indiscriminate enslavement of indigenous peoples. Similar to resettlement policies in Spanish America, the aldeia project in Brazil was supposed to supply a mandatory, rotating draft of wage laborers to the colonial economy. But the plan failed, both as a social experiment and as a reliable source of labor, as disease, flight, and conflicts between Jesuits and private colonists hit the missions hard. A smallpox and measles epidemic cycle raged along the coast in the early 1560s, claiming an especially large toll in the vicinity of Salvador, Bahia. These cataclysmic conditions led several groups to flee from the missions and to attempt to reconstruct the fragments of their social order far away from the Portuguese, in places like the Ibiapaba Hills of Ceará, coastal Maranhão, the mouth of the Amazon, and the middle Amazon Valley. Reencountered by French and Portuguese missionaries and backwoodsmen in the seventeenth century, these groups retained a bitter memory of the conquest.

The political and military realignment of indigenous polities within the colonial context played a significant part in several other episodes during the sixteenth and early seventeenth centuries. By the 1560s, the Tupi-speaking Temiminós had emerged as a powerful group supporting Portuguese efforts to take control over Guanabara Bay. The site was a French colony, established in 1555, and a stronghold of the Tamoio Indians, a Tupi group that had redefined its ethnic boundaries in its opposition to Portuguese rule. The Portuguese dislodged the main French settlement in 1560 but did not gain full control of Rio de Janeiro until 1567, and they still faced pockets of Tamoio resistance well into the 1570s, when this group was reduced to a few hundred slaves.

Rewarded for his role in the conquest of Rio de Janeiro, Temiminó leader Martim Afonso Arariboia struggled to carve out a place for his people within the colonial sphere, but their role as independent allies had shifted to one of colonial subordination, as they became confined to a mission village. In northeastern Brazil, as the sugar economy expanded and began to demand new sources of indigenous labor, the Portuguese and their Tobajara allies in Pernambuco began an important cycle of conquest in the 1570s, starting with the captaincies of Paraíba and Rio Grande do Norte and culminating at the mouth of the Amazon. Although it was not always possible to distinguish between private slave raids and officially sanctioned expeditions against declared enemies, Tupi groups who maintained relations with the French bore the brunt of this northward expansion. The Caetés, a group held responsible for slaying and eating Brazil's first bishop in 1556, faced relentless assaults, especially after a "just war" had been proclaimed against them in 1562, allowing for their legal enslavement and leading to their complete annihilation by the 1580s.

The Potiguars proved to be more powerful adversaries, holding off numerous Portuguese, mestizo, and indigenous forays to the end of the century. While several Potiguar groups sought refuge in the remote backlands, others assented to a peace agreement in 1599, becoming Christian vassals entrusted to Franciscan missions. The charismatic leader Zorobabé reoriented his military skills to serve colonial aims, commanding a mixed force of 1,300 Potiguars and Tobajaras against the Ge-speaking Aimoré, a constellation of groups who continued to resist in Ilhéus and Porto Seguro. In spite of Zorobabé's service to the Crown and to local sugar planters, however, Portuguese authorities still considered him to be a threat and exiled him to Portugal, where he died in prison. Other Potiguar military commanders were to play a significant role in later exploits, fighting for both the Portuguese and the Dutch on both sides of the Atlantic during the West India Company's occupation of Pernambuco (1630–1654) and Angola (1641–1648).

In a sense, the Portuguese occupation of Ceará, Maranhão, and Pará in the early seventeenth century completed the conquest of the Atlantic seaboard, although a few groups (like the Tremembés) were not subdued until much later. A continuation of the northward push from Pernambuco, this process included the expulsion of yet another French colony established on the island of Saint Louis (immediately renamed São Luís) in 1615 and the establishment of Belém at the mouth of the Amazon one year later. But the presence of Tupinambá groups who had migrated away from the Portuguese in the previous century posed the greatest challenge, and their defeat by private colonists and their indigenous subordinates echoed the feats of conquering bands in Spanish America. Not surprisingly, since Portugal and its possessions were subject to Spanish kings during the Iberian Union (1580–1640), the enterprise was couched explicitly in the vocabulary of conquest. In the 1620s, both private colonists and the municipal council of São Luís adopted yet another term that evoked Spanish institutional forms, expressing a wish to hold conquered Indians in *encomienda,* making explicit reference to similar practices in the "Indies of Castile."

During the seventeenth and eighteenth centuries, the location of conquest shifted to the *sertão,* or backlands. Private expeditions, usually without any official sanction, employed a mix of force and persuasion in displacing populations from their homelands and resettling them on rural estates or in missions. These expeditions, commanded by experienced backwoodsmen (*sertanistas*), received material support from colonists interested in acquiring labor, or from religious orders interested in replenishing mission populations. São Paulo and other nearby towns became the staging grounds for scores of overland expeditions, while in the northern colony of Maranhão and Pará, canoe flotillas known as *tropas de resgate* (ransom troops) plied Amazonian waterways for captives and converts. These expeditions rarely possessed direct territorial designs, but they did contribute to the dislocation and devastation of countless indigenous peoples.

Confrontations were more intense in regions where territorial designs were involved, as they were in cattle country or in gold-prospecting zones. Cattle expansion into the northeastern interior led to the so-called Guerra dos Bárbaros (Barbarians' War), a constellation of armed conflicts that raged from the 1680s to the 1710s. Based on their notoriety as backwoodsmen and Indian fighters, royal authorities recruited *Paulistas* (colonists from São Paulo) and their indigenous soldiers to wage a brutal campaign against the Cariris and other rebellious groups. Conquest in this case entailed bloody massacres, the enslavement of captives, and the confinement of shattered societies in missions. On the far western frontier of Mato Grosso, the early eighteenth-century gold rush brought on the stiff resistance of Paiaguás, Guaicurus, and Southern Kayapos. Once again the Crown prescribed harsh treatment, promoting the organization of punitive *bandeiras* (armed expeditions) and thus underwriting some of the most violent confrontations in Brazilian history.

Frontier violence also characterized late colonial territorial expansion, both in the "forbidden lands" on the eastern fringe of the Minas Gerais gold-mining region and on the cattle front to the southwest of São Paulo. Although it seemed somewhat anachronistic, the Crown issued orders in 1808 much along the lines of the old "just war" sanctions, permitting military actions against Botocudo and Kaingang groups and allowing for the enslavement of war captives. One episode in southern Brazil fittingly became known as the conquest of Guarapuava, which shows that at the end of the colonial period, the ideals and practices associated with conquest remained in force. Even after independence, in spite of humanitarian outcry and projects to promote the "civilization" of the Indians, government officials and private interests in various provinces continued to outfit bandeiras and consciously carried the violent tradition of conquest into modern times.

John M. Monteiro

References

Abreu, J. Capistrano de. *Chapters of Brazil's Colonial History, 1500–1800.* Translated by Arthur Brakel. New York: Oxford University Press, 1997.

Davidson, David. "How the Brazilian West Was Won: Freelance and State on the Mato Grosso Frontier, 1737–1752." Pp. 61–106 in *Colonial Roots of Modern Brazil,* edited by D. Alden. Berkeley and Los Angeles: University of California Press, 1973.

Hemming, John. *Red Gold: The Conquest of the Brazilian Indians, 1500–1760.* Cambridge: Harvard University Press, 1978.

———. *Amazon Frontier: The Defeat of the Brazilian Indians.* Cambridge: Harvard University Press, 1987.

Langfur, Hal. "Uncertain Refuge: Frontier Formation and the Origins of the Botocudo War in Late Colonial Brazil." *Hispanic American Historical Review* 82, no. 2 (2002): 215–256.

Monteiro, John M. "The Crises and Transformations of Invaded Societies: Coastal Brazil in the Sixteenth Century." Pp. 973–1023 in *The Cambridge History of the Native Peoples of the Americas.* Vol. 3, *South America, Part I,* edited by F. Salomon and S. Schwartz. Cambridge: Cambridge University Press, 1999.

Schwartz, Stuart. "Indian Labor and New World Plantations: European Demands and Indian Responses in Northeastern Brazil." *American Historical Review* 83, no. 3 (1978): 43–79.

Wright, Robin, et al. "Destruction, Resistance, and Transformation—Southern, Coastal, and Northern Brazil (1580–1890)." Pp. 287–381 in *The Cambridge History of the Native Peoples of the Americas.* Vol. 3, *South America, Part II,* edited by F. Salomon and S. Schwartz. Cambridge: Cambridge University Press, 1999.

See also: Amazon; Bandeirantes; Cannibalism; Catholic Church in Brazil; Colonists and Settlers II—Brazil; Columbian Exchange—Disease; Conquest I, III–VII; Conquistadors; Donatary Captaincies; Dyes and Dyewood; Encomienda; Engenho; Enlightenment—Brazil; Independence II—Brazil; Jesuits—Brazil; Missions; Monarchs of Portugal; Native Americans I–II; Sugar.

CONQUEST III—CARIBBEAN

For the quarter century following Columbus's discovery of 1492, the Spanish conquest of the Caribbean Sea and Gulf of Mexico region spread outward from Hispaniola in the northeast to the mainland (Tierra Firme) in the southwest, with lateral moves into the other Greater Antilles; it then shifted to the northwest to Mexico and Central America, with conquests moving north from Panama and southeast from Mexico. Venezuela and Colombia followed, beginning in 1528. The coasts of Florida and the Gulf coasts were explored in 1519; however, they offered few human or other resources to attract Spanish conquistadors. Christopher Columbus's discoveries and geographical theories largely set this sequence of events in motion.

Columbus's first two voyages established that Cuba, Hispaniola, and, less certainly, Puerto Rico had large numbers of native inhabitants, gold, and various plants whose uses were uncertain but that were presumed to be of medicinal or other value. Jamaica, explored in conjunction with the second voyage, lacked gold. These large islands also seemed to offer ecological conditions suitable for European animals and plants. Columbus's third voyage included the discovery of the South American mainland (which Columbus thought was a great island off the southwestern coast of Asia), a pearl fishery, hints of goldfields farther west along the present Venezuelan and Colombian coasts, and large numbers of native peoples. The Lesser Antilles were too small and sparsely populated to attract Spanish conquistadors, who sought goods for trade and islands with dense native populations to exploit their labor. Intended to prove that the open water southwest of Jamaica led to India,

Columbus's fourth voyage in 1502–1503 instead revealed Honduras and Central America; with these discoveries Columbus found new evidence of gold.

Rodrigo de Bastidas and Juan de La Cosa may have reached the same point in 1501 coming from the east, thereby closing the Caribbean Sea on the south and west, even though Columbus claimed his last voyage had taken him to a point on the Indochinese coast. Bastidas and Cosa had earlier found pearl fisheries, some pockets of Native Americans, and even gold along the northern coast of South America in areas west of Columbus's landfalls on his third voyage. They also had bartered for gold at the Gulf of Urabá, somewhat farther east than Columbus's last discovery. Because of Columbus's stress on sailing southwest to reach India, the resources of the Gulf of Mexico's shores remained unknown to Europeans until 1519, when Alonso Álvarez de Pineda coasted its shores and reported that they had nothing of value until one reached the northern coasts of Mexico. Thus, where Columbus had been, and not been, shaped Spanish knowledge of the resources of the Caribbean proper for a generation.

Hispaniola became the first focus of Spanish efforts. Landing with some 1,200 men in 1494, Columbus and one of his chief lieutenants, Alonso de Ojeda, soon began a military conquest aimed at seizing control of the goldfields and eliminating the cacique blamed for the deaths of the men Columbus had left at La Navidad in 1492. This first aggression began episodic warfare with local rulers, a war that Nicolás de Ovando finally brought to an end with a systematic conquest of the island's peoples in 1502–1504. Columbus's initial victories were followed by the imposition of a tribute per adult of a hawks-bell of gold every three months, or the equivalent in spices or cotton. The tribute in turn led to a census of sorts in late 1495 or early 1496, which indicated over a million Native American inhabitants, a number apparently already reduced by Old World diseases and Spanish cruelty.

By the time of Columbus's arrest and return to Spain in chains in 1499, Spaniards had established labor tributes and begun systematically to work placer mines using this labor. Successive administrations, notably Ovando's, readily reassigned labor pools (usually by cacique) according to political considerations dictated largely in Spain. This instability of tenure created an incentive for miners, and men who had Indians to "rent" to them, to exploit mercilessly a rapidly diminishing native population. In Spain, the government issued laws intended to make the relationship like that of the *encomienda,* a system of control, tribute, and (in exchange) cultural tutelage and military and juridical protection. Although subsequently brought under greater legal and administrative control than ever was the case on Hispaniola, this institutionalized exaction of labor set the pattern until the 1530s and 1540s, when the Dominicans' outcry against the reality of often brutal exploitation of native peoples finally, together with the dramatic decline in their numbers, brought about changes in the relationship between Spaniards and Indians.

Columbus's disgrace provided the opening that allowed the Crown to undo the overly generous privileges it had granted him in 1492. Not only were he and his brother replaced as governors of Hispaniola and his other discoveries, an effort was made to break his claims to the pearl fishery at the Gulf of Paría. The means were the so-called Andalusian, or minor, voyages of 1499–1502 along the coasts of modern Venezuela and Colombia in search of pearls and new goldfields. Alonso de Ojeda, Juan de la Cosa, Cristóbal Guerra, Rodrigo de Bastidas, and others pushed the frontier of knowledge westward to the base of the Isthmus of Panama. These early voyages quickly garnered vast quantities of pearls, but found little gold except at Río de la Hacha (Colombia). Instead, a slave-raiding industry began to feed the needs of the gold mines on Hispaniola.

With the new geographic knowledge at hand from these voyages, the Spanish Crown formulated a plan to explore the unknown area north and west of Honduras in search of a strait that would lead to Asia, and also conquer the mainland, or Tierra Firme. Alonso de Ojeda, Juan de la Cosa, and Martin Fernández de Enciso were given the contract for Urabá and points east (mostly the coast of Colombia) and Diego de Nicuesa was granted Veragua, the area west of Urabá. The Gulf of Urabá divided the grants. Sailing from Spain in 1509, these expeditions quickly fell apart, leaving only 100–200 survivors and reinforcements at Santa María la Antigua de Darien, on the western side of the Gulf of Urabá. Blasco Núñez de Balboa emerged as the leader of this "colony." To the north, Vicente Yáñez Pinzón and Juan Díaz de Solís may have sailed west from Honduras and then north along the coast of Yucatán, perhaps even entering the Gulf of Mexico. But there was no follow-up on whatever they found for almost another decade.

When Balboa informed the Crown in 1513 of the existence of the Pacific Ocean and the potential riches in gold and pearls of eastern Panama, the conquest of the region began in earnest. The man entrusted to bring Spanish rule to the goldfields of Panama, and ultimately of southern Central America, was Pedro Arias de Avila (Pedrarias). A courtier who went to Darien from Spain in 1514 with about 1,400 persons, Pedrarias and his party quickly established a reputation for ruthlessness in their search for gold and food. He also executed Vasco Nuñez de Balboa. This campaign was also the first to use the *Requerimiento* (a brief history of the world establishing that the pope had the right to grant the kings of Spain dominion over the Americas and calling on the native peoples to accept both papal and Spanish royal authority, or incur a "just war" for their disobedience).

In 1519, having exhausted the human and mineral resources of eastern Panama and coveting the pearls reported to exist off its southern, Pacific coast, Pedrarias moved his headquarters to an Indian village on the Pacific (at old Panama City). The same pattern of raiding expeditions for shares of the loot was used to extend Spanish hegemony farther west. Then, in 1522, Gil González arrived with orders to explore the Pacific. In the face of Pedrarias's opposition, he did so, discovering the west coast of Central America as far as the Gulf of Fonseca (Honduras) and beginning the conquest of Nicaragua. Gold and slaves were the main objects of interest to the conquistadors who attacked Nicaragua and Costa Rica. The slaves went mostly to supply the new sugar plantations on Hispaniola.

While the conquest of Panama was thus beginning, Diego Colón, Columbus's legitimate son and heir, claimed his father's privileges and was appointed governor of Hispaniola (1508); he also filed and won his lawsuit against the Crown in 1511. Established at Santo Domingo in 1509, Diego tried to guard the family claim to the Antilles by sending agents to conquer Jamaica (1509) and then Cuba (1511). Juan Ponce de León's occupation of Puerto Rico (begun in 1508) was brought under Colón's government as well. To meet labor needs on Hispaniola, other Spaniards already were slaving in the Bahamas, Lesser Antilles, the islands off the coast of Venezuela, and even the Venezuelan mainland (and occasionally the North American mainland as well).

The move into Cuba proved to be the prelude to the discovery and then conquest of New Spain, modern Mexico. By 1510, mariners and mapmakers knew that Cuba was an island, and not a peninsula of Asia. Exactly when Yucatán and Florida were first observed by sailors is not known. But in 1517, Diego Velázquez de Cuéllar, Colón's governor of Cuba, sent Francisco Hernández de Córdoba on a voyage that explored Yucatán as far as Champotón on its west coast. The discovery of Mayan cities encouraged the organization of a second expedition in 1518; this one was led by one of Velázquez's relatives, Juan de Grijalva. Grijalva's lieutenant, Pedro de Alvarado, explored as far as the Río Pánuco, where he found abundant evidence of gold and highly developed societies. Grijalva also made a first contact with representatives of the Aztec Empire.

Grijalva's discoveries led Velázquez to commission Hernando Cortés and several hundred volunteers to trade and explore; however, he also allowed Cortés some discretion should unforeseen circumstances appear. Not only did Cortés seize control of the expedition when Velázquez tried to replace him before he set sail, but he also arranged for his men to found a town

(Veracruz) and elect him as their military leader. Scuttling all but one ship, which he sent to Spain with news of his discovery and projected conquest, together with a request (and bribe money) for royal confirmation of his independent authority, Cortés marched the bulk of his force inland. Over the next two years (1519–1521), and aided by thousands of native allies and an outbreak of smallpox, Cortés and his men conquered Tenochtitlan and the Mexica-Azteca Empire.

The Venezuelan and Colombian coast came under Spanish occupation in the late 1520s, as expeditions founded settlements and then went inland in search of gold. In 1528 men from Hispaniola founded Coro, Venezuela, which the following year became the base for further conquest, which evolved in 1535 into Nicolas Federmann's expedition into central Colombia. In 1529 Rodrigo de Bastidas led men from Hispaniola to settle Santa Marta; and finally, in 1533 Pedro de Heredia's expedition founded Cartagena. It too became a base for expeditions into central Colombia. As was the case in Yucatán, so too in Venezuela and Colombia the conquest of native peoples dragged on into the 1540s, and in some places even later.

Yucatán and the northern coast of South America were the last significant areas of the Caribbean to be conquered. Florida and the northern Gulf of Mexico had a different history, although a number of expeditions attempted conquest during the early sixteenth century. The Spaniards never controlled the entire Florida peninsula, and except for some attacks on native populations in northeast Florida and Georgia between 1565 and 1602, their "conquest" was entirely a matter of a Spanish settlement and missions. The northern Gulf of Mexico coast finally came under their partial control with the settlement of Pensacola (1698), the founding of missions and San Antonio in eastern Texas (1719), the acquisition of part of French Louisiana (1763), and the military conquest of British West Florida (Pensacola to the Mississippi River) in 1779–1781.

Paul E. Hoffman

References

Anderson, Charles L. *Old Panama and Castilla del Oro: A Narrative History of the Discovery, Conquest, and Settlement by the Spaniards of Panama, Darien, Veragua, Santo Domingo, Santa Marta, Cartagena, Nicaragua, and Peru*. Washington, DC: Sudwarth, 1911.

Chamberlain, Robert S. *The Conquest and Colonization of Yucatán*. Washington, DC, 1948.

Floyd, Troy. *The Columbus Dynasty in the Caribbean, 1492–1526*. Albuquerque: University of New Mexico Press, 1973.

Parry, J. H. *The Discovery of South America*. New York: Taplinger, 1979.

Sauer, Carl O. *The Early Spanish Main*. Berkeley and Los Angeles: University of California Press, 1966.

Sherman, William L. *Forced Native Labor in Sixteenth-Century Central America*. Lincoln: University of Nebraska Press, 1979.

Simpson, Lesley Byrd. *The Encomienda in New Spain: The Beginning of Spanish Mexico*. Rev. and enlarged ed. Berkeley and Los Angeles: University of California Press, 1950.

Vigneras, Louis Andre. *The Discovery of South America and the Andalusian Voyages*. Chicago: University of Chicago Press, 1976.

See also: Borderlands; Caciques; Catholic Church in Spanish America; Colombia; Colonists and Settlers III—Caribbean; Columbian Exchange—Disease; Conquest I–II, IV–VII; Conquistadors; Cuba; El Dorado; Encomienda; Explorers; Florida; Hispaniola; Honduras; Missions; Native Americans III—Caribbean; Panama; Pirates and Piracy; Puerto Rico; Requerimiento; Venezuela; War of the Spanish Succession.

CONQUEST IV—CENTRAL AMERICA

Spanish efforts to conquer Central America began with the ill-fated campaign of Rodrigo de Bastidas in 1501 and continued until roughly 1540, by which time disease had ravaged the isthmus and most of the area had been pacified. Colonization began in earnest in the 1540s, although the borders and Spanish institutional jurisdictions continued to shift until 1570, when the final shape of the Kingdom of Guatemala was determined and its *audiencia* was established, extending from Chiapas through Costa Rica. By that time demographic devastation and dislocation posed serious challenges for both natives and Spaniards in the creation of a functioning colonial society.

The climate and geography of Central America determined much of the region's social and demographic structure both prior to and after European contact. A chain of mountains runs along the Pacific edge of the isthmus of Central America, creating highland areas of mostly temperate, but some cold, climates. These areas are greatest in Guatemala and Chiapas, but can be found throughout the isthmus. Nicaragua, by contrast, offers some of the lowest and most tropical lands in the region. Most of this mountain range provides for a narrow Pacific costal plain, while to the east, low-lying plains, swamps, and forests extend to the Caribbean coasts. The Pacific region tended to be far more densely populated and agriculturally developed than the Caribbean. The Pacific was aided by a mixture of dry and rainy seasons and multiple climatic zones, allowing for more varied and productive agriculture and the development of larger, more complex, and more diversified communities and social structures. Among these communities were the Mayas in Chiapas, Guatemala and northwestern Honduras, the Pipils in southeastern Guatemala and El Salvador, the Lencas in Honduras and El Salvador, the Chorotegas and Nicaraos of western Nicaragua, and the Huetars and Chorotegas in Costa Rica. The Caribbean, by contrast, faced more insistent rains and more limited climatic variations and consequently sustained smaller and less hierarchically organized groups of inhabitants. These included the Payas, Sumus, and Xicaques in Honduras; the Matagalpas, Sumus, and Ramas in Nicaragua; and the Guaymís, Chirripós, and Bribris in Costa Rica.

Central America never rivaled New Spain (Mexico) or Peru for wealth or importance to the Spanish Empire. Except for Honduras and Nicaragua, the region lacked great mineral wealth, and even these areas offered little competition for the rich silver mines of Zacatecas or Potosí. Although dyestuffs (e.g., cochineal and indigo), cacaos, and sugar eventually propelled the region's economy, especially in the eighteenth century, it remained a peripheral region of the empire throughout the colonial period. These problems were exacerbated by Central America's geography, which pointed its economic and demographic development toward the Pacific, whereas the centers of imperial importance faced out toward the Atlantic Ocean. This same geography also made most of eastern Central America too costly to colonize. Indeed, the Spanish never conquered much of the Caribbean region of the isthmus.

Spaniards first encountered the great cultures of the Americas in Central America. Rodrigo de Bastidas is credited with making the earliest contact with the region when he sailed to the southern border of modern Panama in 1501; however, it was Christopher Columbus's fourth voyage in 1502 that made the first great reconnoiter of the Caribbean side of the isthmus. Columbus initially happened upon the Bay Islands of Honduras, where his men captured a large native trading canoe. This capture hinted at the commercial potential of the region, but the rest of Columbus's southward voyage along the eastern shore of the isthmus led away from the more densely populated zones. Exaggerated reports of riches led Columbus to name one of the lands Costa Rica, an implicit claim that whetted the appetites of subsequent conquistadors.

In 1509, the Spanish Crown authorized Diego de Nicuesa and Alonso de Ojeda to settle the isthmus, but their efforts were defeated by disease and native resistance. Nicuesa's expedition holed up in a miserable settlement called Nombre de Dios and awaited reinforcements. Ojeda, injured during the adventure, died upon his return to Hispaniola, leaving his partner Martín Fernández de Enciso to take up the colonization effort. Enciso's men organized the survivors of the failed Nicuesa and Ojeda expeditions and founded the town of Santa María la Antigua de Darién. By 1510, however, Vasco Núñez de Balboa, a stowaway on Enciso's ship, had risen to lead the Darién community. Balboa expelled Enciso and Nicuesa and sought official sanction for his leadership. Balboa reached a detente with native groups, and promoted stability in Darién, which enabled the Spaniard to attempt further exploration. Backed by fresh arrivals from Hispaniola, Balboa sought out the "South Sea" (the Pacific Ocean), where native accounts promised new riches. He reached

the shores of the Pacific in 1513, claiming it and all bordering lands for Spain.

Balboa's discovery opened a critical new phase of Spanish expansion along the western coast of the Americas, and the Crown rewarded him with the title of Adelantado (Governor) of the South Sea. Just prior to Balboa's discovery, however, Spain had named Pedro Arias de Avila (known more commonly as Pedrarias Dávila) governor of Panama. The Crown tried to avoid overlapping authorities by conceding exploration of the Pacific region to Balboa, while charging Pedrarias with the Central American isthmus to the north. Despite this, the two conquistadors feuded over the region's wealth and power, and Balboa eventually fell victim to Pedrarias's schemes to eliminate him. In 1519, in a fashion that proved typical in conquistador power struggles, Pedrarias charged Balboa with treason, and after a hurried trial, Balboa and four of his key supporters were beheaded. With Panama now firmly under his control, Pedrarias established a new capital in the somewhat cooler climes of Panama City and turned his attention to the rest of Central America.

In 1522, the Crown granted Gil González Dávila a concession to explore northward from Panama. The colony's growing role as the gateway to Pacific expansion also established it as the base for Central American conquest campaigns. Although González Dávila was disappointed by Costa Rica's failure to live up to its alluring name, his fortunes turned as he reached Nicaragua, where he encountered sedentary Nicarao and Chorotega communities and significant use of gold. Although the Chorotegas forced González Dávila to flee, the possibility that he might return to claim the governorship of Nicaragua led

Pedrarias to order Francisco Hernández de Córdoba to settle the territory on his behalf in 1524. Hernández de Córdoba did so, but after founding the towns of Granada and León, he sought to claim the territory for himself. Pedrarias responded by marching on Nicaragua and capturing and executing his erstwhile protégé. By 1524 word had reached Hernando Cortés in Mexico of Central American treasure and of threats to his continued southward conquest. Although the first expeditions southward came at the behest of Cortés, his hand-picked representative, Cristóbal de Olid, followed typical conquistador patterns and claimed independence from him. In response, Cortés mounted an expedition to bring the region under his control and punish his disloyal lieutenant.

Hernando Cortés's right-hand man, Pedro de Alvarado, led the campaign that led to the establishment of the Spanish Kingdom of Guatemala. Just as native allies and European disease had been fundamental to Cortés's success in defeating the Aztecs, so too were they for Alvarado. After he arrived in Guatemala, Alvarado's army of native soldiers was bolstered by an alliance with the Cakchiquel Mayas, who helped him to defeat their rivals, the Quichés. From there Alvarado fought to control the rest of Guatemala and El Salvador, meeting stiff resistance from the Pipils and even his onetime Cakchiquel allies. Further expansion was also limited by Alvarado's confrontations with Pedrarias, who by 1526 had control of Honduras and Nicaragua. In 1527, the Crown established two "captaincies general," one in Guatemala under Alvarado and another in Nicaragua under Pedrarias. The Crown also created the Kingdom of Guatemala, submitting to its authority the territories of Chiapas, Guatemala, Honduras, El Salvador, Nicaragua, and Costa Rica, although Costa Rica remained outside of Spanish dominion until the 1561 campaign of Juan de Cavallón. Panama's role as the conduit for the bullion emerging out of the Viceroyalty of Peru ensured that it joined this jurisdiction.

A few priests and friars followed the early conquistadors into Central America, but they mostly ministered to the Spanish themselves. Gil González Dávila's claim, in 1523, to have baptized more than 30,000 natives in Nicaragua, for example, suggests both bluster and an effort to paint the region's peoples as numerous, organized, and compliant. Certainly these early representatives of the Catholic Church made meager efforts to convert natives or prevent their abuse and enslavement at the hands of the first conquerors and *encomenderos,* whose royal grants of indigenous labor and tribute (*encomiendas*) made them the wealthiest and most powerful men in the colonies. By the late 1530s, however, a new generation of churchmen had arrived, one that intended to plant the institutional roots of the Church more firmly in the isthmus; many actively opposed Spanish cruelty and the difficulties this cruelty created for their Christianizing mission. The most famous of these men was the Dominican friar Bartolomé de las Casas, whose experiences in Nicaragua led him to return to Spain to condemn the Spanish military conquest and to argue for the New Laws of 1542, which limited the encomienda system and outlawed Indian slavery. Las Casas returned in 1543 as bishop of Chiapas, just one of several new reformist bishops in the region, including Cristóbal de Pedraza of Honduras (1542) and Antonio Valdivieso (1543). The bitterness of the struggles between the earliest conquistadors and these reformers was evident in the murder of Valdivieso by the son of Nicaragua's then-governor Rodrigo de Contreras. From his arrival, Valdivieso had condemned encomendero greed and abuse to the Crown, forcing Contreras to return to Spain.

Although the larger Pacific and highland communities of Central America had been brought under military control by the 1540s, the lowland Caribbean zones remained almost entirely outside of Spanish authority. Even in pacified zones, native groups periodically rebelled. By this point, most of the original conquistadors had died or moved to new areas in hopes of greater wealth and opportunities than Central America could provide. After years of fighting between competing Spanish conquistadors and with Central America's numerous and dispersed native peoples, the region was devastated, and economic opportunities seemed few. Demographic data on the size of the native population on the eve of Spanish contact are scarce, but estimates range from 5.6 million to 13.5 million inhabitants. However, by the end of the sixteenth century, disease, enslavement, and fighting had combined to dramatically reduce the population, albeit with wide regional variation. Estimates indicate the native population of Chiapas was reduced by 80 percent, the lowest decline in Central America. In Pacific and highland Nicaragua, by contrast, the decline in native population approached 97.5 percent.

Justin Wolfe

References

Herrera, Robinson A. *Natives, Europeans and Africans in Sixteenth-Century Santiago de Guatemala.* Austin: University of Texas Press, 2004.

MacLeod, Murdo J. *Spanish Central America: A Socioeconomic History, 1520–1720.* Berkeley and Los Angeles: University of California Press, 1973.

MacLeod, Murdo J., and Robert Wasserstrom, eds. *Spaniards and Indians in Southeastern Mesoamerica: Essays on the History of Ethnic Relations.* Lincoln: University of Nebraska Press, 1983.

Newson, Linda A. *Indian Survival in Colonial Nicaragua.* Norman: University of Oklahoma Press, 1987.

Sherman, William L. *Forced Native Labor in Sixteenth-Century Central America.* Lincoln: University of Nebraska Press, 1979.

See also: Audiencias; Cacao; Cah; Catholic Church in Spanish America; Colonists and Settlers IV—Mexico and Central America; Columbian Exchange—Disease; Conquest I–III, V–VII; Conquistadors; Costa Rica; Dyes and Dyewood; El Salvador; Encomienda; Gold; Guatemala; Hispaniola; Honduras; Native Americans IV—Mesoamerica; New Laws of 1542; Nicaragua; Panama; Potosí; Religious Orders; Silver; Slavery I–IV; Sugar.

CONQUEST V—MEXICO

The climatic event of the military conquest of Mexico was the fall of the Aztec capital, Tenochtitlan (now Mexico City). The subjugation of the remaining cities was anticlimactic; most submitted peacefully, and even those independent of the Aztecs were too weak to effectively defend themselves from Spanish conquest. Tenochtitlan's fall in 1521 ended the ninety-three years of Aztec imperial domination that had begun in 1428 with the overthrow of the Tepanecs.

Leading perhaps 450 soldiers when he landed in 1519, Hernando Cortés met the Aztecs on the Veracruz coast, where they supplied him with food and shelter. But after Cortés rejected Moctezuma's order not to come to Tenochtitlan, and the governor's request to move his camp five or six miles away, the Aztecs withdrew. Within three days, the Spaniards were approached by local Totonacs, and Cortés learned that their king disliked the Aztecs, to whom they paid tribute. Setting his course irrevocably, Cortés allied with the Totonacs, destroyed all but one ship to prevent desertion, and accepted a commission from the city council of the city he established, Villa Rica de la Vera Cruz, to lead an expedition inland. To cement this patently political gambit, Cortés sent the last ship to Spain to deliver all the gold and wealth collected thus far, rightly assuming that if he was successful, his disobedience of Cuban governor Diego Velazquez, on whose orders the expedition had been launched, would not be heeded.

Conquering Mexico demanded help, and two months later, Cortés marched inland with over 300 Spanish soldiers and 400 Indian porters, leaving as many as 150 infirm Spaniards in hastily constructed fortifications. As he passed through towns, he "freed" them from paying tribute to Moctezuma.

Cortés passed through Tlaxcala, east of the Valley of Mexico, where after a series of battles that left over forty-five Spaniards dead, the rest wounded, and food and arms diminished, an alliance was struck, most likely initiated by the Tlaxcaltecs, not Cortés. Tlaxcala was at war with the Aztecs, and they recognized the Spaniards as assets, few as they were in number. Spanish weapons could penetrate opposing formations, allowing their forces to flood through, turn the opposition's flanks, and defeat them.

Cortés stayed in Tlaxcala for seventeen days, then marched south to Cholollan,

most likely at the Tlaxcaltecs' behest, as it was not on the route, but had recently switched alliances from Tlaxcala to Tenochtitlan. He was peaceably received, but there, in what Cortés claimed was self-defense against treachery, he massacred the Chololtec leadership, and the town re-allied with Tlaxcala. Two weeks later, the Spaniards marched into the Valley of Mexico, entering Tenochtitlan on November 8, 1519, where they were amicably received, housed, and fed.

Moctezuma and his advisers had known about the Spaniards since 1518, when the previous expedition landed on the Gulf coast, but had taken no actions against their return, and that decision had divided the leadership. Moctezuma knew Cholollan's king had been killed, but given his own lack of support, he could not afford to alienate the rest of his allies. So when Cortés approached, he did not stop him.

Tenochtitlan was far larger than any city in Europe; its 200,000 residents perched on an island in a vast saline lake system, where connecting causeways could be severed by removing their bridges. So why did Cortés enter? He was vulnerable, but he could not return to Cuba after having openly violated Velazquez's orders, and he would lose his Indian allies. There was no turning back, so Cortés entered the capital, and within a week, he had seized the king and ruled through him for over seven months.

But the actions Moctezuma was forced to take alienated his own people, and Cortés did not enjoy the secure control he had expected. The king appeared weak to the nobles, if not the people, and his authority further eroded after, at Cortés's urging, he seized and imprisoned the rulers of several important nearby cities.

The situation came to a head when Pánfilo de Narváez landed on the Gulf coast with 1,100 soldiers and orders from Governor Velázquez to arrest Cortés and return him to Cuba. In late May, Cortés left Pedro de Alvarado in charge of 80 men in Tenochtitlan and marched to the coast with 266 men. Having defeated Narváez and the combined forces, he quickly marched back to Tenochtitlan, where relations between the Spaniards and the Aztecs had turned violent.

Claiming a plot against the Spaniards, Pedro de Alvarado had blocked the three entrances to the main courtyard during a festival and massacred thousands of unarmed nobles inside. As word spread, the people had risen up and attacked, driving the Spaniards back into their quarters, where they were besieged.

When Cortés arrived on June 24, with 1,300 Spaniards and 200 Tlaxcaltecs, his entry was unimpeded. But once in the city, he too was trapped. When force failed, he took Moctezuma up to the rooftop to calm the people, but to no avail. Spanish accounts claim that Moctezuma was fatally struck by a stone thrown from below, but Indian accounts insist that when it was recovered, Moctezuma's body bore Spanish dagger wounds. Certainly it is the case that, unable to control his people, the Aztec ruler was a far greater liability to Cortés than an asset. With their supplies exhausted, the Spaniards crept out of the city at midnight on June 30, under cover of a rainstorm. The alarm was raised midway through their escape, but Cortés and 450 Spaniards successfully made their way across the Tlacopan causeway and out of the city. They were fortunate. Almost 900 Spaniards were forced back into their quarters and killed over the next few days, as were 1,000 Tlaxcaltecs, Moctezuma (if he was not already dead), and other captive kings and nobles.

Cortés's party battled their way north around the valley, before finally reaching Tlaxcala where they recuperated. Within three weeks, they were attacking Aztec tributaries near Tlaxcala. The Aztecs sent reinforcements, but this defensive strategy was doomed in the face of the Spanish-Tlaxcaltec offensive.

Tenochtitlan was in turmoil: Cuitlahua had been chosen to succeed his brother, Moctezuma, and the kings of other cities were replaced as well. But Cuitlahua lacked time to consolidate his rule by a show of military prowess, and instead remitted tribute, which did not build an image of strength. Also, smallpox spread from an infected member of Narváez's party throughout central Mexico, killing some 40 percent in a year, and reached the Valley of Mexico by mid-October. Among its victims was Cuitlahua, who died in early December. So while the surviving Spanish leadership remained intact, the political elite of Tenochtitlan and many other cities was in disarray. Successions were contested, Spanish support was sought by weak incumbents or contenders, and the Spanish often tipped the balance to install leadership favorable to themselves.

During his recovery, Cortés must have considered the task before him; his original strategy of controlling Tenochtitlan from within was no longer feasible. He recognized that he would have to besiege it, and that meant controlling the lakes across which the city's food and water flowed. But to do that, he had to obtain a secure base in the valley and then cut off Tenochtitlan from outside support. He began by securing the road to Vera Cruz, along which a vital though intermittent flow of men and materiel moved, enough supplies to reequip his force and enough men over the next year to double their numbers.

Repairs in Tenochtitlan, the agricultural season, smallpox, and political disruptions throughout the valley all hindered the Aztecs, who adopted a defensive strategy. Waiting in Tenochtitlan ensured cheap and hard-to-interdict logistical support, the largest possible army, and unrestricted mobility and striking power anywhere in the valley, while undermining the Spaniards' striking power and complicating their logistical problems.

When Cuitlahua died, his nephew Cuauhtemoc was chosen as successor, although he was not crowned until February. Against this uncertain leadership, Cortés's forces reentered the Valley of Mexico on December 28. Cortés marched to Tetzcoco, the second city of the empire, after allying with Ixtlilxochitl, pretender to the city's throne. He was welcomed by its reigning king, Coanacoch, who then fled to Tenochtitlan with his supporters, leaving the Spaniards and their allies in charge of an ideal base of operations. Tetzcoco had enough land and people to support the Spanish forces, was strong enough to thwart virtually any Aztec attack, was distant enough from Tenochtitlan to prevent surprise attacks yet close enough for the Spaniards to launch theirs, and offered direct access to the deepest parts of the lakes.

Spanish and Aztec forces clashed throughout the valley, but Cortés's main endeavors focused on three assaults. The first, against Ixtlapalapan at the western end of the peninsula that jutted into the lakes, failed, so in the second, Cortés began an encirclement north around the lakes to Tlacopan, while in the third, he marched south of the valley, before reentering the southwest corner and attacking Xochimilco's rear. The Aztecs reinforced these cities by canoe and repulsed Spanish forces at both Tlacopan and Xochimilco. But these two campaigns effectively cut off support from beyond the valley, and every Spanish success brought more pledges of loyalty from surrounding cities.

In late May of 1521, Cortés launched a direct assault on Tenochtitlan, dispatching armies under Pedro de Alvarado, Cristobal de Olid, and Gonzalo de Sandoval, each with fewer than 200 Spaniards supported by 20,000–30,000 Indian allies. They severed the city's western causeway from Tlacopan, and the southern one that forked southwest to Coyohuacan and southeast to Ixtlapalapan, and en route they destroyed the aqueduct that carried water into the capital. Control of the lakes was essential to interdict supplies and troops and to protect Spanish forces exposed on the causeways. To this end, Cortés launched thirteen 40-foot brigantines assembled in Tetzcoco. With sails, oars, and cannons as well as armed soldiers, the ships quickly dispatched the Aztec armada sent against it, severed the causeways, and entered the hitherto protected waters between, where they scattered the canoe-borne attackers. Once the armies reached the juncture of the southern causeway, Sandoval's force withdrew and assaulted the northern causeway at Tepeycac, the city's last major link to the shore.

Battles were fought on the causeways, but the war was over allies. Success and failure shifted allied support, almost decisively on June 30, when 68 Spaniards were captured in one battle and sacrificed. Cortés's allies departed, and his forces were attacked with renewed vigor, but they weathered the assaults by withdrawing to defensive positions; when the Aztecs failed to destroy them, their Indian allies gradually returned.

Though depleted by months of battle and worn by the thirst, starvation, and disease that decimated their capital, the Aztecs fought on, but the Spanish forces slowly ground forward, crossing the causeways and entering the city. There, urban warfare began, with the Aztecs fighting from in and atop buildings, and the Spaniards responding by razing everything they passed. The fighting continued, reaching the great marketplace of Tlatelolco around August 1, and with the capture of Coanacoch, the Tetzcocan forces loyal to the Aztecs defected to Ixtlilxochitl and the Spaniards.

Seven-eighths of the city was now in Spanish hands. Combat was hand to hand. Soon thereafter, Cuauhtemoc requested negotiation, and a lull came in the fighting. But with no progress in the negotiations, Cortés eventually renewed the assault, and on August 13, the Spaniards overran the last Aztec defenses. With no more options, the Aztecs finally surrendered. Cuauhtemoc and thirty nobles and kings fled the city in a fleet of fifty canoes, but were captured by a brigantine. Tenochtitlan was in ruins, the streets were filled with the dead, and the Tlaxcaltecs began a four-day rampage, looting and killing throughout the defenseless city. Of the Spaniards, 900 survived the conquest.

Mexico was conquered from within, not abroad. The Spaniards were important, but they took full credit even when they were only the most visible element. The Aztecs did not lose their faith; they lost a war. And it was a war fought overwhelmingly by other Indians, who certainly took full advantage of the Spanish presence, but who exploited their own unique understanding of Mesoamerican political dynamics, which Cortés could never master. The war was more coup or rebellion than a conquest. Conquest came later, after the battles, as the Spaniards usurped the victory for which their Indian allies had fought and died.

Ross Hassig

References

Cortés, Hernán. *Letters from Mexico.* Translated by Anthony Pagden. New York: Grossman, 1971.

De Fuentes, Patricia. *The Conquistadors: First-Person Accounts of the Conquest of Mexico.* Norman: University of Oklahoma Press, 1993.

Díaz del Castillo, Bernal. *The True History of the Conquest of New Spain.* 5 vols. Translated by Alfred Percival Maudslay. London: Hakluyt Society, 1908–1916.

Hassig, Ross. *Aztec Warfare: Imperial Expansion and Political Control.* Norman: University of Oklahoma Press, 1994.

———. *Mexico and the Spanish Conquest.* London: Longman Group UK, 1994.

Lockhart, James. *We People Here: Nahua Accounts of the Conquest of Mexico.* Berkeley and Los Angeles: University of California Press, 1993.

Sahagún, Bernardino de. *The War of Conquest: How It Was Waged Here in Mexico: The Aztecs' Own Story.* Salt Lake City: University of Utah Press, 1978.

See also: Altepetl; Atlantic Economy; Cah; Colonists and Settlers IV—Mexico and Central America; Conquest and the Debate over Justice; Conquest I–IV, VI–VII; Conquistadors; Encomienda; Native Americans IV—Mesoamerica; Trade—Spain/Spanish America; Weapons.

CONQUEST VI— SOUTHEASTERN NORTH AMERICA

Between 1513 and 1565, the vast northeastern borderland of New Spain known as *La Florida* became the focus of repeated Spanish military expeditions. As soldiers, sailors, adventurers, and missionaries representing the Spanish Crown explored and attempted to settle the southeastern part of what is now the United States, they encountered considerable native resistance from well-organized and powerful chiefdoms. Most of the early expeditions ended in resounding failure. Even worse was the Spaniards' destructive impact on the cultural landscape of the Southeast, as they left behind a legacy of pillage, rape, warfare, enslavement, and disease.

The earliest reconnaissance of mainland North America probably occurred before 1513, but was unsanctioned by the Crown and therefore went unrecorded. Official Spanish exploration of southeastern North America began in 1513 when Juan Ponce de León, the former governor of Puerto Rico and a veteran of Columbus's second voyage, received a royal *asiento*, or charter, to search for and settle Bimini, an island rumored to lie north of the Bahamas. Ponce sailed from Puerto Rico in March 1513, eventually making landfall on Florida's northeast coast. He named the region La Florida because he made his discovery during the Easter season, the Feast of Flowers *(flores)*. In the days that followed, he sailed down the peninsula, west along the Florida Keys, and then up the Gulf coast, possibly as far as Tampa, before heading home. His company had at least two hostile encounters with the Calusas of southern Florida. In each case, the local inhabitants drove the invaders back to their ships.

During the next fifty years, the Spanish Crown repeatedly offered concessions and rewards to a succession of men who attempted to establish a permanent presence in southeastern North America. Royal charters typically specified the rights and responsibilities of conquistadors in relation to the Crown as well as any benefits they would receive if the expedition were successful. As the conquest of Central and South America proceeded after 1519, new objectives were added to mere control of La Florida and its inhabitants and the extraction of marketable resources. When the French and English established their own presence in the Caribbean after 1550, Atlantic coast settlements that could provide protection and services for the Spanish treasure fleets became crucial. In addition, the prospect of linking New Spain (Mexico) and the Atlantic coast of La Florida by an overland road protected by fortified missions and settlements grew increasingly attractive. None of these ambitions were realized prior to the establishment of Saint Augustine in 1565, though the Spanish explored much of the Southeast in their quest to accomplish these elusive goals.

Ponce de León was typical of the explorers who led military expeditions, or *entradas,* into La Florida. All reached its shores as veterans of Spanish exploits elsewhere in the Americas. They operated within a conceptual framework that assumed their own technological and cultural superiority over the natives and sanctioned the use of violence to achieve religious and cultural conversion and, ultimately, control over the landscape, its resources, and its inhabitants. They valued

Pánfilo de Narváez (center) led an expedition to Florida in June 1527 to erect a presidio and establish a community. Narváez's expedition proved disastrous, as his overland expedition failed to rendezvous with the ships. The expedition was subject to Indian attacks and soon ran short of food, and all but a few men were lost at sea during an attempt to sail to Mexico on makeshift vessels. (Bettmann/Corbis)

La Florida primarily for its agricultural potential and the lucrative products it might yield. Their primary interest in the Indians related to their potential use as a labor force suitable for extracting these profitable resources. Roman Catholicism was important as the justification for their authority and as the key to incorporating the local inhabitants into a Spanish world.

The first entradas were primarily coastal ventures. In the 1510s, several slavers and explorers reconnoitered the Atlantic and Gulf coasts, and in 1521 Ponce himself returned to South Florida, where he died in the first abortive Spanish attempt to establish a colony. The same year, slavers Pedro de Quejo and Francisco Gordillo made landfall on the South Carolina coast, where they established peaceful trade relations with local Catawban speakers before luring 60 aboard ship and forcibly abducting them. The slavers' glowing report to their sponsor, Lucas Vásquez de Ayllón, prompted him to mount a colonizing expedition of 600 men, women, and children, plus black slaves, in 1526. They established San Miguel de Gualdape on the Georgia coast, but it lasted only three months. Heat, insects, and insufficient food led some colonists to impose themselves on a nearby village, where they quickly wore out their welcome. Their native hosts slew them, then attacked the Spaniards' coastal settlement. The survivors fled to Hispaniola. Two years after Ayllón's ill-fated endeavor, Pánfilo de Narváez began an exploration of the northern Gulf coast. His army of 400 men and 40 horses landed near Tampa Bay, intending to travel overland along the coast to New Spain. When misfortune and illness halted Narváez's progress in Appalachee territory in northwestern Florida, he ordered his men back to sea, where most of the company was subsequently lost. Only five, including Álvar Núñez Cabeza de Vaca (1528–1536), survived and eventually returned to Mexico in 1536 after eight years' captivity among Texas natives.

Four years after Cabeza de Vaca's return, Hernando de Soto undertook the first extensive land exploration of La Florida (1539–1543). Accompanied by the largest, most destructive force yet seen in the region, de Soto marched up the Florida peninsula and ultimately across much of the interior Southeast. During its four-year trek, de Soto's army visited many native villages, often taking hostages to use as bearers, guides, and interpreters, and compelling native women to serve the men as personal servants and sex partners. When corn and supplies were not forthcoming, the conquistadors plundered, taking what they wanted by force. Native disgust with the Spaniards reached its climax in two major battles in Alabama and Mississippi in late 1540 and early 1541. During these confrontations, the Spanish both inflicted and suffered considerable loss of life. In early 1542, de Soto became ill and died on the west bank of the Mississippi River; his diminished party finally made its way back to Mexico a year later.

The unfavorable outcome of de Soto's expedition prevented significant interest in La Florida for almost two decades. Fi-nally, seventeen years after the return of de Soto's party, another major expedition was sent out under Tristán de Luna y Arellano, a thirty-year veteran of the Crown's service in New Spain. His party of 1,500 soldiers and settlers landed on the Gulf coast in 1559, planning to march over-land to the Atlantic and establish a colony at Santa Elena. After setting up their main base at Pensacola Bay, some moved inland, where they found that much had changed since de Soto's time. Many formerly populous, thriving towns were deserted, the inhabitants having died from disease. By early 1561, the entrada was plagued by internal dissension, inadequate supplies, and poor planning, prompting Mexican authorities to replace Luna. His successor, Ángel de Villafañe, tried to move the colony to Santa Elena, but failed, and Philip II officially brought the venture to an end in September. Although Spain made two further attempts to effect a settlement in La Florida before 1565, neither succeeded.

To a great extent, the Spanish conquest of La Florida foundered on its own advance publicity, as stories of the strange white men and their often offensive behavior traveled ahead of the entradas along native trade routes. The hostility the conquistadors encountered was a direct consequence of Spanish strategies and tactics, which were designed to move them forward with as much local logistical support and as little native resistance as possible. From the Spanish perspective, this approach often necessitated commandeering local corn supplies and native bodies to serve as bearers, guides, and interpreters. If they could not be obtained peacefully, the Spaniards took them by force, confident in their innate superiority and their God-given authority to enforce native compliance.

The effectively organized, centralized chiefdoms of La Florida were not passive victims, however, and they employed a range of responses based on their own needs and perceptions. When given sufficient time to prepare, they greeted the Spaniards with a pomp and ceremony familiar to and appreciated by the conquistadors. When it appeared that the intruders might prove useful allies in existing local rivalries, native leaders tried to enlist Spanish aid through diplomatic negotiation. When cooperation seemed the best method to speed the Spaniards on their way or to buy time until a better response could be made, the natives complied or appeased the conquistadors through deception or misinformation. When all else failed or it seemed most expedient, natives resorted to force, often with great success.

Ultimately, the most effective weapon in the explorers' arsenal was an unintentional one, disease. European pathogens accompanied the Spaniards everywhere, with devastating results for many native communities. Evidence suggests that the demographic collapse of the North American population began with the arrival of the first Spanish explorers in the early fifteenth century. Infectious diseases for which the native inhabitants had no immunity often traveled ahead of actual contact along indigenous trade routes. Catastrophic population loss likely prompted restructuring and relocation of surviving communities before the first permanent European settlements were established in the 1560s; it undoubtedly diminished the natives' ability to resist and became the most enduring legacy of conquest in the Southeast.

Nancy L. Hagedorn

References

Hoffman, Paul E. *A New Andalucia and a Way to the Orient: The American Southeast during the Sixteenth Century.* Baton Rouge: Louisiana State University Press, 1990.

Howard, David A. *Conquistador in Chains: Cabeza de Vaca and the Indians of the Americas.* Tuscaloosa: University of Alabama Press, 1997.

Hudson, Charles M. *Knights of Spain, Warriors of the Sun: Hernando de Soto and the South's Ancient Chiefdoms.* Athens: University of Georgia Press, 1997.

Quinn, David B., ed. *New American World: A Documentary History of North America to 1612.* Vol. 2, *Major Spanish Searches in Eastern North America. Franco-Spanish Clash in Florida. The Beginnings of Spanish Florida.* New York: Arno Press and Hector Bye, 1979.

Thomas, David Hurst, ed. *Columbian Consequences.* Vol. 2, *Archaeological and Historical Perspectives on the Spanish Borderlands East.* Washington, DC: Smithsonian Institution, 1990.

See also: Asiento; Atlantic Economy; Borderlands; Bourbon Reforms; Colonists and Settlers VI—Southeastern North America; Columbian Exchange—Disease; Conquistadors; Defense—Colonial Spanish America; Explorers; Fleet System; Florida; Native Americans VIII—Southeastern North America; Pirates and Piracy; Slavery IV—Borderlands; Weapons.

CONQUEST VII— SOUTHERN CONE

The success or failure of conquest in the Americas, as well as the societies that emerged in the wake of conquest, varied according to the mineral wealth and the indigenous peoples the conquistadors encountered. The silver deposits and settled indigenous populations of the core areas of Spanish America, namely Mexico and Peru, retained close ties to Spain and attracted large numbers of Spanish settlers. Local society became a mixture of Iberian, indigenous, and African peoples, yet showed many of the economic, social, and political characteristics of Europe. Imperial rule and the Catholic Church formed the glue that held together the growing network of cities, agricultural estates, transatlantic traders, and a society that soon included Spanish women. These core regions represented the European ideal, that is, societies that functioned according to European norms, geared toward the extraction of wealth and its transportation across the Atlantic to Iberia.

Outside the core lay what can be considered the fringes of Spanish settlement. Fringe areas generally had no valuable export commodity and attracted mostly male settlers with little wealth or social status. Practices that became outdated or even outlawed in the core areas, such as the *encomienda* system of exacting tribute from the native population in return for protection, often continued in the fringe regions. In marked contrast to the growing official presence in the core regions, fringe areas were often ignored by the colonial government; they became the provinces of missionary orders and were secured by military outposts. An important point to remember, however, is that the distinction between these two areas was fluid, easily influenced by the discovery of valuable local products or a change in the tastes and demands of the European market. Fringe areas could transform themselves into core regions, and core areas could decline to the status of fringe settlements.

The impetus that drove the Spanish conquest of the Americas waned following the establishment of settlement centers in Mexico and the Andes. Conquistadors sought mineral wealth and the settled indigenous populations that might provide the labor needed to work the Spaniards' mines and fields. Non-Andean South America appeared to offer little of either commodity in the sixteenth century. It is true that, even where obvious signs of wealth were lacking, rumors of enormous riches continued to spur Spaniards to finance and participate in further conquests of South America's interior. However, with the exception of the Guaranís, the indigenous peoples that these speculators encountered were non- or semisedentary people, and they were generally hostile to the European interlopers. Many of the expeditions ended in disaster, though several resulted in at first tenuous, then lasting settlements. The conquest of the regions that subsequently became the Southern Cone countries of Argentina, Chile, Paraguay, and Uruguay followed the above patterns, as expeditions originating in Spain and the Americas advanced southward from the Andes and along the rivers that led inland from the Atlantic coast.

The conquest and subjugation of Chile's indigenous peoples continued into the eighteenth century. For much of the colonial period, Chile was considered a frontier and was home to military garrisons. Initial attempts at conquest followed Francisco Pizarro and Diego Almagro's defeat of the Inca Empire. Conflict between the two conquistadors, as well as the desire for further wealth, convinced Almagro to lead an expedition south in 1535. Almagro's force was much larger than that of either Hernando Cortés or Francisco Pizarro, and was made up of Spaniards who had taken part in the conquests of Peru, Mexico, and Central America, as well as Indian auxiliaries and

African slaves. The expedition was hindered by desertions, the loss of pack animals and horses, and a shortage of food and pasture for the animals. In 1536, Almagro returned to Peru in order to contest Pizarro's claims to the spoils of the Inca Empire. Pizarro had him executed in 1538. The failure of Almagro's expedition dissuaded others from immediately following in his footsteps. Moreover, Chile's indigenous population was now aware of the Spanish presence and would not be intimidated by the new invaders. Despite these circumstances, in 1540 a former lieutenant of Pizarro gave up the wealth he had accumulated in Peru in exchange for the right to conquer Chile.

Pedro de Valdivia and his successors ultimately pacified much of Chile, but it was a brutal and costly operation. In February 1541, after an eleven-month journey south from Peru, Valdivia founded the settlement of Santiago and became governor of Chile. It had been an arduous trek, in which the participants had battled Indians, the Atacama Desert, and each other. Still, early successes against the indigenous population did not mean that their presence was welcomed. Less than a year after its founding, Santiago was attacked and burned to the ground by local Indians. The settlement survived thanks to the brutal actions of Valdivia's mistress, Inés Suárez, and a priest who accompanied the expedition. They ordered seven hostage caciques executed and their heads thrown among the attacking Indians.

The 1552 discovery of gold in Chile prompted a distribution of large encomiendas and the use of Indian labor in mining. Chile witnessed the arrival of more than a thousand colonists, many of whom began to engage in farming and ranching.

In the center and in the north, mining supported a society that became predominantly Hispanic, and included import merchants, professionals, artisans, Spanish women, and significant numbers of freedmen and slaves. Disease and miscegenation meant that mestizos represented a majority of the rural population by the mid-seventeenth century. Life was different in the south. Between 1598 and 1612, and again in 1655, attacks by Araucanian Indians forced the Spanish to abandon almost all the settlements south of the Bío-Bío River. Frontier forts, subsidized by Lima, were necessary to maintain the frontier with the Araucanians, who resisted Spanish rule throughout the colonial period. The Araucanians adapted quickly to Spanish weapons and tactics, and by 1600 they had more horses than the frontier garrisons and towns. Their lack of a central institutional leadership made defeat of the Araucanians difficult for the Spaniards. Ongoing conflict and the spread of European diseases meant that the Chilean population did not return to its 1540 levels (about one million) until the 1840s.

Spanish settlement of what is now Argentina occurred from several different directions. The northwest owes its origins to Peru, the west to Chile, the north to Paraguay, and the east to the sea. European exploration of the area began under Juan Díaz de Solís in 1516. Ferdinand Magellan followed in 1520 on his voyage around the globe. Sebastian Cabot, who sailed beyond the Paraná delta to establish a small fort at Sancti Espiritus, made a further reconnaissance of the area. Cabot traded for silver (*plata*) and thus named the wide estuary that flows into the Atlantic the Río de la Plata (known in English as the River Plate). The Spanish were to find that the only silver in the region originated in Potosí. Nonetheless, competition over the region increased between the Portuguese and Spanish Crowns, leading both to contemplate the establishment of a permanent settlement.

In 1534, King Charles I (Holy Roman Emperor Charles V) granted Pedro de Mendoza the right to equip and lead a force to conquer the territory on the east coast of South America. Two years later, Mendoza arrived on the banks of the Río de la Plata with a force of 1,600 men to found the port of Nuestra Señora Santa María del Buen Aire (now Buenos Aires), named for the patron saint of mariners (Rock 1987, 10). The eventual failure of the settlement was, in part, due to its size. Having arrived too late during the southern summer to plant crops, the men relied upon fish from the estuary and the willingness of the local Indians to help; both proved insufficient for their needs. Starvation and Indian attacks pushed the group to the point of cannibalism, and in 1537 Mendoza's deputy led an expedition up the Paraná in search of a happier environment. Pedro de Ayolas established friendly relations with the Guaraní Indians and in 1537 built the settlement of Asunción del Paraguay. Life was abundant in Paraguay, and the Guaranís offered the Spanish gifts of women, food, and Indian labor. In 1541, Asunción welcomed the rest of the Spaniards from Mendoza's original encampment. Mendoza himself had died on the return journey to Spain in 1537.

Paraguay witnessed a mixture of Spanish and Guaraní traditions during the sixteenth century. The Guaranís, a branch of the Tupis, were a sedentary people living around present-day Asunción and east of the Paraná River. To the west of the Guaranís, in the Chaco, lived seminomadic hunters such as the Guaycurus, their traditional enemies. As they did elsewhere in the Americas, the Spanish settled among the sedentary people of the region, the Guaranís, and gave them assistance in their battles with their neighbors. Unlike their experience with other sedentary peoples, however, the Spanish were not able to impose the encomienda system and to merely replace Indian leaders with their own and exact tribute from the native population. There were no mines and no existing system of exacting tribute. Instead, Spanish men entered Guaraní society as headmen. They received women as gifts, and since it was the women and their relatives who performed agricultural labor, they became the basis for Spanish survival in Paraguay. Subsequently, most of the "Spaniards" in Paraguay were mestizos, and Guaraní foods, customs, and even language became those of the Spaniards. In a parallel manner, Spanish ideals and religion entered native society, creating a cultural mix unique in Spanish America. This stable society in Paraguay contributed to the reestablishment and expansion of settlements in Argentina.

Exploration into northwest Argentina followed the conquest of Peru. In 1535 Diego de Almagro passed through the region on the way to Chile. Diego de Rojas, who had been with Cortés in Mexico, followed in 1547. A permanent settlement in Tucumán was established in the 1550s, as the Spaniards sought both an outlet to the sea and new supplies of Indian labor. Several towns were founded in the 1550s, but only Santiago del Estero survived the Indian attacks of 1562. Three years later, San Miguel de Tucumán was founded north of

Santiago del Estero. Tucumán came to resemble a core rather than a fringe region, as it soon began to supply the needs of Potosí. Spaniards there raised livestock and crops, provided mules for transportation, and produced wool and textiles for clothes. After 1560, initiatives for settlement also came from Chile. Settlers sought to capture Indians for labor and to secure a route for Spanish troops from the Río de la Plata, troops that might aid them in their conflict with the Araucanians in southern Chile. Mendoza and San Juan were founded as a result of these initiatives.

The continued growth of Potosí, rather than the Chilean initiatives, drove further the conquest and settlement of Argentina from the interior toward the coast. Mining interests supported the founding of Salta, La Rioja, and San Salvador de Jujuy in order to protect the route to Chile, as supply points for the mines, and as part of a plan to establish outlets on the Atlantic for silver. As these cities became more established, the Spanish settlement in Paraguay took the opportunity to resettle Buenos Aires. In 1580, Juan de Garay led an expedition south from Asunción toward the Río de la Plata, founding Santa Fe en route. Ten Spaniards and fifty-six mestizos successfully resettled Buenos Aires, able now to rely on supplies of food from upriver and on the herds of wild horses and cattle descended from those left behind by the earlier settlers. In 1587, Corrientes was founded on the Paraná between Santa Fe and Asunción. These settlements hoped to benefit from the flow of silver out of Potosí, and to establish a trade in cattle hides.

On the eastern bank *(Banda Oriental)* of the Río de la Plata, the presence of fierce Tupian and Charrúa peoples contributed to the scant attention that Spaniards and Portuguese paid to the interior of Uruguay until the late seventeenth century. As in neighboring Argentina, native peoples in the Banda Oriental were aided in their defensive abilities by the presence of wild Spanish horses. After 1680, the Banda Oriental became the focus of imperial rivalries when the Portuguese established a trading fort in Colônia do Sacramento, directly across the river from Buenos Aires. Spain countered with a defensive fort in Montevideo, which belatedly became the center of Spanish settlement in Uruguay. Spain attracted settlers with grants of land, and Montevideo became the seat of a town council (*cabildo*).

Alistair Hattingh

References

Burkholder, Mark A., and Lyman L. Johnson. *Colonial Latin America.* New York: Oxford University Press, 1994.

Lockhart, James, and Stuart B. Schwartz. *Early Latin America: A History of Colonial Spanish America and Brazil.* Cambridge: Cambridge University Press, 1983.

Loveman, Brian. *Chile: The Legacy of Hispanic Capitalism.* New York: Oxford University Press, 2001.

Rock, David. *Argentina, 1516–1987: From Spanish Colonization to Alfonsín.* Berkeley and Los Angeles: University of California Press, 1987.

See also: Argentina; Borderlands; Cabildo; Catholic Church in Spanish America; Chile; Cities; Civil Wars; Colonists and Settlers V—Southern Cone; Conquest I–VI; Conquistadors; Defense—Colonial Spanish America; Encomienda; Horses; Independence I—Argentina; Jesuits—Paraguay; Missions; Native Americans V—Central and Southern Andes; Paraguay; Potosí; Women—Colonial Spanish America.

CONQUISTADORS

The identities, experiences, and life stories of the Spaniards who participated in the conquests in the Americas vary. Nevertheless, a typical conquistador can be constructed from the general patterns of conquistador biographies. He tended to be a young man in his late twenties, semiliterate, from southwestern Spain, trained in a particular trade or profession, who sought opportunity through patronage networks based on family and hometown ties. Armed as well as he could afford to be, and with some experience already of exploration and conquest in the Americas, he was ready to invest what he had and risk his life if absolutely necessary in order to be a member of the first company to conquer somewhere wealthy and well populated. He was not in any sense a soldier in the armies of the king of Spain.

Although the conquistadors are often misleadingly referred to as professional soldiers—and they were certainly armed, organized, and experienced in military matters—most acquired their martial skills not from formal training but from conflict situations in the Americas. Expedition members tended to be recruited in recently founded colonies, creating a relay system of conquest that meant that most participants already had some military experience in the New World. One example is that of the Spaniards who participated in the famous capture at Cajamarca of the Inca emperor Atahualpa. Of the 101 Spaniards at Cajamarca whose pre-1532 experience is recorded, 64 had prior conquest experience, and 52 had spent at least five years in the Americas (Lockhart 1972, 38). But none of this amounted to formal training.

The conquistadors' lack of formal training was paralleled by a lack of formal ranking; Spanish forces in Europe at the time were led by commanders from the high nobility and organized into various ranks. In contrast, conquistador groups were headed by captains, the sole named rank and one that could be held by more than one man, with the other men divided only into those on horseback and those on foot—the latter rising to the former simply through the purchase of a horse. The record of the division of spoils at Cajamarca listed the men in two categories only, *gente de a cavallo* (people on horseback) and *gente de a pie* (people on foot).

Conquistadors did not identify themselves as soldiers under orders, but rather as individual men on foot or on horseback, representing hometowns in Spain, aided by networks of kinship and patronage, and motivated by a search for economic and social opportunity. The best-known captain to lead a conquest expedition in the Americas, Hernando Cortés, wrote a series of letters to the king during and after his 1519–1521 war against the Mexica (Aztec) Empire. These letters, published in Cortés's lifetime and still in print today in many languages, give the impression that the conquistadors were driven by a sense of loyalty to crown and church. This image of the conquistadors was constructed for the benefit of the king, who was well aware of the personal ambitions and motives of the conquerors.

Perhaps more revealing are the words of conquistadors who were not famous captains. Francisco de Jerez, for example, emphasized that the members of conquest companies "were neither paid nor forced but went of their own will and at their own cost" (Jerez 1985 [1534], 60). Gaspar de Marquina was a page to Governor Pedrarias in conquest-era Nicaragua and

Ferdinand Cortés and Hernando de Soto in the Inca settlement of Cajamarca. (Library of Congress)

then, like Jerez, followed Francisco Pizarro and Diego de Almagro into the Inca Empire. Marquina wrote to his father that he went to Peru because it was a place where "there's more gold and silver than iron in Biscay, and more sheep than in Soria, and great supplies of all kinds of food, and much fine clothing, and the best people that have been seen in the whole Indies, and many great lords among them" (Lockhart 1972, 460).

Marquina was not a professional soldier, but a page, a fully literate, high-ranking servant to two of the early conquistador-governors of Spanish American colonies. He came to "the Indies" of his own free will, hoping to return to his father in Spain a wealthy man and, most likely, take up a career as a notary or merchant. He pursued that opportunity through his connection to important patrons. Like most Spaniards who fought in the violent invasions of the early sixteenth century, however, he died before he could return to Spain. (Marquina had been killed in a skirmish with native Andeans by the time his father received his son's letter and the gold bar that accompanied it.)

Most Spaniards joined conquest expeditions not in return for specified payments, but in the hope of acquiring wealth and status. They were "free agents, emigrants, settlers, unsalaried and ununiformed earners of *encomiendas* and shares of treasure" (Lockhart and Otte 1976, 3). An encomienda was a grant of Native American labor; the holder, or *encomendero,* had the right to tax in goods and labor the natives of a given community or cluster of towns. Such grants allowed the recipient to enjoy high status and often a superior quality of life among his fellow colonists. As there were never enough encomiendas to go around, the most lucrative grants went to those who had invested the most in the expedition—and survived to see it succeed. Lesser investors received lesser grants (a few dozen, instead of thousands, of indigenous "vassals") or simply a share of the spoils of war.

To one extent or another, all participants were investors in commercial ventures that carried high risks, but also the potential for the highest of returns. Spaniards called these ventures "companies." Although powerful patrons played important investment roles, it was the captains who primarily funded companies and expected to reap the greatest rewards. As the governor of Panama, Pedrarias de Avila, told the king of early conquest expeditions into Nicaragua and Colombia, "it was done without touching your majesty's royal treasury" (Lockhart and Otte 1976, 12). The spirit of commercialism infused conquest expeditions from start to finish, with participants selling services and trading goods with each other throughout the endeavor. The conquerors were, in other words, armed entrepreneurs.

Marquina refers to himself as a page, *paje,* and a dependent, *criado.* An Englishman of the day would have called him either a "servant" or a "creature," although no English word fully conveys the way in which a criado was both subordinate and a real member of the household. The identity of Marquina's patrons and other details of his life also give us a sense of his social status within the broad category of criado. Conquistadors' self-identities did not necessarily match those given to them by others, and they shift according to circumstances. However, records in which the conquerors identified themselves still help us to know who the conquistadors were. For example, following the founding of the city of Panama in 1519, the 98 Spanish conquistador-settlers were asked to contribute to such a record (Avellaneda 1995, 91). Of these, 75 responded. Only 2 of the 75 men claimed to be professional soldiers. Sixty percent claimed to be professional men and artisans, occupations from the middle ranks of society. A similar analysis of the conquerors of the New Kingdom of Granada (today's Colombia) is less precise as to occupations and probably exaggerates the numbers of middle-ranking men. Nevertheless, the data clearly show that men of some means or property, professionals, and entrepreneurs of some kind predominated.

Comparable information on Peru's conquistadors is likewise patchy, but sufficiently revealing. Of the 168 men at Cajamarca, 47 gave their occupations; again, they were not professional soldiers but professionals and artisans who had acquired various battle experiences and martial skills. The 17 artisans included tailors, horseshoers, carpenters, trumpeters, a cooper, a swordsmith, a stonemason, a barber, and a piper/crier. The same kinds of artisans also accompanied Francisco de Montejo on his first expedition into Yucatán in 1527, along with the usual professional men—merchants, physicians, a couple of priests, and a pair of Flemish artillery engineers. An unspecified number of the artisans and professionals invested in the company were confident enough of its outcome to bring their wives (although, following customary practice, these Spanish women probably remained with the merchants at the last Caribbean port before Yucatán was reached).

In addition, Conquest records often contain information on the age and birthplace of conquistadors; it is available, for example, for 1,210 members of the original expeditions to Panama (84 men), Mexico (743), Peru (131), and Colombia (252) (Lockhart 1972; Avellaneda 1995; Thomas 2000; Restall 2003, 33–37). The makeup of each expedition was similar, with an average of 30 percent from the southern Spanish kingdom of Andalusia, 19 percent from neighboring Extremadura, 24 percent from the core kingdoms of Old and New Castile, and the remainder from other regions of the Iberian peninsula. Other Europeans were rare, restricted to the odd Portuguese, Genoese, Flemish, or Greek man. In age, the conquerors ranged from teenagers to the occasional sixty-year-old; the average age of the men who went to both Peru and Colombia was twenty-seven, with the vast majority in their twenties or early thirties.

In terms of education, again the range was broad, from men who were completely illiterate and uneducated to the occasional man of considerable learning. Although the availability of and attention given to conquistador narratives certainly give the impression that the conquerors were handy with a pen if not well read, the fully literate were among the minority in Spain as among conquest expeditions. Literacy rates among the conquerors and early settlers were slightly higher than average rates in Spain, if only because few farmers and other plebeians were among the migrants. The classic eyewitness narratives—Bernal Díaz and Cortés on Mexico, Gonzalo Jiménez on Colombia, Francisco de Jerez and Pedro Pizarro on Peru—are classics in part because they are rare. Most conquistadors wrote or dictated "merit" reports in a formulaic style. Despite the common misconception that literacy gave Spaniards an advantage over Native Americans, members of conquistador companies could probably read and write no better than the most literate Native American societies, such as the Mayas.

Nor was the correlation between social status and literacy among conquistadors as close as might be expected; the colonial chronicler Juan Rodríguez Freyle, a Santafé de Bogotá native, claimed that some city council members of the New Granada settlements used branding irons to sign documents. Among the ten leaders of the famous 1532–1534 invasion of Peru, including the four Pizarro brothers, four were literate, three were semiliterate (they could sign their names), and three were illiterate (including Francisco Pizarro).

Spanish men were not the only people who fought with invading companies. A small number of Spanish women accompanied the conquistadors; of the thousand-odd Spaniards who entered Mexico with Cortés, Pánfilo de Narváez, or other captains in the 1520s, 19 Spanish women participated to the degree that we might call them *conquistadoras,* and there is evidence of at least 5 of them actually fighting. Spaniards also brought with them African slaves and servants, their numbers increasing from less than a dozen in each company to many hundreds per expedition after 1521. Black conquistadors tended to be ignored in Spanish histories of the conquests, yet they were not only ubiquitous but much valued as fierce fighters. Finally, the title of conquistador was appropriated soon after the conquest by Maya, Zapotec, and other indigenous elites who had allied with Spanish invaders and won certain privileges in the new colonial system. Their role was crucial, as without the many thousands of indigenous soldiers who fought as *indios amigos* (Indian allies), the Spanish conquistadors would not have lived to found colonies in the Americas.

Matthew Restall

References

Avellaneda, José Ignacio. *The Conquerors of the New Kingdom of Granada.* Albuquerque: University of New Mexico Press, 1995.

Cortés, Hernán. *Letters from Mexico* [1519–1526]. Edited by Anthony Pagden. New Haven, CT: Yale University Press, 1986.

Díaz del Castillo, Bernal. *The Conquest of Mexico* [ca. 1570]. Edited by J. M. Cohen. London: Penguin, 1963.

Jerez, Francisco de. *Verdadera relación de la conquista del Perú* [1534]. Madrid: Historia 16, 1985.

Lockhart, James. *The Men of Cajamarca.* Austin: University of Texas Press, 1972.

———. Lockhart, James, and Enrique Otte. *Letters and People of the Spanish Indies: The Sixteenth Century.* Cambridge: Cambridge University Press, 1976.

Restall, Matthew. *Seven Myths of the Spanish Conquest.* New York: Oxford University Press, 2003.

Thomas, Hugh. *Who's Who of the Conquistadors.* London: Cassell, 2000.

See also: Artisans; Chroniclers; Civil Wars; Colombia; Colonists and Settlers I–VI; Columbian Exchange—Disease; Conquest and the Debate over Justice; Conquest I–VII; El Dorado; Encomienda; Explorers; Mexico; Native Americans I–VIII; Peru; Race; Slavery I–IV; Women—Colonial Spanish America.

CONSTITUTION OF CÁDIZ

In March 1812, the Cortes of Cádiz adopted Spain's first written constitution, the Constitución Política de la Monarquía Española. In effect until May 1814, and reapplied during the "Liberal triennium" of 1820–1823, this magna carta introduced constitutional governance to Spain and Spanish America.

The regency governing Spain during its War of Independence against Napoleon Bonaparte (1808–1814) convened a *Cortes* (parliament), which decided to promulgate a constitution in December 1810. The Cortes appointed a committee of ten peninsular and five American deputies, including liberals, moderates, and royalists, as well as priests, lawyers, bureaucrats, and a baron. Working from a draft constitution prepared for the Junta Central that had governed Spain in 1808–1809, the committee presented two-thirds of a draft constitution to the Cortes plenary for discussion, amendment, and adoption on August 25, 1811. Over the next seven months, deputies discussed the constitution's 10 sections in order, addressing each of 384 articles individually.

The constitution ended ancien régime absolutism by establishing a constitutional monarchy, individual rights and liberties, and separation of powers. Its first two sections defined Spain as a sovereign nation with a constitutional monarchy and as a single entity comprising peninsular and overseas provinces. They also outlined regulations for nationality and citizenship, and established Roman Catholicism as the national and sole religion. The three subsequent sections (titles 3–5), much like the U.S. Constitution, defined the composition and responsibilities of separate branches of government: the Cortes (legislative), the king (executive), and a Supreme Court and provincial judiciaries (judicial). Subsequent sections regulated the institutions of provincial government (6), taxation (7), the military (8), public education (9), and rules for observing and modifying the constitution (10). Elections received substantial attention, with 69 articles dedicated to procedures for parish, district, and provincial electoral bodies to follow when selecting city councilors and deputies to provincial councils and subsequent Cortes.

Known familiarly as la Pepa, the Constitution of 1812 blended tradition with innovation. Although Spain was at war with Napoleon, Spain's deputies borrowed two important concepts from France. From the Declaration of the Rights of Man (1789) came the idea of national rather than royal sovereignty. From the Code Civil (1804) came the principle of distinguishing a person's civil status (nationality) from political standing (citizenship), which allowed definition of all those born in Spanish territory as "Spaniards," while limiting voting rights and office-holding to "citizens," who had to be of European or American (including Indians), and not African, origin. Although found by royalists to be too liberal, in addition to retaining Roman Catholicism as Spain's official religion, the Constitution provided exceptions to the theory of equality before the law by failing to abolish slavery or the slave trade, by retaining certain church and military privileges *(fueros),* and by reserving four seats each for the church and nobility in the royally appointed forty-member Council of State. Provincial government, too, combined royally appointed governors with municipal and provincial councils elected by residents. American deputies, a minority in the Cortes, were disappointed at being unable to achieve free trade within the empire, the enfranchisement of *castas* (castes), or acknowledgment that their full population (greater than peninsular Spain's when counting Indian and African populations) should determine the bases of American representa-

tion in future Cortes. In addition to influencing Spain's subsequent constitutions, the Constitution of 1812 established a blueprint for government that influenced Spanish American legislatures after independence.

Jordana Dym

References

Chust, Manuel. *La cuestión americana en las Cortes de Cádiz.* Valencia: UNED, 1999.

Rodríguez, Mario. *The Cádiz Experiment in Central America, 1808–1826.* Berkeley and Los Angeles: University of California Press, 1978.

Rodríguez O., Jaime E. *The Independence of Spanish America.* Cambridge: Cambridge University Press, 1998.

Suanzes-Carpegna, Joaquín Varela. *La teoría del estado en los orígenes del constitucionalismo hispánico: Las Cortes de Cádiz.* Madrid: Centro de Estudios Constitucionales, 1983.

See also: Abolition and Emancipation; Atlantic Economy; Cortes of Cádiz; Enlightenment—Spanish America; Independence I–VI; Laws—Colonial Latin America; Liberalism; Napoleonic Invasion and Spanish America; Trade—Spain/Spanish America.

CONTRABAND

In general, traffic in prohibited goods, or violations of commercial policy. Some students of colonial trade distinguish between two kinds of illicit commercial activities, describing the breach of prohibition regimes and external trade as contraband, and tax evasion as smuggling. Official discourse in the Iberian imperial systems commonly referred to all commercial transgressions as contraband. In theory, both the Portuguese and Spanish Crowns enjoyed commercial monopolies over their American colonies. Colonial subjects in the New World were expected to import only from their respective metropoles, export their primary products directly to the Iberian Peninsula, and traffic and trade along approved routes and in specified ports. In practice, however, Portugal and Spain could never fully impose their mercantile will on their colonial subjects, who chronically, systemically, and often quite profitably violated restrictions against trade between colonies and across imperial divides.

Contraband existed in all parts of the Americas throughout the colonial period, although it was more prevalent in some places and certain periods than others. In general, contraband's existence depends on legal frameworks for trade regulation and state actions to enforce these controls. In the Ibero-American case, mercantilist subordination defined the colonies' commercial relationship with their respective metropoles from early in the colonial period. Acts that constituted smuggling took shape once the monopoly trade systems were established and enforcement implemented, that is, by the middle of the sixteenth century. Trade between colonies within the same imperial system was discouraged, and trade outside of the imperial system, either with northern European rivals or their American colonies, was prohibited. The elaborate systems of trade included a multitude of taxes imposed on goods sent from Iberia to the New World, as well as tariffs that often made prohibitively expensive the finished goods and other European commodities marketed to American consumers. The high prices for legal goods, the limited number of approved points of exchange, and the irregularity of supply made it difficult for many to comply with official trade policy. Some ports outside of the core colonies went for decades without seeing a licensed ship. Some colonial subjects sought to take advantage of these restrictions by trading in untaxed goods under the cover of the legal transatlantic trade, while others chose to trade outside of the imperial monopoly trade structure entirely.

Tax fraud within the legal transatlantic trade became a regular practice much earlier than external trade. The very merchants and colonial bureaucrats who operated and regulated the legal trade were often the most deeply involved in this form of contraband. The strategies for profiting from bending or breaking tariff schedules and quota stipulations were varied and were performed at most if not all the stages in the transatlantic trade. Merchants underreported total volumes or values of their merchandise, thereby paying taxes on a fraction of the taxable goods. The introduction of untaxed merchandise was pervasive, from the sailors who snuck aboard a few bolts of cloth among their personal belongings, through the ship captains and merchants who loaded and transported barrels or chests of unreported or banned goods, to the very builders of oceangoing vessels. Ship construction itself was used as a smuggling technique: tonnage determined some taxes assessed on a vessel's cargo, so ships were often built bigger than what their builders claimed and what showed on the tax rolls, and thus the tonnage of ships was often underreported. Sometimes goods were loaded onto merchant vessels after taxes had been levied and paid. This activity took place at night, off the coast of the Iberian Peninsula, or sometimes even at sea. Additional furtive loading took place in the islands of the eastern Atlantic where Iberian ships made stops for basic supplies before heading for their American destinations.

Unreported calls at ports along sailing routes also provided the opportunity to buy and sell off the books. Sanctioned and taxed goods on legitimate vessels could make their way into unsanctioned markets through faked forced landings at places like Martinique, Jamaica, Saint Eustatius, Rio de Janeiro, and Curaçao. Arrangements with local officials allowed for additional tax-evasion techniques. Customs officers in cahoots with smuggling merchants or crew members identified and confiscated unreported goods that represented a fraction of the total smuggled merchandise. The confiscation and auction of captured merchandise also served as a smuggling strategy. Arrangements were made so that confiscated goods were sold to the original owners or their agents. Complicit customs officials would then be recompensed. Port authorities also altered travel papers and reports to mask unauthorized landings or clandestine cargo. Ships returning to Lisbon or Seville from American ports likewise performed similar deceptions, both along the way and at their final ports of call.

The structure of colonial government and bureaucratic service encouraged this type of extralegal trade, especially in the Spanish American empire. Over time the Spanish Crown increasingly sought quick, consistent solutions to its chronic financial difficulties. Venality spread throughout the colonial bureaucracy. By the eighteenth century, the highest and lowest offices in Spanish America were for sale, and in some cases the prices were high and the waiting lists long. Military officers and career colonial administrators paid the Crown many years in advance to reserve their posts as governors and viceroys, and they often borrowed from Carrera de las Indias merchants the money for the post as well as the funds to cover travel for themselves and their entourages. Colonial officials arrived in the Indies deep in debt and willing to turn a blind eye to extralegal commercial activities in order to reimburse their creditors and make some money during their short time in office. In most New World colonies, this attitude meant allowing some degree of contraband under the guise and protection of the legal transatlantic trade. In some parts, colonial officials faced a more complicated challenge. The contraband trade that went on around them, often involving them, joined subjects of the Portuguese and Spanish Crowns with subjects of their European rivals.

Smuggling across imperial divides became a regular part of commercial life in Iberian America much later than the surreptitious tactics carried out within the legal trade. The conditions for regular trade with foreign colonies or with subjects of rival European states did not present themselves until nearly two centuries after the initial conquest by Spain and Portugal. The rise of consistent interimperial contraband depended on a number of factors, all of which turned on efforts made by Spain's and Portugal's European rivals to challenge, undermine, or penetrate Iberian territorial and economic positions in the New World. Silver drove much of this activity. The violent attempts to capture shipments of silver and other precious metals that characterized European rivalries of the sixteenth and early seventeenth centuries began to give way in the second half of the seventeenth century to more peaceful and ultimately more profitable strategies for penetrating Ibero-American markets.

The Dutch were the first to make the transition and provided the model soon imitated by other Europeans. In the last decades of the seventeenth century, the Dutch transformed their island colony of Curaçao from a staging ground for raids against Spanish American coastal settlements and convoys into the entrepôt of the south Caribbean. This new role first took shape during the second half of the seventeenth century with the slave trade. Over the next several decades, the inventories bought and sold on the island expanded to include textiles, finished goods, firearms, food, and spirits from Europe, and specie, sugar, cacao, tobacco, indigo, hides, and other products from the Americas. Dutch merchants based in Curaçao traded throughout the Caribbean, but they dominated along the northern coast of South America and in the southern islands of the Caribbean Sea. The Dutch established a similar center for the eastern Caribbean on Saint Eustatius. The trade with the Spanish colony of Venezuela proved particularly fruitful, and by the beginning of the eighteenth century, Venezuela had become Curaçao's principal trading partner in the thriving Caribbean transit trade.

In Jamaica the English followed the Dutch example. Taken from Spanish control in 1655, the island became not only a successful sugar-producing colony, but also a major center for smuggling that rivaled Dutch Curaçao in the eighteenth century. English smugglers sailing out of Jamaica dominated the trade with New Spain and Central America, and under the guise of the *asiento,* the slave-trade contract granted by the Spanish Crown to the English South Seas Company after the War of the Spanish Succession, carried out extralegal trade in Spanish America's principal legal ports and trade fairs.

European demand for American primary products like tobacco, cacao, sugar, and indigo helped consolidate the smuggling system. After steadily increasing over the later seventeenth and early eighteenth centuries, this demand grew at an unprecedented rate between 1720 and 1750. The rising demand was no secret, nor was the wealth generated by the growing economies of Spanish America's periphery. After the War of the Spanish Succession, the Bourbon monarchs sought to assert effectively the mercantilist claims and policies the Habsburgs had put into place centuries before. The economic, political, and military reforms aimed to orient the rising economies of Venezuela and the Río de la Plata toward Spain. The contraband trade in cacao in the first case and Peruvian silver in the second belied the Spanish Crown's claims to commercial hegemony and threatened the monarchs' claims to sovereign control.

Venezuela and the Río de la Plata were the two most prominent examples of a growing trend throughout Latin America during the eighteenth century. The two colonies had for generations been relegated to the defensive backside of the Spanish American systems of trade and defense. Chronic neglect of these peripheral colonies had led their occupants and administrators to develop their own strategies for survival. Ironically, violation of monopoly trade regulations maintained places like Tierra Firme, Central America, and the Río de la Plata as viable parts of the Spanish Empire, and by the eighteenth century transformed them into thriving export economies. For example, for years the Spanish Crown considered the Río de la Plata's role as strictly defensive. It protected the backdoor entrance to the silver-rich Upper Peru. But the Crown provided few resources, and the commercial restrictions imposed upon the colony made it virtually impossible to fulfill its role in the imperial system through legal means. It was contraband, trading with the very Europeans who were seen as threats to territorial control, that kept the Río de la Plata functioning as a Spanish colony and that forced a major shift in imperial policy.

Portugal also sought to tap into the illegal trade in Peruvian silver through the Río de la Plata. The Colonia de Sacramento was founded in 1680 as part of the Portuguese Crown's attempt to exert formal control over the illegal penetration of the Spanish Empire that had been carried on by Portuguese subjects for years. The steady trade through the Río de la Plata, as witnessed by the constant presence of English ships at the river's mouth, spurred the urban growth of Buenos Aires and influenced the economies of the interior as well. Industries arose to provide services and supplies to the illegal trade in silver that joined Upper Peru with the Argentine interior, Buenos Aires, and beyond.

The Bourbon and Pombaline reforms of the second half of the eighteenth century tried to impose political and economic control over areas that had developed with a great deal of autonomy. This centralization was often deeply resented, especially in places like Caracas and Buenos Aires, where the Creole elite viewed economic prosperity as having been achieved in spite of metropolitan neglect and restrictions. Smuggling in these places was a long-standing tradition, understood as an unwritten prerogative developed in response to economic necessity. This resentment eventually contributed to some elite members' willingness to embrace radical political alternatives as a means to reestablish control over what they considered rightfully theirs.

Jeremy Cohen

References

Aizpurua, Ramón. *Curazao y la costa de Caracas: Introducción al estudio del contrabando de la provincia de Venezuela en tiempos de la Compañía Guipuzcoana, 1730–1780*. Fuentes para la Historia Colonial de Venezuela, no. 222. Caracas: Biblioteca de la Academia Nacional de la Historia, 1993.

Arauz Monfante, Celestino Andrés. *El contrabando holandés en el Caribe durante la primera mitad del siglo XVIII*. 2 vols. Fuentes para la Historia Colonial de Venezuela, nos. 168 and 169. Caracas: Biblioteca de la Academia Nacional de la Historia, 1984.

Feliciano Ramos, Héctor R. *El contrabando inglés en el Caribe y el Golfo de México (1748–1778)*. Seville: Publicaciones de la Excma. Diputación Provincial de Sevilla, 1990.

Grahn, Lance R. *The Political Economy of Smuggling: Regional Informal Economies in Early Bourbon New Granada*. Boulder, CO: Westview, 1997.

Klooster, Wim. *Illicit Riches: Dutch Trade in the Caribbean, 1648–1795*. Leiden: KITLV Press, 1998.

Moutoukias, Zacarías. "Power, Corruption, and Commerce: The Making of the Local Administrative Structure in Seventeenth-Century Buenos Aires." *Hispanic American Historical Review* 68, no. 4 (1988): 771–801.

Pijning, Ernst. "Controlling Contraband: Mentality, Economy and Society in Eighteenth-Century Rio de Janeiro." Ph.D. dissertation, Johns Hopkins University, 1997.

See also: Asiento; Atlantic Economy; Bourbon Reforms; Brazil; Cacao; Caracas Company; Defense—Colonial Spanish America; Habsburgs; Independence I–VI; Monarchs of Spain; Monopolies; Pirates and Piracy; Ships and Shipbuilding; Silver; Sugar; Tobacco; Venezuela; War of the Spanish Succession.

CONVERSO

The term *converso* refers to anyone who converted from a non-Christian faith to Christianity. More specifically, the term is used for Jews who converted to Christianity during the Middle Ages and the early modern period in Europe. Jewish conversion on the Iberian Peninsula happened between 1391 and 1497, largely due to pressure from anti-Jewish Christians.

Though newly Christian, many conversos did not receive acceptance within the Christian society of Spaniards and Portuguese, nor did members of Jewish society willingly interact with them. Most Jews disliked the conversos because they were perceived as having rejected the Jewish faith. Many "Old" Christians (the name given to those without a Jewish heritage) did not like them because they believed that the conversos were insincere in their conversion. These Old Christians thought conversos had converted to receive the social advancement available to Christians.

Nevertheless, conversos came to hold positions as priests, friars, chaplains, city councilors, and doctors. People of prominence throughout Iberian society had converso blood. Saint Teresa of Ávila's grandfather was found guilty of being a Judaizer (a Christian who practices Jewish customs) by the Spanish Inquisition. Upper-class Christians and Jews intermarried for money and political position. King Ferdinand of Aragon was a descendant of Jews, and many visitors to the court of Queen Isabella commented on the Jewish quality of the queen's court and the queen herself. To prevent the converted Jews from reverting to their previous religion, the Catholic monarchs, Ferdinand and Isabella, instituted the Inquisition. Originally both conversos and Old Christians were subject to the Inquisition. By 1540 conversos had basically disappeared from inquisitorial cases; instead they were persecuted through prejudice.

The question of purity of blood and what to do with conversos was debated among the intellectuals of Iberian society, many of whom were conversos themselves. In an attempt to join with the affluent society and prove their faith in Christianity, many converso intellectuals turned their rhetoric against Jews. Statutes that required *limpieza de sangre* (literally, "cleanness of blood"; that is, blood without Jewish or Muslim "impurity") were issued for certain jobs. Though some individuals and institutions ignored these laws, others used them as justification to persecute conversos.

Many conversos opted to flee the peninsula due to political and social oppression. Latin America became a desired location because of its cultural similarity to Spain and Portugal. Passage to Spain's viceroyalties in the New World was limited by law to Old Christian Castilians. Though other people did migrate to the colonies, they had to use illegal methods or receive special permission from the Crown. A life in the New World allowed a fresh start for some conversos, since they left their previous communities and could practice Christianity without the stigma of having converso blood. The greater physical space among the populace in the New World allowed those who wished to continue to practice Judaism to do so in greater secrecy. This does not mean that conversos or Jews enjoyed a safe haven in the New World. On the contrary, during the sixteenth century conversos believed to be insincere in their conversion were persecuted by the Mexican Inquisition.

Jonathan Truitt

References

Beinart, Haim. "Conversos and Their Fate." Pp. 92–122 in *Spain and the Jews: The Sephardi Experience 1492 and After,* edited by Elie Kedourie. London: Thames and Hudson, 1992.

Gojman de Backal, Alicia. "Conversos." In *Encyclopedia of Mexico: History, Society and Culture,* 2 vols., edited by Michael S. Werner. Chicago: Fitzroy Dearborn, 1997.

Kamen, Henry. *The Spanish Inquisition: An Historical Revision.* New Haven, CT: Yale University Press, 1997.

Martz, Linda. "Relations between Conversos and Old Christians in Early Modern Toledo: Some Different Perspectives." Pp. 220–240 in *Christians, Muslims, and Jews in Medieval and Early Modern Spain,* edited by Mark D. Meyerson and Edward D. English. Notre Dame, IN: University of Notre Dame Press, 1999.

See also: Catholic Church in Spanish America; Comissários; Familiares; Inquisition—Luso-America; Inquisition—Spanish America; Islam; Jews—Colonial Spanish America; Migration—From Iberia to the New World; Moors; Race; Religious Orders; Viceroyalties.

CORREGIDOR/ CORREGIMIENTO

The *corregidor* and his political, organizational, and jurisdictional unit, the *corregimiento,* functioned as a regional layer in the colonial administration of the Spanish Empire in the New World, between the viceroy and *audiencia* (high court) at the top and the Amerindian pueblos and Spanish towns at the bottom. This system of provincial administration came to America from the Kingdom of Castile, where it had been introduced toward the end of the fourteenth century and given its juridical basis in 1500. In Castile the corregidor intervened in municipal government; in America he domesticated the provincial

government, as a centralizing agent of the Crown in order to correct (*corregir*) local government, administer justice, and maintain public order. In America corregidores were initially introduced to check the power of the *encomenderos* (those who, as holders of grants called *encomiendas,* had the right to exact tribute in goods and labor from a specific group of natives), to keep them from becoming a New World aristocracy and a threat to royal authority, and to protect Native American communities from the more exploitative practices of the encomenderos. Corregidores collected the tribute paid out by the Amerindian communities to their encomenderos and to the Crown and oversaw the labor services provided by the Amerindians to the local community.

In Mexico the functions of corregidores and *alcaldes mayores* tended to converge, and over time the terms became synonymous and interchangeable. Initially the term *alcaldes mayores* designated officials of several territories that had been grouped together under their rule as an *alcaldía mayor.* By 1535 there were at least 100 of these two kinds of officials in Mexico, and by 1570 there were upwards of 70 alcaldías mayores and 200 corregimientos. As the Amerindian population declined, however, corregimientos were suppressed, and their territories and jurisdictions were attached to the nearest alcaldía mayor, so that alcaldes mayores became by far the dominant provincial officials in Mexico.

In Peru and Colombia, the operative provincial bureaucrat for both Spaniards and Amerindians was the corregidor. The office was introduced in Peru in the 1560s and 1570s with the creation of eighty-eight corregimientos and in Colombia in the 1590s. Opposition from encomenderos and other members of the provincial elite was significant. The responsibilities and functions of both alcaldes mayores and corregidores were the same and similar to those of a governor, though usually with a smaller territory. They oversaw town councils, administered justice in the first instance, and made sure provincial life and government conformed to Spanish norms. Peninsulars usually held office for five years, while New World–born designees were in office for only three. Viceroys could make interim appointments of one to two years.

In those areas formerly ruled by the Inca, the corregidor was a position in great demand because of the huge profits that could be made in exchanges with the Amerindians. Even after the Spanish conquest, Amerindian institutions and customs still prevailed and were used to deliver vast amounts of labor, goods, and services to the local elite—encomenderos, native lords, and church and government officials at the town and pueblo level. Riding herd on the local elite was the corregidor, and his ability to regulate this exchange offered him a chance for personal enrichment. In Mexico and Peru competition for the position was intense, and fabulous sums were paid out for the office, sometimes years in advance. Corregidores made as much as 100,000 pesos in profit from the *reparto de mercancía* (distribution of merchandise), that is, the "forced" sale of merchandise to Amerindian communities.

Most historians view the corregidor as an exploitative official who forced unwanted and overpriced merchandise on the Amerindian communities. The official and the institution have a long and nefarious record in the historiography and have contributed much to Spain's Black Legend, which suggests that Spaniards were particularly cruel, especially toward Native Americans. Recent scholarship, however, suggests that many Amerindians willingly received the money or merchandise advanced. From this point of view, the reparto de mercancía was an innovative system that solved the market limitations of a pre-Columbian indigenous economy and of a premodern Iberian bureaucracy. It made life easier for peasant producers, government officials, and Iberian merchants by offering them economic advantages that were not otherwise available.

Whatever the case, the system generated much controversy among Bourbon reformers like José de Gálvez, who believed the corregidores and alcaldes mayores to be corrupt. As minister of the Indies (1776–1787), Gálvez replaced most of them with a smaller group of powerful regional officials, known as intendants. At the same time, Gálvez prohibited the "forced" sale of merchandise. This structural "reform" at the regional level throughout much of the Spanish Empire has generated an enormous debate among historians. Traditionally scholars have tended to accept arguments for "reform," perhaps because the word carries a positive connotation. It is true that in the late colonial period, Indian rebellions or communities on the road to empowerment and new elites on the rise invariably clashed with local officials and were critical of the older system. Whether most scholars will continue to accept the resulting negative documentation against corregidores and alcaldes mayores as true remains to be seen.

Maurice P. Brungardt

References

Bakewell, Peter. *A History of Latin American Empires and Sequels, 1450–1930.* Oxford: Blackwell, 1997.

Baskes, Jeremy. *Indians, Merchants, and Markets: A Reinterpretation of the Repartimiento and Spanish-Indian Economic Relations in Colonial Oaxaca, 1750–1821.* Stanford, CA: Stanford University Press, 2000.

Lockhart, James, and Stuart B. Schwartz. *Early Latin America: A History of Colonial Spanish America and Brazil.* Cambridge: Cambridge University Press, 1983.

Lohmann Villena, Guillermo. *El corregidor de indios en el Perú bajo los Austrias.* Madrid: Ediciones Cultura Hispánica, 1957.

Moreno Cebrián, Adolfo. *El corregidor de indios y la economía peruana del siglo XVIII (los repartos forzosos de mercancías).* Madrid: Instituto Gonzalo Fernández de Oviedo, 1977.

See also: Administration—Colonial Spanish America; Audiencias; Bourbon Reforms; Catholic Church in Spanish America; Cities; Conquest and the Debate over Justice; Encomienda; Intendants/Intendency System; Repartimiento.

CORTES OF CÁDIZ

The Cortes, a modified descendant of the medieval Spanish parliament, met in the southern Spanish city of Cádiz from 1810 to 1814, producing Spain's first written constitution in 1812.

When it became clear that neither a Supreme Central Junta (1808–1809) nor an appointed Regency (1809–1810) could unite Spain's regions in the fight against Napoleon Bonaparte, the Regency summoned a Cortes to help govern in the absence of Spain's king, Ferdinand VII. After considering convening a traditional parliament representing the estates of cities, noblemen, and clergy, authorities instead announced on January 24, 1810, elections for a unicameral body to include elected representatives from Spain's free and occupied peninsular territories and its overseas possessions in the Americas and Asia.

The Extraordinary Cortes (1810–1813) met first on the Isla de León (September 24, 1810–February 20, 1811), moving to Cádiz (February 24, 1811) as Napoleon's troops closed in; there it remained until its closing on September 14, 1813. The subsequent Ordinary Cortes (1813–1814) began in Cádiz (October 1, 1813), removed to León from mid-October to early November, and from January 15 to May 4, 1814, met in Madrid until Ferdinand VII returned and dissolved the Cortes and rejected its constitution. With few large public buildings, the Cortes met principally in churches and in theaters.

The Cortes included representation from Spain's peninsular and overseas territories. Historians believe that about 300 permanent and temporary deputies attended, with about a third representing districts from what are now Mexico, Central America, Puerto Rico, Cuba, Argentina, Chile, Venezuela, Peru, Colombia, Santo Domingo, and the Philippines. Deputies included approximately 90 clerics, 60 lawyers, 20 academics, 45 military men, 50 bureaucrats, and a dozen landowners. Youthful (mid-20s to mid-40s) liberal deputies predominated at the Extraordinary Cortes, while there was a slightly older, conservative majority in the Ordinary.

Although initially convened to advise the Regency, at the opening session on September 24, 1810, Cortes deputies pronounced their body a constituent assembly and declared that sovereignty resided "essentially" in the Spanish nation, rather than the king. By early December, calls to draft a Spanish constitution succeeded, and a committee representing all the tendencies of the Cortes—peninsular and American, secular and religious, liberal, moderate, and royalist—worked from a draft prepared by

Antonio Ranz Romanillos for the Suprema Junta Central. After heated debates, in March 1812, the Cortes adopted the *Constitución Política de la Monarquía Española.* The constitution established Spain as a constitutional monarchy; made Roman Catholicism the national religion; separated legislative, executive, and judicial power; established civil and political rights for individuals; and emphasized equality before the law. The Cortes also passed substantial legislation regulating elections, separating military and civil administration, abolishing the Inquisition, ending the practice of entailing estates (*señorios*), defining responsibilities of new bodies like elected city councils and provincial deputations, ending forced labor for Indians (the *mita*), approving habeas corpus, and declaring Spain's American territories an "integral" part of the monarchy rather than colonies. On the other hand, the Cortes could not agree to end certain privileges for the church and military *(fueros),* provide political rights to Spaniards of African heritage, end either slavery or the slave trade, or establish full free trade. Debates over granting freedom of the press produced the term "liberal" in its modern sense of "progressive," and overall legislation of the Extraordinary Session was consonant with constitutional ideas introduced in France and the United States, while respecting the traditional Spanish heritage.

Jordana Dym

References

Chust, Manuel. *La cuestion nacional Americana en las Cortes de Cádiz.* UNED: Alzira-Valencia, 1999.

Rodríguez, Mario. *The Cádiz Experiment in Central America, 1808–1826.* Berkeley and Los Angeles: University of California Press, 1978.

Suárez, Federico. *Las Cortes de Cádiz.* Madrid: Rialp, 1982.

See also: Abolition and Emancipation; Administration—Colonial Spanish America; American Revolution; Atlantic Economy; Constitution of Cádiz; Enlightenment—Spanish America; Independence I–VI; Inquisition—Spanish America; Laws—Colonial Latin America; Mita; Monarchs of Spain; Monopolies; Napoleonic Invasion and Spanish America; Slave Trade.

COSTA RICA

This former Spanish colony is located on the isthmus of Central America between Nicaragua and Panama. Costa Rica was reportedly named by Christopher Columbus, who briefly visited the Atlantic coast of the region on his fourth and final voyage to the Americas in 1502. However, some sixty years passed before permanent Spanish settlement was undertaken there.

The colony of Costa Rica was situated on the periphery of one of Spain's more peripheral colonial realms, the area under the jurisdiction of the Audiencia (High Court) of Guatemala. Few settlers were attracted to the "Rich Coast," despite its name, given a dearth of both profitable exports and exploitable native labor. Therefore, the Spanish conquest of Costa Rica (proceeding from Panama in the 1520s) was slow, not completed before the 1570s, and even then there were extensive frontier regions beyond Spanish control. Costa Rica had the smallest population of any Central American province during the colonial period: on the eve of independence an estimated 63,000 inhabitants lived there, scarcely more than 5 percent of the total population of the audiencia.

Costa Rica's geography is marked by a central plateau, with the central valley lying within that plateau. This feature powerfully shaped patterns of settlement, as more settlers were attracted to the agreeable climate of the valley than to the hotter and wetter lowlands on either coast. The population of the central plateau was, however, further isolated from the colonial capital by this geography.

Culturally, most of the indigenous people inhabiting what is now Costa Rica lay outside of the Mesoamerican "high culture" area, sharing more features in common with the Chibchan cultures of northern South America. Available evidence suggests the native peoples of Costa Rica at the time of contact were organized into small tribes and chiefdoms that had no advanced farming techniques, practicing slash-and-burn agriculture instead. Because of their small numbers, customary Spanish institutions for controlling native labor (such as the *encomienda* and *repartimiento*) proved generally ineffective.

Native Americans in Costa Rica, as elsewhere, resisted Spanish intrusion. One area the Spaniards found difficult to subdue was the Talamanca region in the southern part of the province. This mountainous terrain provided a refuge for Indians who sought to escape Spanish demands of labor and tribute. Rebellions in Talamanca, in 1610 and again 100 years later, helped to keep the Spaniards at bay. Efforts to pacify the indigenous population included the work of Franciscan missionaries who moved into such frontier regions.

After the Spaniards' initial search for quick mineral wealth was abandoned, the province became a site for tobacco production and cattle raising. Some of these goods were sent to provision the indigo-growing regions in and around El Salvador. Overall, however, most inhabitants of colonial Costa Rica lived and worked in the context of a strictly local economy.

The one significant export crop produced in colonial Costa Rica was cacao. The bean used to make chocolate became a viable export after cacao plantations were developed in the Matina Valley region of the Atlantic coast during the second half of the seventeenth century. The decline of existing plantations on the northern Pacific coast of the audiencia coincided with rising demand in Europe to create an opening for Costa Rican cacao. The development of this potentially profitable crop led to the most substantial use of black slave labor in the history of the province. African slave imports into Costa Rica were minuscule compared to other regions; even so, black slaves and their more numerous mulatto and *zambo* (half black, half Indian) descendants provided most of the labor needed for cacao production.

The cacao bean did not, however, produce substantial wealth for Costa Rica, as competing producers were better situated to dominate the market. Among other problems, Costa Rica's Atlantic coast cacao plantations were vulnerable to the depredations of the Zambos-Miskitos, Indian and Afro-Indian inhabitants of the coast who were based further north on the Mosquito shore. The Zambos-Miskitos, supported by British settlers in the region, played a key role in undercutting Spanish claims to authority in the Atlantic coast region, engaging in contraband trade and even assassinating a Costa Rican governor in 1756.

Central America's independence from Spain in 1821 marked a clear turning point, but it was accompanied by little of the controversy seen elsewhere in the

Americas. Costa Rica was a member of the United Provinces of Central America from 1823 to 1838. As this Central American federation crumbled, Costa Rica was just beginning to realize the potential of a new export crop: coffee. By the end of the nineteenth century, coffee accounted for the vast majority of Costa Rica's export revenue, and provided the cornerstone for an expanding trade with Britain and other industrializing countries. The development of Costa Rica's coffee economy was powerfully influenced by the province's colonial heritage. For example, the same shortage of labor that had limited colonial settlement in Costa Rica inhibited the growth of the coercive patterns of labor exploitation associated with coffee production in countries like Guatemala and El Salvador.

The people of Costa Rica are commonly described as being more "European," racially and culturally, than other Latin Americans. Although Costa Rica did have a small native population at contact, and their numbers declined continuously throughout the colonial period, the number of Spanish colonists who arrived during that period was also relatively small. The growth of the province's population during the colonial period was largely a result of miscegenation: "whites" in Costa Rica were already outnumbered by people of mixed race by 1700, and one hundred years later those *castas,* as they were called, made up 75 percent of the province's population. After independence, the most significant influx of immigrants consisted not of European migrants, but rather of West Indian blacks who came to the Atlantic coast to work on the railroad and banana plantations.

On the other hand, Costa Rica might assert a "European" cultural inheritance, though certainly not a Spanish one, on the basis of the country's largely successful and stable embrace of liberal democracy. The country experienced only one brief stint of military rule, in the early 1900s, and then abolished its army after a revolution in 1948. These features do indeed distinguish Costa Rica in a region characterized throughout the twentieth century by a strong tendency toward military dictatorship.

Doug Tompson

References

Gudmundson, Lowell. *Costa Rica before Coffee: Society and Economy on the Eve of the Export Boom.* Baton Rouge: Louisiana State University Press, 1986.

Hall, Carolyn. *Costa Rica: A Geographical Interpretation in Historical Perspective.* Boulder, CO: Westview, 1985.

MacLeod, Murdo J. *Spanish Central America: A Socioeconomic History, 1520–1720.* Berkeley and Los Angeles: University of California Press, 1973.

Wortman, Miles L. *Government and Society in Central America, 1680–1840.* New York: Columbia University Press, 1982.

See also: Audiencias; Bananas; Cacao; Coffee; Contraband; Dyes and Dyewood; Encomienda; Independence III—Central America; Mulatto; Native Americans IV—Mesoamerica; Religious Orders; Repartimiento; Tobacco.

COTTON

Two species of cotton, each with several varieties, are native to the Americas, *Gossypium hirsutum* (North American Southwest, Mexico, Central America, Florida, and the Greater Antilles) and *Gossypium barbadense* (Galapagos Islands, the Andes, Brazil, and Lesser Antilles). The plant was domesticated in ancient times for its fiber, seed, and oil. Beginning in the preclassic period, cotton cloth became an important commodity in the systems of tribute and trade that accompanied urbanization and early state formation. The painted accounts preserved in the *Codex Mendoza,* for example, reveal the large quantities of cotton mantles sent as tribute to Tenochtitlan (Mexico) by subject towns in the early sixteenth century. Christopher Columbus reported cotton cloth in the inventories of Maya trading canoes that he intercepted off the coast of Central America. And Hernando Cortés used native cotton batting for armor during the conquest of Mexico.

Until the late eighteenth century, primarily indigenous peoples produced cotton fiber and cloth. Plants were cultivated in household gardens and *milpas,* or gathered in wild stands of cotton found in coastal lowlands. Thread and bolts of cloth (*mantas*) were collected by the Spanish as tribute, expropriated through the coercive systems of exchange known as the *reparto de efectos* or the *repartimiento de mercancías* (distribution of goods), or sold in regional markets by Indian merchants. These finished goods were made by women, using ceramic and wooden spindles and backstrap looms.

In the second half of the eighteenth century, systems of cotton cultivation and textile manufacturing were transformed with the onset of the Industrial Revolution. Mechanized looms were gradually introduced into Latin America, and textile manufacturing shifted to urban artisan shops and male workers. As demand for raw fiber increased in Europe, the cultivation of cotton in Mexico and elsewhere moved to plantation agriculture and commercial farms. Dependence on indigenous production ended. In Brazil, for example, after the Pombaline reforms, cotton growing was promoted in Maranhão, Pernambuco, and parts of the Bahia, using African slave labor. By the 1790s, a third of British cotton imports were from Brazil.

Nonetheless, cotton production languished in Latin America for much of the nineteenth century, except in the 1860s, when the Civil War in the United States opened opportunities in global markets for cotton producers in Mexico, Peru, and especially Brazil. Mexico could not meet domestic demand for cotton fiber in this period, even though textile manufacturing was industrializing rapidly after 1870. Cotton cultivation in Latin America finally made substantial gains in the twentieth century, first with government campaigns to diversify agriculture during the Great Depression and then with the so-called Green Revolution of the late 1950s and 1960s, when pesticides and chemical fertilizers were promoted more aggressively. Today, Brazil is the largest producer in the region.

Kevin Gosner

References

Berdan, Frances F. "Cotton in Aztec Mexico: Production, Distribution, and Uses." *Mexican Studies/Estudios Mexicanos* 3 (1987): 235–263.

Bulmer-Thomas, Victor. *The Economic History of Latin America since Independence.* Cambridge: Cambridge University Press, 1994.

Fryxell, Paul A. *The Natural History of the Cotton Tribe.* College Station: Texas A&M University Press, 1979.

Salvucci, Richard J. *Textiles and Capitalism in Mexico: An Economic History of the Obrajes, 1539–1840.* Princeton, NJ: Princeton University Press, 1987.

See also: Artisans; Coca; Codices; Coffee; Columbian Exchange—Agriculture; Dyes and Dyewood; Enlightenment—Brazil; Henequen; Milpa; Native Americans IV—Mesoamerica; Repartimiento; Women—Colonial Spanish America.

COUNCIL OF CASTILE

The Royal Council of Castile was an institution that advised Spanish monarchs regarding public affairs and counseled them in the government and administration of the kingdom, which from 1492 until 1524 also included Spain's territories in the New World. The council was created at the initiative of King John I in the Cortes of Valladolid in 1385. It then began to function as a permanent and organized bureaucratic entity, with its own attributions and fixed personnel, comprised of four prelates, four knights, and four citizens. These councilors, together with the king, intervened in all important matters regarding the government of the kingdom except those areas that exclusively pertained to the monarch: the administration of justice, the concession of land, graces and favors, royal pardons for the crime of homicide, and the provision of palace offices and public positions.

Over time, the structure of the council varied, with a progressive increase in size; thus, in 1426, there were over sixty-five councilors. The increase in size brought with it new responsibilities, the most important of which involved the incorporation of jurists, or university-trained experts in the law, upon whom the incipient modern state increasingly came to rely. As early as 1406, Henry III replaced the citizens with doctors in law, fixing the number of councilors at sixteen. Nevertheless, following the chaos and administrative inefficiency of the reign of Henry IV, the Catholic Monarchs, Isabella and Ferdinand, established the most effective and enduring reform. With the administrative and institutional restructuring carried out in the Cortes of Toledo in 1480, the Royal Council of Castile became the central organ of the government and the model for the political system. Beyond elevating the council to the supreme tribunal of Castile, the Catholic Monarchs included among its functions advice in the designation of offices and concession of favors, as well as the supervision of Castilian local government, international relations, royal finances, and internal security. Isabella and Ferdinand converted the Council of Castile into a permanent consultative institution established in the residence of the Crown, with a composition that gave preference to legal experts who were trusted by the monarchs. Their strategy was to prevent the council from falling under the control of the powerful Castilian high aristocracy. The council consisted of a prelate as president, eight or nine university graduates, and three knights, who, in daily meetings, would dispatch reports and resolve political matters. The council's presidency became the most important and prestigious state office.

The structure described barely changed under the rule of the Habsburg dynasty (1517–1700), from Charles I (who as Holy Roman Emperor was known as Charles V) to Charles II, although the number of royal councilors increased considerably in the seventeenth century as a result of the sale of public offices. Nor did the royal council cease to be the axis of Spain's internal government in the eighteenth century, in spite of the relevant role that the secretaries of state achieved in the centralizing policies of the new Bourbon dynasty (from Philip V to Charles IV), whose monarchs relegated other state councils to honorific roles or made them disappear. From that point until its disappearance in 1834, the Council of Castile consisted of a lay president, twenty-two ministers, three university graduates, and seven notaries.

The Council of Castile assumed the governance of the Indies until 1524; however, because of the vast territory of Spain's colonial possessions and the administrative complexity of an overseas empire, the Crown decided to establish a new administrative body, the Council of the Indies.

Carlos Alberto González Sánchez

References

Bakewell, Peter. *A History of Latin America.* Oxford: Blackwell, 1997.

Gan Giménez, Pedro. *El consejo real de Castilla.* Granada: Imprenta Román, 1970.

García de Valdeavellano, Luis. *Curso de historia de las instituciones españolas: De los orígenes al final de la Edad Media.* Madrid: Alianza, 1998.

See also: Administration—Colonial Spanish America; Atlantic Economy; Bourbon Reforms; Council of the Indies; Habsburgs; Monarchs of Spain; Trade—Spain/Spanish America.

COUNCIL OF THE INDIES

This was created by Charles I (better known by the name he bore as Holy Roman Emperor, Charles V) on August 1, 1524, as an advisory body to administer Spain's overseas territories. Following Columbus's first voyage, Queen Isabella of Castile, who had sponsored the expedition, used Juan Rodríguez de Fonseca, a member of the Council of Castile, to oversee colonial matters. When Rodríguez de Fonseca died in 1524, Charles determined to replace the minister with a council. The conquest of Mexico and the development of the Spanish Caribbean made it obvious to Charles that his American territories required closer supervision.

The early Council of the Indies consisted of a president, four or five councilors, a *fiscal* (royal attorney), a secretary, a comptroller, scribes, and an usher. Later the Crown added a treasurer, cosmographer, additional attorneys, and technical experts. In 1604 the Crown added a second secretary and divided the council into two sections, one for the Viceroyalty of Peru and the other for Mexico. During the 1500s, councilors generally were either lawyers or clerics, men with legal training (*ministros togados*). By the seventeenth century, the number of councilors had grown to ten, and it continued to swell under the rule of the later Habsburg monarchs. Councilors with no legal expertise (*ministros de capa y espada*) received appointments, a sign of growing venality and favoritism. Before the eighteenth century, few councilors had any firsthand knowledge of the New World, the Crown fearing that American ties might make them personally interested in the outcome of policy decisions and less loyal to the Crown.

The monarch, of course, had sovereign power over the American colonies, but the council's competence extended into all colonial administrative arenas. A "royal and supreme council," it had independent jurisdiction over all colonial matters, free from interference by other royal councils and institutions. The Council of the Indies prepared legislation for the monarch's approval, sent out special inspectors (*visitadores*), and organized reviews (*residencias*) of the principal outgoing colonial officials. Civil suits appealed from the colonial *audiencias* (high courts) received their final hearing by the council, and it was also the final court of appeal for both civil and criminal cases from the Casa de Contratación (House of Trade). Financial, commercial, military, and ecclesiastical matters also fell under its purview. Supervising royal patronage in the colonies, the council recommended individuals for appointments to political and ecclesiastical offices. Formally constituted subgroups of the council had special responsibilities: for example, the Cámara of the Indies took charge of patronage; the War Committee (*Junta de Guerra*) of the Indies oversaw military matters, particularly defense of the colonies. The council flourished in co-operation with strong, energetic rulers such as Philip II, but became overly bu-reaucratic and languid during the 1600s with the weak, later Habsburg monarchs. It also served as the model for the Por-tuguese colonial council established in 1604, when that nation was ruled by the king of Spain.

The council's status and responsibili-ties changed with the arrival of Philip V and the Bourbon dynasty. By 1717, Philip had placed colonial administration under a secretary or minister of the Indies. This al-leviated one of the greatest problems of the conciliar system: the lack of individual re-sponsibility for policies and decisions. The council retained its jurisdiction over pa-tronage and appeals from the colonial courts. Bourbon monarchs increasingly ap-pointed councilors with colonial experi-ence in the late 1700s.

Trying to govern Spain during the Napoleonic invasion and occupation of the peninsula, the Cortes of Cádiz abolished the Council of the Indies in 1812, but Fer-dinand VII restored it in 1814 when he re-turned to the throne. It survived until 1834, even though nearly all of Spain's overseas empire had won independence more than a decade earlier.

Kendall W. Brown

References
Burkholder, Mark A. *Biographical Dictionary of Councilors of the Indies, 1717–1808.* Westport, CT: Greenwood, 1986.

Haring, Clarence H. *The Spanish Empire in America.* New York: Harcourt, Brace and World, 1963.

See also: Audiencias; Bourbon Reforms; Casa de Contratación; Habsburgs; Laws— Colonial Latin America; Monarchs of Spain; Napoleonic Invasion and Spanish America; Ordenanza del Patronazgo; Viceroyalties; Visita.

COUNCIL OF TRENT

This was the general council of the Catholic Church convoked by Pope Paul III in 1545 to respond to the Protestant Reformation and reform movements within the Catholic Church. Its decrees aimed at modifying ecclesiastical practices and reforming the customs of the faithful. In Spanish America, the council's decrees gave impetus to the ascendancy of the parish clergy over the monastic orders, which had carried out much of the initial evangelization of the indigenous popula-tion, and required bishops by means of reg-ular parish inspections to monitor and cor-rect the religious practices of the laity, including new Indian converts.

The council was held in the northern Italian city of Trent and lasted until 1563. It consisted of twenty-five intermittent ses-sions that spanned eighteen years and the reigns of five popes. Political wrangling among various popes, Holy Roman Em-peror Charles V (Charles I of Spain), and Francis I of France often caused delays and suspensions of the council's work. In spite of political trials, prelates and theologians from across Europe attended the council and, despite much contentious theological debate, formulated numerous decrees re-forming and codifying ecclesiastical disci-pline, church doctrine, and lay devotional practices. Because of the wide-ranging nature of its decrees, the Council of Trent is considered the most significant church synod of the early modern period.

The council's response to calls for change from Protestant and Catholic reformers largely depended on the target of their critiques. In general, the Council of Trent responded positively to reformers' criticisms of ecclesiastical laxity. The council strengthened the authority of bishops to regulate the conduct of both the regular and secular clergy within their dioceses, mandated the foundation of diocesan seminars to better train priests, and called for the end of administrative abuses, such as simony, nepotism, and clerical nonresidence within benefices. In terms of theology, however, the prelates at Trent tended to uphold traditional positions in the face of critiques. For example, Trent condemned Martin Luther's proposition of justification through faith alone, and defended the necessity of good works for salvation. It reaffirmed the status of the seven Catholic sacraments, codified the doctrine of transubstantiation (the belief that the body and blood of Christ are truly present in the bread and wine after consecration during the mass), and maintained the sacramental nature and celibacy of the priesthood. The council sought a middle ground on the issue of lay piety. Rather than condemning devotional practices such as pilgrimages and the veneration of images and relics, as some reformers had advocated, Trent sanctioned them. However, it did attempt to subordinate such lay devotions to the sacraments and replace local patron saints with more universally recognized holy figures, such as Christ, the Virgin, and Saint Joseph.

The Council of Trent did not resolve all issues raised for debate. Most significantly, delegates at Trent could not agree on the question of papal vis-à-vis episcopal and conciliar authority, leaving the contentious issue pending.

The Council of Trent had a profound impact on Catholicism in Europe and the Americas. Especially in Spanish territories, provincial councils, or regional synods, soon promulgated the decrees of Trent at the local level. Provincial councils were convoked in Salamanca, Valencia, Granada, and Mexico in 1565. Peru soon followed in 1567. Bishops such as Juan de Palafox y Mendoza of the diocese of Puebla de los Ángeles (1639–1652) began to exert authority over religious orders and founded seminaries for clerical formation. Still, decrees aimed at reforming lay devotions, many of which in the Americas were influenced by indigenous customs, met with mixed success. Although the laity increasingly centered their devotions on Christ and the Virgin, the faithful continued to engage in extraliturgical practices that Tridentine Catholics found unorthodox.

Brian R. Larkin

References

Alberigo, Giuseppe. "The Council of Trent." Pp. 211–226 in *Catholicism in Early Modern History: A Guide to Research,* edited by John W. O'Malley. Saint Louis, MO: Center for Reformation Research, 1988.

Christian, William A., Jr. *Local Religion in Sixteenth-Century Spain.* Princeton, NJ: Princeton University Press, 1981.

Schroeder, H. J., ed. *The Cannons and Decrees of the Council of Trent.* Rockford, IL: TAN, 1978.

See also: Catholic Church in Spanish America; Clergy—Secular, in Colonial Spanish America; Diabolism in the New World; Idolatry, Extirpation of; Jesuits—Iberia and America; Papacy; Protestant Reformation; Religious Orders; Saints and Saintliness; Syncretism; Virgin of Guadalupe.

CREDIT—COLONIAL LATIN AMERICA

In colonial Latin America, credit networks functioned at all levels of society and were key to colonial economic, political, and cultural systems. Transatlantic trade as a whole rested on credit mechanisms. Credit facilitated subsistence, production, consumption, and governance in a colonial world without formal banking institutions and with chronic specie shortages. Credit, embedded in ubiquitous patron-client relationships, was important for social mobility and crucial for business success. Pawning, or *empeño,* was a common credit mechanism for poor and middling groups. Grocery retailers and employers extended lines of credit to their regular customers, and credit at *tiendas de raya,* or company stores, was also common on haciendas, in large-scale textile workshops (*obrajes*), and in mining towns. Individuals, including elite women, made personal loans and extended mortgages. Using local officials, specifically *corregidores,* as middlemen, merchant creditors financed agricultural production in many indigenous communities. In cities, merchants financed local artisans, providing them with raw materials and business capital on credit. Large-scale obrajes that produced woolen and cotton textiles also depended on credit for working capital. Urban and rural property owners, including *hacendados* (hacienda owners) and mine owners, secured mortgages from merchants, ecclesiastical lenders (especially convents, monasteries, and the Inquisition), and lay brotherhoods, or confraternities (*cofradías*). Colonial governments, too, borrowed both from the Church and from local merchants. The government also borrowed from Indian communities, as did merchants and hacienda owners.

In the eighteenth century, Spain's Bourbon monarchs introduced new commercial and public credit mechanisms. At the same time, they limited ecclesiastical lending opportunities. Catholic usury prohibitions generally restricted interest rates on money lent, whoever the lender, to about 6 percent annually. However, a variety of subterfuges were used to charge more for credit. While historians agree on the ubiquity of credit in the colonial economy, there is little consensus on whether credit had positive or negative effects on borrowers and the economy in general.

Credit was not only obtained at the macro level. In places such as Potosí, Chucuito, and Quito in the sixteenth and seventeenth centuries, Spanish and Andean women forged petty credit networks, including pawning relationships. And in Mexico City, pawning credit was a necessary lubricant for the economy, as small business owners and artisans hocked goods with other store owners, shoemakers, and goldsmiths. More than two-thirds of retail business capital might be tied up in *prendas,* or pawned goods, most of them securing loans of less than half a peso. Pawning credit differed from some other forms of popular credit—like the company store—in that no debt was incurred because collateral goods secured loans. Yet the pawning process was similar to credit accounts in stores in that it represented a link between households and the colonial political economy. By the 1750s, regulations for *pulperías* (corner stores) in New Spain required neighborhood grocers to accept goods in pawn from regular customers, especially women, as a means of providing for their families. In 1775, as part of the Bourbon reforms, the Monte de Piedad, a state-sponsored pawnshop, opened in Mexico City, providing low-interest loans to the largely white population who owned silver and imported cloth goods to leave as collateral. The average loan at the Monte de Piedad was 10 pesos, though loans of up to 1,000 pesos secured by elaborate jewelry and table service items were also made. More than 90 percent of goods pawned at the Monte de Piedad were redeemed within six months. Many Creole households maintained appearances through financial hardships in the Bourbon era by converting their stock of material wealth into a revolving credit line.

Credit was also necessary to daily life outside cities, with merchants and retailers advancing credit to laborers in need of subsistence provisions. Historians debate whether the credit system in hacienda, obraje, and mining stores constituted gouging or welfare during droughts and lean times. Similarly, the *repartimiento de bienes* (forced distribution of goods), by which local government officials brokered the advance of merchant credit to indigenous agricultural producers, has traditionally been seen as an abusive system that trapped producers into debt cycles. The forced sale, often on credit, of imported goods, mules, and oxen at inflated prices by the same brokers was even more onerous for peasants. Some Andean scholars argue that this cycle of abuse sparked rural rebellions in the eighteenth century. The institution was outlawed in 1786, though it continued illegally. A revisionist study of cochineal production in Oaxaca in southern New Spain argues that repartimiento proffered necessary credit to indigenous producers, who were voluntary and not coerced participants in the market economy.

Artisan production relied on credit, with materials paid for in installments, inventories pawned, and workshops mortgaged. Textile obrajes, too, were financed through mortgages and capital advances. Financial and family ties among merchants and artisans crossed the Atlantic, and some lasted for generations. One cloth wholesaler from Toledo made diverse investments in foreign and domestic trade in the early seventeenth century. He formed a retail partnership with a silk maker in Mexico City, to whom he contributed 2,500 pesos' worth of silk and merchandise; he imported and reexported 5,000 pesos in Chinese silk, extended 1,000 pesos in credit to cap makers and tailors in Mexico City, and invested in cochineal dye from Guatemala. Wholesale merchants both issued and honored bills of credit for affiliates, advanced goods, and made cash loans at 5 percent interest to provincial merchants. Merchant networks from import wholesaler to humble retailer depended on loans secured by promissory notes that were backed by future merchandise sales. However, though it was vital to the economy, the credit chain was also highly vulnerable: if one major player failed to meet obligations, shock waves could be felt up and down the economic ladder. The strength of the largest wholesale firms mitigated to some extent the risks inherent in mercantile credit.

Merchants also supplied credit beyond commercial circles to the mining, weaving, and agricultural sectors. In the Viceroyalty of Río de la Plata in the eighteenth century, merchants dominated the economy through import-export trade credit networks, investment, and money lending at all levels. In New Spain, Peru, and Río de la Plata, family ties shaped the mercantile credit networks and lent them stability.

Ecclesiastical institutions, lay religious brotherhoods, and Indian communities dominated mortgage lending until the middle of the eighteenth century. Numerous studies illustrate that convents were embedded in credit networks throughout the colonial world. For example, from the sixteenth century in Arequipa, the Santa Catalina convent and the Mercedarian order were major creditors to the landowning elite. In Brazil's Bahia in the seventeenth and eighteenth centuries, connections with the Convent of Santa Clara do Desterro allowed families to alleviate financial insecurity with regular access to credit. In Cuzco, the *censos* of the Santa Clara convent as well as credit provided to the convent created reciprocal relationships between the institution and the elite, binding them in a "spiritual economy." And in New Spain, too, convents offered credit to landowners, obraje owners, and merchants, in the process acquiring real estate. Indian trust funds (*Cajas de Censos de Indios*) also held mortgages; the Indian Caja of Lima, managed by non-Indian state-appointed officials, loaned out over a million pesos between 1757 and 1781, with haciendas the most mortgaged properties. Though some historians portray land-based credit as burdensome on productive units, others argue that credit mechanisms tied to land helped overcome an insufficient currency supply and provide cash for local investments.

Large-scale agricultural and mining enterprises depended on intricate credit connections, which were dominated by merchants. Hacienda owners were embedded in multiple levels of credit relations. They extended credit to laborers in their stores, and they secured credit for themselves to finance grain production, in part through mortgaging their haciendas with merchants or ecclesiastical lenders. Hacendados were also tied into an elaborate credit system that linked loans of working capital (*avíos*) supplied to landowners by urban merchants to bonds that guaranteed the delivery of grain to merchants who would then market it. Silver mining in New Spain and Peru depended on credit that was channeled by city merchants through local officials to the mining towns. Although silver drove the colonial economy, the state left the provision of necessary credit to the private sector, which charged dearly for credit. The exception was the mercury monopoly; a mining revival followed a stable flow of credit arranged by officials in Lima to finance mercury-mining operations in the 1720s.

The colonial state itself was a regular borrower; throughout the colonial period the Royal Treasury met expenses through a variety of forced loan mechanisms. Religious orders and the Indian trusts lent to the Spanish government, as did the Monte de Piedad in New Spain after the 1770s. In the eighteenth century, the merchant guilds (*consulados*) became more important lenders to the state and were more effective than traditional providers of public credit in getting the state to service the debt. Ecclesiastical property was increasingly confiscated by a debt-laden Spanish Crown in the early nineteenth century, a process that destroyed much of the private credit reserves in the viceroyalties.

Marie François

References

Baskes, Jeremy. *Indians, Merchants, and Markets: A Reinterpretation of the Repartimiento and Spanish-Indian Economic Relations in Colonial Oaxaca, 1750–1821.* Stanford, CA: Stanford University Press, 2000.

Burns, Kathryn. *Colonial Habits: Convents and the Spiritual Economy of Cuzco, Peru.* Durham, NC: Duke University Press, 1999.

Cope, R. Douglas. *The Limits of Racial Domination: Plebeian Society in Colonial Mexico City, 1660–1720.* Madison: University of Wisconsin Press, 1994.

François, Marie. "Cloth and Silver: Pawning and Material Life in Mexico City at the Turn of the Nineteenth Century." *The Americas* 60, no. 3 (January 2004): 325–362.

Hoberman, Louisa Schell. *Mexico's Merchant Elite: Silver, State, and Society, 1590–1660.* Durham, NC: Duke University Press, 1991.

Quiroz, Alfonso W. "Reassessing the Role of Credit in Late Colonial Peru: Censos, Escrituras, and Imposiciones." *Hispanic American Historical Review* 74, no. 2 (1994): 193–230.

See also: Atlantic Economy; Banks and Banking; Bourbon Reforms; Catholic Church in Brazil; Catholic Church in Spanish America; Confraternities; Corregidor/Corregimiento; Estancia; Hacienda; Obraje; Repartimiento; Trade—Spain/Spanish America.

CREOLES

As persons of exclusive Spanish lineage though born in the Americas, Creoles were distinguished from *peninsulares* (also called *gachupines*), that is, Spaniards born in Spain. Several colonial-period documents from New Spain also refer to *criollos negros,* or black creoles, who were black Africans born in the Americas. However, without the qualifier *negro,* "Creole" refers to an American-born person of Spanish lineage. Because of their distinction from European-born Spaniards, Creoles developed a strong sense of group identity, which manifested as a protonationalist sentiment, and helped inspire the struggle for political independence from Spain.

The first Spaniards to occupy the Americas were conquistadors whose offspring were mestizos, that is, people of Spanish and Amerindian parentage. As time passed, more Spanish women came to the Americas, and together with their Spanish husbands, produced Creole offspring. Though many Creoles enjoyed a relatively high level of social and economic status, generally speaking, peninsulars achieved even higher levels of status. Peninsulars rationalized this distinction, in part, by arguing that the tropical and subtropical climate of the Americas adversely affected the intellectual and moral conditions of those who were born there or resided there for long periods. Consequently, peninsulars and other Europeans generally considered themselves worthy of greater social standing and political privileges in the Americas than those born there.

By the late seventeenth century, Creoles began to develop a sense of group identity and a quiet resentment of peninsulars. In the written record, some Creole authors, including Carlos de Sigüenza y Góngora (the seventeenth-century astronomer and savant from New Spain) and Agustín de Vetancurt (also from New Spain), wrote about the cultural and intellectual achievements accomplished in ancient Mexico and New Spain. They also glorified the pre-Hispanic past, likening it to the Roman past, and they claimed that

Creoles were the legitimate cultural descendants of it.

The eighteenth century experienced the development of the *sistema de castas,* that is, caste system, which ordered the inhabitants of Spanish America into a social hierarchy. Based on notions of lineage and social status, the sistema de castas adopted Linnaeus's taxonomic system to assign social position to lineage. For example, those of Amerindian or African lineage were placed at the bottom of the social hierarchy, while mulattoes and mestizos ranked higher. Spaniards occupied the highest tier of the sistema de castas. And though Creoles were not distinguished from Spaniards in this system, in practice peninsulars were more highly regarded than Creoles and enjoyed greater political privileges.

By the mid-eighteenth century, the Bourbon reforms had reshaped the political, religious, and economic face of Spanish America. Under Bourbon rule, peninsulars were given the highest administrative positions in the Americas, further estranging Creoles in the process. At the same time, Creoles began to form an even stronger sense of solidarity and identity, which paved the way for eventual independence movements. Although many Creole families enjoyed elevated social and economic status, their exclusion from high governmental positions gave them the sense of being second-class citizens in a land they considered their own. By the early nineteenth century, Creole disillusionment and solidarity led to successful independence movements in much of Spanish America. In their quest to create national identities, many Creole leaders, artists, and authors incorporated native, mestizo, and mulatto imagery and cultural heritage, such as the Virgin of Guadalupe and the pre-Hispanic past, into their nationalist agendas, claiming them as integral components of a new Spanish American identity.

James M. Córdova

References

Boyer, Richard. "Negotiating Calidad: The Everyday Struggle for Status in Mexico." *Historical Archaeology* 31, no. 1 (1997): 64–72.

Kuznesof, Elizabeth Anne. "Ethnic and Gender Influences on 'Spanish' Creole Society in Colonial Spanish America." *Colonial Latin American Review* 4, no. 1 (1995): 153–179.

Pagden, Anthony. "Identity Formation in Spanish America." Pp. 51–93 in *Colonial Identity in the Atlantic World, 1500–1800,* edited by Nicholas Canny and Anthony Pagden. Princeton, NJ: Princeton University Press, 1987.

Pratt, Mary Louise. "Reinventing América/Reinventing Europe: Creole Self-Fashioning." Pp. 172–197 in *Imperial Eyes: Travel Writing and Transculturation.* London: Routledge, 1992.

See also: Art and Artists—Colonial Spanish America; Bourbon Reforms; Conquistadors; Constitution of Cádiz; Cortes of Cádiz; Independence I–VI; Mestizaje; Migration—From Iberia to the New World; Mulatto; Nationalism; Race; Science and Scientists—Colonial Spanish America; Science and Scientists—Modern Latin America; Women—Colonial Spanish America.

CRIME

Historically in Latin America, the presence of crime within society reflects a number of issues and concerns, including economic realities and imbalances, attitudes about gender, the role of popular culture and the activities of the plebeian classes, desires for social control, and debates regarding the treatment of criminals and criminal activity. During the colonial period, the fear of widespread disorder experienced by the minority elite class, economic stresses and insecurities experienced by lower-class groups, and broader resistance to colonial institutions themselves shaped both the place of crime within society and reactions to it. The violence of the independence era and the decades of chaos that followed provided a perfect context for the perpetuation of criminal activity, which often went unchecked until the emergence of liberal economic agendas toward the end of the nineteenth century, when ideas about political, economic, and social progress demanded order and stability. In the contemporary world, the reasons for crime have not lost their force, as the economic consequences of modernization, first under rapid industrialization, and later with the adoption of neoliberal economic policies, have exacerbated the social tensions within Latin American society.

Colonial elites in Latin America, who were always in the minority, consistently feared violent uprisings by the lower classes, and social disorder continued at the forefront of concerns about the stability of the colonial project. These concerns were especially high in urban areas, where the concentration of elites was highest, and the proximity and daily interaction with members of the plebeian classes were especially close. These fears in a sense were justified. The conquest of the Americas was fundamentally a violent event, and the establishment of colonial institutions and order created a context of economic stress and insecurity for a large segment of the population. Criminal activity for some was simply a means of survival in a world that provided limited economic opportunities.

During the colonial era, elites who were responsible for upholding the law and meting out punishments defined crime, but the types and severity of criminal activity varied widely. On one end were violent crimes, such as murder, assault, rape, and armed robbery, which, while a reality of colonial life, accounted for only a small percentage of criminal arrests. Much more common were property crimes committed by the poor, stemming from their inability to support themselves and their families. Theft, the sale of stolen merchandise, gambling, prostitution, and nonpayment of debts acted as survival strategies for the economically disadvantaged, a necessity in an era lacking welfare protections for the poor. Another common class of crime comprised plebeian activities such as drinking (to excess), common-law marriage, gambling, and petty theft, deemed criminal by elite classes because they tended to perpetuate social disorder, but seen as perfectly acceptable activities in the eyes of the masses. Finally, domestic violence, primarily against women, contributed to the criminal landscape of the colonial era. Though a certain amount of domestic violence was tolerated, based for example on the right of the patriarch to maintain his control over female family members, limits to the use of physical violence were recognized, and transgressions of those limits did not go unpunished.

Colonial officials, recognizing the precarious nature of elite control, created a number of institutions to aid in the maintenance of social order and stability. Municipal police forces monitored city streets in urban centers like Mexico City. The presence of military forces also provided another reminder of state power. The Inquisition, as a social institution, monitored the activities of colonial residents and reinforced colonial obedience to civil and divine laws. During the late eighteenth century, in an attempt to bring more order and efficiency to the colonial world, Bourbon reformers greatly expanded the criminal justice system in Mexico City, primarily through increases in the manpower of the police and court systems, in an attempt to defuse social conflict and lessen the possibility for open rebellion against colonial authorities. These reforms generally worked, as members of the lower classes in the imperial capital felt that they had a legitimate space to air their grievances and protect themselves against criminal injustices, thus making them less likely to resort to violence to have their voices heard.

The wars of independence, followed by the transition from colony to modern nation, was a period fraught with violence, disorder, and instability, in which criminal activity found a safe haven. The resulting disorder and chaos of the early to mid-nineteenth century only further exacerbated the problem, as struggles between liberals and conservatives, political indecision, and economic decline provided a context in which criminal behaviors thrived. In rural areas, banditry became commonplace, a reflection of a lack of law and order. Resistance to forced military recruitment was also a factor, as new states rapidly expanded their military forces and presence in an attempt to establish state dominance. Increasing economic stresses in the cities, brought on by a lack of any kind of growth and development, meant that the traditional crimes of the colonial era associated with unemployment and daily survival, such as petty theft and the sale of stolen goods, continued unabated.

At the same time, however, new issues regarding the rights of individuals and increasing concerns over the lack of social order and control helped to reshape prevailing attitudes about crime and the nature of those who participated in activities deemed dangerous and socially disruptive. Naturally, state formation after independence included the development and consolidation of judicial institutions and practices that found their roots in the colonial era. New liberal ideas about the individual and equality before the law forced elites in particular to reconsider the existing legal terrain. Still, given the context, criminal activity rose dramatically in the early decades of the nineteenth century, and the fears of public disorder and chaos led to stiffer mechanisms of social control in countries like Mexico, Peru, and Argentina. In this particular context, new criminal classifications arose to deal with increasingly chaotic urban realities. In Mexico for example, laws against vagrancy became increasingly popular, as a catchall category for the various crimes committed by insurgents, unemployed workers, and criminals in general.

By the late nineteenth century, liberal oligarchies constituted the government in most Latin American nations, and the new ideology of positivism shaped the discourse of progress and the creation of institutions and programs aimed at achieving modernity. Important in this context was the belief that rational solutions, based in science and technology, could provide solutions to a host of social ills and obstacles to development, including crime. Indeed, according to scholars such as Pablo Piccato, positivism played a crucial role in shifting the discussion of crime and the criminal act to a discussion of criminality and the criminal state. It also provided the foundation for modern police systems and penitentiaries. Throughout the region, the rising demands of capitalist economic production, coupled with the consolidation of elite political hegemony, meant that law and order were more important than ever. In Brazil, the state pressed new modern police forces into service to preserve a social order characterized mainly by slavery and slave relations. In urban centers such as Mexico City and Rio de Janeiro, local law enforcement struggled to contain the resentment and outright defiance of growing populations of lower-class workers frustrated and angry over physical and material changes brought on by modernization that threatened their ability to survive on a daily basis. Certainly, the failure of the liberal economic agenda to provide a reasonable standard of living for both urban and rural workers meant that property crimes continued to act as a safety net to help guarantee basic survival. In rural areas, new groups, such as the *rurales* in Mexico, worked to protect foreign properties and economic investments against insurgent forces and frustrated workers.

Along with the obsession with law and order that dominated the landscape of the late nineteenth century, gendered aspects of crime also crept into the larger discourse surrounding the nature of criminals and their activities. Though the connection between order and progress was emphasized, it did not always mean the same thing for women as it did for men. Indeed, colonial concepts of female honor and the need to protect it superseded emerging attitudes about the importance of equality before the law and the need for punitive actions in maintaining an orderly society. Crimes typically connected to women, such as abortion and infanticide, were often understood not in the modern context of criminal activity, but rather in the colonial context of defending female honor and

moral order. What was important in dealing with these types of crimes was not the notion of punishment, vengeance, or even rehabilitation, but rather the defense of a moral order, based in part on entrenched gendered attitudes about both men and women, which society deemed necessary for the maintenance of social order and thus economic progress. While Latin American nations were changing in terms of the economic and political institutions, some colonial attitudes regarding the constitution of society remained stagnant.

As Latin America moved into the twentieth century, the dynamics of economic growth and political change, as well as the social consequences of these processes, continued to shape the reality of crime and responses to it. Certainly, the economic programs of rapid industrialization, which began in earnest after 1930, created new economic opportunities for some. But inherent weaknesses in rural economies, especially after World War II, meant that the cities increasingly were viewed as a land of economic opportunity, and rural-to-urban migration resulted in population explosions in urban areas. For the most part, the economic desires of new immigrants could not be met, and thus the cycle of unemployment and the drive for basic survival meant the reliance of some on criminal activities. This reliance has continued with the shift to neoliberal economic structures since the 1990s, as Latin America struggles to find its way in a new global economy. It is within this context that the drug trade with the United States has flourished, and with it the accompanying violence and challenges to social order and stability.

In the realm of gender, economic changes of the twentieth century have also resulted in violent responses, as traditional social relationships are increasingly questioned. For example, new opportunities for women within the neoliberal agenda have challenged persistent gender norms and the patriarchal structure that has historically defined Latin American culture. In Ciudad Juarez, along the border between Mexico and the United States, hundreds of young women have been murdered since the early 1990s; these crimes can be understood as a consequence of economic modernization. The maquiladora system, which dominates the economic landscape of the city, provides jobs for young women, along with a newfound economic and physical independence. The majority of the victims in the Ciudad Juarez cases have been maquiladora workers, and it has been suggested that their murders are in part a social reaction to the lessening of male dominance and patriarchal control within northern Mexican society. In the end, the social consequences of various political and economic changes cannot be underestimated; the presence of crime in Latin America, how it is defined and understood, provides a significant context in which to understand the history and development of the region.

Sharon Bailey Glasco

References

Aguirre, Carlos A., and Robert Buffington, eds. *Reconstructing Criminality in Latin America.* Wilmington, DE: Scholarly Resources, 2000.

Holloway, Thomas. *Policing Rio de Janeiro: Repression and Resistance in a 19th-Century City.* Stanford, CA: Stanford University Press, 1993.

Johnson, Lyman L., ed. *The Problem of Order in Changing Societies: Essays on Crime and Policing in Argentina and Uruguay, 1750–1940.* Albuquerque: University of New Mexico Press, 1990.

Salvatore, Ricardo, and Carlos Aguirre, eds. *The Birth of the Penitentiary in Latin America: Essays on Criminology, Prison Reform, and Social Control, 1830–1940.* Austin: University of Texas Press, 1996.

Taylor, William. *Drinking, Homicide, and Rebellion in Colonial Mexican Villages.* Stanford, CA: Stanford University Press, 1979.

Vanderwood, Paul. *Disorder and Progress: Bandits, Police, and Mexican Development.* Wilmington, DE: Scholarly Resources, 1992.

See also: Administration—Colonial Spanish America; Alcohol; Bandits and Banditry; Bigamy, Transatlantic; Bourbon Reforms; Conquest I–VII; Contraband; Culture; Drugs; Independence I–VI; Inquisition—Luso-America; Inquisition—Spanish America; Laws—Colonial Latin America; Liberalism; Native Americans I–VIII; Positivism; Poverty; Prostitution; Race; Rebellions—Colonial Latin America; Slave Rebellions—Brazil; Slavery I–IV; Women—Brazil; Women—Colonial Spanish America; Women—Modern Spanish America; World War I; World War II.

CUBA

The Spanish first arrived in Cuba in 1511. As with other Caribbean islands, the indigenous peoples of Cuba were quickly conquered, enslaved, and eventually exterminated by the conquistadors. After the conquest of Mexico and the South American mainland, Cuba, along with the rest of the Caribbean, was largely ignored by imperial authorities. Until Mexico's independence, Cuba was under the authority of the Viceroy of New Spain. Havana remained an important port city for transatlantic commerce and for imperial defense. The rest of the island was sparsely inhabited by independent cattle ranchers and small-scale farmers. Much of the island's commercial activity centered on the city of Havana, especially after the all-important bullion fleets arrived. In the interior regions, early colonists received land in the form of *mercedes* (land grants from the Crown) or *realengos* (the right to use Crown land). In practice, there was little difference between these two forms of land tenure. Over time, strong localized traditions of exclusive individual usufruct rights characterized rural relations of production. Subsistence production coexisted alongside primitive sugar production, tobacco growing, cattle ranching, and, along the coasts, smuggling and contraband. With the expansion of large-scale sugar production in the nineteenth and twentieth centuries, usufruct land tenure was eliminated in favor of the legal right to divide, sell, and rent land. Other lands in the sparsely populated eastern half of the island were occupied by runaway slaves or by legally freed former slaves: these people rarely had legal title to land, but many families had occupied the same plots for decades. Vestiges of usufruct land tenure persisted to the 1930s, especially in the remote and mountainous parts of eastern Cuba.

Relations between Cuba and Spain experienced a dramatic change in the late eighteenth century. Imperial rivalry among Spain, England, and France resulted in the British occupation of Havana in 1762. This event forced Spain to pay more attention to Cuba. More significant, from an economic perspective, when Spain regained Cuba in 1763, the Cuban elite had had a taste of freer trade and access to new markets. Imperial reformers in Madrid and Havana encouraged the shift to open markets and to a commercially oriented economy. With the Haitian Revolution (1791–1804), Saint Domingue was no

longer the world's major sugar producer: hundreds of refugees entered Cuba, many with the capital and expertise necessary to invest in Cuban sugar production. By the 1820s Cuba was the world's single largest sugar producer. The resulting colonial revenue to the Spanish treasury made Cuba Spain's most important colony, especially after the loss of Spain's empire on the mainland. That loss also led to a massive influx of loyalist refugees to Cuba from Mexico, Venezuela, Peru, and other former colonies; this migration reinforced Cuba's identity as a Spanish stronghold.

Cuba's new prosperity was based on sugar production, and sugar production was based on slavery. Between 1762 and 1860, Cuba's population increased from 150,000 to 1.3 million; approximately 600,000 of those people were slaves brought to work on the sugar estates. Before the 1860s, economic prosperity brought loyalty, and while there certainly were Cubans who wanted independence from Spain, the independence movement was marginal within Cuban politics. Most white Cubans could not imagine Cuba without slavery, and slavery could not be maintained by the Cuban elite alone. Cuban prosperity and the maintenance of slavery required a powerful external power. Indeed, the problem for the Cuban elite was that Spain was not powerful enough to guarantee Cuban prosperity. Spanish imperial policies provoked considerable resentment among wealthy merchants and planters, many of whom felt that Cuban wealth was sapped by a mother country that was a hollow shell of its former imperial self. As a consequence, many Cubans believed that annexation to the United States was the best guarantee for a secure future: Cuba could be part of the American slave South, and political annexation to the United States would complement the economic reality that most Cuban trade was with the United States, despite Spain's attempt to monopolize the Cuban market.

In the 1860s, Cuba's relations with Spain changed once again. The American Civil War eliminated the prospect of a secure future for slavery in the Americas. Postwar American governments were too preoccupied with the social and political implications of Reconstruction to annex a multiracial society still dominated by slavery. The increase of abolitionist activity throughout Europe and the Americas added to planter anxiety about the future. Slavery's days were numbered, and the question was not whether abolition would occur but how it would take place and what kind of workers would replace slave labor. In Cuba, some powerful groups hoped that some form of provincial autonomy for Cuba within the Spanish orbit might be negotiated. From a Spanish perspective, keeping Cuba was more important than ever before: Spanish conservatives and liberals alike believed that if Spain were going to industrialize, it needed a stable and wealthy Cuba to purchase manufactured goods and to provide revenue to the treasury. Industrialization, many believed, rested on colonialism, and Spanish prosperity depended on Cuban prosperity.

Yet neither the Cuban elite nor the Spanish state had the time to solve the problems they confronted. In Spain, civil war, *pronunciamentos,* and revolution undermined reform at home and abroad. After 1868, Spanish political and economic policy toward Cuba was increasingly militaristic, and restrictive trade policies were intensified. Within Cuba, a combination of slave resistance, the growing international momentum against slavery, a divided political class, and Spain's domestic crisis encouraged antislavery groups and pushed more people into the ranks of the independence forces. In October 1868 Cuba's first war for independence, known as the Ten Years' War, was initiated by disgruntled plantation owners, slaves and former slaves, and a new generation of nationalist youth from all social classes. After ten years of war, neither side could win a decisive victory, and in February 1878 the Pact of Zanjón was signed. Under this agreement Cuba was to have better representation in Madrid, slaves who fought for the rebels were to be freed, and leaders of the revolt could leave Cuba safely.

In reality, however, the Pact of Zanjón was more of a truce than it was a peace agreement. None of the fundamental issues that caused the Ten Years' War had been addressed, and many Cubans believed it was only a matter of time before war would erupt again. Even though Cuban slavery ended in 1886, political and economic tensions continued to mount. By the early 1890s, Cuba was caught between a weak colonial power and a sugar economy almost entirely dependent on the North American market. Cuba's second war for independence began in 1895, but this time it did not end in a stalemate; in 1898, Spain was defeated by a combination of Cuban arms and American intervention. Spanish tactics during this conflict were especially brutal: scorched-earth campaigns and large concentration camps to prevent civilian contact with insurgents caused great hardship among the Cuban population. Such tactics only served to recruit more fighters for the cause of Cuban independence. Meanwhile, in the United States, pressure was growing on the government to intervene militarily in Cuba. Though some Americans certainly supported the principle of Cuban independence, other powerful economic and political interests eyed Cuba as a potential source of wealth and investment opportunities. When the Americans intervened in 1898, Spanish forces were already on the defensive and confined largely to the cities. America's "splendid little war" defeated a demoralized Spanish army and navy and robbed Cuban fighters of their victory.

One of the great ironies of Cuba's relations with Spain is that more Spaniards went to Cuba after Spain lost the island than during the entire colonial period. Throughout the colonial period, Cuba did not attract many Spanish immigrants. Imperial officials, wealthy merchants and planters, and soldiers dominated the Spanish community. It is true that between 1868 and 1898 well over 200,000 Spanish soldiers were stationed in Cuba, and many remained on or returned to the island after their military service. But it was with the large-scale transatlantic migrations of the early twentieth century that Spaniards came to dominate much of Cuban society at all levels. Between 1900 and 1930, 800,000 Spaniards migrated to Cuba. After 1902, Cuban governments encouraged Spanish immigration because they hoped that Spanish workers and farmers would help bring prosperity to the war-ravaged island as well as counter what the Cuban elites believed was the "uncultured" influence of Afro-Cubans and Afro-Caribbean migrant workers. After the abolition of slavery, Cuban sugar producers struggled to find an alternative form of labor. Between 1886 and 1915, war, economic uncertainty, foreign intervention, and high debt loads meant that Cuban producers typically felt they were on the verge of ruin.

It was only after World War I, when a massive amount of American capital was invested in sugar production, that the industry gained a solid basis. The labor problem was solved when, after 1915, Cuba began to bring in hundreds of thousands of migrant workers from Haiti and the British West Indies. Cuba stands out as the only Latin American nation in the twentieth century that received large numbers of both white (mostly Spanish) and black (West Indian) immigrants. It was also the only tropical country in the world that received large numbers of European (mostly Spanish) immigrants. As a result, issues of racial, ethnic, class, and national identity were forged within a unique set of circumstances. Each immigrant community in Cuba had its own advantages and disadvantages when it came to the migration experience. Spaniards had the advantage of being desirable immigrants, even if they were resented by many Cubans because they dominated the job market and commerce. Cheap Afro-Caribbean labor, according to traditional thinking, was needed to work in the cane fields, but their cultural practices were condemned. Spanish immigration to Cuba was a critical, if contradictory, aspect of Cuban national formation: Spanishness was both a desired racial attribute and at the same time a representation of the colonial past.

Many Spaniards migrated within existing family and employment networks. Spaniards were influential as shopkeepers, tradespeople, café owners, merchants, and small-scale property owners. Several prominent and wealthy Spanish landowners, merchants, and bankers remained in Cuba after 1898, but this elite group was small in comparison to those of humble origins. The majority of Spanish immigrants to Cuba were from Galicia, Asturias, and Catalonia, and cultural centers were formed along these regional lines. Most Spaniards settled in urban areas, though some purchased land in Santa Clara and Camagüey. Spaniards were prominent in the trade union movement, as well as in the anarchist and early Communist movements. Partially in response to Spanish migration, Cuban nationalist sentiment grew in the 1920s and 1930s. Between 1933 and 1940, a series of nationalist laws compelled foreigners to become Cuban citizens or return to their country of origin. Given the turmoil in Spain in the 1930s, it is understandable that many Spaniards adopted Cuba as their new country.

Robert Whitney

References

Álvarez Estévez, Rolando. *Azúcar e inmigración en Cuba, 1900–1940*. Havana: Editorial de Ciencias Sociales, 1988.

Casanovas, Joan. *Bread, or Bullets: Urban Labor and Spanish Colonialism in Cuba, 1850–1898*. Pittsburgh: University of Pittsburgh Press, 1998.

Fernández, Áurea Matilde. *España y Cuba: Revolución burguesa y relaciones coloniales*. Havana: Editorial de Ciencias Sociales, 1988.

Maluquer de Motes, Jordi. *Nación e inmigración: Los españoles en Cuba, siglos XIX–XX*. Oviedo, Asturias: Júcar, 1992.

Moya, José C. "Spanish Immigration to Cuba and Argentina." In *Mass Migration to Modern Latin America*, edited by Samuel L. Baily and Eduardo José Míguez. Wilmington, DE: Scholarly Resources, 2003.

Schmidt-Nowara, Christopher. *Empire and Antislavery: Spain, Cuba, and Puerto Rico, 1833–1874*. Pittsburgh: University of Pittsburgh Press, 1999.

See also: Abolition and Emancipation; Atlantic Economy; Bourbon Reforms; Cimarrones; Colonists and Settlers III—Caribbean; Conquest III—Caribbean; Contraband; Cuban Revolution; Defense—Colonial Spanish America; Fleet System; Guerrillas; Haitian Revolution; Independence I–VI; Migration—From Iberia to the New World; Monopolies; Native Americans III—Caribbean; Race; Seven Years' War; Slave Rebellions—Caribbean; Slavery II—Caribbean; Slave Trade; Spanish Civil War and Latin America; Sugar; Tobacco; Viceroyalties; World War I.

CUBAN REVOLUTION

The 1959 Cuban Revolution, in part a response to the legacies of Spanish colonization and U.S. intervention, led to a radical realignment of the island's development.

The nationalism that inspired the revolution derived from Cuba's long struggle for independence from Spain. Wars in 1868–1878 and 1879–1880 had ended in bloody failure before U.S. assistance led to independence on May 20, 1902. Some feared Cuba was exchanging Spanish dominance for that of the United States. José Martí shared that fear, and he also argued that independence was only guaranteed if all Cubans stood to benefit. Cuba gained its independence; however, continued U.S. involvement after the war did limit Cuba's freedom. The Platt Amendment constrained Cuba's relations with foreign powers, and Cuban industries could not compete with the preferential treatment enjoyed by U.S. manufacturers.

Successive governments in Cuba failed to confront these issues, and it was that failure that led to a radical nationalist revolution in 1959. It is true that Fulgencio Batista had instituted reforms in the 1930s and overseen the promulgation of a constitution promoting social justice and democracy in 1940, but the Batista government that the rebels overthrew in 1959 had become corrupt and repressive. For two years, Fidel Castro's rebels fought their way from the mountains of the Sierra Maestra, through the Cuban countryside, to Havana. Along the way they won the support of the peasantry, the workers, and the Cuban middle class. From an initial group of twelve, the forces of Castro's movement of the 26th of July (so named from the day it began) gained widespread support throughout Cuba.

The socialist outcome of the revolution was a result of the cold war context in which it occurred. The revolution enjoyed enormous popular support through the 1960s and 1970s, spurring the pace of radical reforms and alarming the propertied classes and the United States. The revolutionary government reduced rents, increased wages, gave land and credit to peasants, and abolished legal discrimination against Afro-Cubans. Landowners protested the confiscation of their lands and U.S.-owned utility companies resented the reduction of their rates. When the United States threatened to reduce Cuba's sugar quota, the Soviet Union purchased the sugar. Cuba also bought Soviet oil. When U.S. oil companies refused to refine the oil, Castro promptly nationalized foreign refineries. Further nationalizations resulted in the United States breaking diplomatic ties in January 1961.

The 1961 CIA-organized Bay of Pigs invasion and the 1962 Missile Crisis drove Cuba further from the United States, both economically and politically. Cuba relied on Eastern Bloc economic support through the 1980s, but it was also able to find economic outlets and political sympathy elsewhere in Europe. In 1966, Spain became Cuba's closest trade partner after the USSR, allowing General Franco to show his independence from the United States. European youth identified with Cuba's defiance of the United States and the image of Che Guevara watching over 1960s protests. Cuba and Guevara supported revolution more directly elsewhere, sending troops to Africa and Latin America.

Alistair Hattingh

References

Balfour, Sebastian. *Castro*. London: Longman, 1999.

Pérez, Louis. *Cuba: Between Reform and Revolution*. Oxford: Oxford University Press, 1988.

Pérez-Stable, Marifeli. *The Cuban Revolution: Origins, Course, and Legacy*. Oxford: Oxford University Press, 1999.

See also: Cold War—Spain and the Americas; Communism; Cuba; Guerrillas; Nationalism; Oil; Spanish-American War; Spanish Civil War and Latin America; Sugar.

CULTURE

The various developments in the study of culture in Latin America have had a profound influence on scholarly understandings of the interactions between Iberia and the Americas. Few subjects in contemporary Latin America are as intellectually productive and irreplaceable, and yet as rife with disagreement, as the idea of culture. Although mid-twentieth-century U.S. anthropologists developed a whole social science discipline around the study of culture, the late twentieth century witnessed a veritable explosion of wider academic and public debate over the culture concept's theoretical scope, practical applications, and political influence. Anthropologists originally defined culture as the "complex whole" of a people's myths, ritual ceremonies, and forms of social organization. More philosophically, the anthropological definition of culture also implied the ways that different people make sense of the world. In Latin America today, the culture concept is widely considered indispensable to the study of politics and urban change, as well as the study of indigenous movements, the ideological basis of social mobilization, the definition of a habitable human environment, ethnic and gender norms, the significance of public art, state education, government policies, sexuality, and identity.

The study of culture in Latin America first coalesced during the early twentieth century, when ethnographic fieldworkers questioned the validity of evolutionary theories that categorize all societies within a single, all-encompassing hierarchy of evolutionary development—from the "archaic," or "primitive," to the "complex," or "advanced." Working against these evolutionary frameworks, twentieth-century anthropologists refashioned the idea of culture into a technical concept, with reference to the individuality and unique character of each people or society, including their languages, myths, kinship systems, politics, and distinctive ways of life. For most anthropologists, culture corresponded to an elemental or fundamental aspect of the human condition.

Ethnographic fieldwork, not surprisingly, depended upon the study of culture. The typical ethnographer would set out for a distant part of Latin America to live among a people (for example, among the Yanomamis who reside in Venezuela and Brazil, or the Aches who inhabit marginal forested areas of Paraguay), only to return from such diverse localities to write about their myths, rituals, and social formations in cross-cultural perspective. The anthropological notion of culture thus served a highly instrumental empirical purpose, allowing the transatlantic region's diversity of forms of ethnic, linguistic, and social organization to be studied without placing any of its peoples or customs in a prearranged (and Eurocentric) hierarchy or natural order.

However, scholarly debates over ethnographic fieldwork methodologies also gave rise to the ethic of cultural relativism, which holds that no single people's moral values or aesthetic ideals can be applied to judge the values and ideals of another people. The Borroro tribal culture in eastern Brazil was to be viewed by anthropologists as distinct from the culture of the Inca civilization in Peru's highlands, which in turn was different from the Spanish conquistadors' culture, and so forth. Each needed to be analyzed according to its own cultural traditions. Although ideas and goods could be exchanged between cultures, each individual culture studied by anthropologists was considered an autonomous unit of analysis that must be understood on its own terms.

On one hand, the principle of relativism obligated the ethnographer to embrace rational scientific methodologies, or inductive modes of social analysis. To illustrate, if anthropologists in Brazil noted that race was not a topic Brazilians ordinarily mention in daily conversation, the ethic of cultural relativism held that the ethnogra-

Yanomami Indian shaman in village of Irokai-teri, Venezuela. (Robert Caputo/Aurora/Getty Images)

pher should not deduce that forms of race-based discrimination, although visible or observable by the cultural standards of the ethnographer, were equally important to Brazilian culture.

On the other hand, anthropologists' embrace of the principle of relativism did not entirely do away with prejudice or bias in the study of culture; in fact, new types of ethical quandaries arose. For instance, many twentieth-century ethnographers in Latin America grew to self-identify with the culture they researched and described. On several occasions, ethnographers witnessed killings and other illegal activities during their fieldwork. In these situations, ethnographers tended to consider themselves professionally obligated to privilege the wider cultural beliefs of the societies, subgroups, or persons they studied in rela-

tion to such violent or illicit activities. In sum, the ethic of cultural relativism guided twentieth-century ethnographic fieldworkers to investigate the broader social conditions and worldviews that legitimate, condone, or repress cultural acts of any sort, rather than judging them outright.

Throughout the middle of the twentieth century, Latin American anthropologists regularly employed the culture concept to analyze pressing geopolitical issues. For example, the Bureau of American Ethnology's seven-volume *Handbook of South American Indians* (1946–1959) brought together hundreds of articles on indigenous cultural history in order to archive or preserve cultural knowledge that appeared to be disappearing under the pressures of modern society. Anthropologists developed theories of indigenous cultural organization based upon levels of sociopolitical development and complexity, using the standard anthropological model of bands, tribes, chiefdoms, and states to fit all indigenous peoples into specific styles or modes of cultural organization. Although indigenous cultures in Latin America were the main subject of early twentieth-century anthropological research, one observes roughly from the time of the *Handbook*'s publication a marked increase in ethnographic fieldwork projects to investigate modernization as a cross-cultural process.

During the 1950s and 1960s, anthropologists began to use the term *folk culture* to describe Latin American people who self-identified as neither fully indigenous nor completely urban. Nevertheless, anthropologists continued to view the integration of indigenous groups within national culture as a fundamental geopolitical problem; in Latin American anthropological writings, the persistence of the contrast between indigenous and modern culture(s) held sway until the late twentieth century. At the same time, anthropologists began to investigate the process by which country people migrated to cities and incorporated themselves as subjects of modern nation-states, a phenomenon described as Latin America's "folk-urban continuum." Mestizo culture (that is, cultures of mixed-race peoples) quickly turned into a subject of anthropological investigation in monographs that analyzed so-called *cholo, montubio, ladino,* and *caboclo* peoples (mixed-race). As a result, mid-twentieth-century anthropologists made important scholarly contributions to the critique of national culture and its symbolic attachments to powerfully discriminating myths, rituals, and elite-based race ideologies.

The anthropological focus on culture shifted once again when ethnographers in Latin America began to systematically analyze cultural economies. As urban ethnography gained prominence, anthropologists began to differentiate between typologies of peasantry and working-class cultures. Studying urban life in impoverished zones, anthropologists investigated what they termed the *culture of poverty.* The culture of poverty model contentiously hypothesized that urban dwellers living in marginalized neighborhoods uphold notions of personal dignity and self-worth in daily activities (such as communal alcohol drinking and quickly spending one's salary on family, friendships, and love relationships) that economically prohibited individuals from developing financial savings, improving community resources, or moving out of blighted neighborhoods. Thus, members of working-class families in Mexico City typically found themselves subjected to cultural pressures to remain within a perpetually degrading economic life cycle; culture, in such a perspective, turns into the key measure of socioeconomic illness or malfunction. In a similar vein, the study of cultural materialism attempted to diagnose the relative productivity or inutility of different cultural practices in Latin America.

Throughout the mid-twentieth century, anthropologists debated the scientific validity and wider public value of cultural materialist theories. But ethnographers also analyzed culture increasingly in terms of working-class people's unequal access to socioeconomic power, or their distance from state and government representation. To do so, ethnographers gravitated to social history. The change in thinking about culture was emblematic of the growing influence of Marxist sociological theories. Ethnographers began to view culture as a product of the broader patterns of socioeconomic development. For example, the colonial history of the transatlantic sugar trade (and the emerging international market in sweet foods) could be analyzed from the perspective of local hacienda plantation development and labor-exploiting social relations between different castes or classes; the history of the sugar trade linked cultural activities in the centers of power (for example, British tea gatherings, which required sugar consumption) with cultural activities in the colonial peripheries (for example, the rise of black slavery in Puerto Rico as an institution dedicated to sugar production).

This new focus on culture as a byproduct of transatlantic political and economic processes challenged what anthropologists had previously considered to be the elementary forms of cultural life. Rather than concentrating exclusively on the myths, rituals, kinship systems, or psychological worldviews of local peoples, anthropologists began to focus more specifically on state and regional government measures, and the ways peoples lived with or reacted to such organizational changes. In other words, ethnographers moved away from analyzing culture in itself to considering the manner in which transnational histories and socioeconomic processes created new sets of hierarchical cultural relationships.

While late twentieth-century anthropologists and critics accordingly have grown distrustful of nonhistorical definitions of culture, emphasizing the traditional concept's capacity to oversimplify the religion, customs, or behaviors of a society by translating such ordinary social phenomena into timeless models, most anthropologists, historians, and critics continue to find cultural viewpoints the key to describing the complexity, richness, and diversity of the human experience in Latin America. Few anthropologists today view culture as an ahistorical, autonomous, or individual entity, choosing instead to focus on the historical processes by which inequality (that is, unequal access to social, environmental, and governmental resources) may inform the basis of cultural difference itself. Many modern ethnographers systematically investigate how ordinary people use the concept of culture to describe their historical opposition to national political agendas. From the rise of Bolivia's street protests to assert that people's access to water is a cultural right to the spread of Brazil's lower-class dance forms such as samba and *capoeira,* anthropologists throughout Latin America lend special attention to new cultural movements as emerging forms of political involvement.

Contemporary anthropologists may eschew the study of essential indigenous culture(s); however, the methodologies of cultural interpretation have proven especially useful to historians who analyze the processes by which European notions of civil and religious behavior were imposed upon indigenous peoples during the colonial era. By studying the ways that Iberian missionaries and government magistrates wrote about indigenous peoples in colonial society, and by drawing analogies to the ethnographic problems of interpreting another culture, contemporary historians have shifted the grounds of historical analysis to shed more light on colonial rituals and daily colonial interactions between Latin American people from different ethnic, race, and class backgrounds.

Whereas much historical work prior to the twentieth century tended to focus on Europeans' "discovery" and "conquest" of the Americas, the incorporation of the culture concept within historical research led historians to interpret more subtle signs of indigenous cultural response(s) to colonization, especially the local reformation or transformation of indigenous religions. Cultural historians thus concern themselves with the interpretive problems and paradoxes of cultural analysis. If the Spanish and Portuguese colonization of New World territories and people implied a clash of cultures, then the so-called European discovery (*descubrimiento*) of America described by colonial Iberian chroniclers, but viewed through the contemporary lenses of cultural analysis, was rather something like a subtle form of cultural concealment (*encubrimiento*): the official documents and diaries written by Iberian chroniclers, however they may have described events that actually took place, also made indigenous societies into reflections of their own cultural biases and presumptions. Addressing these textual problems, cultural historians analyze the subtle play of European and indigenous worldviews, and the unexpected transformation(s) of these worldviews, in the unfolding of both colonial historical events and daily life.

Among early Spanish and Portuguese colonists, the dominant cultural perspective or way to understand the endeavor of colonization was deeply influenced by the phenomenon known as the *Reconquista* (Reconquest). The beginning of Ibero-American territorial expansion in the New World (1492) coincidentally took place the year after Jewish and Islamic groups were coercively expelled from the Iberian Peninsula. As a result, most early colonial texts drew from medieval and Renaissance cultural crusader worldviews to champion the expansion of Christianity into the pagan lands of the New World. Conquistadors, missionaries, and colonists thus viewed their own participation in the subjugation of American people and territory as a form of religious and economic reclamation, and Iberian settlers tended to consider their postconquest entitlements to indigenous land and labor as a form of ransom (*rescate*), or just repayment for having subjugated pagan areas. The forms of colonial government implemented upon the conquest of a new territory involved Old World Iberian models of cross-cultural integration; individual conquistadors or colonizers frequently gained territorial deeds and noble status in exchange for protecting and converting indigenous laborers and black slaves.

Historians and anthropologists have amply demonstrated that initial forms of Iberian colonization intimately involved spreading a culture of terror. Indigenous peoples, through a bureaucratic process called *congregación* or *reducción,* were forcibly relocated from native hamlets, towns, and cities into the newly arranged Spanish and Portuguese settlements. In other words, the first act of European colonization after open warfare and hostilities had subsided involved the forced resettlement of indigenous people. In new colonial towns, indigenous labor and spiritual obligations in the *encomienda* system, an Iberian institution whereby elite members of the conquering parties would receive "entitlement" to native people's labor and services in return for physical and spiritual "protection." In essence, the institution of encomienda demanded one's conversion to Christianity, along with regionally varying forms of debilitating labor requirements such as agricultural work, mining, and urban construction. Therefore, what is observable in the early colonial historical record as the pacification of indigenous people more often than not involved Spanish and Portuguese colonial measures that inspired fear of torture or execution (public whippings, garroting, and the like) among newly colonized populations. Given that few Spaniards or Portuguese could initially speak native indigenous languages in a newly conquered region, the impoverished forms of communication with colonized peoples only heightened the latter's fear of violent European reprisals.

Over the span of a generation, however, the culture of terror that characterized much of the initial exchanges between Iberians and indigenous people quickly led to more quotidian forms of urban cultural interaction and daily life. The key to local colonial order, in most cases, involved the imposition of Catholicism upon indigenous and enslaved groups, and the efforts to relocate natives into colonial towns. The evangelical customs of the colonial Church borrowed heavily from medieval and early modern notions of Christian practice, especially the importance of participation in the ceremonies of the Church to prove one's fidelity to the Catholic faith. Among the politically compromised indigenous groups, successful performance of religious rites became the most practical route to achieving higher social standing. Catholic ceremonies were obligatory events, and the

worship of biblical and saintly images was used as a measure of individual and group dedication to the colonial civic-religious order.

The culture of colonialism was marked by a strong emphasis on the Christian calendar of saint's-day celebrations, and the ceremonial coparticipation of the marginalized masses. New organizations, such as religious brotherhoods, convents, and monasteries, were developed in every major city and became the principal vehicle and expression of civic-religious integration. Each organization was also responsible for running annual cycles of Christian and governmental rituals. Though peninsular citizens and Old Christians (without Jewish or Moorish ancestry) of noble backgrounds enjoyed hierarchical privileges within these civic associations, individuals from different ethnic, class, and gender backgrounds were also included within the fold of such institutions. The overarching result of colonial-era Christianization, which involved wide-ranging cultural participation in church-based organizations, was the creation of a decidedly Catholic civil society and the culture of Latin American Catholicism that political commentators have described with greater or lesser degrees of sophistication from colonial times to the present.

Despite the widespread missionary success of Christian evangelization, many indigenous cultures in Latin America retained elements of pre-Columbian religious practices. The study of indigenous syncretism has been perhaps the most industrious branch of Latin American cultural history. Whereas historians during the 1980s and 1990s generally concentrated on indigenous syncretism as an example of resistance to colonial rule, more recent scholarship has focused more specifically on the interplay of local colonial pressures to adopt some specific cultural practices over others. For example, indigenous groups' mixing of Catholic and native religious practices or worldviews attests to the fact that Catholic local religion was not simply imposed by Iberian colonists. To a certain degree, indigenous individuals and enclaves were active participants in their own Christian indoctrination.

In terms of the changes to indigenous languages that occurred as a result of colonialism, the agency of indigenous groups can also be historically analyzed. Missionary groups typically employed the pre-Columbian language that was regionally prevalent as a kind of lingua franca in their attempts to communicate with indigenous communities who spoke in different, mutually unintelligible tongues. As Iberian colonists advanced throughout Central and South America, however, indigenous peoples devastated by warfare and Old World pathogens formed themselves into new societies with ad hoc political associations. A process of ethnogenesis—that is, the cross-cultural negotiation and creation of new ethnic and linguistic identities—was already under way during the early colonial era, and it was not always controlled or directed by colonial governments; indigenous people formed new linguistic and political groups as a way to organize themselves in response to the bureaucratic demands imposed by European colonial order. The cultural histories of indigenous groups in Latin America, in a similar fashion, focus on the development of languages, myths, rituals, and sociopolitical circumstances of native peoples, in cross-cultural context.

What distinguishes cultural studies in Latin America from other fields of research is a dependence on interdisciplinary academic discussions and debates. The field broadly includes anthropologists, literary critics, novelists, political theorists, sociologists, philosophers, and historians among its various practitioners and proponents. In cultural studies journals, one may find an essay on sixteenth-century Mexican female religious poets alongside an essay on the representation of gang life in current Colombian cinema, or a theoretical essay tracing the idea of translation in famous writers in Latin America such as Gabriel García Márquez and Jorge Luis Borges. The guiding thread that connects most cultural studies research is nevertheless an emphasis on the representation of historically marginalized peoples or practices, and the politics of new or emerging forms of cultural experience.

Christopher Eric Garces

References

Chance, John K., and William B. Taylor. "Cofradías and Cargos: An Historical Perspective on the Meso-American Civil-Religious Hierarchy." *American Ethnologist* 12, no. 1 (1985): 1–26.

García Canclini, Néstor. *Hybrid Cultures: Strategies for Entering and Leaving Modernity.* Minneapolis: University of Minnesota Press, 1995.

Lockhart, James, and Stuart B. Schwartz. *Early Latin America: A History of Colonial Spanish America and Brazil.* Cambridge: Cambridge University Press, 1983.

Mills, Kenneth, William B. Taylor, and Sandra Lauderdale Graham, eds. *Colonial Latin America: A Documentary History.* Wilmington, DE: Scholarly Resources, 2002.

Pagden, Anthony. *The Fall of Natural Man: The American Indian and the Origins of Comparative Ethnology.* Cambridge: Cambridge University Press, 1982.

Steward, Julian, ed. *Handbook of South American Indians.* 7 vols. Washington, DC: U.S. Government Printing Office, 1946–1959.

Taussig, Michael. *Shamanism, Colonialism, and the Wild Man: A Study in Terror and Healing.* Chicago: University of Chicago Press, 1987.

See also: Alcohol; Architecture—Brazil; Architecture—Colonial Spanish America; Architecture—Modern Spanish America; Art and Artists—Brazil; Art and Artists—Colonial Spanish America; Art and Artists—Modern Spanish America; Catholic Church in Brazil; Catholic Church in Spanish America; Chroniclers; Cinema; Colonists and Settlers I–VI; Columbian Exchange—Disease; Confraternities; Congregaciones; Conquest I–VII; Encomienda; Environment; Gay Rights and Movements; Idolatry, Extirpation of; Islam; Jews—Colonial Latin America; Jurema; Languages; Mestizaje; Mita; Moors; Music and Dance I–V; Nationalism; Native Americans I–VIII; Popular Festivals; Race; Religious Orders; Repartimiento; Saints and Saintliness; Slavery I–IV; Slave Trade; Sugar; Syncretism; Terrorism; Women—Brazil; Women—Colonial Spanish America; Women—Modern Spanish America.

```
303.482    Iberia and the
IBE        Americas.
```

$270.00   35017000762305

DATE			